HANDBOOK OF NORTH AMERICAN BIRDS

Sponsored by American Ornithologists' Union and

New York State Museum and Science Service

HANDBOOK OF

NORTH AMERICAN BIRDS

VOLUME 2

Waterfowl (first part)

WHISTLING DUCKS
SWANS
GEESE
SHELD-DUCKS
DABBLING DUCKS

EDITED BY RALPH S. PALMER

New Haven and London, Yale University Press, 1976

Library of Congress catalog card number: 62-8259
International standard book number: 0-300-01902-5

Designed by John O. C. McCrillis
and set in Caledonia type.
Printed in the United States of America by
The Vail-Ballou Press, Inc., Binghamton, N.Y.

Published in Great Britain, Europe, and Africa by
Yale University Press, Ltd., London.
Distributed in Latin America by Kaiman & Polon, Inc., New
York City; in Australasia by Book & Film Services, Artarmon,
N. S. W. , Australia; in India by UBS Publishers' Distributors
Pvt., Ltd. , Delhi; in Japan by John Weatherhill, Inc., Tokyo.

$144.00   C. Aiclew   9-20-90 (J.S.)

CONTRIBUTORS TO VOLUMES 2 & 3

Authors, illustrators (*), and those who are both (**) have signed their contributions with initials as follows:

AD	ALEXANDER DZUBIN	JAH	JOSEPH A. HAGAR
AJE	ANTHONY J. ERSKINE	JPR	JOHN P. RYDER
AWS	ARLIE W. SCHORGER	KCP	KENNETH C. PARKES
BK	BRINA KESSEL	LGS	LAWSON G. SUGDEN
BM	BROOKE MEANLEY	LKS	LYLE K. SOWLS
CDM	CHARLES D. MacINNES	MCH	MERRILL C. HAMMOND
CHN	COLLEEN H. NELSON*	MFJ	MARY F. JACKSON
DSF	DONALD S. FARNER	MTM	M. T. MYRES
ETS	ELLEN THORNE SMITH	MWW	MILTON W. WELLER
FCB	FRANK C. BELLROSE	RDJ	ROBERT D. JONES JR.
FGC	F. GRAHAM COOCH	RMM	ROBERT M. MENGEL*
FM	D. FRANK McKINNEY	RSP	RALPH S. PALMER**
FWP	FRANK W. PRESTON	SDR	S. DILLON RIPLEY
HAH	H. ALBERT HOCHBAUM	TWB	THOMAS W. BARRY
HH	HELEN HAYS	WEB	WINSTON E. BANKO
HLM	HOWARD L. MENDALL	WHE	WILLIAM H. ELDER

ACKNOWLEDGMENTS

Those acknowledgments made in the front matter of volume 1 apply equally to volumes 2 and 3.

The locations I have visited in accumulating information on waterfowl extend from Bering Sea eastward around the globe to central Asia and from the Canadian higharctic down to Mexico. There has been time afield, alone or in company of local experts, and at research stations, aviaries, museums, universities, and in libraries. Such absences from the monotony of office work are pleasant to recall. The combined input reflects the contacts made and opportunities realized—and others missed.

Some species accounts are the work of a very few individuals and credit clearly belongs to them and to those persons whom they cite. So much has happened recently in waterfowl research, however, that other accounts have evolved through a process of drafting, deleting, revising, refereeing, modifying, and updating. Thus it becomes less clear sometimes to whom credit is due for a particular statement or viewpoint as it appears in this book. I am grateful to those who have assisted in any way at any stage in the process.

Contributors to the waterfowl volumes have attempted to assimilate and organize a great deal of what is known about waterfowl that occur in North America, in some instances through 1973. There are oversights and omissions. There is also a welcome and very significant increment of original material to plug holes that existed in early drafts and expand the overall coverage. Now that information is accumulating at an unprecedented rate and concepts are being revised even before they have become widely established, whether various matters are communicated adequately or correctly becomes a nagging problem. Authors (like editors) constantly revise their opinions and change their minds. Example: the usual concept of territory does not fit the Anatidae; a flexible concept continued evolving even while this work was in preparation. So treatment varies not only with subject but also with author, not necessarily always being consistent, even where that would be possible, nor always correct. Then, too, there is a direct ratio between the number of persons consulted on any matter and the number of alterations and compromises proposed. When a manuscript is sent out for review, many an expert sees its contents another way, or would switch the sequence of treatment, or wants more emphasis on his specialty. Readers always want more information. "And further, by these, my son, be admonished; of the making of many books there is no end; and much study is a weariness of the flesh" (*Ecclesiastes* 12:2).

I have been fortunate in acquiring various scarce Russian publications from the late Professor Hans Johansen, of Copenhagen, and many of the more recent ones through the long-continued kindness of the late Professor Leonid A. Portenko, of Leningrad, and in having Leon Kelso as a translator. Special thanks are due the Canadian Wildlife Service for loan of various unpublished translations, to Mrs. Roxy Laybourne for overseeing the translation of a paper from the Japanese, and to Paul A. Stewart for translating a long German paper.

I find it rather difficult to explain the nature and extent of having become imprinted on others who, metaphorically speaking, have painted enduring canvases with a proper brush. One develops a humble—at times awesome—respect for the energy and enthusiasm of Millais, the broad erudition of J. C. Phillips, the cheerful industriousness of Bent, the expertise of Schiøler joined with the great talent of Larsen, the dependability and discipline of Jourdain, Tucker, Ticehurst, Witherby, and Meinhertzhagen (in Witherby 1939), the insights and common sense of Tougarinov, the summing up without exceeding the facts by Isakov and Ptushenko (in Dementiev and Gladkov), the precision of the Kurodas, the empathy of Delacour, and dedication of Scott. They are prominent among the many who have influenced the shape and contents of these waterfowl volumes.

Albany, New York   R.S.P.
December 1973

CONTENTS

(List of literature cited in this volume
is combined with that of volume 3
and precedes the index in volume 3.)

x

COLOR PLATES

All plates of downy waterfowl are in this volume, but note that, except for whistling ducks and dabblers, text for the species illustrated on the last two plates is in volume 3.

INTRODUCTION

GENERAL REMARKS

The general remarks in volume 1 apply to volumes 2 and 3 also, with the emendation that there is more information of a statistical nature now available on waterfowl, which is utilized to a considerable extent. Because of advances in knowledge, and because of the special characteristics of waterfowl, some new introductory matter is necessary. Most of this consists of clarification or definitions which in some measure are at variance with or supplement the approach used in volume 1.

But first, the information explosion. As related to waterfowl, this had its real beginnings in the 1930s. It is now a deluge of tomes on particular facets of the subject and an outpouring of other items ranging from papers in technical media through in-house progress reports to memoranda circulated in multiple copies. There are files of valuable but unanalyzed data. Although a physical distinction between published (however defined) and unpublished might be formulated, it would not be very relevant any more. The distinction is blurred. One needs to be cognizant of the fugitive stuff because some of it is valuable. Even the material in technical sources is excessive in quantity (why independently redescribe one tracheal apparatus half a dozen times?) and uneven in quality. Although control at the source is essentially a philosophical question, one must recognize that there is considerable justification for a number of papers along fairly similar lines on some waterfowl topics, because of regional variation within some aspects of the total biology of waterfowl that relate to local problems of maintaining their welfare. Yet the Anatidae are already the best-known avian family. At least in the Northern Hemisphere, they also are the most administered, in numerous ways are economically the most important, and continue to be the most studied. The upshot is that, even with present data-retrieval methods, nobody, nor any agency, has convenient access to extant information. One obvious result has been a trend toward symposia on single species, but these have not always been as fruitful as anticipated.

Because of the species included, these volumes tend to be more management oriented than their predecessor. Nevertheless, one should seek elsewhere for particular information on such topics as controlling waterfowl damage to agricultural crops, habitat improvement, hunting methods, aviculture, domestication, parasites, diseases, lead poisoning, biocide studies, navigation, internal anatomy, genetics, and so on. Furthermore, in the Nearctic, a sort of jargon has evolved which, because of the vagaries of language, may never become established on a Holarctic or broader basis. For example, appropriate information can be communicated without such labeling as "harvest" (a euphemism for retrieved hunting kill) or "productivity" (estimated annual shootable population increment), and without calling a ♀ Mallard a "hen," although both sexes are also "ducks."

1

HIGHER TAXONOMIC CATEGORIES

Within the modern Anseriformes, the arrangement of the Anatidae in subfamilies, tribes, and broad genera, as monographed in 3 volumes by Delacour (1954, 1956, 1959), appears to be generally satisfactory and now is widely adopted. The allocation of "aberrant" forms continues to be debated, but the proposed transfer of a monotypic genus *Thalassornis* as far as from the stifftail tribe to the whistling ducks is exceptional. Some of the earlier suggested departures from Delacour were discussed by him in a final chapter of an additional volume (Delacour 1964), for the most part without adopting them. For various departures that were proposed in the 1960s and for an interesting short history of the classification of the Order, the reader is referred to C. G. Sibley and Ahlquist (1972). Generally speaking, in a relatively homogeneous group such as the waterfowl one encounters somewhat different—but certainly just as many —difficulties in defining and arranging more and smaller genera as when dealing with fewer and larger ones. The latter approach, which emphasizes relationships rather than differences, seems preferable.

SPECIES TREATMENT

The main purpose of these volumes is to present accounts of species. In the case of those occurring regularly in any numbers in the Nearctic area, the goal is to have all topics relating to a species integrated and complete enough so that the reader can determine what a bird of either sex, or of any annual increment to the population (cohort), looks like and is doing at any time of year. This has been achieved rather satisfactorily sometimes, but in other cases only a start has been made.

DESCRIPTION   **Plumage**   This word, capitalized, is used in a special arbitrary sense: as the exact equivalent of "feather generation." In behavior studies, a bird may be described as flapping its wings or making a short flight; however, when Wing-flap and Short flight are stereotyped (as displays), this is indicated by capitalizing. The use of *Plumage* is an extension of this principle; the use of plumage (not capitalized) is avoided, the total vestiture of a bird being termed its feathering.

Sequence   After an initial diagnosis, the definitive or "final" Plumages of ♂ and ♀ are described first, irrespective of whether the birds are capable of breeding when this Plumage is first acquired. That is, the definitive cycle is described first. In our Northern Hemisphere, in waterfowl having more than 1 Plumage/cycle (and excepting the stifftails), the "display" Plumage (which does not consist of the entire feathering) is acquired in fall. Commonly (*Bucephala* is an exception) this Plumage is succeeded, in the ♀, by the corresponding portion of Basic Plumage in spring, i.e., before "breeding" (meaning nesting and its attendant biology) begins. The ♀ is not in "display" Plumage when "breeding." There still is much misunderstanding about such simple matters.

The name of a Plumage is followed, in parentheses, by a statement of the feathering it includes, thus defining it. I believe that, on this scale, this is more or less an innovation in ornithological literature. Then usually there follows the approximate period of time the Plumage normally is worn—the dates of molting by which it is acquired and later succeeded by the next feather generation. After a Plumage is described, any feathering that is retained from a previous generation (Plumage) is mentioned, thus completing the inventory of what the bird is wearing (its total vestiture). One then can visualize the appearance of the bird in its entirety.

Next follows description on day of hatching, or reference to a colored illustration.

Then the predefinitive Plumages are described in temporal sequence, from the earliest (Juvenal) onward. Here a choice lies between describing all Plumages for one sex and then all for the other, or describing each successive cycle for both sexes. The latter alternative is followed, the idea being that—at least in waterfowl—it is preferable to keep the descriptions of the sexes, when of approximately the same chronological age, close together. After all, considerable waterfowl literature relates more to cohorts than to sexes. (For full discussion see chapter 2 in *Avian Biology*, ed. by D. S. Farner and J. R. King, N.Y.: Academic Press, 1972.)

Tertials is a term applied collectively to several innermost secondaries, which usually differ from the others in some respect. In waterfowl, however, there is no consistent difference, nor any boundary, delimiting them; therefore, in the present text, these feathers usually are referred to simply as the innermost secondaries.

Age In some waterfowl studies, particularly in analyses of band-recovery (or ringing) data, the fixed point in time is the beginning of the calendar year. A bird arbitrarily is designated a first-year bird or a yearling in the balance of the calendar year in which it hatched; then it is a 2-year-old during the next calendar year, and so on. The alternative is to use, as the fixed point in time, the known or assumed date of hatching; after that, the bird is a yearling for 12 months, a 2-year-old the next 12 months, and so on—i.e., the actual chronological age is known or estimated. To avoid confusion, the latter is used except where otherwise stated in this volume; dating, where given, is based on actual or assumed chronological age. It is recognized, of course, that birds hatched throughout a long season tend to get into much closer synchrony later on, as though they were nearer the same actual age.

Illustrations Almost all of the text figures plus half the color plates are based on layouts prepared by the editor, using any relevant source material but with emphasis on his own photographs. The layouts, with reference material and instructions attached, were forwarded to R. M. Mengel. After the text figures had been done, Xerox copies were made. Any corrections deemed advisable were indicated on these copies, which then were returned to the artist, who altered his originals accordingly. The colored figures of downy young on day of hatching were done direct from life, over a period of more than a decade, by Colleen H. Nelson. She then made up the composite plates by copying these originals.

Color terminology The color chart and names included in volume 1 are used throughout. The colors are correct in all copies of the chart except that "rufous" is consistently too pale.

Measurements There is a problem with WING. It is measured from the flesh at the "bend" to tip of the longest primary feather, but there are several methods: **1a** flattened or **1b** straightened (against a straight measuring surface); **2** over the curve of unflattened wing, i.e., an arc; and **3** across chord of the arc—along an imaginary straight line from bend of wing to tip of longest primary of unflattened wing. Since the long feathers tend to be curved in 2 different planes (but less so in waterfowl than, for example, owls), flattening the wing removes the curve in one plane, while straightening the feathers is

3

an attempt to remove it in both planes. The wing when flattened does not measure quite the same as when measured over the curve, but the difference is rather slight. The third method (chord), by definition, produces a shorter measurement. Generally speaking, it is better to standardize by using the first method (flattening) on all birds, making departures in special cases, and in any paper or volume that includes measurements, stating the method used. And although it is difficult to flatten waterfowl wings satisfactorily, especially of the larger birds, this method is used in the present volume in all series of measurements initialed ETS. But frequently, following measurements by ETS, another series from the literature is cited, in which measurements were made in some other way and this method is stated, thus calling the reader's attention to differences in method. When citing someone else's work, it has not always been possible to be certain of the method used. One does, however, come to associate names with methods. Examples: Schiøler and the present volume—flattened; Witherby—over the curve; Friedmann, J. C. Phillips—across chord.

Hybrids These, in a strict sense, are crosses between species. If the Common Mallard and North American Black Duck are considered separate species, a cross between them is a hybrid; if they are regarded as subspecies of a single species, the progeny of a mixed mating are termed intergrades. It is inexact and antiscientific to describe "crosses" between breeds of domestic fowl (*Gallus gallus*), or even between regional populations within a wild species, as in flickers (*Colaptes*), as hybrids. Such usage is rejected here.

VOICE   Most waterfowl give the impression of having a rather limited repertoire of distinct vocalizations. The more typical calls are fairly well known and their characteristics can usually be communicated via verbal description with reasonable effectiveness. Yet it has become evident, in some *Anas* species, for example, that, depending on the situation, the ♀ may have perhaps a dozen or more vocalizations that can be defined. That is, if they were recorded on tape and then played, with the particular circumstances of occurrence of each described, they might be labeled. That is not to say, however, that a written description of each would be meaningful or useful to readers of these volumes.

DISTRIBUTION   According to the late James Lee Peters of the Museum of Comparative Zoology at Harvard, "birds have wings and sometimes use them." His statement has continued relevance.

After some maps of waterfowl distribution had been prepared, similar to those used in volume 1, the editor decided to disregard them and to use various approaches depending on circumstances. In the present volumes (unlike their predecessor), for Holarctic species the maps usually are restricted to the Nearctic portion of the range. The accompanying text, written for all species by the editor, assumes more importance because it includes significant information supplemental to the maps; it is not restricted to the Nearctic. Again, in waterfowl there are special problems. A species often has a divided winter range, narrow main lines of travel, and sometimes quite restricted nesting areas. The Pintail is mapped rather traditionally, showing overall nesting and winter distribution and where these overlap. The Tundra Swan map emphasizes restricted areas of normal occurrence seasonally, including during migrations. Two Blue/Snow Goose maps are of the latter sort and, although they are based on much more information than that of the Tundra Swan and have already gone through one revision, they may be partially obsolete by the time this volume appears. The Canada Goose has a separate map for each subspecies recognized, showing usual winter range, nesting range, and intervening occurrence—and sometimes, when feasible, occurrence during molt migration and the related molting. The complexities of waterfowl mapping are such that several maps or several overlays could be used for each species; in our current state of knowledge, however, fewer maps and more text seem appropriate—the more so because distribution is changing constantly.

In North America north of Mexico, plus Hawaii, nearly 19,000 persons participated in the 1971 Christmas bird count, and the number of birds reportedly seen included 583 species and over 64,500,000 individuals. This included, of course, large numbers of waterfowl. Mentioning these figures is a crude way of indicating that information on waterfowl occurrences, for example, now consists of so many scattered items derived from such varied conditions and sources that it is neither practical nor desirable to cite all the material that influences the preparation of maps and/or text. To do so would at least quadruple the number of entries in the list of literature cited at the end of volume 3.

MIGRATION   By and large, migration **routes** or aerial **paths** are wider than **corridors,** although they may coincide sometimes. The corridor concept of F. C. Bellrose is especially applicable to species that have narrow traditional lines of travel. In some of the popular literature the term flyway has come into use as a synonym of migration route. This is erroneous, since a flyway is a very large area containing nesting, migratory, and wintering occurrence of a conglomerate of species and is so designated for administrative purposes.

In the text, no adjustment in reported information is made to allow for the fact that the **International Date Line** passes through Bering Strait; i.e., dates on the American side must be advanced by one day to obtain the corresponding date on the Siberian side.

BANDING STATUS   The main figures given pertain to the joint efforts of the Canadian Wildlife Service and U.S. Fish and Wildlife Service: number of birds banded, number of recoveries, and main places of banding in diminishing order of number of individuals banded. Since Greenland is included in the present treatise *in toto*, the results of Danish ringing (banding) in that area are given. No attempt is made to give complete coverage for additional areas, but there is some further information. For example, it seems worthwhile to mention some of the work done in the Palearctic on species that also occur in the Nearctic region.

REPRODUCTION   Activities related to reproduction that occur in any season are included. The fact that waterfowl displays and pair formation commonly occur on winter range—far distant from nesting areas—is only one of the reasons why this general topic must reckon with most or all of the year. Durable pair bonds, long main-

5

tained, and sometimes renewed family bonds, and related matters, extend coverage around the calendar.

Displays, when defined, are named in SMALL CAPS; elsewhere the display name has its first letter capitalized. These are entirely arbitrary devices. (Compare with Plumage, discussed earlier.)

HABITS   If older treatises are consulted, it will be found that much of what customarily was reported under this heading actually relates to reproduction. Information on other activities which are more or less characteristic of a particular species proves to be elusive and rather limited. Of that which exists, a considerable amount is omitted—for example, published figures on depths of diving have not been compiled. A miscellany of information is included; sometimes duplication is minimized by devoting much space under one species to a topic, and then cross-referencing. Example: adverse seasons in the arctic are treated mainly under the King Eider.

Waterfowl numbers   One becomes wary of precise figures, or even of rounded numbers, of individuals in various species. Estimates or counts are very inclusive and accurate for a few waterfowl, but decidedly otherwise for most. Winter inventories, assuming they are taken the same way annually, are a very useful index of relative numbers. Sometimes they are treated as neat figures in the popular press, but they are not precise and all-inclusive. A recent mystery as to the seasonal whereabouts of such supposedly conspicuous birds as some 50,000 wintering white geese (Greater Snows) is something to ponder. In the literature on the Palearctic there are concurrent "counts" of numbers of a species that are at variance to the extent of millions of individuals.

FOOD   It has been evident for some time that the summaries of information prepared for this volume were inadequate in coverage, especially of the non-English literature, as of the time they were prepared. They have been supplemented considerably, and some accounts have been more or less updated. But even if they were complete, they might better be regarded as rough inventories, sometimes mainly of undigestible items or portions of items swallowed. Now that it is recognized that soft foods may be digested very rapidly, hence may be missed unless a bird is shot when actively feeding and its digestive tract immediately preserved, a reappraisal of just what is ingested at various ages and seasons has begun. The older work has lasting value as background material, but the direction of studies has shifted.

ORDER ANSERIFORMES

WATERFOWL   These are some characteristics of the modern species, which comprise a single avian family: they supplement the characteristics—mainly anatomical—that were listed in *Handbook* 1 19 where this Order was placed next to the Phoenicopteriformes (flamingos). Many facets of the anatomy and biology of waterfowl were covered at length by various authors in Delacour (1964).

Nearly worldwide in distribution, in various habitats but generally associated with water. Sexes essentially similar in appearance and 1 Plumage/cycle in the Magpie Goose (*Anseranas*), whistling ducks, swans, and geese, but often strikingly different in other species, most of which are known to have 2 Plumages/cycle; 1 (*Clangula*) has 3. The Basic Plumage is "conservative" in an evolutionary sense, i.e., different species are nearest alike when wearing it. Males tend to be larger than ♀ ♀ . The wing quills are dropped once/cycle—successively in *Anseranas* (flight maintained) and near simultaneously in all others so far as known (flying species become temporarily flightless)—except in *Biziura* and in some (probably all) *Oxyura,* in which they are dropped twice/cycle; furthermore, this matter has not been investigated in all of the stifftail tribe.

Nasal glands are well developed in saltwater dwellers. The bill in waterfowl is more or less lamellate,—but modified to serrate in *Mergus*—and is covered with a soft skin; the terminal nail varies from obscure to very prominent, even hooked. Except for geese and whistling ducks, most have marked sexual dimorphism in tracheal apparatus; this includes an elongated, convoluted trachea in *Anseranas* and a bony bulla in at least most ducks except the stifftails, in which there is an air sac connected to the trachea and which varies structurally with species. Most species have the front toes fully webbed, but this is reduced in a few (greatly in *Anseranas*); the hind toe, lobed or otherwise, is set higher than the front toes.

In most nontropical species at least, pair formation occurs long before nesting and often far from nesting areas. The pair bond varies from lifelong (swans, geese, at least some whistling ducks) to very brief or nonexistent (as in Muscovies). There is a very high order of social and family organization in some (geese, swans), with long-maintained family bonds. Many are very long-lived. Most nest on the surface of the ground, solitarily to colonially, but a few use terrestrial cavities and some others use tree cavities. Probably most, aside from whistling ducks, surround the eggs with a protective nest down from the venter of the ♀ . A few species are partially, and at least one wholly, parasitic in egg laying. Incubation is by the ♀ only, with some exceptions, periods 22–35 (mostly 23–28) days. Very few species are double- or multiple-brooded.

Depending on the species, waterfowl eat a wide range of plant and animal foods and their bills are specialized variably, depending on nature of food and manner of feeding. Most of them ingest considerable grit. Many dive expertly, 1 (*Clangula*) to depths exceeding 50 meters. Some use only the feet in diving, others their more-or-less-opened wings also. Many nontropical species are highly migratory. Quite a number have an additional so-called molt migration—to a molting place where they become flightless. A few species are flightless. A few are very awkward on land.

The Anseriformes are an ancient group. Fossil waterfowl are known from the Cretaceous (*Gallornis*) and Eocene (*Romainvillia, Eonessa*), and fossils assignable to

7

present-day subfamilies of the family Anatidae date from the Oligocene. As to N. Am., the fossil and prehistoric species were catalogued by Wetmore (1956) and those of the Pleistocene again by Wetmore (1959). There is a worldwide descriptive catalog of fossil forms by Howard (in Delacour 1964) and, again worldwide, a catalog that lists both fossil remains and those from archaeological sites by Brodkorb (1964a). There are about 150 modern species, many of which are known from the Pleistocene.

FAMILY ANATIDAE

SWANS, GEESE, DUCKS   Within the Anseriformes this is the only modern family; see above. The present volume includes 18 of the genera, which are discussed next; then the 63 species accounts follow one another uninterruptedly through volumes 2 and 3.

Subfamily Anserinae

Tribe Dendrocygnini

Dendrocygna WHISTLING DUCKS   Eight species. An ancient and homogeneous group of somewhat gooselike waterfowl; neck fairly long; legs long, the tarsi reticulate in front; downies have distinctive patterns—contrasty and clear-cut; 1 Plumage/cycle; slight to no sexual dimorphism in feathering; few and simple displays; durable pair bonds (probably in all species); drakes, at least in some species, participate in care of young; both sexes have whistling voices. All species were figured in color on a single plate in Delacour (1954). There are captive crosses within the genus, but none known, even in captivity, with other waterfowl. Most are maintained easily in captivity. In our area: 3 species, including 1 accidental.

Tribe Anserini

Cygnus TRUE SWANS   Largest waterfowl; tarsi short and reticulated; neck as long or longer than body; the trachea, which lacks a bulla, forms a loop inside the sternum in some species; downies of all species, including the Black-necked and Black Swans of the S. Hemisphere, are remarkably similar in coloring—white or very pale; from hatching (in *C. atrata*) or after early life, the lores are bare; 1 Plumage/cycle; early Plumages are more or less gray-brown or gray; definitive Plumages are white or black and white. Swans are long-lived and have lifelong pair bonds. It seems preferable to treat the swans as 1 genus (with subgenera), rather than as 2 genera. Captive crosses within the genus, also with a number of species of geese, are well known. All the swans breed in captivity. The 2 species *cygnus* and *buccinator* comprise a superspecies and only *columbianus* has recognizable subspecies. Four species now occur in N. Am.: *cygnus* (local), *buccinator* and *columbianus* (widespread), and *olor* (introduced).

Anser TRUE GEESE   Nine species. Northern Hemisphere distribution. Smallish to very large waterfowl (only the swans are larger); bill high, narrow, laterally serrated, and (except *A. cygnoides*) more or less highly colored; legs and feet brightly colored; downies are more or less bicolored but not strongly patterned; 1 Plumage/cycle; sexes similar; feathering varies from mostly white to somber to contrastingly patterned (includes black); as in swans, pair bonds are durable and family bonds often of long duration; displays are few and simple; the true geese are highly social, also "clannish," i.e., there are more or less discrete units; some have compli-

cated migrations; all walk well and most are primarily terrestrial feeders. Two species
(*A. anser* and *cygnoides*) have been completely domesticated and all others have bred
in captivity. Hybrids between *Anser* species are fertile, but rarely are crosses with
other geese or other waterfowl. The Emperor (*A. canagicus*) forms a good bridge
between *Anser* (subgenus) and *Chen* (subgenus)*. Five species in our area.

  Branta BRANT AND ALLIES Five species. Northern Hemisphere, including
Hawaii. Very similar to the true geese but differ morphologically as follows: bill
smoother (serrations reduced or concealed) and very dark (to black); legs and feet
black; feathering richer in coloring, with more elaborate pattern that includes black
and white; head–neck conspicuously and contrastingly patterned; downies more distinctly patterned; 1 Plumage/cycle; sexes similar. They are very similar to the true
geese in their general biology but are more rapid in movements and have somewhat
higher-pitched and harsher voices. The Canada Goose (*B. canadensis*) is unique
among waterfowl because of its tremendous geographical size variation; the Hawaiian
Goose (*B. sandvicensis*) is unique in the tribe in being a tropical-island resident. All
species except the Brant (*B. bernicla*) breed readily in captivity. Hybrids (mostly in
captivity) are within the genus, also with *Anser*, *Cygnus*, and allegedly a few other
waterfowl. Three species are native to our area, and another (*B. ruficollis*) may have
occurred as a straggler.

  Subfamily Anatinae

  Tribe Tadornini

  Tadorna SHELD-DUCKS Seven species. One or more species native to all
continents (and New Zealand), except N. Am. Moderate- to large-sized ducks; somewhat gooselike proportions, with relatively long legs; quite flattened (ducklike) bill;
downies have striking black and white pattern; in all species studied, 2 Plumages/cycle;
rich coloring, including patterned wing, and slight to pronounced sexual
dimorphism—all species figured in color on pl. 13 in Delacour (1954) and the genus
was discussed by Delacour (1970); lifelong pair bond; the nest is in concealed places,
such as holes; not colonial; more or less omnivorous; breed readily in captivity, where a
number of species have crossed. One species now probably is extinct. Four of the
others comprise a superspecies. One species has straggled to our area; another, although recorded, may not have occurred naturally.

  Tribe Anatini

  Anas TRUE DABBLING DUCKS Over 40 species. Nearly cosmopolitan, including occurrence on some oceanic islands. Small to moderate-sized ducks; rather
short-tailed (with a few exceptions) and short-legged; hind toe not lobed; wings more or
less pointed; on the secondaries a metallic (but sometimes pale) speculum; sexes differ
in voice; downies are bicolored, dark above and brownish, buffy, or even white

*This is contrary to the A. O. U. *Check-list* committee (*Auk* **90** 413–14, April 1973), which
maintains *Chen* as a genus. The *Handbook* sections are authored by individuals. In the present
matter the viewpoint adopted is accepted and used by various waterfowl authorities and we believe it will continue to prevail. RSP FGC

ventrally—all, in effect, tending to be variations of the downy Mallard (*A. platy-rhynchos*) pattern; 2 Plumages/cycle in all species studied; the various species forage in, or at least prefer, shallow fresh or brackish water; most have seasonal pair bonds (sometimes renewed) and the ♀ tends the young, but in some tropical and southern species the bond is maintained longer and the drake remains with the family. The most comprehensive way to describe the genus is to refer to the 174 pages, or nearly all, of vol. 2 (1956) of Delacour, devoted to it. He then recognized 38 species (but later excluded *Calonetta*), achieving this low number in part by lumping *A. diazi*, *A. ful-vigula*, and some others as subspecies of *A. platyrhynchos*. (See "Distribution" of Common Mallard for discussion of this matter.) There are some clear-cut groups within the genus, notably the wigeons. Practically all species do well in captivity. There are numerous interspecific, and some intergeneric, wild hybrids, and a much longer list of those occurring in captivity. The Common Mallard is the ancestor of all domestic strains of ducks, excepting Muscovies. Seventeen species occur in our area, of which 4 are stragglers.

Tribe Somaterini

Polysticta SMALL EIDER   One species. Primarily Bering Sea and adjoining areas. A small marine duck, differing from the large eiders in many respects, such as: bill all dark and of "normal" ducklike shape, but lateral portions of upper mandible are fleshy and the nail at end is not well defined; drake's tracheal bulla disproportion-ately small and trachea increases in diameter distally; very different color pattern, the drake's back being black in Alt. Plumage, and all Plumages of both sexes include some brown; scapulars downcurved; speculum metallic; legs and feet very dark. Has not bred in captivity. No known hybrids.

Somateria LARGE EIDERS   Three species. Holarctic distribution. Middle-sized to large marine ducks; bill more or less attenuated, highly colored at least season-ally, with nostrils near midpoint, and large and definite nail; the tracheal bulla of drakes is fairly sizable, with an expanded chamber; downies are quite somber-colored, each species with a distinctive head pattern; 2 Plumages/cycle, with the modified long scapulars in both sexes molted once/cycle; no speculum; in the definitive cycle, ♀ ♀ are more or less barred black and browns in both Plumages, while the drake is predomi-nantly black in Basic and black and white in Alt.; innermost secondaries down-curved—strikingly in the drake; rather elaborate displays; highly colonial (*mollissima*) to typically a scattered nester (*spectabilis*). At least 2 species have bred in captivity (but *spectabilis* rarely). Known wild hybrids are of *spectabilis–mollissima* parentage. In Iceland and a few other places *mollissima* has, seasonally, a symbiotic relationship with man. All 3 species occur in our area.

Tribe Aythyini

Aythya BROAD-BILLED POCHARDS   Eighteen species. Widespread on con-tinents (except Africa and S. Am., where only a local visitor) and on some islands. Compact diving ducks with broad bills, large feet set well back (waddling gait ashore), and short tails. The drake has a rather elaborate tracheal bulla, angled rather than rounded, and with external membranous windows. Downies have bicolored pattern, darkish to very dark dorsally, buffy to yellowish to white ventrally, and no facial stripes; 2 Plumages/cycle; striking sexual dimorphism in some, but in 1 group both sexes are ♀-like (browns predominate)—reduced sexual dimorphism; coloring variable in Alt. Plumage, but large areas of feathering tend to be quite uniformly colored—black (or very dark), browns, white in drakes, muted browns or grays plus white in ♀♀; sex for sex, the species tend to be very similar in Basic Plumage; secondaries may be pale or mostly white, but no metallic speculum; seasonal pair bonds; moderately elaborate displays, the Head-throw in particular differing with species; most are at least semicolonial nesters; several hybridize in the wild, the resulting crosses sometimes resembling a species within the genus but other than either parent; most species have bred in captivity. The broad-billed pochards consist of 4 distinct groups; 8 species are on our list, 5 being widespread, 2 local but evidently regular, and 1 rare (2 individuals captured over a century ago).

Tribe Cairinini

Aix NORTHERN WOOD DUCKS   Two species. Nearctic and e. Palearctic. Small trim ducks with small bill having large nail; eyes large (both species prefer shaded waters, such as forest streams and ponds); they perch readily in trees; the drake's tracheal bulla is left-sided and thin walled; downies are sharply and contrastingly patterned; 2 Plumages/cycle, Basic and Alt. being very different in drakes and very similar in ♀♀; drakes have very "ornamental" Alt. Plumage, i.e., elaborate pattern and variegated coloring, hence are considered the most beautiful of waterfowl; the innermost secondaries are modified (truncated), being enlarged as dorsal "sails" in 1 species; fairly elaborate displays; solitary tree-hole nesters; at least 1 species (*sponsa*) is double- or multiple-brooded in warm climates; the 2 species have hybridized in captivity, possibly also in a feral state; both breed readily in captivity. One species in our area.

Cairina GREATER WOOD DUCKS   Three species. Subtropical and tropical areas around the globe. Large, broad-winged, short-legged, tree-perching ducks. The drake's tracheal bulla is left-sided and irregular in shape (so far as reported). Downies have a simple bicolored pattern (so far as known); evidently 2 Plumages/cycle, although authors claim only 1 (no careful study has been made); sexes quite similar in appearance; wing very patterned, the upper coverts being distinctively colored; ♂ much larger than ♀; a bony knob at bend of wing; drakes, seasonally, have caruncles or a swelling at base of bill; sedentary flocking habits; prefer marshes and ponds; hole nesters; scant data on reproduction; evidently multiple sexual nexus (successive polygamy or promiscuity) to single sexual nexus (seasonal monogamy?), depending on species; the Muscovy (*C. moschata*), in domestication, is heavier than in the wild, occurs in various color strains, and hybridizes readily with domestic strains of Mallard (the crosses are sterile). All 3 species do well in captivity, where they are aggressive toward other waterfowl. One species, the Muscovy, occurs locally in our area in a feral state.

Tribe Mergini

Melanitta SCOTERS   Three species. Circumboreal. Moderate-sized to rather large marine diving ducks, capable of deep diving, and with awkward gait

11

ashore. The bill of drakes is swollen or modified and elaborately patterned and/or colored, which is reflected on a reduced scale in ♀♀; in both sexes, bill coarsely serrated and with very large nail. Downies are very plain-colored and with blended pattern, more or less sooty with white cheeks and part of venter, at least the upper breast being dark; 2 Plumages/cycle; often prolonged molting; drakes mostly (to entirely) black in Alt. Plumage, ♀♀ largely gray-browns or darker in all seasons; marine most of year, but nest (except in a few places) inland near fresh water, in more or less scattered groups; complicated migrations; fairly elaborate displays; extremely varied voices; drakes of 2 species have a large, more or less bony tracheal swelling and small and slightly asymmetrical bony bulla, the other species (*nigra*) has part of the trachea slightly enlarged proximally and a hardly noticeable enlargement of the bony junction with the bronchi; as to hybrids, 1 species is said to have crossed with *Bucephala* and to have formed a pair bond with *Somateria;* all are difficult to maintain in captivity. All 3 species occur in our area.

Camptorhynchus LABRADOR DUCK   Northern Atlantic coastal region of N. Am. Rather smallish duck, about the size of the Wigeon. Bill with a kind of overlying plate at top base, concealed coarse serrations, hooked nail, and distal margins of upper mandible fleshy and pendulous; the drake's tracheal bulla had a large round chamber on the left side; evidently 2 Plumages/cycle; feathers of cheeks (drake in Alt. Plumage) stiffened and bristly (as in some eiders); pattern and coloring of feathering somewhat scoterlike; see Humphrey and Butsch (1958) for some further information. Extinct.

Histrionicus HARLEQUIN   Iceland, Greenland, ne. and nw. N. Am., and e. Siberia, in winter farther southward. Small stoutish duck, adapted to turbulent and rushing waters, at sea and inland; bill short, narrow, with small membranous lobe at gape; the drake's trachea has a constriction, also a large rounded bony bulla without membranous windows; downies have a rather simple bicolored pattern without dark breast band; 2 Plumages/cycle; great sexual dimorphism in Alt. Plumage, the drake having very complicated pattern and elaborate coloring, the other Plumages in the species being somber grays and gray-browns with somewhat patchy head pattern; a terrestrial and not an obligate cavity nester; highly social; quite difficult to maintain in captivity; no known hybrids.

Clangula OLDSQUAW or LONG-TAILED DUCK   Holarctic. Small tundra-nesting marine duck, capable of diving to very great depths—see Kuroda (1959) for anatomical specializations; small stout bill with broad nail; unusual among our ducks in that the margin of feathering extends from the gape in a nearly straight line diagonally forward up side of upper mandible; the drake's trachea is enlarged and flattened proximally, while the bony bulla is large, expanded to the left, quite kidney-shaped, and with a single very large external membrane; downies have a fairly simple bicolored pattern which includes a dark breast band; much sexual dimorphism; so far as known, the only waterfowl having 3 Plumages/cycle—and concomitant complicated molting; fairly complicated pattern—of near-black, browns, grays, and white in Alt. and plainer in Basic and Suppl. Plumage; central tail feathers greatly elongated in the drake, slightly in the duck; displays, as yet, not well known; usually a scattered nester. Few have lived very long in captivity, where a drake is said to have crossed with *Anas castanea.*

Bucephala GOLDENEYES and BUFFLEHEAD Three species. Holarctic. Rather smallish to diminutive diving ducks (a few stifftails are the only ones smaller than the Bufflehead); inland in summer and mostly on shallow salt water in other seasons; bill fairly high at base, with large nostril and considerably hooked nail; in the goldeneyes there is a midtracheal swelling and the bulla at inner end is large, decidedly asymmetrical, and with an elongated membranous window, but in the Bufflehead the trachea lacks the swelling and the bulla is rather simple and not markedly asymmetrical; downies have a clear-cut bicolored pattern—sooty cap, upperparts (with some white spots), and breast band, the remainder white; 2 Plumages/cycle; the ♀ is "delayed" and gradual in molting into Basic head–body, i.e., not prior to nesting; much sexual dimorphism—drakes with clear-cut pattern of very dark metallic coloring plus white, ♀ ♀ more blended, browns, grays, white; all species have brightly colored feet; displays are elaborate and well known; the high degree of territoriality in this genus probably is related to competition for nesting cavities—see discussion by Erskine (1972a); all are obligate tree-cavity nesters, except *B. islandica*, which will nest in a variety of situations in the absence of natural tree cavities. The 2 goldeneyes have crossed in the wild and *B. clangula* allegedly with several other genera; a drake *B. albeola* is said to have formed a pair bond with a ♀ *B. clangula*, also to have crossed in captivity with 1 *Aythya* species. All 3 species can be maintained in captivity, where 1 has bred quite often, another a few times. All 3 species are in our area.

Mergus MERGANSERS Seven species—5 N. and 2 S. Hemisphere— including 2 believed extinct. Elongated, streamlined waterfowl adapted to chasing such rapid and agile prey as small fishes; bills are long, slender, almost tubular, with backward-pointing conical serrations, except that the bill is more "ducklike" in shape in the Smew; in all species in which the tracheal apparatus is known, there is more or less of an enlargement in the trachea, while the drake's bony bulla is remarkably large and asymmetrical, with a large circular membranous window; downies of several species have considerable brown in their heads, but others are neutral-colored (includes the Smew), and all known species are dark dorsally with lateral white spots and white venter; 2 Plumages/cycle in all species occurring in N. Am. (and probably the others); in our species the ♀ tends to have a somewhat delayed and prolonged Prebasic head–body molt, i.e., a trend in the same direction as ♀ *Bucephala*; much sexual dimorphism in N. Hemisphere species, the drake in Alt. having contrasty clear-cut pattern that includes very dark plus some to a great deal of whitish or white; the ♀ ♀ have more or less brown heads, gray upperparts, and white venter; head feathering enlarged or crested in both sexes in Alt. Plumage; 2 S. Hemisphere species are more somber, with greatly reduced sexual dimorphism; displays of our species are well known; long incubation period, as in *Bucephala*; hybrids are within the genus, or with *Bucephala*, also allegedly with 3 additional genera in captivity. Not easily kept long in captivity where, however, 3 species have bred. Three species are widespread in our area; a fourth occurs in small numbers and possibly may breed.

Tribe Oxyurini

Oxyura RUDDY group and MASKED DUCK Seven species. Widely distributed on 5 continents. Small to diminutive "foreshortened" ducks with comparatively

13

stiff, long tails and somewhat upturned bills (at least seasonally blue in drakes); they not only dive expertly but also settle beneath the surface like grebes; primarily vegetarians, in quiet (usually fresh) water. Drakes lack a tracheal bulla, but probably all have an inflatable air sac, opening into the trachea and structurally different in the various species. Downies are rather plain in coloring, but most have contrasty facial striping; they have large legs and feet; 2 Plumages/cycle known in several species and probably occur in all; unlike any other waterfowl occurring in N. Am., the 2 head–body molts, in the duck as well as the drake, occur in opposite seasons and Alt. is worn in the nesting season; it also is known that in 3 Ruddy species the wings are molted twice/cycle, a condition so far known in only one other waterfowl, the Musk Duck (*Biziura lobata*) of Australia; much sexual dimorphism in coloring; in Alt. Plumage, drakes have much black on their heads and reddish brown on their bodies; ♀ ♀, also drakes in Basic, tend to have a finely broken dorsal pattern; the displays of at least 1 species (*O. jamaicensis*) are well known; the eggs, probably in all species, are very large for the size of the parent bird and clutch size is rather small; one species allegedly has crossed (in captivity) with *Aythya;* at least several species do well in captivity. One species is widespread in our area and another is local and breeds.

14

Fulvous Whistling Duck

Dendrocygna bicolor (Vieillot)

Fulvous Tree Duck of 1957 A.O.U. list. Smallish, somewhat gooselike, primarily terrestrial and wading duck having long neck and legs. All postdowny stages: lower neck to vent almost entirely a single color (tawny-cinnamon or somewhat fulvous). At least in definitive stages, feathering furrowed on side of neck. The sexes and all flying stages much alike in appearance; ♂ av. slightly larger. Tracheal apparatus rather simple though sexually dimorphic, as yet not adequately described; Heinroth (1918) mentioned it rather briefly under the name *D. fulva* and Johnsgard (1961c) illustrated one from a drake. Length of this duck 17½–20 in., wingspread to about 37, wt. probably seldom reaches 2 lb. No subspecies. *D. bicolor* and *D. arcuata* (latter occurs from Java and Philippines through parts of Australia) form a superspecies (Delacour 1954).

DESCRIPTION   One Plumage/cycle in both sexes. At what stage the rather slight sex differences in appearance first become evident is unknown. Some individual variation in coloring in both sexes and all postegg stages; beginning with Juv. Plumage it is most notable in presence (and amount) or absence of brownish red on wing coverts.
▶   ♂ ♀ Def. Basic Plumage (entire feathering), FALL to FALL; the earliest (basic II) acquired earlier (in summer) than later Basics in which the molt occurs mainly in Sept. in our area; duration of flightless period unknown, probably 3 weeks. **Bill** nearly unicolor, dark bluish slaty; **iris** dark brownish. **Head** crown nearer fuscous than chestnut (with very slight crest at occiput), its sides and part of upper neck tawny-olive with feathers margined buffy, chin nearly white; feathers from rear of crown down nape

15

blackish, forming a well-delineated stripe which is continuous in ♀ but usually interrupted on rear of head of ♂; remainder of foreneck and sides of neck whitish buff, the latter (where furrowed) with broken dark diagonal lines. **Upperparts** mantle blackish brown, the feathers with broadly rounded (toward squarish) tawny-buff ends; sides of rump and the upper tail coverts light buffy, center of rump black. **Underparts** lower neck to vent some variant of tawny-cinnamon or fulvous, the feathers inconspicuously tipped pinkish buff; on sides and flanks the feathers that overlap the folded wing are "ornamental"—long, with tapering ends, upper vane white, a dark median streak, and lower vane clouded brownish gray; under tail coverts mainly whitish. **Tail** blackish. Legs and **feet** deep bluish gray. **Wing** lesser and middle coverts usually are predominantly dark reddish brown with distal coverts of these 2 series mostly black, rest of upper wing surface black or nearly so, wing lining black. In overall appearance the ♀ has less vivid coloring than the ♂.

As in swans and geese, the flight feathers and greater primary coverts of wing are dropped almost simultaneously at onset of Prebasic molt.

AT HATCHING   See col. pl. facing p. 370. White and dark grays; no light stripe above eye; upperparts lighter than in any other whistling duck; back unspotted (usually) or with 2 or 4 white spots. Pale phase (uncommon): dark areas of head dark gray, back silvery gray.

▶   ♂ ♀ Juv. Plumage (entire feathering) fully developed at age 9–10 weeks (see "Reproduction" for some details) and, except for long-retained greater primary coverts and flight feathers of wing, quite rapidly replaced beginning some weeks (precise information lacking) thereafter. Dorsal line of lateral profile of bill nearly straight, with "practically none of the concavity so pronounced in mature birds" (Dickey and van Rossem 1923). When ducklings are about a third full size, the Juv. feathering begins to appear on pectoral–scapular area, anterior portion of flanks, and sides of face. Fully developed Juv. differs thus from succeeding Plumages: paler overall; coloring more muted; the darks are brownish, not clear black; lightest areas off-white (somewhat buffy); light feather tipping on mantle narrower, with muted coloring, and varies from poorly delineated to no demarcation whatever; various feathers (most evident on dorsum) decidedly narrower in shape (ends not broadly rounded) and with comparatively loose texture. Upper coverts of wing vary with individual from having none to considerable muted reddish brown coloring.

▶   ♂ ♀ Basic I Plumage (entire feathering, except for retained Juv. greater primary coverts and flight feathers of wing) acquired in LATE FALL, usually about mid-Oct. into Nov., and retained into following SUMMER, about July. As Def. Basic except: brown feather tipping on mantle somewhat darker; feather shapes (most evident on dorsum) and texture intermediate between Juv. and Def. Basic (nearer latter); the worn, dullish, Juv. wing quills are diagnostic as long as they are retained.

Measurements 8 ♂ (from Cal., La., and Texas): BILL 44–50 mm., av. 46; WING 209–220, av. 217; TAIL 47–51, av. 50; TARSUS 54–60, av. 57.5;   4 ♀ (Cal., Texas, Argentina): BILL 45–49 mm., av. 47; WING 212–220, av. 216; TAIL 48–55, av. 51.5; TARSUS 54–59, av. 55 (ETS).

Another series 14 ♂ (Cal., Mexico): BILL 44–48.5 mm., av. 46.4; WING (across

16

chord) 196–224, av. 210.1;   14 ♀ (La., Texas, Cal., Mexico): BILL 45–48.5 mm., av. 46.8, WING (across chord) 202–225, av. 210.9 (Friedmann 1947).

Weight few data; a pair in breeding condition May 30 in La.: ♂ 747.7 gm., ♀ 771.4 (Meanley and Meanley 1959); 2 "adult" ♀ Dec. 26 in Fla.: 712 and 731 gm. (Owre 1962); on Oct. 14 in Mich. an "im." ♀ 580 gm. and an "ad." ♀ 590 (G. Hunt 1963).

Twenty-four ducklings from artificially incubated eggs weighed, on day of hatching, 24.3–33.4 gm., the mean and standard error being 27.8 ± 0.47, and standard deviation 2.29 (Smart 1965a).

Hybrids not reported in wild birds; in captivity has crossed with 5 other whistling duck species.

Geographical variation in the species nearly nil. Birds of the northernmost of the 3 disjunct (so far as now known) portions of New World range were described by Wetmore and Peters (1922) as having bill smaller and narrower and part of feathering paler (not invariably). Friedmann's (1947) study of the species throughout its world range demonstrated no appreciable differences in dimensions or coloration in any part of range. Although he maintained that the bill is smaller and narrower in the area whence these characteristics had been reported previously, a glance at his table of measurements reveals that bill size is generally variable. Using other New World specimens, Hellmayr and Conover (1948) found that all the N. Am. examples had narrow bills, but so did 8 others (from Colombia, Venezuela, and Paraguay) out of 12 from S. Am. They recognized no subspecies, nor did Delacour (1954), J. Bond (1956), or more recent authors. RSP

FIELD IDENTIFICATION   Data for our area. General appearance dark; brownish body with light area on rump, very dark wings without white patch. Flight pattern generally quite irregular—bunches of birds with no evident organization.

In flight, appears somewhat gooselike, wingbeats not rapid and noise not loud (unlike some other whistling ducks); legs extend beyond tail; long neck frequently appears to sag somewhat; upper tail coverts form conspicuous pale crescent. When alighting, stretches neck downward as do other whistling ducks, the bill nearly touching feet (Head-low-and-forward posture). When standing, tawny or fulvous ventral feathering; darkish bill, feet, and long legs; long neck; creamy white areas on certain feathers combine to form stripe along sides and flanks. In at least most of our area, not known to perch in trees.

The sexes, at least when both are present, are distinguishable in all seasons by their calls (see below). When a flock contains older age-classes of both sexes and the birds are in good view, drakes may be identifiable as such—they are somewhat larger, more vividly colored, and the dark line on crown–nape generally is broken at upper nape (it is unbroken in ♀).

A bird of ricefields, marshes, and shallows; rarely seen where water is deep. Social in all seasons. In nesting areas, tends to fly in wide circles, often swinging low over observer. In nonbreeding season the flocks vary in size, usually under 500 but occasionally to several thousand.

In s. Texas one could hardly confuse this bird with the Red-billed Whistling Duck, as latter has conspicuous white wingpatch. There and elsewhere, birds in flight at a distance possibly could be mistaken for geese or Glossy Ibises. BM

VOICE Data from La. and Texas. Noisy during daylight and darkness. Characteristic call, whether birds flying or not, a high-pitched, usually 2-syllabled (accent on 2nd) whistle, *pit-tu*, or *kit-tee* or *pee-chee*. As noted among captives, it is slightly higher pitched in ♀. It seems to have several functions, especially rallying, greeting, and alarm. A standing bird giving this call stretches neck to full height and frequently throws head upward, bill pointing vertically (Head-back posture), repeating this action with each successive call. Often a series of very short high-pitched notes follows the 2-syllabled call.

A 2nd common call, very soft and with little carrying quality, is used by birds on ground for expression of mild excitement or friendly response to presence of recognized individual. This *cup-cup-cup-cup* (duration variable) varies in pitch, frequency, and volume, depending on emotional state of caller. A captive ♀ produced a conversational effect in uttering this call and variations.

Sometimes these ducks, an instant after taking wing, utter a squealing whistle —hence the vernacular name "Mexican squealer." They cannot quack.

Still another quite distinct note is soft drawn-out *weep*, often repeated several times, probably associated with mating display.

Young maintain an almost continuous chatter. BM

HABITAT Around the world this duck occurs where summers are hot and winters mild, preferring rather shallow fresh and brackish waters. It spends much time afloat, dives readily (even the ducklings), and is a ground nester. In some areas it seems to avoid forests, but not in others. The following data pertain to *Handbook* area.

Characteristically associated with extensive prairie (formerly tall-grass) areas of contiguous ricefields during the breeding season in La.—3,000 in Jefferson Davis and Evangeline parishes in 1956 (B. Meanley), and Texas—3,500–5,000 in Brazoria Co. (Singleton 1953). Records to date show that in La. it nests in that cultivated marsh type only, where it was locally common by the 1960s. Also nests in ricefields in San Joaquin Valley, Cal., but major nesting habitat there is native marsh dominated by tule *(Scirpus)* and in Imperial Valley principally in cattail *(Typha)*. In lower Rio Grande Valley (Cameron Co., Texas), breeding birds frequent ponds and resacas usually containing cattail and water hyacinth *(Eichornia crassipes)* (B. Meanley); for additional s. Texas data, see Cottam and Glazener (1959).

For nesting in La. it evidently selects ricefields that produce a variety and abundance of preferred grass seeds (includes rice) and that provide good cover plus shallow water. Rice seed is available in spring, late summer, and fall; seeds of *Paspalum distichum, Echinochloa colonum, E. walteri, Brachiaria extensa, Cyperus iria, Caperonia palustris, Polygonum hydropiperoides*, and other aquatics mature during summer. In 1962, Vermilion Parish was the leading rice-producing parish and it was doubtful that any whistling ducks nested there (McCartney 1963).

In La., highest nesting density was 6 nests on 400 acres of adjoining ricefields in 1955. Same locale in 1956 had approximately 20 pairs in a 5-sq.-mi. area (B. Meanley).

In early fall in La., this duck concentrates in extensive paille fine *(Panicum hemito-*

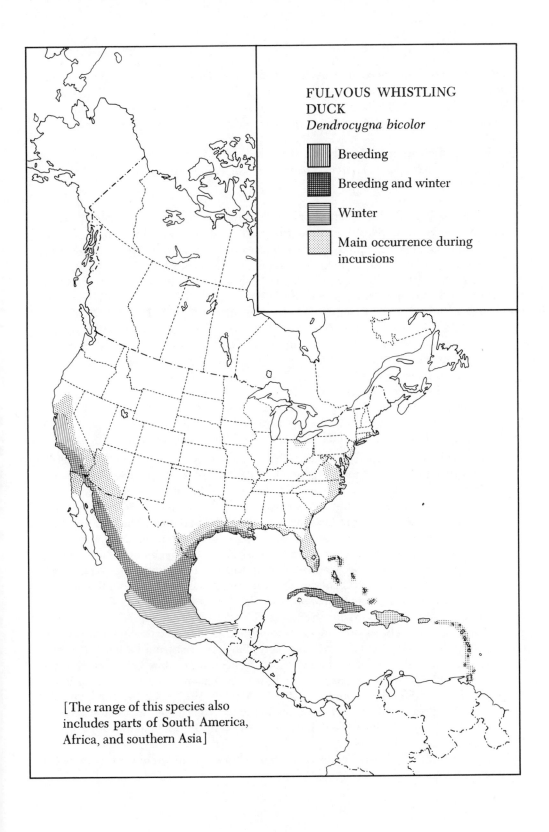

FULVOUS WHISTLING
DUCK
Dendrocygna bicolor

Breeding

Breeding and winter

Winter

Main occurrence during
incursions

[The range of this species also
includes parts of South America,
Africa, and southern Asia]

mon) marshes along the coast, especially in marsh ponds where water shield *(Brasenia schreberi)*, a known food, occurs, as in Lacassine Refuge in Sept. Four birds at Pass-a-Loutre (Mississippi Delta) in Nov. 1956, were observed in a freshwater marsh of *Phragmites communis, Zizaniopsis miliacea*, and *Alternanthera philoxeroides* (R. Beter).

Recorded occasionally in spring and fall at Sabine Wildlife Refuge in sw. La., in brackish marsh of *Spartina patens, Distichlis spicata, Juncus rosmerianus*, and *Scirpus californicus* (R. Rudolph). BM

DISTRIBUTION (See map.) For older data on world range, see especially J. C. Phillips (1923a). A propensity to wander beyond usual range is not limited to N. Am.

An undoubtedly incomplete listing of places in N. Am. n. of Mexico where this species has occurred away from known breeding range is as follows. CANADA B.C. (in 1905), s. Ont. (1962), and New Bruns. (1961); details in Godfrey (1966). In CONTER-MINOUS U.S. may appear almost anywhere. Wash., Ore. (flock in Feb. 1970); nw. Cal. (7 on Dec. 8, 1962, at Ft. Bragg) and other occurrences well away from breeding range in the state; Nev., Utah, Ariz., New Mex., states up the w. side of the Mississippi to include Minn., and many states e. of the river, including Tenn. (4 records); scattered inland occurrence in Va. and N.C.; a grouping of records at w. end of L. Erie, and occurrence all along the Atlantic coast (except for N.H.) into Canada.

Some of the scattered occurrences (of singles and flocks) distant from usual range date back many decades. Examples: pair near Prescott, Ariz., in Nov. 1864; several at Washoe L., Nev., early in 1877; flock of 11 (5 shot) near Alberni, B.C., in Sept. 1905; 10 at Gray's Harbor, Wash., Oct. 3, 1905; taken in Bermuda on Oct. 10, 1900.

The "explosion," mapped by J. Baird (1963), McCartney (1963), and H. Jones (1966), and recorded by other authors, began in late 1949–early 1950. The route was mainly along the Gulf Coast and across to e. Fla., then up the Atlantic seaboard. There were appreciable numbers in Fla. beginning in winter of 1960–61; about 2,000 were present in the winter of 1971–72 at the Loxahatchee Nat. Wildlife Refuge. The origin of those nesting on Virginia Key, near Miami, in the late 1960s is not determinable; apparently at first there were escapees from Crandon Park Zoo, later augmented by wintering birds of presumed natural occurrence. Twenty were seen in Puerto Rico on Dec. 21, 1960 (Biaggi and Rolle 1961). There were widespread movements again the next autumn, with 21 birds in New Bruns. on Nov. 4 and 30 in R.I. on Dec. 23. In 1962–63 there was a series of reports for the Lakes Erie–Ontario area.

Since flights have been autumn–early winter movements and there have been records for other seasons also, beginning about 1961, at least from Ocean City, Md., southward, it is assumed that the latter occurrences are for birds that survived the winter outside the usual range. The "explosive" movement has continued; for example, 2 of these ducks at Scarborough, Me., on May 20, 1972 (1972 *Am. Birds* **26** 738). Again Fla.—presumably wild pairs nested in the L. Okeechobee area in the 1960s. A bird of this species was found dead Dec. 16, 1964, at Ft. Jefferson in the Dry Tortugas (Robertson and Mason 1965).

For some historical data on changes in numbers occurring in our area, see below under "Habits."

Extralimital Apparently only a straggler in Baja Cal.; whether it occurs on the Mexican Plateau seems to be unknown but is rather unlikely. For the W. Indies there are many data in J. Bond (1965, 1966), briefly as follows. This duck has spread comparatively recently to the W. Indies, where it was widely distributed in the winter of 1960–61. The first breeding record for Cuba was in 1964. It was unknown in the Lesser Antilles until 1962, when it was noted on Barbados (all 4 New World *Dendrocygna* now are recorded from there); the Lesser Antillean birds were virtually wiped out, for they were shot soon after they arrived. The great increase in numbers in Cuba may have been a causal factor in the extraordinary spread of this bird throughout the Bahamas and Antilles from 1960 to 1965.

Three of these ducks were seen in the s. Sargasso Sea in lat. 23°03′ N, long. 60°00′ W, on Oct. 25, 1964 (Watson 1967).

Range in S. Am. may prove to be less discontinuous than heretofore believed, especially when more is known about any seasonal movements. See Meyer de Schauensee (1966) for S. Am. distribution.

Limits of occurrence in w. Africa still not well known, perhaps also of dispersal in s. Africa. Local breeder on Madagascar. Very few records for peninsular India; 3 for Ceylon.

Recorded from a **Precolumbian site** in Venezuela; see Brodkorb (1964a). RSP

MIGRATION Some birds apparently are rather local in their seasonal travels, but others definitely are migratory in s. U.S. in spring (late March through April) and in fall (Sept. onward).

In July–Oct. of 1969 and 1970, a total of 195 marked individuals was released in 3 se. Texas counties; many joined wild flocks; 6 were recovered over 50 mi. away—4 went eastward and 2 southward in Sept. or later; a bird recovered in Oct. in Veracruz supports the assumption that the U.S. Gulf Coast birds winter in s. Mexico (Flickinger et al. 1973).

See the preceding section for dispersal movements. RSP

BANDING STATUS Total number banded was 743 up to 1964 and there were 46 recoveries to 1961; main places of banding were Cal. and La. (data from Bird Banding Laboratory). RSP

REPRODUCTION Major sources of information are Meanley and Meanley (1959) for La., Cottam and Glazener (1959) for Texas, Dickey and van Rossem (1923) for Cal., and McCartney (1963), who worked in La. but also summarized information for all U.S. breeding range.

Age when **first breeds** 1 year. **Somewhat colonial;** several pairs usually nest in a relatively small area within extensive uniform habitat (see "Habitat" for nesting density).

Most breeders **arrive** in breeding areas at least 4–6 weeks prior to first nesting attempts. Although some birds may be paired before arrival, behavior of many thereafter indicates that for them it has not been accomplished. The birds feed, sleep, and move about largely in groups—not in pairs. Individuals and odd numbers of birds freely leave one group for another and are accepted with mild or no protest.

Pair formation Few data; 2, 3, or 4 birds in prenesting period join in a flight characterized by much twisting, turning, and sharp banking from side to side. On one occasion, 3 ♂ (identified as such by voice) followed a ♀ on the ground; she maintained 3–10 ft. lead and, if ♂ ♂ stopped following, she moved closer to them until they again began to follow. Whenever a calling ♀ flew over a field, many ♂ ♂ standing on the ground immediately answered the call. Display on ground (greeting may be a function): bird with head and neck stiffly erect approaches at fast walk until within inches of 2nd bird; former puffs out breast, holds neck and head in partial S-shape, and utters *weep* call; then, with bill to ground, simulates feeding. Pair-bond form may prove to be lifelong monogamy in all *Dendrocygna*. All the whistling ducks are considered to be notably lacking in displays, the only striking ones for the Fulvous being described below.

Copulation Birds usually on water. They engage in brief mutual HEAD-DIPPING, then the drake suddenly mounts and treading lasts only a short time, then both birds call loudly and drake slips off to one side. Then, side by side, both birds tread water very fast, raising their bodies to steep angle, breasts puffed out, necks in tight S shape with bills on breasts, and both lift the wing on side away from partner—a STEP-DANCE. The birds may be in contact or a few in. apart. This was described by Finn (1919) and described and also illustrated both by Meanley and Meanley (1958) and Johnsgard (1965).

Nest usually in dense vegetation over water—like that of King Rail or Purple Gallinule, except lower—or placed on levees. In ricefields, rice is main nest material: leaves, uprooted plants (in early nests), even unripened grain heads (late nests). One nest in a ricefield was made entirely of *Brachiaria*. No down is added, but occasionally a few dropped feathers are present. Dimensions of a nest in La.: outside diam. 32 cm., overall height or depth 30 cm. Nests are flimsy at first and early eggs may drop through the bottom. After clutches are laid, most nests have a partial or complete canopy. Several also observed to have ramps, one 4 ft. long. In Cal., nests are built of grasses, sedges *(Scirpus)*, and cattails (Dawson 1923), but Barnhart (1901) mentioned nests on dry ground and one was 500 ft. from water. In s. Texas birds nested in dense stands of water-loving plants, but when favored areas were too dry they nested on young or matted stands of *Paspalum*, the nests being exposed in all but 1 instance (Cottam and Glazener 1959).

There is an old report (Burrows, in Bent 1925) of nesting in hollow trees in lower Rio Grande Valley (Texas) at heights of 4–30 ft; it has been questioned by Rylander and Bolen (1970). [Within its wide range, this duck nests in treeless to well-forested areas. In some localities where seemingly suitable trees are available, it nests on the ground. It reportedly uses tree cavities, also old "outside" nests of other birds (evidently adding at least some plant material), and even is reported to build its own nest on a tangle of branches. For further details see J. C. Phillips (1923a).]

A late nester (the usual time anywhere in U.S. for **full first clutches** being about June 10–15) but laying did not start in Texas in a dry summer until late June. Egg dates: La., 12 records May 25 (first egg in nest) to Aug. 20; Texas, 9 records May 16–Sept. 10; and Cal., 23 records for April 28 (very exceptional) to July 13. Part of these data are from

22

Bent (1925). Captive yearlings, kept by J. Lynch in La., did not lay before July; their egg production reached a peak in 3rd week in Aug. and a few eggs were laid in Oct. (McCartney 1963), which raises the interesting point as to just when these ♀ ♀ were flightless during molting.

Clutch size in La., 12–14 eggs (Lynch 1943); in s. Texas 11 first clutches of 6–16 (Cottam and Glazener 1959); 12–16 in Cal. (Dawson 1923). "Dump nest" of 23 eggs in La. (Meanley) and 62 in Cal. (Barnhart 1901). In Cal., eggs of this duck have been found in nests of Ruddy Duck and Redhead (Shields 1899). Eggs usually are laid at rate of 1/day.

One egg each from 18 clutches (9 from Texas, 9 from Cal.). Size length 54.40 ± 2.70 mm., breadth 40.40 ± 1.34, radii of curvature of ends 15.03 ± 1.31 and 12.07 ± 0.95; shape nearly elliptical, elongation 1.34 ± 0.049, bicone −0.095, asymmetry +0.099 (FWP). Shell surface rather rough, color nearly white.

Incubation shared by ♀ and ♂; Delacour (1954) suggested ♂ spends more time at nest than ♀. Eggs are left uncovered by the departing sitter. In s. Texas, Cottam and Glazener (1959) felt that the birds spend little time on nest during warm hours of day until near hatching. In La. 2 birds have been observed flying to a nest and 1, 2, and 3 birds have been observed flying from a nest and also 1, 2, and 3 birds have been flushed within 10 ft. of a nest.

Incubation period 24 days under domestic hen (Dickey and van Rossem 1923, Meanley and Meanley 1959, McCartney 1963) and 26 days in an aviary (Johnstone 1957a).

Hatching dates for 20 clutches in La. in 1961 and 1962: last week of June (3), 1st week of July (1), 2nd week (6), 3rd week (7), last week (2), and in 3rd week of Aug. (1) (Lynch, in McCartney 1963).

Nesting success   Only 3 of 10 nests in La. were successful. The 10 were believed to have been first clutches, which are especially vulnerable to predation by man in the area studied; data on replacement clutches would raise the percentage of success. Eggs lost from predation (by man mostly, also raccoons, opossums, skunks) and severe weather. On the protected Welder area in s. Texas, 11 first clutches totaled 122 eggs; of these, 85 (69.7%) hatched in the 8 nests in which at least some eggs hatched (Cottam and Glazener 1959). The next year, 1958, nesting habitat was drier, nests were more exposed, and losses greater—1 nest in 6 was successful (Cottam and Glazener).

Young are tended by both parents. Ducklings dive "with skill and dexterity of a grebe" (Cottam and Glazener). In La., with draining of ricefields preparatory to mechanical harvesting, the families of ducks move to nearby fields which remain flooded and the ducklings are particularly vulnerable to predation when thus forced to travel overland to reach water. When afloat, they generally remain well hidden in vegetation. Development of a captive ♀: at age 4 days—egg tooth lost; 35 days—quills appeared on wings and tail (feathers through tips of sheaths), legs changing color to "adult" bluish gray; 40 days—Juv. feathering appearing on upper back, flanks, and foreneck; 60 days—remnant of cheek stripe of downy stage still present, nearly complete Juv. feathering (but flight feathers of wing and tail still growing); 63 days—cheek stripe absent, first flight at this age. Wt. in gm. of this bird: 28.4 (at 4 days), 32.3 (6 days), 34.7 (8), 223.8 (33), 523 (60).

At least in our area, this species almost certainly is single-brooded; the prolonged laying season is a result of renesting after loss of earlier clutches plus presumably late laying by yearlings. BM

HABITS   There are many older data in J. C. Phillips (1923a) and Bent (1925), more recent information in Delacour (1954) and Meanley and Meanley (1959), and both the new data and the bibliography in McCartney (1963) are very useful. The following information is for La. unless otherwise indicated.

This duck is active both day and night, large flocks foraging noisily even in darkness. Flight intention is signaled by lateral Head-shaking. Not wary; flushes reluctantly, but night-foraging flocks do not allow close approach.

In March and April they make nightly raids on water-planted ricefields. On April 21, 1956, Meanley observed them leaving a coastal marsh on such forays, in tight bunches of 20–30 noisy birds, at 7:30 P.M. An estimated 1,000 birds headed for one field. They are known to feed on other crops also—oats in La., corn and sorghum in Texas. Since all the birds of an area may join in a single flock, this creates an illusion of vast numbers.

Prior to beginning of nesting in late spring, they spend much time in fields of young rice. Frequently they alternate between these fields and wet pastures previously used for ricegrowing and which have an accumulation of weed seeds. During summer, many (50–75) feed in favorite feeding fields, often making several trips of 2–4 mi. to the field daily. Preferred fields commonly contain more weeds than rice and have many potholes.

For some information on habits of young of this species, see Rylander and Bolen (1970).

After the nesting season, flocks of 50–500 frequent inundated rice stubble and potholes in the fields of standing rice for feeding (mostly on weed seeds); sometimes they associate with the Blue-winged Teal.

In La., Texas, and Cal. there have been complex and changing agricultural practices in rice culture—manipulation of water levels; altering the flora to a near monoculture, with various methods of planting and harvesting; application of biocides, fertilizers, and treatment of seeds with insecticides. Rice treated with aldrin drastically reduced the numbers of this duck in the Gulf Coast area by the 1970s. See McCartney (1963) for some details and for relation to the Red-billed Whistling Duck. In La., other factors affecting the population of this duck include: disturbance, or deliberate destruction, of nests by man; gathering of eggs for hatching under domestic fowl (15 broods seen in 14 barnyards in one parish in 1955); occasional flying against overhead power lines (probably at night); and predation by the skunk, raccoon, opossum, and dogs.

The birds walk about in wet pastures, feeding on weed seeds; they swim or walk in shallow water of ricefields or marshes, stripping grainheads of native plants. In deeper water they feed on the surface or by tipping like dabbling ducks, also commonly by diving—a springing upward and then headfirst plunge, but only a shallow dive. In general, this species is more of a swimmer and dabbler than a wader. Much time through midday is spent loafing and sleeping on ricefield levees or in pastures. They are not known to perch in trees in La. nor, in fact, throughout most of U.S. range.

Although said to be capable of fast flight, small groups and pairs in particular fly slowly, generally at low altitude. They are much given to circling about, particularly just prior to alighting. This duck decoys readily to an imitation of its voice. It is easily killed, having brittle bones—"the humerus and femur can easily be broken by one's thumb and forefinger" (Dickey and van Rossem 1923).

As a game species in N. Am., the Fulvous Whistling Duck is of some importance in parts of coastal Mexico, although it is not abundant. In addition to local hunters, others have gone there from the U.S. in order to take advantage of liberal waterfowl hunting regulations. This species needs special protection there—both legal restrictions on its capture and establishment of a coastal waterfowl refuge (A. S. Leopold 1959).

Fulvous Whistling Ducks are kept in semidomestication in both of the Americas and elsewhere.

The following summary of changes in numbers is based mainly on McCartney (1963).

La.: apparently scarce in any season before 1900; in the following quarter century numbers increased in fall–winter; in all probability this duck bred in the state earlier than the first authenticated breeding in 1939; a population peak was reached in early 1940s (documented by Lynch 1943) and a marked decline occurred subsequently. (Also see below.)

Texas: early records were mainly for lower Rio Grande Valley, from which this duck largely disappeared beginning around 1900; after about 1912 it occupied the rice belt and by early 1950s it again was a common summer resident in s. area; now it also breeds along entire coast, but population in the state is less than formerly. In both coastal Texas and La. a great decline was evident by the early 1970s, from ingesting biocides used in treating rice seed.

Nev.: has long occurred, and probably breeds, in w.-cent. sector. BM RSP

FOOD   Data mainly for our area. Largely vegetable (seeds and structural parts of plants, cultivated grains) and aquatic insects. Based on stomach contents of 3 specimens, food consisted of 97.3% vegetable and 2.7% animal material (Fish and Wildlife Service).

Vegetable   Filamentous algae 6% and seeds of: borage (*Allocarya*) 29%, jungle rice (*Echinochloa colonum*) 27%, paspalum (*Paspalum*) 23%, spurge (*Ditaxis*) 6%, and miscellaneous seeds 6% (Fish and Wildlife Service). A stomach from Merced Co., Cal., contained finely comminuted grass and other vegetable material (J. Grinnell et al. 1918).

The principal foods, based on examination of 200 droppings and 20 gizzards in La. were: from dry-planted fields, *Fimbrystilis* sp. 65%, *Paspalum distichum* 25%, *Eleocharis* sp. 10%; from water-planted ricefields, *Oryza sativa* 78%, *Brasenia schreberi* 11%, *Ranunculus* 11%; on rice stubbles and mature rice fields (100 droppings), *Echinochloa colonum* and *E. walteri* 45%, *Paspalum distichum* 30%, *Oryza sativa* 15%, and miscellaneous grasses and sedges 10% (Meanley and Meanley 1959).

Visits cornfields to obtain the grain (Lawrence 1874). In Asian portion of range said to feed extensively on rice. Opinions differ as to its economic effects on ricefields of Texas and La. Stated on the one hand to damage severely the rice in "milk" stage (Carroll 1932), to eat only the newly sown rice and not the sprouted grain (Hasbrouck 1944b), and to rarely damage the rice, being very beneficial in consuming the seeds of weeds in the ricefields (Lynch 1943). See "Habitat" and "Habits" in the present volume, also McCartney (1963) for further information.

Animal   Water scavenger beetle (*Tropisternus*), back swimmer (*Notonecta*), predaceous beetle (*Hydroporus*), and water boatmen (Corixidae). AWS

26

Black-billed Whistling Duck

Dendrocygna arborea (Linnaeus)

West Indian Tree Duck of 1957 A.O.U. list. Long-legged and somewhat gooselike duck—largest of the whistling ducks (length 19–22 in.)—with black bill and black spots on ventral feathering. Sexes nearly alike; Juv. Plumage more muted, with less distinct markings. The tracheal bulla, which is the same in both sexes, is diamond-shaped and has a shallow keel; it was described and figured for both sexes by A. Newton and E. Newton (1859). No subspecies.

DESCRIPTION   **Head** crown and nape nearly black, the feathers of occiput (in ♂ only?) elongated to form an appreciable crest; sides of head brownish paling to white of chin and upper foreneck; feathering on sides of neck furrowed in definitive stages; lower neck mixed black and white. **Upperparts** dark brownish, the feathers with narrow and much paler terminal edging. **Underparts** breast toward tawny, paling to nearly white abdomen which is spotted black; under tail coverts white with large black spots; feathers of sides and flanks boldly marked black and white. **Tail** blackish brown. Legs and **feet** muted greenish or lead-colored. **Wing** dark on both surfaces, the speculum area grayish, lining sooty black. For color illus. of this duck, see Delacour (1954). Downy: light areas rich yellow; pale band between dark crown and bill.

Measurements of specimens taken in various localities and seasons. 11 ♂: BILL 51–56 mm., av. 54.4; WING 257–274, av. 267.5; TAIL 77–84, av. 81.5; TARSUS 68–75, av. 70.6;   12 ♀: BILL 49–56 mm., av. 53.7; WING 251–278, av. 265; TAIL 75–83, av. 80.5; TARSUS 65–72, av. 69.8 (ETS). Wing across chord of curve: ♂ 250–277 mm.; ♀ 248–273 (H. Friedmann). **Weight** no information except see Smart (1965a) for newly hatched young. RSP

DISTRIBUTION   Resident in Bahamas and Greater and n. Lesser Antilles, the specific islands listed by J. Bond (1956). **In our area** 1 taken in Nov. 1907, in Bermuda, originally recorded by Bradlee and Mowbray (1931) as *D. autumnalis*. Escapees occur in the Miami, Fla., area, especially on Virginia Key (at nearby Crandon Park Zoo the birds are free flying).

Erroneously reported from Tabasco (s. Mexico) and Brazil.

For records from **prehistoric sites** in Puerto Rico, see Wetmore (in Bond 1958) and Brodkorb (1964a). **Fossil**, apparently of late Pleistocene age, in Barbados (Brodkorb 1964b). RSP

OTHER TOPICS   For further information see especially J. C. Phillips (1923a), Westermann (1953), and Delacour (1954). RSP

Red-billed Whistling Duck

Dendrocygna autumnalis

Black-bellied Tree Duck of 1957 A.O.U. list and of some authors; others prefer Red-billed, which has been in the literature since at least 1751. Smallish, somewhat gooselike terrestrial and wading duck, having long neck and legs. After early life, has reddish pink bill, extensive clear-cut areas of nearly uniform coloring (browns, grays, white), and geographical variation in color of belly (from black to gray); legs and feet pinkish. Juv. plainer, but all flying stages have large white or whitish wing area. The tracheal apparatus, which is sexually dimorphic, has been mentioned briefly by several authors (including Heinroth 1918); as in *D. arborea*, the bulla is entirely osseous. Sexes similar in appearance and size. Length 20–22 in., wingspread to about 37, usual wt. about 1¾ lb. Two subspecies.

DESCRIPTION   *D. a. autumnalis.*   One molt/cycle in both sexes, Basic II being definitive. Extent of individual variation still little known. A somewhat generalized description based on examination of specimens plus Cain's (1970) data on pen-reared and wild birds follows.

▶   ♂ ♀ Def. Basic Plumage (entire feathering), ALL YEAR, with intervening molt (includes flightless period) usually in early fall (Aug.–Sept.) in our area. **Bill** reddish pink with bluish nail; **iris** dark brownish; **head** and upper half of neck medium gray except crown (a slight crest at occiput) and hindneck deep olive brownish; eye ring and chin white; remainder of neck (feathering not furrowed) to lower **breast** rufous-chestnut, grading to more cinnamon-chestnut **mantle**; rump and upper tail coverts black; **underparts** belly blackish; posterior abdomen and under tail coverts white with nearly black bars and spots; **tail** black; legs and **feet** vary (with individual? or season?) from scarlet pinkish to whitish pink; **wing** outer primary black, the others white for

28

more than basal half and distally black, the secondaries blackish, lesser coverts pale brownish, middle ones nearly white (toward ashy), greater coverts white, and wing lining black.

AT HATCHING   See col. pl. facing p. 370, also photo in Bolen et al. (1964). Light areas muted and pale to vivid yellow (individual variation); rarely a yellowish line adjoining top base of bill. (In the closely related *D. viduata* the pattern is less distinct and there is a pale spot, not a line, above and in front of eye. *D. arborea* is larger, the yellow areas vivid, and a pale band adjoins top base of bill.) The 2nd down begins to appear among the natal down at 10–12 days posthatching; as the latter grows, the former fades and the ducklings appear grayish brown at 17–25 days.

▶   ♂ ♀ Juv. Plumage (entire feathering), in pen-reared stock begins to appear at about 25–28 days, develops rapidly from 3rd to 9th week, and is not fully grown until at least age 100 days. Most of the Juv. feathering is lost at age about 16–20 weeks, but not all of it on the venter until age 35 weeks, and the wing is retained much longer.

A drab Plumage. **Bill** upper mandible mostly dusky, lower mostly grayed yellowish; **iris** very dark; much of **head** and upper neck smoke gray, with thin white eye ring, and a narrow dark stripe from crown down hindneck; **upperparts** back light chestnut, rump feathers blackish with light ends, **underparts** breast buffy brown; belly light grayish, the feathers each with at least 2 blackish spots; **tail** blackish brown, the feathers with notched ends; legs and **feet** lead-colored with pinkish suffusion. **Wing** quite similar to definitive, but various feathers narrower, coloring muted (more of the wing patch is off-white).

The notched Juv. tail feathers first appear at age 25–28 days, are fully grown by the 8th week, and are being molted beginning in the 12th (sometimes the 11th) week posthatching.

Flying is possible when the longest primary has an av. length of 69 mm. and the shaft is hard (age 56 days or older); its av. length reaches maximum, 125 ± 3.2 mm., at about 100 days posthatching.

▶   ♂ ♀ Basic I Plumage (all feathering except wing), acquired gradually; in pen-reared birds begins to appear in 13th–14th week, first on head and tail (central feathers first), then neck, breast, back, and venter. When in heavy molt into Basic I, at 16–19 weeks, a bird appears spotted. Molting finally is completed, at about 35 weeks posthatching, when white-tipped Juv. feathers of the pelvic region are replaced by all-black ones (but some individuals in Basic I have white spotting on black belly feathers). This Plumage, with which the Juv. wing is retained, is worn for nearly a year.

Basic I has same colors and pattern as later Basics, but various feathers (as scapulars) are often somewhat narrower (intermediate in shape between Juv. and Basic II).

Early during molting out of Basic I (when the Juv. wing is lost), there is a flightless period lasting 20 days. See Cain (1971) for a tabulation of age characteristics from hatching to age about 21 mo.

Measurements   10 ♂ (from Texas, Mexico, and Costa Rica): BILL 47–53 mm., av. 50.4; WING 231–251, av. 242.8; TAIL (of 9) 66–72, av. 68; TARSUS 58–64, av. 60.6;   10 ♀ (Texas, Mexico, Costa Rica, Panama): BILL 50–57 mm., av. 52.9; WING 223–249, av. 240; TAIL 66–74, av. 70.5; TARSUS 54–63, av. 59.5 (ETS).

Bolen (1964) published meas. of 21 "adults" taken in s. Texas in 1963; the mean for wing (across chord) for 11 ♂ was 239.40 (spread 233–248); and for 11 ♀ was 235.35 (229–247.5). WING (across chord) 4 ♂ (Texas) 234–244 mm., av. 240.5; and 4 ♀ (Texas and nearby Tamaulipas in Mexico) 234–241 mm., av. 236.5 (H. Friedmann).

Weight Bolen (1964) gave the following data for spring–summer in s. Texas: 9 ♂ 728.2–951.8 gm., mean wt. 799.52; and 8 ♀ 831.8–978.7, mean 893.36; and another series weighed, in early May, to nearest oz. in the field and converted to gm.: 35 ♂ 680.4–907.2 gm., mean wt. 816.48; and 37 ♀ 652.1–1,020.6, mean 839.16. Although ♀ ♀ were heavier than ♂ ♂, this may be seasonal and due to enlarged ovarian tissues.

Thirty incubator–hatched ducklings, after 4 hours of drying, av. 28.6 ± 2.10 gm. (Cain 1970).

Hybrids none in wild reported. In captivity it has crossed with at least 3 other species of whistling ducks.

Geographical variation in the species: northerly birds av. larger. Friedmann's (1947) proposal would require 4 named populations: 2 with lower part of neck, all around, like back, subdivided into (a) belly dark brown (Texas and ne. Mexico) and (b) belly black (Ariz. and Veracruz s. to w. Panama); and 2 having lower part of neck, all around, and breast brownish gray, abruptly contrasting with brown of back, subdivided into (c) upper back and breast brownish gray with suffusion of tawny or hazel (n. Colombia, s. Panama, nw. Venezuela, and W. Indies) and (d) upper back and breast gray with no or very little tawny suffusion (e. Venezuela to the Guianas, s. to n. Argentina). Hellmayr and Conover's (1948) study, with which Delacour (1954) concurred, demonstrates that individual variation is so extensive that it is preferable to have only 2 named populations—in effect, Friedmann's 2 main categories without dividing each, as in Peters (1931). RSP

SUBSPECIES **in our area** *autumnalis* (Linnaeus)—descr. and meas. given above; **extralimital** *discolor* Sclater and Salvin—southerly, see preceding paragraph. RSP

FIELD IDENTIFICATION Data for our area, where occurrence is almost entirely in s. Texas, April–late Oct., occasionally in winter.

Sexes alike. Slightly gooselike appearance. In flight, wingbeats slower than those of our other ducks; white wing patch very conspicuous; legs extend beyond tail; long neck sometimes droops somewhat. They fly in lines or groups, not wedges. When alighting, the neck is stretched downward sharply until bill nearly touches feet, then raised.

Standing bird recognized by long neck and long pinkish legs, pinkish to rather reddish bill, brownish back, black belly contrasting sharply with cinnamon-brown breast, and the usual whistling duck stance—long axis of body angled steeply upward (not held horizontal).

When swimming this duck appears as though its center of gravity were very far forward, the base of the neck being low in water. When alert on the water, however, the body is in more "normal" position for a duck.

Pattern of flight, standing profile, and many aspects of habits and behavior resemble those of the Fulvous Whistling Duck, (which see). Where the 2 sometimes are seen in flight together in s. Texas, the white wing patch of Red-billed, white upper tail coverts of Fulvous, and quite different calls, distinguish them. The Red-billed appears larger and its flight sometimes seems more lumbering. Both species are less wary than other ducks.

As noted outside our area, half-grown downies bear a resemblance to ♀ Masked Duck, but head-neck pattern is different (Slud 1964). BM

VOICE   A noisy duck. Usual call diagnostic: high-pitched, soft musical whistle, described as descending 4-syllable *pee-chi-chi-nee*, the first syllable long drawn and high pitched (Delacour 1954); as *weeseeweesee* Haverschmidt 1947); and as *peya-cha-cha-chanee* (present author); more musical than voice of any other whistling duck. Volume and carrying quality are less than those of the penetrating squeals of the Fulvous Whistling Duck. Uttered during flight, also while standing or swimming. Stance of standing bird when calling essentially as in Fulvous, but head usually not thrown upward so far or so vigorously.

Other calls given in flight may be written *chit-chit-chit* and *cheet-cheet*.

A single note, *yip* or series of them, given when taking wing. The same, in short series, indicates alarm. In distraction display, a frantic *oo-eek* similar to ordinary call of N. Am. Wood Duck (Slud 1964).

When loafing, these ducks often utter twittering sounds. BM

HABITAT   This is a tropical lowland duck, in general preferring shallow lagoons with floating vegetation and areas of exposed mud. Not on salt water. An arboreal nester. Usually found in more arid regions than the Fulvous; both species occur together in some intensively cultivated areas, as in lower Rio Grande Valley in Texas. Following paragraphs pertain to Texas.

Red-billed occurs on shallow ponds or lakes that may be completely devoid of emergent vegetation, but more often contain water lilies (*Castalia* sp.), water hyacinths (*Eichornia crassipes*), and cattails (*Typha*) and are bordered by woodlands or dense thickets or open agricultural land.

Much of original nesting habitat in lower Rio Grande Valley has been cleared for cultivation. Preferred area usually is a thicket near or bordering a lake or pond and composed of the characteristic thorny trees and shrubs of this semiarid region, with nest trees along border or in openings. Dominant growth: ebony (*Pithecollobium flexicaule*), mesquite (*Prosopis chilensis*), retama (*Parkinsonia aculeata*), hackberry (*Celtis laevigata*), huisache (*Acacia farnesiana*), and cacti (*Opuntia* spp.). Five species of the dove family nest in these thickets.

Most of Rio Hondo population in Cameron Co. nests in an open grove of ebonies (and several hackberries) where all accompanying vegetation has been removed so as to allow cattle to graze. This grove covers about 10 acres and is on the border of a small lake; 5–10 pairs usually nest there. For additional information, see Bolen et al. (1964). BM

DISTRIBUTION   (See map.) It was suggested by Cain (1973) that decreasing temperature northward may limit breeding distribution by restricting the amount of productive energy available for egg formation. Reportedly migratory at both latitudinal extremes of the species' range, but at least at n. extreme a few winter occurrences are known. Within its general range, distribution is not as continuous as the map would indicate. Quite often kept in semidomestication. Also, a common aviary bird within its range and elsewhere and some individuals undoubtedly escape.

D. a. autumnalis—incomplete data for our area are as follows. Main range in 1964 was 4 counties in s. Texas, but has spread and increased since then. By 1971 it had nested successfully in Bee Co. (well n. of Corpus Christi) and was increasing in numbers. There are recent sightings in New Mex. Has occurred rarely in se. and cent. Ariz. in summer, has nested at 3 localities, and 2 families were wintering near Nogales in

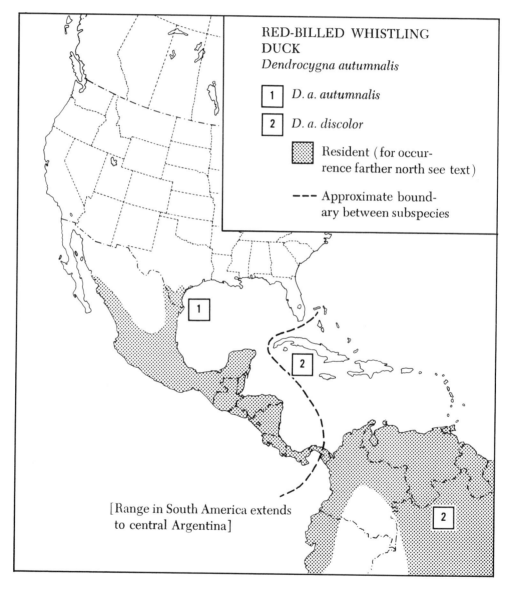

RED-BILLED WHISTLING
DUCK
Dendrocygna autumnalis

1 *D. a. autumnalis*

2 *D. a. discolor*

Resident (for occurrence farther north see text)

--- Approximate boundary between subspecies

[Range in South America extends to central Argentina]

32

Dec., 1960 (Monson and Phillips 1964). More recent Ariz. reports include these for 1970: several birds near Phoenix in late May, 13 near Tucson on May 17, and 26 near Nogales on May 25. In Cal. at least 3 records by 1970. In La., 2 individuals were seen on a pond near New Iberia in June 1969.

In Fla., a sighting in March, 1952, on the Tamiami Trail, possibly pertained to an escaped aviary bird. In the late 1960s what were probably zoo escapees nested on Virginia Key near Miami.

D. a. discolor—W. Indian places of occurrence were listed by J. Bond (1961a). The following probably are assignable to this subspecies. In Puerto Rico, only in small numbers in recent times (Wetmore 1938); no recent record (J. Bond 1959). This duck was brought to Jamaica long ago and older records may pertain to introduced birds (J. Bond 1956); has occurred there recently, mainly in winter and early spring (J. Bond 1966). Birds were released in Cuba in Pinar del Rio Prov. in 1931 and in the Zapata Swamp (J. Bond 1956).

Straggler to Albemarle I. in the Galapagos (Lévêque et al. 1966).

Recorded as **fossil**, apparently of late Pleistocene age, from Barbados (Brodkorb 1964b) and from **archaeological sites** in Puerto Rico and Venezuela) references in Brodkorb 1964a). RSP

MIGRATION   There is flocking and at least some travel over most of the range of the species, but with seasonal near-absence only at extreme limits, as in Texas. Lehmann's (1957) report of temporary flocks of a thousand or more birds in Dec.–Jan. in Colombia suggests that the ducks may gather from some distance. In the dry season in Costa Rica, they occur "almost literally in clouds" (Slud 1964). Following applies to *Handbook* area.

Spring arrival in lower Rio Grande Valley usually in April; av. date April 17 based on 17 records 1949–56 (L. Goldman). Hundreds present by mid-April in 1970 in Corpus Christi area.

Fall departure usually in Oct., but a few sometimes remain into Nov. (R. Montgomery). Where they are concentrated for nesting, the entire group (including prebreeders) may leave together in fall (L. Goldman).

Winter small flocks are occasionally seen in lower Rio Grande Valley; in 1955 seven birds on Jan. 11 (H. Reeves), 3 on Feb. 8, and 24 on Feb. 20 (L. Goldman). Where those Texas birds that leave spend the winter is unknown—perhaps along cent. and s. Gulf Coast plain of Mexico, as this species is seen there regularly at that season (W. Jennings). BM

BANDING STATUS   Through 1964 a total of 528 had been banded in Texas, with no recoveries or returns (Bird Banding Laboratory). RSP

REPRODUCTION   Age when **first breeds** probably 1 year. Usually colonial, at least several pairs nesting in fairly close association. Following are s. Texas data, except where otherwise indicated.

Birds return to traditional breeding area—at least 30 consecutive years to Montgomery Ranch at Rio Hondo, Texas. They may arrive in a single flock.

Displays   HEAD-LOW-AND-FORWARD is a common threat posture used by both "adult" and "juvenile" individuals (Bolen et al. 1964), and, in interspecies encounters, the Fulvous yields to the larger and more aggressive Red-billed (Cottam and Glazener 1959). Displays leading to pair formation are simple, mutual, and include NECK-STRETCHING, HEAD-DIPPING, and DIVING, (Bolen et al. 1964). Pair bond form is **lifelong monogamy.** Dickey and van Rossem (1938) stated that, in El Salvador, it is "not improbable" that the birds are mated all year; Delacour (1954) suggested that they are continuously mated. Bolen (1971a) had data on 6 instances of pair bond mainte-nance for at least 2 consecutive years and noted that homing tendencies seem equally strong in both sexes. At Rio Hondo, Texas, birds were paired and ready for nesting by May 20 in 1957 (B. Meanley).

Copulation   Three observations by Meanley on May 23. No precopulatory display. Postcopulatory display, described by Meanley and Meanley (1958), consisted of mates strutting a few steps side by side, breasts puffed, head and neck in tight S-shape; oc-curred in water too shallow for churning with feet; only once an attempt to lift a wing on side away from partner after manner of Fulvous Whistling Duck. Bolen et al. (1964) stated that the wing away from partner is raised but remains folded and, occasionally, the birds face one another instead of assuming side-by-side position.

For a week or longer prior to nesting, **sites** in trunks of old ebonies are inspected by 1 or more pairs daily, in morning or evening. Sites are mainly in ebony and hackberry, but willow (*Salix* sp.) and elm (*Ulmus* sp.) occasionally are used. Entrance to cavities av. approximately 4 ft. from ground or water, with extremes at 10 in. and 20 ft. In El Salvador, said to use cavities to a height of 50 ft. (Dickey and van Rossem 1938). A ground nest in Bermuda grass (*Cynodon*) at Rio Hondo in June (R. Montgomery). Cavities are bare, or may have a few chips (Meanley), but in El Salvador, according to Morales (in Dickey and van Rossem 1938), some down always is present (there is no true nestdown in *Dendrocygna*). Bolen et al. (1964) added live oak (*Quercus vir-giniana*) and mesquite (*Prosopis glandulosa*) to trees used and gave detailed informa-tion on nests studied in 1962. Seventeen were in trees, of which 7 were in "closed" cavities (entrance on face of trunk, as in woodpecker nests) and 10 were in "open" cavities (exposed hollow in top of broken-off trunk); 3 were on the ground. Ten dead trees standing in water were used and 6 of the 7 sites ashore were in live trees. Tree-sites ashore were within 50 ft. of permanent water, except 2 were a quarter mile dis-tant. Mean height of entrances was 270.7 cm. above water and 162.5 over ground. A nearby exposed perching place is important and, ashore, an herbaceous understory is preferred to brushy growth. Ground nests were well concealed, apparently without regard to distance from water; one was described as a "well constructed, although shal-low basket of woven grasses about 20×17 cm. in size." No lining is added. For photo of a ground nest, see Bolen (1962). Suitable nestboxes, which increase nesting success, were described by Bolen (1967).

A long **nesting season** (includes renesting). Texas egg dates: 16 records May 3–Oct. 18, with 8 of these in the period June 20–July 14 (Bent 1925). A recent May 14 record (R. Montgomery). Downy young as late as Sept. 3 (R. Montgomery); brood of 11 dow-nies perhaps 10 days of age on Sept. 30 (Cottam and Glazener 1959); in El Salvador, young only a short time out of nest on Sept. 9 (Dickey and van Rossem 1938). On the

34

other hand, Wetmore (1943) saw 2 downies in s. Veracruz (Mexico) early in April.

Renesting In Texas, in 3 cases the same mates remained paired and, after their first clutches were taken (2 on June 7, 1 on June 10), the first 2 pairs were renesting on Aug. 5 and 8, the third on July 27 (Bolen 1971a).

Clutch size 12–16 eggs (Bent 1925). One **egg** each from 20 clutches from Texas **size** length 53.61 ± 2.30 mm., breadth 39.13 ± 1.26, radii of curvature of ends 14.38 ± 0.95 and 10.70 ± 0.96; **shape** between elliptical and subelliptical, elongation 1.36 ± 0.038, bicone−0.095, asymmetry+0.129 (FWP). Shell smooth, **color** nearly white (faintly brownish).

A combined laying of 52 eggs in May, 1956, at Rio Hondo (R. Montgomery), another of 26 that same season in lower Rio Grande Valley (W. Jennings); also one of 41 and another of 65 were reported by Bolen (1971a). As a result of such **communal laying,** 140 of 335 eggs reported by Bolen et al. (1964) remained untended in tree cavities. A tabulation of the fates of 428 eggs in s. Texas in 1962 showed that nearly half (48.6%) were untended in communal nests and part of the additional losses was caused by man, raccoon (*Procyon lotor*), opossum (*Didelphis virginiana*), and rat snake (*Elaphe obsoleta*); a total of 83 eggs (19.4%) hatched (Bolen et al. 1964). Cain (1972) suggested that large broods from incubated "dump nests" in s. Texas may have a high rate of survival if the weather is favorable for a period after hatching.

In Live Oak Co., Texas, on June 16, 1967, a nest contained 6 eggs of North American Aod Duck and 9 of Red-billed Whistling Duck; the former supplied nest down and incubated the eggs; 4 Wood Duck and 8 Whistling Duck eggs hatched about July 3 and all 12 young left the nest box (Bolen and Cain 1968). Thus these species compete for nest sites where their nesting ranges overlap.

Incubation by the ♀ ♂ in turn (R. Montgomery, Delacour 1954, various papers by Bolen); **period** for the species 27 days (Delacour); noted as 28 in Texas (R. Montgomery), as 25, 27, 28, and 30 in Texas by Bolen (in Cain 1970); and hot summer days may cause some embryonic development prior to actual incubation (Cain) The period in an incubator is 29–31 days (Cain).

The **ducklings,** having long sharp nails and stiffened tails, can climb the walls of nest cavities (Bolen et al 1964; also see Rylander and Bolen 1970). They jump from nest entrance to ground or water 1–2 days after hatching and thereafter are tended by both parents. They travel on water like geese: a parent leads, then come the young, and the other parent is at rear (photo in Bolen 1962); infrequently, ducklings climb onto the back of a parent in a manner reminiscent of swans (Bolen et al. 1964.) The wt. of individuals in large broods is significantly lower than of individuals in smaller ones, details in Cain (1971). Some pen-reared ducklings **attained flight** at age 56 days and wild ones were seen flying for the first time when between 56 and 63 days old (Cain 1971). Parents and young remain together after the latter have attained flight (Bolen et al. 1964), the duration of this bond between generations being unknown.

Single-brooded so far as definitely known but, since the nesting season is prolonged, there is a possibility that this duck may be double-brooded sometimes. BM

HABITS Texas data unless otherwise indicated.

Found in pairs or assemblies of pairs in breeding season and in sizable flocks (presumably including paired birds) in other seasons. There is a certain amount of mutual preening and nibbling, perhaps pair bond maintenance activity. There is a slight excess of drakes at all ages from hatching onward (Bolen 1970). This species is more of a wader than the Fulvous Whistling Duck.

The Fulvous Whistling Duck is the only species with which the Red-billed has been observed to deliberately associate. Occasionally they depart together in flight. The Fulvous answered the call of the Red-billed coming in to alight on same pond. But at times the Red-billed is aggressive toward the Fulvous. Waterfowl in the same habitat, and which are ignored, include: Mottled Duck, Shoveler, Common Gallinule, and American Coot.

When not feeding, a flock of off-duty breeders spent most of the day loafing and sleeping among water hyacinths (*Eichorniaz*) and flying back and forth between several small lakes within a 2 sq. mi. area. In Surinam, Haverschmidt (1947) reported that they sleep high up on solitary trees or groups of trees in or at edges of lagoons. In some parts of the species' range, they perch in trees mostly during the breeding season (Delacour 1954). In April in El Salvador, some water-killed trees at a lake were "crowded with tree ducks to the last available inch of space" (Dickey and van Rossem 1938). In Costa Rica they sometimes perch on "bush scrub," hardly ever in trees (Slud 1964). During the prenesting period (May) at one s. Texas breeding locality, they perched in trees only when seeking or inspecting nest sites. Several pairs gathered in nest trees, with some chasing about on branches. When inspecting a cavity, each member of the pair in turn entered while the mate perched on a nearby branch or on the ground at the base of a tree (B. Meanley).

A tendency to perch in other than nest trees depends somewhat on the presence of dead trees or of snags in ponds or lakes where the birds spend much of their time. In s. Texas reported to sometimes alight momentarily on dead limbs of trees bordering lakes before descending to a resting place in bed of water hyacinths (L. I. David). They seldom alight on water deeper than the length of their legs (Bolen et al. 1964). They may descend on emergent or stranded vegetation; where this is absent, they usually alight on the shoreline and walk into water.

These ducks are relatively inactive at night during the prenesting season at Rio Hondo, Texas. After evening foraging in grain stubble, 8–10 pairs returned to beds of water hyacinth and remained quiet for long periods. The most active feeding period was 6–7 p.m. (standard time), as observed in late May, when several pairs (sometimes accompanied by Fulvous Whistling Ducks) flew from favorite resting ponds several hundred yds. to sorghum (*Sorghum vulgare*) stubble. In El Salvador, they are very active at night and especially when there is moonlight (Dickey and van Rossem 1938), presumably in summer.

In s. Texas, according to Bolen et al. (1964), the birds tend to congregate adjacent to grainfields, then "enter en masse as if in response to a signal." But, if others already are feeding, later arrivals (individuals, groups) go in directly. When feeding, they are in assemblies and "move together about the fields."

The same authors also described the water areas where the birds occur and estimated the s. Texas population at 416 pairs in 1962. They had increased greatly by 1970.

Pairs have been observed to feed during any hour of the day in pastures or fallow fields, particularly those containing seeds of *Panicum texanum;* also in shallow ponds, upon the vegetative parts of submerged aquatic plants (by immersing head and neck, also by up-ending; and upon undetermined food in beds of water hyacinth (B. Meanley). At L. Corpus Christi, Texas, they feed in beds of water star grass (*Heteranthera* sp.) (Bolen et al. 1964). Sennett (1878) described actions of this duck in cornfields in lower Rio Grande Valley: "When corn is nearly ripe, it alights on the stalks, strips the ears of their husks, and pulls the grain from the cob, making this its chief food during the season."

During certain seasons, in some areas, this species is known to do considerable nocturnal feeding. In Dutch Guiana during the rainy season (May–June), great flocks visit the ricefields at night (Haverschmidt 1947). Flooding of grain fields and other feeding areas by irrigation or after a heavy rainfall influences the feeding habits of whistling ducks. In San Luis Potosi, Mexico, the Red-billed congregated in cornfields and meadows after heavy rains (R. Newman); they did likewise in sugarcane fields in Mexico when irrigation was in progress (W. Jennings). In s. Veracruz in Mexico they came to cornfields in large numbers in late May–early June to feed at night after crops had been cleared and the ground burned over for June planting (Wetmore 1943). BM

FOOD Various field observations are mentioned above. Bolen and Forsyth (1967) reported on food eaten by 22 of these ducks (22 gizzards, 11 crops) in s. Texas. They had eaten plant material (seeds only) 92%, animal matter 8%, and the amount of grit per bird ranged from 0.8 to 2.4 gm.

Plant Sorghum and Bermuda grass predominated, other plants being smartweeds, millets, water star grass, and a single incidence of corn.

Animal Insects and mollusks; a snail (*Physa anatina*) seemed singularly important.

Early in the season the birds fed at stockyards on grains, then Bermuda grass in May, and sorghum in midsummer–fall, but late summer diet was supplemented by water star grass. See Bolen and Forsyth's paper for percentages of foods and various other details.

Food of Ducklings In Texas, the food of five 21-day-old young primarily consisted of *Echinochloa colonum* seeds plus a small amount of *Verbesina alba* seeds; the crops of all of them contained some animal matter. Six 35-day-old young each had eaten *Sagittaria* tubers, trace amounts of *Heteranthera dubia* seeds, and their crops contained some animal matter. The younger birds had eaten insects (of 14 families), spiders, snails (*Physa*), and one had eaten a bivalve (*Sphaerium*). The 6 older birds had eaten insects (9 families), snails, oligochaetes, a tick, and a freshwater shrimp. The few data indicate that ducklings of this species "apparently rely less heavily on animal foods than many other waterfowl species" (Bolen and Beecham 1970). AWS

Mute Swan

Cygnus olor (Gmelin)

A knob at top base of bill (smaller in ♀; its growth begins in first year); tail wedge-shaped (central feathers longest); all feathering white in definitive stages. From hatching through Juv. stage largely not white, except in **color phase.** Regarding sternum and tracheal apparatus, Yarrell (1845) wrote: "The keel [sternum] is single, unprovided with any cavity; the windpipe descends between the branches of the forked bone, and curving in the form of part of a circle, passes upwards and backwards to the bone of divarication [which is not a swollen bulla in either sex], and from thence by short tubes [bronchi] to the lungs." The inner portion of the trachea plus the bronchi were figured in Heinroth and Heinroth (1928).

The ♂ is larger within these dimensions: length 54–62 in., wingspread 82–94, usual wt. 18–24 lb.

No subspecies, at least in present-day birds.

DESCRIPTION   One Plumage/cycle. The shape of various feathers, especially the scapulars, changes with each of at least several early Plumages, from tapering and narrow (Juv.) through intermediate shapes to parallel sided and broad, with broadly rounded (almost squarish) ends; see illus. for Tundra Swan on p. 74. Basic III here is treated arbitrarily as earliest definitive on assumption that soft parts and feathering are relatively stable from the time when this Plumage is worn.

▶   ♂ ♀ Def. Basic Plumage (entire feathering), ALL YEAR, white, often with ferrous staining, especially on head and neck. **Bill** of ♂ reddish near base, grading to orange distally; of ♀, muted orange; in both, the bare loreal skin and base, the knob, nostril margins, lateral edges of bill, and the nail black; a flesh-colored area on underside of bill toward tip. In winter, bill color becomes more vivid, at least in ♂, and his knob enlarges. **Iris** brownish. All **feathering** white. Legs and **feet** black in other than white-phase birds, but brownish in both sexes of the latter. A molt of all feathering

38

begins in summer. In successful breeders (usually they are older, i.e., in a later Plumage than Alt. III), the ♀ begins molting first, with all wingquills dropped well after its onset (when her brood is a few weeks old); the ♂ becomes flightless later—about 2–3 weeks in feral stock in Rhode Island (Halla 1966). Counting from date of loss of a primary feather, its succeeding feather is cornified after 58 days (Heinroth 1906). The flightless period in mature birds thus is about 8 weeks. At about the time the ♂ regains flight, the brood first attains flight. Prebreeders, nonbreeders, and failed breeders all molt earlier than successful breeders.

AT HATCHING bill blackish with yellowish nail, lores covered with down (frontal down extends about 6 mm. farther forward than loreal down); iris brownish; upperparts pale brownish gray, paling to white on sides and underparts (entire down is white in white-phase young); legs and feet blackish gray (brownish in white-phase birds). The young appear much the same throughout their downy period.

▶ ♂ ♀ Juv. Plumage (entire feathering), worn in entirety briefly. This Plumage develops gradually, with not much growth of primaries before the 7th week; at age 4½ mo., zoo birds could barely fly (Heinroth and Heinroth 1928). (Possibly feral and wild birds may develop somewhat more rapidly.) The lores become nearly bare and blackish; bill mostly dark gray, without a knob. "Normal" phase—feathering a blend of various drab browns; darkest on crown, nape, and much of dorsum; palest on foreneck and part of venter; nowhere white; the tail comparatively short, the feathers with notched ends. Legs and feet nearly black. White phase—all feathering white, bill light brownish, feet brownish.

There is a satisfactory monochrome illus. of Juv. in Scott et al. (1972); the figs. labeled "Juv." in standard treatises (Schiøler 1925, Witherby 1939, others) are of birds that are at least advanced into Basic I.

▶ ♂ ♀ Basic I Plumage (all feathering except most of wing), acquired mostly within a span of 2–3 weeks beginning at about 4½ mo. posthatching; retained (with most of Juv. wing) through WINTER into EARLY SUMMER. Then the head–body begin molting, but tail and wing not until some weeks later. "Normal" phase: head and neck quite evenly brownish gray or a neutral gray, paling very close to bill and on lower neck; upperparts various grays and some browns, the pattern tending to become patchy in part because of bleaching and wear (lighter areas become almost white or white); underparts breast and venter usually a pale grayish (may fade to white); tail very pale, fading to white, the feathers not notched. This is the first winter feathering, in which the birds are more or less gray, or some individuals quite brownish, and usually somewhat patchy in pattern by midwinter. The bill partly develops its bicolored pattern and the knob becomes evident on the ♂. Legs and feet black. White phase—all feathering white; legs and feet brownish.

▶ ♂ ♀ Basic II Plumage (entire feathering). In feral stock on Long I., N.Y., some individuals begin head–body molt in very late spring (into white feathering), while others show no sign of losing any grayish or brownish Basic I until at least late May. Some yearlings are flightless by very early July. After the flightless period, the new wing quills become functional some time in Aug. or very early Sept. (individual variation). By then the head–body–tail have molted into much of the next Basic. All feathering is white in Basic II, regardless of color phase earlier in life.

39

▶ ♂ ♀ Basic III Plumage (entire feathering), also succeeding Basics, all **feathering** white in both phases. The scapulars and other feathers are broad distally. The knob on the bill continues to grow and enlarges seasonally; by this stage or later it reaches a ht. of 17–25 mm. in the ♂ and 14–20 in the ♀; legs and **feet** continue to differ in coloring between the phases. Molting is later in successful breeders than in all other categories.

NOTES The preceding paragraphs give approximate av. course of events for feral birds in e. N. Am. The variables—individual, sexual, seasonal, annual—are difficult to study in birds that molt from white to white. Among feral birds on Long I., some individuals having much darkish feathering already have decidedly orange-yellow bills and others in all-white feathering, and in the same season, have bills essentially gray and have black feet. Early changes in bill coloring apparently are not closely correlated with age and in older birds the seasonal increase in bill color and in enlargement of knob begin well after conclusion of molting.

A young ♂ killed in Albany Co., N.Y., in early winter had white feathering, beginnings of a knob (7–8 mm. high), and predominantly grayish bill; within a month after it had been made into a museum birdskin, it appeared more "adult" because the bill had become nearly scarlet-orange as it dried out.

From study of feral stock in R.I., it was determined that color phases are due to a single sex-linked gene. "Gray was dominant to white and the gene frequency of the recessive allele (white) was determined to be .293" (R. Munro et al. 1968).

Measurements (of Danish birds) 10 ♂: BILL (from knob) 70–85 mm.; WING (meas. with tape along outside curve) 560–622; TARSUS 98–120; 9 ♀: BILL (from feathers) 73–90 mm.; WING (outside curve) 535–570 (Schiøler 1925).

Weight ♂ 10–12 kg. (22–26.4 lb.) and ♀ 9–10 kg. (19.8–22 lb.) (Heinroth and Heinroth 1928). The maximum that Hilprecht (1956) listed was a fall ♂ in E. Prussia at 22.5 kg. (49.5 lb.). Portmann's (1945) graph of wt. increase of cygnets showed that they attain about 75% of mean adult wt. in 150 days. At Little Compton, R.I., in 1963, on June 12 three ♂ cygnets weighed 15, 13, and 12 oz.; on Aug. 31 they weighed 20 lb., 16 lb. 7 oz., and 19 lb. 10 oz. respectively (Halla 1966).

Color phase white at all ages, legs and feet brownish or sometimes pinkish gray (not black) from Juv. stage onward. Some broods contain both phases.

Hybrids none in wild reported. In captive and semicaptive stock the number of species in different genera that the Mute Swan has crossed with, as listed by Gray (1958), are: *Cygnus* 3, *Anser* 3, and *Branta* 1.

Geographical variation none reported in present-day birds. Serebrovsky (1941) named *Cygnus olor Bergmanni* [sic] from the Pleistocene of Binagada, near Baku, in Azerbaijan, the type being part of a pelvis. It was described as larger than present-day birds and differing in certain respects otherwise. I have not found it mentioned by later Russian authors. RSP

FIELD IDENTIFICATION In our area. When swimming or standing, Mute Swans generally hold the neck curved gracefully and bill pointed downward somewhat. Even at a great distance, the graceful appearance is diagnostic in comparison with the vertical "broomstick" neck of our native swans. A territorial ♂, especially, often arches the wings, thus giving a very bulky appearance. For details of younger birds, see "Description"; older birds are all white (if not stained), have bill partly scarlet-orange, and a knob on the forehead. Mated birds are in pairs all year, but pairs may combine in flocks (which also may contain unmated birds) when off territories. Prebreeders usually are in flocks. The Mute Swan flies low on short flights, the individuals arranged in an oblique line, and their swishing "wing music" is an especially impressive sound if the birds pass close by. They are said to fly silently sometimes. RSP

VOICE Generally silent, but not "mute." The keeper of the Abbotsbury Swannery (Dorset, England) claimed that this bird utters at least 8 "different" sounds (Moynihan 1959). Wild birds, especially in early spring, have a far-carrying call: ♂ higher-pitched *kiurr;* ♀ more guttural and rolling than voices of our native swans. Sometimes this call is uttered in flight. The swish of wings, audible a great distance in calm air, may be a substitute for a contact call. Birds disturbed on territory, especially near the nest or brood, have an explosive exhaling which begins with a shrill component. There are lower-intensity variants down to a hiss. The ♀ is said to summon her brood with a call like the bark of a puppy (Moynihan). The small young have a peeping call somewhat like that of ducklings. See Hilprecht (1956) and Moynihan (1959) for further information; also see "Reproduction." RSP

HABITAT See the following section.

DISTRIBUTION **In our area, introduced** (early dates unknown; see "Habits" for some historical data) and presumably also has escaped from captivity; well established as a **feral** bird, increasing in numbers, and extending its range locally. Widely kept as an ornamental species.

Main places of occurrence as a feral bird are part of R.I., Long I., (N.Y.), and near Traverse City in Mich. (where they are fed in winter). Many R.I. birds occur seasonally (especially in late fall, but there is some going and coming in winter and spring) in nearby Mass. and e. Conn. estuarine habitats. This swan occurs in various seasons and has nested on Block I. in R.I. and on Martha's Vineyard and Nantucket in Mass. Winterers in w. Conn. evidently come from Long I., and some from Long I. also evidently go at least as far sw. as Barnegat Bay, N.J., possibly as far as coastal Va.

Feral Mute Swans have nested a few times in Ont., notably at Bradley's Marsh in Kent Co. In Mich., presumably the Traverse City birds are the source of recent scattered winter records both in Mich. and in several counties in Wis.; it nested as far n. in Mich. as Antrim and Traverse cos. in 1971. In Conn., it nested inland near New Haven in 1970. In Del., 4 of 5 pairs at a single locality had young in 1970; this colony has increased rapidly.

It is expected that breeding range will increase somewhat on the Atlantic seaboard, but extension from there inland in the northerly sector is limited by waters remaining frozen at the time nesting ordinarily begins.

On the Atlantic seaboard there are records of wintering as far n. as Portsmouth, N.H., and in York Co., Me.

Mute Swans in warmer parts of their breeding range, where waters generally remain open through winter, tend to be rather local in their movements; many from cooler parts of Eurasia, however, migrate considerable distances. In both N. Am. and Eurasia, there are individuals that make long flights, generally in fall, less commonly (and prior to molting) in spring. Thus the Mute Swan has a vast total recorded range, in much of which it occurs very seldom. This swan may appear almost anywhere in at least temperate N. Am. Example: 4 spent the winter of 1956–57 at Regina, Sask., were present subsequently, and Godfrey (1966) noted that they had been reported nesting there.

Palearctic region Truly wild, feral, and escaped captive birds seldom are distinguished clearly in the literature. According to Ticehurst (1957), this swan was indigenous to parts of England, but already was semi-domesticated as early as the 12th Century.

Presumably wild birds, from the continent, also occur. Swans banded in se. England have been taken on the continent, at various places n. to include the entrance to the Baltic; no Mute Swan banded elsewhere in Britain has been taken abroad (R. Spencer 1971). In France, apparently by the end of the 17th Century, it had been introduced and become acclimatized in rivers around Paris (Mayaud 1962). In the 1960s it was extending its breeding range in Europe, especially in the n. Baltic area. It has occurred in winter on the s. edge of the e. Mediterranean, in the Nile Delta, around the Persian Gulf, to the n. rim of the Arabian Sea, in Korea (rarely), and on the perimeter of the Yellow Sea (regularly?).

Introductions and **transplants** have been many, even to very distant places. Introduced in New Zealand in 1866 and 1868, where it is now local as a feral bird on both North and South I. (The Black Swan, *C. atratus*, was introduced from Australia in 1864 and vastly outnumbers the Mute.) In Australia, the Mute has been introduced to ponds and lakes, mainly within cities as an ornamental species, but also on more natural waters in n. Tasmania and in sw. W. Australia. Although it has become established, it has not extended its range (the Black Swan may be an influence), but possibly it may become established ultimately as a wild bird (Frith 1967).

Recorded as **fossil** from the Pleistocene of Ireland, England, Denmark, Germany, Portugal, Italy, and Azerbaijan, and from an **archaeological site** in Denmark; see Brodkorb (1964a) for references. RSP

MIGRATION **In N. Am.** On the Atlantic seaboard, established breeders tend to remain on individual territories through winter if adequate food is present and waters do not freeze. The majority, however, are forced to move by freeze-up, usually in late Nov. or in Dec., to nearby sheltered brackish- and saltwater areas. There are various wintering localities, on mainland and is., from se. Mass. counterclockwise to Md. Breeders return to their territories when weather permits, from early Feb. onward, usually in first half of March. The swans at Traverse City, Mich., have only very local seasonal movements.

As studied by Willey (1968), in the period 1962–67 inclusive, the R.I. swans were found to travel rather short distances—usually to localities extending w. to Groton, Conn., and e. to the easternmost part of the Westport R. estuary in Mass. In addition, marked birds reached Long I., N.Y., and, as of 1967, Md.

Molt migration Prebreeders are in flocks and widely scattered in spring, but on approach of summer the R.I. birds return to ponds within the state to molt. This swan thus is present in the state in greatest numbers at the end of summer (Willey 1968).

Palearctic region There is now a considerable literature on the travels of this bird. See Hilprecht (1956) for data from banded birds. For Britain, recent useful papers include Perrins and Reynolds (1967) and Minton (1968, 1971). RSP

BANDING STATUS In R.I., the number banded 1962–67 inclusive was 776 (includes 475 in 1966–67), and, in that period, 199 were recaptured (Willey 1968).

In Britain, 20,519 had been banded by the end of 1969 and there were 6,511 recoveries (R. Spencer 1971). Others have been banded elsewhere, notably in Scandinavia. RSP

REPRODUCTION Available N. Am. data (Halla 1966, Willey 1968) are supplemented here by a limited amount from the many existing data from abroad. Most of the older information on this swan was from captives, with later information from feral ones, there being essentially none for birds that are not conditioned to some degree of association with man.

Age when first breeds In England, 2 ♀♀ bred at age 2 years and ♂♂ began at 3 years, but many of both sexes not until older; most individuals not nesting until age 5 years were ♂♂ ; see Minton (1968) and papers he cited for details. In zoo birds, the usual pattern is for a 3-year-old to be mated, to build a nest, and for some to lay eggs (rarely fertile), but successful breeding ordinarily begins a year later (Heinroth and Heinroth 1928). These authors mentioned a ♀ that was mated while in gray feathering. In feral birds in R.I., youngest known-age breeders were 3 years old and a pair at this age incubated 8 eggs and raised 6 cygnets to flight age (Willey 1968).

In both free and confined birds, in some circumstances, established breeders probably prevent prebreeders from acquiring suitable territory and becoming breeders, i.e., breeding is inhibited. In R.I., the number of known active Mute Swan nests increased from 35 in 1965 to 61 in 1967 but there were other mated pairs exhibiting nesting behavior but not successfully building or laying (Willey 1968).

At least rudiments of **display** occur in young from their 1st winter on and more or less temporary pair bonds are common after the birds molt into white feathering. Older prebreeders have clear-cut displays, used in pair formation and maintenance of a bond. These normally occur on water, the birds in twos and generally within or near assemblies; after pairs become territorial, they may form in assemblies elsewhere later, as when forced to move by weather. There is some display all year, although mostly in winter. HEAD-TURNING mutual, necks straight up, bills horizontal, heads moved from side to side; in a variant the bills point downward. BILL-TOSSING mutual, necks straight up, bill tossed rapidly (as in geese), in vertical plane as though head attached by a hinge. FALSE PREENING head rubbed along coverts and secondaries of folded wing; often mutual. DIPPING of bill (in air), ranging to submerging entire head and neck in water; often mutual. At times a pause and, with necks upstretched, heads are held side by side momentarily (probably homologous with intertwining of necks in *C. columbianus*). As these displays proceed, the actions of partners tend to become synchronized. Betweentimes, there are various comfort movements (preening, shaking

43

the feathers) or even up-ending as though foraging. See Huxley (1947) and Boase (1959) for further details and the latter for illus.

The cob (♂) frequently chases the pen (♀), in flight, on water, and may even continue pursuit if she walks ashore.

Threat display (toward other Mute Swans, toward man, dogs, any swans, geese) is referred to as BUSKING—wings partly raised above the back, the inner feathers spread somewhat and primaries remaining folded, the neck rests on back, the bill is pressed against throat; an exhaled snoring hiss is uttered. Sometimes, in threat, the wings are extended and flapped. (See especially Poulsen 1949 for additional details.) After the intruder is repelled, the ♂ returns to his mate and then there is a TRIUMPH CEREMONY—both arch their wings, they touch breasts, rub cheeks, waggle bills, and shake their feathering in a particular sterotyped manner, meanwhile uttering snoring calls. The ♀ may initiate this display, generally near nest or brood; the ♂ joins her and both utter snoring noises. The Busking attitude occurs also as a mutual ceremony of paired birds.

Copulation on water, exceptionally ashore. Both birds engage in Dipping, then the ♀ signals readiness by settling her body in water and stretching neck fully forward along or just above the surface. The ♂ mounts and the ♀ utters a prolonged exhaling sound. Sometimes there is little or no pre- or postcopulatory display. Full version of latter: REARING both birds rear up and tread water, usually while facing (or sometimes side by side) and, with breasts and cheeks in contact, they utter snoring or trumpeting sounds. Then both settle on the water, bathe, preen, and shake their feathers. See Hilprecht (1956) for illus.

Territory size varied from 0.5 to 11.8 acres in 12 territories in R.I. Some pairs permit nearby nesting by other species of waterfowl, but others do not. Defense commonly continues through summer, even into fall. If other individuals enter defended territory and are physically unable to escape, usually they are killed by the aggressive owner. The same occurs at times if other waterfowl enter the territory. (From Willey 1968.) In captivity they have been known to kill ducks and then eat them (W. B. Stone and Marsters 1970).

Pair bond form is **lifelong monogamy;** other forms are known to occur occasionally among feral birds and captives. According to Heinroth and Heinroth (1928), remating after loss of mate is not long delayed, but Poulsen's (1949) findings, also from study of zoo birds, were to the contrary. In feral birds in England, repairing sometimes was delayed 2 or 3 years, or in a few cases evidently a bird remained unmated. The whole subject of pair bond variation was discussed at length by Minton (1968).

Nest site preferably an islet, or secluded stretch of shore, or built up in shallow water or a marsh; at ponds, the entire pond is defended by the ♂ as territory (in which all activities of the season normally occur). In semidomestication at the famous Abbotsbury Swannery in Dorset, England, there are many scores of pairs on 25 acres (Bannerman 1958). The same site is used by the same pair for many years. On U.S. Atlantic seaboard, the feral birds, if they have not remained all winter, reoccupy the old nest or site from early Feb. into late March (depends on season). Here, at first, the ♀ makes **nest-building** movements (with or without materials) and, usually around mid-March, building in the true sense begins. She stands beside or in the nest, gather-

44

ing material (reeds, sticks, and debris) within reach, and adds it to the heap; the ♂ gathers material from below the water's surface, or floating, or nearby ashore, and places it within reach of his mate. In R.I., one ♂ uprooted nearly a half acre of pickerelweed (*Pontederia cordata*) (Willey 1968). The resulting nest heap usually is 5–6 ft. in diam. and the ♀ forms a depression in this for the eggs; material is rearranged and added throughout incubation.

On U.S. Atlantic seaboard, **laying** generally starts the very last days of March or early in April; hence, barring some catastrophe, the best time to census nesting pairs is in the first half of May. Eggs usually are laid on successive days, early in A.M., and at first are left uncovered in absence of the ♀. Presumably viable eggs have been found on the U.S. Atlantic seaboard from about March 25 to June 15.

Clutch size usually 5–7 (2–11) eggs in U.S. In R.I. in 1962–65 inclusive, 77 nests contained 493 eggs or 6.4/nest (Halla 1966). In a study in England, clutch size showed little difference in respect to age of the ♀ (Perrins and Reynolds 1967). **Egg** size (sample size not stated) in R.I. **length** av. 103 mm., **breadth** 75, and weight 258–365 gm., av. 295 (Halla 1966). This agrees well with Palearctic data in Schönwetter (1960). **Egg color** at first very pale bluish green, but soon becomes soiled and rather brownish.

At least some ♀♀ evidently do some sitting prior to completion of the clutch (which may at least partly explain variation in reported incubation period). If, in absence of the ♂, the ♀ also leaves a nest having a completed clutch, she first covers the eggs with nesting materials, which includes some down and contour feathers. **Incubation** by the ♀, but ♂ often on nest when the ♀ is away feeding or occasionally for some hrs. even when she is close by. Elements of some displays previously described occur at Changing-over (or so-called Nest-relief ceremony). Generally, the ♂ remains nearby, on guard. **Incubation period** 35 (34–38) days in a zoological garden (Heinroth 1911).

If nesting is disrupted early during incubation, the pair may nest again at a different site in the same territory (Halla 1966), but no data on size of **replacement clutches**.

Hatching dates in R.I.: cygnets have been seen as early as May 7, but peak of hatching occurs in 3rd week of May (Halla 1966). **Hatching success** in 1958 on Long I., N.Y.: 13 ponds, each having a pair with brood, had a total of 49 cygnets (counted when downy)—2 broods (of 7 each), 2 (of 6), 1 (5), 1 (4), 1 (3), 5 (2), 1 (1) (J. Elliott). In R.I., of 493 eggs in 77 nests, 367 (74.4%) hatched and 319 cygnets reached flying age (Halla 1966). Av. size of young broods was 4.5 in 447 English broods and 4.2 in 59 Scottish broods (Eltringham 1963); see Minton (1968) for further data.

Young go to water the day after hatching, the first ones to leave being tended by the ♂ while the ♀ remains until the last cygnet departs. She may remain 2–3 days, then roll out or cover any unhatched eggs (Halla 1966). The family swims with young bunched or strung out behind the ♀ and with the ♂ closely following. Sometimes the cygnets climb (from the side) and ride on ♀'s back.

For at least 10 days the young birds are unable to up-end for food and so rely on their parents to pull up vegetation from the bottom and place it on the surface near them; after they can feed independently in shallow water, they still depend on parents to gather food from the bottom where the water is deeper (Halla). The nest remains a focal point for a long time—for loafing, for brooding the young, and for spending the night (Halla). In R.I., territoriality wanes in Sept. and family groups begin wandering; by

Oct. 1, all cygnets are on the wing and many family groups break up at this season (Halla), so that the parents begin the next nesting season without young. In mild winters, however, the family may remain and use the nest site until the beginning of the next nesting season, when the young depart and join a herd of prebreeders (Halla).

Zoo birds barely **attain flight** in 4½ mo. (Heinroth 1911), but it may occur somewhat earlier in feral ones. See Portmann (1945) and Halla (1966) for wt. data on young of known age, and Heinroth and Heinroth (1928) for photographs. RSP

HABITS   N. Am. data are emphasized here. Unlike our native swans, the introduced Mute readily becomes **semidomesticated.** Many people desire and encourage its presence. Yet the Mute is aggressive toward other large waterfowl and can be dangerous toward man because of the blows it strikes with its wings if it is molested within its territory. Also, if the birds become accustomed to being fed and the food supply runs out, they become very belligerent. And in addition, there are nuisance problems: injured swans wandering about, birds walking on public thoroughfares, and so on. In the long span that feral molters are flightless and therefore confined to an area of water, they eat vast amounts of food and pass a tremendous quantity of fecal matter, to the detriment of water quality. When feeding, they uproot and destroy much aquatic vegetation. Molters leave great numbers of feathers. (Summarized from Willey 1968.)

R. H. Flengel —

The Mute Swan **feeds** at any hour during daylight and apparently to some extent on moonlit nights. In a 7-day experiment, Willey found that a swan consumed 329 gm. of dry wt. or 3,789 g,. (8.4 lb.) wet wt. of aquatic vegetation/day; yet 2 swans lost an av. of 3.9 lb. during the entire period.

In England a reason for possessing Mute Swans is that they are "royal birds and so lend a certain air of distinction, well-being and importance to their owner" (Ticehurst 1957). In N. Am. their **greatest value** to man is aesthetic and, rather oddly, they seem to be considered most aesthetic when in aggressive posture, the so-called Busking.

Flight intention is indicated by holding the neck vertical; an exhaling sound may be uttered. Poulsen (1949) stated that wild ones, on large lakes in Sweden, become alarmed and take wing at a distance of a thousand meters. This distance is modified (decreases) as a result of association with man. The Mute flaps along the surface when taking flight, then the birds usually form in oblique lines. Wingbeats 2.7/sec. downwind and 3.2–3.3 cruising (Meinertzhagen 1955). On low (short-distance) flights they sometimes collide with overhead wires and cables, although less often in N. Am. than in Britain (where there are far more swans). Older birds **feed** by immersing the head and neck, also by up-ending, but seldom dive. Older preflight cygnets dive readily. This swan, like other species, has a trait of extending a leg backward above water, then bringing the foot forward to conceal it in flank feathers. When shaking the feathering, first the tail is swung from side to side, then the shaking spreads over the whole body, ending at the head (Poulsen 1949). Mute Swans occasionally are seen "somersaulting" on the water, an activity noted also in other northern swans and various geese.

Wild and feral birds gather in large numbers (and may include Tundra and Whooper Swans) in winter at some Eurasian localities, especially in hard winters. In N. Am. and abroad, such **assemblies** contain pairs and unmated birds, but at some localities in warmer parts of the range there are pairs of Mutes on adequate territory that probably are solitary most of their lives.

In summer on Long I., a sizable flock of prebreeders on a pond faced the wind when moving forward, the birds evenly spaced, all moving with military precision (J. Elliott).

There seems to be no record available as to when the Mute Swan first was brought to N. Am.; captives certainly were present earlier than the 216 imported in spring of 1910 and 328 in spring of 1912, which were mentioned by J.C. Phillips (1928). There is a museum specimen from Boston Market, 1875 (Griscom and Snyder 1955).

Following are some data for conterminous U.S.

MASS. The birds have spread from R.I. to the mainland and is. and occur in numbers, mainly in winter, in the se. part of the state.

R.I. Estates at Newport had birds that were not pinioned and these are believed to be the source of feral stock, which increased greatly and spread beginning in the 1950s. The first known nest of a feral pair was at Little Compton in 1948 and there were 2 nests at Newport in 1951. The Mute nested on Block I. about 1958 and became resident. On ponds near lower Narragansett Bay a herd of 100–150 in Oct. and Nov. was not unusual by the late 1950s. When waters froze in Dec., the herds, which already had begun to diminish in size, disappeared, leaving behind small groups which fed at openings in the ice and on open water of the bay, also sometimes elsewhere along the coast. By midwinter, even these disappeared. Presently (late 1960s) most of the swans evidently do not travel very far (see "Migration"). Breeders return to territories in late Feb. or in March. Prebreeders in the 1950s occupied at least one pond not bordered by potential nesting habitat. In 1962–67 inclusive, the greatest number of swans seen annually varied from 296 (Aug. 1962) to 519 (Oct. 1967); there were 61 active nests in 1967 (Willey 1968).

Factors that diminish breeding success include vandalism (a large egg is a tempting trophy) and killing of cygnets by snapping turtles. One pond lost 22 cygnets, when they were about a month old, to the turtles. As to older swans, if food supply at a molting place is inadequate to sustain them for the time they must remain, they become weakened and are victims of parasites and disease. In 1968, in 3 areas, they suffered

47

from a fungus which caused rotting of the feet. In 1967, prolonged rains and concurrent high tides flooded nests and caused heavy loss of eggs and young. (Summarized from Willey 1968.)

As in Britain and Europe, there is speculation that the swans "eat out" ponds and otherwise render these places less useful to other waterfowl. This subject has not been given much attention in this country, but has been reported on at length for se. Sweden by Berglund et al. (1963).

CONN. Occurs in coastal waters primarily, and in winters—a few score birds by the late 1950s and perhaps a maximum of several hundred by about 1970.

N.Y. Mainly on Long I., where more numerous eastward, also a few feral pairs in nearby mainland counties. Probably they are descendants of birds released near Oakdale (M. Cooke and Knappen 1941). Some winter counts: 399 (in 1956), 350 (1957), and 301 (1958, incomplete). In mid-July, 1958, there were 59 prebreeders at one pond and 155 at another. On Jan. 17, 1959, about 570 Mute Swans were counted on Long I., of which 315 were in Shinnecock and Moriches Bays; over 500 were in Moriches Bay on Dec. 26, 1959 (Bull 1964). In the Jan., 1967, winter waterfowl survey, the figure (rounded to nearest hundred) for Long I. was 700. So far as known, there are now no feral breeders along the lower Hudson, although a few bred there formerly.

N.J. Birds have escaped from several estates; a considerable number of feral birds were established by 1940. They nested in the 1950s at ponds near the coast and occasionally inland, at least as far as Sussex Co. Some go to Barnegat Bay in winter (as do some birds from elsewhere). The winter count for the state in early 1957 was 118 birds.

CHESAPEAKE BAY In Talbot Co., Md., 2 pinioned pairs escaped in March, 1962; as feral stock, the swans increased to about 150 birds in a decade.

OHIO Near Akron, a flock was wing-clipped annually from 1911 until 1934 when allowed to migrate, which probably accounts for birds reported seen or shot during Dec. of 1934 in Pa., Ohio, and W. Va. (M. Cooke and Knappen 1941).

MICH. Traverse City; the birds that nest thereabouts spend the winter in West Bay, where they are fed corn. The latest count at hand is 180 for winter of 1960–61. By the end of the 1960s there were scattered occurrences in various seasons in Mich. and Wis., including breeding records for n. Mich.

The above is based on sources cited plus data from J. Baird and the late J. Elliott. For further general information on the species, see Hilprecht (1956) and Scott et al. (1972). There is an interesting volume on swans and swan keeping in England by Ticehurst (1957). The Mute Swan has an important place in mythology and folklore (see especially Armstrong 1958), in art, and in literature (even including the limerick!). RSP

FOOD Except for what has been mentioned above, there are no N. Am. data. The earlier European and British literature mentioned aquatic plants, grassses, leaves, seeds, and roots of cultivated grains, algae, insects and their larvae, snails, worms, tadpoles, frogs, and occasionally small fish. More specifically: vegetable starwort (*Callitriche aquatica*), pondweed (*Potamogeton*), eelgrass (*Zostera*), arrowhead (*Sagittaria*), waterweed (*Anarchis alsinastrum*), algae (*Elodea, Chara, Lemna*). A favorite food of young is *Lemna* (Naumann 1905a). Some recent papers, not summarized here, are: for Sweden, Berglund et al. (1963), and for Britain, Eltringham (1963) and especially M. Gillham (1956). For a compilation from various sources, see Hilprecht (1956). AWS

48

Whooper Swan

Cygnus cygnus (Linnaeus)

Profile of head plus bill is wedge-shaped, the middorsal line of bill and forehead form-ing a nearly straight line; tail rounded; entire feathering white in definitive stages. After early age: bill black distally, the lores and sides of base yellow to nostrils (some-times not quite to, sometimes below and slightly beyond), also some yellow extends forward from base on underside. Younger stages are described below. In external characters, readily separable when in hand in all ages from Tundra Swan (*C. colum-bianus*) by difference in bill–head shape; from Trumpeter (*C. buccinator*) by smaller overall size, smaller feet, and (possibly not always) in definitive stages by greater amount of yellow on lores and bill. No tracheal bulla. Trachea forms simple loop within the sternum and there is no bony upward bulge (into body cavity) to indicate its pres-ence below; for an excellent illus., see Thomson (1964). "The depth of the insertion [posteriorly, of the loop] is not, however, so considerable in females or young males" (Yarrell 1845). Sexes similar in appearance. Within these spans, ♂ av. larger: length 48–58 in., wingspread 82–94, wt. usually 15–22 lb. No subspecies. The Whooper and the Trumpeter form a superspecies.

DESCRIPTION   One Plumage/cycle. Two/cycle, mentioned in Dementiev and Gladkov (1952), apparently refers to differences in timing of wing and body molting during the single molt, the renewal of body feathering sometimes continuing even into winter. Differences in shapes of corresponding feathers in succeeding predefinitive Plumages are as in other *Cygnus* (see Tundra Swan especially). Basic III Plumage is here treated arbitrarily as earliest definitive.

▶   ♂ ♀ Def. Basic Plumage (entire feathering), ALL YEAR, all **feathering** white, sometimes with much ferrous staining. **Bill** black except for yellow lores and individual variation in amount of yellow on basal half (sometimes extends across top base, with or without black margin at forehead; see pl. 70 in Schiøler 1925). **Iris** brownish. Legs and **feet** black. In Prebasic molt of all feathering (with flightless period), differences be-tween sexes in successful breeders, also between age-classes, etc., probably corre-spond to those mentioned for the Mute Swan, but growth of new flight feathers is more rapid. As in other swans, wing quills and greater primary coverts are dropped almost simultaneously well after beginning of the body molt. According to Heinroth (1906), the new primaries grow about 9 mm. daily and a Whooper is "nearly full-winged" 40 days after loss of the previous quills.

AT HATCHING and throughout downy stage: upperparts pale gray, paling to white on sides and underparts; downy area on side base of bill (over lores) extends in point nearly to nostril; bill, legs, and feet flesh color.

▶   ♂ ♀ Juv. Plumage (entire feathering), begins to be replaced about as soon as it is fully grown, except part of wing long retained. Loreal skin becomes nearly bare (free of down); this area and proximal part of **bill** muted rose, grading to dusky distally. **Feath-ering** largely medium grayish brown, paling to white around and below eyes; under-parts paler than upperparts. Legs and **feet** pale flesh.

▶   ♂ ♀ Basic I Plumage (entire feathering, except for retained Juv. wing), begins replacing Juv. in fall, in some individuals largely acquired by early winter, in others it

49

is acquired more gradually in fall–winter. Lores and proximal part of **bill** become dingy whitish, grading into black of distal portion. **Feathering** of upperparts near smoke gray, some feathers tipped or edged white, various feathers dark along shaft, scattered ones all white; underparts paler (to white); tail white (these feathers often not acquired until well along in winter). Legs and **feet** become light bluish gray.

▶ ♂ ♀ Basic II Plumage: in summer at age slightly over a year, a molt of all feathering. All incoming **feathers** are white so far as known. About the time this molt is finished, **bill,** legs, and **feet** generally attain definitive coloring, the yellow and black areas of the bill sharply defined.

Measurements 9 ♂: BILL 101–112 mm.; WING (measured with tape along outside curve) 577–628; TARSUS 112–120; 8 ♀: BILL 94–103 mm.; WING (outside curve 562–595 (Witherby 1939). For additional meas., see tabulation in Hilprecht (1956).

Weight usually 7–10 kg. (15½–22 lb.), but ♂ to 13.5 kg. (29¾ lb.) according to summary in Hilprecht (1956). A fat "adult" ♂ taken in early Nov. on Amchitka I. (Aleutians) weighed 12.7 kg. (27.9 lb.) (Kenyon 1961). In Iceland in Aug., 3 breeders av. 9.4 kg. and 4 prebreeders av. 7.9 (Kinlen 1963).

Hybrids No doubt all among captive stock, with *C. buccinator, C. columbianus, Anser anser,* and presumably *C. olor,* were listed by Gray (1958).

Geographical variation Icelandic Whoopers reportedly are somewhat small, but no more so than some individuals from elsewhere, and few have been measured. The Whooper and the Trumpeter are not conspecific (Wetmore 1951, Parkes 1958, present author), contra Delacour (1954). RSP

FIELD IDENTIFICATION A trim white swan, often stained yellowish or reddish brown; lores and much of basal half of bill yellow; bill appears longish even for a

R.Ṁ.Ṁengel —

50

swan, and thick toward base. Compare with Trumpeter and Tundra Swans (bill–head profile like that of former); also compare voices. Grayish young, described above, might be mistaken for geese. In the Old World, where the Whooper and the Bewick's race of Tundra Swan occur (they usually have about the same amount of yellow on bill), they can be confused if bill color is relied on. The Whooper is usually larger, its neck more slender, its facial profile heavy and ungraceful, and birds on water (or ♀ on nest) have the neck kinked back at base and then going straight up—as though out of forepart of back (as in Trumpeter) rather than extending up near very front of body (as in Tundra Swan)—and voice is less musical. Some further details in Mauersberger (1958). RSP

VOICE   Often heard calling. Usually a double buglelike note, 2nd part higher pitched, and sometimes a pause of variable duration between them; sometimes a rapid series of these double notes. In alarm, a loud harsh *krow*, lower, gooselike, and deeper in ♂. Many variants of calls, including a range of "conversational" notes. Voice is hard to verbalize. Christoleit (1926) is the usual source of information, but there are additional data in Witherby (1939), Hilprecht (1956), and Mauersberger (1958). (See under Tundra Swan for comparison with that species and with the Trumpeter.) RSP

HABITAT   In **summer,** prefers weedy-margined and usually shallow waters within the forest zone and even out on the steppes, also tundra ponds and lakes. In **winter,** shallow freshwater (including lakes on the outer Aleutians) and sheltered saltwater areas, the latter more generally when fresh waters freeze. RSP

DISTRIBUTION   ALASKA   This is the wintering swan of the outer Aleutians (Kenyon 1961, 1963). There are 3 records for St. Paul (Pribilofs): mid-Nov. (seen), early Dec. (captured), and May 14 (captured). Occasional in summer (molting individuals?) on n. side of Seward Pen.

COMMANDER IS.   Regular migrant, more frequent in autumn, and rare in winter (Johansen 1961). (To the north in Siberia this is the only swan that nests e. of the Kolyma R.; it has not been found nesting on the Chuckchee Pen., but some go there (mainly to the w. part) to molt in summer. It has visited Wrangel I. occasionally.)

CONTERMINOUS U.S.   One was taken in Washington Co., Me., in 1903; details in R. Palmer (1949).

GREENLAND   Undoubtedly bred in the s. part long ago; subsequently an occasional visitor, sometimes in small flocks; see Hørring and Salomonsen (1941) for some records. Schiøler (1925) gave meas. of 7 birds from Greenland, all in white feathering but, with a single exception, inactive sexually, as appeared from dissection. Probably they were summering prebreeders, from Iceland.

ICELAND   This swan breeds on the central plateau and on many lowland areas, both inland and close to the sea; it is increasing in numbers. Some remain through winter, but most of them migrate to Scotland and Ireland. Evidently a few visit Greenland.

ELSEWHERE IN EURASIA   There has been an expansion of breeding range northward in the present century, concurrent with warming of the climate and increased protection. Limits of winter range vary depending on severity of the season. For overall distribution, see Dementiev and Gladkov (1952), Bannerman (1958), and Vaurie (1965).

Changes in breeding distribution in Fennoscandia during about 130 years were discussed by Fjeldså (1972). For Japan, see especially O. L. Austin, Jr., and Kuroda (1953); near Niigata, on the w. coast of Honshu, about a thousand Whoopers are fed in winter (Matthews 1972).

Usually some birds remain s. of breeding range. There are a few summer occurrences in the Faeroes, where this swan is a migrant (it was exterminated as a breeder in the beginning of the 17th century). Some are regularly present in Scotland and occasionally attempt to nest, rarely with success (Atkinson-Willes 1963).

Recorded as **fossil** from the Pleistocene of Ireland, England, Denmark, France, Monaco, Italy, Malta, Switzerland, Germany, and Finland; from **archaeological sites** in Denmark and Switzerland; see Brodkorb (1964a) for details. RSP

MIGRATION   There are few data for the outer Aleutians. Early **fall** dates are Nov. 8 on Amchitka and Nov. 9 on Adak; **spring** R. D. Jones saw 3 groups (2, 7, and 8 birds) on Feb. 11 on Atka, which possibly were early migrants; other sightings are spread through March to one for April 2 on Amchitka and April 7 on Adak. Nov., Dec., and May occurrences in the Pribilofs have been mentioned earlier.

EURASIA   A few birds remain in summer s. of breeding range, as noted above, and a few in winter remain far n. of usual winter range at places where there is open water. Most of the birds make long migrations.

In **spring** the birds begin leaving winter quarters as early as mid-Feb. They move on and gather at staging areas and then, within a brief time and correlated with rise in temperature, the majority depart, making long high-altitude flights over traditional routes. At that time the land below still is snow covered and few waters show even the first hint of spring thaw. The birds are scattered across breeding range beginning in April.

Molt migration   Breeders molt where they rear their young, within the general nesting area. The presence of sexually inactive birds in Greenland (see "Distribution") is presumptive evidence of molt migration of prebreeders from Iceland.

Fall migration is late, the birds tend to linger until freezing of waters forces them to move. Usually they are gone from n. waters by sometime in Sept. or nearly Oct. Then they linger at traditional places (lakes, coastal waters) along the way, so that migration extends at least through Nov. In severe seasons they are concentrated farther s. and there is further movement during winter if continued cold weather forces the birds to change quarters. There is a Pacific route (to Japan, many going via Sakhalin I.), inland routes, and one via the White Sea, then overland, and down to the s. Baltic (s. Sweden, Denmark) and w. Europe. The Baltic route was demonstrated by banding recoveries listed in the first (1961) *Information Bull.* of the Bird-ringing Center in Moscow.

See especially Dementiev and Gladkov (1952) for places and dates of occurrence in various seasons.

In Iceland, partly resident and partly migratory; swans remain on lakes and large rivers as long as there is open water. Thus there are large concentrations on small unfrozen areas. If these freeze (or if food becomes scarce?), the birds move to sheltered coastal waters. Although individuals banded (some as cygnets and others full-grown when molting) in Iceland have been recovered in the Brit. Isles (Ireland mainly), it is uncertain whether that portion of the Icelandic stock that migrates is large enough to account for all the Whoopers wintering in Great Britain and Ireland (Atkinson-Willes 1963). RSP

BANDING STATUS   None banded in N. Am. Most banding of this swan has been done in Iceland, where the time to band both preflight young and flightless older birds is the middle 2 weeks of Aug. RSP

REPRODUCTION   Age when **first breeds** unknown—probably varies as in the Trumpeter Swan (which see). There are displays, in assemblies of prebreeders, leading to pair formation. Practically all displays known for the Mute Swan have homologues in the Whooper, the most striking difference being frequent use of wings extended (not arched or folded) in various displays of the latter. Pair bond form evidently is **lifelong monogamy.** Although the Whooper is an early spring migrant, undoubtedly there is a "waiting period" until nesting places are in suitable condition for occupancy, as it is not a correspondingly early nester. Prebreeders usually (but not always) spend the winter within the breeding range, generally in assemblies sometimes numbering several hundred birds. Breeders: a single pair at a small body of water, or widely scattered pairs at larger waters. **Nest site** on an islet or ashore or even a considerable distance from water, generally commanding a wide view of surroundings. Nest frequently used in successive years, with annual additions (mostly plant debris) gathered at the site; not much ventral body down and few feathers are added beginning within the laying span. In Eurasia, full **clutches** in May (late April to early June), depending on latitude, altitude, and season; in Iceland, also in May and vary with locality and season. If summer begins exceptionally late in Iceland, the Whooper fails to breed (Yeates, in Bannerman 1958). In Finland, since it takes 130 days from beginning of laying until young attain flight, early fall freezing of ponds and lakes can cause heavy losses of preflight birds (Haapanen et al. 1973).

The Whooper lays a smaller **replacement clutch** if the first is destroyed (Dementiev and Gladkov 1952). First clutches usually contain 4–6 eggs (2–8 reported), in Iceland usually 4. Egg size (83 eggs from Iceland and n. Eurasia) length 105–126 mm., av. 112.5; breadth 68–77, av. 72.6; and a fresh egg weighs about 331 gm. (Schönwetter 1960); **shape** subelliptical to long elliptical; **color** when fresh, creamy white, some tinged bluish (Whiterby 1939). Said to be laid on alternate days. The ♀ incubates with ♂ nearby on guard. **Incubation period** of captives has been reported as 31 days (Eckhardt 1918); it is 34 days in the wild (Haapanen et al. 1973).

Young are tended by both parents and the family tends to remain in the general vicinity where the brood was hatched. Mean brood size was 2.81 cygnets in 32 Icelandic broods (Kinlen 1963); in June in Finland, broods av. 3.7 young—see Haapanen et al. (1973) for many data. Statements that the young attain flight in about 2 months apparently originate from Hantzsch (1905), who probably was guessing. More dependable figures are 87 (78–96) days for the Whooper, as compared with 90–105 for the Trumpeter and 135 for the Mute Swan, as given by Haapanen et al. (1973).

For additional data see Airey (1955), authors in Bannerman (1958), Dementiev and Gladkov (1952), Hilprecht (1956), Poulsen (1949), Scott et al. (1972), and Witherby (1939). RSP

53

SURVIVAL   Few useful data. Haapanen et al. (1973) discussed losses of preflight young in Finland and also speculated that the annual mortality rate of prebreeders subsequently may be higher than that of breeders. RSP

HABITS   A shy, truly wild swan, although captives breed quite readily. Essentially a freshwater bird. Active, sometimes covering considerable distances afoot when foraging ashore, and quite noisy at times. Feeds at any hour, in tidal areas depending somewhat on tide and, at night, on moonlight. A surface feeder and also up-ends in shallow water; a grazer ashore. Like our other swans, often flies low when making short-distance trips to and from feeding places; migrants fly high, often passing unseen, in oblique lines, chevrons, or in small groups (families?) at times having no evident formation. Recorded flight speeds 31–40 mph (Meinertzhagen 1955). No musical sound from wings, only a slight swishing noise. Assemblies, not only of prebreeders in summer, but also of mixed age-classes in winter, sometimes consist of up to several hundred birds, and other species of swans may occur with them. In winter and in migrations there is apparently a tendency toward segregation of older prebreeders from breeders with or without broods. For further information, see authors cited at end of preceding paragraph; for data on increase in wintering population in Britain, see Boyd and Eltringham (1962) and Hewson (1964).

A Jan., 1967, count of Whoopers in the Brit. Isles, Europe, U.S.S.R., N. Africa, and sw. Asia gave a figure of 36,900 (Atkinson-Willes 1969). RSP

FOOD   **In our area** the digestive tract of the bird shot in early Dec. at St. Paul I. (Pribilofs) contained black sand, vegetable debris, and 31 seeds of *Ruppia* (Wilke 1944); that of an "adult" ♂ killed Nov. 9 at Silver Salmon Lake on Amchitka I. (Aleutians) contained finely ground aquatic vegetation (Kenyon 1961).

Elsewhere   Green parts of plants, seeds, fruits, and roots, aquatic insects and their larvae, worms, small mollusks and frogs, and fish rarely. Clover (*Trifolium repens* and *T. fragiferum*) found in stomachs in Germany (Naumann 1905a). Stomach of specimen collected in Iceland in July contained: grit 60%, leaves of water buttercup (*Ranunculus paucistamineus*) 30%, seeds of cotton grass (*Eriophorum scheuzeri*) 10% (B. Roberts 1934). Manna grasses (*Glyceria fluitans* and *G. aquatica*) utilized in winter in Scotland (Witherby 1939). Flying to fields in Scotland, and more recently in England, to eat decaying potatoes left scattered there has become a regular habit only recently (Pilcher and Kear 1966). There is some information on food by season in Iceland in G. Timmermann (1949) and a general summary for the species in Hilprecht (1956). AWS

Trumpeter Swan

Cygnus buccinator Richardson

Nearly straight, evenly sloping forehead–bill profile; tail rounded; entire feathering white in definitive stages—these being characters shared with the Whooper (*C. cygnus*), but the Trumpeter av. larger and has little (usually no) yellow on lores and basal part of bill. Bill somewhat broader distally than in Tundra Swan (*C. columbianus*); also, anterior edge of nostril to tip of bill 50 mm. or more in Trumpeter (22 measured) and 49 or less in Am. specimens of Tundra Swan (28 measured) (Banko 1960); variation in color of lores and upper mandible are described below. Downy stage and at least Juv. Plumage largely not white, except in **color phase.** See Truslow (1960) for excellent photos of Trumpeter Swans. Young Tundra and Trumpeter Swans differ in facial profile, size (notably of feet), etc.

No tracheal bulla. The trachea, after making a rearward loop within the sternum, also makes a forward, dorsal loop that is protected by a bony case that bulges into anterior end of body cavity; further details in Yarrell (1832) and especially J. Murie (1867); there is a diagram showing relation of trachea to sternum in Banko (1960) and a photo of trachea plus undissected sternum in Wildfowl Trust 13th *Ann. Rept.* (1962).

Sexes similar in appearance, ♂ av. larger. Length to 59 in., wingspread possibly to 84 (a dead ♂ at least 6 years old—length 57 in., wingspread 83—meas. by R. S. Palmer); wt. of full-grown birds usually 18–27 lb. No subspecies. The Trumpeter and the Whooper form a superspecies.

DESCRIPTION   One Plumage/cycle. Feather shapes differ, progressively, from tapering and with rounded ends (Juv.) to evenly broad and rather squarish terminally (Basic III onward), as in other *Cygnus*. Basic III is here treated arbitrarily as earliest definitive, all feathering being white and feather shapes not altering from this stage onward. Beginning with Prebasic II, most molting occurs in summer, it continues and part of it (notably of greater wing coverts) is delayed or "offset" until much later. Dating is based on information from Mont., except where Alaska is specified.

▶   ♂ ♀ Def. Basic Plumage (entire feathering), SUMMER to SUMMER, except at least a small portion of feathering retained and molted at a later time. **Iris** brownish. **Bill** upper mandible and lores usually all black, but some individuals have orange-yellow loreal spot and some have indistinct irregularly shaped grayish spot behind nostril, or same rarely tinged yellow (Banko 1960); lower mandible black distally with individual variation in extent of salmon red or ruby, which is usually limited to basal portion (as in *C. columbianus*). All **feathering** white, often with much ferrous staining. When in Basic II or even Basic III, legs and **feet** still commonly are more or less muted orange-yellow; afterward, often black, but gray common, and some are olive-yellow to varying extent. It has been suggested (LaNoue, in Banko 1960) that feet and legs may be yellow in spring. (There is no information on whether, as in the Mute Swan, white-phase young continue to have light feet when older.)

Molting   The Trumpeter may have several molts, beginning with Prebasic II, that start early in June and are presumably more or less synchronous in the sexes before the birds breed. In successfully breeding pairs, the ♀ begins molting first (June–July), her

55

mate later (July–Aug.), so that mates only briefly or occasionally are flightless at the same time. Rarely, an individual of either sex is flightless in Sept. or as late as early Oct. (Based on Banko 1960.)

Alaskan data: The ♀ begins wing molt 7–21 days after her eggs hatch; the ♂ begins from some time before (usually) to after hatching. On the Kenai Pen., ♂ ♂ usually start early in the incubation period. In both sexes, first there is a loss of the alula and often many secondaries (and loss of flight), then the primaries drop during a period of a few days. Both sexes of prebreeders and breeders are flightless for at least 30 days. The major part of molting evidently requires over 2 mo.; a few body feathers, some tail feathers, and the greater secondary coverts on the wing are retained and molted later, probably after arrival on winter range. (These data mostly from H. A. Hansen et al. 1971.)

AT HATCHING and throughout downy stage, gray (usual) phase—iris brownish; bill muted pink basally grading to dark distally, nail on bill more or less triangular posteriorly (not curved as in Tundra Swan), the lores covered with down which extends considerably farther forward on top than on sides of bill; the downy cygnet is pale grayish dorsally, paling to white ventrally; legs and feet muted orange-yellow. White-phase young have white down, the unfeathered parts as in gray young.

▶ ♂ ♀ Juv. Plumage (entire feathering) well developed at age 10 weeks (Ward, in Banko 1960), also in Alaskan birds, but wing quills still growing and so flight not attained until at least age 13 weeks, some not until 15 weeks (90–105 days) (H. A. Hansen et al. 1971). Entire **feathering** (except in white phase) some variant of buffy brownish, paling on underparts. After the feathering is grown, the bill gradually darkens. Most of this feathering is molted during FALL, or from then into WINTER, the tail beginning in winter, and some wing coverts beginning in winter.

In Alaskan birds, the feathering develops as follows: age 4 weeks—scapulars, flanks, tail; 5 weeks—sides, belly, part of cheeks and neck; near 6 weeks—lores become bare (of down), tail feathers erupt from sheaths; 6 weeks—belly, breast, and cheeks fully feathered, secondaries erupt, tail coverts well developed, sheaths of primaries and their coverts visible; 7 weeks—upper back, most of neck, crown, the secondaries 105 mm. long, primaries 100 mm., 8 weeks—primaries 160–180 mm., little natal down remains except some on nape, lesser wing coverts, and middle of back to rump; 9–10 weeks—completely feathered, but may have some down still adhering, flight feathers of wing not fully grown (H. A. Hansen et al. 1971).

▶ ♂ ♀ Basic I Plumage (all feathering except most of wing), acquired through FALL into winter and retained into SUMMER (to age about 1 year). The **feathering** partly gray (most of head, neck, and upperparts) and the remainder white or nearly white. While this Plumage is being acquired, pinkish blotches sometimes are present on the dorsal midsection of the otherwise blackish upper mandible. Legs and **feet** some shade of gray to black, but sometimes suffused orange-yellow. The new (pale grayish) Basic I tail feathers appear over a span of time beginning in winter or even not until spring. Most of the wing is retained Juv. feathering.

▶ ♂ ♀ Basic II Plumage (entire feathering), mostly acquired by a molt in SUMMER (begins at age about 1 year), with flightless period from near onset of molting, and retained until the following SUMMER. Some feathers on the body (especially rump) and

56

wing (mostly greater coverts) are retained well beyond the summer period of molting, probably until some time in winter,—i.e., a small portion of this molt (and succeeding ones) is "offset" in time from remainder. All **feathering** white. Some individuals have muted orange-yellow legs and part of **feet** (seasonally?).

Color phase white at all ages. In Yellowstone Park over a 4-year period, 13% of cygnets were white; also 3 seen in 1956 in Fremont Co., Idaho; none ever reported from Red Rock Lakes, Mont. (Banko 1960).

Measurements Friedmann (in Banko) gave these figures for "adults": 5 ♂ (Idaho, Wyo., Wis., Mich.): BILL 104–119. 5 mm., av. 112.5; WING (across chord) 545–680, av. 618.6; TARSUS 121.5–126, av. 122.9; 3 ♀ (Mont. and "North America"): BILL 101.5–112.5 mm., av. 107; WING (across chord) 604–636; av. 623.3; TARSUS 113–128.5, av. 121.7.

Another series:—4 ♂ (Mont., N.D., Ill.): BILL 104–115 mm., av. 111; WING (nearly flattened) 631–679, av. 649; TAIL (of 3) 188–223, av. 202; TARSUS (of 3) 128–130, av. 129 (ETS).

An appendix to H. A. Hansen et al. (1971) lists various meas. of each of 117 birds, from the Copper R. valley, Alaska, by sex and age-class ("cygnet," "yearling," "adult").

Weight to nearest lb. of molting flightless birds at Red Rock Lakes, Mont.: 8 ♂ 20–27 lb., av. 23; 14 ♀ 16–23 lb., av. 20 (Banko 1960); these birds probably would have been heavier when not molting. From Kortright (1942): 6 ♂ 21–38 lb., av. 28; 4 ♀ 20–24½, av. 22 lb. 9 oz.

For flightless (molting) yearlings, Banko (1960) gave minimum wt. among 8 ♂ as 18 lb., among 4 ♀ as 15 lb. (See under Tundra Swan for comparative wt. of large examples of that species vs. small Trumpeters.)

Data from Copper R. valley, Alaska. "Cygnets weighing less than 8 oz. at hatching reached 19 lb. in 8 to 10 weeks" (H. A. Hansen et al. 1971). In an appendix these authors gave wt. (and date weighed) of each of 102 individuals, including the following: 9 heaviest ♂ "adult" 10,886–13,154 gm., av. 12,247 (27 lb.); 3 heaviest ♀ "adult" 10,206–10,433 gm., av. 10,357 (over 22¾ lb.); 7 heaviest "yearling" ♂ 10,886–12,247, av. 11,598 (about 25½ lb.), and 3 heaviest "yearling" ♀ 10,433–10,886, av. 10,735 (23⅔ lb.).

Hybrids reported only among captives. Has crossed with the Mute Swan (*C. olor*), both subspecies of Tundra Swan (*C. columbianus*), and Canada Goose (*Branta canadensis*); references in Gray (1958).

Geographical variation The eggs and newly hatched cygnets are larger in Alaska than in conterminous U.S.; details in H. A. Hansen et al. (1971). Sex for sex and age for age, Alaskan Trumpeters may be slightly larger, but there are inadequate data from conterminous U.S. for comparison. There seems to be no mention of white-phase cygnets occurring in Alaska.

The Trumpeter is not conspecific with the Whooper. RSP

FIELD IDENTIFICATION In N. Am. The main problem is to distinguish the Trumpeter from "Whistling" (Am. subspecies of Tundra) Swan, since the likelihood of having to distinguish the former from the Whooper is slight because of different distribution.

Various characteristics overlap with Tundra Swan, making positive identification at a distance difficult even when possible. Larger size of the Trumpeter is difficult to judge afield. Trumpeters, afloat or ashore, resting or in mild state of alertness, generally have the neck kinked back at base so that it appears to rise from the forepart of the back (as in Whooper) rather than from very front of body (as in Tundra Swan). At short range, the Trumpeter's straight, "heavy," facial profile appears quite unlike the shallower bill plus rounded head of the Tundra Swan. No yellow on lores or bill is indicative of the Trumpeter, but not positively diagnostic. Singularly different voices provide the surest basis of identification. The Trumpeter has a tendency, however, to be silent when in small groups, also when associating with large numbers of noisy Tundra Swans.

In spring of the year after they hatch, Trumpeters are quite gray dorsally (Basic I Plumage), while Tundra Swans of the same age have white or nearly white bodies. Then, after molting in summer, all feathering is white in both species.

♂ Alert
(note axes of
body)
♀

(postures after
deVos 1964)

About 17.5 cm.
(7 inches)

Head-bow
♀
♂

(after
O. Murie
1954)

Length of track (from rear of "heel" to tip of middle nail) in a fully grown Trumpeter measures well over 6 in.; it is less than 6 in the Tundra Swan. The foot of a dead ♂ Trumpeter (measured by RSP) would have produced a track 6¾ in. long; fig. 170 in O. Murie (1954) showed a length (along middle toe) exceeding 7 in.; and M. Monson (1956) stated that the footprint of an "exceedingly large" individual in Alaska measured 7¾ in.

In Alaska, when Trumpeters build their nests, shaped like rounded haystacks, in shallow water where emergent vegetation grows, the birds add the surrounding vegetation to the heaps—thus creating a "moat" averaging about 25 ft. in diam. It is readily identifiable from an aircraft. On the other hand, the Tundra Swan accumulates a volcano-shaped heap ashore, on open terrain (H.A. Hansen et al. 1971).

When a mated pair has firm footing, the sexes may be distinguished sometimes by a difference in posture—bill horizontal in ♂, tilted slightly downward in ♀. WEB

VOICE   Usually 1 or 2 trumpetlike syllables as *ho* or *ho-ho* (sounded rather than pronounced). Rather like Sandhill Crane. They contain a very broad band of sound frequencies. When mates are alarmed, ♀'s call is higher pitched than ♂'s, so that 2 calls (♂ then ♀) sound like one two-toned call (de Vos 1964). Trumpeting thus is synchronized between mates. Many "conversational" variants of trumpeting. When displaying, calls are rapidly repeated forceful to muted trumpetings sounded mutually, these frequently ending in prolonged wailing notes. A synchronized vocal effort by a flock commences with a few staccato trumpetings, builds up gradually to crescendo as frequency of calls and number of participants increase, with climax being followed by a few scattered trumpeting notes. Flocked prebreeders, and flocks containing these and breeders, are active vocally; breeders are moderately quiet from onset of incubation until at least well along in rearing period.

Both sexes have gurgling and burping sounds and both hiss. A soft hissing by a pinioned ♀ when gathering nest material (de Vos 1964).

Calls, "conversational" notes, and synchronized effort often as heard at night from flocked birds, especially March–May and on moonlit nights in summer–fall. Holman (1933), quoting R. Y. Edwards, stated that, prior to starting north, the swans "sing" all night with a peculiar cadence; then they leave the next morning. Calls are often audible well over a mile, a synchronized flock effort possibly up to 3 miles. A distinctive noise of wings striking water on takeoff also is audible a half mile or more under favorable conditions.

Young have higher-pitched, flutelike, calls changing to hoarse off-key variant of "adult" voice at age 7 mo. (P. Ward); also muted gurgles. WEB

HABITAT   A bird of sheltered, shallow, preferably fresh waters. In GREATER YELLOWSTONE area in conterminous U.S. **Summer** ponds and lakes at least partly bordered with areas of cattail, rushes, etc., and with submerged aquatic plants for food; this might also be described as ideal muskrat (*Ondatra*) habitat. Some nest in areas of marsh away from the near vicinity of extensive open water. **Winter** well-vegetated fresh waters that remain unfrozen (kept open by warmth of water or by current).

Supplementary feeding is provided at some wintering places, at least in Yellowstone area.

ELSEWHERE   In Alaska and Canada, in **summer** at ponds varying from less than an acre in size to very large ones, or lakes, preferably with wide shallow margins, submerged and emergent aquatics, and sedgy shorelines. Beaver impoundments. Also islands of some waters having wooded shorelines. In **migration** fresh, brackish, and to some extent sheltered saltwater areas. **Winter** unfrozen ponds, lakes, and sluggish moving waters, inner brackish reaches of coastal fjords and bays, and on marshy meadows. Inland at Lonesome Lake, B.C., where supplemental feeding is provided. Probably inland and intermingled with Tundra Swans from s. Wash. into Cal.; see discussion by H. A. Hansen et al. (1971). RSP

DISTRIBUTION   (See map.) Range and population now greatly reduced. Early records indicate that former greatest breeding abundance was in n.-cent. Canada, that region extending from Hudson Bay to the Rocky Mts. and northward toward the upper edge of the forest zone. Reduction of population and shrinkage of range began shortly after Caucasian settlement. Original settlers along the e. seaboard killed wintering swans for food and for the down and feathers, and commercialization followed. By 1772 and lasting until nearly 1900, swan skins (principally of this species) were a standard article of trade of Hudson's Bay Company. Nesting groups apparently never were numerous in n. conterminous U.S. where the species was, and still is, at s. limits of breeding range. Extant records (50+) for s. of Canadian boundary indicate, however, that significant numbers bred in the following regions: Flathead Valley of w. Mont., Greater Yellowstone region of sw. Mont. and ne. Wyo., in s. Minn., s. Wis., and in Iowa. (For additional Midwest data, see Schorger 1964 and 1968).

Breeding   At present, the principal area s. of Canada is Red Rock Lakes National Wildlife Refuge and adjacent waters in extreme sw. Mont., Yellowstone Nat. Park in nw. Wyo., and contiguous U.S. Nat. Forest and other areas in Wyo., Idaho, and Mont. Trumpeters also breed at Malheur Nat. Wildlife Refuge (se. Ore.), Ruby Lake Nat. Wildlife Refuge (e.-cent. Nev.), and Lacreek Nat. Wildlife Refuge (s. S.D.) where 57 cygnets were transplanted from Red Rock Lakes in 1960–62 and 62 cygnets were hatched and reared to flight age by late 1967. Gabrielson et al. (1956) mentioned birds transferred from Red Rock Lakes to the Nat. Elk Refuge (Jackson, Wyo.) as having established a small breeding colony. Pinioned Trumpeters were transplanted from Red Rock Lakes in 1963, and free-flying birds in 1964 and 1966, to the Turnbull Refuge in ne. Wash.; the first reported nesting of pinioned birds occurred there in 1967, and of free-flying ones near the refuge in 1968 (Johns and Erickson 1970). The Trumpeter has wintered there—a total of 32 in the winter of 1971–72.

In Canada, the largest known nesting unit is near Grande Prairie (Peace R. dist. of w. Alta.) where limited habitat supports perhaps 20–30 breeding pairs (including all age-classes, a total of 104 present in late Sept., 1968). Two pairs were found breeding near Brooks, Alta., in 1961. Swans, presumably Trumpeters, bred in 1952 near Stony Rapids in n. Sask. (Nero 1963). Easternmost recent record: at least 1 pair since 1948, and 2–3 in 1968, in the Cypress Hills area of Sask.; Nieman (1972) reported 1 pair there until 1961, when an additional family was observed, and a 1971 survey revealed 16

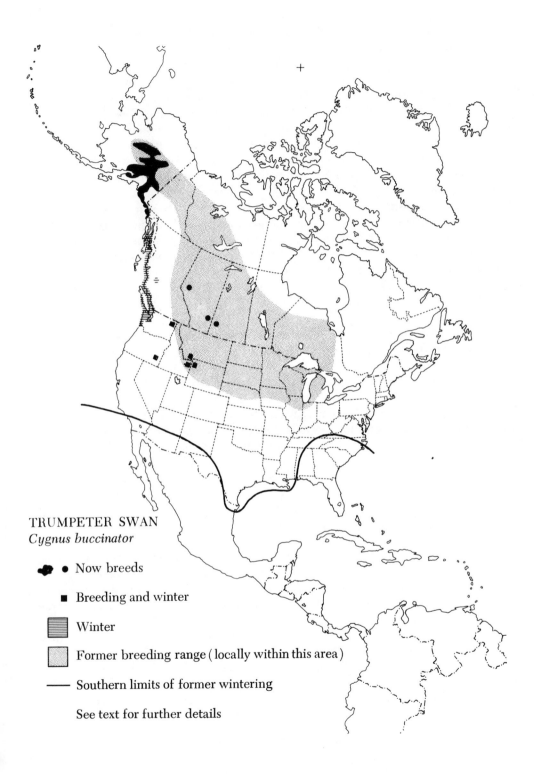

TRUMPETER SWAN
Cygnus buccinator

- Now breeds
- Breeding and winter
- Winter
- Former breeding range (locally within this area)
— Southern limits of former wintering

See text for further details

birds and included 3 breeding pairs. Some have been released at Swan Lake, near Vernon, B.C., where a cygnet was reared in 1968. Five cygnets were released at Delta. Man., in 1972.

It is possible that some Trumpeters go to unknown places in what was breeding range in former times, in the Mackenzie Dist., but there is no positive evidence.

In Alaska there was an estimated minimum of 3,400 Trumpeters (including all age-classes) in late summer of 1968. Main nesting areas are shown on the accompanying map; some probably are scattered elsewhere. There appears to have been considerable change in breeding distribution within the past 100 years (H. A. Hansen et al. 1971). The proposed Copper R. Highway will pass through what is currently (1973) an area supporting more nesting Trumpeters than any other.

Winter The birds at most locations in conterminous U.S. and some in Alta. are largely resident (and some are fed grain through the winter). Trumpeters remain in the Greater Yellowstone region, mostly in areas listed here in decreasing order of extent of use: Island Park area in ne. Idaho, Red Rock Lakes Refuge, and Yellowstone Park. Some move s. into s. Idaho and Utah. There were no Trumpeters at Red Rock Lakes Refuge on Jan. 8, 1972, but many returned on Jan. 24. One, banded in early Aug., 1967, at Red Rock Lakes, was recovered Dec. 27, 1968, a considerable distance ne. at Ryegate, Mont.

Lonesome Lake, some 70 mi. se. of Bella Coola, in interior B.C., has long been a wintering locality; see especially R. Edwards (1951). The estimated 500 that now spend the season there (and are fed grain) are mostly from Alaska. In 1972 there were too many birds for the open water area and too many to feed.

Alaskan Trumpeters are known to winter on sheltered waters on the fringe of the Gulf of Alaska and southward. They have wintered as far n. as the Kenai Pen. and near Seward, Alaska, but probably most are scattered, in small flocks, along the rugged coastline and around islands of B.C. (good counts in recent winters of 700–800). The actual whereabouts at this season of less than a third of them is known, however. Some occur farther s., among wintering Tundra Swans in the Puget Sd. area, along the lower Columbia R., and occasionally beyond into Cal.

Recent Jan. inventories for the administrative divisions known as Pacific and Central "flyways" include these numbers of Trumpeters: 1968—700 and 100, 1969—800 and 100, and 1970—600 and 100.

The most recent information at hand is from I. D. Smith and Blood (1972), as follows. In 3 winters, 1969–71, the number of wintering swans on Vancouver I. increased 129%; the proportion of cygnets each winter was 22%, 26%, and 25%; there was a minimum of 1,076 Trumpeters in the winter of 1970–71; and the birds prefer sheltered estuaries during the cold season.

Recorded as **fossil** from the Pleistocene of Ore., Ill., and Fla., and from **archaeological sites** in Pa., Ohio, Ill. (several localities), Iowa, Wis., and Kodiak I. (Alaska); see Brodkorb (1964a) for references, also Jehl (1967) for Ore. RSP

MIGRATION Formerly, when the population was more widespread, many Trumpeters migrated long distances n. in early spring and s. in late fall. Present seasonal movements in the Greater Yellowstone region are limited to local flights between breeding habitat and contiguous wintering areas. Family groups apparently comprise a flight unit for local movement, but these and unrelated birds may join in loosely formed flocks of modest size. Local flights typically are low, the birds in no particular formation. A recent observation, plus analogy with other swans, suggests a pattern of V-formation or modification of this may be formed at higher altitudes by larger flocks on longer journeys. The birds fly locally at any hr.; there is almost no information on time of departure on long migratory flights—probably early forenoon. Formerly, Trumpeters associated with migrating or wintering Tundra Swans in the Pacific Northwest and apparently they are doing so at present. In the Greater Yellowstone region they occur seasonally in company with large numbers of migrating or (few) wintering Tundra Swans.

Spring Observations in the Greater Yellowstone region confirm early reports that this swan historically departed from wintering areas early and, breaking into smaller flocks on approaching breeding areas, arrived early (ahead of spring thaw?) in boreal breeding habitat. Also, they departed late in fall, hence arrived late at wintering areas. Some occurrences of migrants at various locations were listed by Bent (1925), but whether these represent normal flights or stragglers is unknown.

In se. Alaska, there were 50+ Trumpeters near Cordova on Feb. 27, 1959, an early date (they may have wintered not far distant down the coast). For the Kenai Pen., earliest date is March 31, 1959. The birds at Lonesome Lake, B.C., begin leaving in late Feb. or early March. In general, it appears that April is the month of much northward movement, and many Trumpeters are preceded by Tundra Swans. Depending on timing of the thaw (it is much earlier near the coast than in the interior), the birds probably reach inland localities in Alaska during the last half of April and until some time in May.

Summer No molt migration is known. Breeders molt in the general vicinity of nesting territories; younger prebreeders, whether migratory or essentially sedentary, occur in flocks and molt in summer, on shallow lakes, not distant from traditional breeding areas. Older (paired) prebreeders evidently are more or less scattered, some perhaps even when molting.

Fall In Alaska there is movement from the interior in Sept., as total freeze-up occurs there by the first week in Oct. By mid-Oct. they generally are gone from the Kenai, except for an occasional family which remains for the winter. On the coast, at the Copper R. delta, autumn lingers late and so do the swans, many remaining until about mid-Nov. Presumably they moved there leisurely, ahead of freeze-up. A shift of birds down the coast presumably occurs from Sept. until very late in the year, timing and distance varying depending on severity of the season. They arrive at Lonesome Lake, B.C., beginning Oct. 20–25.

The Peace R. (Alta.) birds apparently accompany the last of the Tundra Swans on fall passage and, from banding evidence, are known to join some of the Red Rock Lakes birds that spend the winter in Fremont Co., Idaho.

Stopover locations of flocks, in past times when the population was larger, are unknown; records suggest, however, shallow lakes, bays, and sloughs of major river valleys. In Alaska the Kenai Pen. is a stopover location for some migrants, evidently also the Copper R. basin. L. Minchumina (cent. Alaska) was used in spring and fall in 1924; there is no recent information (but it is a nesting locality). Preliminary results of Canadian banding and color-tagging accomplished since 1954 show fall movement of Grande Prairie (Alta.) birds into w. Nebr., nw. Wyo., and Greater Yellowstone area (R. Mackay 1957). There are fall and spring sightings in Missoula Co., Mont. (Hoffmann et al. 1959). This swan migrated from B.C. into Wash. (A. Brooks 1926), this movement substantiated (J. Munro and Cowan 1947) and probably has continued. For example, a recent winter record, Dec. 4, 1966, in Grays Harbor Co., Wash. (G. Alcorn 1968).

The above is based mainly on Banko (1960) and H. A. Hansen et al. (1971), with some additional information. WEB

BANDING STATUS A total of 369 were banded Sept. 6, 1945–Dec. 31, 1957, at Red Rock Lakes Refuge, with 16 recoveries and 27 returns in that period, all in the area where banded or nearby. Shooting was the cause of death in 5 known cases and ranked high in suspected causes of mortality of the balance of recoveries (11). In addition to the above, 23 Trumpeters from Red Rock Lakes were banded and then released at Malheur Refuge (se. Ore.), 7 at Ruby Lake Refuge (ne. Nev.), and 31 at Turnbull Refuge (ne. Wash.). This listing is incomplete.

The total number banded through 1964 was 740 birds; main places of banding were Mont., Alaska, Alta., and Ore. (data from Bird Banding Laboratory). RSP

REPRODUCTION Main sources of information are Banko (1960) for Red Rock Lakes Refuge, Mont., and H. A. Hansen et al. (1971) for s.-cent. Alaska.

Age when **first breeds** varies, depending on density of birds in relation to available habitat of extablished breeders. For example, at Red Rock Lakes where limited breeding habitat is occupied by older birds, high numbers of cygnets have been followed by high numbers of breeders 5 years later. On the other hand, pinioned cygnets transferred to Lacreek Refuge (N.D.), where there were no other Trumpeters, formed stable pair bonds at 20 mo. of age and began their first successful nesting before attaining age 3 years (2 years 9 mo.) (Monnie 1966).

Pair formation It is probable that Trumpeters engage in pair formation activity in their 2nd winter, probably all of them by the following winter, regardless of length of interval thereafter before they first nest. Since younger cohorts contain more birds than older ones (there is less time for attrition), it follows that nonproductive mated pairs, i.e., mated prebreeders, can be numerous on summer range.

There are **displays** of prebreeders and of mated birds in any season. These often have somewhat of a group character in prebreeders and, in some degree, in breeders outside breeding season. Also there are displays, such as a "greeting," by birds as others alight nearby, illustrated in Banko (1960).

Captive prebreeders form various temporary attachments culminating in a stable bond. Then mates keep close company and, on water or on firm footing, face each other, their necks curved gracefully, their more or less opened wings undulating or beating in unison. In Alaska on June 12 a pair stood, the birds facing each other, wings arched but not fully spread, and proceeded to rotate in a circle while their heads bobbed in rhythmic motion; this continued for about 5 min. before observers interrupted it (M. Monson 1956). This may have been bond-maintenance behavior. Also, on winter range at Lonesome Lake, B. C., 2 birds swim toward each other till breasts touch, then slowly entwine their long necks.

Pair-bond form is believed to be **lifelong monogamy.** A record of 3 wild "Adults" accompanying a single brood in 2 successive seasons suggests persistence of an aberrant bond; a trio relationship has been noted in pinioned Trumpeters and is not rare in feral Mute Swans. This contrasts with over a thousand recorded cases of pair-only breeding-season associations in wild Trumpeters. In Alaska, a banded ♀ of unknown age mated with a ♂, also of unknown age, in the year following loss of her mate.

At Red Rock Lakes, pairs or small groups (probably families) visit and rest on frozen open marshes (subsequent breeding areas) as early as Feb., miles from the nearest open water. Pairs are observed regularly on such areas in March and April before the ice melts. Size of **territories** varies with population level and habitat. In 1957, eleven shoreline mi. of *Carex* habitat surrounding Upper Red Rock Lake (2,880 acres of open water) held 6 nests; the 1,540 acres of *Scirpus* marsh and *Carex* shoreline of Lower Red Rock Lake held 10 nests; the *Carex* island and shoreline habitat of Swan Lake (400 acres) contained 7 nests. Variation thus ranged from 480 down to 57 acres/nest. Studies of 35 territories in Alta. revealed that all but 2 were on separate lakes; some lakes of well over 1,000 acres were large enough only for one family (R. H. Mackay). In study areas in Alaska, there were only 4 known instances of more than a pair at a single body of water, the exceptions all being at large lakes (H. A. Hansen et al. 1971).

Usually 1 bird (probably ♂) defends territory; in some circumstances both participate. Defense usually is against other Trumpeters; aggression toward geese, herons, and pelicans has been noted but is uncommon compared with instances of tolerance. Aggressive display consists of partially extended half-raised quivering wings, extended neck, and staccato trumpetings; a somewhat erect body posture also is maintained when the bird is on firm footing, and occasionally on water by treading. This attitude usually is assumed by 2 facing birds, but a similar display occurs outside the breeding season by as many as 3–5 Trumpeters in a more or less circular grouping. Aggressiveness also consists of chasing, feather pulling, treading, and aerial pursuit—in territorial defense, or after 3 or more birds participate in the above display. In Alaska, nesting swans (both mates) display aggressively toward an aircraft (float plane) on the water, but switch to escape behavior as soon as anyone comes into their view. One nesting bird, however, forced an observer to retreat hastily.

In certain activities, as noted by de Vos (1964) in pinioned breeders, the sexes can be distinguished, as in the following. WATER-TREADING by ♂ only, body up at steep angle, wings lifted but not spread, head–neck arched down; and HEAD-BOW ♂ has neck curved under so that tip of mandible touches the ground; then head is moved forward gradually while the tip of the upper mandible is kept in contact with the ground; the ♀ has her head aimed straight down, the bill sometimes open when the mandible reaches the ground.

TRIUMPH CEREMONY   After repelling an intruder, the defender returns to the mate and they engage in mutual display; the defender swims with half-opened trailing wings and with neck folded back on the body, and his mate does likewise. This also occurs sometimes, evidently as an "ego booster," preliminary to attacking an interloper.

Nest site   In a 4-year period at Red Rock Lakes, 82 of 109 sites under observation were reoccupied, 4 being used every year (whether by the same individuals was not determined). These sites were mapped in Banko (1960). In the Greater Yellowstone region, the nest sometimes is partially screened, but usually is quite openly located on a marshy island or near the shallow shoreline of a lake, slough, or in an open marsh. The nest is elevated, usually being on one of a preceding year, and originally having been built on a muskrat house or semifloating bog mat with a cleared moat surrounding it. Materials at the site are utilized in building—rootstalks, stems, and leaves of *Carex*, *Scirpus*, *Typha*, and other marsh emergents; the lining is composed of similar items, but somewhat less coarse; feathers and down are present only incidentally. Both members of the pair from a standing or sitting position pluck and then deposit desired plant materials on the nest with comparatively rapid selection and with movements of head and neck. A completed structure resembles a flattened haycock, about 4 ft. in diam. and 2 ft. high.

Alaskan data from H. A. Hansen et al. (1971): old **nests** often are renovated and reused from year to year as determined from observations of banded birds; also, disturbance will cause desertion or movement to another location. The nest may be more or less afloat (built on emergent vegetation), or in shallow water, or (much less often) ashore. The ♂ uproots materials (clears a moat around the site) and places these at the base of the nest, where the ♀ can reach them. Duration of building varies, whether repairing an old nest or constructing an entirely new one (which may occur close to a formerly used site). A pair spent 2 weeks building a new one, but the first egg was laid only 6 days after construction began. There is very little down in the nest.

Copulation (data from pinioned birds at Delta, Man.). Mates swim slowly "in a synchronized fashion" and this is followed by mutual rapid DIPPING (of bill in water) and blowing into water (bird blows bubbles as the head is withdrawn gradually from the water); during the last (of usually 4–5) Dipping movements, the ♂ often crosses his neck over the ♀'s. Then the ♀ extends her neck and lowers her body into the water and the ♂ mounts from the side and with neck curved. The ♀ then is largely submerged. The ♀ raises her wings and head slightly before copulation and the ♂'s wings may be lifted slightly at the same time. The ♂ then pinches the ♀'s nape with his bill tip. At moment of dismounting, both birds assume an erect posture on the water, necks fully extended upward, breasts touching, the ♂ waving open wings. Calls are given at this moment. While treading water and with breasts raised and in contact, heads are lowered slowly, necks curved, and the folded wings are erected briefly over the back. They then flap wings in unison, waggle tails, and bathe. (Data from F. McKinney, also de Vos 1964.)

Egg dates (obtained by dating back from hatching dates) In the Greater Yellowstone area, laying normally commences in late April or early May and is completed about mid-May. The schedule is about the same in the Copper R. basin of Alaska, but later in the interior. **Clutch size** at Red Rock Lakes (70 clutches): 1 (of 2 eggs), 4 (of 3), 10 (4), 25 (5), 20 (6), 7 (7), 2 (8), and 1 (9). In the Copper R. basin, clutches of 1–7; mean clutch size varied from 4.4 (in the very late spring of 1964) to 5.5 (in 1965); for details and additional data, see H. A. Hansen et al. (1971). The eggs av. larger than those of the Tundra Swan, but there is great overlap in size. **Egg size** At Red Rock Lakes (109 eggs from 21 nests, meas. to nearest 0.5 mm.): length 104–123 mm., av. 110.9; breadth

66

68–77.5, av. 72.4 (Banko 1960). In s.-cent. Alaska (146 eggs): length 109.8–125 mm., mean 117.4 ± 8.8; breadth 69.8–81, mean 75 ± 1.0; the meas. and wt. of each of these eggs is given in an appendix in H. A. Hansen et al. (1971). **Shape** subelliptical to long elliptical; shell granular, **color** white until stained brownish. An egg is laid approximately every other day, i.e., it requires nearly 2 weeks to produce a large clutch. No parasitic laying is known. No replacement clutches are known and there is only 1 known instance of renesting. **Incubation** is by the ♀, who is not a constant sitter until the clutch is completed. The ♂ remains close by, on guard, most of the time. The ♀ covers her eggs and joins her mate, to bathe (and feed?) and presumably to relax. After incubation has begun, the covered eggs remain warm even if the ♀ is absent for hours.

Incubation period 33–37 days, both at Red Rock Lakes and in s.-cent. Alaska. In an av. clutch, hatching requires about 24 hrs. In the Greater Yellowstone region, where hatching occurs from about June 1 onward, **hatching success** is poor—at Red Rock Lakes 31 of 61 eggs (51%) in 12 nests hatched in 1949, 48 of 73 eggs (66%) in 13 nests in 1951, and 114 of 178 (64%) in 36 nests in 1955. In some years, as many as half the eggs laid failed to hatch; infertility and death of embryos were main causes of failure. On the other hand, hatching success was 55–90% during 6 years at Grande Prairie, Alta. In the Copper R. basin in Alaska, hatching success in 38 clutches (179 eggs): 1 or more eggs (total of 99, or 55.3%) hatched in 29 nests. On the Kenai Pen., 83 nests had 450 eggs and 371 (82.4%) hatched.

At Red Rock Lakes, 2 newly hatched cygnets weighed 7 and 7½ oz. on June 19, increasing in wt. (in captivity) to 15¼ lb. and 15 lb. 6 oz. by Sept. 2 (75 days). Wild fat preflight cygnets weighing over 18 lb. have been recorded rarely at this locality. In Alaska, cygnets weighing less than 8 oz. reached 19 lb. in 8 to 10 weeks; correlation of wt. to age is good up to 8 weeks, but after that the cygnets vary markedly (H. A. Hansen et al. 1971).

Preflight period At Red Rock Lakes, an av. of 2.6 cygnets left 12 nests in 1949. On the Kenai Pen. in 1957, an av. of 4.1 young in 13 broods was observed 7–14 days after hatching. At least in conterminous U.S., the first week of life is hazardous—some cygnets are trampled, others may become lost or deserted or entangled in vegetation and drown, still others are victims of leeches, and some have an unendurable number of internal parasites. In Alaskan studies, cygnet mortality within the first 8 weeks posthatching ranged annually 15–20%. Cygnets have been seen riding on the back of a parent (Hammer 1970), but this is not a usual trait such as it is in the Mute Swan. Young Trumpeters are closely attended by both parents until the former reach flight age; there are few exceptions. The parents will, however, desert readily, without defense or display, when escaping man. As observed in Alaska, if families are disturbed, they may leave the natal area and travel overland, through marshy habitat or even dense forest, to another lake; various instances were described by H. A. Hansen et al. (1971), who stressed the need of lack of disturbance during the brood season.

In 1965 in the Copper R. basin, 30 broods contained 151 cygnets at hatching and still contained 121 by Sept. 9, an exceedingly high survival (80%) to that date. In 1966 on the Kenai, of 121 cygnets in 28 broods, a total of 86 (71%) survived to flight age; and in 1967, 18 broods contained 71 cygnets, of which 55 (77%) reached flight age (H. A. Hansen et al. 1971).

Preflight young spend considerable time exercising their wings. **Age at initial flight** about 110 days in the Greater Yellowstone region, but has been noted to vary considerably, even within a brood, due to individual variation in development. In Alaska, some are able to fly before age 13 weeks and some not until 15 weeks (90–105 days posthatching). Because of the length of time required for rearing a brood to flight age, if the nesting season begins late and freeze-up comes early, preflight young may be trapped by ice. This hazard exists throughout the breeding range, even in the Greater Yellowstone area. A strong family bond persists at least into late winter. Also, 3 broodmates banded in 1955 were shot virtually together in late Oct., 1956, which indicates cohesion of a brood after separating from the parents. WEB

SURVIVAL   Some information on preflight young is given in the preceding section. In the Greater Yellowstone region, 6- to 10-week-old cygnets have an estimated life span of 6 years (assuming no interchange of birds with other regions); this is based on 16.5% annual turnover 1952–57 (total swans censused the previous year, minus "immatures" and "adults" censused in subject year, divided by total swans censused on the previous year). From Banko (1960). WEB

HABITS   Clannish. Breeders and prebreeders are moderately gregarious, except when many are widely distributed in pairs in summer. Flocks behave as loose aggregations of related individuals rather than well-integrated units. The Trumpeter associates with the Tundra Swan during migrations and in winter; also, in winter, with various ducks and geese. There seems to be no indication of territoriality outside the nesting–rearing season, although there is aggressive behavior. Prebreeders, probably younger ones especially, occur in small groups and loosely formed flocks; in summer they molt on large shallow lakes within the general breeding area. Older, paired, prebreeders evidently are more or less scattered in summer.

Flight intention may be indicated by pumping the head and neck while calling. Escape distance undoubtedly is greater during the flightless period of molting, but specific data are lacking. A very rapid swimmer when flightless and pursued, and also travels rapidly on solid or semisolid terrain under these circumstances. In deeper water, flightless older birds frequently resort to diving if sustained rapid swimming fails; maximum underwater distance about 50 ft. and depth to 5 ft. Escaping preflight cygnets sometimes attempt to dive, but may fail to submerge.

The Trumpeter flies at approximately 2 wingbeats/sec. (M. Edson), as determined from motion picture film. There are no data on speed.

The following behavioral notes are from de Vos (1964), from observations on pinioned birds. SHAKE (or preen)—as in other swans, starts with lateral waggling of the tail and spreads forward, finally to head and neck; wings are vibrated vigorously; head flicked once, quickly, near end of Shake. HEAD-FLICK an essentially rotary movement. FOOT-SHAKE foot extended backward and shaken a few times; most often occurs just prior to sleeping. DIPPING commonest movement; continuous up to at least 10 min. sometimes; head and neck submerged and rapidly withdrawn so that water runs over the back. (Most "bathing" consists of Dipping.) WING-THRASHING sometimes preceded by fast swimming; neck bent, bird "leans" to one side (as though partly capsized) and thrashes partly opened wings rapidly. (Rolling of body always is accompanied by thrashing.) PUDDLING rapidly with feet, "apparently to stir up food" (de Vos), but main use perhaps is to remove silt and mud from food plants (W. Banko). Done regularly.

Cygnets and birds of any age possess considerable adaptability to man's activities, if these are experienced regularly and without undue disturbance. They are docile in captivity and breed when given adequate quarters, although strife may develop if they share confinement with other large white fowl. They have a retentive memory over many years, of fright experiences.

Hudson's Bay Company sold some 108,000 swan skins, mostly of Trumpeters, in London between 1823 and 1880; this northern trade, which was discussed at considerable length in Banko (1960), surely was a prime factor in eliminating this species from a large segment of its breeding range. Some former breeding areas in conterminous U.S. have been lost because of drainage, ditching, and ploughing. Losses of swans from lead poisoning, starvation, hunting, and other factors, also were discussed by Banko. Of 103 individuals at Red Rock Lakes Refuge, captured when flightless in 1956 and fluoroscoped, a total of 15 (14.6%) were carrying lead shot (Banko 1960).

The total Trumpeter population frequently has been stated to have been fewer than 100 individuals about 1916, but this low figure did not include the birds of Alaska and any in Canada. These, until very recently, were generally believed to have been Tundra Swans. Even so, with more adequate reporting, the total population of Trumpeters was believed to have been less than 2,000 individuals in the early 1960s. In Aug., 1968, an aerial survey in Alaska counted 2,844 Trumpeters, where the total number that fall may have been 3,500–4,000 birds. At that time there also were about 100 known to be in Canada and over 900 in conterminous U.S.

The Greater Yellowstone aggregate of birds had a 10% annual increment 1932–52, increasing from 69 birds (incomplete ground census = 80 statistically projected) to 571 (aerially censused). In the period 1955–63, numbers leveled off (peak of 641 in 1958) and declined slightly. The general trend has been one of increase in breeding pairs, which have filled usable habitat, as birds matured, but fewer cygnets raised (only enough to replace annual losses). Population stabilization thus is related more to decrease of fecundity rather than increased mortality of prebreeders and breeders. From projection of fecundity data, these regional units were expected to stabilize at 600–700 individuals, assuming no further expansion in breeding range. These figures, however, had been exceeded by late 1968. In Alaska, "little growth potential remains" in much of the summer range of the Trumpeter (H. A. Hansen et al. 1971).

The much publicized wintering flock at Lonesome Lake, B.C., formerly fed on

69

aquatic plants in fast water at the lake's outlet, but a landslide in 1930 raised the lake level. The swans now are fed about ½ lb. of wheat per bird daily, from very early Dec. to the end of March. Orphaned cygnets do not accept this handout and gradually starve. (The few Tundra Swans wintering there also usually do not survive until spring.) For photos of this flock, see R. Edwards (1951), *Life* magazine **68** no. 13:48–56 (April 10, 1970), and *Alaska* magazine **39** no. 3:36–38, 55–56 (March 1973); for earlier history, see H. Chapman (1942).

Food is gathered in water by submerging the head and part of neck, or all of neck and part of body when up-ending. The birds do not dive to feed. The feet are used frequently and vigorously when obtaining underwater rhizomes and tubers, resulting in extensive excavations in the soft bottom. Food gathering is the most time-consuming daily activity, occupying long periods in any season, or short periods if abundant grain is provided. Feeding of territorial pairs usually is limited to territory, but occasionally a bird (the ♂ ?) flies elsewhere—sometimes several territorial diameters away—to feed.

Prebreeders usually feed in loosely formed flocks, or sometimes widely dispersed. (This section is based to a large extent on Banko 1960, which see for further information.) WEB

FOOD   Except for first few weeks of life when diet includes foods of animal origin, natural food is composed almost entirely of stems, leaves, seeds, rootstalks, and tubers of freshwater aquatic plants, so far as known (no data from tidewater wintering areas in se. Alaska and B.C.). In Yellowstone Park, cygnet droppings during the first 3 weeks of life av. 95% animal matter, with snail shells (*Lymnea stagnalis*) appearing in the droppings in Aug., along with increasing quantities of digested plant remains. Yellowstone Park cygnets change from animal to vegetable items after about 5 weeks of age [a month-old cygnet had eaten 3 freshwater shrimp (*Eubranchipus*), fragments of *Carex*, and small piece of *Chara*]. At Red Rock Lakes, stomachs of 6 cygnets estimated 3–4 weeks old contained 80–100% unidentified leaf and stem fragments of aquatic plants; seeds of *Carex* (chiefly) and other aquatics made up principal balance with only 1 stomach containing a trace of animal matter. At Bremner R. in Alaska, examination of feces on nest indicated heavy consumption of insects and crustaceans by cygnets; at one site, young were feeding on *Equisetum fluviatile* before age 2 weeks (H. A. Hansen et al. 1971).

Older records indicate that wapato, or duck potato (*Sagittaria* sp.), was a preferred food of this swan, epecially along Columbia R. where in 1806 Lewis and Clark noted both *C. buccinator* and *C. columbianus* "fed on that root," and where later *Sagittaria variabilis* [*S. latifolia*?] was noted as being a favorite food. If this is scarce, they utilize roots of other plants and, in higher latitudes, tender underground runners of grasses.

In Yellowstone Park the following are known foods: pondweed (*Potamogeton filiformis*) and water milfoil (*Myriophyllum verticullatum*); muskgrass (*Chara* sp.), waterweed (*Elodea canadensis*), duckweed (*Lemna triscula*), tule (*Scirpus* sp.), spatterdock (*Nymphaea polysepala*), bur reed (*Sparganium angustifolium*), and wapato (*Sagittaria cuneata*); filamentous green algae, *Carex* spikes, *Potamogeton* sp., *Nuphar* sp., and trace of animal matter (Trichoptera) from examination of 17 samples of droppings collected at Grebe Lake on Sept. 2.

At Red Rock Lakes, a Dec. stomach contained 443 *Potamogeton pectinatus* tubers and fragments of rootstalks (100%), a June stomach contained 597 of these tubers plus rootstalk and leaf fragments (96%), with remaining percentages of *Ranunculus aquaticus*, *Ceratophyllum* sp., filamentous algae, and seeds, principally *Carex* and *Potamogeton*. Two April stomachs (abnormal; the birds died of lead poisoning) contained chiefly leaves and stems of white buttercup *Ranunculus* (*trichophillus*?) and moss *Fissidens* (*grandifrons*?), both of which probably are less desirable food items.

Information on winter foods in Greater Yellowstone region is lacking, but these foods probably differ significantly from those of other seasons (difference in availability).

Reported to feed ashore occasionally, one author mentioning that the Grande Prairie population fed in grainfields fronting the lakes. Field feeding seldom observed in Greater Yellowstone habitat, but observed in wet meadows during spring breakup when it did occur. Observations on birds wintering on fresh water in B.C. indicate: seeds of yellow pond lily (*Nuphar polysepala*) and water shield (*Brasenia schreberi*), tubers of sago pondweed (*Potamogeton pectinatus*), and stems and foliage of similar species are attractive; *Fontinalis* sp. and *Scirpus* sp. are taken when preferred foods are not available; stems and roots of grasses and sedges, seeds of *Ceratophyllum demersum*, *Polygonum* sp., *Carex* sp., *Eleocharis* sp., and *Prunus emarginata* were identified from stomachs of 8 "adults" and 2 "juveniles" that had died from lead poisoning.

In captivity, *Scirpus* and *Lemna* have been taken naturally; the leaves and stems of *Sagittaria*, chopped *Typha* leaves, and mowed lawn clippings have been readily accepted as supplement to or as main source of green bulk food.

The above summarized from Banko (1960), which see for further details. The note in Delacour (1954) stating that this swan feeds preferably on wild celery, which is abundant in the lakes of Alta., is erroneous, as this plant is rare. Probably *Alisma gramineum* or *Sagittaria* was intended. WEB AWS

Tundra Swan

Cygnus columbianus

"Whistling" Swan (of New World) and "Bewick's" (of Old) are tundra-breeding geographical representatives (subspecies) of the same species.

Head rather rounded, with comparatively "shallow" bill (in lateral view its dorsal profile typically, but not invariably, at least somewhat incurved) and, although its lateral outline also is variable, usually it is more spatulate (sides curve out more, distally) than in either Trumpeter or Whooper. Tail rounded. Entire feathering white in definitive stages. By about age 2 years, lores and upper mandible usually have become black except: usually with yellow area on lores ("Whistling"), or lores and much of basal half of the upper mandible usually yellow ("Bewick's") and this generally terminates approximately at the nostril. At least in "Bewick's," variants include (rarely) individuals with yellow legs and more or less red in bill; a few individuals have the iris pale blue instead of dark brown. (Also see comparison in opening paragraphs under Trumpeter Swan.) For predefinitive stages of New World birds, see beyond. No tracheal bulla. Trachea forms a simple loop within the sternum, its presence posteriorly indicated within the body cavity by a bony upward bulge or ridge (very variable in size) along "floor" of sternum. For many further details and excellent text figs., see Sharpless (1832); there are more recent illus., among the best being fig. 64 in T. S. Roberts (1932) and fig. 21 in Banko (1960) for nominate *columbianus* and a fig. on pl. 3 in Schiøler (1925) for subspecies *bewickii*.

Sexes similar in appearance, ♂ av. larger. These data are for Am. birds, which av. larger than those of Eurasia: length 47–54 in., wingspread usually under 80 (but reportedly to 97!), wt. usually 12–18 lb. Two subspecies recognized, 1 in our area.

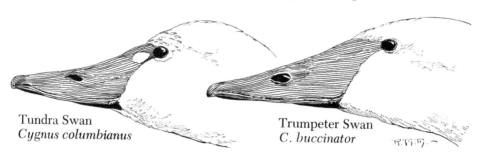

Tundra Swan
Cygnus columbianus

Trumpeter Swan
C. buccinator

DESCRIPTION *Cygnus columbianus columbianus.* One Plumage/cycle. Basic II arbitrarily is treated as earliest definitive, being all white; feather shapes and soft-part colors may undergo some slight further change. There is a gap, however, in dependable information between earliest cycles and those of birds old enough to have bred several times; the next paragraph describes the latter.

▶ ♂ ♀ Def. Basic Plumage (entire feathering), MIDSUMMER or later to following MIDSUMMER or later (except at least some wing coverts; see below); all **feathering** white, often with ferrous staining. **Iris** dark brownish, eyelids usually dark, occasionally more or less yellow. Naked **lores** black, not invariably with small elongated yellow area; **bill** not invariably all black—some individuals (with or without yellow on lores) have side base of lower mandible salmon red or toward a muted magenta (also the interramal area of lower mandible). Legs and **feet** black. In successful breeders, molting (with wing quills dropped near-simultaneously close to its onset) usually begins in the ♀ from within a few days to up to about 2 weeks after her brood hatches, i.e., later than in the ♂. The molting of parent swans is not synchronous; usually 1 adult can fly while the young are flightless (T. Barry). The earliest time for any breeders to become flightless (they remain so probably for at least a full month) is about the 3rd week in July; it must be later sometimes, since there are instances of birds in all-white feathering still flightless at least into early Sept. Failed breeders begin molting earlier than successful ones.

As observed in nominate *columbianus*, part of the wing molt is offset (delayed). Birds dyed with picric acid in winter go n. in spring and return in fall still showing a line of yellow-dyed upper coverts in the wing (W. J. L. Sladen). That is, these are the last feathers of the wing to be molted—after fall migration.

NOTES   Captive *bewickii* were "nearly full-winged" 32 days after loss of the previous quills (Heinroth 1906).

There has been a surmise that head–neck possibly are molted twice/cycle; birds dyed in winter, however, retain the color into summer and there is only 1 molt in the remainder of the year.

Scott (1966) made an illustrated formula or key for identifying particular individual *bewickii* by pattern of the bill and relative amounts of yellow, palish magenta, and black (which vary with individual). He noted that some individuals showed minor changes in pattern from year to year. Ogilvie (1968a) also reported an instance of increase in black and corresponding reduction of yellow.

AT HATCHING   See col. pl. facing p. 242. The lores are covered with down, which extends as far forward on top as on sides of bill; posterior margin of nail on bill more or less rounded. There is some individual variation in shade of the pale dorsum, even among siblings. For detailed description of downy *C. c. columbianus*, see Parmelee et al. (1967); for a brief one of *C. c. bewickii*, see Johnstone (1957b).

▶   ♂ ♀ Juv. Plumage (entire feathering), probably fully developed by age 9–10 weeks and, soon after, begins to be succeeded by Basic I (but the Juv. wing is long retained). Lores begin losing their down about the time the Juv. feathering is completed and then, like more than basal half of bill, are fleshy pink, muted rose, or lavender, with gape and remainder blackish. Iris brownish. **Feathering** variants of brownish gray, darkest on head, lightest (dingy whitish) on rump and underparts; some birds become stained, hence darker. Legs and **feet** grayed to vivid flesh color (individuals vary).

▶   ♂ ♀ Basic I Plumage (all feathering except wing), soon begins to replace Juv. (see above), some individuals acquiring much Basic I during late fall–early winter, others more gradually through winter, occasionally into spring. At least early in the span during which Basic I is acquired, the feathering still extends farther forward on top midline of bill than it does later when in definitive feathering. By winter, the **bill** varies (with individual) basally from a palish grayed magenta to muted orange-scarlet, grading to black tip on both mandibles. Incoming **feathering** mostly white, but a grayish or even gray-brown cast to head, neck, and parts of dorsum is typical. At a distance, in spring–early summer, this distinguishes yearling prebreeders from those a year older (the latter have white heads and necks). **Tail** white and generally not acquired until some time in winter. Legs and **feet** muted magenta with black webs, but usually have become very dark or black by spring. **Wing** Whether there are any new coverts is unknown.

▶ ♂ ♀ Basic II Plumage (entire feathering), summer to summer, **feathering** white. The molt by which this Plumage is acquired, the one by which it is lost, and any others that occur prior to breeding, begin early, often in latter third of June.

Shapes of long scapulars

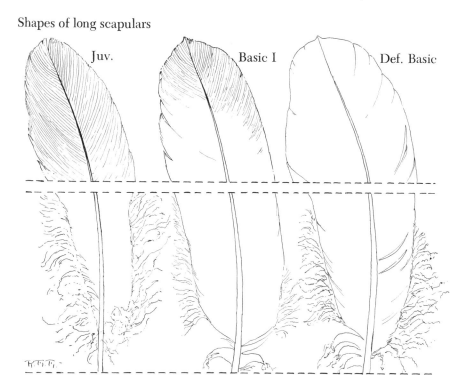

Juv. Basic I Def. Basic

Measurements of "adults" 8 ♂ (Alaska, Md., Va., N.C.): BILL 97–107 mm., av. 102.6; WING (across chord) 501–569, av. 538; TAIL 162–181, av. 170.8; TARSUS 105–117.5, av. 111.9; 15 ♀ (Alaska, Cal., Md., Va., N.C., and captivity): BILL 92.5–106 mm., av. 99.9; WING (across chord) 505–561, av. 531.6; TAIL 146–186, av. 165.3; TARSUS 99.5–115, av. 107.2 (Friedmann, in Banko 1960).

Weight (age-classes and seasons not indicated) of 35 ♂ av. 15.8 lb. (7.17 kg.), max. 18.6; 42 ♀ av. 13.6 (6.17 kg.), max. 18.3; and an unsexed bird at 21 lb. (A. L. Nelson and Martin 1953). Other available information, as in Kortright (1942), is in close agreement.

Comparison of maximum-sized Am. Tundra Swans with minimum-sized Trumpeters: Tundra Swans over 2 years old—max. in 7 ♂ was 19.5 lb., and in 21 ♀ was 19 lb.;

minima for Trumpeter—in 8 ♂ was 20 lb. and in 14 ♀ was 16 lb. In birds just over a year old, max. for Tundra—in 2 ♂ was 17 lb. and in 7 ♀ also was 17 lb.; min. for Trumpeter—in 8 ♂ was 18 lb. and in 4 ♀ was 15 lb. (Banko 1960). All these are wts. of live birds when flightless in molt; they are heavier when not molting.

On day of hatching, 8 incubator-hatched downies weighed 170.6–189.3 gm. (Smart 1965a).

Hybrids, known for certain only among captive stock, have occurred between this species and at least 4 other species of *Cygnus* (*atratus*, *olor*, *cygnus*, and *buccinator*), also domestic goose (*Anser*) and *Branta canadensis*; for references, see Gray (1958).

Geographical variation in the species: in N. Am., size av. larger, with reduced amount (sometimes no) yellow on lores (but full extent of this variation unknown); in Eurasia, size av. smaller, the lores and more or less of basal portion of bill usually yellow (but pattern and relative proportions of yellow and black highly variable). Especially in Eurasia, individual variation is greater and geographical variation in size less than authors usually have implied or stated; see below. RSP

SUBSPECIES **In our area** *columbianus* (Ord)—av. larger, typically with less (in some, no) yellow on lores; full descr. and meas. given above; N. Am. and has wandered to e. Asia.

Extralimital *bewickii* Yarrell—size av. smaller; lores and individually varying amount of yellow (usually much) on basal area of upper mandible. For meas., see Delacour (1954), Hilprecht (1956), who also gave wt., Vaurie (1965), and appendix in Scott et al. (1972). Breeds across n. edge of Eurasia, except extreme e. and w. areas.

"In specimens of Bewick's Swan obtained in the eastern part of the range the bill is on the average longer and wider than in western birds; those features do certainly not characterize all the eastern individuals of Bewick's Swan. In some specimens from Novaya Zemlya the bills are large, and those birds can not be distinguished from specimens obtained near Yakutsk; some east-Siberian swans have on the contrary small bills, not differing from those of the western type. In any case, in the eastern part of the range large-billed specimens certainly prevail, without being strictly localized geographically. Specimens with bills of an intermediate size are to be met with throughout the range. Under such circumstances, the east-Siberian race described under the name . . . *jankowskii* Alph. can not be recognized" (Tougarinov 1941).

After examining and measuring Eurasian breeding birds, Vaurie (1965) arrived at the same conclusion. RSP

FIELD IDENTIFICATION In N. Am. All-white swan with black bill and feet; often a small amount of yellow on lores (visible only at close range). Young in 1st fall–winter are dingy or patchy, their bills more or less muted pinkish or wine-colored basally. In flight or not, hardly to be confused with much smaller, comparatively stoutish, white *Anser caerulescens* (Snow Goose). Latter has at least some black in wing. Our white swans and geese often have much rust-colored staining, on head and neck especially. The Tundra Swan is noisy; its yelping, hooting, and shouting (remotely resembling voice of Snow/Blue Goose) may be heard long before the birds come into view. Migrants fly in long diagonal lines and broken chevrons, like geese; irregularly shaped bunches are more typical of small groups or families during low-altitude flights for short distances. Very gregarious.

Can be confused with the Trumpeter, but an experienced observer generally can distinguish them at considerable distance, the Tundra having softer voice, rounder appearing head, shallower bill. The Tundra Swan in N. Am. does not invariably have yellow on lores, nor does the Trumpeter invariably lack it. Tundra and Trumpeter occur together at various migration stopover and wintering localities. See under the Trumpeter for comparison of their tracks.

Trumpeter and Whooper (in N. Am., latter in Aleutians mainly), when at ease—afloat, ashore, incubating—have neck curved back at its very base, then going straight up as though out of forepart of back. In the Tundra Swan this "kink" is lacking and so the neck goes upward from very front of body, a posture duplicated by the other 2 swans when they stretch their necks up fully because they are suspicious, alert, excited, or about to take wing. Various illustrations of swans are misleading. For example, Fuertes (in Eaton 1910, pl. 22) painted the "Whistling" (Am. race of Tundra) Swan in gracefully arched neck plus arched-wing Mute Swan posture and later (in Forbush 1925, pl. 20) portrayed it in kinked-neck or "at ease" posture of Trumpeter and Whooper; in Witherby (1939, pl. 76) the Mute, "Bewick's" (Eurasian Tundra), and Whooper all are correctly portrayed, although the last is in "alert" (Tundra Swan!) rather than "at ease" kinked-neck posture. Various field guides show the correct anatomy and coloring of these various swans, but are deficient as regards postures. There are, of course, intermediate neck positions, but Larsen's fine illus. of these (in Schiøler 1925) point toward the distinctions just mentioned. The diagnostic differences in posture may be seen in various photos in Hilprecht (1956).

First-fall Tundra Swans generally have darker necks and more vividly pinkish bills than Whoopers of similar age. Under fair field conditions, an experienced observer can distinguish Tundra and Whooper in all flying ages by voice and/or appearance. RSP

VOICE   Sounds identical in Nearctic and Palearctic birds. Variations on *hoo* or *wow*, each note preceded by a kind of whistling (as though exhaling) sound audible only at rather close range. Calls vary from soft gooselike "conversational" babble of feeding flocks to loud trumpetlike calls or "shouting" in flight or in display—but always softer, more musical, lower pitched, and less buglelike than in Whooper and Trumpeter, and always can be recognized by an experienced observer. Less harsh than calls of the larger subspecies of Canada Goose. When a large number are active, they can be heard for a distance of at least 4 miles under favorable conditions. (These data from I. C. T. Nisbet.) Also see summary by Hilprecht (1956). RSP

HABITAT   *C. c. columbianus*—in **summer,** at and near tundra ponds, lakes, and sluggish rivers, less often near sheltered tidal waters; tends to avoid areas near exposed marine coasts. **Outside breeding season,** mainly extensive shallow fresh and brackish water; much less frequent on salt water. Migrants occur at ponds, lakes, flooded lowlands, slow-moving stretches of rivers, and estuaries.

   C. c. bewickii—in general, as above, but has changed winter habitat radically in European portion of range. All writers before 1935 described it as preferring salt water (or at best brackish water in areas where food was abundant, such as the Zuyderzee), and as being the most maritime of swans. Its 19th century haunts in w. Ireland and the Hebrides all were on salt water; there are even accounts of it riding out gales on the open sea when sheltered fresh water was available. Until 1938 all but a few English records were from the coast, but now it is exceptional for this swan to stop on salt water there. This change may be slightly exaggerated by the fact that most of the old records were from peripheral areas, which the birds visited mainly during hard frosts when most fresh waters were frozen, but insofar as it is real it is probably due to the following causes: **1** virtual disappearance of *Zostera* from former marine wintering areas during the 1930s. **2** desalinification of the Ijsselmeer (Holland) in 1932, which was followed by spread there of the birds' favorite food plants and may have accustomed the birds to fresh water; and **3** possibly also climatic changes—fresh waters now freeze less regularly than formerly. This paragraph is based on Nisbet (1955, 1959), whose later paper contains a useful list of references. RSP

DISTRIBUTION   (See map.) *Cygnus columbianus columbianus.* Wide breeding range, from Bering Sea to Baffin I. The majority, when breeding, is concentrated in ALASKA, especially in the vast Yukon–Kuskokwim delta, valleys around Bristol Bay, and inland from the shores of Kotzebue Sd. In Bering Sea, Hanna (1917) probably was correct in identifying as *columbianus* the swans seen in summer on St. Matthew I. Beyond to the north, a few pairs nest on the w. half of St. Lawrence I. (Fay and Cade 1959, Fay 1961); also note mention of Chuckchee Pen., below, under stragglers. The Tundra Swan breeds on the Alaska Pen.; it is not known as a migrant at the distal end, at Izembek Refuge, although it nests there (and on Unimak I.) and occurs the year round. Presumably those occurring into winter are injured or otherwise temporarily incapacitated birds which thus remain in the only part of their Alaskan breeding range where they could survive past Oct.

   In CANADA concentrated in parts of Mackenzie and Anderson r. deltas, most numerous a short distance in from the coast and numbers dimish from there toward tree line. Elsewhere across its summer range, breeders are scattered on areas of wet

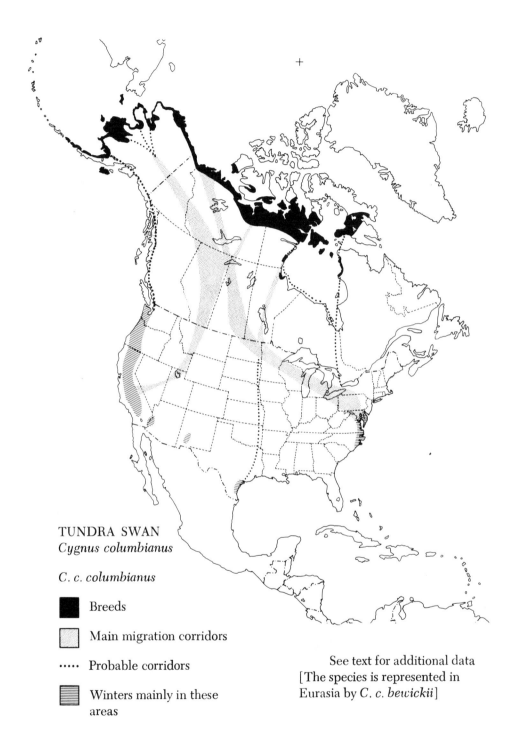

TUNDRA SWAN
Cygnus columbianus

C. c. columbianus

■ Breeds

▨ Main migration corridors

···· Probable corridors

▤ Winters mainly in these
areas

See text for additional data
[The species is represented in
Eurasia by *C. c. bewickii*]

tundra (some within tree line), away from rocky terrain. In se. Hudson Bay its nests on the Belcher Is.; in ne. Hudson Bay it nests in from the mainland coast at a number of localities, listed by Heyland et al. (1970), from near Port Harrison n. to C. Wolstenholme. Just off the Cape, it was first reported in 1866 to breed on the Digges Is. As to Mansel, Coats, Southampton, and part of Baffin I., see the distribution map. A pair nested in n. Baffin near Navy Board Inlet in 1970.

Especially as a migrant and winterer, this swan was hunted intensively and numbers declined until the period in which it was given full legal protection. Much rarer than formerly at Churchill, Man. (Taverner and Sutton 1934), but increasing recently. The large numbers that formerly wintered along the Gulf Coast of Texas probably were exterminated by shooting in the previous century; Dalquest and Lewis (1955) stated that there were no records for Texas over a span of 50 years, then 2 recent ones. In the late 1960s it was wintering regularly in small numbers in s. Texas. In Ala., 7 sightings Nov. 3–March 25 (Imhof 1958) and more subsequently. Some reuse of former migration corridors and reoccupation of former range is occurring.

The swan of the outer Aleutians is the Whooper (*Cygnus cygnus*) and those wintering in tidal waters of se. Alaska and B.C. (also at an inland locality in B.C.) are mostly Trumpeters (*C. buccinator*). In **winter** as in summer, Tundra Swans are concentrated at a few localities—estuarine waters of Chesapeake Bay and Currituck Sd. and interior valleys of Cal. Others are scattered elsewhere, from extreme s. B.C. down into Cal.; e. of the Rockies, from n. Nev., n. Utah, and s. Texas, to e. localities s. to n. Fla.

NOTE   The few Tundra Swans that attempt to winter with Trumpeters in the B.C. interior at Lonesome Lake seldom survive the season.

Straggler to the Labrador coast, Nfld., N.S., New Bruns., n. New Eng. (various records from colonial times onward), Bermuda, Cuba, and Puerto Rico. There are several Mexican records, the southernmost being far down in the interior in the State of Guanajuato. Has occurred in the Commander Is., several times (includes 3 collected) in coastal Anadyrland (Portenko 1939), perhaps breeds on the Chuckchee Pen., and perhaps is the subspecies that has been seen on Wrangel I. (Portenko 1972).

Palearctic distribution (of *C. c. bewickii*) is omitted here, except to note that the species generally is regarded as not occurring as a breeder in an area from w. of the Kolyma drainage eastward. Probably it has straggled much farther eastward, however.

Fossil in the Pleistocene of Fla. and Cal. and remains are known from widely scattered **archaeological sites;** for a listing for the species, of both Nearctic and Palearctic localities and published references to these, see Brodkorb (1964a). Swan bones have had various uses in the past, hence may be expected in many archaeological digs. A recent addition to the list of localities is in the Brooks Range in Alaska (E. S. Hall 1969). RSP

MIGRATION   In N. Am. The birds that nest in a particular area have traditional routes and summer and winter destinations (see distribution map). Segments of some aerial corridors still are not known with certainty. In both spring and fall, small numbers or even single birds may be expected away from main routes of travel. Also, flocks sometimes encounter a severely unfavorable weather front and are forced down, exhausted, at places they otherwise do not visit; occasionally the birds reverse their direction under these circumstances.

79

Ideal conditions for departure from wintering and stopover places are adequate rest and food beforehand and favorable weather, particularly light tail winds in early evening (Sladen et al., in Kuhring 1969). Mass departure generally occurs late in the day, but occasionally also in the morning. This is preceded by flocks making trial flights, seeming to depart, but soon returning. When they do leave on their long journey, birds of the youngest cohort, especially, may drop out, turn back, and not leave until weeks later.

This swan is an interior migrant, going long distances over most of its routes, then resting and feeding at traditional places. Migrants fly very high, by day and night, in flocks of about 5–200, the birds usually in diagonal lines; often they pass unseen. Flight speed (ground speed) av. about 50 mph. Prebreeders go to the summer quarters of breeders and remain, generally no great distance from nesters, through the season.

It is probable that analysis of all extant information would eliminate some uncertainties mentioned below.

Spring Both e. and w. winterers begin leaving winter quarters around mid-March (occasionally some local movement even in late Feb.) and departures continue until past mid-April; a few birds may linger into early May.

EASTERN-WINTERING BIRDS (Md.–N.C.) The largest subpopulation; trend nw. in a wide corridor. Major stopover places are: 1 ne. L. Erie (Long Pt. area) and especially the w. end of the lake and thereabouts; 2 Saginaw Bay; 3 w.-cent. littoral of L. Michigan and waters in e. Wis.; 4 Devil's Lake region in ne. N.D.; 5 Peace–Athabaska waters of n. Alta.–Sask. boundary; and 6 waters of inner deltas of Anderson and Mackenzie rivers. A small number (a few hundred in late 1960s) continue westward to destinations on the arctic slope of Alaska, thus traveling the farthest of any of our Tundra Swans.

The number of swans dwindles along the above corridor, because flocks leave it and head more directly northward toward their destinations. Presumably the birds that stop on ne. L. Erie go toward e. Hudson Bay and the e. Canadian arctic. Others, that leave the corridor at points at least as far w. as N.D., go n. (a large flight up through Man. beginning in early May) toward w. Hudson Bay and arctic areas beyond. Others probably go from the Peace–Athabaska area n. to the cent. Canadian arctic.

R.T. Piengel—

Banded birds that winter in Chesapeake Bay have been found at the other end of the corridor at localities from the Mackenzie delta e. to Coppermine in N.W.T.; birds dyed at Chesapeake Bay have been sighted along segments of the corridor; a radio-tagged bird was followed along part of the corridor and its travels were described and mapped by Sladen et al. (in Kuhring 1969).

It has been known since colonial times that Tundra Swans occur as far ne. as s. Mass., notably at ponds on Martha's Vineyard and Nantucket. There are more occurrences, and of more birds, in fall than in spring. Possibly there is an overland route between this area and e. Hudson Bay.

Where the few swans nest that now occur in s. Texas in winter is unknown; somewhere well e. in the Canadian arctic would seem logical, but possibly they come from w. Alaska.

Arrival dates are highly variable, depending on rate of advance of the spring season. In the Peace–Athabaska delta region, the swans usually begin arriving about mid-April with more until perhaps mid-May. Depending on season and on time of arrival, the stay of a particular flock probably varies from rather brief to longer than 3 weeks. In the Mackenzie and Anderson r. deltas, spring arrival is timed to coincide with the first meltwater pools on the ice, usually about mid-May (T. Barry). This swan has been recorded May 29 on Banks I. and June 1 on s. Victoria I. In an average year, migration continues until about June 10 on the mainland and to past mid-June in the Canadian arctic archipelago and in arctic Alaska.

WESTERN-WINTERING BIRDS are concentrated mainly in the San Joaquin and Sacramento valleys of Cal., with others in ne. Cal., se. Ore., and a few (regularly?) in extreme s. interior B.C. and a few also (irregularly?) e. of the Rockies in Nev. and Utah. The great majority of the birds in Cal. fly eastward over the Rockies. The Bear R. Refuge in n. Utah is a major gathering place, used in April–early May. Then the swans go n. via e. Idaho, w. Mont. (Freezeout Lake is a stopping place in early April), Alta. (early April–early May), then nw. across the ne. corner of B.C., across Yukon Terr., and down the Yukon–Kuskokwim drainage (beginning about May 1) toward the Bering Sea coast of Alaska. Quite likely, some of these birds travel far enough eastward in Alta. to associate with easterly winterers at the Peace–Athabaska stopover area.

The comparatively small remainder of the westerly birds, instead of crossing the Rockies, goes up interior valleys of B.C. and presumably continues onward fairly near the coast of se. Alaska. In the late 1960s, some 8,000 swans generally arrived about April 10 on Cook Inlet, Alaska, presumably birds from this westernmost segment. And presumably they arrive comparatively early on the Bering Sea coast of Alaska.

Fall So far as known, the swans use essentially the same corridors as in spring. Some linger within breeding range until new ice forms on inland waters, ordinarily by about mid-Sept. If the nesting season was late and freeze-up on schedule, young swans, still not having attained flight, may perish at freeze-up (as happened in 1959 in w. Canadian arctic). The first stages of the fall journey are somewhat more leisurely than those of spring, the birds moving on as freeze-up overtakes them.

EASTERLY WINTERERS The arctic Alaskan and nw. Canadian birds gather in the lower (inner) Mackenzie drainage; flocks rest and feed on small lakes e. of the river. Then they move down to the delta of L. Athabaska, as also presumably do those from the cent. Canadian arctic. Many thousands stop at lakes Claire and Richardson in ne. Alta. In an av. season, numbers build up in that area until very early in Oct. It is probable that many swans from the Alaskan Bering Sea coastal area also visit here. The swans linger late and, on departing, easterly winterers go se. along the traditional corridor. Some thousands stop in N.D.; between there and the Atlantic coast there is apparently at present no place where large numbers stop regularly. In a mild winter some may remain at inland localities n. at least to Minn. and Mich. Some pause on L. Erie, others on various smaller waters.

As of 1971, at least in fall, a few dozen of these swans migrate along s. Hudson Bay and down through James Bay.

WESTERLY WINTERERS Apparently, from the Peace–Athabaska region, part of the birds go down through e. Alta. and begin arriving at Bear R. Refuge usually beginning in the 2nd week in Oct. and peak numbers (over 41,000 in 1969) are present in the 2nd half of Nov. Apparently other swans, from the Alaskan Bering Sea fringe, fly via the Alaskan interior and then southward e. of the Rockies (reverse of a major line of travel in spring), and contribute heavily to the buildup at Bear R. Refuge. Then the birds go w. over the Rockies to Cal., although a few may remain in Nev., Utah, and even as far n. as Idaho in mild winters.

Swans banded in the Yukon Delta have been recovered in e. Alta, Utah, Nev., and one in sw. Ga.

There is little information on the westernmost segment, which presumably travels over sparsely inhabited terrain. Birds banded in the Yukon Delta have been recovered in extreme s. B.C. and in n.-cent. Cal.

Generally speaking, Tundra Swans begin arriving at winter quarters on both sides of the continent beginning about mid.-Oct., with large increments arriving during the next 4 weeks. After early Dec., movement usually consists of local shifting about, if the food supply dwindles or the season is severe.

The above account has its obvious deficiencies—little mention, for example, of birds of the e. Canadian arctic.

The majority of unusual occurrences of this swan are caused by adverse winds (which force migrants to halt or turn back), unusually cold winters (which result in a scattering of southerly occurrences), prolonged warm fall season (which delays migration), and various factors—late and cold spring, unusually cool summers, scarcity of nutritious food, etc.—that prevent acquisition of adequate body reserves for making sustained long flights.

For Palearctic *bewickii* there is no single coverage of migration, the subject being touched upon in papers in various languages. RSP

BANDING STATUS The total number banded in N. Am. through 1964 was 1,168 individuals and there were 24 recoveries through 1961; main places of banding: Mackenzie Dist., Ore., Alaska, and Md. (data from Bird Banding Laboratory). There has been considerable banding in subsequent years. There has been some banding of *C. c. bewickii* at various places, the number British-ringed through 1969 being 199, with 8 recoveries. RSP

REPRODUCTION (*C. c. columbianus* unless otherwise indicated.) Age when **first breeds** probably variable; minimum of 2 or 3 years (see Trumpeter Swan for effect of crowding of individuals on age when breeding begins in that species). Pair bond probably **lifelong monogamy**, once a firm bond is established. In *C. c. bewickii*, as observed on winter range in England, in 7 years no pair bonds were dissolved; also, if a bird lost its mate, sometimes it was not seen remated until the 3rd winter afterward (Scott 1970). Displays both by prebreeders and breeders, occur in winter and continue during pauses in spring migration. Especially in winter, displays are rather communal in nature—a pair or group begins calling and wing waving and this becomes contagious in the flock. Various authors have written at some length on displays of *bewickii* (see Hilprecht 1956), but there are few data for nominate *columbianus*.

Mutual **displays**, including vocal accompaniment, as observed in England (*bewickii*) and at L. Erie (*C. c. columbianus*), are identical (I. C. T. Nisbet). Two (occasionally 3) "adults" on land or water: the birds face one another, necks stretched slightly forward so that heads are close or even crossed, the wings half to fully spread and may be in motion continually; the birds utter all the while a loud clear call, higher pitched and more incisive than their usual calling. In an intense form of display, necks are held almost straight up and bills jerked up and down to the fullest possible extent. After a few sec. to a half min., the birds separate and appear to feed quietly. In squabbles, one bird drives off another with loud calls and neck extended stiffly forward—at about 45° by a swan on water, but more gooselike and nearer horizontal on land. "Young" are submissive to "adults." A few actual fights have been observed, the birds swimming or standing breast to breast, buffeting each other with wings. These activities occur at least Jan.–March in England (little time spent observing outside this span) and observed in March on L. Erie (Nisbet). Also see Scott (1966) for individual and group dominance in *bewickii*.

On the Texas coast in winter, N. L. Davis (1895) reported Tundra Swans in a flock on water "curling their long necks around each other, all making a strange honking noise, peculiar to themselves." There is a description by Larsen (in Schiøler 1925) of a pair of *bewickii* twining necks, ♂ seizing ♀'s "shoulder," and turning around and treading her; later they both flapped wings.

On nesting territory the ♂ or ♀ will chase intruding individuals by aerial flight, often at a steep flight angle, with neck slightly arched and head held high. The pursuer often pulls out some tail coverts of the pursued before the chase ends. Then the resident pair, on territory, have a mutual Triumph display with wings at least partly spread and shaking.

Yearling prebreeders, as they are excluded from nesting territories, gather in flocks of increasing size beginning in early June, at choice feeding beds of *Potamogeton filiformis* at Anderson R. delta, Kugaluk R., and in the Mackenzie delta. By early July, such flocks contain up to 1,800 individuals and then these break into smaller groups of less than 20 birds that begin to molt by July 20. There are indications that 2-year-old prebreeders establish territories in June, but do not attempt to nest. (Data from T. W. Barry.)

Nest sites preferably are on islets in tundra ponds and lakes, but others are ashore and not always close to water. The location is dry, as on a raised spot—even a low hill—or, in swampy tundra, on a hummock; generally it commands a sweeping view. In optimum habitat, several pairs may have nests very widely spaced but still in view of one another.

83

Nest a flattened mound, to over 6 ft. diam. and up to 2½ ft. high. Mosses, sedges, grasses, willow and even driftwood are used in construction, depending on what is available close to the site. Wads of moss, grass, and sedge usually are folded and poked into the nest, and the nest can thus be distinguished by these folded tufts or wads. There is a fairly deep depression for the eggs. The same site is used in successive years. Sometimes the surrounding area is cleared of vegetation by the nest-building ♀, probably assisted by the ♂. At a locality on s. Victoria I. where no swans were seen on June 5, the huge nest had been built and 3 eggs had been laid and were being incubated on June 13 (Parmelee et al. 1967). At the time the clutch is being laid, usually there is a little **nest down** intermixed with the nest materials. Although some more is added during incubation, the total is small—even less than in Snow Goose nests. The ♀ usually pulls the mixture of mosses and down over the completed clutch before she leaves the nest. Gebauer's data (in Delacour 1954) on roles of ♀ and ♂ in captivity are at variance with these statements.

Maximum number of eggs/clutch in 20 clutches was 5 (MacFarlane 1891); usual **clutch size** 4 or 5 eggs; the upper limit apparently is 7 (Bent 1925, T. Barry), as indicated below.

One **egg** each from 19 clutches (Alaska to Hudson Bay): **size** length 105.18 ± 4.87 mm.; breadth 68.42 ± 2.50; radii of curvature of ends 22.62 ± 2.68 and 18.19 ± 2.17; **shape** usually intermediate between long elliptical and subelliptical; elongation 1.53 ± 0.064; bicone −0.078; asymmetry +0.100 (FWP). Shell nearly smooth, without gloss, **color** whitish cream.

From w. to e., some **dates for clutches** or incubating birds are: ALASKA just outside Wales area—clutch of 4 on June 1, of 3 on June 2 (A. Bailey 1943); near St. Michael—eggs June 14 (E. W. Nelson 1887); Hooper Bay area—among earliest waterfowl eggs deposited, often by May 20 (Brandt 1943) (and he may have referred to a late season). CANADA Mackenzie delta—clutch of 5 on June 10, of 6 advanced in incubation June 21 (Porsild 1943); near mouth of Anderson R.—earliest egg on May 27 and av. date of clutch initiation is June 2 (T. Barry); Richards I. in Mackenzie delta—a swan incubating 4 eggs on May 30 (Barry); Banks I.—birds sitting on 2 nests seen within the period June 20–24 (Manning et al. 1956); s. Victoria I.—3 eggs early in incubation on June 13 (Parmelee et al. 1967); Adelaide Pen.—clutch of 4 not pipped July 14, another of 4 hatched by same date (Macpherson and Manning 1959); Southampton I.—an Eskimo found about 20 nests at C. Low before June 1 and took 2 clutches of 3; elsewhere on the island a clutch of 3 fresh on June 3, and of 3 each on June 21 and 27 (Sutton 1932). Although these various dates are useful, it must be remembered that time of laying at any particular locality varies a great deal.

In a late season, many swans nest late and have fewer eggs, or do not nest at all. In the Yukon–Kuskokwim delta, the av. clutch size in the very late spring of 1964 was 3.3 eggs (41 clutches) compared with 5.0 (42 clutches) in the early season of 1967 (Lensink, in H. A. Hansen et al. 1971). In the Anderson R. delta region, clutches of 1, 2, and 3 eggs predominated in the late seasons of 1957 and 1964, and there were clutches of 5, 6, and 7 in the early season of 1963 (T. Barry).

Eggs of *bewickii* have been found on s. Novaya Zemlya by May 29 and in the delta of the Kolyma by June 2. These are early dates.

84

Incubation by the ♀, the ♂ on guard at a station close by, may be usual; however, incubation by the ♂ has been noted in several pairs at Anderson R. (T. Barry). **Incubation period** of captives was given as 5 weeks by Gebauer (in Delacour 1954), but Tougarinov (1941) gave 29–30 days, presumably for wild *bewickii*. In England, at the Wildfowl Trust, 30 days for a captive ♀ (Johnstone 1957b); and in 2 seasons the same ♀ sat for a full incubation period on eggs that did not hatch, then renested and successfully hatched 2nd clutches (Delacour 1964).

Rearing period The downies are unable to dive until they are about 10 days old; older flightless young, and flightless parents, dive well when pursued (T. Barry). In the Churchill, Man., area, a pair with young apparently had traveled at least 2 mi. overland from the nest (Pepulak and Littlefield 1969). Parents move broods to larger lakes or rivers, probably to avoid an early freeze-up of small, still, waters. Nevertheless, an estimated 3–5% of preflight young are frozen each year in the Mackenzie and Anderson r. deltas. Most of the young there can fly by Sept. 2. The latest date for still flightless young is Sept. 20 and the last family group was seen in the Mackenzie delta on Oct. 9. (Data from T. Barry.)

On Southampton I. in the cold summer of 1945, most cygnets that hatched froze before they could migrate (Manning 1949).

Flight is attained at an estimated 9–10 weeks; undoubtedly there is considerable individual variation. The family remains together during fall migration, through winter, and to a large extent during spring migration; see D. Q. Thompson and Lyons (1964) for spring data; then breeders go to territories from which prebreeders are excluded. Then the latter sometimes are found, in groups, sometimes in areas quite remote from where any breeding territories are known to exist. Young swans (*bewickii*) in their 2nd winter have been known (Scott 1966) to rejoin their parents who then also were accompanied by young in their 1st winter. RSP

HABITS (Subspecies *columbianus* unless otherwise indicated.) In the boreal summer, prebreeders are quite terrestrial and, like breeders, their wariness greatly increases during the flightless period.

Outside the period of breeding and molting, the birds are restless, active, and noisy. They are very gregarious, in herds of hundreds or even many thousands, with groups constantly arriving and departing. As in geese, the family is a cohesive unit in winter. Large groups are very shy, families much less so, and detatched singles are quite unwary. If standing or swimming birds are alarmed, flight intention is indicated not only by upstretched necks, but also by an arching of the inner portion of the wings. This produces a more arched (higher) lateral body profile and, especially as viewed directly from the rear, a fairly conspicuous cleft down the middle of the back. The birds take flight with ease from water or land and probably spend more time on the wing than other N. Hemisphere swans. Various recorded flight speeds range 18–55 mph, including 45 mph air speed when pursued by an aircraft and 50–55 max. air speed as noted from aircraft (C. H. Blake). During 11 hr. and 10 min. of flight, a radio-tagged bird had an av. ground speed of 51 mph. (Sladen et al., in Kuhring 1969).

In the Anderson–Mackenzie delta region, from the time when the first meltwater pools are on the ice until breakup in early June, the swans feed exclusively on strands of

Potamogeton filiformis; the dark strands of this pondweed absorb heat and thus thaw free, in narrow tubes of water, in the ice (T. Barry).

This swan gathers submerged vegetation (by up-ending if depth of water is suitable) or plant materials on tidal flats or ashore, sometimes feeding far from water. Diving is not a regular habit. When a group is feeding, some individuals are on guard constantly. A grubber as well as a grazer ashore, often pulling up and eating the whole plant. As also recorded for subspecies *bewickii* by Brouwer and Tinbergen (1939) and Nisbet (1959), Am. Tundra Swans sometimes paddle with their feet before feeding, presumably to clear the mud from their food plants. Also, underwater grubbing creates pits or "swan holes" which are a considerable annoyance to anyone wading where they occur.

Various geese and ducks swim among the feeding swans and feed on fragments of the vegetation uprooted by the larger birds. Baldpates (*Anas americana*) and several *Aythya* do this commonly.

Since the majority of swan skins in the northern trade in the previous century probably were of Trumpeters, they are discussed under that species.

Swans and swan eggs are taken by Eskimos whenever the opportunity to do so occurs. In the Yukon–Kuskokwim delta area the Eskimos in 1964 took about 5,600 swans (Bartonek et al. 1971). Perry R., where the Tundra Swan has bred in numbers (at least formerly) has the native name Koguak ("place of swans") and the local tribe is called Kogmiut ("swan people").

The very greatly reduced Am. population of Tundra Swans was given legal protection in 1918, but recovery in numbers was slow for a long time afterward. Even now, the taking of swan eggs and the hunting of flightless molting birds by Indians and Eskimos are significant mortality factors in some areas. Furthermore, Sherwood (1960) discussed illegal shooting first among mortality factors in w. conterminous U.S., with lead poisoning next in order. At Tule and Lower Klamath refuges numbers for the years 1948 and 1954–59 inclusive varied from about 9,200 to 20,000 swans, with estimated annual mortality there from ingesting lead shot ranging from 1.0 to 3.3% of the birds. Usual symptoms of lead poisoning are gradual weakness and emaciation, as compared to no emaciation in heavy mortality from fowl cholera such as occurred at Lower Klamath in 1958 (Rosen and Bankowski 1960). For further data on lead poisoning, see Quorthrup and Holt (1940), Sherwood (1960), and Trainer and Hunt (1965).

In spring, migrants alight some years on the Niagara R. (N.Y.–Ont.) above the falls. Those that get into the swift current are fated to be swept over the falls to their destruction. Various known instances of this, from 1750 onward, were summarized by A. H. Wright (1913). The instance on Mar. 15, 1908, when over a hundred swans were swept over the falls, was described graphically by Savage (1908). Fleming (1912) reported additional instances. In spring of 1955, easterly birds migrating northward encountered a severe weather front and many were forced down, exhausted, in w. N.Y. and in Ont.; some lingered on lakes all summer. In 1966, summer arrived late and was cold; the swans were not able to accumulate adequate energy reserves for making long nonstop flights. Lean birds, young and old, stopped at scattered localities along what are usually nonstop segments of the easterly fall corridor.

Graphs in Glover and Smith (1963) showed the w. wintering subpopulation as having increased from about 10,000 in 1949 to over 40,000 in 1962–63; within that span of time the e. subpopulation was around 30,000 in 1950, rose to 90,000 in 1955, dropped to the former level in 1958–59, and was about 50,000 for some time thereafter. Year-to-year fluctuations seem to be very great, probably reflecting the influence of weather on the annual increment of young. The continental population was estimated at over 120,000 late in 1966 and continues to fluctuate but evidently to trend upward. Through the 1960s, the number of breeders plus summering prebreeders in Alaska averaged over 60,000 individuals.

No total figures are at hand for Palearctic *bewickii*, but the population is only a fraction of that of nominate *columbianus*.

Under special permit, with season limit of 1 swan/hunter, the first recent open season was Oct. 13–26 inclusive in 1962 in Utah. Some 320 swans were bagged—a figure not a great deal larger than the presumed illegal kill in that state alone in some prior years. The number bagged in subsequent open seasons were as follows: 392 (1963), 335 (1964), 336 (1965), 246 (1967), and 520 (1968). In each year, about as many also were reported hit, including birds downed and not retrieved. From a Tundra Swan one gets well over a pound of feathers and, unless the bird is young, some fairly tough and not especially tasty meat.

In the Chesapeake Bay region the increasing numbers of swans are damaging to soft-shelled clams (*Mya*), reducing the commercial catch of this shellfish; the swans also compete with ducks and geese for the available supply of submerged aquatic vegetation. By the late 1960s, in late winter, flocks of swans regularly were spending time in cornfields on the E. Shore of Md. and the northern neck of Va. The same has occurred in Cal. The change in habits, evidently resulting from depletion of usual foods, was causing some pressure for restricted legal hunting.

NOTE   The name "Tundra Swan" is appropriate for the species *Cygnus columbianus*, whose Nearctic subspecies is called "Whistling Swan" and whose Palearctic subspecies is variously called "Bewick's Swan," "Tundra Swan," or something else, depending on language and author. Swan names have a rather garbled history in the English language. To call the 2 subspecies of *Cygnus columbianus* American and Eurasian Whistling Swans respectively would appeal in N. Am. (because "Whistling" is retained), but this is not the most appropriate name on a Holarctic basis. The following 2 paragraphs were contributed by A. W. Schorger at the editor's request.

The 2 Am. swans were clearly recognized by Lewis and Clark (P. Allen 1814). As to the smaller species, the call "begins with a kind of whistling sound, and terminates in a round, full note, louder at the end: this note is as loud as that of the large species; whence it might be denominated the whistling swan." A year after this information was published, Ord (in Guthrie 1815) listed Whistling Swan, *Anas columbianus*, without a description. Sharpless (1832) gave an excellent description of the bird as a new species, *Cygnus americanus*, which he called the American Wild Swan. Two years later Nuttall (1834) used Wild or Whistling Swan. The latter name soon passed into general usage.

It is possible that Am. use of "Whistling" was influenced by the English vernacular names of the Whooper. Willughby (in John Ray 1678) described this bird and called it Wild Swan, Elk, or Hooper. As to the voice, he quoted a man as having heard "an unusual and most sweet murmur composed of most pleasant whistlings and sounds." Few ornithologists can detect whistling; however, A. H. Evans (1899) stated that "The

87

note is trumpet-like or whistling." In Pennant (1785) the Whooper becomes the Whistling Swan which occurs also in America. The habitat of the Whooper was given in 1790 as Europe, Asia, and N. Am. (Latham 1790). The Am. Tundra or Whistling Swan is sufficiently similar to the Whooper so that their supposed identity is understandable. In the early 1700s, Lawson (1709) distinguished 2 kinds of swans in N.C., the larger called the "Trumpeter" and the smaller the "Hooper." The name Whistling Swan commonly was applied to the Whooper (*C. cygnus*) up to the end of the last century. Forbush (1925) prefixed "American" to "Whistling Swan" which avoids possible confusion. Delacour (1954) maintained separate names in English for 3 subspecies of *C. columbianus* (includes 1 now not recognized), without providing an inclusive one for the species. RSP

FOOD   *Cygnus columbianus columbianus.* Very largely stems, seeds, and bulbous roots of aquatic plants; also seeds and young shoots of cultivated grains. The small amount of **animal matter** consists mainly of the larvae of aquatic beetles and dragonflies, worms, and mollusks. Frogs, tadpoles, and fish reported by Yorke (1891). A swan collected near Camp Harney (Ore.) had eaten 20 mollusks having shells about ½ in. long (Bendire 1875).

Plants   In e. U.S., foxtail (*Alopecurus*) (Bent 1925) and other grasses; wild celery (*Valisineria americana*); pondweeds, especially sago (*Potamogeton pectinatus*); smartweeds (*Polygonum persicaria*); square-stem spike rush (*Eleocharis quadrangulata*); arrowhead (*Sagittaria*); coontail (*Ceratophyllum demersum*); mermaid weed (*Prosperinaca*); in small amount, muskgrass (Characeae), bulrush (*Scirpus*), and horsetail (*Equisetum*) (Martin et al. 1951). In upper Chesapeake Bay region, principally wild celery, wigeon grass (*Ruppia maritima*), sago pondweed, and a few bivalves (*Mya arenaria, Macoma balthica*) (R. E. Stewart and Manning 1958, R. E. Stewart 1962). Stomach of a swan killed in Md. in Nov. contained a seed of bulrush and a ball of wild celery about an inch in diam. (Judd 1902).

In w. conterminous U.S., grasses; sago pondweed (*Potamogeton pectinatus*); horsetail (*Equisetum*); and bur reed (*Sparganium*); Columbia R. Valley, tubers of arrowheads (*S. latifolia* and *S. arifolia*) (McAtee 1914). Stomach of a swan taken in Cal. in Dec., aside from a large amount of gravel, contained almost entirely *Potamogeton pectinatus*: fibers 26%, ground seeds 8%, and 541 whole seeds 65%. Crops and gizzards of 50 specimens from the great Salt Lake valley contained almost exclusively the seeds and tubers of sago pondweed (Sherwood 1960). Rice and barley eaten in the stubble (Moffitt 1939). Occasionally destructive to grainfields in winter (J. Grinnell et al. 1918).

From summer range there is no information from digestive tracts. However, in low-artic and subarctic areas, the birds spend much time on slow-moving and quiet waters, obviously feeding on the dense beds of *Potamogeton*. The growth of the previous year is available from the time when there is a layer of meltwater on the surface of the ice; by mid-July, new growth reaches the surface of the water, where it forms dense mats beginning in Aug. AWS

White-fronted Goose

Anser albifrons

Medium-sized rather slender goose, mostly in the medium to dark range of general coloring. Definitive stages: bill usually a variant of pinkish (in Greeland birds orange), its dorsal profile normally somewhat concave, the feather margin at side base of upper mandible tends to be curved outward (it is nearer straight in the Greylag, *Anser anser*), and nail whitish; a white "front" adjoins bill at top and sides (some white on chin also is common), very rarely extending back on forecrown to over the eyes (as it does normally in the Lesser Whitefront, *A. erythropus*); relatively inconspicuous eyering; underparts vary greatly but usually belly and lower sides at least considerably blotched very dark, hence "specklebelly"; feet more or less orange. Juv. has dark sides and flanks, unmarked palish belly, and lacks white facial "front." As in geese in general, no tracheal bulla; for description of the trachea, see Latham and Romsey (1798).

Sexes essentially similar in appearance, ♂ av. larger. In the species as a whole, including all size variation, length 25–34 in., wingspread 50–65, wt. 4½ to perhaps 9 lb. Most mature birds, however, do not have a wingspread greater than 58 in. and weigh 4½–7 lb.

There are 4 Whitefront subspecies. Three are in our area; 1 nests in Greenland and 2 in N. Am., and the latter 2 are more or less redefined in this volume, as follows. The name *gambelli*, which in recent decades has been restricted to relatively few individuals at upper limit of size in the species, is used for a widespread population of individuals that av. large. The name *frontalis* is restricted to small birds of part of ne. Asia and part of w. Alaska; those of each side of Bering Sea migrate via the corresponding side of the Pacific to winter range. The nominate subspecies is entirely extralimital, nesting across n. Eurasia to somewhere in the vicinity of the Kolyma drainage; most of these birds migrate westward toward or to the ne. Atlantic.

DESCRIPTION *Anser albifrons gambelli*, which breeds in parts of Alaska and Canada, is treated in detail here; some information is drawn from other subspecies. One Plumage/cycle. Various feathers differ in shape in each of the earlier Plumages, the shape becoming essentially stabilized beginning with Basic II which may be regarded as earliest definitive.

▶ ♂ ♀ Def. Basic Plumage (entire feathering), worn from about JULY—AUG. to the following JULY—AUG. (overlapping in the single molt) by breeders, but molting begins earlier (in JUNE) in prebreeders. **Bill** pinkish orange (rarely orange), **iris** brownish. Coloration of eyelids varies with individual from orange through yellow (latter in estimated 10% of individuals) to brownish, evidently with some seasonal variation. **Head** white area (its size varies with individual) adjoins sides and top of bill, the chin often with some white anteriorly; remainder of head individually varying from medium drab brown to much darker, and darkest at border of white "front"; the neck usually at least quite dark, the feathers on sides pointed, giving a furrowed effect. **Upperparts** mantle like head or lighter and with gray bloom in new feathering, the feathers with sharply defined pale brownish or whitish terminal edges; lower back and most of rump same (or with paler rump), but feathers without light tips; upper tail coverts white (sometimes

89

some are grayish along their shafts). **Upperparts** breast paler than neck, the belly vari-able (to whitish) and usually having irregular patches, separate or merging, which are nearly black and extend up on sides; except for such patches, sides and flanks olive brownish, the uppermost feathers with light edging that forms a whitish line where these feathers overlap the folded wing; vent to base of tail white; **tail** feathers brownish gray, broadly tipped white; legs and **feet** variable, from somewhat reddish orange to orange-yellow, more muted seasonally. **Wing** greater primary coverts dark olive grayish, tipped white; primaries dark, nearly black, the shafts paler and the vanes (inner usually darker than outer) paling toward base; secondaries very dark; under-surface of wing almost evenly darkish.

At Kindersley (Sask.) in fall of 1961, live-trapped Whitefronts were examined and classified as to amount of dark area on venter, from 0 (belly gray, unmarked) to 5 (al-most entirely black); the figures for "adult-appearing" [Basic II onward] individuals were as follows: 211 ♂: 0 (1 bird), 1 (1 bird), 2 (36), 3 (89), 4 (70), 5 (14); and 216 ♀: 0 (0), 1 (7), 2 (59), 3 (91), 4 (52), 5 (7). There was a definite tendency for ♀ ♀ to have more or larger intervening light areas than ♂ ♂. In *A. a. albifrons*, according to Scott and Boyd (1954), variability of belly markings is not directly dependent on age or sex and, evidently, there is a tendency for markings to be of the same size on an individual in successive years. A captive N. Am. bird, observed for 10 years, always had an un-marked belly (J. Lynch).

In yearling prebreeders, Prebasic II molt starts by some time in June as the birds near age 1 Year. Ordinarily, considerable head–body molting proceeds quite rapidly, then the birds become flightless; they regain flight about 3½ weeks later. In some indi-viduals, molting continues after flight is regained, even being prolonged into fall; sometimes it appears to be interrupted, then completed in winter–early spring so that entire Basic II feathering is not acquired until such individuals are over 18 mo. old. When the birds become breeders and breed successfully, flightlessness begins when the brood is about 2 weeks old; that is, often around mid-July. Failed breeders com-mence molting earlier.

Several partially white individuals have been seen in fall in Sask. (A. Dzubin). Al-binistic, buffy, and melanistic individuals have been noted in *A. a. albifrons* (Oliver 1970 and sources he cited).

AT HATCHING   The goslings of *gambelli* from near the e. limits of nesting, at Perry R., are the lightest known from N. Am., being strikingly paler than dark *frontalis* of the Yukon–Kuskokwim delta. Birds from these 2 areas are shown together in a mono-chrome illus. in H. C. Hanson et al. (1956). For dark young *frontalis* in color, see plate facing p. 242 in this volume and another in Brandt (1943). Regardless of geographical or other variation, a lighter and more or less yellowish "front" shows on the head of down-ies of this species.
▶   ♂ ♀ Juv. Plumage (entire feathering), perfected soon after flight is attained, usu-ally in AUG., and much of head–body feathering generally replaced by Basic I by MID-WINTER; most of the wing is retained into the following summer. General coloration of upperparts rather variable, usually a sort of olive greenish with silky sheen. Also differs from birds in Basic Plumages as follows: **bill** muted yellowish, orange yellowish, or grayish, often with pale magenta tinge and some blackish; no white "front" on **head**,

the head–neck brownish or gray-brown, in some a thin line of black feathers around base of upper mandible, sometimes some white on chin, sides of neck smooth (no furrowing); feathers of **mantle** narrower and with rounder ends, their light tips variably buffy, hence less contrasty; upper tail coverts brownish with some white intermingled; **underparts** the feathers of upper sides and flanks medium or lighter olive brownish, grading to wide palish margins, but on lower sides the color merges gradually (compare with Basic I, which also has unmarked venter) into the white or whitish belly and this unmarked light area extends to tail; **tail** feathers tapering, with notched ends (where the down broke off); legs and **feet** dingy yellowish; **wing** primaries shorter, more pointed, than their successors (which are Basic II, not Basic I), the secondaries and upper coverts narrow and with rounded ends.

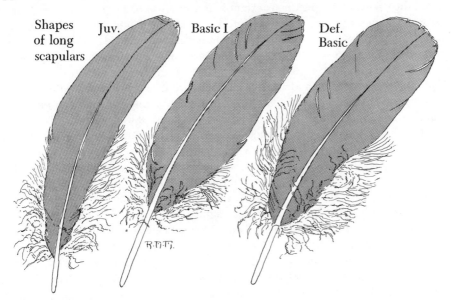

Shapes of long scapulars   Juv.   Basic I   Def. Basic

▶ ♂ ♀ Basic I Plumage (entire feathering except, on wing, includes only some new coverts), acquired from early Sept. to well along in winter or even later (generally much of it present by EARLY WINTER); **upperparts** the new long scapulars have well-defined and evenly narrow and conspicuous whitish margins; underparts feathers of sides and flanks medium olive brownish grading to wide pale brownish buff borders; the darkish coloring contrasts with (rather than grades into, as in Juv.) the white or pale grayish **belly** (the ratio of white- to gray-bellied individuals is about even); sometimes the breast is faintly marked somewhat darker (more often in ♂ ♂).

When the young Whitefronts are 10–12 weeks old (early Sept. or later), the first white flecking appears in the facial "front" and the amount increases (mixed with black in some individuals); generally less than half the white is in by early Nov., but most of it has appeared on practically all individuals by late March. There then is much individual variation in its extent. While the white is increasing, bill color changes, usually at ages 13–16 weeks, from predominantly muted yellowish orange toward fleshy pink (and there are variants); this change may occur about a week earlier in ♂ ♂ than in ♀ ♀.

The timing of growth of new body feathering is more or less synchronous with that of head–neck; a good deal is acquired by early winter, but molting continues, slowly, after that; some birds even retain some Juv. body feathering until onset of Prebasic II molt in summer. The notched Juv. tail feathers usually are not all succeeded by squarish-ended Basic I feathers until sometime in winter and retention of some of the former into spring is not rare. The retained Juv. portion of the wing shows much wear before it is molted when the young birds are about a year old.

▶ ♂ ♀ Basic II Plumage (entire feathering)—earliest definitive stage—most individuals have the venter blotched blackish, this usually becoming visible by about June 15–25, i. e., yearlings molt earlier than older (breeding) cohorts.

Measurements Those published are of limited usefulness. Some are of selected series of the very largest specimens extant in museums (mostly captured remote from breeding range); others are series of winterers and/or migrants, often including individuals from places where 2 subspecies might occur; still other data are inadequately reported or are for so few individuals that they are only indicative and not representative. See, for example, the compilation by H. C. Hanson et al. (1956).

Todd (1950) gave locality and meas. for 23 Whitefronts, none from breeding range. If one omits the 1 Mexican and 5 Cal. birds as possibly being *frontalis* and makes the reasonable assumption that the others (Kans. 1, Man. 2, Sask. 14) most likely came from other Alaskan stock or from Canada, then their meas. may be representative of present-day *gambelli* as treated in this volume. These "adults" measure—12 ♂: BILL 49.5–57 mm., av. 53.5; WING (of 11, across chord) 398–445, av. 425; TAIL 114.5–139, av. 127; TARSUS 62–76, av. 70.8; 5 ♀: BILL 47.5–55.5 mm., av. 51.2; WING (across chord) 396–437, av. 420; TAIL 124–129, av. 126.3; TARSUS 63–75, av. 69.4 (Adding Todd's 6 other birds lowers the averages slightly.)

The largest individual Whitefronts taken in the past may exceed in size almost, or all, of those now occurring in the wild. Examples of these, from Cal. (probably from easterly Canadian breeding range)—"adults" 10 ♂: BILL 54.2–61.4 mm., av. 58.2; WING (flattened) 443–495, av. 465; TARSUS 77–87, av. 81; 4 ♀: BILL 52.5–56.6 mm., av. 55; WING (flattened) 442–450, av. 446; TARSUS 77–82, av. 78 (H. C. Hanson et al. 1956). For WING meas. across chord, of very large individuals, see Swarth and Bryant (1917) and Elgas (1970).

Weight of "adults" from Inaru R. (arctic slope of Alaska) June 2–3: 15 ♂ 2,100–2,935 gm., av. 2,498 (5½ lb.); 15 ♀ 1,980–2,543, av. 2,169 (4¾ lb.) (E. Schiller).

Of the various series of Whitefronts live-trapped and examined at Kindersley (Sask.), these represent 2 of the 6 trapping intervals in fall of 1962: ♂ "adult" 46 taken Sept. 14–15, 2,399–3,130 gm. (mean 2,676) and 43 on Oct. 18, 2,330–3,220 (mean 2,731); 36 ♀ "adult" taken Sept. 14, 2,010–2,830 gm. (mean 2,442) and 43 on Oct. 18, 1,920–2,790 (mean 2,468); first-fall birds 26 ♂ taken Sept. 18, 1,820–2,680 (mean 2,194) and 23 on Oct. 24, 2,170–2,900 (mean 2,480); 38 ♀ taken Sept. 14–18, 1,650–2,370 gm. (mean 2,017) and 34 on Oct. 18–24, 1,950–2,540 (mean 2,246) (A. Dzubin, H. Miller, J. Sweet).

Among 120 "adult" ♂ examined in fall, 1959–63, at the same locality by Dzubin and coworkers, the 6 largest av. 3,260 gm. (7 lb. 3 oz.).

The above data, plus other scattered fragments, lend some support to the concept

92

that the largest Whitefronts still come from Canadian and interior e. Alaskan breeding range and that arctic Alaskan birds may be slightly smaller but are within the overall range of variation of *gambelli*.

The wts. given in Kortright (1942) and A. L. Nelson and Martin (1953) perhaps are indicative of overall variation in Whitefronts in fall in N. Am.; it is probable that their series were not restricted to any one subspecies.

Hybrids and presumed hybrids were listed by Gray (1958); of these, at least the species here indicated by an asterisk have crossed in the wild with the White-front: *Anser anser*, **caerulescens* (both Blue and Snow), *canagicus, cygnoides, *erythropus, *fabalis* (includes *f. brachyrhynchus*), *indicus, Branta bernicla, leucopsis, *canadensis*, and *Chloephaga poliocephala*.

In addition to definitely known *albifrons × fabalis* hybrids, similar appearing birds have been seen several times in the wild in Britain (H. Boyd). A ♂ specimen from Holland, having banded bill and orange-yellow legs (*Anser "carneirostris"*) was listed as a hybrid *albifrons × fabalis* by Voous (1945). Shackleton (1956) reported an apparent *albifrons × erythropus* having been seen in Britain; to this report P. Scott appended mention of 2 such mixed-species pairs seen in winter flocks in Britain, plus a specimen which probably is a hybrid. In captivity, *albifrons* and *caerulescens* cross quite readily and the progeny usually are fertile. Two presumed natural crosses of *albifrons* with either Blue or Snow *caerulescens* were studied carefully (but not collected) near Coleville, Sask., Oct. 5, 6, and 11, 1962, by A. Dzubin.

Captives of known parentage, age, and sex, of *albifrons × caerulescens*, and crosses of these hybrids with *Branta canadensis*, were described in detail by Salomonsen (1946).

Geographical variation in the Whitefront, frequently discussed—often on a regional basis—over the past 60 years, appears to be of lesser dimensions to those few investigators who have understood the extent of individual variation both in size and coloring.

The only well-differentiated and easily definable population consists of the birds that breed in a portion of w. Greenland and go to winter range in the Brit. Isles (mainly to Ireland). They av. middle-sized, are darkest in overall coloring, have the most extensive amount of black ventrally, and the bill is distinctly colored.

In Eurasia, going eastward, a supposed gradient of increase in overall size, heaviness of bill, and darkness of coloration, has been claimed but is of limited application. Tougarinov (1941) stated that large-billed individuals occur and are more frequent going eastward. Yet the birds from the Kanin Pen. across Eurasia to the vicinity of the Kolyma are decidedly variable; they av. middle-sized and usually are comparatively gray. The meas. of 9 "adult" ganders and 4 ♀♀ taken on breeding range between the Indigirka and Kolyma Rivers, as reported by S. Uspenskii et al. (1962), are very close to those of westerly birds examined both in U.S.S.R. and on winter range in England.

Eastward beyond the Kolyma, the geese are smaller, variable in color but often palish, and they migrate via the Pacific to a separate e. Asian winter range. An extension of this subpopulation of small and partly palish birds occurs on the N. Am. side of Bering Sea, in Alaska in the Bristol Bay region and the vast Yukon–Kuskokwim delta. These also migrate via the Pacific, but down the N. Am. side.

From the Seward Pen. in Bering Sea coastal Alaska eastward in N. Am., Whitefronts currently have scattered nesting areas over a distance of about 2,000 mi. Omitting the 2 areas assigned above to small birds, the geese of the other 12 nesting areas presently av. comparatively large in size but are variable; they tend toward browns in general coloring, with dark heads and necks, and many are relatively large billed (large bills are an integral part of the characteristics of large individuals). At least nearly to the present time, the very largest individuals probably occurred at e. extremity of Canadian breeding range and must at some time have had at least a reasonably discrete winter range (Cal.? La. and vicinity?). Gavin (1947), who saved no specimens, reported that he had found Whitefronts weighing "about" 9 lb. nesting in the Perry R. region (astride the n. end of the Mackenzie–Keewatin boundary) and smaller ones weighing about 5 lb. nesting only 6 mi. away. H. C. Hanson et al. (1956) reported finding large Whitefronts at Perry R. in 1949, but none measuring up to the largest known individual birds. (See under *gambelli* in the section on "Subspecies" for an attempt to reconcile these matters.)

The darkest downy Whitefronts so far reported from N. Am. come from the breeding range of *frontalis* (as defined herein) in w. Alaska; strikingly paler ones have been taken far to the eastward in the Perry R. region, while goslings that are somewhat intermediate but tend toward the latter (see Elgas 1970) have been taken at Upper Yukon flats in interior e. Alaska. A comparison of breeding Whitefronts and their downy goslings, from the various breeding areas in Alaska and Canada, would be rewarding. RSP AD

SUBSPECIES For speculation on origin, dispersal, and subspeciation of the Whitefront, see Johansen (1956); there also is a discussion of probable isolation during the last glacial maximum by Ploeger (1968). There is a brief comparison of subspecies by Salomonsen (1948) and important N. Am. data in Todd (1950).

Since one of the subspecies of Whitefront straddles the Bering Sea, breeding in both ne. Asia and w. Alaska, and another travels from winter range in the Palearctic (Brit. Isles) to summer range in the Nearctic (w. Greenland), it is desirable to consider the species on a Holarctic basis while attempting to shed some light on that portion of it occurring in our area.

A. a. albifrons (Scopoli)—Palearctic. Whitefronts in w. Asia shifted northward after the last glacial maximum and have extended their breeding range westerly as far as the Kanin Pen. and easterly to somewhere in the vicinity of the Kolyma drainage. They migrate westerly and southerly, mostly to Europe and the Brit. Isles; see especially Philippona (1972) for detailed information.

These whitefronts are comparatively moderate in size; many are relatively grayish overall; they have comparatively short bills. A wide range of individual variation includes both rather large and/or dark individuals; the larger ones are large billed. For meas. (WING over curve?) and wt., by sex and age-class, of birds on winter range in England, see Beer and Boyd (1963). Their data for "adults" include: ♂ bill (of 74) 42.8–53.2 mm., mean 47.1; and wing (of 73) 377–464, mean. 423.4;   ♀ bill (of 64) 40–50.5 m., mean 44.9; and wing (of 60) 379–438, mean 399.7. For comparison, these authors also cited data from Schiøler (1925) and Ptushenko (in Dementiev and Gladkov

1952). As would be expected, the Juv. wing (of 1st-winter birds) measures shorter, sex for sex, than the Basic wing of older birds. It is of interest that the upper limit of winter wt. among ganders they examined—3.34 kg. or about 7 lb. 5 oz.—is a fairly close match for present-day large birds from part of N. Am.

frontalis (Baird)—Palearctic and Nearctic. These birds survived the last glacial maximum in refugia in ne. Asia, perhaps also on the land bridge which now is beneath Bering Sea, and in part of Alaska (or possibly also extending into nw. Canada). At the present time their breeding range in ne. Asia is not very extensive: from the Kolyma drainage or thereabouts eastward to include the w. part of the Chuckchee Pen.; then, on the Am. side, they breed in the Yukon–Kuskokwim delta and Bristol Bay areas of Alaska. The Asian birds migrate to Korea and Japan, the Am. ones to Cal. and some beyond into Mexico. Collectively, they are small in av. size; some are relatively pale, but others vary to dark overall; on the av., they have considerably more black on the venter and a more than proportionately smaller white facial front than is typical of the species elsewhere in Alaska and in Canada.

There are surprisingly few useful data on size and wt. because investigators seldom have singled out birds from the appropriate breeding areas and reported on them. For example, H. C. Hanson et al. (1956) had few data for tabulation. These are summer "adults" from the coastal fringe of the Yukon–Kuskokwim delta, meas. by J. W. Aldrich: 8 ♂ BILL 45–53 mm., av. 49.5; WING (across chord) 380–415, av. 399; TAIL 113–124, av. 119; TARSUS 69–80, av. 75.5; 5 ♀ BILL 46–53 mm., av. 49.2; WING (across chord) 380–405, av. 395; TAIL 106–126, av. 118; TARSUS 70–75, av. 72.4. These same individuals were included in a larger series from "Alaska" by Elgas (1970). The meas. just given are very similar to those of 9 ♂ and 17 ♀ from Japan and Korea, i.e., ne. Asian *frontalis* taken on winter range, as given by Kuroda (1929).

The specimen later designated as type was taken at Ft. Thorn, New Mex.

gambelli Hartlaub—Nearctic, straggling to the Palearctic. The provenance of large (and the very largest) Whitefronts in N. Am. has been the subject of much speculation. The solution may be one of the following alternatives. 1 With deglaciation after the last glacial maximum, Whitefronts expanded eastward from Alaskan breeding range and, in some period, evolved into larger individuals going eastward. (Among mammals, the grizzly, a ground squirrel, and some small rodents have had a pattern of easterly spread from Beringia.) 2 There were Whitefronts n. beyond the ice in the Banksian refugium in the w. Canadian arctic and birds from there subsequently, on the mainland, spread both westward (into Alaska) and eastward (in Canada). 3 There were Whitefronts in N. Am. s. of the continental ice and subsequently they shifted northward and expanded their range laterally.

There is much in favor of the third hypothesis. For example, the largest and least migratory Canada Geese are believed to have existed s. of the ice and only very small ones in northern refugia. By analogy, some Whitefronts fit this pattern and, after shifting northward, at least part of them were comparatively short-distance migrants to some northerly winter range more or less apart from other Whitefronts. Again by analogy, those musk-oxen of the N. Am. mainland were s. of the ice and subsequently shifted northward into the cent. Canadian subarctic and arctic; they and the Whitefront both have a rather similar species-specific habitat preference—dry terrain with woody scrub growth and herbaceous ground cover interspersed. At any rate, large Whitefronts presently occupy scattered breeding areas in parts of Alaska and Canada; it would appear that, until very recently, the very largest nested at the e. periphery of Canadian breeding range and migrated to northerly winter range in conterminous U.S.—not to the major wintering areas beyond in Mexico.

As is known for other geese, it is likely that the warm period which is terminating at present has resulted in much shifting of the distribution of Whitefronts in various seasons—shifting of individuals among breeding units, geese of lesser size sharing breeding range with very large ones (as at Perry R.), and overlapping of birds from widely scattered units on migration routes and on parts of winter range. A resultant mixing, and consequent interbreeding appear to have resulted in a genetic leveling out of individual size so that birds as big as some taken in the past no longer may occur. (Some Canada Geese are in an earlier stage of such a process; some units of diminutive *hutchinsii* and larger *parvipes* currently interbreed to an extent that the geese of some breeding units are not really assignable to either "parent" subspecies.)

In the present century, at least, some of the very largest individual Whitefronts evidently migrated sw. to Cal. via the same general route used by Ross' Goose. There, obviously they were different from small Yukon–Kuskokwim birds that arrived via the Pacific. The big ones, when in Cal., acquired the local name "tule geese" and, under the name *gambeli* [note spelling], were discussed by Swarth and Bryant (1917). This narrow concept, to fit only the biggest individuals, was reflected in "Tule Goose" in the 4th edition (1931) of the A.O.U. *Check-list* and again in the 5th edition (1957) but minus vernacular name. But the so-called Tule Goose as thus defined progressively has become a more elusive entity with passage of time.

Within overall Whitefront breeding range in N. Am., very large individuals have been taken in Alaska at Hooper Bay and in Canada in N.W.T. at mouth of the Mackenzie, also on the coast e. of Ft. Anderson, and at Perry R. and Repulse Bay. As a migrant, taken in se. Oregon and most recently a gander live-trapped Sept. 23, 1963, in sw. Sask. In winter (or some might be migrants): Sutter Co., Cal, source of majority of all records, also in Solano Co.; other records include near Obregon (Sonora, Mexico), near Brownsville (Texas), and there are reports of occurrence near the La. coast. (A bird from near Tucson, Ariz., does not qualify.) In Japan: a captive taken about 1925 and a sighting in 1964, according to Kuroda (1968).

Rarity is cause for great concern and attendant publicity. Speculation as to where the "Tule Goose" might breed focussed for some time on the Canadian arctic archipelago. Then Twomey (1956), in a popular article, claimed to have found breeding birds somewhere in the Mackenzie delta. No more has been heard of this. Still later, interest shifted to the Upper Yukon flats in interior e. Alaska (far within overall Whitefront summer range), where large, but not outstandingly large, Whitefronts nest. Thus the "Tule Goose," as narrowly defined and as included in various treatises, never has acquired a discrete known breeding range and distribution in various seasons consists mostly of scattered occurrences of extra large Whitefronts in N. Am. and, allegedly, in Japan.

From evidence and theory, it would appear that extra large Whitefronts are rare in the wild. Yet reports of "Tule Geese" may recur, especially from Cal., where small

Pacific migrants and recognizably larger birds (probably from Canada) may be found in the same locality. Large Whitefronts, from interior and n. Alaska and from Canada, usually are quite brownish overall (discounting adventitious coloring), have large white facial fronts, and usually a reduced amount of black ventrally. Some meas., but none from summer range, where given earlier under "Description."

The name *gambelli* of Hartlaub antedates the name *frontalis*. Hartlaub had 3 birds, still extant, including an "adult" from Texas which subsequently was designated as the type specimen (Kuroda 1929). None of Hartlaub's birds was of outstanding size. It is rather unfortunate that the type locality for both of the names just mentioned are remote from Whitefront breeding range.

flavirostris Dalgety and Scott—Nearctic breeding range and Palearctic winter range. The Greenland birds are of lesser size than *gambelli*. Their general coloration is dark, slaty (absence of browns); bill orange. Other supposed characteristics, such as narrowness of light margins on dorsal feathers and extensiveness of black on underparts, are matched by exceptional examples of *gambelli*. Juv. birds have bill grayish with dark nail, feet muted brownish yellow (Fencker 1950). Some mensural data were published by Dalgety and Scott (1948), Salomonsen (1948), Delacour (1954), and Vau-

A. a. flavirostris
(Greenland)

A. a. gambelli

gambelli—definitive
feathering

gambelli—Juv.

R. R. Triengel—

rie (1965), but adequate information, by sex and age-class, still is lacking. From Delacour: ♂ BILL 45–57 mm., WING (flattened?) 410–455, TARSUS 73–77; ♀ WING (flattened?) 392–420 mm. From Vaurie: 18 ♂ BILL 45–56 mm., av. 52; WING (flattened) 410–442, av. 428. Wt. 4–6 lb. Migrates from breeding range in w. Greenland via vicinity of Iceland to England, Scotland, and (mainly) Ireland; on reverse journey, may stop en route in Iceland. Has occurred in e. N. Am. (evidence includes 3 banded individuals recovered) and a few, especially young birds, perhaps straggle here quite regularly. See Parkes (1960) for partial summary of Whitefront occurrences, including records of *flavirostris*, on the Atlantic seaboard of N. Am. There have been more Whitefront records for this area subsequently, some very likely of this subspecies.

NOTE If one must apply English names to Whitefront populations (subspecies), the word "tule" should be omitted. The birds may be referred to as Eurasian (nominate *albifrons*), Pacific (*frontalis*), Interior (*gambelli*), and Greenland Whitefront (*flavirostris*). AD RSP

FIELD IDENTIFICATION In Nearctic area. A member of the "gray goose" group, but it is not very gray. Flies in lines and chevrons. Very agile on the wing; flocks, when descending, often sideslip steeply downward. Associates with various other geese, but maintains its own groups and family units. Most are darkish, rather trim, in appearance. Beginning before age 1 year, these geese have a white "front" (which may be obscured by ferrous staining) adjoining base of bill, and the latter is in the range orange-yellow-brownish in N. Am. birds, orange in Greenland birds, and commonly quite pinkish in the Eurasian birds that winter in Europe and the Brit. Isles. Underparts vary from plain whitish or grayish (exceptionally) to same heavily marked black. Legs and feet more or less orange, but some seasonal variation. Juv. birds lack the white "front" and have plain underparts; their legs and feet vary from dingy toward yellow, bill variable (usually darkish) and with some blackish. This combination of characters is diagnostic. Young, especially of Greenland birds, might be confused with the Pinkfoot (see under Bean Goose), but they differ in proportions and otherwise. The dark belly markings begin to appear at age very close to 1 year.

On the N. Am. Atlantic seaboard, as in the Brit. Isles, very dark Whitefronts typically are of Greenland origin. RSP

VOICE Usual contact call is high pitched, pleasant, and rather melodious—a "laughing" goose. The call is uttered quickly, usually 2 syllables *kow lyow, lyo lyek, kr lik*, etc. Various "conversational" sounds have less carrying power. Very large individuals have a comparatively coarse harsh voice (Swarth and Bryant 1917, Delacour 1954).

Fencker (1950), in his study of breeding Greenland Whitefronts, noted that the gander's voice, at least in summer, is pitched higher than that of the goose, i.e., the sexes can be distinguished. He also stated that, in territorial fights, the gander utters trumpeting notes. These are variants of the same calls that are uttered in Forward display or Triumph ceremony (neck forward and head lowered) by mates when they rejoin after an intruder has been repelled. Birds in subarctic Canada at Perry R. in summer often uttered a call similar to the Triumph call of the Greylag (*Anser anser*) (H. C. Hanson et al. 1956). An alarmed parent with small young utters a low rally call and the goslings gather close by. Yearlings (and any older prebreeders), while they remain in the vicinity of nesters, set up a noisy chorus if alarmed; this warns nesters and is distracting to potential predators.

For much information on the development of voice in the individual and on its functions, see Würdinger (1970). RSP

HABITAT In N. AM. **Breeding** Primarily subarctic and low-arctic; nests from open areas within the forest zone northward to a few arctic is. On high dry terrain, such as ridges, slight elevations, mounds, etc., in inner portions of deltas, or near other watercourses, also where there are ponds and shallow pools. Ground cover typically is quite low—scrub willow or birch, heaths, sedges, grasses.

There is a rather well-defined zonation of breeding distribution of various geese. In Alaska, from the Bering Sea coast inland, the sequence is: Brant, smallest Canada Geese, Emperor Goose, and Whitefront. The sequence on the Alaskan arctic slope and in part of Canada is: Brant, Snow/Blue Goose (if present), Whitefront, smallish Canada Geese, and (where present) Ross' Goose. On s. parts of arctic is. where the Whitefront nests (Victoria, Jenny Lind, King William): Brant, Lesser Snow (if present), and Whitefront. Well inland on the continent (as at Upper Yukon flats in e. Alaska) and at southerly places (as Coppermine and Thelon headwaters in Canada), Whitefronts nest on drier areas within well-watered, broad, rather tundralike, expanses. Although there is not space for elaborating here, the zonation is controlled by topography, vegetation types, and predation. The zoning concept was treated briefly by Barry (in Linduska 1964).

It may be noted that Whitefronts nest far enough away from the sea for the localities to be influenced by inland climate: the snow cover may be considerable but it clears rapidly; ground cover is not high but often is dense.

In **migration** areas of extensive shallow water, croplands, pastures, open terrain with numerous ponds and potholes, interior and coastal marshes. In **winter** much the same.

GREENLAND In **summer** entirely low-arctic, inland on rolling tundra with ponds and marshy areas (southerly), also on marine is. and islets (northerly). In **winter**, when in Ireland, sedgy bogs are preferred.

EURASIA Zonation of **breeding** distribution of geese depends on many of the same variables as in the Nearctic, but one of the complications is more species of geese. If all were arranged in a linear sequence going inland (not all occur in any one sector), the order would be about as follows: Brant, Emperor Goose (low coasts) and Barnacle Goose (cliffs near coasts), Lesser Snow (inland on Wrangel I., formerly also middle portions of mainland deltas), Bean Goose, Whitefront, Red-breasted Goose, and Lesser Whitefront. (Bean Goose plus both of the Whitefronts seem to be ecological counterparts of various populations of Canada Goose in N. Am.). In **other seasons**, habitat in Eurasia essentially as in N. Am. RSP

DISTRIBUTION (See map.) In the Nearctic, exclusive of Greenland, the Whitefront has some 14 major breeding areas. Perhaps ⅔ of the birds occur in Alaska. In Canada, the number of birds becomes very small e. of King William I. and the Queen Maud Gulf lowlands, but a few Whitefronts nest beyond the places bordering the nw.

coast of Hudson Bay and n. to inner Repulse Bay. Although some individuals shift within the overall range, birds of a breeding unit tend to have their particular places of occurrence in all seasons; see below under "Migration" for data on distribution away from summer range.

Groups of summering prebreeders may be expected both within and some distance from breeding areas. Limits of winter occurrence of the species in N. Am. extends from s. B.C. in Canada down to Tabasco and Oaxaca in extreme s. Mexico. The possibility that occasional occurrences of any subspecies in various seasons may be escaped aviary birds should not be overlooked.

In our area there are the following subspecies, going from w. to e.:

frontalis breeds in Alaska in the Bristol Bay region and, mainly, in part of the vast Yukon–Kuskokwim delta. They are Pacific migrants, to Cal. and some beyond into Mexico.

On geographical grounds, the following most likely are birds of this subspecies. Rare **straggler** in the Aleutians (O. Murie 1959); May, June, and Sept. sightings and a May specimen from the Pribilofs (Fay and Cade 1959). The provenance of these is more doubtful: occurs occasionally on St. Lawrence I. (Fay and Cade 1959); recorded in the Hawaiian Is. at Hawaii in 1891 and 1963, Molokai in 1895, and at Midway Atoll in 1962.

On the Asian side, *frontalis* nests in some numbers as far eastward as the w. part of the Chuckchee Pen., but evidently does not breed in the e. and s. parts. It is an occasional visitor to Wrangel I. As a migrant, it is regular in spring and rare in autumn in the Commander Is. (Johansen 1961). This subspecies occurs in Korea and winters in Japan.

Heavy human predation on eggs and on molting flightless birds was continuing in e. Siberia (Dementiev and Gladkov 1952, but see especially S. Uspenskii et al. 1962). Such losses on summer range presumably have contributed to the serious decline in numbers of Whitefronts wintering in Japan.

gambelli—the major **breeding** areas at the present time are, in Alaska, the Kotzebue Sd.–Selawik R. area, arctic coastal plain, Koyukuk R. area, Minto flats, and Upper Yukon flats; in Canada, Old Crow flats, Mackenzie–Anderson r. tundra, parts of se. Victoria I. and of Jenny Lind and King William I., Queen Maud Gulf lowlands (includes Perry R. region), and a sizable area well inland near headwaters of Back, Coppermine, and Thelon Rivers. There are scattered small units in Canada both e. and s. of these major ones.

Older evidence did not indicate that this goose bred in the Thelon Sanctuary (inland, astride the Mackenzie–Keewatin boundary), but it has become quite plentiful there (Kuyt 1962, various observers). Whether this indicates a shift in birds or reflects the general increase in Whitefronts at easterly places is unknown.

North of breeding range, presumably it is *gambelli* that Manning et al. (1956) reported as seen occasionally on Banks I.

While en route between breeding and wintering areas, this goose occurs abundantly on its various routes or "corridors," but also may be expected occasionally almost anywhere in conterminous U.S. w. of a line drawn approximately from the e. end of L. Superior down through e. Ala. Farther eastward, Whitefronts of at least 2 subspecies have occurred at scattered places and along the Atlantic seaboard (see below under

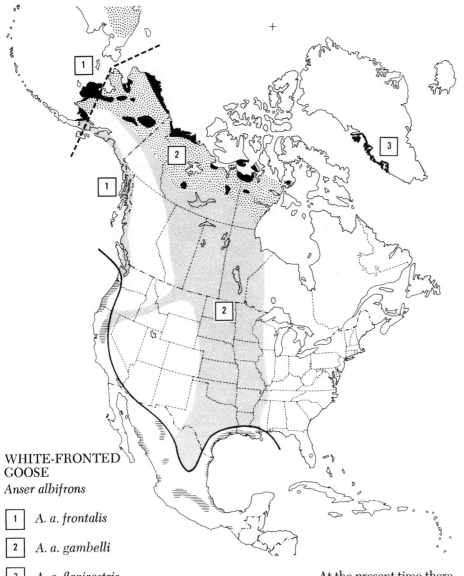

WHITE-FRONTED
GOOSE
Anser albifrons

1	*A. a. frontalis*
2	*A. a. gambelli*
3	*A. a. flavirostris*

🐾 Breeding areas

▦ May breed scatteringly

▨ Main occurrence in migrations

⌣ Upper limits of usual winter occurrence

▥ Principal wintering areas

At the present time there appears to be no discontinuity between breeding ranges of *frontalis* and *gambelli*.

The Greenland birds (*flavirostris*) migrate to winter range mainly in Ireland.

The Whitefront is widely distributed in Eurasia (includes *Anser a. albifrons*).

flavirostris). A bird banded in its 1st fall on Sept. 28, 1962, in sw. Sask. was shot Dec. 23, 1968, at Sagaponack on the s. shore of Long I., N.Y.

It may be *gambelli* that now is fairly regular in small (increasing?) numbers on the Fla. Gulf Coast s. of Tallahassee, especially at St. Mark's Refuge. The Whitefront (subspecies?) has occurred in Cuba. Many Whitefronts winter in Mexico s. of the latitude of Cuba and there is a record for Campeche (w. side of Yucatan Pen.).

In Japan: an alleged specimen and a sighting.

flavirostris—as a result of amelioration of the climate, has extended its **breeding** range northward in w. Greenland into s. parts of the Upernavik Dist, (Fencker 1950), which may be temporary. It **winters** regularly only in the Brit. Isles. At present small flocks in nw. England, at least 1 regular haunt in Wales, in Scotland the main area is Islay (about 3,500 birds), and in Ireland mainly Wexford Slobs (5,000–7,000), the total wintering population in 1972 being of the order of 12,000–15,000 individuals (Merne 1972). Has straggled (banded bird) to Norway. A Baffin I. record presumably is of this subspecies. A Whitefront, evidently this subspecies (see Todd 1963), was taken near Hopedale, Labrador. An adult ♀, molting with Canada Geese, was captured on July 23, 1967, in ne. Ungava (Que.) at lat. 60°51′ N, long. 77°30′ W (J. D. Heyland). It has straggled to lower Que., N.B., Prince Edward I., N.S., and there are several Nfld. records; various occurrences, though not all, on the U.S. Atlantic seaboard pertain to this subspecies, including a record for N.J. (J. Bond 1960), "Washington, D.C., market" (A.O.U. *Check-list* 1957), and a sighting in Currituck Sd., N.C. (see Parkes 1960). There continue to be sightings of Whitefronts, not always as dark birds as those of Greenland, along the Atlantic seaboard and down to include the Fla. Gulf Coast. A Whitefront was seen April 30, 1971, in Genessee Co., Ala.; a flock of 5 was seen in N.C. in late 1971 and a flock of 5 in Pa. in March, 1972.

Extralimital *albifrons*—the most useful map of Eurasian breeding range is in S. Uspenskii (1965a), showing westernmost concentration of breeders on the s. island of Novaya Zemlya (on the mainland it nests w. onto the Kanin Pen.) and easternmost concentration in Indigirka delta in Yakutia (and it breeds at least some distance farther eastward). In the Brit. Mus. (Nat. Hist.) there are 2 eggs from a clutch of 4 taken on June 21, 1898, at C. Chance in Franz Josef Land (C. J. O. Harrison 1962). Uspenskii mapped upper limits of breeding as on the n. island of Novaya Zemlya and on Kotelny in the New Siberian Is. For information on migrations and on wintering in Asia, see Dementiev and Gladkov (1952); for migration and winter distribution in Europe, see Philippona and Mulder (1960) and especially Philippona (1972). In Britain there has been a loss of winter habitat, changes in winter distribution, and a decline in numbers concurrent with an increase in Holland (Ogilvie 1968b). Recoveries of British-banded Eurasian Whitefronts are scattered on the continent from France to Denmark, thence eastward widely in the U.S.S.R. e. of the Urals, and n. to include Vaigach I., both is. of Novaya Zemlya, the Yamal Pen., and sw. corner of the Taimyr Pen., also s. to include Italy and Greece (R. Spencer 1969).

In the Nearctic area, *Anser albifrons* is recorded as **fossil** in the Pleistocene of Ore., Cal. (several localities), and New Mex., and is reported from **archaeological sites** in Alaska and 1 in Cal.; the references to these localities, plus others in the Palearctic, were listed by Brodkorb (1964a). RSP

102

MIGRATION   Nearctic data. Travels of the Whitefront extend over more than 50°
of latitude, more distance than covered by any of our other geese. The birds tend to
take a fairly direct course, but with some deviation so as to follow inland waterways or
sections of coast. Spring and fall routes apparently coincide to a considerable extent.
Migrants commonly occur with other geese, especially Ross' and the Lesser Snow
component of *Anser caerulescens*, but each kind keeps more or less by itself. Whitefronts make long flights between certain stopping places. As in Eurasia, sometimes the
birds shift from or abandon long-used routes; tens of thousands now travel via e.
Alta.–w. Sask. where they were unknown until at least 1935 (Whitefronts were fewer
then). The following account is condensed and somewhat schematic; mention of stopping places and local routes is kept to a minimum.

As related to migration, there are these major aggregations in continental N. Am.: **1**
Yukon–Kuskokwim birds plus those farther s. around Bristol Bay—Pacific migrants. **2a**
those elsewhere in Alaska (Koyukuk R., Seward Pen.–Selawik area, arctic coastal
plain, Minto Flats, Upper Yukon Flats) and eastward to Liverpool Bay in Mackenzie
Dist.—continental interior migrants to s. Alta.–Sask., thence to the Gulf of Mexico
coast or nearby, and many beyond far into Mexico. **2b** easterly birds (principally se.
Victoria I., s. King William I., Queen Maud Gulf continental lowlands, and Back,
Coppermine, and Thelon river headwaters)—which overlap the preceding in migration, but tend to keep more easterly and to terminate their travels around the n. Gulf of
Mexico coast.

The divisions are by no means clear-cut because, for example, an interchange of
birds evidently occurs between summering units and Todd (1950) surely was correct
that some large easterly Canadian birds have a diagonal (southwesterly) migration, like
that of Ross' Goose, to interior Cal. (where Pacific migrants also occur).

1 Pacific birds (Nearctic subpopulations of *frontalis*). **Spring**   The birds of w. coastal Mexico and interior of Cal. (majority in latter area) migrate n. slowly at first, passing
up through the interior and also along the coast of Ore. in March and throughout April.
In very late April and the first quarter of May the first (small) flocks generally reach the
Yukon–Kuskokwim delta of Alaska and by about the 20th the remainder generally have
arrived.

Fall   Most of the birds have left breeding range by mid-Sept. They cross the Alaska
Pen. and pass down the Pacific coast to coastal Ore. and remain there some 2–3 weeks.
Then they move overland, crossing the Cascades, and spread out and forage in the
Tule–Klamath basin and vicinity. In Oct. they move s. in the interior to **winter** quar-
ters in the Central Valley of Cal. A few thousand continue on s. through the Imperial
Valley of Cal. and beyond to winter range along the w. coast of Mexico. All birds prob-
ably are on winter range by early Dec.

2a and **2b**   Interior-traveling *gambelli* from the various breeding areas are combined here, since they cannot be distinguished where their occurrence and timing
overlap. **Spring**   The birds tend to fly lower than in fall. They begin leaving s. interior
and e. coastal Mexican winter range gradually, in Feb. They are abundant around
Beaumont, Texas, in late Feb.– early March. They are abundant in Nebr. in latter half
of March (peak about March 20), where they forage in fields harvested the previous
fall. There are peak numbers in S.D. about 10 days later. Large numbers move on

103

about April 1 and, by about April 20, Whitefronts are scattered across marshy areas and pothole country from cent. Alta. into w. Man. After foraging for some 2 weeks, they again move on. In some years, at least, the vanguard reaches n. interior Mackenzie Dist. in the last week in April. The flight up from the prairies is long, either nonstop or with brief stops, and the final staging areas at which they arrive are places where the season is much more advanced (influenced by interior weather) than on those breeding areas that are a short flight farther on and nearer the coast (influenced to some extent by marine climate). They scatter on breeding areas about mid-May (earlier or considerably later, depending on season). In Alaska, probably they are on interior nesting areas beginning somewhat earlier, with later arrivals continuing into June; they reach the Seward Pen in May and others evidently are scattered inland on the Alaskan arctic slope in very late May or the beginning of June.

Summer Whitefront pairs are scattered when nesting. Many young of the previous year stay close to their parents until the time approaches for the next cohort to hatch; others depart (thus behaving like 2-year-olds); still others remain and become flightless. Older prebreeders (mostly 2-year-olds) usually are paired, tend to keep in groups by themselves, and have a molt migration; that is, they leave the nesting areas early and, in assemblies which may number hundreds or even thousands of birds, inhabit marshy areas and shallows where food is abundant. Often they are joined by failed breeders and, still later, by some successful breeders (which are the last to become flightless) with their goslings. Travel to molting areas, by breeders (which are largely earthbound because of their goslings and soon become flightless themselves) is overland and by swimming, the distance varying from a few to perhaps scores of miles. Like other *Anser* species, molting Whitefronts are by preference more terrestrial than aquatic; yet many of them move considerable distances on the water, downstream on rivers and through deltas. Most of the 1- and 2-year-old birds are again on the wing by very early Aug., successful breeders considerably later.

The pattern just outlined has modifications or variants. For example, there are scattered families and small parties of molting birds. Depending on topography and vegetation, molting areas may be located from within to well away from nesting areas. Various molting places are traditional, i.e., used year after year.

Fall migration begins rather early and the birds are believed to fly higher than in spring. Beginning some time in Aug., the youngest cohort with the parent birds (those slightly over a year old now tend to keep apart) occur in assemblies at lake margins, on river bars, etc. They are noisy. The groups make daily flights for a while to feed on uplands; then they depart. Some of the birds generally linger until freeze-up, regardless of how late this occurs. A few small groups (older prebreeders) make long flights s. to winter range early, but the vast majority have a pattern as follows.

Beginning about Aug. 10–15, many geese (prebreeders) from parts of Alaska and Canada move toward and converge at favored stopping places such as the Hay Lakes–Peace R.–L. Athabaska area. More arrive over a span of several weeks, including breeders with young beginning in the latter half of Aug. Vast numbers may remain in the area for weeks, or flocks may depart over a long span of time, or the majority may soon move on. Toward the end of Sept. there are peak numbers in the s. ⅔ of Alta. and in Sask. (the Kindersley Dist. is a major staging area) and, if the weather continues mild, a great many may remain there even until very late Oct. Then, if the geese are

104

in good physical condition, most of them fly nonstop to the Gulf Coast of Texas and La. In seasons when they are in poor condition, they make frequent stops along the way. By some time in Nov. the vast majority are on the Gulf Coast; by some time in Dec., probably many more than half of these birds have moved on to **winter** quarters, which extend far down in Mexico. Those that do not move on to Mexico evidently are from easterly Canadian breeding range.

flavirostris—in **spring** the Greenland birds do not leave Ireland in quantity until April; en route, most of them probably visit Iceland. They approach sw. Greenland (very late April through May) and then, for the most part, travel n. up the w. interior or, frequently, along the w. coast. Small flocks come first. **Fall** The birds are believed to depart in early and mid-Sept. and to travel se. nonstop over the icecap. They continue over the Atlantic, skirting or barely touching sw. Iceland, to winter quarters in sw. Scotland and (mainly) Ireland. (The Faeroes are not a stopping place in either fall or spring.) RSP

BANDING STATUS   In the Nearctic area. The total number banded in N. Am. through 1964 was 17,308 and, through 1961, there were 1,241 recoveries; main places of banding: Sask., Cal., Alaska, and Mackenzie Dist. (data from Bird Banding Laboratory). At Kindersley, Sask., 1961–64 inclusive, 6,555 were leg-banded and an additional 1,123 also were otherwise tagged; for an analysis of returns from these for the hunting seasons of 1961–66 inclusive, see H. W. Miller et al. (1968). The Danish banding program in Greenland resulted in a total of 961 A. a. flavirostris being banded in 1946–58 inclusive (Salomonsen 1966) and the work has continued. There have been many published recoveries; for example, see Salomonsen (1965 and 1967).

The number banded in Britain through 1969 was 582 and there have been 190 recoveries.

Other reports relating to rather extensive banding in the Palearctic region are not summarized here. RSP

REPRODUCTION   For the Nearctic area there are only scattered fragments of information, including Fencker's (1950) brief paper on Greenland birds. The following is based on information on the species as a whole, but with emphasis on N. Am.

On winter range in England, studies of Whitefronts that nest in the Barents Sea region (nominate *albifrons*) have revealed that banded yearlings and 2-year-olds are not accompanied by offspring and that a smaller proportion of birds in their 3rd calendar year have families than do those a year or more older (Boyd 1965 and papers he cited). That is, some of these Whitefronts **first breed** when about 24 mo. old, many not until a year older. In *frontalis* in N. Am., a small percentage of 2-year-olds breed successfully, at least in some years. Most birds of this cohort are paired in their 2nd winter and an unknown percentage may be sexually mature and copulate before visiting nesting areas. It is possible that such birds commonly are prevented from acquiring nesting territory by established breeders, unless there are vacancies as a result of earlier mortality among the older birds.

Boyd (1954) found that **pair formation** occurs in the span fall–spring, a gradual process, the bond being firm when the 2 birds engage in joint attack or defense against another Whitefront. The majority are paired in 2nd winter (before age 2 years), but this

105

includes some temporary alliances. In n. Canada at Perry R., H. C. Hanson et al. (1956) collected a mated pair of Whitefronts, the goose being a yearling and the gander a "mature adult." Other examples of age disparity between mates are known.

Pair bond form is **lifelong monogamy** once a firm bond is established.

The pattern in spring evidently is not that of a long terminal flight to nesting areas and then a waiting period there; instead, the flocks halt when only say 1–2 hrs. flight away, where there are quiet waters and places to roost. By about this time there is 24-hr. daylight for most Whitefronts. On waters at these final staging areas the older birds presumably copulate (which they are not seen to do later on nesting areas); the associated behavior probably is similar to that of *Anser anser* as described by Heinroth (1911). The timing of subsequent events varies depending on the season. Pairs and accompanying yearlings make reconnoitering flights (the goose leading) to nesting areas, in order for the goose to determine when a site is suitable for occupancy. This may happen soon, or there may be quite a delay, until the snow cover clears. As soon as a site is acceptable, laying begins promptly. Two-year-old birds, more or less by themselves, go to breeding areas but most of them soon depart for molting areas.

Limits of **territory** appear to be flexible. In optimum habitat, or where space is limited as on an island, the geese nest within view of one another, a few pairs/sq. mi. being a rather high density. Often they are much more widely dispersed and a gander will leave his guardsite and go a considerable distance to confront an intruding gander or "escort" an intruding pair through the territory. Yearling prebreeders, by themselves or with the gander, sound the alarm and fly to meet an approaching predator; their distraction behavior serves to protect the nest.

The **nest site**, chosen by the goose, usually is a slightly elevated spot—a slight rise in ground or a hummock—which becomes dry early and commands an unobstructed view of the surroundings. On low is. in the Kolyma delta that often are flooded in spring, the geese were found nesting sometimes on upturned roots of a stranded tree, sometimes on piles of driftwood or other rubbish (Thayer and Bangs 1914). The goose finds or makes a shallow depression; then, through the laying period, she forms a nest around the eggs from any material available at the site; she adds a relatively small amount of feathers and down during the latter part of laying and continues this activity for a while thereafter. The **nest down** is pale grayish; feathers that are intermingled are fairly large, white, grayish, black, or a mixture of these (and in Eurasia they can be confused with those of the Lesser Whitefront).

Eggs usually are laid 1/day, but a skipping of 1 to several days in the laying span is known to occur. During that span, the eggs are kept more or less covered and the parent birds spend the hours of continuous daylight away from the nest, resting and feeding.

Across the middle of the species' Nearctic summer range, from w. Alaska to Greenland, in an av. season (if such exists), one may expect to find many **clutches** completed by about June 5; at least a week should be subtracted from this for sw. Alaskan areas and probably interior southerly Canadian areas, and at least a week added for localities along the n. limits of nesting. Dating varies everywhere, depending on the season. **Clutch size** 4–7, usually 5–7, eggs. In *gambelli* from nw. Mackenzie Dist., the upper limit was 7 in about 100 clutches examined (MacFarlane 1891). In *frontalis* in the

Yukon–Kuskokwim delta in 1969–72, mean clutch size in 77 nests was 4.53 eggs and, in 5 other studies there in 1942–72, the mean for 211 clutches was 4.9 (P. Mickelson). In *frontalis:* **egg size** in 1969–72, some 24 mi. se. of Hooper Bay, Alaska, 294 eggs (mean and SD): length 80.9 ± 2.76 mm. (extremes 71.9–90.4) and breadth 53.5 ± 1.63 (48.1–57.6) (P. Mickelson). **Shape** usually between subelliptical and long elliptical (but quite variable); the shell smooth and with almost no gloss, its **color** almost white (creamy or very pale buff) when clean.

The goose incubates, beginning when the clutch is complete; the gander stands guard fairly close by; the yearlings serve as lookouts until, well along in incubation, they depart to molt. **Incubation period** usually given as 26–28 days, this confirmed for nominate *albifrons* by de Vries (1944) and apparently underestimated for *flavirostris* by Fencker (1950) as "about 22–23 days." The goose has periods of absence, to drink and feed, during the hours of continuous daylight; she loses considerable wt. during incubation and the gander, who is more mobile but keeps largely to his guardsite, loses less. Fencker stated that, in Greenland birds, the bill becomes pale yellowish and the legs and feet pale orange-yellow.

For an excellent photo of 5 downy *frontalis* in a nest, see Brandt (1943).

From about the time the **goslings** are dry and ready to leave, the gander takes charge and leads the brood; the goose follows.

When the young are small, if any prebreeders thereabouts set up a commotion on sighting a potential predator, the parents lower their breasts, elevate their rear ends (white area becomes conspicuous), and give a low rally call. The goslings gather close by. After about a week of local and largely terrestrial living, the family becomes more mobile and moves away in the direction of a molting place. By this time, at any sound of alarm, brood members scatter widely and hide in vegetation. If on the water, they dive expertly. The traveling done by the family is, in effect, a modified molt migration for the parent birds—one becomes flightless when the goslings are about 2 weeks old, whether or not they have reached a molting area. By about this time, the goose has grown considerable new down on her venter. Traveling groups vary in size, since various families use the same routes and so intermingle, separate, re-form, etc. **Age at first flight of** *flavirostris* goslings evidently was underestimated as about 5 weeks by Fencker (1950) and in *gambelli* is closely estimated as 42–45 days.

In nominate *albifrons*, according to Boyd (1954), parents and nearly all 1st-winter young live in family parties. That is, normally, 2 breeders and up to 7 young. If a parent is lost, the group retains its cohesion. Also, in some instances, probably the offspring of the previous year join the parents and younger birds. That is, the youngest birds are about a year old before they part from their parents and then, after a period of separation (see "Migration"), may be with them again. In *gambelli* in fall in Sask., the bond among parents and members of the youngest cohort is strong, as determined experimentally with color-banded wild birds by H. W. Miller and Dzubin (1965). RSP

SURVIVAL   In N. Am., av. life expectancy from date of hatching probably is about 4 years, although there are records of individuals of this species surviving more than 16 years.

The westerly component of continental interior migrants—the birds that nest in n.

107

half of Alaska and e. to just beyond the Mackenzie delta—was declining in numbers in 1961–69, although the more easterly birds were increasing. An analysis of banding data on the former gave the following "preliminary annual mortality rates" for the period 1961–63: 0.441 for all "immatures" and 0.313 for all "adults." The "weighted average" 1st-year rate was 0.34 for all cohorts. The av. production was 25% during these same years. These data are from H. W. Miller et al. (1968), who discussed methods of analysis and also listed the pertinent domestic and Palearctic literature on survival in the species.

In w. Siberian birds (nominate *albifrons*) that migrate to Gloucestershire, England, a third of the young are lost before their first winter and 1st-year mortality is well in excess of 50%. The estimate of adult mean annual survival rate is 0.72 ± 0.11 and for Greenland *flavirostris* is 0.66 ± 0.04, according to Boyd (in Le Cren and Holdgate 1962). In the former the av. annual mortality rate is $27.0 \pm 3.6\%$, assuming that the rate does not vary with age of the birds (Boyd 1965). Studies of these birds on winter range also revealed that those that breed in their 3rd calendar year are less successful than older birds and that there is a possibility that production of young may fall off with increasing age after "no more than four years of maturity" (Boyd 1965). Also see Boyd (1957 and 1959) for various other details. RSP

HABITS   Much useful information on the Canada Goose and Blue/Snows, for example, has accumulated over a long span of time; the Whitefront in N. Am., on the other hand, has been the object of very little attention or research until recently. Its population in our area, exclusive of Greenland, was believed to be about 225,000 birds and increasing in the mid-1960s, but stabilized or decreasing by the early 1970s. Spring counts in Nebr. and other midwestern states showed 201,000 in March 1974; adding 100,000 (or maybe as many as 150,000) from there westward to the Pacific gives a total in spring in N. Am. of perhaps 350,000 individuals.

The Whitefront associates with other geese, notably the small Canadas and white and blue morphs of *Anser caerulescens* in N. Am. and the Pinkfoot and other Bean Geese in Eurasia. Whitefronts more or less maintain their own flocks, within which the fundamental social unit is the family—the parents and at least all members of their youngest brood. A common short-distance threat display, used in maintaining family unity, individual distance when feeding, etc., is similar to that of other *Anser* and at least some *Branta*: a vibrating of the furrowed neck feathers (which are furrowed in the Whitefront). Alarm or flight intention is signaled by lateral Head-shaking, which displays the white facial front conspicuously.

For interesting observations of maintenance of alignment of individuals in a spring flock of *frontalis* during a period of activity subsequent to alighting, see J. Munro (1936). For many details of behavior of flocks, families, and individuals of nominate *albifrons* in England in winter, see Boyd (1953). He found that the flocks are unstable, that the majority of persistent groups are families and paired birds, and he worked out the order of dominance from large families down to unattached young individuals. Both parents use similar threat and attack behavior, but the gander is more active and successful in encounters. Conflicts stem from sexual rivalry (in pair formation activities), interference with freedom of movement, and preservation of family cohesion.

108

Over 15,000 Whitefronts died in Nebr. in April, 1975 from fowl cholera.

When the geese resort regularly to a shoreline or mudflat, as they do between feeding periods, the surface soon is trampled to a remarkable extent and droppings are everywhere. Where they feed, the birds thoroughly denude the area—a "goose pasture"—of easily obtainable food in a relatively short time, but they also fertilize it and there seems to be no evidence that they injure the plant cover sufficiently to prevent regeneration. This goose is a grazer primarily, also a gleaner, and a grubber, depending on circumstances. Longhurst (1955) reported large individuals grubbing up tubers and rhizomes of *Scirpus* from mud under as much as 1½ ft. of water in Cal. in Dec. On winter range, daily routine generally includes a period of feeding in the early daylight hours, then a flight to a resting place at water. As noted in Sweden, when the geese are arriving at a resting place they call to one another and sideslip downwards steeply, a special behavior (Markgren 1963). In N. Am., high-flying flocks of fall migrants have been seen to make a sudden and very spectacular near-vertical descent on reaching a stopping place. (So-called aerial somersaulting occurs in various geese and swans.) See Markgren's paper for many data on winter behavior and ecology of the Whitefront and for the various relevant literature, which he cited.

A monograph by Philippona (1972), devoted almost entirely to the nominate subspecies (of Eurasia), contains many valuable data. RSP

FOOD   Largely **vegetable**—grasses, sedges, aquatic plants (mostly emergent), and berries—and to a slight extent insects and mollusks. Little specific information. Like other geese, they swallow considerable grit—sand and gravel.

In N. Am., in Alaska feeds largely in spring and fall on berries (Ericaceae) (E. W. Nelson 1887), and in summer on young grass shoots and, to some extent, on aquatic insects and their larvae. Not known to eat mollusks (Turner 1886). Two stomachs obtained in May on the Pribilof Is. contained grass 99% and leaves of saxifrage and chickweed 1% (Preble and McAtee 1923). The stomachs of 6 adults collected during the breeding season in the Perry R. region in n. Canada contained the stems, branches, and rootstalks of *Equisetum* and the stems, blades, and heads of *Eriophorum* (H. C. Hanson et al. 1956).

The following pertain to winter range. In Cal., largely grass and sprouting grain (Dawson 1923); also tubers and rhizomes of *Scirpus robustus* (Longhurst, 1955). Elsewhere, Audubon (1835) found that they ate acorns and beechnuts that fell along the margins of ponds. The only evidence of animal food was the shells of snails. Texas specimens contained in their stomachs rice *(Oryza sativa)*, Bermuda grass *(Cynodon dactylon)*, bur clover *(Medicago hispida)*, and algae (Glazener 1946). Feeds extensively on waste grain in stubble fields on winter range in Cal. and Texas.

For the Greenland birds, little is known from summer range. There they eat chiefly grass (Salomonsen 1950). At a wintering locality in Wales, the roots of cotton grass *(Eriophorum angustifolium)* are eaten almost exclusively, but as winter proceeds this food becomes less palatable and they eat the shoots of white beak sedge *(Rhynchospora alba)* (Cadman 1953, 1956; Pollard and Walters-Davies 1968).

For some data on the nominate subspecies, see J. W. Campbell (1947) for 3 stomachs from England, Naumann (1905a) for Germany, Markgren (1963) for much information from s. Sweden and mention of other localities, and Dementiev and Gladkov (1952) for U.S.S.R. In England, on short winter days, the birds spent over 90% of the day feeding and got 650–800 gm. of fresh food—over 25% of body wt.—and digestion is inefficient; first-winter birds fed faster than older ones by walking faster, being less selective, pecking faster, and spending less time on the alert, which probably gives them an advantage in most winters (M. Owen 1972). AWS

110

Bean Goose

Anser fabalis

Dark goose, smallish to above medium sized (much geographical and individual variation), in definitive stages distinguished from closely related species by having combination of bicolored bill (black, with more or less of midsection pinkish or rather orange or yellow; rarely without black) and head and neck uniformly quite dark, the essentially plain lower breast and belly appreciably lighter than dorsum. In all postdowny stages some individuals have a very narrow white area adjoining sides and top of bill (much less than is usual in the Whitefront). Bean Geese in their first year are superficially like young Whitefronts, but differ in proportions and in some details of color. For description of tracheal apparatus (of *A. f. brachyrhynchus*), see Frère (1846). Sexes similar, ♂ av. larger; in the species as a whole, length 24–35 in., wt. 3½–9½ lb.

Some authors recognize 6 subspecies, but only 4 (includes the Pinkfoot as 1) are recognized here; the Pinkfoot breeds within our area and 2 e. Asian subspecies have occurred as stragglers.

DESCRIPTION *A. f. brachyrhynchus*. The Pinkfoot. Smallest Bean Goose. Sequence of Plumages as in the Whitefront.

As in various of the larger geese which require a long time to mature, there is much individual variation in rate of Plumage development during 1st fall into spring. The usual pattern consists of rapid replacement of considerable Juv. feathering in fall, then a continuing and gradual molt plus activation of additional follicles into spring. The process is more rapid in some individuals (largely completed by midwinter) and lags or is never fully accomplished in some others (some Juv. feathering still retained in late spring). Subsequently (in Prebasic II and later molts), the same pattern recurs in at least some individuals—bulk of molt early, then some molting continues into winter or even spring. There is no satisfactory evidence that various follicles are activated twice/ cycle, i.e., that 2 Plumages/cycle exist, although this has been claimed for the species by several authors.

▶ ♂ ♀ Def. Basic Plumage (entire feathering) ALL YEAR—the preceding and succeeding Basic Plumages overlap in molt approximately from late July through Aug. (includes flightless period) and the molt often continues into early winter. The timing of the molt varies with locality and season in breeders and begins correspondingly earlier by about a month in prebreeders. As observed in breeders, there is actual loss of flight prior to dropping the wing quills (after onset of Prebasic molt); the geese are believed to be flightless for about 26 days. In a normal year in Iceland, where the season averages much earlier than at other Pinkfoot breeding areas, they are again on the wing about Aug. 5–10.

Bill banded, black at base and tip with intervening area pink (rarely orange); occasionally it is wholly pink, but usually ³/₅ or more is black. **Iris** medium brownish. **Head** and neck dark ashy brown; many individuals have a very small amount of white adjoining base of bill at sides and top; feathers on sides of neck pointed, the resulting furrowing not conspicuous. **Upperparts** have a bluish gray "bloom" in new feathering, but become rather brownish when worn, the individual feathers with very conspicuous

111

whitish or pale brownish terminal borders; lower back and upper rump dark ashy gray, the lower rump and upper tail coverts usually all white. **Underparts** upper breast, sides, and flanks medium ashy brown, and along upper sides the whitish feather margins overlap so as to form a pale line overlying folded wing; lower breast and part of belly paler; vent to tail white. **Tail** feathers dark ashy brown with edges and tips white (more white on outer ones). Legs and **feet** pinkish. **Wing** remiges dark grayish brown, the innermost secondaries lighter and quite conspicuously bordered white distally; most upper coverts (which have broad squarish ends) are dark grayish brown with conspicuous light brownish or whitish distal margins.

AT HATCHING olive greenish with yellowish on part of head (forehead, cheeks, chin), on throat, bar along wing, a spot on body behind wing, and underparts. Bill toward medium slaty with pale nail; iris dark; legs and feet medium to dark grayish. Older goslings, after true body down grows, are rather pale grayish with only a tinge of greenish.

▶   ♂ ♀ Juv. Plumage (entire feathering), perfected at about age 6–7 weeks, then much of it generally lost quite rapidly (see beginning of this section) except at least most of wing always retained into following summer. **Bill** grayish with pinkish tinge. A brownish and blended (not contrastingly patterned) Plumage, the pale borders of feathers on dorsum and sides quite brownish (not whitish); neck smooth (no pointed feathers); various feathers (most obviously on upperparts) tapering, narrow, and with rounded ends; tail feathers also tapering, with notched ends; wing coverts comparatively narrow and with rounded ends.

▶   ♂ ♀ Basic I Plumage (much of or even all head–body and possibly some wing coverts; at least most of Juv. wing, and in some individuals considerable other Juv. feathering, is retained). Much of this Plumage comes in rapidly beginning when the birds are about 7 weeks old, in FALL. Both ends of the **bill** darken and the midsection becomes more colored. **Head** and neck brownish; any pointed neck feathers generally come in toward the end of the molt, in spring. Generally not all the **tail** feathers that are going to be acquired are grown before midwinter. **Upperparts** more slaty (less brownish) than Juv.; sides blotchy (feathers somewhat slaty with brownish margins), grading to spotty effect more ventrally, the sides and **underparts** thus becoming markedly different from those of a 7–8 week old bird. Legs and **feet** become suffused with pinkish.

In this Plumage, various early-incoming feathers are more intermediate in shape between those of Juv. and Def. Basic than are the later-incoming ones, which are more like the latter and so differ more in shape from any Juv. feathers that may have been retained.

Measurements of specimens taken on winter range in Britain:—8 ♂: BILL 45–49 mm., av. 47; WING 407–458, av. 433; TAIL 115–143, av. 132.5; TARSUS 67–78, av. 74;   5 ♀: BILL 43–47 mm., av. 45; WING 420–433, av. 425; TAIL 119–134, av. 128; TARSUS 70–78, av. 73 (ETS). A larger sample, with WING measured over curve (Coombes, in Witherby 1939), shows greater spread in meas. As is to be expected, the Juv. wing is shorter than the Basic wing; see tables in Schiøler (1925).

Weight   For summary and discussion of various published data, plus additional information by sex and age-class, see Elder (1955). The following, from Beer and Boyd

112

(1962), pertains to 2,844 birds examined mainly in Oct., but some in Nov., on winter range in England and Scotland; the figures are the means with range in parentheses: "adults" 750 ♂ 2.77 kg. (1.90–3.35) and 796 ♀ 2.52 (1.81–3.15); first-autumn birds (age 3–4 mo.) 671 ♂ 2.39 kg. (1.41–3.08) and 627 ♀ 2.17 (1.45–2.80). In 1959, a year of poor breeding success, the wts. of "adults" and "young" that fall on winter range were significantly reduced.

Flightless "adult" Pinkfeet in Spitzbergen weighed slightly less (♂ 5.7% and ♀ 7.0%) than their Oct. wt. in Britain (Beer and Boyd).

Hybrids   In Iceland a ♀ was seen mated to a Barnacle (*Branta leucopsis*) gander; the 4 eggs were robbed, probably by a gull (Wildfowl Trust 5th *An. Rept.*, p. 88. 1952). For the species: a "few" wild hybrids with the Whitefronts have been recorded (Delacour 1954). (Also see under White-fronted Goose.) In captivity, the Bean Goose has crossed with a number of other waterfowl species.

Geographical variation in the species. Johansen's (1956) speculation on the evolutionary history of Bean Geese is summarized in part in this paragraph. Ancestral stock was split during a glaciation into birds in unglaciated ne. Siberia and others that were forced to retreat to other refugia more southerly in Eurasia. The former became differentiated into "tundra geese" (smaller and stockier, the short bill having high base and oval nail); the latter became differentiated as "forest geese" (larger and elongated, the long narrow bill having rounded nail). During a subsequent interglacial, the tundra birds spread westward and there they now av. smaller, the westernmost breeding sub-populations are the smallest birds,—i.e., the Pinkfeet of Spitzbergen, Iceland, and e. Greenland—while breeding birds of s. Novaya Zemlya are presumed to trend toward Pinkfeet in morphological characteristics. The forest geese from southerly refugia moved n. in Eurasia and occupied breeding areas within the boreal forest zone.

a forest bird	tundra bird	Pinkfoot (tundra)
(*middendorfi*)	(*serrirostris*)	(*brachyrhynchus*)

A common idea of geographical variation implies considerable randomness of mate selection occurring on breeding range, but it is extremely limited in *Anser* (and some other waterfowl). The various flocks or units of Bean Geese have their traditional breeding places, migration routes or corridors, and winter quarters; pair formation is a gradual process and mate selection tends to be restricted to within a flock in which individuals have long and close contact, including on winter range. Then the geese, when nesting, are essentially in separate units, occurring in scattered areas of preferred habitat and subject to the pressures of their particular local environment.

Even within a framework of such limitations, there is sufficient mingling so that a clear-cut demarcation between tundra and forest types of Bean Geese does not now exist in Eurasia. Also, various morphological characters in the species tend to vary in-

113

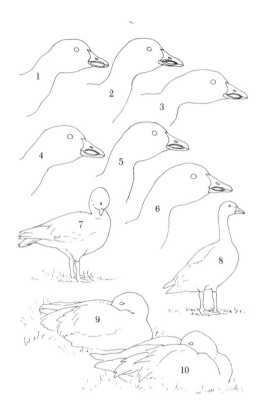

Lesser Snow/Blue Goose

Anser c. caerulescens

1 Blue—age 50-70 days.
2 Blue—age about 85 days.
3 Blue—age about 115 days.
4 Blue—age 5-6 months.
5 Blue—age about 10 months.
6 Blue—Def. Basic Plumage. The nail on the bill has become increasingly better defined until, finally, there is a definite groove where top of bill meets edge of nail. Note various accumulations of rusty (ferrous) staining on head.
7 Lesser Snow—Def. Basic Plumage.
8 Blue—white-bellied individual in Def. Basic Plumage.
9 Lesser Snow—Juv. Plumage.
10 Blue—Def. Basic Plumage. Compare shapes of dorsal feathers with those of the Juv. Lesser Snow (whose feathers are identical in shape with those of the Juv. Blue Goose). (For day-old downies in color, see plate facing p. 242.)

114

R. M. Mengel—

dependently, occurring in different combinations, so that there is great individual variation. For example, there are individuals having the light area of the bill pink and the legs and feet also pink (A. "neglectus") and others having similar bill coloring but with orange-yellow legs and feet (A. "carneirostris"). Many of the geese in a vast inland area (Yenessei drainage and vicinity) have a mixture of "forest" and "tundra" characteristics and variation also is great on the Gydan and Yamal Peninsulas and vicinity. (Beyond the Yenessei, but especially from the Lena R. eastward, large areas of tundra–alpine environment occur far s. of the northerly limit of trees, down nearly to lat. 60° beyond the Lena.) In all probability, flocks or other units that differ from one another in averages of morphological characteristics (i.e., may be of 2 different sizes, etc.) nest in fairly close proximity.

The molt migration of prebreeders has caused much past confusion. Many prebreeding forest geese depart from (or fly beyond) the nesting areas of their parents and spend the summer to the northward in the vicinity of breeding tundra geese; prebreeding tundra birds also move to molting localities, even to various is. n. of the breeding range of the species. Thus summering prebreeders may be very different birds from the breeders at the same locality; the former often have been confused with the latter.

Krashkin (1962) studied an interesting, but not entirely adequate, series of 79 specimens of breeding (not prebreeding or molting) Eurasian tundra birds. His findings included: 1 BILL length and WING length increase steadily from w. to e., 2 in the same direction the number of relatively small individuals decreases and number of large ones increases, and 3 from opposite ends of Eurasian range there are individuals alike in size but differing in sum total of external characters. He concluded that the tundra birds have overall clinal variation across Eurasia, without trenchant divisions and with mingling of local units, and that the name A. f. fabalis should be used for all the tundra birds from Scandinavia to Kamchatka inclusive. RSP

SUBSPECIES The Bean Goose was revised by Johansen (1945) and Delacour (1951), with some additional information in Delacour (1954). A few authors still treat the island-breeding Pinkfoot as a species, but it is here regarded as a tundra subspecies of Bean Goose. Because of the nature and extent of geographical variation and amplitude of individual variation, mentioned above, a passably acceptable application of the subspecies concept to the birds of the Eurasian mainland and near vicinity is as follows: tundra birds may be divided very arbitrarily into a western and an eastern subspecies, while true forest birds comprise a single (eastern) subspecies. This reduces the number of continental subspecies of A. fabalis to 3, then adding the island-nesting A. f. brachyrhynchus brings the total to 4, as in S. Uspenskii (1965a) whose map of breeding distribution is followed.

In our area middendorfi Severtzov [sibiricus (Alpheraky) of some authors]—a large elongated form with long neck and long narrow bill; very variable morphologically; has large breeding range within the forest zone in e. Asia. BILL 64–87 mm., WING 440–462; visible DEPTH OF LOWER MANDIBLE 7–10 (Delacour 1951). One was taken on St. Paul I. (Pribilofs), Alaska, April 19, 1946 (Gabrielson 1947).

brachyrhynchus Baillon—the Pinkfoot. Smallest of all Bean Geese; an island-breeding tundra form. Full descr. and meas. given above. Breeds in e. Greenland, in Iceland, and Spitzbergen; winters mainly in the Brit. Isles; reported in continental

N. Am. A ♀ shot at Rowley, Mass., Sept. 23, 1924; 1 was seen at Bombay Hook, Del., Nov. 1, 1953 into Jan., 1954 (Cutler 1955); whether it was an escapee, is debatable; 1 supposedly was seen on Long I., N. Y., in the winter of 1971–72.

serrirostris Swinhoe—the larger tundra birds of e. Asia (but on the Chuckchee Pen. not recorded e. of a line approximately from C. Vankarem down to Kresta Gulf). Usually has reduced yellowish area on bill (compared with westerly nominate *fabalis*); highly variable in size and other characteristics. BILL 65–76 mm.; WING 420–525; visible DEPTH OF LOWER MANDIBLE 8–13 (Delacour 1951). See under "*sibiricus*" in Dementiev and Gladkov (1952) for additional meas.; also see Sdobnikov (1959a) for meas. and wt. of a small series. According to Johansen (1961), a regular spring and rare autumn migrant in the Commander Is. A ♂ was taken at Gambel on St. Lawrence I., Alaska, on May 8, 1952 (A. Bailey 1956, Sealy et al. 1971); a ♀ was taken on St. Paul I. (Pribilofs), Alaska, May 26, 1961 (Sladen 1966).

Reported sightings of single individuals (subspecies?) include: (near Gambel on May 19, 1959, and May 16, 1966 (Sealy et al. 1971);) on Amchitka, in the Aleutians, in late May or early June, 1971 (Cornell Lab. Ornithol. *Newsletter* no. 62: 5. 1971).

Extralimital *fabalis* Latham—the w. Eurasian birds, highly variable morphologically and not entirely tundra-breeding, in size av. smaller than the e. Eurasian birds known as *serrirostris*. Included here in *fabalis* are the birds that have been subspecifically labeled "*johanseni*" and also those called "*rossicus*," even though the flocks and other units may have some av. differences from others considered "typical" nominate *fabalis* and have their particular places and seasons of occurrence. Such inclusion requires a slightly broader definition of the nominate race than previously suggested in the non-Russian literature. RSP

FIELD IDENTIFICATION   The species. Moderate-sized to smallish dark geese. Head and neck appear very dark, remainder of bird mostly lighter in varying degrees, with plain underparts. Sometimes a very small amount of white adjoining base of bill (not a conspicuous amount as in the Whitefront). Bill usually bicolored, having black distal portion and base, with orange, yellow, or pinkish midsection, sharply delimited, but proportions of dark/light vary greatly. Generally speaking, color of hind limbs approximates that of light area of bill, but there are exceptions. Birds in their 1st fall–winter, if by themselves, are very difficult for the inexperienced observer to identify; a person familiar with various species of *Anser* and their age categories distinguishes Bean Geese by dark head and neck plus overall proportions of the birds.

They fly in lines, chevrons, and strings, quite often in large flocks. General habits about as in Whitefront, but they have somewhat different environmental preferences.

The Pinkfoot—as above; light area of bill and the hind limbs normally pinkish. Smallish, stocky geese. Upperparts appear slaty bluish (brownish in worn condition), contrasting decidedly with dark head and neck. Young in 1st fall–winter appear more compact than at least most Whitefronts and they have relatively shorter and smaller bills. The 2 species associate in parts of their ranges. RSP

VOICE   Bean Geese often are silent. Usual honk, of 2–3 syllables, evidently varies in the species depending on size and sex of the individual. When the tundra birds of w.

Eurasia are compared with the smaller Pinkfoot, the former is said to have a lower and more reedy *ung-unk*. The gander's voice is higher pitched than that of the goose. In Iceland a pair of Pinkfeet, in flight after being frightened from the nest, uttered a high-pitched *ee-wink ee-wink*, much thinner and more squeaky than the winter calls (Yeates 1955). RSP

HABITAT   Total **breeding** habitat of the species: moss-lichen, grassy, sedgy and scrub tundra, even southward in the forest zone in open expanses, also along water-courses there. **Winter** habitat includes low-lying coasts, also deltas, estuaries, lakes, marshes, and various terrain within daily foraging flight of these places.

The Pinkfoot breeds on arctic terrain, in some places so rocky and so sparsely vege-tated as to be virtually a desert. See for details: e.-cent. Greenland (Salomonsen 1950), cent. Iceland (Scott et al. 1953, Sladen 1960, Gardarsson 1972), and s. Spitzbergen (Løvenskiold 1964). In Iceland, the relatively well vegetated Thjorsarver Delta in the central part of the island has about 75% of the breeding birds; other units are scattered in less favorable environment.

Outside the breeding season as above for the species generally; often on cultivated lands not distant from water. RSP

DISTRIBUTION   **In our area** the only **breeding** Bean Geese are the western-most subpopulation of the Pinkfoot (*A. f. brachyrhynchus*), of e. Greenland (they go to Palearctic winter range); 2 additional subspecies are recorded as **stragglers** from e. Asia; the records are given above under "Subspecies."

Elsewhere   Aside from the combined subpopulations of the Pinkfoot, winter range of the species is rather difficult to delimit. In the past, as at present, limits vary depend-ing on mildness or severity of weather and, no doubt, on predation or disturbance by man. Only about 1,400 were found wintering as far n. as within the U.S.S.R. in Jan., 1967. The species has been reported as wintering in parts of n. Africa, in Asia Minor, Palestine, Caucasus region, Caspian Sea, and se. Iran, but now perhaps is absent or not regular. Present status on the Iberian Pen. is not well known. This goose was known in ancient Egypt, which may indicate that it wintered farther s. some 5,000 years ago.

No attempt is made here to summarize all records of **stragglers**. *A. f. brachyrhyn-chus*, for example, has been reported from Franz Josef Land, from s. U.S.S.R., also at several places on the Indian subcontinent as listed by Ripley (1961). In the Atlantic, *brachyrhynchus* reportedly has occurred s. to Terceira (Azores) and Lanzarote (Canaries), but one taken off Terceira in 1968 was a forest bird (and a Madeira record is for a tundra bird, nominate *fabalis*).

For a listing of Palearctic records of the species as **fossil** in the Pleistocene and also from **archaeological sites,** see under *A. fabalis, A. neglectus,* and *A. brachyrhynchus* in Brodkorb (1964a). RSP

MIGRATION   Emphasis here is on the only breeding stock in our area, the Pinkfeet of e. Greenland; data mainly from Salomonsen (1950), whose information has been further bolstered by subsequent banding recoveries.

GREENLAND **Spring**   The birds begin leaving England–Scotland in April. They arrive in Angmagssalik Dist. of e. Greenland from early to end of May, sometimes in

117

"enormous skeins." They cross Iceland en route. Probably they are of regular occurrence in the Faeroes in spring and again in fall.

Molt migration   Prebreeders, soon after they arrive at breeding areas with their parents, move some distance away to molting places. Main requisites there are adequate food (which is practically nonexistent in some breeding areas) and safety while flightless (ashore, on fresh water, or the sea). Taylor (1953) gave some evidence that Icelandic prebreeders have a molt migration to ne. Greenland; Christensen et al. (1965) provided additional important information that such a flight occurs. Perhaps 15,000 Icelandic birds molt in Greenland (Kerbes et al. 1971).

Fall   When the goslings attain flight, and their parents regain it after the molt, families make local flights and have favorite places where they congregate for a while prior to departure. Latest recorded occurrence in a Greenland breeding area is Sept. 8. The geese are seen in passage in Angmagssalik Dist. in Sept. and the majority spend the winter in Scotland and England where they arrive mid-Sept. to mid-Oct. A few reach the n. shores of Europe. (Icelandic Pinkfeet also go to Britain, while Spitzbergen birds occur around the s. rim of the North Sea, mainly from Denmark to n. France.)

Winter   There is considerable shifting about, to a large extent depending on weather. See, for example, Holgersen (1960) for the birds from Spitzbergen.

ELSEWHERE   For various additional data on Bean Goose migration, these are localities and sources: Japan (O. L. Austin, Jr., and Kuroda 1953), U.S.S.R (Dementiev and Gladkov 1952), w. U.S.S.R. plus Europe and Britain (Mathiasson 1963), Finland (Lampio 1961, Waaramäki 1970), Spitzbergen (Løvenskiold 1964 and authors cited by him), and Iceland (banding recoveries in various vols. of the journal *Brit. Birds* and various mention in Wildfowl Trust *Reports*).

Very important molting places in Asia (within limits of breeding range) include cent. Yamal and w. Taimyr Pen. and the delta of the Indigirka (S. Uspenskii 1965a), also the Lena delta (Portenko 1959); some go n. of regular breeding range to the New Siberian Is. (Pleske 1928). RSP

BANDING STATUS   None in N. Am. Pinkfeet have been banded on winter range and at the 3 general breeding areas, Greenland, Iceland (many banded there), and Spitzbergen. A considerable number of Bean Geese that breed in w. Eurasia also have been banded, almost entirely on winter range in w. Europe, the number banded in Britain through 1969 being 11,826, with 3,286 recoveries. Numerous recoveries for the species have been published, scattered through literature in several languages. RSP

REPRODUCTION   *A. f. brachyrhynchus.* Information mostly from Iceland, not much being known from elsewhere. Main sources: 5th (1953) and 7th (1955) *Reports* of the Wildfowl Trust, also Scott and Fisher (1953), plus some Greenland data from Salomonsen (1950).

Pair formation occurs mostly on winter range, after fairly long association of prospective mates. Very likely many 2-year-olds have formed a more or less stable bond. Pairbond form is **lifelong monogamy.**

Usually **first breeds** at age about 32 mo. (Boyd 1956), but some when younger as they become 2-year-olds. They arrive at breeding areas in Iceland in May, in flocks, the breeders already paired. For excellent photos of Icelandic breeding habitat, see Kerbes et al. (1971). The span from arrival to onset of laying probably is a few days at most. At Constable Pt., Scoresby Sd., Greenland, in 1929, A. Pedersen found the "adult" population to be of usual size, but the season was retarded and the geese did not breed there that year. (Undoubtedly there also are localities where the summer residents consist solely of molting prebreeders.)

Nest site a dry spot, almost always where the goose has a reasonably good view of surroundings and, within about 15 ft. of it, a guard site for the gander. Some nests are on ledges of cliffs; many are in tundra marshes, commonly on top of low frost mounds; some are near pools or streams, but water nearby is not essential. In Greenland usually well within large deltas, the site being a vegetated hillock of sand or shingle; also terraces and ledges on sides of valleys, low islands, and on open heath (here only solitary pairs). The goose builds the nest, using materials at the site plus her down; there is preference for a site used a former year. The **nest down** is brownish gray, some with lighter centers; any included feathers are small and gray, tipped lighter, giving a somewhat silvery appearance (Witherby 1939).

Copulation on water away from territory (probably just before arrival there).

Most clutches are completed about May 25 in a normal year in Iceland (certainly later in Greenland and Spitzbergen). Nineteen **clutches** (Iceland): 6 (of 3 eggs), 3 (of 4), 5 (5), 4 (6), 1 (7) (Boyd 1956). Thirty-six Icelandic **eggs size** av. 80.1 × 52.5 mm.; **shape** variable, generally between subelliptical and long elliptical; surface rather coarse grained, **color** dull whitish. Usually laid 1/day. Incubation begins on completion of the clutch. The goose, joined by the gander, leaves her eggs once daily to feed and defecate. A captive ♀ began laying May 14 and was not seen to leave the nest until June 14 (Pitt 1944). There is so little vegetation in some areas that probably the geese get almost no nourishment until they move away with their brood. Her pear-shaped droppings are seldom over 30 yds. from the nest, while the gander leaves a patch of short, broken, droppings at his guard site. **Incubation period** closely estimated as 28 days.

The goslings remain in the nest about a day; then the family moves away, often to water, to seek adequate food. The parents with their downies tend to form aggregations so that, after the goslings are a few days old, individual broods cannot be distinguished. In Greenland, young are led to grassy plateaus; then, after about a month, the families often travel to the fjord coast and there join with others.

Breeders become flightless while with their preflight young. If the geese are ashore and are pursued when flightless, they flee to higher ground, being able to run uphill at astonishing speed. In some places they take to water (sometimes to the sea in Greenland and Spitzbergen).

Little is known about persistence of the family bond in the Pinkfoot, in fact for Bean Geese generally, but the pattern probably is very similar to that of the better-known Whitefront. RSP

SURVIVAL A. f. brachyrhynchus that winter in Britain: mortality of young from hatching to mid-Oct. evidently is of the order of 60%; mortality between 1st and 2nd Octobers of life about 42%; mean annual mortality thereafter about 26%, although this

119

varies widely from one year to another (Boyd 1956). Estimated mean annual survival rate 0.74 ± 0.02 (Boyd). RSP

HABITS   The species. A less vocal bird than the Whitefront and Greylag.

Goose pastures   The microclimate and plant succession at summer feeding places have been mentioned in passing by several authors; for cent. Taimyr, they were discussed more fully by Tikhomirov (1959), in part as follows. When the geese arrive, they find some food (notably *Oxytropis*) where the thaw begins on south-facing slopes and tops of hillocks. When more level areas are snow free and plants begin to grow, the geese feed in cotton grass–moss plant communities. At first the cotton grass (*Eriophorum*) is rooted in still frozen soil and the birds actually have been seen to lose their balance and to fall over when trying to pull it loose. After the soil is thawed, the geese uproot the cotton grass and eat all parts, except that they discard old, coarse growth. The disturbance of the shallowly thawed surface produces a characteristic ragged or tattered appearance. Subsequently, surface water washes the discarded portions into shallow depressions in the ground; the extent of goose foraging can be gauged by the amount of such accumulations.

Pulling the cotton grass increases aeration of the soil, more drying of its upper layer, and deeper thawing; the altered pattern of heat exchange can result in increased soil creep on slopes. The plant community alters from cotton grass–moss through a moss stage, to patchy sedge–cotton grass–moss, or patchy sedge–moss with only scattered cotton grass plants. The cycle goes on, and probably has done so for thousands of years, the geese selecting mainly cotton grass and also fertilizing the areas with their fecal matter.

There is another cycle, on freshwater shores. The geese (especially prebreeders) congregate when molting, feed heavily, and leave their abundant droppings. Such plants as *Arctophila*, *Dupontia*, *Pleuropogon*, and *Carex stans* may be eliminated by the geese, temporarily.

Pinkfeet
(*A. f. brachyrhynchus*)

definitive   Juv.

Elevated shores of tundra waters, where *Puccinellia* and *Dupontia* are plentiful, are favorite "goose pastures." At one stage, as a result of goose activity, the surface topography is altered to tiny hummocks 10–12 cm. high.

Wintering Bean Geese in s. Sweden are, according to Markgren (1963), rather more generalized feeders than Whitefronts. There they prefer uncultivated grassland, hayfields to a lesser extent, and ploughed and/or harvested fields to a minor extent. Their food is partly pulled, partly cut, by the bill. The birds spread out, in small groups, and keep moving so that they never clean out a meadow. They rest at midday on their feeding areas, but prefer to go to open water or out on ice for the night. In Britain they resort to meadows, pastures, and arable land, and tend to make longer flights between roosting and feeding areas than other British-wintering geese.

The Bean Goose still is numerous in parts of its range. Stories of its abundance long ago in Japan are "almost unbelievable," but the wintering population has dwindled steadily for a long time (O. L. Austin, Jr., and Kuroda 1953). The numbers of Pinkfeet (*A. f. brachyrhynchus*) wintering in Britain from 1950 onward were discussed by Boyd and Ogilvie (1969); in view of a continuing increase, they forecast 90,000 birds by 1975. RSP

FOOD *A. f. brachyrhynchus*. Almost entirely **vegetable**, animal matter forming only a trace. Stomachs of 2 birds taken July 31 and Aug. 6 in ne. Greenland contained respectively an amphipod and an insect, but mainly grasses and sedges with their seeds: sedge (*Carex*) 54.5%, meadow grass (*Poa*) and undetermined Gramineae 32.5%, bulblets of arctic smartweed (*Polygonum viviparum*) 3%, debris of 3 species of moss 2.5%, and undetermined plant material 7.5% (Cottam and Knappen 1939). Aside from grass, there has been found in stomachs the leaves of sorrel (*Oxyria*), also *Dryas octopetala*, and leaves and seeds of *Polygonum viviparum* (Degerbøl and Møhl-Hansen 1935, Løppenthin 1932, Pedersen 1942.) In an Icelandic colony, food seems to have been grasses and *Equisetum* stems, also sedges and grasses (Scott et al. 1953). In Spitzbergen, only plant remains in stomachs (Römer and Schaudinn 1900). Among identifiable plants were grasses, stems, leaves, and roots of *Cerastium edmonstonii*, various species of saxifrage (*Saxifraga*), and horsetail (*Equisetum arvense, A. alpestre*) (Le Roi, in Koenig 1911). Young had eaten buds and leaves of willow (*Salix reticulata*).

In Scotland, the birds eat almost every type of crop available, not selected in proportion to availability; grass is eaten as long as the birds are present; spilled grain mainly in autumn; decaying or abandoned potatoes in harvested fields in autumn, winter, and early spring; and growing corn mainly in late spring; the chief conflict with agriculture occurred when the birds ate young grass in spring (I. Newton and Campbell 1970).

For other Bean Geese, no summary is attempted here. Suggestive, however, are references cited above under "Habits." Also see Kapitonov (1962) for autumn data on *A. f. serrirostris*, while Middendorff (1853) mentioned large flocks of forest geese feeding on blueberries (*Vaccinium*) on mossy moors in ne. Asia in Sept. AWS

Snow Goose/Blue Goose

Anser caerulescens

There are color phases or **morphs** in the smaller subspecies (and very rarely in the larger?), individuals varying from white with part of wings black (Lesser Snow) through intermediates to dark (Blue Goose), the last having head and neck white, body mostly dark brownish gray, and part of wing very dark; and a larger (Greater Snow) counterpart of the white phase. For the single species, 3 vernacular names are retained and used here where applicable, and a 4th is mentioned tentatively.

Moderate-sized to rather large, fairly short-necked goose; broad area on side of mandibles ("grinning patch" or "smile") conspicuous from hatching onward; bill high at base, wrinkled (not warty), the feather margin on side forming a forward-curved line; "furrowing" of feathers on sides of neck not usually apparent except in times of stress (mainly during pair formation and when nesting); to greatest extent in definitive stages, innermost secondaries ("tertials") and their greater coverts are lengthened and downcurved; head and neck, especially, often with ferrous staining; ♂ av. larger than ♀. For comment on tracheal anatomy, see Humphrey (1958a).

Lesser Snow/Blue: length 26–30 in., wingspread about 52–61, wt. usually 4–6¼ lb. (♂ av. under 5½); Greater Snow: length 29–33 in., wingspread about 53–64, wt. usually 6–10½ lb. (♂ av. 8 lb.). The smaller subspecies mainly, and the larger subspecies entirely, in our area.

DESCRIPTION *A. c. caerulescens* Lesser Snow/intermediates/Blue. See col. pl. facing p. 114. One Plumage/cycle. Basic II approaches definitive condition, although fullest development of feather shapes generally, and of modified inner wing feathers especially, probably begins with Basic III. (Also see comment under Basic II below.)
▶   ♂ ♀ Def. Basic Plumage (entire feathering), LATE SUMMER to LATE SUMMER (overlap of Basics at intervening molt). In all categories: **bill** pinkish scarlet (some seasonal variation), more toward orange at base, with whitish nail; **iris** medium brownish; eyelids vary—whitish to ruby, even violet-magenta; **tarsi** and toes muted pinkish scarlet, soles yellowish, nails black.

CATEGORIES 1 White (Lesser Snow)—feathering white except: greater primary coverts pale or medium gray; alula varies with individual from white to medium gray and there is more or less correlation with number of dark flight feathers (minimum—white alula + 7 black primaries; maximum—medium gray alula + all primaries + 4 outer and several innermost secondaries black); dark flight feathers lighter at base; usually some dark on innermost elongated secondaries. 2 Extreme white-bellied Blue—head, neck, and underparts white, sometimes with narrow grayish or fuscous band on upper breast; upperparts, including wing, much as in category 5 (described below) except modified innermost secondaries white; tail and rump vary, white to pale gray. 3 Intermediate white-bellied Blue—like preceding except solid band of dark gray or fuscous across underparts from lower foreneck to foresternum; innermost secondaries not always white; tail and rump mainly light gray. 4 White-bellied Blue— sizable white area on belly, extending back to vent; otherwise like following. 5 Blue (Blue Goose)—**head** and neck white, occasionally with broken black line from crown

122

down hindneck; **upperparts** base of hindneck to beyond center of back dark slaty brownish or fuscous, many feathers with pale grayish subterminal area and pale brownish red tip; scapulars similar but paler; lower back to tail varies from nearly white (in few birds) to mainly pale bluish gray like upper wing coverts (most birds); **underparts** lower throat to belly very like upper back; abdomen, flanks, and under tail coverts pale gray mixed with whitish, but whitish replaced in some birds by sooty black; **tail** feathers pale brownish to medium gray, broadly edged with white or whitish; **wing** primaries and secondaries black or nearly so, lighter toward bases, and latter edged smoke gray to white, some inner ones somewhat modified as plumes and the innermost few similar, but dark medial color grades laterally to dark brownish and with broader whitish edging; coverts light to bluish gray, the inner greater coverts being the most modified as plumes of any of the wing feathers, and their dark medial color grades to conspicuous white edging; under wing coverts pale gray or light bluish; axillars almost white or white.

Plumage acquired by Prebasic molt of all feathering, the flight feathers of wing dropped at or near onset of molting. Successful breeders ($♀$ about 3–4 days in advance of $♂$) begin molting when their goslings av. 21 days old and the parents have a flightless period of about 21 days. Thus they molt about 3 weeks later than yearlings and 2-year-old prebreeders. Breeders that lose eggs or young (failed breeders) begin molting at an intermediate time. With successful breeders, timing is such that the parent birds regain flight close to the time when their young first attain it.

NOTES   A very few Lesser Snow individuals that were color-marked with dye in late fall in Cal. still showed some dye in the following late Oct. and Nov. (Kozlik et al. 1959), which indicates that their intervening molt was incomplete at the time they returned again to winter range.

Based on further analysis of data from the Boas R. (Southampton I.) breeding unit, the 5 categories of feathering given above were expanded to 8, and each defined, by F. Cooke and Cooch (1968). These authors theorize that the gander (when a gosling) is "imprinted" to the appearance (pattern, etc.) of one or both of his parents and so, subsequently, selects as a mate a $♀$ similar in appearance to one or both parents—i.e., this is the mechanism whereby polymorphism is maintained. There is a single-gene difference between "white" and "blue" with the allele responsible for "blue" dominant over "white." The genetics of color phases were discussed most recently by Cooke and Mirsky (1972).

AT HATCHING   See col. pl. facing p. 242. Categories are numbered here to correspond with the 5 parental categories given above, with which they correlate quite closely. **Iris** brownish in all. **1** Golden—bill light gray with buffy yellowish nail; general color of the down is greenish yellow (somewhat grayish on back and wings); medium brownish markings on crown, nape, and a line of same through eye; indefinite yellowish patches on back and wings; medium brownish area from thigh through flank; hind limbs mostly light grayish. **2** Dark golden—like preceding, except brownish areas on head and neck much darker; line through eye nearly black and some have blackish eye ring; general frizzled appearance. **3** Dusky—general color dusky olive green with overall yellowish cast, but darker (blackish) on head and upperparts; pale yellowish chin patch and narrow line of same from bill to eye; bill and feet mostly sooty black;

general coloration bleaches rapidly to give patchy appearance at age 3 weeks. **4** Dark—like 3 except yellowish cast reduced and no yellowish line from bill; bleaches as preceding. **5** Darkest—bill blackish with whitish nail; except for pale chin patch, the head, neck, and upperparts dusky brown to sooty black; underparts somewhat lighter (brownish olive); hardly any yellowish cast; legs and feet blackish. The down bleaches uniformly.

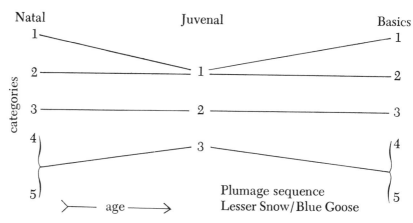

▶ ♂ ♀ Juv. Plumage (entire feathering), fully acquired at age 60–70 days; begins to be succeeded by Basic I at about 85 days. **Bill** blackish gray with somewhat lighter tip; **iris** brownish; legs and **feet** dark gray, sometimes with greenish cast. Innermost secondaries and longest overlying coverts not at all or slightly modified, depending on individual.

CATEGORIES   1 Pale—grayish brown upperparts grade into white underparts. Succeeds #1 natal. Forehead whitish; stripe from bill to eye, the crown, hindneck, and mantle medium brownish gray with lighter feather edgings mainly on back; primaries blackish; greater coverts and secondaries dark, at least the former grading to broad white borders; rest of feathering white or nearly so. Some individuals, darker in overall appearance, were #2 natals. 2 Quite dark—rather like "adult" Blue, but head and neck as dark as upper body and browner. Were #3 natals. Line along feather edge on sides of upper mandible white; chin patch white; back, rump, and tail never as light as whitish-backed definitive-feathered Blues; ventral color between light and medium gray. 3 Dark—essentially like preceding except no white line at side base of bill; lower back and rump bluish gray intermixed with white; tail as in definitive-feathered Blue; most of ventral surface as dark as upper back. Succeeds natals #4 and #5.

The Juv. feathering pushes out the 1st (natal) down, which then wears off the feather tips.

▶ ♂ ♀ Basic I Plumage (all feathering except: Juv. flight feathers of wing, sometimes some tail feathers, and possibly some feathers of head–neck occasionally. Begins to succeed much of Juv. in FALL (see above), usually fully acquired by some time in WINTER (but much individual variation in timing, including duration, of molting) and worn until about JULY (at age slightly over 1 year). Data here are for Blues, other categories presumably being similar. At age 85 days, scattered white feathers appear on head; 115 days, many light spots on head, molting and replacement on underparts noticeable from this age onward; 150–180 days, head mostly white, bill mostly pinkish (associated with molting is an increasing amount of pinkish in bill and feet, accompanied by gradual sloughing and abrasion of skin).

NOTE   As observed at McConnell R. (e. Keewatin), there is tremendous variation among individuals, even within broods. Of 4 yearling siblings (Blues) wearing attached neckbands and still together on June 22, 1971, one was indistinguishable in the field from an "adult" Blue, one had a nearly pure white head, and two had much dark on the head and upper neck. Nearly all yearling Lesser Snows can be identified in summer, when in flight, by a darkish cast of secondary coverts and by dark feathers on the back. On the ground they usually (but not always) have some brownish feathers visible at base of the neck, particularly behind. Perhaps 75% of yearling Blues (neckbanded) have noticeable dark speckling on the head; some have only a few white feathers. (Data from J. Prevett.)

▶   ♂ ♀ Basic II Plumage (entire feathering), SUMMER to SUMMER (age about 13–25 mo.), very close to definitive. As observed in both Lesser Snows and Blues, some dark feathering, especially on head and neck, sometimes comes in with the white. These individuals may have a more perfected definitive feathering later, but a few such birds probably have blackish traces on crown and neck throughout life. Molting was discussed above.

Some age characteristics   Birds slightly over a year old (early autumn) that have attained feathering approaching definitive still have the nail and adjoining portion of the maxilla appearing continuous (no complete separating groove), usually some black blotches on both mandibles, penis small and not fully enclosed in sheath, or oviduct closed. Bursa of Fabricius noticeable until 2nd autumn, with closure at age 17–20 mo. (Higgins 1969). By age 2 years, nail clearly defined from maxilla by groove, no black blotches on bill, penis sheathed entire length, or oviduct open.

As in other waterfowl, the feathers differ in shape in the early Plumages from somewhat tapering and with narrow rounded ends (Juv.), through intermediate shapes, to wide and parallel sided with rather squarish ends (definitive)—most evident on dorsum, especially the scapulars.

Color phases in all age-classes of *A. c. caerulescens* are described above. For censusing in the field, definitive-stage categories 1–2 are combined as Lesser Snow and 3–5 lumped as Blue. In breeding range, the proportion of the latter diminishes to zero going from e. to w. Going in that direction, the following paragraphs give: breeding locality and geographical coordinates of its approximate center in 1968–72, year, number of breeders (thus omitting the largest cohorts, i.e., prebreeders), and percentage of Blues—usually for 2 different years—then change in overall numerical status. (This does not include all breeding areas and, for example, the coordinates are not exactly as in some published papers.)

BAFFIN I.   Koukdjuak R. (66°40′ N, 73°00′ W), 1955—75,000 (50%) and 1968 —50,000 (60%), decreasing since 1967; C. Dominion (66°10′ N, 74°00′ W), 1955— 100,000 (85%) and 1968—150,000 (80%); Bowman Bay (65°30′ N, 73°30′ W), 1955— 165,000 (97%) and 1968—250,000 (90%), decreasing since 1967. [In 1955 there were colonies at Cory Bay—3,000 (30%)—and Garnett Bay—3,000 (35%)—but they seem to have disappeared. In 1960 at Nettilling L. there were 30,000 (60%), all prebreeders at a molting area.]

SOUTHAMPTON I. East Bay (64°00′ N, 82°10′ W), 1955—75,000 (20%) and 1968—50,000 (30%), now fairly static; Bear Cove (63°40′ N, 85°45′ W), 1957—2,000 (30%) and 1968—5,000 (30%), fairly static; Boas R. (63°40′ N, 85°45′ W), 1952—35,000 (20%), 1961—100,000 (30%) and 1968—60,000 (30%), decreasing since 1963.

EXTREME S. HUDSON BAY C. Henrietta Maria (55°10′ N, 82°30′ W), 1960—17,000 (38%) and 1972—45,000 (75%), increasing.

W. HUDSON BAY (n. to s.). Wolf Creek (61°45′ N, 94°15′ W), 1959—1,000 (14%) and 1972—75,000 (26%), increasing; Maguse R. (61°20′ N, 94°10′ W), 1954–61—nonexistent and in 1968—13,000 (26%), becoming established; McConnell R. (called Eskimo Pt. in Cooch's published papers) (60°50′ N, 94°25′ W), 1954—15,000 (14%) and a total count of nesting pairs from aerial photos in 1972—310,000 individuals (26%), a twentyfold growth, still increasing, and with satellite areas forming away from the main colony, total numbers now far in excess of those on Wrangel I., U.S.S.R.; Tha-anne R. (60°30′ N, 94°40′ W), 1954—1,000 (14%) and 1972—3,000 (26%), becoming established; La Pérouse Bay (58°40′ N, 93°10′ W), under 500 prior to 1963 and in 1972—5,000 (25%) based on a count from aerial photos, now fairly static.

N. MACKENZIE–KEEWATIN Perry R. (also called Queen Maud Gulf or cent. Canadian arctic birds; scattered colonies from Adelaide Pen. W. to Bathurst Inlet) (67°00′ N, 100°–102° W), 1960—12,000 (10%) and 1970—24,000 (5%), increasing.

NW. MACKENZIE Anderson R. (69°45′ N, 129°30′ W), 1960—5,000 (0%) and 1971—8,000 (0%), stabilized; Kendall I. in Mackenzie delta (69°30′ N, 135°15′ W), 1960—5,000 (0%) and 1971—7,000 (0%), stabilized; BANKS I. Egg R. (72°30′ N, 124°50′ W), 1960—140,000 (trace and 1971—200,000 (trace), show increase to 1971 and then some decline.

ALASKA Small numbers peripherally, less than 5,000 (0%).

U.S.S.R. Wrangel I. (74° N, 180° W), in 1960, according to S. Uspenskii (1965a), 400,000 or more mature individuals (0%); numbers now very low because of tardy and cold summers 1969–74 inclusive (no young in some years, as in 1972); also, reindeer are detrimental to the habitat.

Proportions of color phases were changing rapidly on the w. side of Hudson Bay at McConnell R. and on Baffin I. in the C. Dominion–Koukdjuak colonies, at estimated rate of 1–2% per annum toward Blue, until the 1960s, while at McConnell R. between 1961 and 1965 the proportion of Blues increased 15% to 25%, then little change through 1970 (varied between 24% and 28%); also the number of breeding birds increased there to possibly 100,000 individuals (J. Prevett). For details of assortative mating, see Cooch and Beardmore (1959), F. Cooke and Cooch (1968), also beyond under "Reproduction." For various useful historic and other information on most of the above-mentioned colonies, see Cooch (1963).

Preliminary estimates, from an aerial photographic survey June 5–28, 1973, by R. H. Kerbes, of the Hudson Bay–Southampton–Baffin colonies indicated a million breeding individuals. The proportion of Blues was about 25–30% on w. Hudson Bay and Southampton I. and 60–80% at C. Henrietta Maria and on Baffin I., about as expected. Estimated numbers of breeding birds: C. Henrietta Maria 26,000 [decrease from 45,000 in 1972 (see above) probably due to Baffin birds returning to Baffin I. in 1973], La Pérouse Bay 4,000, McConnell R. (including Tha-anne R., Wolf Creek, and Maguse R.) 350,000, Southampton I. (including Boas R., East Bay, and Bear Cove) 250,000, and Baffin I. (including Bowman Bay, C. Dominion, and Koukdjuak R.) 370,000.

Aberrant individuals reported include entirely white Lesser Snows and others with reduced amount of black in the wings; according to McIlhenny (1932), an occasional Blue Goose is all white except the wings.

Measurements   Lesser Snows from scattered N. Am. localities, 12 ♂: BILL 52–63 mm., av. 57.5; WING 411–468, av. 440; TAIL 128–143, av. 135.5; TARSUS 74–90, av. 82.6;   9 ♀: BILL 54–58 mm., av. 55; WING 404–426, av. 415; TAIL (of 6) 126–141, av. 133; TARSUS 72–81, av. 78.8 (ETS).

Another series of Lesser Snows, WING meas. across chord and tail to nearest 5 mm.; these birds also from scattered localities; "adult" ♂: BILL (of 45) 51–62 mm., av. 58; WING (of 45) 395–460, av. 430; TAIL (of 34) 115–165, av. 130; TARSUS (of 35) 78–91, av. 84;   ♀: BILL (of 40) 50–60 mm., av. 56; WING (of 43) 380–449, av. 420; TAIL (of 37) 115–165, av. 130; TARSUS (of 37) 75–89, av. 82;   "immature" [= 1st fall–winter with the shorter Juv. wing] ♂: BILL (of 24) 50–61 mm., av. 56.5; WING (of 24) 380–430, av. 410; TAIL (of 23) 105–165, av. 120; TARSUS (of 24) 74–92, av. 83;   22 ♀: BILL 50–62 mm., av. 55; WING 385–420, av. 405; TAIL 110–125, av. 120; TARSUS 77–88, av. 82 (Kennard 1927).

For many additional meas. of Lesser Snows, by sex and age-class, see Trauger et al. (1971).

For meas., by sex, of a small series of Lesser Snows from Wrangel I., see S. Uspenskii et al. (1963).

Blues "adults" from scattered N. Am. localities, 11 ♂ : BILL 54–61 mm., av. 58; WING 406–441, av. 423; TAIL 120–133, av. 126.5; TARSUS 80–88, av. 84;   7 ♀: BILL 53–57 mm., av. 55; WING 382–431, av. 414; TAIL 112–134, av. 124; TARSUS 77–82, av. 80 (ETS).

Fully mature Blues, 98 ♂ : BILL 51–62 mm.; flattened WING 395–460;   84 ♀: BILL 50–61 mm.; flattened WING 387–450 (F. G. Cooch).

Weight data from 5-year period 1952–56, for Blues in fall, taken to ¼ lb., at James Bay and vicinity: ♂ 476 fully mature 4¾–7½ lb. (mean. 6.0 = 2,542 gm.) 613 age about 3 mo. 3½–7 lb. (mean 5.0 = 2,724 gm.); ♀ 408 fully mature 4¼–7¼ lb. (mean 5.6 = 2,860 gm.), 601 of age about 3 mo. 3–6½ lb. (mean 4.6 = 2,088 gm.). Also see Cooch et al. (1960).

Lesser Snows, Oct. 19–23, 1964, in Sask., mean and standard deviation: "adults" 27 ♂ 2,670 ± 15.42 gm. and 26 ♀ 2,501 ± 16.75; "immature" (first fall) 51 ♂ 2,337 ± 16.45 gm. and 38 ♀ 2,144 ± 16.26 (A. Dzubin, H. Miller, G. Schildman).

For additional wts. of Lesser Snows, by sex and age-class, see Trauger et al. (1971).

Breeders usually arrive n. in good condition, the ♀ heavy with large egg follicles. While she is incubating, the gander loses only about ½ lb., as he obtains considerable food, but the sitting goose loses about 25% of her wt. (Also see beyond under egg losses.) After hatching, the goose gains, but the gander (as family guardian) loses about

127

17%, then gains as duties lessen. Then ♂ ♀ have a marked decrease from time molt begins. With termination of molting and reactivation of pectoral muscles, ♂ ♀ gain wt. steadily in the feeding period before and also during early stages of migration. There are few data for later on.

Prebreeders have a wt. decrease after arrival n., where nutritive food is then scarce, and another slump during molting.

Weight of incubator-hatched goslings, with mean and standard error: 10 Lesser Snow 61.4–95 gm. (79.3 ± 3.60) and 19 Blue 71.9–96.7 gm. (85.8 ± 0.48) (Smart 1965a).

Hybrids in the wild with small Canada Geese have been reported several times; see especially photos in H. K. Nelson (1952). At Lake Harbour (s. Baffin I.) in 1957, apparent (large) Canada Goose × Greater Snow hybrids were seen (F. G. Cooch). At McConnell R. (lat. about 60° N) on the w. side of Hudson Bay, a ♂ Lesser Snow was mated to a ♀ Canada (*B. c. hutchinsii*) and they had 4 goslings, July 18, 1970 (J. Prevett). Thirty *A. caerulescens* × *B. canadensis* (evidently *B. c. hutchinsii*) hybrids, sighted in 5 years and at various places, were reported by Prevett and MacInnes (1973); they suggested that egg-laying in each others' nests could result in the goslings being imprinted on the foster species, which could lead to occasional hybridizing. At Squaw Creek Nat. Wildlife Refuge (Mound City, Mo.), H. Burgess obtained specimens and photos of Lesser Snow × Ross' Goose hybrids; a considerable number of intermediates between these species now are known (see under Ross' Goose). Near Kindersley, Sask., 2 probable Whitefront (*Anser albifrons*) × Lesser Snow crosses have been examined (Dzubin 1964). In Texas, 3 different *A. c. caerulescens* × Whitefront hybrids plus a Blue × ♀ Whitefront pair with 4 first-winter young were seen in the winter of 1969–70; the young varied from very similar to young Whitefronts (2 individuals) to one with white-speckled head as in young Blue (J. Prevett).

In captivity, *Anser caerulescens* has crossed with various geese; according to Delacour (1954), hybrids with other *Anser* species are fertile, with *Branta* sterile. See Salomonsen (1946) for descriptions of certain captive hybrids and other combinations, of known parentage and sex.

Geographical variation in the species—see below. FGC RSP

SUBSPECIES   The 2 are so different in size as to have relatively slight overlap in meas.; length of BILL from feathers almost always is diagnostic. At the present time, apparently they are intergrading in the Clyde R. region of Baffin I. Also, a considerable number of the smaller birds has been noted in recent decades within autumn and winter range of the larger ones. Furthermore, an inland locality on Baffin I. is both a molting area for prebreeding Lesser Snow/Blues and a staging area for Greater Snows.

NOTE   The type locality of *Anser caerulescens*, which usually is given as Hudson Bay, should be restricted to "northeastern Manitoba" (L. Snyder 1963), probably York Factory (F. G. Cooch).

A. c. caerulescens Linnaeus. Lesser Snow/Blue—the smaller, more graceful, birds; 2 color morphs and intermediate stages; details given above; much larger (mainly low-arctic) breeding range; most of winter range more southerly and westerly.

A. c. atlanticus (Kennard). Greater Snow (and Greater Blue?)—larger, less graceful;

more northerly (high-arctic) and smaller breeding range, the most northerly nesting of all true geese (but matched by Brant); more limited (to part of Atlantic seaboard) and less southerly winter range.

Downies vary to correspond with the 2 palest (yellow) categories of Lesser Snow/ Blue downies, and with intergradation between them.

L. Snyder (1957) stated that "there is no Greater Blue Goose." In 1973, J. D. Heyland collected 2 birds that match the Greater Snow in all meas., but are identical with the Blue Goose otherwise. These are: 1 mature ♂ in molt (it was accompanied by a dark-phase 4-week-old gosling) on Bylot I., Aug. 10; 2 first-fall ♀, at Ile-aux-Oies [Goose I.], on the St. Lawrence R. about 60 mi. e. of the city of Quebec. Specimen numbers (Que. Wildlife Serv. coll.): 708 ad. ♂, 680 1st-fall ♀, and 709 gosling ♀. Are these extremely large ordinary Blues or is there a Greater Blue morph of the Greater Snow?

Measurements of Greater Snows, wing and tail to nearest 5 mm. and former evidently meas. across chord; from scattered localities, "Adults" 20 ♂: BILL 59–73 mm., av. 67; WING 430–485, av. 450; TAIL 135–160, av. 140; TARSUS 86–97, av. 92; 10 ♀: BILL 57–68 mm., av. 62.5; WING 425–475, av. 445; TAIL 130–150, av. 140; TARSUS 80–91.5, av. 85.5; "Immature" [1st fall–early winter] 8 ♂: BILL 62–69 mm., av. 65; WING 420–440, av. 430; TAIL 120–140, av. 130; TARSUS 84–91, av. 88; 15 ♀: BILL 58–69 mm., av. 63; WING 390–445, av. 425; TAIL 110–130, av. 120; TARSUS 71–89, av. 83.5 (Kennard 1927).

The following meas. (include flattened wing), by J. D. Heyland, are of hunter-killed Greater Snows at C. Tourmente, Que., in Oct.–Nov. of 1967. White-feathered birds 23 ♂: BILL 60.4–70.8 mm., mean 65.5 and SD 2.8; WING 440–485, mean 468.5 and SD 11.5; TAIL 125–148, mean 137.9 and SD 6.4; 23 ♀: BILL 59.7–71.3 mm., mean 64.4 and SD 2.4; WING 430–470, mean 449.3 and SD 12.1; TAIL 118–143, mean 130 and SD 6.0; first-fall birds 74 ♂ BILL 53.9–71.0 mm., mean 64.5 and SD 4.7; WING 417–470, mean 445.7 and SD 11.3; TAIL 105–135, mean 121.7 and SD 6.6; 69 ♀: BILL 51.2–68.0 mm., mean 61.1 and SD 2.9; WING 378–455, mean 429.2 and SD 10.1; and TAIL 100–134, mean 121.0 and SD 6.2.

Seventy-nine live "adults" (not sorted as to sex) on Bylot I. BILL 57–71 mm., av. 64.1; 79 of age about 3 mo. (also not sexed) at C. Tourmente, Que. BILL 54.7–70.7 mm., av. 62 (Lemieux 1959a).

Weight 21 ♂ av. 7.3 lb. (max. 10.4) and 13 ♀ av. 6.2 (max. 6.5) (A. L. Nelson and Martin 1953).

In Oct., 1968, at C. Tourmente, Que., mean wt. of first-fall birds: 87 ♂ 6.2 lb. and 85 ♀ 5.5 lb.; and birds from older cohorts: 10 ♂ 7.6 lb. and 18 ♀ 6.8 lb. (J. D. Heyland). RSP

FIELD IDENTIFICATION   Sexes similar in appearance. White birds (both subspecies) are white with black wing tips. Blue phase (of smaller subspecies) has white head and neck, darkish body, light rump and tail. See above under "Description" for intermediates between smaller whites and blues. All birds of the species have a blackish "grinning patch" on side of bill, visible some distance, also (after first winter) pinkish legs and feet. Often much orange (ferrous) staining, especially on head and neck.

On water, the birds look chunky compared with swans. Diminutive Ross' Goose is colored like Snows but is much smaller than the Lesser Snow, has stubby bill, only a hint of a "grinning patch," and different voice.

In the species, downies vary in color (see "Description"), but even they have a pronounced "grinning patch." Age for age, they are larger than Ross', have larger bills, shorter down, and larger feet.

First-fall Snows/intermediates/Blues somewhat reflect older stages, the white birds having pearly gray upperparts, the Blues being very dusky overall, and all have dark bill and feet until into 1st winter when pinkish begins to appear. Then, in 1st winter–spring, appearance of most individuals alters toward definitive coloring and pattern. Young Whitefronts are trimmer, usually have yellowish legs and feet, and lack a "grinning patch."

Flocks fly in various configurations—broken wavey lines, chevrons, and curves. During migration and winter they usually are in large, even enormous flocks which consist mainly of aggregations of families. Where the dark birds occur, smaller whites and intermediates occur also. Whitefronts and small races of Canada Geese are among the more common associates outside the breeding season, to some extent Ross' Goose also. FGC

VOICE   Lesser Snow/intermediates/Blue—both sexes, from age over about a year, give loud nasal *whouk* or *houk*, characteristically clipped at end; uttered any hour or season, in flight or not. For a spectrogram of this call, see Sutherland and McChesney (1965). Younger prebreeders are relatively quiet. During high-altitude migration, flocks are believed to be mostly silent except for an occasional high-pitched call. Feeding call or "conversation" among members of a family group consists of a prolonged series of very guttural *gah* notes, uttered when alighting or on the ground. A parent with preflight goslings utters long series of *uh-uh-uh* notes very quietly and rapidly; strays were observed to rejoin parents while it was uttered. When alarmed during nesting season, breeders utter a deep hoarse *kha-ah* or *kaw* (Sutton 1932, recent observers). Variants: **1** warning, somewhat like groan, given with closed bill, heard only at close quarters; **2** alarm on approach of man (or other predator such as a large gull), in higher pitch, often long drawn out and inflected upward, audible 300 yds. Either variant can be imitated by man to induce the goslings to follow a person.

The Greater Snow, when compared in captivity with the Lesser, is distinguishable by lower pitch and greater resonance (author, J. D. Heyland, H. A. Hochbaum).

As with swans and geese generally, in certain stress situations, Blue/Snows have an exhaling sound.

For development, mechanics, and functions of voice, see Würdinger (1970). FGC

HABITAT   In **breeding season** Lesser Snow/Blue—mainly low-arctic, on is. n. of continents (Wrangel, Banks, s. Baffin, and others) and, in continental N. Am., also down to the very edge of the forest zone (s. Hudson Bay, James Bay). Typically inland and commonly on relatively featureless terrain; generally near ponds, shallow lakes, streams, or on is. in braided deltas. Prefer to nest on slight ridges, knolls, and hummocks, which are clear of snow early and generally are not flooded during the spring thaw. Some colonies consist of many thousands of nests, some more or less bunched, others scattered, and with unoccupied intervening areas. Prebreeders and molting postbreeders prefer moist inland meadows where forage is plentiful.

Greater Snow—high-arctic, inland from the sea (some are well inland on Ellesmere I.); some nesting areas are quite level terrain, as between hills; others are sheltered sides of ravines (as on Bylot I.), on slopes and some nests on cliff ledges (Axel Heiberg I., Greenland); or variable, from relatively flat terrain to slopes, the nests generally on ridges, hummocks, and knolls, commanding an unobstructed view of the surroundings (Baffin I.). Loose aggregations of 25–300 nests are typical on Bylot, evidently elsewhere also. Prebreeders and molting postbreeders with young assemble on meadows, margins of shallow fresh waters, or any nearby water.

Outside breeding season In early fall, after new flight feathers have grown, the geese often make daily flights to drier terrain and uplands, to grub for roots and to feed on berries. At least the Lesser Snows of Wrangel I. feed similarly at their fall stopover places in Alaska.

The Greater Snow is more of a brackish- and saltwater bird than most units of the smaller subspecies. Its estuarine spring and fall stopover place near St. Joachim, Que., was described fully by Lemieux (1959b). In spring in this area, it also visits farmland where it tramples wet fields and pulls up cereal seedlings. In spring and autumn, both subspecies tend to avoid muskeg and forested areas; they stop usually on shallow-water marshes (fresh and brackish), wet prairie, and sandbars. In winter, units differ; examples of the smaller birds: B.C. and vicinity—mainly on and near marine waters and beaches; Cal. and farther s. and e.—mainly inland, largely on grassland, cultivated fields, and marshy areas.; La.—coastal fringe of fresh- and brackish-water marshes, and go to marine beaches for gravel; in w. La. and e. Texas—on ricefields (which are flooded seasonally, after the birds leave) and improved pastures during 2 years of 3-year rotation. That is, beginning in the 1950s, Lesser Snows have shown a preference for feeding on cultivated lands rather than in native marshes, and depredations on improved pastures and on rice crops were severe in La. by about 1970. A late shooting season was declared in 1970 in an attempt to alleviate the situation. Greater Snow— mainly on marine inlets and bays, often near marshes and on very shallow tidal waters. FGC

DISTRIBUTION The smaller birds (*A. c. caerulescens*) presumably survived the last glaciation in Beringia (E. Siberia–Alaska) and the larger ones (*A. c. atlanticus*) in the Banksian refugium (w. Canadian high-arctic); the most recent discussion is by Salomonsen (1972). Presumably the geese migrated to winter range s. of the glacial ice. Subsequently the ranges of the subspecies have altered greatly and now are beginning to overlap.

The species has occurred widely (see map), practically throughout N. Am. s. into Mexico, but most birds keep to narrow flight paths or "corridors," such as shown on the migration diagrams. There are some known changes in routes; additional ones, plus some shifting of nesting and wintering places, are to be expected; in fact, in the decade during which this book was written, the data for this section have required major revision at least twice and additional very recent changes are known. For various details of Canadian range, see Godfrey (1966).

In Canada, these factors undoubtedly will result in changes in distribution of the geese in the future: 1 the cooling trend of the climate which began before 1960 and is forecast to last at least several decades; 2 exploration for oil, gas, and minerals will disturb colonies and migration stopover places; and 3 a major hydroelectric water impoundment already is in the making on the e. side of James Bay and others are planned—their direct effects are not readily predictable, but definitely there will be an impact on the life of the Indians who have used the geese as an important source of food.

In the conterminous U.S., there appears to be a tendency for some of the geese not to go as far south as formerly, a matter (and some possible consequences) alluded to under "Migration."

The 2 subspecies do not now have entirely disjunct ranges in N. Am.; the main overlap consists of some of the smaller birds wintering, migrating, and even occurring within the nesting range of the larger ones.

A. c. caerulescens—Lesser Snows nested long ago at scattered localities on the Asiatic mainland tundra from e. Chuckcheeland w. to the mouth of the Pyasina R. (w. Taimyr Pen.), perhaps even farther westward at the mouth of the Ob. As a result of egging, of regular and prolonged fowling at nesting and especially molting areas and, with fowling elsewhere in other seasons no doubt contributing, the birds were becoming rare at some mainland localities even very early in the 1800s. They were disappearing from the delta of the Kolyma in the 1820s and perhaps bred hardly anywhere on the mainland by the 1850s, except for a colony on the Chuckchee Pen, down to about 1940. They also disappeared from the Lyakhov Is. They no longer occur in winter in the sw. Caspian area and, in Japan (where formerly abundant) they now are very rare.

The remaining Asiatic location is Wrangel I. where, in 1958, there was one major nesting area plus smaller ones and scattered pairs, in places remote from human habitation. They have increased on that island since then; much the largest of 3 large colonies occupies some 10,000–12,000 hectares in a dry sheltered basin, transected by the headwaters of the Tundrovaya R., in the center of the island. (It is of interest that Asiatic winterers were eliminated early from the Lesser Snow population; the N. Am. winterers from Wrangel I., on which hunting pressure on winter range was negligible until rather late in the 1800s, not only survived but still contains a quarter million geese—the largest unit until recently exceeded in number by the McConnell R. birds.)

A few Lesser Snows (mainly prebreeders?) have been reported over the years in summer on the Asiatic mainland and on is. other than Wrangel and, by some time in the 1960s, small numbers had been found nesting at these localities (e. to w.): Aion I. (mouth of Chaun Bay), the Chaun Bay mainland coast, Kolyma delta, and Indigirka lowlands. For further historical data, in Russian, see Vorobev (1963), S. Uspenskii (1963a), and the long account in Portenko (1972); for brief summary in German, see S. Uspenskii (1965a); and for English translation of another paper, see S. Uspenskii (1967). Some Lesser Snows have been reared in captivity and there have been proposals (S. Uspenskii 1967) to use these, also to place the eggs of Snows in nests of other geese, in attempts to reestablish the species at various localities.

In Alaska there are scattered small colonies on the arctic coastal plain, usually within 2–3 mi. of the sea, from the delta of the Colville w. to the Barrow region. These birds evidently come overland from the Gulf of Alaska, but some may be an extension of colonies in the Mackenzie delta area. At any rate, Lesser Snows nest at places intermediate between Wrangel I. and the nw. Canadian colonies. In fall, some Wrangel birds have returned via arctic Alaska, banded individuals having been taken in the Mackenzie Delta area and also far to the southward in the continental interior (Teplov and Shevareva, in Dementiev 1965). Nesting Lesser Snows were much more plentiful on the Alaskan arctic slope in the past, but reindeer depredations (they eat some nests and eggs and trample others) and reindeer herders may have destroyed some colonies (A. Bailey et al. 1933). Although at least formerly remote and seldom visited by Eskimos, C. Halkett was a famous locality for killing flightless molting Lesser Snows (Anderson, in A. Bailey 1948). "Nonproductive" (prebreeding?) birds were molting there with Brant in 1966 (King 1970). It was estimated that not more than 1,000 Lesser Snows were on the arctic slope in 1966 (King). The number was under 5,000 in the early 1970s.

Lesser Snows also have nested sw. of Barrow in Alaska and down to Bering Sea localities; these nesters are "dropouts" from the spring Pacific–Bering flight to Wrangel I. They have nested, for example, in the Wales area on the Seward Pen.; some molting birds (including "immatures") were banded in the Yukon Delta in 1951 and, slightly farther s., this goose nested on the mainland e. of Nunivak I. in 1950. Evidently it is a sporadic nester in the Yukon–Kuskokwim delta area.

Various nesting areas in the Mackenzie delta region were described by Hohn (1959); they are on the route to Banks I. Recently a few also have been found nesting n. of Banks I. on Melville I. In the cent. Canadian arctic, the mainland localities (which have been increasing in number and size) in the Queen Maud Gulf region have been described by J. P. Ryder (1971a).

The **development of some colonies** in the Hudson–James Bay area is as follows. In s. Hudson Bay, several hundred migrants terminated their spring flight at C. Henrietta Maria in 1947; the colonies that have developed there, described by Lumsden (1959), had increased to a total of 45,000 birds by 1972. To the westward, some 26 mi. e. of Churchill, Man., nesting began later, in an estuary in La Pérouse Bay, and there were about 5,000 birds by 1970; the locale was described by F. Cooke (1969). In James Bay, there was a new colony of some 50 pairs on Akimiski I. in 1959. (Some prebreeders molt on the shores of James Bay.) The nesting of these geese well up and near the e. side of Hudson Bay, between lat. 59°30' and 61° N but concentrated in the area 60° to 61° N and w. of long. 77° W, is on the route to Baffin I. and apparently very recent; there were perhaps 50–70 pairs/year in 1966–68 inclusive. Both Lesser Snows and Blues were present and 46 birds (included 35 goslings) have been banded (J. D. Heyland). Thus it is evident that various new colonies have been started by "dropouts" along spring migration corridors. (This, of course, does not explain how northernmost colonies are founded.)

There is a continuing theme in the Russian literature that foxes limit the expansion of some colonies and prevent establishment of new ones; when small colonies are near nesting Snowy Owls, the owls harass the foxes, but small colonies do not survive through periods of owl scarcity—so it is claimed.

C. J. O. Harrison (1962) stated that there is a clutch of 5 eggs in the Brit. Mus. (Nat.

133

Hist.) taken at Great Slave L. on June 26, 1884. Lesser Snows (cripples?) have produced young at places far distant from normal nesting range—Tule L. In Cal. in 1946 and the Malheur Refuge area in se. Ore. in 1960.

Records of Blues, also Snows of both subspecies, are widely scattered in Britain, also in Europe from Norway and Finland to Greece, as summarized by Bruun (1971); possibly all are escaped captives (but also see hybrids below under Greater Snow).

Icelandic records of Lesser Snow (June 1896 and later) and Blue (July 1954) possibly were not "natural" occurrences in the sense that they might have been British escapees that joined with Pinkfeet or Barnacle Geese and then accompanied them on northward migration (F. Gudmundsson).

The Lesser Snow has occurred in w. Greenland (Upernavik to Nanortalik) and, in e. Greenland, an occurrence in Scoresby Sd. There are over a dozen records (6 of specimens preserved) for Greenland, including pairs in spring and young birds in autumn.

Seen annually in small numbers (Lesser Snow/Blue) to southernmost peninsular Fla. (records well scattered in that state) in recent years; a skull, dating from 1859, and recently a ♀ found alive, on the Dry Tortugas.

According to Gundlach (1876), the Lesser Snow formerly wintered in numbers in Cuba and occurred in the Antilles. It still occurs in Cuba (rare?). For other known Antillean occurrences, see J. Bond (1956). A bone from a midden on St. Croix.

In the Azores a Lesser Snow was shot at Terceira in Oct., 1967, and there is also an older report which may pertain to this goose.

In the Hawaiian Is., recorded on Maui in 1904, 1942, 1966, 1967, and 1970, and on Oahu in 1904, 1958, and 1959 (Berger 1972).

There is a single specimen record each for Korea and Kashmir.

The presently known **limits of occurrence of Blues** may be of interest: e. to N.S. and cent. Nfld.; n. to Greenland limits mentioned earlier and to Victoria and Prince of Wales I.; nw. to Fairbanks, Alaska (first record: May 4, 1963) and beyond in e. Asia at Wrangel I. (summer, 1973, ♂ photographed); w. to Wash. (records begin in 1967), Ore. (now fairly regular in spring at Malheur Refuge), Cal. (includes localities down to Salton Sea area), and Ariz. (several records, beginning in 1950); s. to Cuba and Gulf Coast Veracruz in Mexico.

Since preparation of this book began, a spring route across N.Y. toward the e. side of Hudson Bay has developed and is getting increased usage; over 1,000 Lesser Snows and 2,000 Blues stopped at the Montezuma Refuge in cent. N.Y. in late April, 1971 and more in subsequent years.

In the Anderson R.–Liverpool Bay region (Mackenzie Dist.) a few Blues occur regularly and one was mated to a Lesser Snow in 1963 and in 1964; to the westward at Kendall I., one was mated to a Snow in 1957; and to the northward on Banks I., up to perhaps a score were seen annually in aerial surveys in 1960–62 inclusive. A single Blue on Wrangel I. is mentioned above.

A. c. atlanticus—as of 1969, this goose **nested** on the following is.: Baffin (n. Baffin—major area; extreme w. Baffin at base of Brodeur Pen.—major area), s. Bylot (major), e. Somerset (minor), Prince of Wales ("no room for doubt" that it nests, Manning and Macpherson 1961), Devon (minor), Bathurst (very few), Ellesmere (major),

Axel Heiberg (major?), and nw. Greenland (minor). The total population in May, 1969, was $66,770 \pm 5\%$ (J. D. Heyland).

Perhaps colonization of nw. Greenland is quite recent, even though the nesting areas there are at lower latitudes than those on Axel Heiberg and many on Ellesmere I. This goose is recorded as having nested in Greenland since the early 1890s. Two Snows (presumably this subspecies) were seen in Peary Land, n. Greenland, in Aug. 1949. [Records for sw. coastal Greenland pertain to the smaller subspecies, see above.] Numbers of migrants are seen at Thule, hence nesting places are farther n. (P. Johnsen 1953). The subject of occurrence and distribution in Greenland has been updated to 1969 by Heyland and Boyd (1970).

At least 10 Whitefront × [Greater?] Snow hybrids, including a group of 7 in the winter of 1960–61, have been seen at Wexford Slobs in Ireland, the main wintering area of Greenland Whitefronts. This suggests mixed pairing in Greenland and that the resulting hybrids migrated with the Whitefronts.

The spring and fall stopover area at C. Tourmente (near St. Joachim, Que.) is known to have been used since at least the 1500s (Giroux 1953).

The Greater Snow **winters** in a small geographical area, mainly N.J. to N.C. coastal areas (mostly in Delaware and Chesapeake Bays, Currituck Sd., and at Pea I. in N.C.).

Occasional **straggler** well inland, there being a few alleged sightings annually, plus a band recovery in e. Texas and another in Ill. or that general region. The few old records for Bermuda may be of Greater Snows.

The species *A. caerulescens* is recorded as **fossil** from the Pleistocene of Ore., Cal., Idaho, and Kans., and from **archaeological sites** in Cal., Ariz., Iowa, Ill., Ga., and the island of St. Croix. For the particular localities and published references, see Brodkorb (1964a). RSP

MIGRATION   Characterized by notably restricted flight lines, great distances between stopping places, and localized nature of nesting, resting, and wintering areas. Flights usually begin at dusk or later. The birds fly high, more so in fall than spring. Often in immense flocks. In the case of paired breeders in spring, there is some slight evidence (from shooting) that the gander flies just ahead of the goose; at least for a while after arrival at breeding areas, the goose probably leads.

In broadest outline, and going from e. to w., the Greater Snow is an essentially discrete population and the Lesser Snow/Blue subdivides into 1 birds of the Hudson Bay periphery plus Southampton and Baffin Is. migrate primarily down the continental interior toward or to La. and Texas; 2 the cent. low-arctic (Queen Maud Gulf) birds, numerically the smallest group, go via interior w. Canada and the midportion of conterminous U.S., some as far as Chihuahua, Durango, and Coahuila in Mexico; and 3 the Wrangel–Banks I.–w. Canadian arctic birds form a nearly discrete subpopulation having the most westerly lines of travel; the Wrangel–Banks birds are intermingled especially on part of winter range in Cal., while some Banks I.–Anderson R. birds go to Chihuahua. The evidence grows, however, that there is more interchange between Lesser Snow/Blue subpopulations than formerly suspected, mainly of ganders.

See migration diagrams, which are based in considerable measure on band-recovery data. They are imperfect for some areas; also, dotted lines indicate certain probable routes. Most Gulf Coast birds now are narrowly concentrated in spring up through the e. part of the Dakotas and beyond in Canada. Soper (1942b) noted spring stopover places in Minn. and Man. which were unused between about 1940 and 1968 but have been reestablished since and in 1972 more than a million birds were seen by H. Blockpoel in s. Man. At Keweenaw Bay (L. Superior), there were almost no geese of any sort in fall from about 1880 to 1948, but Snows have been numerous since in some seasons. Cottam (1935) noted a fall influx of Lesser Snow/Blues along the Atlantic coast; since then, increasing numbers have been reported in the Appalachian region and vicinity and wintering along the Atlantic seaboard. In the latter area in early 1967, Blues outnumbered Snows at Mattamuskeet and Blackwater Refuges, but not elsewhere. A few Lesser Snows occur now, in fall at least, with Greater Snows in the St. Joachim area of Que. Snows migrate in spring and fall across cent. New Eng. and w. to beyond the Hudson valley in N.Y.; in spring the small groups perhaps are Lesser, the large ones in New Eng. are Greater Snows. For spring counts, 1944–54, of Greater Snows in Merrymeeting Bay in Me., see E. J. Baker (1954); even more birds have been noted in Me. in subsequent years.

It would appear that birds of both subspecies are developing new routes and abandoning old ones. In the case of Lesser Snow/Blues especially, if the birds have a late nesting season and then prolonged warm weather in autumn, a great many thousands linger late at places n. of their "normal" winter quarters, perhaps thus starting to establish different wintering traditions.

Area	Year	First arrival	Main arrival	Duration of migration	First nest
Eskimo Pt. = McConnell R.	1954	May 27	May 30	21 days	June 14
"	1959	May 23	May 28	17 days	June 8
"	1960	May 22	May 25	8 days	May 28
"	1961	May 21	May 28	10 days	June 4
Boas R.	1952	May 21	June 1	8 days	June 4
"	1953	May 23	June 3	14 days	June 9
"	1955	May 23	June 1	8 days	June 6
"	1956	May 17	June 3	17 days	June 11
"	1960	May 22	June 1	9 days	June 5
"	1961	May 21	May 28	10 days	June 4
Bowman Bay	1967	May 24	June 14	21 days	June 17
"	1968	May 21	June 9	17 days	June 12

A. c. caerulescens Lesser Snow/Blue **spring** EASTERN BIRDS The av. date that huge flocks leave the Gulf of Mexico coast is March 8 and all have departed fairly soon thereafter. They make a rather long initial flight to the vicinity of Squaw Creek (Mo.), then a series of short flights (25–50 mi.) to the Dakotas, arriving in 2nd half of April. Then to s. Man. about May 1. Then a long flight to James and Hudson Bays, arriving in early May. After resting along the coast, the flight continues in easy stages to nesting areas; they arrive from very late May through the first half of June.

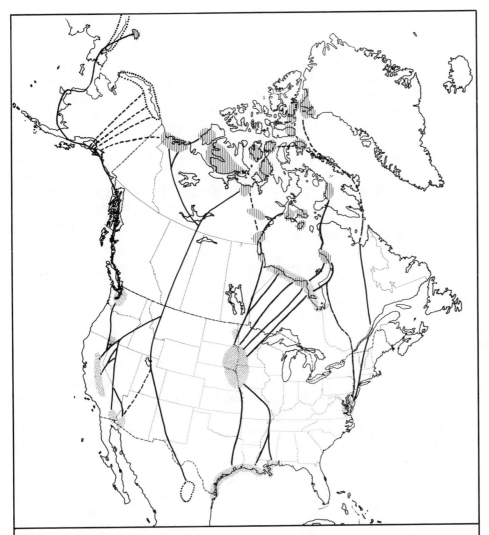

BLUE/SNOW GOOSE
In **SPRING**
Anser caerulescens

A. c. caerulescens, except the
most northerly breeders plus the
major corridor farthest east,
which are *A. c. atlanticus*
(see text)

 Main breeding areas

∴⁖∴ Scattered breeder (small
numbers)

——— Major migration corridors
in late 1960s

- - - Probable corridors

▨ Staging areas en route and
(terminally) wintering
areas

⟨⟩ Probable wintering area

See text for additional
information

WESTERN BIRDS More southerly winterers go n. via an interior route; they depart in very late Feb. and early March mainly, and go via Tule L. (Cal.) and Freezeout L. (Mont.) and e. slope of the Rockies. There were about 100,000 Lesser Snows at Freezeout L. on April 1, 1971. Travel is comparatively leisurely at first. Usually the vanguard reaches s. Alta. about April 12. More arrive and the geese fatten in grainfields there, until early May, and thereafter they travel faster (have few stops). Some spend more or less time in the Hay Lakes–Great Slave Lake region; others move to final staging areas just s. of the n. edge of the mainland. There, along inland watercourses, the birds find some open water and snow-free sandbars or mudflats. (The geese have overtaken and gone beyond the n. advance of the spring thaw.) On these waters, the sight of some geese copulating probably is a stimulus to the others and all paired breeders that are present copulate within a very brief time. The next (terminal) flight is short for many of the geese. The birds reach nw. Canadian mainland breeding areas beginning about May 15–20. Early arrival dates: May 9, 1927, at Aklavik in the Mackenzie delta (Porsild 1943); May 16, 1914, at Herschel I. (W. Brooks 1915); and May 16, 1953, at Banks I. (Manning et al. 1956).

Flocks are still passing overhead, bound for island destinations, at the time when mainland birds are nesting. Prebreeders approaching age 2 years tend to keep in separate flocks from breeders (the latter commonly are accompanied by progeny approaching age 1 year), but there is no strict segregation by age-class.

Usually, when the geese arrive, the nesting areas still are covered with snow. The birds stand about in flocks, wherever there is any meltwater or bare mudflats. As soon as there is a hint of bare ground on ridges, hummocks, and knolls, the flocks break into smaller groups and then pairs take up occupancy of the scattered first traces of snow-free nesting habitat. The timing of the disappearance of snow cover appreciably governs onset of nesting; the rate at which the ground becomes bare governs nesting density (rapid melting results in less crowding of nests).

The more northerly western winterers (the vast majority are bound for Wrangel I.) begin departure somewhat later. On a Pacific coastal route, Lesser Snows occur in small numbers along the coast of se. Alaska, the Alaska Pen., the Yukon delta, and Seward Pen. In se. Alaska the Stikine flats are a concentration area and, beyond, the mouths of the Copper and Susitna rivers. From the latter areas, some Snows are believed to fly overland (probably via several routes) to the Alaskan arctic coastal plain. (Up to 10,000 usually are seen near Ft. Yukon and some hundreds near Fairbanks and in the Copper R. valley; the former must go to some other place to nest than the Alaskan arctic slope.) The bulk of the Pacific travelers, bound for Wrangel I., are believed to pass via the Bering Sea coast, flying fast and high, possibly making long overwater flights; they are not known to have any major staging area in Alaska when northbound. A few thousand arrive at St. Lawrence I. in the last third of May and linger a while before moving on to Wrangel I. At the latter place they begin arriving in the last third of May or in early June, depending on earliness or tardiness of the season. There were large bands at Wales, Alaska, on May 31, 1922 (A. Bailey 1925). For additional information, for both spring and fall for the Wrangel birds, see Teplov and Shevareva (in Dementiev 1965) and especially Portenko (1972).

Summer The terminal stage of spring travel of yearlings tends to be a **molt migra-**

tion from nesting areas to a place some distance away. On Baffin I., Nettilling L. is such a place; on Banks I., prebreeders (mostly yearlings?) are concentrated on the n. part at Castel Bay and Thomsen R. Older prebreeders generally remain closer to breeders, a considerable number even on the periphery of nesting colonies, where their routine more nearly resembles that of breeders; their molting begins earlier than that of breeders, but later than that of yearlings. Breeders become flightless en route from nesting places to rearing areas (often where younger birds are molting); that is, many of them make surprisingly long terrestrial journeys, a molt migration on foot, accompanied by their preflight young.

In 1970 at McConnell R., for several days after most breeders had settled down at nests, small flocks of yearlings continued to fly over the colony in a northerly direction, presumably to areas beyond the n. limits of the colony. Possibly these birds had been orphaned earlier, or recently had separated from breeders in late stages of migration; the majority of the yearlings accompanied breeders back to the nesting area. Many of these occupied sparsely populated parts of the colony, also places along the coast, and around the periphery of the nesting area. A few stayed with their parents at nests until well into the incubation period. (Data from J. Prevett.)

Fall EASTERN BIRDS Prebreeders and failed breeders depart late Aug.–early Sept.; successful breeders with Juv.-feathered young follow, beginning a week later. At first, they go in short stages. At James Bay, a first major influx Sept. 15, then first arrivals leave about Oct. 1 and, by Oct. 15, there is an exodus of all age-classes. The predominance of the Blue morph in autumn assemblies at James Bay has been discussed by several authors. At least to James Bay (and probably to wintering areas), some prebreeders (of age about 15 mo.) go by themselves and fly very high.

At any stopover place, for some days prior to departure, the geese rest and make little effort to feed. At James Bay, winds are consistently southerly with force often over 35 mph. From James Bay to the Gulf of Mexico coast there are 2 patterns: 1 nonstop, direct, high altitude (to about 10,000 ft. known), for 1,700+ mi. in probably less than 60 hrs.; or 2 interrupted, when a great many thousands stop in the n. and cent. tier of states. If because of weather nesting is delayed, then molting is delayed, and there follows less time to regain wt. loss before migrating. Decreased mean wt. is a causal factor for interrupting the fall flight to rest and feed. Beginning in the 1950s, however, there has been an increasing tendency for some units to interrupt migration on an annual basis; the stopping has become a fixed part of the fall itinerary. By the early 1970s there was a concern in La. and Texas, where about 50% of the hunting kill had been usual, that goose shooting would diminish there but would increase farther northward in the cent. states. Most of the birds that go on to the Gulf Coast and other traditional wintering areas arrive in late Oct.–early Nov. See Cooch (1955) for some additional details.

McIlhenny (1932) reported that some of the geese arrive on the Gulf Coast the last week in Aug. and do not remain, then considerably more come in Sept. and some stay. Perhaps these were the early high-altitude migrants and some birds continued on to Mexico or the Caribbean area.

WESTERN BIRDS An unknown (small?) number of Siberian (Wrangel I.) birds travel via n. Alaska and down through the continental interior (a route described below). The

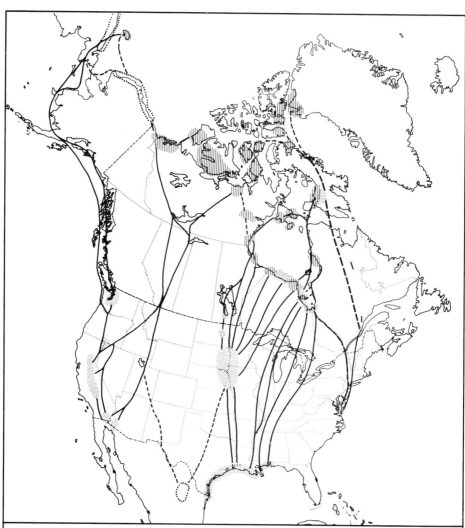

BLUE/SNOW GOOSE
In **FALL**
Anser caerulescens

A. c. caerulescens, except the
most northerly breeders plus the
major corridor farthest east,
which are *A. c. atlanticus*
(see text)

Main breeding areas

Scattered breeder (small
numbers)

—— Major migration corridors
in late 1960s

--- Probable corridors

Staging areas en route and
(terminally) wintering
areas

Probable wintering area

See text for additional
information

great bulk of the Wrangel birds, however, travel as follows. They begin to appear on the Seward Pen. in late Aug. or early Sept. They begin arriving on St. Lawrence I. about Aug. 20, mostly in small flocks, and pass intermittently for a month. Very large numbers are in the Yukon Delta in Sept.—in excess of 50,000 birds near Dall Lake w. of Bethel, some flocks of up to 10,000 birds. They fatten on berries and are highly regarded as a table bird by both natives and whites. There is some variation in timing and numbers, which seem to relate to weather in the nesting season, size of berry crop, and other factors. For example, in years of nesting failure, the birds arrive in Alaska earlier. They stay in the Yukon Delta until driven out by freeze-up, in early Oct. After that, a few are seen on inner end of the Alaska Pen., the Anchorage area, Cordova, and the Stikine R. Some 3,000–4,000 is the most that have been recorded s. of the Yukon Delta in fall; the bulk of the birds fly rather directly to Wash. and Ore. The delta, then, is a major fall staging and fattening area for Wrangel I. Snows. (Data from Jim King.) The Skagit area (nw. Wash.) is a stopping place for some of the birds. They arrive at Tule Lake (in Cal.) beginning in Oct.

The birds from the Alaskan arctic slope, Mackenzie delta area, Banks and Victoria is., and Queen Maud Gulf go s. in the interior, e. of the Rockies. Their schedule is roughly as follows. Prebreeders regain flight first and begin leaving molting areas about Aug. 15–20. A very few of these make long, early flights southward. The others (all age-classes) fly to staging areas (some breeders evidently swim there, accompanied by preflight young). Very large assemblies occur, for example, in the outer Mackenzie delta, where the geese fatten on emergent and terrestrial vegetation and also make daily flights inland to feed on berries, cotton grass tubers, and lesser amounts of other plant materials.

The length of time spent at staging areas and availability of nutritious food are reflected in wt. of the geese; that is, if they are forced by weather to depart early (rather than in mid- or late) Oct., then they are in poorer condition and so interrupt their subsequent travels several times to feed. If in good condition, i.e., if they remain late, the birds from lower Mackenzie fly very high and nonstop for well over 1,000 mi., to extreme n. Alta. The Hay Lakes region is a major stopping place; if fat, the birds soon move on; if lean, they may remain and feed until freeze-up. They move down onto cultivated fields of cent. and s. Alta. and Sask. (often heavy concentrations from late Sept. to mid-Oct.). They reach Mont., depending on season, from late Sept. to late Oct. Then they cross over the Rockies to Ore. and Cal., where numbers increase in late Oct. and through Nov.; in the latter month they fly to winter quarters in the Sacramento valley and some even beyond as far as Mexico.

NOTE   It is known from banded and color-marked Lesser Snows (see especially Kozlik et al. 1959) that some individuals shift routes—such as from wintering in Cal. one year to occurring in La. and Texas the following year. As mentioned earlier, such change-over is mostly by ganders.

A. c. atlanticus   Greater Snow—spring and fall routes do not differ greatly, so far as known. In spring, however, some birds may go farther e. in New Eng. on the first stage of their journey, a few even as far e. as New Bruns.

Spring   There is a shift northward, up the Atlantic coast from Va. and the Carolinas, beginning about the 3rd week in Feb. Then most of the birds congregate in several

141

enormous assemblies; these depart in March, fly over New Eng. to near Quebec City, then veer e. to the St. Joachim area on the St. Lawrence. They arrive usually March 20–April 5 (earliest recorded arrivals on March 11). They remain about 1½ mo.; they depart usually May 23–29 and are thought to fly a few mi. eastward along the river and then go n. overland. At that time, interior Ungava is largely snow covered and there is very little open water. Probably they arrive at all nesting areas from early June onward, but occasionally are first seen at some southerly nesting areas in very late May. (In the far north there is snow-free terrain and fresh waters thaw long before marine waters open.)

Summer There is some movement afoot, i.e., terrestrial **molt migration** toward coasts.

Fall The geese probably leave the various more northerly areas by very early Sept., when freshwater ponds and the soil freeze. Yet the arrival of the main flock on the St. Lawrence is 4–6 weeks later. It is hard to imagine that the birds from widely scattered nesting areas could arrive *en masse* on the St. Lawrence unless they departed *en masse* from a northerly place. The scattered greater Snows apparently more or less gather at the base of the Brodeur Pen. (nw. Baffin I.) and on part of Bylot I., and also may feed and rest for a time somewhere to the southward in interior Baffin, prior to beginning a nonstop mass flight down across Ungava. In the St. Joachim area of Que., migration consists of 2 parts. First, a vanguard of 2,000–3,000 geese (mostly prebreeders). They are said to arrive beginning in early Sept., but in 1954–68 inclusive the date varied from Sept. 21 (in 1958) to Oct. 9 (1966). The main flock began arriving as early as Oct. 5 (1964) to as late as Oct. 19 (1968). The number of days' difference between the 2 arrivals varied from 44 days (1957) to 17 (1958). Duration of stay at St. Joachim varies, to 2½ mo., until tidal flats begin to freeze. Then the birds apparently leave all of a sudden, in large flocks. They go nonstop to Delaware Bay and later shift more southward. Thus the time of arrival at Delaware Bay and beyond varies, depending on length of stay at St. Joachim. These data are mainly from Lemieux (1959b) and from J.D. Heyland.

NOTE Part of the Greater Snows actually counted on aerial photos taken in fall, 1971, at St. Joachim was not accounted for in censuses later on winter range. The discrepancy was of the order of 50,000 birds. FGC

BANDING STATUS Lesser Snow/Blue—through the year 1972 a total of 131,487 had been banded in Canada and 74,527 in conterminous U.S., for a combined total of 206,014. Places of banding in Canada: Keewatin 83,321; Franklin 22, 016; Sask. 6,436; Mackenzie 5,674; Man. 5,950; Ont. 8,037; and small numbers in Alta. and Que.; in conterminous U.S., most banding was done in S.D. and Cal.

Through 1971 the total number of "direct" recoveries (through 1st hunting season after banding) was 12,081 and "indirect" recoveries (during subsequent hunting seasons) was 21,515, for a combined total of 33,596.

In the U.S.S.R. the number banded on Wrangel I. was 1,200 in 1961, 1,339 in 1962, and 1,983 in 1963; the Ringing Center in Moscow had 452 recoveries of Russian bands and, from within the U.S.S.R., 91 bands from N. Am. (Teplov and Shevareva, in Dementiev 1965).

142

Greater Snow—5,532 had been banded through 1972, mostly in Dist. of Franklin; there were 341 "direct" and 98 "indirect" recoveries, totaling 439.

There has been scattered use of banding data by various authors. Recently, for Lesser Snow/Blues of the Hudson Bay–Southampton–Baffin I. area, analyses of banding data have resulted in numerous unpublished background papers, prepared for use in formulating rational conservation and exploitation policies. FGC

REPRODUCTION *A. c. caerulescens*—this section includes original data, from study of Blues primarily, plus published information from Soper (1942a) and others. Some comparative data on *A. c. atlanticus* also are given.

Most of the geese **first breed** at age 3 years, a few at 2 and, depending on breeding-unit size and structure, and phenology, some may not breed until 4 years. At McConnell R., rarely, 2-year-old ♂ ♂ with mates defend territories in the colony, complete with Triumph ceremony after encounters with nearby pairs, but do not nest; no 2-year-old ♂ ♂ were found breeding but, in some years, 20% or more of ♀ ♀ going into their 2nd year bred (J. Prevett). The smaller subspecies, regardless of color or intermixture, nests in association with Brant in some areas; white-phase birds sometimes with or close to Ross' Goose, as discussed by J. P. Ryder (1969, 1971a). Snow Geese (either subspecies) in our area usually nest within 5 mi. of the sea, in a few places much farther inland; (as in U.S.S.R.) on Wrangel I. and at Egg R. on Banks I.); on low flat plains; *atlanticus* uses drier terrain, with nests on slopes or even cliff edges. **Colonial,** though some small groups appear scattered; occasionally solitary. **Loose aggregations** are more typical of *atlanticus*.

The geese arrive in vicinity of breeding areas in flocks containing family groups (breeders with yearlings) and newly formed pairs. The first birds arrive at dusk (Boas R., 6 years' data; McConnell R., 5 years'), but after that at any hour—and soon there is continuous daylight at most colonies. In some (early) seasons, there is much flying in noisy flocks, often in seemingly random mixture with King Eiders, Sandhill Cranes, various species of geese, and Tundra Swans.

Often, when the birds arrive, **nesting areas** still are covered entirely with snow. The birds stand about, at first in flocks, in the vicinity (or possibly to 50 mi. away, depending on breeding unit), wherever there is open water or bare mudflats. As soon as there is a hint of bare gound, on ridges, knolls, hummocks, and other elevations, the flocks break into smaller groups and then pairs take up occupancy of the scattered first traces of snow-free nesting habitat.

Nesting territory is selected by the ♀; it is used for mutual display, occasionally copulation (it usually occurs before arrival), nesting, and some feeding. The timing of the disappearance of snow cover appreciably controls onset of nesting and the subsequent rate of melting controls density: rapid decrease in snow cover results in less crowding. The latter, in turn, is affected by configuration of the terrain. The area defended by the ♂ diminishes daily until the clutch is complete. At maximum, roughly an acre; minimum, less than 36 sq. ft. Territory size changes as land surface increases. Maximum nesting density (1952, Boas R.) 1,200 pairs/sq. mi., with 23 nests on a 10 × 20 yd. ridge exposed above shallow water, and up to 3,500 pairs/sq. mi. at McConnell R. There was much fighting at this locality. In a crowded area there is con-

143

stant noise, of conflict and Triumph displays, and the resulting stress may contribute to diminished clutch size in retarded seasons.

From the time territory is occupied (or reoccupied), breeders maintain territory until they leave with their goslings, and they generally are waders or terrestrial in habit throughout this span and until they regain flight after their Prebasic molt. If they can avoid it, they neither swim nor (when able) fly.

Territorial defense If threat does not suffice, defense is vigorous, even violent—the sexes pair off, ♂ fights ♂, ♀ fights ♀. Yearlings generally are nearby; some defend in absence of parents and give way to parents on their return. This goose defends against intruders except man and polar bear. When fighting, a bird tries to grasp the other's nape, side of neck, or upper breast; at the same time they pummel each other with their wings. Boundaries are crossed and other geese enter the fray. Fights end all of a sudden, with threats at boundaries, or the intruder takes wing and is "escorted" out of the territory. The resident pair returns to near the nest and has a mutual TRIUMPH CEREMONY, calling, with open bills pointed well upward and wings half spread.

As recorded for the Greater Snow (Drury 1961), in aggressive display, the black wing tips are flashed at the opponent.

Common **feeding** and **resting areas** (undefended) are used near nesting areas until onset of incubation. The birds occur here in groups, resting on snow or bare ground, or standing in water, at times feeding or perhaps getting grit.

As noted earlier, **mixed matings** occur between all Plumage categories of Lesser Snow/Blue. In all our *Anser* and *Branta*, when birds are measured in series, the ♂ series av. larger than the ♀ but there is great overlap. In mated pairs the ♂ is the larger bird—i.e., mate selection is assortative, not random, in this respect. Furthermore, in *A. c. caerulescens*, the incidence of Blue (majority being heterozygous and not pure Blue) ♂ mating with white (Lesser Snow) ♀ is greater than if selection in this respect were random (for details see Cooch and Beardmore 1959, Cooch 1961). Furthermore, it is theorized that **mate selection** is by the gander, who was imprinted on his parents when a gosling and so selects a goose resembling one or both of his parents (F. Cooke and Cooch 1968). Pair bond form usually is **lifelong monogamy;** a new mate is sought only when the original one is lost (determined from banding data) or possibly in some cases when reproduction is unsuccessful due to infertility.

To begin at the beginning, on winter range as the season progresses the birds form in close groups in which **activities leading to pair formation** occur (displays, much vocalizing, fighting). Fighting among ♂ ♂ increases as the time to migrate approaches. Also, "chase flights" occur from early Dec. to about mid-June. A ♀ is pursued by several ♂ ♂. A persistent ♂ tries to get between the ♀ and the other ♂ ♂ and aerial collisions are frequent. The ♂ sometimes seizes the tail of the ♀. During flight, the ♀ tumbles and sideslips. The birds utter piercing monosyllabic calls during pursuit and finally they alight near the spot where the flight originated. On the ground the ♂ jostles for position next to the ♀. A pair is formed when ♂ and ♀ have mutual ("greeting") display, containing many elements of the Triumph display described earlier. A certain amount of pair formation activity very likely occurs among prebreeders on summer range and may continue into winter–spring.

Copulation Some chase flights occur after arrival on nesting grounds. Some of these may represent a terminal phase of pair formation; others are by mates and precede copulation. The following is more common behavior. Pair walks in parallel course; ♂ suddenly faces ♀, assumes near-vertical posture, and does a violent neck stretch (upward). The stretch is repeated with increasing tempo until the ♀ responds similarly and some measure of synchronization of motions is achieved. Then ♂ appears to buffet ♀ with one of his wings and, as she turns to avoid the blow, she is grasped by the nape and forced into a PRONE position. After copulation the birds wash and preen. Copulation occurs rarely after the 1st egg is laid. Typically it occurs, in probably all breeding pairs present, and within a brief span of time, at the final staging area on northward migration (along coast of James and Hudson bays, inland from Mackenzie and Anderson r. deltas, etc.), the birds in water of wading depth or deeper. Many single ♀♀ arrive at nesting grounds, lay a fertile clutch, and may succeed in raising a brood. Generally speaking, however, ♀♀ that have lost their mates are less successful nesters.

Nest   The ♀ selects the site, typically a slightly elevated spot; sometimes she uses it in successive years (banded birds at marked nests). There is some local shifting because of changes in snow cover or water runoff, but there is a tendency to nest in the same vicinity (J. Prevett). A shallow scrape is made, lined with pieces of vegetation and, in due course, some nest down and some feathers; it is more bulky than is typical of Brant. Construction is begun by the ♀ late in the day and completed the next A.M. The ♀ sits and gathers any available material within reach and deposits it behind her; she moves in a circular path or rotates, piling up material in the center; the ♂ stands guard nearby. The first egg, laid in the morning when the scrape is completed, is covered with plant materials by the goose, hence is very well concealed. Material from the site is added to the nest until about the midpoint of incubation, the goose, in effect, building the nest around the eggs. There is no concealment of the nest. A lining—her nest down and some feathers—is added from about the time the 3rd egg is laid until about the end of the 1st week of incubation, but the wind may scatter much of this material (Brant nest down is much more cohesive). The **nest down** is pale gray and there are white feathers intermixed. Nests av. about 20 cm. inside diam. and 9.5 deep; about 60 cm. outside diam. and 14 high; in *A. c. atlanticus* estimated ⅓ larger.

In colonies studied, **laying begins** within 4 days (range 2–7) after arrival of birds at nesting area, thus usually from very late May to the 2nd week in June. On arrival, ♀♀ are recognizable at 200 yds. by abdominal bulge from advanced development of eggs. Dates for first viable eggs: Boas R., av. June 9 (June 4–153, 1952–60; Eskimo Pt. [McConnell R.], May 28–June 11, 1954–65, and May 26, 1971 (C. MacInnes); Bowman Bay, June 11, 1929 and June 6, 1955; Banks I., June 6, 1955. Also Banks I.—many clutches of up to 5 as early as May 31, 1953 (Höhn 1957). Mackenzie delta–Liverpool Bay area—last week in May. Wrangel I., av. June 1, 1959–65. Laying span in a colony is 14 days or less, but at McConnell R. in 1968, a very backward season, it was 20–21 days (J. Prevett). At onset, more "whites" begin at the same time than "blues" or "mixed" pairs; mixed pairs tend to lay later than either "pure" category; consequently, only excessively late breeding seasons have any disrupting effect on their nesting phenology.

Clutch size and parentage (1952–56 inclusive, Boas R.): Blue × Blue 1 egg (7

145

clutches), 2 (51), 3 (155), 4 (399), 5 (243), 6 (51), 7 (10), Blue × Snow 2 (35 clutches), 3 (66), 4 (156), 5 (108), 6 (19), 7 (1); Snow × Blue 1 (2), 2 (7), 3 (55), 4 (107), 5 (82), 6 (10), 7 (4); Snow × Snow 1 (32 clutches), 2 (202), 3 (566), 4 (1,216), 5 (784), 6 (140), 7 (4), 8 (2). From onset of laying in a colony toward the end of the period, there is a definite daily regression in av. clutch size from 6 to 3. If the season is early, Blues will have larger clutches; if late, Snows.

Egg retrieval All 42 Blue ♀ ♀ tested in 1970 at McConnell R. rolled eggs back into nests. Two of 17 did not when the egg was 18–27 in. away, but did so when it was moved to 12 in. Three of 5 did not retrieve eggs at 36 in., but did at 24, suggesting that 95 cm. (36 in.) is near the critical limit beyond which most Blues do not retrieve eggs (Prevett and Prevett 1973).

Nest parasitism It is not common for Lesser Snow/Blues to deposit eggs in nests of other species, but at McConnell R. they have done so in nests of Common Eider, Herring Gull, Sandhill Crane, and evidently the Canada Goose (Prevett et al. 1972). Probably the list could be expanded elsewhere to include, for example, Ross' Goose and Brant.

"Egg dumping" Especially in tardy seasons, when the geese are ready to lay but the environment is not yet suitable for nesting, eggs are "dumped" on the tundra. Many are scattered; others are deposited together—up to 41 eggs at a "dump" site at McConnell R. in 1968. See Prevett et al. (1972) for further details.

Replacement clutches none; if an incomplete clutch is destroyed or flooded out, the ♀ may lay the remainder of her clutch at the same site. Occasionally, another ♀ may occupy the site (total number of eggs deposited greater than usual clutch size), or sometimes several ♀ ♀, in sequence, usurp a nest and add eggs.

Egg losses At McConnell R. in 1965–67 inclusive, the Blues lost 20% of their eggs, mostly late in incubation. Since they defend their nests against predators, the cause of egg loss may be the inexperience of younger breeders or starvation of the geese during incubation. Nesters had very little to eat and lost about 25% of spring wt. Wt. loss is a function of heat loss, in turn controlled by the weather. Adverse weather could result in considerable wt. loss, which may impair steady incubation, i.e., cause the birds to be absent from their nests. Extreme wt. loss can result in death. More than 20 extremely emaciated ♀ ♀ that apparently had starved to death were found on or near their nests. (Summarized from Harvey 1971.)

One **egg**/clutch from 18 clutches of Lesser Snows from widespread localities (Baffin I. to Alaska) **size** length 81.24 ± 2.06 mm., breadth 53.39 ± 1.66, radii of curvature of ends 19.51 ± 1.58 and 14.38 ± 0.99; **shape** variable, usually long oval to subelliptical, elongation 1.52 ± 0.044, bicone −0.030, asymmetry +0.147 (FWP). At Karrak L. in the Perry R. region, N.W.T., 52 eggs length 67.2–80.2 mm., av. 73.1 and SD 2.5, breadth 44.7–51.4, av. 47.5 and SD 1.5; there is little size overlap with the smaller eggs of Ross' Goose (J. P. Ryder 1971b). Shell varies, glossy to dull or chalky; **color** white to creamy, but soon much soiled. Av. wt. of fresh eggs is about 120 gm. Eggs are laid early in A. M. (usually) and at rate of 1/day until 4th egg, then a day skipped before the 5th, frequently another before 6th.

Greater Snow—**clutch size** Baffin I., June 30, 1969, 22 of 1–6 eggs (mean 3.64); Bylot I., July 9, 1969, 32 clutches of 2–6 (mean 3.62) (J. D. Heyland). On Bylot, Lemieux (1959a) reported an av. clutch size of 4.6 in 1957, compared to 3.6 by Heyland in 1969,

146

yet production of young was good in 1957 and better in 1969 when clutch size was smaller; mean size of 34 clutches on Bylot in 1968 was 3.4, yet it was a poor year for reproduction (J. D. Heyland).

Greater Snow—mean meas. of 116 eggs are length 81.2 mm. and breadth 53.5 (J. D. Heyland); also see Lemieux (1959a).

Incubation by the ♀ only, begins with last or next to last egg. Some ♀ ♀ develop an incubation patch from which all down is absent. After the 1st week on eggs, the ♀ rarely leaves the nest; when she does leave, to feed and defecate, she is escorted by the gander.

Incubation period usually 22–23 days (a great many confirming data—Soper, Manning, Cooch, others), reportedly up to 25 days in larger clutches. Cayouette (1955) reported 23 and 24 days for eggs of Blue artificially incubated. Usually no infertile eggs in the wild. For captive *A. c. atlanticus*, a 21-day period was reported (Lorenz, in Armstrong 1954), but in wild birds at Bylot I. it was 23 days (8 nests), 24 (6), and 25 (4) Lemieux (1959a).

Prebreeders Yearlings tend to stay in close association with breeders until early stages of incubation; 2-year-old prebreeders tend to congregate around the periphery of a colony (but many are a goodly distance away—30 mi. on Baffin I., near L. Nettilling) and are joined by failed breeders. Early in incubation, most yearlings go the periphery (or even much farther away), but the 2 prebreeding cohorts seldom completely mix; younger birds tend to congregate in flocks comprised of sibling groups whereas 2-year-olds are in random mixture and some have formed pair bonds (the ♂ ♂ of these pairs have an aggressive display). Again the yearling class: when the birds are slightly older (say 15 mo.) and in gatherings at stopover places in fall, probably any remaining bonds among siblings (or of young reunited with parents) are dissolved. (Also see below.)

Hatching Goslings may depart within 6 hrs. after the last egg hatches or, in rainy weather, may remain up to about 72 hrs. They may not feed for about 72 hrs., roughly, the time required to resorb the yolk sac (but in *A. c. atlanticus* the young feed before 72 hrs., even when they still have considerable yolk; J. D. Heyland). Then they feed at first on chironomid larvae (which usually are temporarily abundant), flowers of *Dryas* and *Salix*, and fragments of *Sphagnum*. In any event, there is little food left in the colony by time of hatching. This early lack of need of food allows goslings to get out of heavily devegetated areas. (According to Lumsden (1959), the geese severely overutilized the available forage in parts of their nesting areas near s. Hudson Bay at C. Henrietta Maria in the 10 years they had nested there.)

Growth Young Blues develop "at an astounding rate" (Soper 1942a); Greater Snows in captivity grow remarkably quickly and remain awake most of the night clamoring for food (Lorenz, in Armstrong 1954). In the wild, the young can feed at any hour in the constant daylight. Age in days and wt. in oz. of Blues: 1 day (2.6 oz.), 5 (5.4), 11 (11.7), 13 (14.6) (preceding figs. for 23 goslings); 17 (21.8), 19 (27.0) (21 birds), 21 (31.8), 23 (36) (20 birds); 25 (40), 27 (46.5) (19 birds); 29 (51) (18 birds). The gander protects the family; the goose tends and broods the young. From the 7th day on, goslings frequently flap their wings. By the time the young are a week old, the gander can recognize his own goslings and chases strays that attempt to join the family; ♀ ♀ seem more ready to accept stray goslings. As the family travels, the parents defend the brood

147

(maintain a "family distance," the area within defended against intruders). The parents recognize their own young and vice versa. At first (7 days) family groups are widely scattered; they gradually assemble in pods of some 200 families of roughly comparable age.

By the time the brood is hatching, birds of the next older cohort (yearlings) are molting. Then, in flocks, these birds travel afoot, in any compass direction, usually up river valleys or along coasts. About 3 weeks later the pods of parents (now flightless and in body molt) with their preflight goslings travel much the same route as prebreeders. They may go up to 40 mi. (This is the general pattern in the colonies studied; there are variants elsewhere.) **Age at first flight** frequently 42 days and no records over 50. Relations of young to parents and siblings have been mentioned in various places in the present account.

Lack of space prohibits summarizing many additional data. There is general treatment of certain topics in Cooch and Beardmore (1959) and Cooch (1961, 1963). The following localities were treated in particular by the authors given: Baffin I. (Soper 1942a), Southampton I. (Sutton 1931, 1932), C. Henrietta Maria region of s. Hudson Bay (Lumsden 1959, Baillie 1963), La Pérouse Bay, Man. (F. Cooke 1969), Queen Maud Gulf mainland (J. P. Ryder 1971a), Victoria and Jenny Lind is. (Parmelee et al. 1967), Banks I. (Höhn 1957, McEwen 1958), Anderson R. area of N.W.T. (Höhn 1959), and Wrangel I. in U.S.S.R. (S. Uspenskii 1963, 1965a, 1965b, S. Uspenskii et al. 1963).

Greater Snow—some data are included above. For much additional information see: Ellesmere I. (Parmelee and MacDonald 1960), Bylot I. (Lemieux 1958, 1959a, 1959b, Tuck and Lemieux 1959, Drury 1961), and Greenland (Salomonsen 1950, Røen 1960, Heyland and Boyd 1970). At Bylot, travel afoot by the geese during molt is toward the coast, where the goslings begin to fly about Aug. 20, approximately 6 weeks after they hatch. FGC

SURVIVAL   See Stirrett (1954) for composition of 1,343 families of Blues at James Bay in early fall, 1952.

Inventories of Blues have shown that in 10 seasons the number of goslings hatched and surviving until Jan. varied from only 6,000 (winter of 1951–52) to 250,000 (in 1948–49), the av. Jan. count containing 154,000 goslings (of age 6–7 mo.) and 244,000 older geese. The mean brood size was 2.16 for the whole period, the seasonal values ranging from 1.6 to 2.7 (Boyd 1959a).

For western-wintering Lesser Snows, as determined from banding data, the 1st-year mortality rate was 49.1%, compared to 22.5% for "adult" ♂ ♂ and 25.0% for "adult" ♀ ♀; the av. annual turnover was 38.1%, with 28.7% of the loss occurring in the hunting season and 9.4% during the remainder of the year (Rienecker 1965). It was mentioned in the same study that most of the 3.8% of band recoveries from Siberian nesting areas were obtained by shooting in May–July on Wrangel I.

For *A. c. caerulescens* collectively, based on censuses and on age ratios, the estimated mean annual adult survival rate is 0.63, and for *A. c. atlanticus* is 0.67 (Boyd, in Le Cren and Holdgate 1962).

For eastern Lesser Snow/Blues, comparison of mean annual mortality rates for pooled banded samples for the early 1950s with those of 1967–71 inclusive suggest that mean rates for adults have increased significantly, while those for immatures have remained relatively stable (A. Dzubin, H. Boyd, W. Stephen MS).

In Lesser Snow/Blues an av. annual loss of roughly 30% of the population may be expected. That is, it is probably safe to generalize that, on the average, an individual survives to breed successfully only once. Av. survival is somewhat longer in the Greater Snow, which is not as heavily hunted.

Like other waterfowl that nest from the subarctic to high-arctic, *Anser caerulescens* has drastically reduced breeding success in inclement seasons. Thus, from colonies in areas where the season is greatly retarded, a particular cohort may consist of so few birds as to be nearly nonexistent. This was so for Lesser Snows of Wrangel I. in 1965; some earlier years of failure there were listed by S. Uspenskii (1965b). The year 1965 also was one of complete failure on Banks I. and the 1959 season in the Mackenzie delta–Anderson R. area was severe if not a complete loss. The year 1972, however, was the first on record in which there was complete or nearly complete failure at all colonies of the species from Wrangel I. eastward to Greenland, with the exception of the very southerly colonies at McConnell R. and farther s. in Hudson Bay. To be more specific about the Greater Snow, which is high-arctic and of limited distribution, the size of cohorts fluctuates violently, quite comparable to fluctuations in Ross' Goose. Greater Snows had a poor season in 1964, near-total failure in 1965, a highly productive season in 1966, almost complete (if not complete) failure in 1972, then high success in 1973, and near-complete failure in 1974. (Also see list of adverse seasons, and their effects n. of lat. 67°, under "Habits" of King Eider.) RSP FGC

HABITS Data for the species, but emphasis on Lesser Snow/Blues. Highly gregarious. Unwary except where persecuted. For example, long ago Zenzinov (cited in S. Uspenskii 1959) stated that in ne. Siberia the birds were so lacking in shyness when molting that they approached human habitations, where they promptly were killed. Older prebreeders probably are somewhat segregated in all seasons from breeders with their youngest brood. Snow/Blues associate readily at times with other waterfowl, especially the Whitefront, Ross' and various races of Canada Goose.

In the north country the Lesser Snow is known as the "white wavey," the Blue as "gray wavey."

Numbers The figures for winter counts, which were made in Jan. until 1969 and in Dec. (while hunting still is in progress) since then, have been widely publicized. They have been utilized many times and in various ways, hence are not repeated here. The reliability of these (they might better be termed indices) have been questioned by many biologists, by some repeatedly. It follows that calculations of rates of hunting kill and other matters, based on these figures, also are questionable. A fundamental problem is that such figures indicate the existence of far fewer Lesser Snow/Blues than do contemporary estimates and, more importantly, recent aerial censuses on summer range.

Some figures on colony size given earlier in this account (under color phases) do not necessarily jibe with previously published ones; as here revised, they are the best currently available and, when totaled, exceed projections based on winter inventories.

Population structure and colony size are influenced by a broad spectrum of biotic and other factors. As an example, the more northerly colonies show wide short-term fluctuations due to diminished or lost cohorts in adverse seasons when late-lingering snow on the lowlands restricts or even inhibits nesting. The accumulating ice and snow on Baffin I. (Bradley and Miller 1972) reflects this climatic trend. Since there is no way yet to forecast reliably how even one major factor, the climate, actually may affect trends in Snow/Blue population, it follows that consistent and frequent censusing may yield only sufficient data on population parameters for arriving at tentative conclusions on which to base hunting regulations and measures for maintaining the stock of geese.

The Greater Snow population was reduced to perhaps only 2,000–3,000 birds in the year 1900. During the 1950s, fall and winter counts varied about 35,000–51,000 (Lemieux 1959b). It was 59,900 at the end of the 1966 calendar year. In Que. in 1970, from aerial photos, there were 84,000 in spring and 137,000 in very late Oct. (included an av. of 3.6 young per breeding pair) (J.D. Heyland); there were over 150,000 (in photos) at C. Tourmente in fall, 1971.

Habits in winter of Lesser Snow/Blues were described in detail by McIlhenny (1932) and Soper (1942a). [Historical note: it was Soper who, in 1929, discovered the nesting grounds of Blue Geese.] Unless disturbed, the birds prefer to feed by daylight, in morning and toward evening. Flocks, often huge, make spectacular flights a few mi. between resting and feeding places. In all seasons they eat gravel, making flights (except in nesting season) to get it. Winter flocks thus are fairly sedentary, but there is some shifting about (generally local) to get an adequate food supply. Pair-formation activities during this season have been mentioned earlier.

At Squaw Creek Refuge in Mo., in early Jan. 1964, over a thousand Lesser Snows died of fowl cholera in a single night (Vaught et al. 1967). In s. U.S., rice seeds are treated with a biocide, dieldrin; geese feeding on rice seedlings pull up the treated seeds and some of the birds have died as a result.

Geese of this species are shearers, grubbers, and berry pickers, not usually grazers. Fairly typical are actions of Gulf Coast wintering birds of the smaller subspecies. Sometimes, for a short period after arrival, they eat heads of grasses. In some places there is a mass effort when dense flocks hover over an area where *Scirpus* grows 5–6 ft. tall and beat it flat with their wings as they descend on it. After alighting, the geese shear off stems, then dig and enlarge holes to get at the rhizomes and eat them in large pieces. They prefer to feed in water a few in. deep, the head being immersed when grubbing. Feeding birds form a line, facing windward, those behind flying over those ahead so that the flock "rolls" across the landscape, often leaving acres of it virtually a muddy desert. With variations, this is a general pattern of all Snows and Blues through winter and on migration. Grubbing for potatoes in Ore. is a new habit of Lesser Snows since about 1920. Snows and Blues are attracted to areas where marsh vegetation has been burned, in search of rootstalks, as in coastal prairies of La. and Texas, where their damage to cattle pasture usually is followed within a year by a new growth of vegetation.

A large aquatic rodent, the nutria (*Myocastor coypus*), introduced and now populous in the Gulf Coast area and elsewhere, is a competitor for food.

Near the end of the wintering period, birds (either subspecies) form huge premigration assemblages. They become lazy, feed little, are noisy, and occasionally parts of the gathering take wing. There is fighting, display, and chase flights. Eggs are dropped rarely in these gatherings and more often at resting areas along spring migration routes.

On March 15, 1970, J. Prevett observed a premigration assemblage of about 25,000–30,000 birds near Anahuac Refuge in Texas. The birds were quiet, fed and fought little, but were continually making short flights. At 3:30 P.M. small flocks started to depart, flying low, to the north, exactly as described by McIlhenny (1932).

In summer, the geese more nearly approximate land grazers; vegetation is plucked and sorted, various mosses being dropped while all parts of the intermingled or under-layer of desired green plants are eaten. Such plucking gives the landscape a ragged appearance.

In the human economy in N. Am. these geese are important to the Indians of n. Man. and Ont. (Hudson–James bay coasts); they use the feathers (for making bedrolls), the fat (in making bannock), and remainder of flesh and even the cleaned intestines (for food, eaten fresh, dried, or smoked). In former times, spoons were made from the sternum. The kill by Indians has been about 35,000–75,000 annually. Some white hunters consider these geese to be rather inferior table birds, hence pass them up if more preferred species are available.

In conterminous U.S., more Snow/Blues now are killed farther n. than formerly, i.e., away from the Gulf Coast, and the peak of kill is occurring later in the year. There is recent evidence, from the work of J. Prevett, that in huge assemblies of geese on refuges in the cent. states there is increased breakdown of family integrity. There also is concentrated hunter activity. The mammoth gatherings of the geese are detrimental to the young birds: with disruption of families they become more vulnerable to hunters. FGC

FOOD   A. c. caerulescens Lesser Snow/Blue—almost entirely **vegetable,** consisting of seeds, stems, and roots of grasses, sedges, aquatic plants, grain and berries. In the far north, rushes and insects, and in spring and autumn, berries, particularly Empetrum nigrum (Swainson and Richardson 1831, Preble 1908). When tundra is covered with snow at time of arrival of the geese at Southampton I., they rest on the edge of ice floes and perhaps eat seaweed and crustaceans; however, as soon as the ridges are bare, they "nibble at lichens, pull up the roots, and swallow coarse gravel" (Sutton 1932). At nesting grounds on Baffin I., roots of tundra grasses (Carex stans and C. membranopacta), arctic meadow grass (Poa arctica), foxtail grass (Alopecurus alpinus), and arctic cotton grasses (Eriophorum scheuchzeri and E. callitrix) (Soper 1942a). Utilization of horsetail (Equisetum) and crowberries (Empetrum nigrum) has been reported.

In migration at James Bay, Scirpus americana and Eleocharis palustris (Hewitt 1950); crops of 106 specimens from that locality contained Equisetum variegatum, Scirpus atlanticus, S. americana, Carex paleacea, C. salina, and C. aquatilis (Stirrett 1954). In Man. resorts to barley and wheat stubble, eating roots, grain, and young shoots of grass and volunteer grain (Soper 1942a). In Ky. preferred spike rush (E. obtusa), eating also roots of wild mustard (Roripa sessiliflora), Italian ryegrass (Lolium multiflorus), and reed canary grass (Phalaris arundinacea) (J. Morse 1950). In Del. in winter, roots and culms of cordgrasses (Spartina alterniflora and S. patens) and salt grass (Distichlis spicata) (Saylor 1941).

On arrival on wintering grounds on La. coast activities confined to seeds, if available, of feather grass (*Leptochloa fascicularis*) and wild millet (*Echinochloa crusgalli*). Subsequently, very largely roots of three-square bulrushes (*Scirpus robustus* and *S. americanus*), cordgrass (*Spartina patens*), and roots and tubers of delta duck potato (*Sagittaria platyphylla*) (McIlhenny 1932). Other plants utilized are: "cutgrass" (*Zizaniopsis miliacea*), cordgrasses (*S. glabra* and *S. alterniflora*), panic grass (*Panicum repens*), cattail (*Typha angustifolia*), salt grass (*Distichlis spicata*), and glasswort (*Salicornia*) (McAtee 1910, Cottam 1935). Also mentioned are the rootstalks and rhizomes of *Typha latifolia*, *Spartina cyanosuroides* and *Scirpus californicus* (Lynch et al. 1947). The stomachs of 28 specimens collected in La. in winter and analyzed in the Biol. Survey showed 100% vegetable matter as follows: *Carex* 2.79%, *Scirpus* 3.75%, *S. americanus* 16.75% and *S. robustus* 10.36%, *Eleocharis* 3.17% and *E. palustris* 5.64%, *Sparganium eurycarpum* 0.25%, Cyperaceae 22.19%, *Oryza sativa* 0.92%, *Triglochin maritima* 9.21%, *Spartina glabra* 3.92%, *Typha* sp. 20.25%, and plant fiber 1.70% (Cottam 1935).

The principal foods on Texas coast are reed (*Phragmites communis*), bulrushes (*Scirpus americana*, *S. robustus*), smartweed (*Polygonum* sp.), sedges (*Carex*, *Cyperus*), salt grass (*Distichlis spicata*), cordgrasses (*Spartina alterniflora*, *S. spartinae*); and on the prairies stems, leaves, and seeds of various grasses (*Buchloe dactyloides*, *Andropogon*, *Paspalum*, *Festuca*, *Panicum*, *Setaria* and *Sporobolus*) (Glazener 1946). Consumes the waste grain on the upland stubble and in rice fields, and shoots of growing grain. Have fed extensively in late winter before migration on rye grass in improved pastures (J. Prevett).

In Bear R. marshes (Utah) glasswort (*Salicornia*) is one of the principal foods (Cottam 1935). Along the Virgin R. (Nev.), ate the stems and tender shoots of a small club rush (*Scirpus*) (A. K. Fisher 1893). Principal foods in winter in Puget Sd. are the rootstalks of bulrushes (*Scirpus pacificus* and *S. americanus*) (Scheffer and Hotchkiss 1945). Bulrush (*S. americanus*) also utilized in Cal. (Moffitt 1938). Here it feeds largely, however, in grain stubble, growing grain, and pastures. One bird had eaten 1,581 grains of barley, another 500 stalks of filaree (*Eordium*) (J. Grinnell et al. 1918).

Animal matter rare. A specimen collected at Buckeye Lake (Ohio) in April had eaten 2 gizzard shad (*Dorosoma cepedianum*) (Trautman 1940).

A. c. atlanticus Greater Snow—almost entirely **vegetable,** seeds, roots and stems of grasses, sedges, and other aquatic plants, with some grain and berries. On breeding grounds in n. Greenland, according to Ekblaw (in Bent 1925), semaphoregrass (*Pleuropogon*) and mare's tail (*Hippuris*) growing in shallow pools. Crowberries (*Empetrum nigrum*) in autumn (Franklin 1823). The stomachs of molting birds contained stems and leaves of grass (Salomonsen 1950).

On Bylot I. in July, 1969, 25 goslings were collected, at ages of about 24–96 hrs. In all cases, vegetation and sand were found in the esophagus and proventriculus. In all but 2 or 3 individuals, there remained a fair amount of yolk sac to be absorbed, i.e., the goslings eat during their first 72 hrs. even though yolk is present. The foods eaten (most was too fragmented for identification) included *Scirpus* (achenes, scales, fruit), *Juncus* (fruits with perianth), and *Equisetum* (branches). [The last has a high silica content in its stems and these would be rather indigestible.] (Data from J. D. Heyland.)

At stopover area on the St. Lawrence R., rootstalks and sprouts of bulrush (*Scirpus americanus*) and in spring resorting to upland fields (E. White and Lewis 1937). From Del. to N.C. coasts, roots and culms of cordgrasses (*Spartina alterniflora* and *S. patens*), bulrushes (*Scirpus*), salt grass (*Distichlis spicata*), and some glasswort (*Salicornia*) utilized (Cottam 1935, Saylor 1941). E. J. Lewis (1863) mentioned extensive use of "sea-cabbage" (*Brassica oleracea?*) in Delaware Bay.

Stomach contents of 19 Greater and Lesser Snows taken in winter in widely separated parts of the conterminous U.S. showed 100% vegetable matter as follows: horsetail (*Equisetum*) 22.23%, cultivated rice (*Oryza sativa*) 2.77%, wild rice (*Zizania aquatica*) 25%, unidentified grasses 28.44%, bulrush (*Scirpus americanus*) 18.75%, and legumes (Leguminoseae) 2.81% (Cottam 1935).

[For various units, some other activities such as grubbing potatoes and effect of feeding activities on the environment have been mentioned in other sections of the present account.] AWS

Ross' Goose

Anser rossii Cassin

Sometimes called Ross' Snow Goose, since it is a diminutive, Mallard-sized counterpart of white (Snow) phase *Anser caerulescens*. Bill stubby (1 to 1 $^3/_5$ in.), high at base, tapering to rounded tip; feather margin at side base forms a nearly straight line; no pronounced "grinning patch," although there is a slight arch in cutting edge of upper mandible. By the time individuals are of breeding age the majority of them have warty protuberances (caruncles), varying in development and color with individual bird and season, on basal half of upper mandible. The downy young are dimorphic in general coloring (details are lacking on whether these variations may correlate with certain variations in the wing in older birds). Tracheal apparatus evidently undescribed (but see Humphrey 1958a for *Anser* spp.). Sexes similar in appearance and, within the following spans, ♂ av. larger and heavier: length 21–26 in., wingspread 47–53, usual wt. 2¼–3¼ lb. No subspecies.

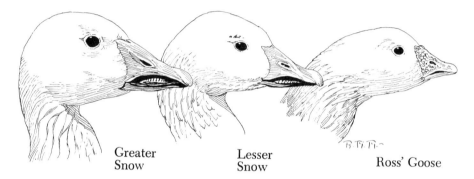

Greater Snow   Lesser Snow   Ross' Goose

DESCRIPTION   One Plumage/cycle; Basic II here regarded as earliest definitive. The bill has not attained "adult" condition in 2nd winter (when Basic II feathering is worn), but probably attains it by following summer (before molt out of Basic II). Note variation in alula coloring (compare with Lesser Snow phase of *Anser caerulescens*).

▶   ♂ ♀ Def. Basic Plumage (entire feathering), SUMMER to SUMMER. **Bill,** not invariably even in breeders, has sizable area of caruncles ("warts"), which are very vascular, on each side of basal portion of upper mandible and generally connected very narrowly across top base. This area usually is grayed greenish in breeding season, but darkens afterward toward grayish blue, lead color, or even purplish. Top center area of upper mandible scarlet-orange (vivid seasonally) in about 90% of individuals and, in the others, it is pinkish or toward rose (but darkening toward magenta in fall) and thus approximates the color of the remaining relatively smooth portion of the bill. The large circular nail is pale grayish or flesh-colored. Lower mandible colored like distal half of upper. **Iris** dark brownish; eyelids (the upper especially) in perhaps 5% of "adults" as well as young have a yellowish tinge reminiscent of the yellow in Whitefronts. **Neck feathering** furrowed. All **feathering** white (seldom with any ferrous staining) except: **wing** primaries black, grading to medium gray basally; greater upper primary coverts and alula usually rather light gray, the feathers often edged and/or tipped whitish,

154

shafts blackish (see beyond for individual variation in wing). Several innermost secondaries ("tertials") and their greater coverts are lengthened and curved downward. Legs and **feet** some variant of pink, nails black.

In Prebasic molt (of all feathering) the flight feathers of the wing are dropped after body molt has begun (and flightlessness actually begins before the long wing feathers are molted); the flightless period lasts about 28 days (duration closely estimated). Successful breeders become flightless later (July 20–25) than prebreeders (about July 15) and failed breeders, the timing in some years undoubtedly being earlier or later than the actually observed dates given here. About a week after an individual becomes flightless, the sheathed "spike" of the new incoming central pair of tail feathers and of the outermost primary are noticeable.

Variation in the bill—in captives at age about 18 mo. (mid-Jan.), bill has somewhat turgid lead-colored basal portion, creased and furrowed and still comparatively soft, not coarse hard "warts" of older birds; and a month later the smoother portion of the bill in ♂ ♂ is more vivid pink than earlier in winter. The individually variable "adult" condition probably is attained within a few months thereafter, i.e., while the birds are still in Basic II feathering.

In fall in Sask., 90 ♂ and 73 ♀ "adults" (may include a few older prebreeders): no "warts" and usually no swelling of base of bill in 10 ♂ and 10 ♀; slight swelling of base in 33 ♂ and 12 ♀; prominent swelling with deep lines throughout swollen area in 20 ♂ and 21 ♀; much lateral swelling but little dorsal swelling and "warts" distinct in 16 ♂ and 17 ♀; extensive lateral swelling with large "warts," but dorsal "warts" small, in 8 ♂ and 9 ♀; unicorn effect—large "wart" on top base of mandible—and extensive swelling and "warting" laterally in 3 ♂ and 4 ♀.

Flight-feather pattern—of other than all primaries black plus all secondaries white occurs in perhaps 10–15% of individuals. "Adults" (may include a few older prebreeders) in mid-Oct. in Sask.: 47 ♂ varied from all primaries and up to 5 adjoining secondaries blackish, to 4 inner primaries and all secondaries white; and 32 ♀ varied from all primaries and up to 3 secondaries plus half of the 4th blackish, to all primaries blackish and up to 4 adjoining secondaries pale grayish.

Alula—feathers may be classed arbitrarily as gray (all or partly gray and with dark shafts) or white. "Adults" (may include a few older prebreeders) in mid-Sept. in Sask.—in 135 ♂ the ratio was 124 gray: 11 white, and in 99 ♀ it was 95 gray: 4 white; also, 2 ♀ had left alulae gray and right ones white. Another series, in fall of 1963, showed ♂ 71 gray: 14 white, ♀ 68 gray: 14 white.

At McConnell R. (near Eskimo Pt. on w. side of Hudson Bay) in 1970, the alulae of 7 ♀ : all white (1 individual), 1 gray feather (2), 2 gray feathers (4); and in 4 ♂ : 1 gray feather (1), 2 gray (1), 2 gray on right and 3 on left (1), and all white on right and all gray on left (1). There was variation in the secondaries (but not recorded) and in primary covert color of these birds; in the ♀ ♀: 3 white plus 7 gray coverts (3), 2 white and 8 gray (3), 1 white and 9 gray (1); and in the ♂ ♂: 2 white plus 1 partly gray plus 7 gray feathers (2 individuals) and all gray (2) (J. P. Prevett).

In 9 captives examined periodically by J. Lynch, the alulae of all were gray or predominantly gray in Juv. Plumage. [There is no Basic I wing, since the Juv. wing is retained and worn with the Basic I head–body.] In Basic II, 4 of the 5 ♂ showed an

155

increase in white, in one of these the alulae now being entirely white. In the 4 ♀, color (gray) and pattern were essentially the same in both feather generations in 2 individuals and in the other 2 the next to longest feather was white in Basic II. Shapes of the feathers varied, with no constant difference between the 2 generations.

Genitalia of ♂—at 19 mo. there is individual variation in development of penis, from ⅔ "adult" size and without sheath to full size and with sheath.

AT HATCHING the down is long and fluffy. The young are dimorphic in color (see pl. facing p.242), often within a brood and, arbitrarily (because of gradation or mixing of one dominant color into the other), they may be sorted into 2 categories. 1 Yellow—bill slaty gray with nearly white nail; iris dark brown; head and neck light yellow with dusky spot in front of eye; upperparts grayed yellowish, paling down sides to whitish yellow underparts; legs and feet muted dark greenish. Individuals vary in general appearance from greenish yellow to light yellow to darkish yellow to blackish yellow. 2 Gray—as preceding except gray replaces yellow. Individuals vary from whitish to pearly gray to dark grayish. The individual variation within each of the categories can be seen at a distance of several hundred feet with unaided eye and until the goslings are about 2 weeks old.

Age for age, bill and feet are markedly smaller in downy Ross' than in Lesser Snow/ Blues.

In 99 broods in 1964 there were: yellow—21 broods (47 individuals) or 21.1%, gray—32 broods (85 individuals) or 32.2%, and mixed—46 broods (66 yellow, 86 gray) or 46.6%. Thus the ratio in monomorphic broods combined was 1 yellow: 2 gray, and in mixed broods 1 yellow: 1 gray. In a sample of 192 downies in their first day after hatching, and which were sexed, there were—yellow, 30 ♂ and 33 ♀ and gray 60 ♂ and 69 ♀; that is, a color ratio of 1 yellow: 2 gray and sex ratio of 1: 1. The dimorphism is deduced to be due to a single gene, 2 allele system with no indication of sex linkage (F. Cooke and Ryder 1971).

▶ ♂ ♀ Juv. Plumage (entire feathering) perfected in latter half of AUG. (with flight attained at age about 42 days), then worn until about DEC., then replaced rather gradually into spring (except Juv. wing retained). A bird in full fresh Juv. Plumage may be described as follows (but also see variation mentioned beyond). General appearance white and pale brownish gray. **Bill** smooth, slaty gray faintly suffused with pink. **Iris** black. **Head** and neck white or nearly white (neck feathers smooth) with medium grayish stripe from bill through eye and continuing so as to join gray on nape; crown and occiput gray and this extends as stripe down hindneck and, becoming paler, encompasses upper **mantle** and upper sides of **breast,** and even paler in scapular area; remainder of body white except for grayish flanks. Legs and **feet** grayish green, somewhat suffused with pink. **Tail** mostly pale or light gray, the feathers comparatively narrow and with notched ends (where the precursor down broke off). **Wing** primaries blackish, lightening somewhat toward their bases; some outer secondaries white with darkish areas in center, then some others white with sprinkling of pale gray-brown, and several innermost ones (which are not elongated) have dark centers and white edges that are faintly spotted grayish; primary coverts pearly gray, alula silvery gray, and some inner greater and middle coverts are partly gray. (Variation in wing pattern not reported.)

156

Prebasic I molt (out of Juv.) evidently begins in DEC. (when birds are about 5½ mo. old) and continues until well along in April. More or less incoming white (Basic I) feathering can be seen on **head–body** by mid-Dec. to late Jan. and the upper mantle is the last darkish (Juv.) body feathering to be lost (usually in Feb.). The scapulars drop and new ones grow in March. The incoming white **tail** feathers have broad ends. Then the molting extends out on the wing so that, by about MID-APRIL, there are new innermost secondaries ("tertials") and new feathers are invading (progressively outward) the covert area. Captives at this stage, examined in the hand by J. Lynch, apparently had no remaining Juv. feathers at all except, of course, in the wing (at least the Juv. primaries and most secondaries are retained until the next molt, in summer).

Prebasic I molt thus is similar to that of Lesser Snow Goose, except that evidently it begins later and, in almost all individuals, is less evident to the human eye because there is less contrast between Juv. and Basic I Plumages in Ross' Goose.

Variation in **bill**—in mid-Sept. to mid-Oct., in ♂ usually gray suffused pink (but varies from all black to all pink), generally being all pinkish by mid-Nov.; ♀ about the same (though less variation observed) and changing perhaps somewhat later. Further details in Dzubin (1965).

Head and **body** in mid-Oct.: "cap" of ♂ usually medium gray, but varied from white (1 bird) to blackish (2 birds) and scapulars same (but with 3 white, 2 blackish) in 44 individuals; tail usually pale to medium gray (but 6 white, none blackish) in 36 examined. And in 36 ♀: "cap" usually medium gray (pale gray to blackish, none white), scapulars same (but also white in 5), and tail pale or light gray, varying to medium gray plus white in 10 birds.

Legs and **feet** by mid-Nov., ♂ essentially all pink, ♀ still usually grayed greenish but becoming grayed pink by late Jan.

Wing in mid-Oct.: in 44 ♂, primaries light to (usually) medium gray to blackish; secondaries except inner ones usually medium gray, but ranged from white (3 birds) to blackish (3); inner secondaries varied similarly (except none white); and 36 ♀, primaries light to very dark gray (usually) or blackish; secondaries except inner ones usually pale gray (15 birds) but ranged to blackish and, in one individual, white; inner secondaries usually pale gray (10 birds), but ranged to blackish and, in 3 individuals, white. In both series the innermost secondaries ("tertials") are highly variable from nearly white to various grays, with or without dark (to black) streaking along entire shaft of feather.

▶ ♂♀ Basic I Plumage (all feathering except part of wing), acquired by molt out of Juv. feathering, as explained in detail above, and replaced in July–Aug. (at age just over 1 year). Although Blaauw (1905) stated that a captive-reared bird began to molt at age 10 weeks, the many live-trapped wild ones aged about 12–15 weeks that were examined by A. Dzubin in Sask., had not begun to molt. Nine of these, retained by J. Lynch in a large waterfowl enclosure in La., did not show molt until into Jan. and this may be a few weeks later than the normal time of onset of Prebasic I molt in the wild. The birds are in full Basic I from about LATE APRIL into EARLY JULY.

Feathering (except part of wing) white, the neck furrowed. Innermost secondaries and their greater coverts are intermediate in length and shape between those of Juv. and of Def. Basic, not yet having attained full length and curvature typical of the latter.

157

In captive ♀♀ at age about 7 mo. (1st winter), the unfeathered cloacal area varies with individual from 1 still flesh-colored, to 2 with dark streaks radiating out from vent, to 3 area entirely dark (blackish purple), almost as dark as ♀ "adult."

Measurements of definitive-feathered birds, 22 ♂: BILL 37–46 mm., av. 41; WING (across chord) 370–400, av. 385; TAIL 110–120, av. 118; TARSUS 67–74, av. 70.5;   20: ♀; BILL 34–41 mm., av. 38.5; WING (across chord) 360–395, av. 370; TAIL 110–120, av. 115; TARSUS 62–70, av. 66 (F. Kennard MS).

Flattened WING in 19 ♂ 360–403 mm., av. 386, and 24 ♀ 355–382, av. 369 (J. Ryder); and another series of 9 ♂ 363–403 mm., av. 385, and 8 ♀ 349–384, av. 369 (ETS).

First-fall (Juv.) birds, compared with first series given above, chord of WING av. about 10 mm. and TAIL 8 mm. shorter, in ♀ the WING to 15 mm. and TAIL to 10 mm. shorter (Kennard).

For additional meas., see table 16 in J. P. Ryder (1967).

Weight of birds in definitive feathering: 18 ♂ 1,165–1,585 gm., av. 1,400 (3.1 lb.), 15 ♀ 965–1,445, av. 1,280 (2.8 lb.); and first-fall birds, 16 ♂ 965–1,415 gm., av. 1,255 (2.7 lb.) and 12 ♀ 910–1,250, av. 1,115 (2.5 lb.) (Kennard). A ♀ on May 27 in Athabaska delta weighed 4¼ lb. (F. Harper).

Live wts. of "adults," Sept. 25, 1962, in Kindersley Dist., Sask.: 31 ♂ 1,320–1,880 gm., av. 1,679, and 32 ♀ 1,270–1,660 gm., av. 1,500 (H. Miller, G. Schildman, A. Dzubin).

For comparison of meas. (including flattened WING) and wt. of Ross', Ross' × Lesser Snow hybrids, and Lesser Snow, see Trauger et al. (1971); their samples included the "adult" Ross' from Kindersley, mentioned above.

Av. wt. of newly hatched young is 65 gm. (64 birds); BILL length av. 15.4 mm. (23 ♂) and 15.1 (27 ♀) (J. P. Ryder).

For a graph of wt. increase of young from hatching to mid-Oct., and wt. of breeders, by sex, from early June into Oct., see J. P. Ryder (1967). Breeders are heaviest at time of arrival in breeding area. Then there is a steady decline, greater in ♀♀ (from regression of genital organs and increasing attentiveness to nest with consequent minimal time for feeding) through laying and incubation. An increase, though not to the earlier high level, follows, then a decline during Prebasic molt, and a leveling off into fall at about 450 gm. (1 lb.) less than spring maximum.

The ♀, during laying and incubation, can lose up to 800 gm. (44%) of her wt.; of this, about 100 gm. are lost by ovary regression (J. P. Ryder 1970).

Hybrids in the wild with Lesser Snows (*Anser c. caerulescens*) have been discussed at length by Trauger et al. (1971). Between 1962 and 1968, 24 hybrids were studied and records of an additional 18 were obtained. Hybrids were observed at breeding areas in the central Arctic (Perry R., Simpson R., Karrak L.) and in the e. Arctic (McConnell R. on w. side of Hudson Bay), also during migration (Sask., S.D., Nebr., Iowa, and Mo.), and on winter range (in La.). They are intermediate in size and other morphological characteristics between the 2 parent species.

At McConnell R., hybrids were seen first in 1969, when a hybrid ♀ and 4 goslings were trapped at banding. Hybrids have been seen there every year since. In 1970, nests of 11 Ross' pairs and 5 hybrid combinations were found: ♂ *rossi* × blue-phase *caerulescens*, ♂ *rossi* × blue-phase hybrid ♀, ♂ *rossi* × white-phase ♀ hybrid, white-phase ♂ *caerulescens* × white-phase ♀ hybrid, white-phase hybrid ♂ × ♀

white *caerulescens*; other hybrid pairs were a Ross' ♂ × Lesser Snow ♀ and a pair of intermediates (hybrid × hybrid) (J. P. Prevett).

Among 10 captive *rossi*, 14 hybrids, and 4 *caerulescens* kept at London, Ont., 5 pairs formed involving Ross' and smaller hybrids (Ross' × hybrid backcrosses) by early June 1971. None of the Blues or large hybrids (Blue × hybrid backcrosses) appeared to have paired. This suggests that substantial numbers of Ross' may form pair bonds when at age approaching 1 year and perhaps breed at about 23 mo. Pair formation behavior was as described (see "Reproduction") for birds in their 2nd winter.

According to Gray (1958), in captivity Ross' has crossed with *Anser anser* (domestic strain), *A. c. caerulescens* (both Lesser Snow and Blue), *A. canagicus*, and reportedly with *Branta canadensis minima* (see C. L. Sibley 1938) and *B. ruficollis* (Wildfowl Trust, 3rd *Rept.*, p. 38. 1951). C. L. Sibley also mentioned a captive cross with the Blue-winged Goose (*Cyanochen cyanopterus*).

Geographical variation none, but individual variation in certain characteristics is greater than heretofore reported. Recent changes in distribution and in numbers of *Anser rossii* and *A. c. caerulescens* have resulted in more contact between them in all seasons; hybridization between them may be a relatively recent phenomenon, and appears to be increasing. If this continues, and especially if the frequency of hybridizing accelerates, *rossii* possibly could become extinct.

(The above section is based on Dzubin (1965), J. P. Ryder (1967), many additional data from these authors, correspondence with J. Lynch, and MS of the late F. H. Kennard.) JPR AD RSP

FIELD IDENTIFICATION Diminutive white goose with black primaries. Often difficult to distinguish from Lesser Snow, which is larger and with which it often associates, although the stubby bill (in relation to head size) is diagnostic when it can be seen. When Ross' and Lesser Snow are near one another, the smaller size of the former is apparent; in close view, the bill of Ross' is seen to be more or less pinkish, usually "warty" basally, and without "grinning patch." Ferrous staining of head—neck is infrequent enough to be unexpected in Ross', but is very frequent and often very pronounced in Snows. Young Ross' in first fall into winter differ from young Lesser Snows in having less and paler gray in their feathering and almost always have a well-defined gray line through eye. Downies, in all their color variations, differ from lighter categories of Lesser Snow goslings in having distinctive long fluffy down and no dark area down nape.

At nesting concentrations where both Ross' and Lesser Snows occur, the former are comparatively easy to distinguish from an aircraft: they are smaller, have short necks, and rapid wingbeat; and molting birds, flapping across the water, also can be recognized (J.P. Ryder 1969). Through fall and into winter, the limited amount of lighter grays of young Ross' viewed from ground or flying aircraft (in aerial censusing), are largely obliterated in strong sunlight; as a result, these individuals appear white, like the older ones. A flock thus appears to contain only white birds. In similar circumstances, the darker grays of young Lesser Snows give them a dirty appearance; that is, members of a flock containing young ("dirty") and older (white) birds do not have uniform appearance.

Swimming Ross' seem very compact, the head being quite close to the body; when

159

alert, the fully upward-extended neck is decidedly shorter and relatively thicker than in Snows. The wingbeat of Ross' is rapid. At times the birds flit up and down or swing from side to side, somewhat after the manner of a twisting, turning, shorebird flock. Generally speaking, flying Ross' appear highly maneuverable and buoyant, Lesser Snows cumbersome and slow flying in comparison.

Ross' associates readily with Lesser Snows (commonly even when breeding; there are few pure Ross' colonies), Whitefronts (especially in migration), and small Canada Geese (with notable frequency on parts of winter range) and, to some extent, with other waterfowl. AD

VOICE   Very different from Lesser Snow (which see). Flying and resting fall migrants utter a high-pitched *keek keek*, or this pair of notes uttered twice. Known to hunters as "squealer" (Tyler 1916). Occasionally a harsh *kork* or *kowk*, on summer and winter range; definitely lower pitched than in Lesser Snow/Blue. See Sutherland and McChesney (1965) for spectrograms of flight call of Ross' and Lesser Snow. A yelping by ganders in winter during pair-formation activities. Spring migrants at L. Athabaska uttered a little grunting honk *hawh hawh* (F. Harper). When nesting and not alarmed, a gruntlike *kug*, weak *luk luk*, or *ke-gah ke-gah*. A high-pitched squeaky call in flight in summer (Barry and Eisenhart 1958). Before attack (territorial defense), a high-pitched squawk, by both members of pair (if both attack); in lower-intensity defense, a low moaning grunt before and after the charge; latter also uttered in Triumph ceremony. Newly hatched goslings, if alarmed, utter a high-pitched squeak. JPR AD

HABITAT   Breeds in colonies in low-arctic environment, usually on is. in tundra lakes, almost always with Lesser Snows. Almost all nesting colonies "lie within the limit of postglacial marine transgression in the central Arctic," but why such areas are preferred is unknown; see discussion by J.P. Ryder (1969). Known nesting environment is nearly flat terrain, a large percentage of it preferably having mixture of dwarf or low woody vegetation plus grassy areas; rocky plus mossy terrain is marginal habitat. Much snow and ice remains into early June and there is a tremendous runoff of meltwater; at Arlone L. the bottom ice continues rising until mid-July and constant summer winds keep the water turbid. Stopover places of migrants in spring–fall include: shallow waters of the Peace–Athabaska delta; saline lakes in Alta. and Sask. and flooded stubble lands and areas of small potholes, the birds also foraging on grassy uplands and in grainfields; more southerly, various kinds of grassy terrain, including wetlands and hay meadows. In winter in Cal., preferably uneven pastureland having scattered rainwater pools, marshy grasslands, and cultivated fields. In Texas and La. in winter, in the habitat of Lesser Snow/Blues with which they associate. JPR

DISTRIBUTION   (See map.) Principal **nesting** area is on the Canadian mainland s. of Queen Maud Gulf in N.W.T. J.P. Ryder (1969) reported and showed (on a map) the location of 35 previously unrecorded colonies there, between lat. 66°21′ N–67°34′ N and long. 97°02′ W–104°15′ W in ne. Mackenzie and nw. Keewatin. There are summer records (but no proof of breeding) to the northwestward beyond, on Banks I. East of the main area, a few breed on Southampton I. at Boas R. delta and East Bay

160

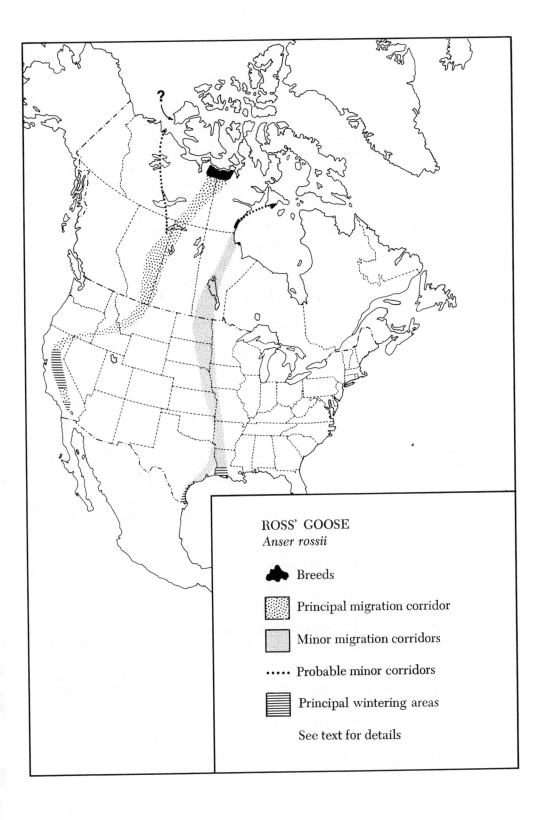

ROSS' GOOSE
Anser rossii

Breeds

Principal migration corridor

Minor migration corridors

•••• Probable minor corridors

Principal wintering areas

See text for details

and, by 1970, a very considerable number in the w. Hudson Bay area in extreme se. Keewatin at McConnell R. (near Eskimo Pt.). In s. Hudson Bay, Ross' evidently began nesting in 1972 in the Lesser Snow Goose colony some 25 mi. e. of Churchill, Man., at La Pérouse Bay (J. P. Ryder and Cooke 1973). Undiscovered colonies possibly exist.

Main **winter** range in the late 1960s was in these counties in Cal.: Glenn, Colusa, Butte, Sutter, and Yolo in the Sacramento Valley and Merced in the San Joaquin Valley. (There were about 21,000 Ross' in the San Joaquin Valley in Feb. 1967.) A few occur at that season elsewhere in Cal., including in the Imperial Valley; also recorded in the Salton Sea area and, formerly, some wintered in the Los Angeles area. The number wintering in coastal La. and Texas increased greatly beginning in the 1960s, reflecting the increase in numbers breeding at McConnell R., mentioned above. There also are winter records for New Mex., Ariz., and interior Mexico.

Occasional birds have wintered as far n. as Minn., S.D., Kans., Colo., and Utah.

On the Atlantic coast, a single bird has been seen at Pea I. Nat. Wildlife Refuge in N.C. in Dec. 1967, March 1968, fall 1970, late Feb.–early April 1971 and, accompanied by an "immature," in winter of 1971–72.

Limits of usual occurrence plus **stragglers** and for all seasons include: Alaska, N.W.T. (Mackenzie Dist., Keewatin Dist., and on Banks I. in Dist. of Franklin), Canadian provinces (B.C. to Ont. inclusive), conterminous U.S. (N.C., Ill., and Wis., plus all states w. of the Mississippi except Ark. and Wyo.), and in interior Mexico (Chihuahua records; banded bird recovered as far s. as Zacatecas). A few probably winter on or near the Gulf Coast in ne. Mexico.

The very large geographical area in conterminous U.S., for which there are literature and specimen records of occurrence of Ross' Goose dating back to 1893, has not been enlarged appreciably by the many additional recent records. Thus, the pattern of widespread occurrence is not a recent development, but the number of individuals recorded—especially beginning around 1960, and down through the cent. conterminous U.S.—has increased greatly. D.L. Trauger (MS) compiled more than 500 records e. of the Rocky Mts. between 1960 and 1968. The fall of 1967 through spring 1968 season alone produced reports of over 200 birds. Prior to 1960, there were fewer than 50 records for the same area. This undoubtedly indicates more and better-trained observers seeking this species, as well as more birds. Comparatively large numbers have been reported in Ore. (Malheur Refuge, peak of 100 in April 1971), Nebr., New Mex. (at least 20 in 1 locality in Dec. 1969, over 100 in the state in fall of 1970), Texas, and Mo. (Squaw Creek Refuge, over 75 in late Nov. 1969), but a significant number also has been observed in the Dakotas, Iowa, Colo., and especially the Texas–La. coastal area. The birds often are associated with Lesser Snow/Blues, Canadas, Whitefronts, and Mallards.

Records over a considerable span of time, for Ont. (Indians at Ft. Severn know this goose and have a name for it) and on down to coastal Texas–La., indicate that easterly breeding birds (at least a few pairs) existed long before any that used this line of travel were discovered nesting. Their numbers increased very greatly in the 1960s, possibly to 6% of the total population of the species; see Prevett and MacInnes (1972) for many interesting details.

NOTES   A pair nested in Iceland in 2 consecutive summers. Both birds were banded

162

and very probably had escaped from captivity in Britain. No young were raised. (Data from F. Gudmundsson.)

A Ross' Goose reportedly reached England with a flock of Greenland Whitefronts in late 1971 and wintered there.

This little goose is reported as **fossil** from the Pleistocene of Ore. and Cal. and from **archaeological sites** on Kodiak I. (Alaska) and Cal.; see Brodkorb (1964a) for references.   JPR RSP

MIGRATION   General pattern as Lesser Snow/Blues, except most of the population uses a single route in spring and in fall (like Greater Snow). On the Canadian prairies there is more latitudinal spread of flocks in fall than in spring. Regularly associates with Lesser Snow over much of route in both spring and fall; usual distance traveled is about 2,300 mi.

Some shifting from traditional route is known, at least in fall in prairie provinces; in a recent instance (e. into Sask.) this was caused by a flooding of feeding marshes in Athabaska delta and a drying of resting areas in cent. Alta. (Dzubin 1965).

MAIN UNIT **spring** Ryder (1967) indicated that flocks arrive at particular localities subsequent to the 32°F isotherm, when the melt has begun and water and food are available. In brief: Feb.–March in Pacific coastal states or nearby, April in Mont., May in Alta., and in early June parents and their yearling offspring arrive at breeding places.

In more detail: the birds leave winter quarters in late Feb.–early March; early stopover places include Pit R. valley (ne. Cal.) and Summer L. (se. Ore.) in last third of Feb. or later, and at least most years in Mont. (mainly e. of Rockies). Stopover in Alta. (Sullivan and Hamilton lakes, to a lesser extent Beaverhill L. e. of Edmonton) April 15–May 1. (Few Ross' are recorded in w. Sask. in spring, but many in Alta.) Later, in Peace–Athabaska area they congregate on a number of lakes. According to Soper (1951), "they appear to reach the Delta about mid-May" and depart about the end of the month (last seen as late as June 10); 1,500 seen there May 28, 1920 (F. Harper) and about 5,000 the following day, mostly in flocks of not over 35, many of the birds in pairs (H. Laing). Probably most then go nonstop to breeding areas. At Perry R. in 1949, some had already arrived by June 3, although 30 were seen arriving on June 18 (H.C. Hanson et al. 1956). In 1963 and 1964, peak arrival at Arlone L. (lat. 67°22' N, long. 102°10' W) was June 8 and 4 respectively. Most arrived in groups of 2–50, not in association with Lesser Snows. In 1963, flocks continued to arrive until the end of June. In 1966, 1967, and 1968 first arrivals were seen on May 30, June 10, and June 4 at a large colony (Karrak Lake), lat. 67°15' N, long. 100°15' W. Peak arrival in those years (estimated): June 3, June 13, and June 8 respectively.

Summer   A molt migration occurs as folows. The yearlings are with parents at first; then, at onset of incubation, they leave (or are driven from?) the nesting territories and retire to communal (undefended) areas and to nearby mainland. This is not a sudden severing of family ties; the young fly around the lake containing the nesting is. and the radius of their circling flight increases so that, by the time the hatching phase starts, these young have left the area and flown to molting places (tundra marshes). There they become flightless, usually in 2nd week in July. They are joined by failed breeders, later (see "Reproduction") by breeders and their goslings, who have a terrestrial migration to these places (where the breeders then go into wing molt).

Fall The birds leave summer quarters just before the temperature drops to freezing. The first flight, to Peace–Athabaska area, is early; arrival of peak numbers probably by mid-Sept. in some years but later that month in others. They linger for some time. According to Dzubin (1965, text and fig.), the peak population farther s. near Kindersley (Sask.) has been noted as early as Sept. 18 (some 2 weeks earlier than Lesser Snows) and as late as Oct. 25–26, depending on year. How long they linger depends on whether the weather remains warm, also on whether the breeding season was late. In an av. year, most Ross' (like Whitefronts) migrate out of Canada by Oct. 15. Again, as in spring, some stop over in Mont. (w. of Great Falls), with peak number in last week of Oct.–first week of Nov. The vanguard usually has arrived in ne. Cal. earlier, in mid-Oct., and there is a buildup until, beginning about mid-Nov., the birds begin drifting southward some 200 mi. into the Sacramento Valley. There are variations. For example, at Tule L. (extreme ne. Cal.), where they usually arrive Oct. 15–20 and stay until mid-Nov., they have lingered very late in some years and in some other years most of them have bypassed this locality. (For many further details for the entire fall season, see Dzubin 1965.)

Winter By mid-Dec. most have moved an additional, final 200 mi. farther s. into grasslands where they remain until late Feb.–March.

EASTERN BIRDS (See earlier under "Distribution.") Many from the w. side of Hudson Bay now evidently use the same routes or accompany Lesser Snow/Blues to Texas–La. coastal areas, but some (banded) even go from there to winter range in Cal.; details in Prevett and MacInnes (1972).

Straggling of individuals and groups occurs, even to places remote from usual routes. Much of this may be explained as being a result of their accompanying other species of geese. Stragglers may accompany Whitefronts in Sask. and move down through Nebr. to Texas where Whitefronts spend the winter. AD JPR

BANDING STATUS In fall seasons 1961–65 inclusive, 2,203 (1,029 first-fall birds and 1,174 older ones classed as "adults") were banded by Dzubin and coworkers in the Kindersley Dist. of Sask. Others have been banded as migrants (mainly in Alta.) and on winter range (mainly in Cal.). On breeding range, 1,693 breeders and 2,225 preflight young were banded 1949–68, almost all by J. P. Ryder in 1963–68 inclusive. Some also have been banded by MacInnes, Prevett, and coworkers on the w. side of Hudson Bay. In the year 1969 the total number of recoveries was about 300, approximately ¾ being from Cal., over half the remainder in Sask., and the others scattered. Band-recovery rate has been less than 5% annually.

Except incidentally by Kozlik et al. (1959), Dzubin (1965), and Prevett and MacInnes (1972), data from banding have not been published. RSP

REPRODUCTION This section is based on studies done in the area known as the Perry R. region in extreme ne. Dist. of Mackenzie. The principal localities are 2 lakes, Arlone (lat. 67°22′ N., Long. 102°10′ W) and Karrak (lat. 67°15′ N, long. 100°15′ W), and the main papers are J. P. Ryder (1967 and 1972).

Ross' Goose **first breeds** at age 2 years (data from banded ♀♀). Unlike *Anser caerulescens*, mating appears to be random (F. Cooke and Ryder 1971).

During warm spells in winter in La., captives at age 19 mo. formed a close group ("winter assembly") and ♂♂ became very conspicuous,with mincing walk, short prancing rushes, rapid sharp yelping calls, bull-neck appearance (fluffing out of neck feathers and pulling back of head), and engaged in much HEAD-DIPPING; ♀♀ did nothing much and were pushed about somewhat by the ganders (J. Lynch). This is the beginning of pair-formation activity.

Many Ross' Geese are paired in spring. In Alta., L. Sugden saw 2 copulations among migrants. Without preliminary display (mutual Head-dipping probably occurs), ♂ mounted ♀ in shallow water, in 1 instance the ♀ becoming entirely submerged. In 1 instance the ♂, after 15 sec., slid off the ♀'s side and then appeared to swim against her side; both partners later fluffed feathers and flapped wings. In the other, they were about 2 ft. apart when they fluffed feathers and WING-FLAPPED. Probably copulation generally occurs during later stages of migration, although Ryder observed it once at a breeding area on June 29, 1967. Any activity, terrestrial or aerial, relating to pair formation, except on winter range or among captives in winter, is unknown. Pair-bond form probably is **life long monogamy.**

The birds appear to be ready to nest when they arrive at breeding areas and, on the average, probably begin construction within 3 days. They are delayed by late-persisting snow at sites, or by meltwater, or high winds. They may be forced into less suitable habitat, or possibly there are occasional seasons that are so tardy that the geese do not nest at all.

On the basis of weather data from Cambridge Bay, not far distant, under optimum conditions the geese at Arlone L. have approximately 93 days (i.e., before the mean daily temperature again drops below 32° F) to complete nesting plus molting through to the time when all age-classes can fly. They need up to 80 days (85%) of this span; later layers, which spend less time producing smaller clutches, may shorten their total required span by as much as a week.

Nest sites, often used in previous years, preferably are in "edge" (mixed) areas of matted birch, rock, and grasses. Less desirable are: "open" (mossy) habitat (suitable for grazing but too exposed to the elements) and areas of low birch (much protection, but no grazing, and goslings may become entangled in the woody growth).

Nest materials, gathered at the site, include small birch or willow twigs, dead leaves, old goose droppings, and plucked moss; often these are built into a bulky structure. Outside diam. usually about 15.5 in. (40 cm.), inside diam. over 6 in. (about 16 cm.), and depth of cavity about 2.3 in. (6 cm.). Decidedly larger nests, of plucked moss, are built in exposed grassy areas, smaller ones in thick stands of birch. Construction occurs concurrently with laying and some maintenance continues through incubation. It is lined with belly down of the ♀, beginning close to the start of incubation. In 55 nests, 2% contained some down prior to laying of the penultimate egg, 16% after the penultimate, and 83% following laying of last egg. The down later becomes mixed with the other materials and this reduces or prevents scattering by the wind.

At Arlone L., in the preferred mixed habitat, there were 6–7 nests/1,000 sq. ft., compared to 0.8 nests/1,000 on mossy terrain. Distance between nests varied 6–39 ft.,

165

depending on habitat. At Karrak L. the nests av. about 15 ft. apart. Gavin (1940) reported them 3–30 ft. apart (many within 6 ft. of one another) and a density of 3.8 nests/acre.

Territory, used for nesting and some feeding, is only about 8–12 ft. in diam. (undefended areas are interspersed among territories); it is defended vigorously by ♂ and ♀ until incubation begins, then the ♂ defends while the ♀ is sitting. Defense posture is as in other *Anser*, neck horizontal, mouth agape. A high-pitched squawk is given by the ♂ (also by ♀ if both attack) if there is near-contact or actual contact with an intruder. Actual fights are very brief. In low-intensity defense, a low moaning groan is uttered prior to and after the charge. In TRIUMPH CEREMONY, ♂ returns to ♀ and, with neck at about 60° upward angle, utters a low moaning sound.

Early, during **laying,** short periods are spent at the nest; other time is spent grazing, and pair flights from the nesting island to the mainland are common. If disturbed, the birds take wing and join in flocks, which alight, and which subsequently break up into smaller groups. As incubation progresses, both ♂ and ♀ tend to stay more and more within the territory. If disturbed at this time, they take to the air and circle in a flock, directly over the nesting island; in 5–10 min. they are back on their territories.

Laying season at Arlone L. was June 9–17 in 1963 and June 4–19 in 1964, peak laying dates being June 11 and 12 respectively. At Karrak L., peak numbers of clutches were begun on June 6, 1966, June 18, 1967, and June 13, 1968. At Arlone L., rate of deposition av. 1.5 days/egg in 56 clutches.

The possible relation of **clutch size** to stored body reserves of the ♀ were discussed by J. P. Ryder (1970). At Arlone L., in 1,675 clutches, the av. was 3.47 eggs/clutch (range 1–8), with 4 the most common and 8 in a few nests only. Fifty nests ranged 2–6 with 4 most common (Gavin 1940). In 1941, several clutches (of 7), 1 (8), and 1 (9) (Gavin 1947). Ten clutches in 1949: 2 (2), 6 (3), 2 (4) (H. C. Hanson et al. 1956). At Karrak L., clutch size in large samples of successful nests varied in 1966–68 from a low of 3.8 ± 0.96 in 1968 to 4.2 ± 1.0 in the relatively early season of 1966 and about 50% of the eggs that hatched in each of the 3 years were in 4-egg clutches (J. P. Ryder 1972). Occasionally there are "dump nests" (10–29 eggs) in a colony. Clutches started later are smaller, as also are those in a retarded season; even a delay of 2 days makes a difference of 1 egg less in clutch size.

Egg size (175 eggs) av. 73.7 × 48.8 mm., with no decrease in size of later-laid eggs in clutches; **shape** near oval (asymmetry of about 0.3); **color** creamy white to white, usually becoming stained; no gloss.

Incubation is by the goose with her head drawn in on her breast, the gander close by on territory; it begins when the clutch is complete or nearly so; **period** 22 ± 1.0 days at Arlone L. in 154 clutches in which the eggs were marked and time of hatching of last was known. At Karrak L., combined mean for 1966–68 inclusive was 21.8 ± 0.90 days; details in J. P. Ryder (1972). Under aviary conditions, the period was 21 days for a clutch of 5 (Blaauw 1903). The ♀ is not a close sitter, the longest incubation span noted at Arlone L. being 46 min.; she covers her clutch with nest down before leaving, which conceals it from gulls and jaegers and retains heat. All eggs generally hatch on the same day. **Hatching period** at Arlone L. was July 3–10 in 1964; peak dates of hatching were July 7–8 in 1963 and July 5–6 in 1964. At Karrak L., hatching periods, with peak in

166

parentheses: June 29–July 9 (July 2), 1966, July 11–18 (July 14–16?), 1967, and July 5–16 (July 10), 1968, in very large samples (J. P. Ryder 1972). In the Perry R. region in 1949, 90% of 260 clutches hatched July 14–17 (H. C. Hanson et al. 1956).

Nesting success At Arlone L. in 1963 nests containing 351 eggs: 3 clutches (12 eggs) failed to hatch, but at least 1 egg hatched in all the others, or 96.7% of nests; in 1964 in 59 nests (230 eggs), nesting success was 83%. In the 2 years combined (152 clutches, 581 eggs), 41 eggs were destroyed, 14 had dead embryos, 8 had no embryo, and 7 were addled. At Karrak L., nesting success was 82.2 ± 5.1% (107 nests) in 1966, 88.3 ± 2.3 (197 nests) in 1967, and 67.6 ± 2.6 (293 nests) in 1968 (J. P. Ryder 1972).

If all eggs are taken from a nest, the birds abandon their territory.

Hatching success These figures are for per cent of eggs which hatched in successful nests at Karrak L.: 89.6 ± 1.6 in 1966, 88.6 ± 1.2 in 1967, and 86.1± 1.2 in 1968 (J. P. Ryder 1972).

The precocious young leave as soon as they are dry (requires about 1 hr.) and go with their parents to water areas of tundra, never to return to the nest. Late-hatching eggs in a clutch usually are abandoned. Both parents (but principally the ♂) guard the brood, often flying up at attacking avian predators—at Arlone L. primarily gulls (*Larus hyperboreus*, *L. argentatus*) and all 3 species of jaegers (*Stercorarius parasiticus*, *longicaudus*, and *pomarinus*). In case of a terrestrial predator, the ♀ tries to call the goslings away; the ♂, with wings outspread and bill open, faces the attacker. When ♀ and young are a safe distance away, he takes flight and joins them.

Growth In captivity, goslings at age 2 weeks still are downy, the bill blackish with white nail, and legs dark greenish; at 21 days there are conspicuous sheathed spikes of all primaries, the secondaries except a few innermost ones, scapulars, and tail; the bill av. 29.7 mm. (8 ♂) and 26.5 (7 ♀), legs and feet are nearly full-sized, tarsus 73.7 mm. (11 ♂) and 68.1 (8 ♀). At 4 weeks they are the size of small domestic fowl, have some down remaining only on hindneck, legs bluish green, bill lighter than earlier, and wt. av. 900 gm. (17 birds). At 5 weeks they are entirely feathered. At 6 weeks, flight feathers are of full length (Blaauw 1905). A captive gosling weighed over 2 lb. at 7 weeks (Barnes 1929).

The parent geese with their broods leave the nesting islands and, at first in family units or small assemblies of these, move toward marshy lakes and rivers. Travel is at least partly overland, the young feeding ashore, mainly on leaves and stems of grasses and sedges. Distance covered varies and may be considerable—some birds reach the Perry R. estuary—and evidently they go in no particular compass direction from nesting to molting place. By 3 weeks posthatching, single families no longer are seen on the tundra; the families and groups have united, sometimes into flocks of up to 200 individuals, and the parent birds have become flightless in molt; the flocks remain on the lakes and rivers (groups of molting yearlings have preceded them there) until, in late Aug., the goslings can fly and the parents have regained flight. For some information on duration of family bond thereafter, see below under "Habits." JPR

SURVIVAL At Arlone L. a few goslings are lost from falling into old Eskimo caches or from becoming entangled in low thickets of birch. Gulls, jaegers, and the arctic fox are known predators. J. P. Ryder (1967) found a balanced sex ratio at hatching and a differential mortality against ♀ ♀ during first 3 weeks of life (137 ♂ : 100 ♀). Number of young/brood declined in 1964 from 2.88 (av. for 99 broods) on summer range to 2.72 (188 broods) in Sask., to 1.65 (65 broods) in Cal.—the last figure after "natural" mortality plus hunting season (J. Ryder, A. Dzubin, J. Lynch). The overall decrease in av. size of brood thus was 42% in their first 6 mo. (For some further data on brood size in fall, see table in Dzubin 1965.)

For older birds, the data still are inadequate for satisfactory analysis. RSP

HABITS Ross' is much like the Lesser Snow/Blue Goose, but is more of an upland and grazing species. A lack of ferrous staining on the head and neck suggests that Ross' does not grub for roots in the manner of *Anser caerulescens*. It is highly gregarious —winter flocks sometimes containing up to at least 5,000 individuals—and social, toward various other geese. Like various other waterfowl, Ross' prefers to rest during midday when not disturbed (as by hunting). It is aggressive, both on summer range and when with Lesser Snow/Blues in winter. In captivity it does not initiate fights, but if attacked by other waterfowl, even large Canada Geese or the Tundra Swan, Ross' fights vigorously and drives off the attacker (J. Lynch). Lesser Snows start nesting slightly earlier than Ross', which gives the former (in mixed colonies) a certain advantage over the latter. MacInnes and Cooch (1963) theorized that the small breeding distribution of Ross' has resulted from competition with the larger *A. caerulescens;* an increase in the latter in the Hudson Bay region would provide donor populations for areas westward into Ross' habitat and the latter eventually may be displaced into an environment to which they are not adapted.

In Sask. in fall, shooting breaks up family groups; then wandering, orphaned, young may be adopted by other families or form in groups of young without adults. Also, in years when nesting is late, large gatherings, predominantly of young birds, are seen there in fall and, possibly from having had insufficient time to accumulate energy reserves, they remain behind when their parents move on and so are adopted by later-leaving families (Dzubin 1965).

This goose has had an interesting history. It was first reported, as "horned wavey" by Samuel Hearne, from observations in 1770; it was not formally described until 1861, when John Cassin named it in honor of Bernard R. Ross, the Chief Factor of Hudson's Bay Co. at Ft. Resolution on Great Slave Lake. Its nesting grounds remained unknown until they were discovered by Angus Gavin, in the summer of 1938, in the Perry R. region. In the 1950s, because of reports of scarcity of this bird on the prairies and in Cal., there was concern that it might become extinct. There were widely quoted estimates that the total population was as low as 2,000 in 1949–52. The wintering population in Cal. was believed to be about 6,000 in 1955; in 1963 it was well censused in fall and afterward in winter at over 25,000 birds; and Dzubin (1965) stated that in 1964 prior to Oct. 1 the population was "no lower than 34,300, and perhaps as high as 44,000." The figures for recent years (see table in Dzubin 1965, also table in Trauger et al. 1971) reflect more and better reporting and a great increase in birds (details in Prevett and MacInnes 1972). (There also has been a great increase in Lesser Snow /Blues and in Whitefronts, the ultimate cause being amelioration of climate.) Recent Jan. inventories of Ross': 31,800 (1965), 30,400 (1966), 31,400 (1967), 39,421 (1968), 20,085 (1969), and 22,720 (1970). Yet there remains doubt that Ross' was as scarce as believed in earlier years, because 1 reliable censusing is a recent development; 2 in Sutter Co., Cal., in 1955, D. B. Marshall personally counted over 5,000 Ross' Geese, one by one; and 3 there have been enough Ross' to produce widely scattered records, away from usual haunts, all through the present century. It is of interest to note, in the inventories given above, the tremendous decline in Jan. 1969, which reflects conditions in the preceding summer when practically no young were reared. Again, in 1972, fall counts in Sask. showed near-total failure to produce young that year—only 9 broods (total of 23 young) among some 20,000 birds and they may have come from some peripheral place such as McConnell R. In 1973 the adult: young ratio showed a highly successful nesting season for the species. (Data from A. Dzubin.)

When associating with Lesser Snows, Ross' is not easily censused, as on winter range in Cal. in Jan.; by mid-Feb. they have a tendency to separate (just prior to migration), Ross' spending more time on higher ground near rainwater pools, the Snows making daily flights to large expanses of water.

Ross' is unwary, at times in migration almost unbelievably so—hence the uncomplimentary vernacular name "galoot" in n. Canada. See Dzubin (1965) for historical data on hunting kill, on special protection given this bird, and mention that an aversion to killing this little goose persists in the prairie provinces because, for the small amount of meat obtained, Ross' is hard to pluck compared with the larger Whitefront and Canada Goose. Legal protection apparently had no effect on Ross,' because hunters could not recognize the bird in life; but many did identify them after they were in hand, hence would discard them prior to any checking of game bags by law enforcement personnel. After the period of total legal protection in conterminous U.S. and Canada, and beginning in fall of 1963, hunters have been permitted to keep 1 Ross' Goose in their bag, in effect "legalizing" the "accidental" shooting of a small goose. Since 1963, hunters in Canada have been permitted to take up to 5 Ross'/day but because the hunting season does not open on white geese until Oct. 7–10, few Ross' are available and few hunters shoot more than 1/day. The kill on Cal. wintering grounds exceeds the Canadian kill by 3–4 times if the distribution of band recoveries to date is any indication. In view of the now known number of Ross,' and assuming it has an av. life span not greatly different from that of the Lesser Snow, the annual loss of individuals (from hatching onward) from the population now must greatly exceed the total population figures given formerly for the species. It is reasonable to assume that the hunting kill is much greater than known at the time Dzubin (1965) summarized existing information. RSP JPR

FOOD When Ross' Geese arrive n., at first they are grubbers of roots of grasses and sedges, if any are available, since there is no new growth of stems and leaves. During incubation, mates feed on sparse vegetation on territory and on nearby undefended areas. Later, traveling families and groups utilize grasses and sedges about tundra pools and, soon afterward, also at tundra marshes where they remain while (and to some extent some time after) the goslings attain flight. They are grazers during migra-

169

tion and winter, preferring green grasses or, in places, such food as sprouted barley.

Spring   During April in Mont., they cropped short green grass of the prairies (R. S. Williams 1886).

Summer   Examination of 26 birds from breeding area in 1963 and 1964 showed that, early in the season, food was primarily roots of sedges and grasses; later, young leaves and spikelets of grasses and sedges, especially by the goslings during their trek on the tundra. Four gizzards from the Perry R. area in 1949: in 2, stems and leaves of *Eriophorum*, in 1 mainly *Eriophorum* and some *Carex*, and in 1 largely *Carex* and some *Poa* (H. C. Hanson et. al. 1956).

Fall   On arrival in Sask. and for 1–2 weeks thereafter, field observations indicate that they graze on sprouted wheat and barley leaves. Also, from some time in Sept. until they depart, they are seen in wheat and barley fields, gleaning kernels of these 2 small grains. Occasionally they feed along the shorelines of saline lakes on green western wheat grass (*Agropyron smithii*), but prominent food in fall is small grain (A. Dzubin).

Winter   Dawson (1923) stated the principal food is grass; recent field observations confirm this. AWS JPR

Emperor Goose

Anser canagicus Sevastianoff

Rather small, short-necked, stocky goose. The stout bill is blunt, with very large nail, and the feather margin at side base of upper mandible approximates in configuration (as viewed on right-hand side of head) the letter S. In all postdowny stages the body is quite dark, unrelieved by any white posterior area (although the tail is white), the individual feathers being very dark or black subterminally and with conspicuous light (to white) terminal margins (partly barred, partly scaly, effect). Definitive stages: head–neck has sharply defined bicolored pattern—most of head white and this continues down hindneck to edge of mantle; chin and front and sides of neck very dark (to black); neck feathering smooth (not furrowed as in various other *Anser*). Juv.: whole head and neck drab grayish. Tracheal apparatus apparently undescribed. Sexes similar in appearance. Within these dimensions the ♂ av. larger: length 25½–28 in.; wingspread 48–57, usual wt. 4–6 lb. No subspecies.

DESCRIPTION   One Plumage/cycle with Basic II earliest definitive.

▶   ♂ ♀ Def. Basic Plumage (entire feathering) ALL YEAR, the incoming Basic overlapping the outgoing one at molt of all feathering which begins in late June or early July in breeders. **Bill** upper mandible mostly pinkish or light violet-magenta with white nail, lower mandible varies with individual from nearly all black (usually) to pinkish with only flecks of black. **Iris** brownish. Feathering of **head**–neck as described above, the white of head especially often with ferrous staining. **Upperparts** very patterned (barred, etc.), the feathers blue-gray, subterminally banded black, and conspicuously margined white (broadest across ends), but pattern becomes indistinct on lower back to tail. **Underparts** have more scaly pattern; more of the feather is dark and grades to darkest subterminally, with white margin (see especially color photo in A. Allen 1951 and also note ferrous staining). Exposed portion of **tail** white, but the feathers are grayish basally. Legs and **feet** orange-yellow, paler seasonally (yellowish). **Wing** primaries medium or darker gray, becoming darker distally, and with white shafts; secondaries medium gray, tipped and externally edged white; upper coverts out to the

Juv.   Def. Basic

R. T. Tjengel —

alula much like mantle, except more dark in each feather, i.e., the dark is not merely a subterminal bar; primary coverts and alula medium to dark gray; wing lining medium gray.

Duration of flightless period, which begins after onset of molting, unknown but probably about 32–35 days. The entire Prebasic molt generally is completed by successful breeders some time in Sept., although individuals occasionally still have some incoming body feathers as late as Dec.

AT HATCHING   See col. pl. facing p. 242. Bill very dark with whitish nail; iris dark, a grayed brownish. Much of head and dorsum medium grayish with smoky sheen; a palish line immediately surrounding eye (spectacled effect); white around base of bill continues down throat and includes underparts. Legs and feet muted olive green, webs much paler (toward flesh). Published color illus. include a drawing in Brandt (1943) and photo in A. Allen (1951). There is considerable individual variation in darkness of head and dorsum of downy Emperors, sometimes even within a brood.

In comparison, downy Black-bellied Brant have darker upperparts, with still darker "cap" on head, slimmer bill, and much of breast dark.

NOTE   The description in Bent (1925) of a gosling that had grown approximately to adult teal size apparently is of a misidentified rather dark Whitefront.

▶   ♂ ♀ Juv. Plumage (entire feathering) fully developed at age closely estimated as 50 days; differs from Basics in having entire **head** and neck medium gray, blackish subterminal markings on **body feathering** and **wing** coverts only indicated. **Bill** mostly dusky bluish, **legs** blackish yellow (Blaauw 1916). As in other geese, etc., body feathers and wing coverts are narrower and more tapering than in later Plumages.

▶   ♂ ♀ Basic I Plumage (all feathering, except most or all of Juv. wing is retained), acquired by gradual molting which begins about as soon as the Juv. Plumage is perfected. Captives acquire it quite rapidly, as Blaauw (1916) stated that, by the end of Oct., young are "similar to the old birds" in appearance and have upper mandible flesh color and blue, lower mandible black, legs orange. More precisely, in Basic I the underside of **neck** tends to have a somewhat brownish cast, not the clear black of definitive feathering.

In the wild, beginning in early Sept., the head (starting at the front) becomes flecked with white; in Oct., much individual variation—some young still are quite dark on head–neck, others already are inseparable at a distance from older age-classes; in Nov.–early Dec. a few individuals still have an occasional darkish feather in white of head–neck. Molting on the body is completed, depending on individual, from Oct. into Dec., exceptionally later; the Basic I tail succeeds the Juv. from Oct. onward into winter.

Various Basic I feathers are intermediate in shape between those of Juv. and Basic II.

At age of approximately 1 year, in last quarter of June or in very early July, prebreeders begin molting and soon become flightless, i.e., lose the Juv. wing and then the Basic I head–body–tail. The vast majority of yearling prebreeders are again on the wing by very late July or early Aug., at which time they are still in body molt.

Measurements of "adults" from Alaska 10 ♂: BILL 36–44 mm., av. 40.9; WING (across chord) 360–398, av. 378.8; TARSUS 70–75, av. 72.9;   11 ♀: BILL 35.5–43 mm., av. 38.4; WING (across chord) 346–374, av. 365.1; TARSUS 64.2–73, av. 67.4 (H. Fried-mann).

Alaskan specimens, Def. Basic WING (flattened) 8 ♂ 382–406 mm., av. 396, and 7 ♀ 371–391, av. 378 (ETS).

Weight summer "adults" from Hooper Bay, Alaska: 6 ♂ 5 lb. 8 oz. to 6 lb. 12 oz., av. 6 lb. 2 oz. (2.8 kg.); 8 ♀ 5 lb. 2 oz. to 6 lb. 14 oz., av. 5 lb. 14 oz. (2.7 kg.) (Brandt 1943). Two ♂ shot on Dec. 1 in Cal. weighed 3 lb. 15 oz. and 4 lb. (Genelly 1955).

Five incubator-hatched goslings weighed 73.5–86.7 gm., the mean being 81.8 (Smart 1965a).

Hybrids unknown in the wild. In captivity has crossed with *Anser c. caerulescens* and *A. rossii* (details in Delacour 1954), also *A. albifrons*.

Geographical variation evidently none. RSP

FIELD IDENTIFICATION Larger than Brant. That the neck is short and thick is especially evident in flight. Wingbeats are comparatively rapid, but the Emperor is not a particularly fast flier. So far as known, generally in flocks of 10–100 individuals (commonly under 50) and the geese fly in uneven, sometimes undulating, lateral or diagonal lines, low over the water. At molting and feeding places and staging areas, flocks combine to form assemblies—to 50,000–60,000 birds at a staging area in spring in Bristol Bay. At times this goose is noisy. Identifiable at long distance by distinctive voice, a 2-syllabled far-carrying call (see below).

Except at close range, older birds appear to have an evenly darkish body, the head–neck divided longitudinally into black and white. Young, on first attaining flight and for a few weeks thereafter, appear evenly gray except for white tail. Definitive-feathered birds roughly resemble the Blue Goose morph of *Anser caerulescens*, but latter has no black on head and neck. Swimming Emperors in sunlight appear light bodied, a silvery or pearly gray, with black of neck conspicuous; when viewed against sunlight, they are dark bodied. Size, manner of flight, orange or yellow legs, and general characteristics of voice, all are somewhat reminiscent of the Whitefront.

Emperors associate with other geese in summer (with Whitefronts, Cackling Canadas, Brant) and in migration (also with Lesser Snows and smallish Canadas), but in winter tend to be more or less by themselves (because of habitat preference).

In fall, the young are distinguishable by their gray heads and necks but, as the season advances and head–neck acquire the bicolored pattern, it becomes increasingly difficult to see any remaining flecks of gray in the white area. If the birds are standing on shore, their legs and bills are seen to be less colored than older birds at this season. Even months later, in April, although very difficult, the young can be distinguished if seen in good light. They are then in Basic I head–body feathering, with dark subterminal markings on feathers less restricted and clear-cut, the pattern appearing to be less definite or orderly. Juv. wing coverts are diagnostic if they can be seen.

Ferrous staining, to a deep reddish orange, probably is most evident on ganders of breeding age. They become heavily stained at small tundra ponds, early in the nesting season, then lose some of it after larger ponds and lakes have thawed. The goose spends very little time at water in this season, hence generally is less stained than her mate (Headley 1967). RSP

173

VOICE   Not much explicit information. Authors agree that it has qualities like those of Whitefront, but is very distinct. Not a honk. A titter and *tehee* in shrill cackle (Laing 1925). Peculiar tinny quality (Harrold, in Swarth 1934). Deep, rather hoarse, strident *cla-ha cla-ha cla-ha* and, when mated breeders take flight in alarm, a ringing *u-lugh u-lugh* with peculiar deep hoarseness impossible to describe (E. W. Nelson 1887). A groaning sound by ♀ alighting beside her nest. RSP

HABITAT   In N. Am. **Nesting** and early **rearing** areas are lowland marsh–tundra, in from the coast and extending inland in vicinity of creeks, etc., to inner limits of tidal action (to 10–15 mi.), perhaps away from tidewater in interior St. Lawrence I. Evidently a preference for remaining fairly close to waters under tidal influence. Nesting and rearing terrain is flooded at times, usually after the hatching period. There are innumerable shallow, often brackish, potholes and ponds and various sizable lakes. Most nests are fairly close to water, where ground cover is matted grasses, sedges, and other herbaceous growth of the previous year.

In the Yukon–Kuskokwim delta region, in relation to the outer (Bering Sea) shoreline, geese nest in this sequence from the coast inland: 1 Brant, 2 smallest Canadas, 3 Emperors, and 4 Whitefronts. Near sheltered tidal waters this zonation is not maintained and Brant are absent.

In **migration** primarily littoral—known in Alaska as "beach goose" (Brant being "sea goose" and Canadas "land goose"). Fall migrants, in thousands, fly to uplands to feed on berries of *Vaccinium* spp. and *Empetrum*.

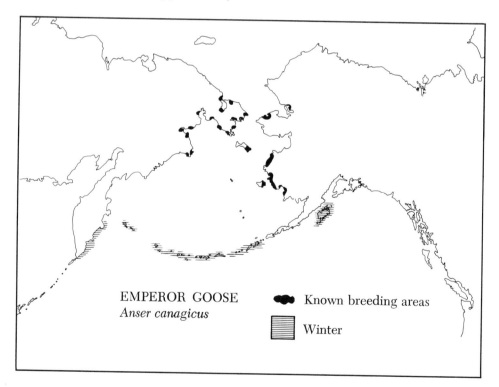

EMPEROR GOOSE
Anser canagicus

● Known breeding areas

▦ Winter

In **winter** typically along reefs, rocky beaches, cliff shores, etc., where food is washed ashore from the clear, kelp-laden waters of the Aleutians, s. side of Alaska Pen., Kodiak I., etc. (Not the glacial outwash plain topography of n. side of Alaska Pen., although this has been described as winter habitat.)

E. Asia—evidently as above, judging from available information; see especially Kistschinskii (1971).

(This section based on various sources, especially data from J. G. King.) RSP

DISTRIBUTION   (See map.) In Alaska, **nesting areas** are as follows.

Nw. side of Kotzebue Sd.—very few.

Seward Pen.—there is extensive apparently suitable habitat along the n. side, from Bering Strait to C. Espenberg. This may have been a major nesting area in the past, but probably there are less than 500 pairs now (1970). Eskimo utilization and probably trampling of nests by the introduced reindeer herds are presumed to be the causes of present low numbers.

Norton Sd. area—very few Emperors nest along the coast from Bering Strait s. to the delta of the Yukon.

St. Lawrence I.—no more than perhaps 2,000 pairs on low tundra of cent. and e. part of the island (Fay 1961). (Also many molting prebreeders are present.)

Yukon–Kuskokwim delta region—the main nesting areas discontinuous, principally from somewhere n. of Kokechik Bay and continuing southward across Baird Inlet onto n. part of Nelson Island; then from margin of s. part of Nelson I. and continuing down to n. shore of Kuskokwim Bay (where distribution is local); and s. shore of Kuskokwim Bay at Carter Spit (where possibly 100 pairs in 1963).

Nunivak I.—does not have much suitable habitat; 20 broods were seen July 26, 1964, on the s. side near C. Mendenhall (J. G. King).

Aleutians—there is a single record for Amak I. (O. Murie 1959); this is near the n. side of outer end of Alaska Pen.

NOTES   Two "adults," taken in mid-July at Barrow, where "Eskimos had never seen one before" (A. Bailey et al. 1933), do not constitute a northerly nesting record.

It is not unlikely that Eskimos and reindeer have affected Emperor nesting distribution not only on the Seward Pen., but also on St. Lawrence I., Nunivak I., and locally elsewhere.

U.S.S.R.—Spangenberg (1960) saw 3 pairs on the lower Kolyma, where local inhabitants claimed that they knew the species and that it nested in small numbers; Vorobev (1963), however, doubted that it nests on the lower Kolyma, in fact anywhere in Yakutia. Nesting concentrations are found beginning much farther eastward, at Kolyushin Bay; from there they nest locally around the Chuckchee Pen., thence sw. around Anadyr Gulf, and to C. Navarin. S. Uspenskii (1965a) mapped 17 nesting localities.

Winter   Probably ⁴/₅ of the N. Am. Emperors are scattered along the Aleutians, the bulk of the remainder in the Trinity–Kodiak–Afognak area and with very few scattered elsewhere around the edge of the Gulf of Alaska. Thus there is an essentially divided winter range in the Am. sector. In mild winters, Emperors linger along the n. side of the Alaska Pen., at localities e. as far as Port Heiden, but are forced to move when waters freeze.

Has occurred fairly regularly inland, in the Klamath Basin in Ore., and there are recent inland records in Cal.; see Wilbur and Yocom (1971) for details.

Asiatic waters—winters in Commander Is. and along the s. half of outer coast of Kamchatka.

Straggler n. beyond the Siberian mainland to Wrangel I., in Alaska n. to Barrow (record mentioned earlier), to places down the N. Am. Pacific coast into Cal. (a number of records for that state, some inland), and to the Hawaiian Is. (Hawaii 1903, Oahu 1957 and 1960, and Kauai 1967), including a flock of about a dozen storm-driven to Midway (H. I. Fisher 1970), date not given but evidently refers to 10 birds on Laysan I. and Midway and Kure Atolls between Dec. 1968 and April 1969.

No fossil record. Known from 7 **archaeologial sites** in Alaska, 6 on is. (southernmost on Kodiak) plus C. Prince of Wales; see Brodkorb (1964a) for references. RSP

MIGRATION Mainly around and also within the perimeter of Bering Sea; includes passage over some fairly wide stretches of water—across Bristol Bay, to St. Lawrence I., perhaps across Norton Sd. (if not via St. Lawrence I.) for birds that go to n. side of Seward Pen. Travels of some Emperors include the full length of the Aleutian chain, but for many the total distance they cover seasonally is much shorter.

Spring Feb.–March—in the last week of Feb., 1966, Emperors disappeared from the shores of Izembek Bay (outer end of Alaska Pen.) and, on March 7, it was discovered that practically all of the birds then present in that general area had gathered in the nw. corner of the bay (Headley 1967), presumably a staging area. Far to the westward, at the Near Is. (outermost Aleutians), in mid-March, the birds begin moving eastward along the Aleutians.

April—early in the month, there is regularly an influx of migrants at various traditional gathering places on outer end of the Alaska Pen., to about 40,000 birds at Izembek Bay and nearby bays and lagoons. After a buildup there, the geese follow the melting of ice eastward from bay to bay along the n. side of the Alaska Pen. Then, from points as far eastward as Egiak Bay, they cross Bristol Bay and are seen in Hagmeister Straits, lagoons near C. Newenham, and along beaches farther northward. Spring was exceptionally late in 1964 and, on May 28, when there was no open water in the Yukon Delta, 60,000 Emperors were in Chagvan Bay (near C. Newenham) (J. G. King). In more favorable seasons, many Emperors arrive beginning in early April on tidewater close to nesting areas of the Yukon–Kuskokwim delta region.

Late April–early May—Emperors (and great numbers of other waterfowl), in "average" seasons, congregate along ice-free shores of Kuskokwim Bay and thereabouts and await the disappearance of snow from the coastal tundra. Flocks of Emperors are scattered along shores in early morning and, as the day advances, bunches of 15–20 fly low over the land and birds drop out and alight on nesting habitat. (At this time there are many mixed gatherings of Emperors, Whitefronts, and Cackling Canada Geese.) The Emperors already have copulated and they begin nesting immediately.

Migration in Alaska continues past the time (late May) when nests in the Yukon–Kuskokwim delta area ordinarily contain full clutches.

Emperors usually arrive at St. Lawrence I. between May 20 and 29 (Fay 1961).

The above indicates the usual pattern in the Am. sector, with dates varying depend-

176

ing on locality and season. In E. Siberia, the geese are migrating in April, with arrivals in Anadyr Gulf beginning in mid-May (Dementiev and Gladkov 1952).

Summer Prebreeders accompany breeders to nesting areas; then they move (or are driven) away and many molt in gatherings in the same general vicinity. However, it was estimated (Fay 1961) that 10,000–20,000 prebreeders molt—including thousands in large assemblies—on St. Lawrence I. (where there are no more than a tenth as many breeders). Thus it appears that young Emperors (from Alaska, Siberia, or both areas?) have a **molt migration** to this island. It is possible that Emperors go to Chuckcheeland via this locality and the yearlings stop here to molt. About Aug. 10–22, when yearlings again are on the wing, they have a strong tendency to migrate northward at St. Lawrence I., both on coasts and across the interior; it is reversed toward the end of Aug. (Fay 1961).

Fall Aug.—on St. Lawrence I., flocking begins in the middle of the month and apparently about half of the birds have left before the first week in Sept. (Fay and Cade 1959). Some remain through Sept. and early Oct., probably breeders with young of the year. Eskimos say that southbound Emperors congregate in the vicinity of Southeast Cape, and some remain as late as Dec. (Fay 1961).

On Nunivak, migrants first appeared on Aug. 20 (Swarth 1934)—evidently prebreeders and/or failed breeders; after mid-Sept., parent birds with their young of the year.

In the Yukon–Kuskokwim delta area, Emperors begin leaving about mid-Aug. and few (of any cohort) are left after mid-Sept. The birds cross Bristol Bay and then proceed (with pauses) westward along the Alaska Pen. The first birds, often small groups consisting of 1 or 2 families, begin arriving in late Aug. at Port Heiden and at Izembek Bay. Many more arrive well along in Sept. Small flocks combine into gatherings of many thousands in the same bays and lagoons where they occur in spring. Thousands make daily flights to drier tundra, to feed on berries. Some flocks cross over the Alaska Pen.; Emperors begin arriving at Kodiak I. and vicinity during the latter part of Sept.

Oct.—freeze-up occurs in the Yukon Delta early in the month, also then or soon after at inner end of n. side of the Alaska Pen. Ahead of freeze-up, later migrants move sw., lingering at Port Moller, Izembek Bay, and False Pass until Nov., by which time great numbers of Emperors already are in the Aleutians. (If sheltered parts of Izembek and Cold Bay freeze, any geese present move to adjoining bays or to s. side of the Alaska Pen.) In 1972 the concentration usually present in the cent. Aleutians in mid-Nov. still had not arrived at the end of the month. The geese begin arriving in the outermost Aleutians in late Oct. and migration continues there into late Dec.

In E. Siberia, by late Sept., the geese are arriving on the outer coast of Kamchatka and in the Commander Is., but some linger late away from winter quarters.

NOTES It seems probable that various flocks cross Bristol Bay farther out in spring than in fall. More commonly in fall, there are over-water flights of a somewhat vagrant nature, probably including birds from St. Lawrence I.

There are various records for the Pribilofs.

Neff (1948) reported that an Emperor, banded on unknown date in the Uelen area (e. end of Chuckchee Pen.), was killed in Cal. on Nov. 21, 1940.

From the distribution map, it would appear about as likely that the birds on n. side of

177

the Seward Pen. are an eastern extension of those of the Chuckchee Pen. as that they are an outpost from farther s. in Alaska. It is quite possible that northerly birds from both sides winter on the Am. side around Kodiak I.

In seasons when heavy snow cover remains on nesting areas at normal time for egg-laying, such nests as are established may contain eggs of 2 or more species of geese. Mixed broods are seen occasionally. Assuming that Emperors hatched in these circumstances become imprinted on, for example, Whitefronts, then the former might migrate with the latter. Yet it is doubtful that this is the explanation of occasional occurrence of Emperors in se. Alaska and to places as far away as Cal.

(The above section is based on various sources, including information from J. G. King and R. D. Jones, Jr.). RSP

BANDING STATUS   A total of 543 were banded in Alaska through the year 1964 and there were 14 recoveries through 1961 (data from Bird Banding Laboratory). The number banded in U.S.S.R. is not reported. RSP

REPRODUCTION   Age when first breeds unknown, probably variable, with minimum of 2 years.

By mid-Feb. at Izembek Bay, families become intolerant of one another. If a bird approaches a family, an adult member (the gander?) initiates an attack, then the others join in. Such behavior is the first sign of territoriality. It is much more in evidence weeks later, after migration, when small flocks containing both breeders and pre-breeders are on waters adjacent to nesting habitat. Before flocks disband, ganders are "extremely jealous and pugnacious, never allowing one of their kind to approach within a number of yards without making an onslaught upon the intruder" (E. W. Nelson 1887). An attacker moves toward its opponent in HEAD-LOW-AND-FORWARD display, the white of head and hindneck in sharp contrast against the gander's dark body. There is no vibration of neck feathers. This plus distraction behavior are the only known displays. Presumably the breeders copulate when on waters adjacent to nesting areas, before first going ashore. Soon the birds make reconnoitering flights low over the tundra and the already mated pairs settle at nesting sites even before the ponds and lakes are free of ice.

Sometime early in the nesting cycle, probably within the laying period or soon after, aggressive activity ceases and an Emperor, a Whitefront, or a Cackling Canada Goose can pass an occupied nest without arousing a response from either member of the resident pair.

After the geese come ashore, prebreeders tend to stay somewhat apart from (or are driven away by) breeders and, in small groups, occur within the general nesting area (for an exception, see "Migration"). A. Bailey (1923) reported "it seems" that off-duty nesters band together with prebreeders to feed; this may be chiefly an activity of the gander, since the absences of the goose apparently are few and brief. It is stated (in Dementiev and Gladkov 1952) that, during incubation, breeding ganders associate in flocks away from the nests, but return when the goslings hatch and then remain with their respective mates and broods. Actually, between feeding periods (when the gander may join others and/or prebreeders and failed breeders), he occupies his guard site; this may be up to perhaps 200 yds. from the nest. If the goose is frightened from the eggs, she is soon seen accompanied by her mate.

Emperors are dispersed nesters, like Whitefronts, with nests commonly over 150 yds. apart and rarely as close as 50 ft. from each other. A preferred type of **nest site** is within 10 yds. of a pond, where grasses are predominant and grow tall and dense later in the season. Others nest varying distances from nearest water. The Emperor is not an islet nester, as is the Cackling Canada Goose. A depression is made, or a natural cavity occupied; then the goose begins laying in this bowl and covers the first eggs with grasses and moss before she departs. Late in the laying period the goose begins to add a lining, of down, some feathers, and plant debris, around the eggs. Construction continues intermittently until some time during the incubation period. The **nest down** is "uniformly pale smoky gray" with pale centers and any breast feathers that are intermingled have a banded pattern (Brandt 1943). The finished nest is nearly flush with the ground surface and, being naturally camouflaged, is difficult to see. The nest down and feathers are diagnostic; the eggs, however, may be confused with those of the Whitefront and Cackler since meas. overlap.

Laying season few specific data. Bent (1925) gave Alaskan egg dates as May 26–July 4, which is about the normal span for viable unhatched clutches. In the Yukon–Kuskokwim delta region, there are full fresh clutches in last half of May in early seasons and later in others. On n. side of Seward Pen., the geese begin laying the first of June (E. W. Nelson 1887). At Anadyr Bay (Siberia), goslings have been found on June 17 (Dementiev and Gladkov 1952), indicating clutches in 3rd week in May. In the Yukon–Kuskokwim delta, Emperors usually complete their clutches a few days earlier than Whitefronts. The earlier nesting begins, the larger the clutches—1966 data from Kolomak R. (Headley 1967); that is, as in other northerly geese, any forced delay (as by weather) in nesting results in regression in clutch size.

Clutch size av. 5 eggs in 78 clutches, 4–6 eggs being common, and 2–8 counted (Headley 1967); up to 11 eggs reported, probably combined effort of at least 2 ♀ ♀ . One **egg** each from 20 clutches from Alaska **size** length 79.11 ± 2.90 mm., breadth 53.46 ± 2.68, radii of curvature of ends 18.22 ± 1.68 and 13.97 ± 1.37; **shape** between elliptical and subelliptical, elongation 1.48 ± 0.70, bicone -0.087, asymmetry $+0.135$ (FWP). In 1969–72, some 24 mi. se. of Hooper Bay, Alaska, 313 eggs (mean and SD) length 78.8 ± 3.56 mm. (extremes 63.3–87.6) and breadth 51.8 ± 1.56 (45.2–55.0) (P. Mickelson). More slender and pointed than eggs of the Whitefront; shell not very hard or strong; it is smooth, without gloss, **color** white but soon soiled (Brandt 1943). It seems to be common for the goose not to cover her eggs before departing.

The **incubating** goose frequently can be approached to within 50 ft.; she assumes a flattened posture with outstretched neck, and so does the gander if he is close by. Then they are relatively inconspicuous. Or, on being approached, the goose may walk away, leaving the eggs uncovered, and the gander may walk away from his guard site also. If this distraction behavior fails, the gander takes flight and often passes over the nest.

Incubation period under aviary conditions 24 days (Blaauw 1916); an observation in the wild of "approximately 25 days" (Brandt 1943); 2 records of 25 days in ne. Siberia (Kistschinskii 1971). Eight nests at Kolomak R. in 1966: 24 days in 4 nests, 25 (in 1), 26

(1), and 27 (2) (Headley 1967). When the eggs are pipping, the gander stays close to his mate almost continuously; both parents tend the brood.

Hatching success (Kolomak R., 1966): 28 nests had a total of 154 eggs; 7 nests failed and in 21 nests 107 eggs hatched (about 70%); over 50% of eggs that did not hatch were destroyed by predators (probably Parasitic Jaegers mainly) and the next largest factor was dead embryos, cause unknown (Headley 1967). There are some scattered, rather inadequate, data on brood counts.

Captive **goslings** grow very rapidly (Blaauw 1916). In their first week of life in the wild (late June–early July), the young require much brooding because of nearly constant cold and rain. They are led to short-sedge habitat, along the banks of rivers and sloughs. In a few instances, when approached, an adult (believed to be the gander) ran from a brood and mate, his head low to the ground, and changed directions frequently in an attempt to decoy the observer away. According to Einarsen (1965), Emperors are noisy, a bird standing conspicuously on a river bank or hummock, raucously scolding, endlessly, or calling its young, even though they are very close by. Later in July the families move up sloughs and feed on intervening mudflats which are flooded by high tides. The goslings by now are able to climb mudbanks and travel across wetlands. By about this time they are frequently joined by birds of the prebreeder cohort, also families join together, and brood counts are no longer feasible. Glaucous Gulls now find it difficult to catch goslings, which are among so many older birds. A brood may feed on a tidal flat, the parents being as far as several hundred ft. distant and on some slight eminence where they can see over the now full-grown vegetation and watch for predators.

In Aug., when Cackling Canadas (which finish their flightless period earlier than Emperors) have gone to dry tundra to feed on berries, Emperors still are on lowlands. By mid-Aug., young Emperors require little parental care. Age at **first flight** closely estimated as 48 days (Headley 1967), the young being on the wing in latter half of Aug. Soon after they attain flight, and their parents have grown new wing feathers, families feed to some extent on dry terrain as do the Cacklers. In late Aug. and in Sept., large numbers make foraging flights from stopover places during migration along the n. side of the Alaska Pen. to uplands to feed on berries. The parents with their youngest cohort (and some probably also joined by strays and orphans) will remain an entity through fall, winter, and until the next nesting season begins.

Yearling prebreeders become detached from their parents when the latter again are nesting. In summer, some presumed prebreeders are seen in pairs; that is, some yearlings may form at least temporary pair bonds. The yearlings molt earlier than breeders accompanied by young of the year; before the end of their 2nd winter, probably most of them have formed permanent (lifelong) pair bonds.

(This section is based on various sources, but especially Headley 1967.) RSP

SURVIVAL   No useful information.

HABITS   Gregarious, at times also social, the flocks intermingling with other geese.

Around the seasons   In summer, in nesting and early rearing period, primarily grazers, on *Carex* (principally), *Elymus*, etc. In late summer, the same plus green al-

180

gae. Somewhat later, they begin to feed on berries as well as marine vegetation. In Sept., for example, they go to uplands near Izembek Bay and their fecal deposits are of crowberry (*Empetrum*). In some localities they eat berries of *Vaccinium vitis-idea* and *V. uliginosa*. Swarth (1934) noted that, on Nunivak, they fed on berries and a gander had face, throat, and intestinal tract dyed blue from eating them. They seem responsive to the cycle of the tides in all seasons, more obviously outside the nesting–rearing season. They feed among rocks and kelp beds at low tide and, after storms, flocks gather to feed among heaps of kelp washed ashore (Kenyon 1961). Also see O. Murie (1959) for habits in the Aleutians. The birds there sometimes appear to be grubbers, rather than grazers, when seeking preferred items on tidal flats. On Adak they have been seen ashore, on snow-free grassy areas, and probably were grazing. They also feed while afloat; an important winter food is eelgrass (*Zostera*), with sea lettuce (*Ulva*) of lesser importance.

Kenyon (1961) suggested that the **total population** of Emperors may be of the order of 200,000. In the U.S.S.R. their numbers were declining steadily (Dementiev and Gladkov 1952), to only a few thousand by the early 1960s, with no hunting then allowed.

Predation   Jaegers, especially the Parasitic, eat eggs of the Emperor Goose and tear up the nests. Many jaegers, not yet of breeding age, spend the summer in areas where Emperors are nesting and are hunting constantly. An Emperor will spread its wings and jump at, or even fly after, a jaeger. If the latter hunt in pairs, while one is distracting the goose the other gets some eggs (Headley 1967). The Glaucous Gull can be a severe predator on small goslings, if they become separated from the parent geese or are unable to climb mudbanks. Some goslings fall into holes and cannot get out. Foxes (red, arctic) and the mink, when numerous, probably take a heavy toll in the nesting season.

In former times at nesting–molting areas in Alaska large numbers of preflight and of older molting birds were taken by Eskimos for food. Some of the skins were manufactured into clothing. There was still (late 1960s) some local native utilization of Emperors. Near villages, eggs were collected, especially from Scammon Bay down to Kwinhagak. There still are a few summer "drives" of flightless geese, including the Emperor, at a very few localities. But the total take of eggs and birds probably is not detrimental to the overall population. For many further details, see Klein (1966).

The Emperor now is getting considerable sport-hunting pressure. It is more vulnerable to both human and nonhuman predation than either Canada Goose or Brant, being much less wary. At Izembek Lagoon, Bald Eagles have been seen to take them in flight, apparently without difficulty; foxes stalk them through the dense grasses bordering beaches. And it is the most frequent goose in hunters' bags, despite the presence of both Brant and Canadas. The Emperors fly low, in small flocks, around the perimeter of the lagoon, paying little attention to what is going on, and coming within easy gun range. (Data from R. D. Jones, Jr.)

A disagreeable odor of both skin and flesh has been attributed to a diet of marine animals, but is caused instead by sea lettuce, a marine alga. When they have been eating this, they are not particularly desirable birds; young of the year, which have been feeding on eelgrass and berries, however, are excellent birds for the table. RSP

FOOD   Formerly, supposed to feed largely on *Mytilus edulis* and other shellfish; now known to be almost entirely a **vegetarian.** Various food items and their seasonal usage have been mentioned in preceding sections. The Emperor's diet is largely marine plants, with a small amount of animal matter, some of it probably ingested accidentally when eating plant materials. Grasses, sedges, and berries, in season. Thirty-three stomachs, representing mainly spring and early summer seasons, examined in the Biological Survey, showed 91.58% vegetable and 8.42% animal food (Cottam and Knappen 1939).

Vegetable   Algae (Chlorophyceae mainly, Phaeophyceae a trace) 30.73%, pondweed (*Potamogeton pectinatus*) 1.52%, eelgrass (*Zostera marina*) 12.36%, Gramineae and Cyperaceae 24.94%, miscellaneous plants 0.48%, and undetermined plant fibers 21.55%. Sea lettuce (Ulvaceae) comprised the sole food of 5 stomachs from the Pribilof Is. (Preble and McAtee 1923). In Cal., eelgrass (Talmadge 1947), and birds seen picking at tubes and heads of slimy kelp (L. Williams 1946). Also heath berries (*Vaccinium* spp.) and crowberry (*Empetrum nigrum*) (various authors). In the Aleutians, green shoots of *Elymus* and rhizomes of *Equisetum* have been reported (O. Murie 1959).

Animal   Mollusks (*Siliqua* and *Mytilus edulis*) 3.66% crustaceans (*Telemesus cheiragonus*) 2.81%; miscellaneous vertebrates, Cottidae, *Lemmus*, and Microtinae 1.76%. AWS

Canada Goose

Branta canadensis

Head and neck black with large white area on cheeks, usually continuous across chin, but sometimes partly or entirely interrupted by a black chin stripe; body coloration gray-brown to variably brown, the light feather borders arranged to form bars on dorsum in all Basic Plumages. Neck feathering smooth (not furrowed); white "crescent" on lower rump; usually all white from vent to tail and extending up on flanks; tail blackish. Iris dark brownish; bill, legs, and feet black. Overall coloring varies, depending on population and individual, from medium or lighter to a very dark shade. Size varies from largest of true geese (length 34–43 in., rarely longer; wingspread to 6 ft., rarely longer; wt. rarely to over 20 lbs.) through intermediate sizes down to smallest (length 23–25 in., wingspread to 43, wt. of mature ♀ occasionally only 2 lb.). For discussion of tracheal anatomy, see Humphrey (1958a) and Würdinger (1970). Sexes similar or nearly so in appearance (♂ said to av. more uniformly colored and with paler underparts in some of the largest Canadas); ♂ av. larger. The species is treated below under 8 trinomials, 4 less than in Delacour (1951, 1954).

DESCRIPTION *B. c. canadensis*—the large and rather light-colored Atlantic birds. One Plumage/cycle. Basic II may be regarded as earliest definitive, there evidently being no subsequent change in feather shape.

▶ ♂ ♀ Def. Basic Plumage (entire feathering) SUMMER to SUMMER or into fall. **Head** cheek to cheek white, seldom interrupted in this subspecies by a black chin stripe; blackish tipping on some of the white cheek feathers (finely speckled effect) occurs occasionally (but is normal in Juv. Plumage); blackish of neck ends abruptly at base. **Upperparts** mantle rather variable, generally medium gray-brown; the individual feathers darken distally and then terminate with a sharply defined, comparatively narrow, whitish margin; such margins, which are so arranged as to give a decidedly barred effect, are conspicuous in new feathering but are less evident later. Pale coloration, nearly white, of upper breast continues (usually rather narrowly) across mantle up against base of black neck, a characteristic of this subspecies only. Rump to tail very dark, interrupted by a very conspicuous white crescent. **Underparts** breast generally pale brownish gray, the feathers with white ends (upper breast appears white); sides and belly light to medium grayish brown, the very pale feather ends giving barred effect. Legs and **feet** black. **Tail** black. **Wing** primaries and secondaries blackish brown, upper coverts much like back, axillars and under wing coverts medium grayish (individual variation includes some white intermingled, particularly along leading edge of wing).

The Definitive Prebasic molt is better reported for other subspecies than nominate *canadensis*, but all Canadas apparently are similar, except the smaller the bird the shorter the duration of molting. Following is a composite account.

Flight feathers of wing and greater primary coverts are dropped simultaneously after onset of body molt. The molting includes entire feathering except that, 6–7 weeks earlier, breeding ♀ ♀ preen the loosened feathers and down from their bellies to line their nests and the new growth there, present soon after normal incubation ends (included

183

area variable in size, feathers less pigmented, paler) is retained; these details are for *B. c. interior*, in H. C. Hanson (1959). The wing quills are dropped some time in the rearing period, generally earlier (up to a week) by the ♀ than her mate. Duration of flightlessness in a large Canada (*B. c. interior*) is estimated at 32 days (H. C. Hanson 1965) and in the largest birds at 39–40 days (Balham 1954, H. C. Hanson 1965). By the time the new quills are about half their ultimate length and growing rapidly, the entire remainder of the bird (except as just stated for the ♀) is in massive molt of both feathers and down. The tail goes into molt about then, but occasionally its timing is slowed or interrupted (full new tail not until into winter). Occasionally some upper wing coverts are the very last feathers to be molted.

The molt comes earliest (by at least a month in large Canadas) in prebreeders, the timing being virtually independent of seasonal phenology. Failed breeders, although not as early as prebreeders, precede successful breeders. Flightlessness is of shorter duration in prebreeders. Adults are capable of flight when the new primaries are about $5/6$ their ultimate length, but normally will not fly at this stage unless severely disturbed. The time when the parent birds again can fly and the time their brood first attains flight tend to coincide, being (usually) slightly earlier in the former.

AT HATCHING in nominate *canadensis* **bill** slaty, **iris** dark; **head** and neck vivid yellow, except large olive brownish crown patch that continues as line down nape, also an indistinct darkish area through eyes. **Upperparts** medium olive brownish. **Underparts** breast and upper belly yellow, paling to grayed yellowish abdomen and grayish olive beyond vent. Legs and **feet** muted greenish olive. **Wing** upper surface dark olive brownish with yellow trailing edge. As goslings grow, the down fades and is intermingled with incoming true body down, the result, especially after further bleaching, being a "soiled" grayish appearance.

▶ Juv. Plumage (entire feathering; worn briefly, then most of it replaced quite rapidly, the tail late in molt, and much of wing retained into following summer). This Plumage covers the gosling by age 5–6 weeks, but is not fully developed at least until flight is attained, probably at approximately 8 weeks, as estimated for *interior* by H. C. Hanson (1965).

Compared with Def. Basic: coloring more blended, somewhat darker general appearance than in later Plumages, and there are fewer feathers. Dark of **head**–neck near-black and without sheen, the white cheek areas generally tinged brownish, or frequently speckled finely, more on chin, with blackish brown (dark tips to the light feathers). Up against the base of the blackish neck the feathers usually are light all around, i.e., dark coloring is interrupted between hindneck and anterior mantle.

Upperparts feathers smaller, narrower, with rounded (not squarish) ends, and more drab brownish in coloring with less well defined and less contrasty lighter ends that are widest in this Plumage. Part of lower rump whitish, the feathers terminally washed or marked with brownish. **Underparts** breast and much of belly consistently paler, with somewhat mottled effect (rather than barring); the feathers are not much more than half as wide as those of Def. Basic and are softer. Ventral coloration blends into white of rear abdomen and under tail coverts (not a sharp demarcation as in all succeeding Plumages). Sides and flanks appear somewhat mottled. Legs and **feet** black. **Tail** feathers without sheen, somewhat brownish (not black), comparatively narrow, and with notched tips (where the precursor down broke off). **Wing** flight feathers shorter, narrower, blackish brown. Plumage acquired by Juv. feathers pushing out natal (first) down.

In the very large *B. c. moffitti*, development of pen-reared birds through their first 60 days (downy plus Juv.) was described and illus. by Yocom and Harris (1965). These Canadas have been reported to attain flight in the wild at ages from 7 to 9 weeks and in captives at a full 9 weeks. Wild *B. c. interior* fly at 9 weeks (H. C. Hanson 1965), penned captives when a few days older. There are no accurate data on nominate *canadensis,* but probably young in the wild are capable of flight at approximately the same age as *B. c. interior*.

▶ Basic I Plumage (entire feathering, except flight feathers of wing and greater primary coverts), gradually replaces Juv. through FALL (largely acquired by Oct., often much earlier). Besides replacing Juv. feathers, there is activation of additional follicles so that there are more feathers. The Basic I feathers, as most readils noted on breast, are intermediate in width and shape between those of Juv. and Def. Basic. Coloring as in latter. A gradual molt of tail, beginning (usually) with outer feather; some individuals have complete Basic I tail some time in fall (at age 5 mo.) or early winter, a few drop no Juv. feathers until toward spring and then lose them quite rapidly, and possibly a few retain some or all Juv. tail feathers until the next (Prebasic II) molt in SUMMER. So long as any Juv. tail feathers with their notched tips are retained, they are sufficient to identify the bird as under a year old.

Criteria of different ages through to sexual maturity, in addition to those of feathering and of timing of molt given above, include: decrease in size (to closing) of bursa of Fabricius (see especially Higgins 1969), changes in coloring and surface configuration of cloaca, changes in penis and clitoris, opening of oviduct, and development of knobby "bump" in ♂ ♂, from fighting, near bend of wing. For details and illus. of these in *B. c. interior,* also references to earlier studies, see H. C. Hanson (1962b).

Measurements, including those of nominate *canadensis,* are given beyond under each subspecies here recognized.

Weight see "Subspecies." The Canada Goose has the wt. cycle of a waterfowl whose migrations are done piecemeal, i.e., leisurely—the geese still are fat on arrival on breeding grounds (where there is little food early in the season), and thus are prepared for the ensuing lean period. The cycle: maximum wt. during spring migration, then a decline from approximately the time of nest construction to end of incubation (minumum wt. then), afterward a gain during molting and through fall (nearly to spring peak), then a fairly high level in winter if food is adequate. Young birds may lose some wt. during their first fall migration. The cycle is not merely fatness vs. leanness; see H. C. Hanson (1962a).

Hybrids are rather rare in the wild. The most frequent appear to be crosses between *B. c. hutchinsii* and both color phases of *Anser caerulescens* (H. K. Nelson 1952, Prevett and MacInnes 1973). Each "dumps" eggs in the other's nests and the resulting young may become imprinted to the other species. The Canada has crossed with the Brant (*Branta bernicla nigricans*) (Ransom 1927) and the Whitefront (*Anser albifrons*) (S. F. Baird 1873), "possibly" with the Whitefront (Kuroda 1953), and suspected with Whitefront (Eckert 1970). A bird seen in Pa. in 3 consecutive winters was suspected of being a cross of *B. canadensis* with either "domestic goose" (*Anser anser* derivative) or the Pinkfoot (*Anser fabalis brachyrhynchus*) (Lech 1968). Captive-produced crosses may escape to the wild. Bailey and Niedrach (1965) mentioned a captive ♂ Lesser Snow and ♀ Canada which produced 7 free-flying young. Published reports of captive Canadas crossing with domestic geese date back at least to Howley (1884).

Two presumed hybrids with *Anser anser* were seen wintering in Sweden (Nord and Bolund 1964); the 2 species now share certain nesting areas there.

Gray (1958) listed various swans and geese, also the Muscovy Duck, with which the Canada has crossed or reportedly crossed in captivity.

In N. Am., "Crested Canada Goose" is a true-breeding strain whose origins evidently include both domestic Greylags (*Anser anser*) and Canadas.

Geographical variation   This topic, at least in its broader aspects, can be elucidated somewhat by hindsight and guesswork—an attempt to reconstruct the later evolutionary history of the species. Rand (1948a) was the first to suggest this approach.

The Brant and Canada Goose appear to have had a common origin; then the former evolved in the Palearctic, the latter in the Nearctic (Johansen 1956). At the time of the last glacial maximum, *canadensis* stock was divided. **1** East of the ice, in cool maritime habitat somewhere on the Atlantic coastal area. **2** South of the ice, within the continent, from the e. side of the Rockies eastward toward the Atlantic seaboard. **3** West of the ice, on the Pacific coast. **4** An early derivative, probably of the same stock as the Atlantic birds, occupied (when breeding) an area somewhere in the Canadian arctic, perhaps beyond the mainland (and possibly shared with part of ancestral *Anser caerulescens*). The last-mentioned Canadas probably had a more easterly migration route than present-day *hutchinsii;* there are 3 separate finds of *hutchinsii*-sized bones from the Pleistocene of Fla. **5** An earlier derivative of the same stock as the Pacific birds occupied (as breeders) unglaciated terrain in the Bering Sea region.

It is of much interest that, aside from the Aleutian–Bering birds, most of the geese now nest on terrain that was under ice at the time of the last glacial maximum.

The geese have been "liberal" in size evolution and "conservative" as regards coloring. The groups, as numbered above, evolved into (1 and 4) gray, pale-breasted birds, (2) toward gray-brown, and (3 and 5) variably to very dark. In this schematic arrangement the smallest dark and the smallest light birds are, within the species, not closely related (contra. Ploeger 1968 and all other previous authors). The diminutive easterly geese are a relatively old entity that shows greatly diminished individual size in response to a short boreal summer season. The milder inland environment of the intervening mainland presently is occupied by a smallish goose (*parvipes*) that may be a later derivative of the same stock that was s. of the ice and within the continent. It appears to have become modified (peripherally), as will be mentioned later.

Using the same numbering as earlier, events during and after the "retreat" of glacial ice have been as follows:

1   The Atlantic birds, still maritime, have shifted northward and now breed from Nfld. to n. Labrador.

2   South of glacial limits (a) easterly birds shifted northward into muskeg country, a few even beyond onto tundra. Their northward advance was split by James and Hudson Bays; both moieties now show clinal variation to smaller individuals at their present extremes—westerly ones in and near nw. Man., easterly ones on s. Baffin I. (b) From nearer midcontinent, part of the birds moved n. with the "retreating" ice, evidently via the corridor that opened in the Mackenzie valley region. Those that remained farthest southerly have become comparatively sedentary and presently are the largest of all true geese; to the north and northwest the geese show a clinal decrease in size and are progressively more migratory, "leapfrogging" southward over the others.

Within the continent, the evidence from pollen studies and other sources indicate that there was, in late glacial times, repeated oscillation from grassland to forest, presumably allowing the geese to colonize large areas during a favorable episode, only to be severely restricted by a succeeding, unfavorable one. There was rapid evolution in size of the birds and the stocks became fragmented. At the present time, for example, the nesting geese of the Great Basin av. slightly smaller than prairie nesters, perhaps in response to altitude (shorter season?) or somehow as a consequence of their present terrain having become ice free at a later time.

3   The dark birds of the Pacific coast, which have remained more or less maritime in habitat preference, shifted northward and presently are strung out (clinally smaller northward), hemmed in as breeders between montane forest and the sea. The northerly ones have a "leapfrog" migration over the southerly ones. These dark geese (*occidentalis*) are roughly the equivalent, in size and ecological niche, of the pale Atlantic birds (nominate *canadensis*).

4   Whether the birds of the lower Yukon drainage and those of the Aleutians have had long parallel histories, or whether one is more recently derived from the other, is pure speculation. They are closely related. In postglacial time the mainland birds presumably have shifted to the present low coastal tundra; the island birds may have had more terrain made available by the postglacial warming of the climate.

5   The small pale birds of the Canadian arctic shifted southward, now being preponderantly mainland dwellers, but with island outposts from s. Victoria I. around to include Southampton, Coats, and sw. Baffin I.; their colonization of cent. w. Greenland presumably is very recent.

In line with a multiple-stock hypothesis, there are situations where 2 stocks, or a derivative of each, have established geographical contact, or a zone of overlap, and not merely on summer range. Examples: (1) ancestral *parvipes* and *minima* stocks, as breeders and/or in other seasons, interbreeding to produce the so-called "*taverneri*" of n. interior Alaska; (2) *parvipes* and *minima* at the present time, locally in the Yukon–Kuskokwim delta region, i.e., on breeding range where they maintain separate identities; (3) *parvipes* of the interior and *hutchinsii* of the mainland perimeter in Canada, a continuing contact and in various seasons, resulting in a spectrum of individuals that grade imperceptibly from one "pure" stock to the other; (4) close to the w. coast of Hudson Bay at about lat. 60° N, northerly *interior* and southerly (atypical) *hutchinsii*, keeping separate identities; on sw. Baffin I., *hutchinsii* and *interior*, the latter probably having arrived more recently, and keeping separate identities. This list could be expanded greatly by adding contacts that occur outside the nesting season.

This migratory goose conforms to Bergmann's rule in winter. That is, the birds sort out more or less in reverse of summer distribution—largest Canadas inhabit the coldest part of winter range, and are limited northward to places where winters are long but "open," and small birds go to warm and/or more southerly localities. The geese now wintering farthest n. in Europe are very large Canadas, not native species which are birds of lesser size.

If a large Canada, such as nominate *canadensis*, may be regarded as having the norm in general proportions, then the largest ones are elongated (body long narrow oval, neck attenuated) and at least some of the small (down to the smallest) Canadas are foreshortened (body toward elliptical in lateral profile, short neck, beak stubby in proportion to its height at base). Some other characteristics, such as relative length of wings, legs, and details of bill, vary within limits from this general trend, i.e., there are rather long-legged and also decidedly long-winged small birds. (Also note variation under "Voice.")

Occurrence of a black stripe through the white on chin is much more frequent northwesterly, especially in darker-pigmented birds, and evidently in ♂ ♂. A white collar at base of black neck is more frequent and widest in some northwesterly populations. Both of these characteristics occur in birds of various sizes.

Color of downy young so far as known has a certain relationship to color of parents. Offspring of lighter Canadas have much yellow on head, neck, and underparts, with more or less olive on upperparts; in the dark Canadas the yellow is reduced and grayed, the dorsal coloring dark and muted. All have a round dark cap and entirely black bill. Legs and feet are light-colored in the yellow downies and dark in the dark downies.

(Dark speckling on white of cheeks not limited to predefinitive Plumages, white spots and patches in black of head–neck, presence of white feathers in wing lining common in definitive feathering, at least in some populations, and differences in number of tail feathers, are individual variation.)

Aberrant coloring occurs regularly but in low frequency, as noted mainly in nominate *canadensis* and in *B. c. interior*. Most common is a bird whose body is pale cream, with black of head–neck replaced by pale khaki. All-white birds also are reported; these are not albinos, since the bill, legs, and eyes are apparently of normal color. Both of the above tend to occur in all members of a family. Additional variant individuals have irregular white patches on the head and neck; in extreme examples the black may be entirely replaced by white, with body of normal color. RSP

SUBSPECIES   Despite more than 60 years of sometimes acrimonious debate, the allocation of Canada Geese to subspecies has remained both logically and heuristically unsatisfactory. In morphometric studies calipers are handy, but small size differences in such large and variable birds should not be overemphasized. Many Canadas nest in remote areas and specimens from regions of critical interest are few or lacking. There is a wealth of banding information from wintering flocks, but a scarcity from various nesting areas. In addition, there has been local extinction after Caucasian settlement, the escape of captive birds, and deliberate introduction and transplanting of stocks of questionable origin; such factors have forever obscured whatever pattern of breeding distribution formerly existed. As to the geese in other seasons, refuges, hunting, and changes in land use have altered migrations and wintering traditions, in the process affecting former continuities and discontinuities of distribution.

Cackling
(*minima*)

Richardson's
(*hutchinsii*)

Aleutian
(*leucopareia*)

Dusky
(*occidentalis*)

Lesser
(*parvipes*)

Interior
(*interior*)

Giant
(*moffitti*)

Atlantic
(nom. *canadensis*)

R. M. Mengel

NOTE that "subspecies" (singular) and "population" (unqualified) are synonymous here. In much of the wildlife literature, "population" (when unqualified) refers to whatever birds are being discussed—an entire subspecies, a major subdivision thereof, a local breeding unit, or birds occurring at a particular migration stopover locality, wintering area, etc. "Flock" also has been used in more than one sense, including for some entities just listed; the present writers tend to restrict this, in waterfowl, to (a) the birds at or from a single breeding locality and (b) an assembly, usually small, of individuals.

For obvious practical reasons, this goose is studied afield by subpopulation (portion of a subspecies) or smaller unit, down to single-flock size; it is not studied by subspecies except when all the birds included therein occur (at least at some season) in an area small enough to investigate. Each subpopulation or smaller unit has some degree of uniqueness of life history and/or morphology of its individuals. Furthermore, many of the geese are "managed" by unit—i.e., hunting kill is regulated, refuges are provided, etc.—because such units have their particular schedules and places of seasonal occurrence. In short, they are "management units," spatially discrete in some places and seasons, often joined in others.

Various subpopulations and smaller units, when studied, tend to acquire vernacular names of their own; the question of subspecies is avoided, except that in published studies trinomials commonly are inserted, more or less as artifacts supposedly required by convention. Some examples of unit names: Tule–Lower Klamath birds (breeding area, very large birds, fragment of *moffitti*), South Atlantic birds (winter range as defined in 1950, large geese, subpopulation of *interior*), Wilson Hill flock (breeding locality in N.Y., large to very large birds which behave for the most part as a single flock—*interior* and *moffitti* intermixed). Certain other useful naming is not explicit in terms of units; example: tallgrass prairie birds (for migration route, or "corridor" of Bellrose 1968, of smallish to very small geese—part each of *parvipes* and *hutchinsii* plus intergrading individuals).

The present authors recognize 8 subspecies. An alternative to such treatment would be to "split" major populations of *B. canadensis* by elevating subpopulations or smaller units to subspecific rank. The latter course gives undue emphasis to comparatively small averages of biological uniqueness, greatly increases the number of individual birds that are difficult or impossible to assign to a trinomial, and progressively increases the arbitrariness of just where to draw a line between naming and not naming. The last could be the most serious in the present context, since it raises similar problems in certain other geese and ducks.

canadensis (Linnaeus)—Atlantic Canada Goose. Described in detail at beginning of this account. Diagnostic character: whitish of anterior breast extends upward and usually continues at least narrowly across very forefront of dorsum adjoining base of black neck. It is sometimes more evident in live birds than in museum skins and it is not the white basal collar mentioned under some other subspecies. Juv. birds, because their coloring is more blended or "clouded," appear slightly darker than definitive-feathered ones, but the light encirclement of anterior end of body is indicated.

Measurements of "adults;" 7 ♂ : BILL 53–58 mm., av. 56; WING (across chord) 444–485, av. 466.3; TAIL 131–149; av. 143; TARSUS 88–95, av. 90.8; 7 ♀ : BILL 51.5–56.5

mm.; av. 53.9; WING (across chord) 435–488; av. 465; TAIL 134–158; av. 147.3; TARSUS 81–88.5; av. 85.9 (Aldrich 1946).

"Wings [flattened] of specimens examined: 465–495 mm. (males), and 455–465 (females); culmens 53–59 and 51–54 respectively" (Hellmayr and Conover 1948).

Weight few dependable data; ♂ about 7–10 lb. (occasionally to 13), ♀6–8 (occasionally to 10); young in first fall probably seldom over 7 lb.

Breeds principally in interior Ungava, where widespread and most numerous on the lake plateau and thinning out toward Ungava Bay; breeds eastward to the Labrador coast and adjacent is.; breeds s. in Que. to Anticosti I. Widespread in interior Nfld.— now perhaps 6,000 breeding pairs. Presumably this subspecies was the one that, in colonial times, bred (in small numbers?) in the Maritimes and parts of New Eng., and within recent decades in Me. Very recent records for these areas relate possibly to

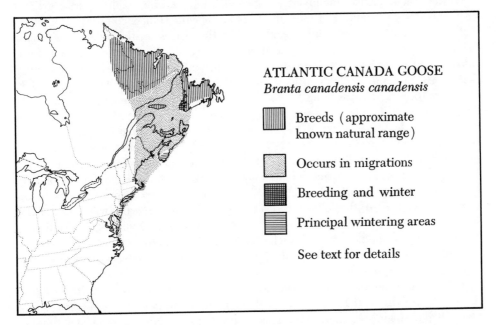

ATLANTIC CANADA GOOSE
Branta canadensis canadensis

Breeds (approximate known natural range)

Occurs in migrations

Breeding and winter

Principal wintering areas

See text for details

crippled birds and escaped pen-reared stock plus restocked birds, at least in Me., Vt., and Mass., some restocked birds being nominate *canadensis* and others *B. c. interior* (see Donovan 1971).

Nesting in Nfld. may have begun with escaped captive stock, presumably augmented by other pairs from the wild. Todd (1963) referred to them as "ultra-typical" in Plumage characters. Most of them nest at present on the interior "barrens" on islets and beaver houses in shallow ponds, also ashore near watercourses. The soil and waters are acid and poor in nutrients.

Migrations In fall large numbers of the northerly (Ungava) birds come down along the Labrador coast. Part of the Nfld. birds remain on sheltered waters on the sw. coast; the others, about 25,000, move on. South of Nfld., as the geese move down the Atlantic coast, overwintering assemblies remain at these places: N.S. (in several counties),

191

N.H. (coastal waters), Mass. (Plymouth Bay and Monomoy I.), N.Y. (e. Long I.), N.J. (Brigantine Refuge and vicinity), and N.C. (Pea I. and vicinity). In spring the birds move up the coast. At least at this season, Merrymeeting Bay, Me., is an important stopover place; from there they go northward overland, evidently stop on the N. Shore of the Gulf of St. Lawrence, then continue on to interior Ungava.

Molt migration By some time in June and in July there are flightless birds (undoubtedly prebreeders) on interior lakes in Nfld. and widely scattered in interior Ungava and eastward to coastal waters. At least 10,000 are concentrated inland from the outer coast of Labrador near Rigolet, in The Backwater and the Double Mer; others are concentrated farther northward, near Nain. Presumably all of these are nominate *canadensis*, molting within or not distant from the breeding range of this subspecies. (The birds that have a molt migration to nw. Ungava are *B. c. interior*.)

Winter range Nfld., mainly at Stephenville and Codroy, total to perhaps 2,500 birds; in N.S. at localities in Queens, Shelburne, and Halifax counties, plus other localities in mild winters (Tufts 1962); and at the places on the Atlantic seaboard beyond into N.C. that were listed earlier under "Migrations." Winters occasionally s. into Ga. and a very few inland sometimes in e. part of Fla. panhandle or on the nearby Gulf Coast. Probably ¾ of the entire population (which is much smaller than that of *B. c. interior*) occurs in winter from N.J. into N.C. Thus the winter range somewhat overlaps that of *B. c. interior*, but nominate *canadensis* favors tidewater localities.

Straggler (this subspecies?) to Bermuda, probably to peninsular Fla., the Dry Tortugas and Cuba—specimens Dec. 11, 1966 and April 7, 1972; another W. Indian record is unsatisfactory (J. Bond 1967 and 1973). There are a few inland occurrences in e. U.S. to as far w. as Mich. of individuals showing whitish anterior encirclement of body typical of nominate *canadensis* (but variant individuals of *interior* approach this condition). Occurrences in the following places have been listed (arbitrarily?) under the nominate subspecies by various authors: Norway, Faeroes, Denmark, Holland, and France. It is most unlikely that all such occurrences pertain to nominate *canadensis*.

Captive geese on the e. end of Long I., N.Y., descendants of decoy stock, are fairly typical nominate *canadensis*.

Although **introductions** abroad commonly have been referred to nominate *canadensis*, it is now evident that they are mostly *moffitti*, some perhaps being *interior*. In Great Britain (England mainly) the species has been introduced at various times— known presence dating from 1678—and established as **feral** breeders. (It is possible also that, rarely, vagrants have occurred naturally.) Although it seems probable that early introductions may have been of nominate *canadensis*, the present birds resemble large prairie geese and so are discussed beyond under *moffitti*.

hutchinsii (Richardson)—Richardson's Canada Goose. May be an early derivative of the same ancestral stock as the pale Atlantic birds (nominate *canadensis*). They are very small in size and rather light-colored, with pale breast; the bill appears stubby (for example, when compared with "typical" *parvipes*); white of cheeks usually continuous across chin; seldom even a hint of a white collar at base of black neck. Downies from Southampton I. are buffy yellowish; the olive brownish area on hind part of crown is large and well defined (Todd 1963); the buffy yellow shows well on a plate in Sutton (1932). Extent of individual variation in downies unknown.

Measurements Southampton I. "adult" ♂ BILL (of 127) 32.3–43.8 mm., mean 37.4; WING (of 21) 363–412, mean 391; TARSUS (of 127) 65.8–80.2, mean 74.2; ♀ BILL (of 115) 31.7–39.3 mm., mean 35.6; WING (of 24) 349–392, mean 371; TARSUS (of 115) 60.7–76.8, mean 69.8 (MacInnes 1966). These meas. were taken from living birds and MacInnes indicated he sometimes was not sure within 2–3 mm. of where to begin measuring the bill. W. E. Godfrey measured 47 Southampton breeding geese (included 41 taken by MacInnes): BILL 20 ♂ 32–39.5 mm., av. 35.8, and 27 ♀ 31–37.5, av. 33.9 mm. These are in close agreement with meas. of 10 ♂ and 8 ♀ also from Southampton, reported by Sutton (1932).

For meas. of 24 summer specimens from Adelaide Pen., see Macpherson and Manning (1959).

Down the w. coast of Hudson Bay the geese show an increase in size, the larger birds at McConnell R. (lat. 60°50′ N) being, in this respect, a fair match for many that are included in the present treatise in *parvipes*—"adult" ♂: BILL (of 102) 33.7–47 mm., mean 40.4; WING (of 18) 361–435, mean 407; TARSUS (of 102) 65–84, mean 75.3; ♀: BILL (of 90) 33–45.1 mm., mean 38.5; WING (of 12) 373–416, mean 389; TARSUS (of 90) 62.4–78.1, mean 70.3 (MacInnes 1966). (Note comment above on bill meas. by MacInnes.)

Weight in summer of Southampton birds: 9 ♂ 3 lb. 12 oz. to 5 lb. 10 oz., av. 4 lb. 12

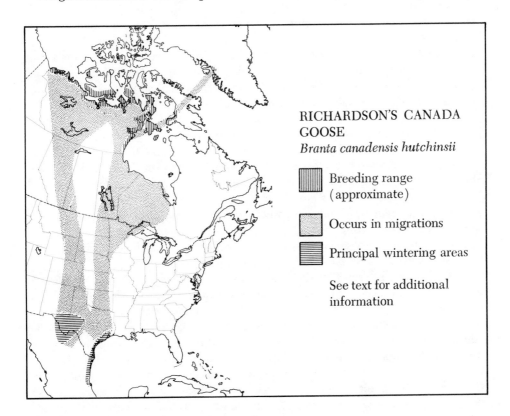

RICHARDSON'S CANADA GOOSE
Branta canadensis hutchinsii

Breeding range
(approximate)

Occurs in migrations

Principal wintering areas

See text for additional information

193

oz. (about 2,150 gm.); 6 ♀ 3 lb. 9 oz. to 5 lb. 1 oz., av. 4 lb. 2 oz. (about 1,870 gm.) (Sutton 1932). From Adelaide Pen.: 6 ♂ 2.1–2.7 kg., av. 2.4 (about 5⅓ lb.); 10 ♀ 1.6–2.5 kg., av. 2 (about 4 ²/5 lb.) (Macpherson and Manning 1959). Usual winter wt. of breeders probably is about: ♂ 4½ lb., ♀ 4 lb.

The larger McConnell R. birds, when lean in summer: 9 mated pairs ♂ 2.1–2.61 kg., av. 2.41 (about 5⅓ lb.), ♀ 1.64–2.15 kg., av. 1.84 (4 lb.) (MacInnes 1966).

Breeds on nw. and throughout sw. part of Victoria I., on Jenny Lind I., King William I., n. Adelaide Pen., Melville Pen., on w. side of Hudson Bay locally down to lat. 60°50′ N, Southampton I., coast of sw. Baffin I., and (regularly?) in Jakobshavn Dist. of cent.-w. Greenland. (Birds at a few other localities also may be *hutchinsii*.)

Migration spring and fall, over prairie routes (as mapped), sharing these with interior-migrating subpopulations of *parvipes*.

Molt migration little useful information. MacInnes (1962) noted that most prebreeders at McConnell R. (se. Keewatin) went elsewhere (destination unknown) to molt; others remained nearby in company with prebreeding Blue Geese. On Adelaide Pen., some prebreeders and presumed failed breeders remained there through the summer (Macpherson and Manning 1959). Perhaps known occurrences n. of breeding range (Banks I., Bylot I., Umanak Dist. in Greenland) pertain to birds that went to these places to molt.

Winter *hutchinsii* and some *parvipes* apparently are more or less together (compare maps); the former, however, tend to go farther southward so that many occur in Mexico.

Stragglers only to points distant from usual range are mentioned here, the listing undoubtedly being incomplete. Northward—see above under "Molt migration"; eastward—to Atlantic coast, at least Me. (Gross 1947, with photo), Pa., Md., and N.C. (see J. Bond 1951 for certain specimens); southward—to St. Mark's Refuge in Fla. (reported as *parvipes*), and in Mexico s. of Chihuahua and in Durango in the interior and Jalisco on w. coast; westward—as reported by Aldrich (1946), an "immature" each from Solomon (Alaska), Klamath Falls (Ore.), and Washoe L. (Nev.).

There are various other reports and occurrences of "probables." For example, Sheppard (1951) reported a flock of 23, either *parvipes* or *hutchinsii*, seen March 16–17, 1950 on the Niagara R. in Ont.

NOTE Atlantic coastal (and some other) gunners have a long-standing tradition of applying the name "Hutchins's Goose" and "Lesser Canada Goose" to any small Canadas including smaller individuals of the large Canadas. The older literature—Forbush (1925), for example—reflects this confusion.

interior Todd—Interior Canada Goose. Different units evidently vary in av. size of individuals, from smaller to larger than nominate *canadensis* and with general coloring somewhat browner and darker; dark of mantle continues uninterrupted to the black neck (seldom a partial or complete pale encirclement of anterior end of body); feather edges on dorsum av. darker and so contrast less with adjoining coloring; breast varies from between light and medium grayish toward slaty gray; occasionally a partial or complete black stripe within the white on chin (more frequent in westerly subpopulations). See Elder (1946a) for individual variation in coloring in westerly *interior*, such as occurrence of white collar at base of black neck, white in wing and head, dark in under

194

tail coverts (present in 17.5% of individuals examined), and lightness of breast. Sub-specific characters of av. coloring are evident in Juv. Plumage.

Downies are somewhat muted, i.e., darker, less vividly colored, than in nominate *canadensis*.

Measurements of Mississippi Valley migrants at Horseshoe L. (Ill.), "adults" (birds in their 2nd fall and older) 109 ♂: BILL 46–61 mm., av. 56; WING (across chord) 448–531, av. 491.6; TAIL 135–165, av. 150.6; 90 ♀: BILL 43–56 mm., av. 49.8; WING (across chord) 438–509, av. 466.4; TAIL 132–162, av. 142.4 (H. C. Hanson 1951a). In these meas., spread and av. markedly exceed those of a small series of ♂ *interior* from scattered localities, and wing meas. in ♀♀, as given by Aldrich (1946).

As in waterfowl generally, the Juv. wing is shorter. Range and mean WING length (across chord) by sex and age-class: "adult" 110 ♂ 506.5 ± 1.3 (SD 13.6 ± .92) and 92 ♀ 481.4 ± 1.4 (SD 13.3 ± .98); Juv. 114 ♂ 485.7 ± 1.2 (SD 13.1 ± .87) and 98 ♀ 460.5 ± 1.5 (SD 14.7 ± 1.1) (H. C. Hanson 1951a). In the observed range there was about 80% overlap between "adult" ♂ and Juv. ♂. See Hanson's paper for various additional data.

Weight seldom exceeds 10 lb. in ♂ and 9 in ♀. Especially useful papers, all relating to birds using the Mississippi Valley route, are: Elder (1946a) for 1,028 fall–winter birds, Friley (1960) for 6,650 fall birds, Raveling (1968) for 559 individuals weighed Oct. 12–March 9, and H. C. Hanson's (1962a) long and detailed paper on the wt. cycle by ages and sexes. Friley gave av. wt. of 6,650 fall birds as 7.97 lb.; of these, ♂♂ classed as "adult" av. 9.04 lb. and ♀♀ 7.82; first-fall birds ♂♂ 7.90 and ♀♀ 6.86. Raveling showed that, as expected, breeders of either sex lost wt. in late winter, but that pre-

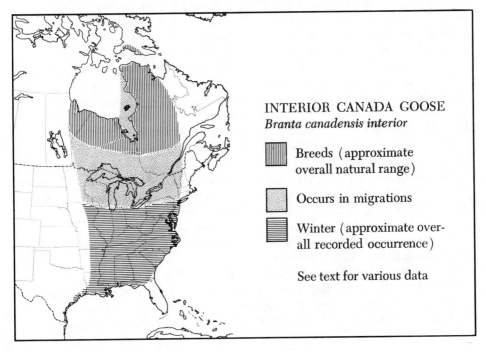

INTERIOR CANADA GOOSE
Branta canadensis interior

Breeds (approximate overall natural range)

Occurs in migrations

Winter (approximate over-all recorded occurrence)

See text for various data

breeders (both first-fall and older) of either sex maintained their wt. in that season in a situation in which they were able to obtain adequate food.

Breeding range w. and n. Ungava, on is. and mainland of e. coast of Hudson Bay, probably most commonly in low country on the mainland from Port Harrison northward; they are thinly scattered in muskeg and open forest of the more elevated interior of the peninsula, with southerly and easterly limits unknown; they also breed on sw. Baffin I., in effect an extension northward beyond n. Ungava; also on is. in James Bay; they are most numerous westward in the muskeg zone around James and s. Hudson Bay to approximately 100th meridian (in Man.)—and possibly breed beyond to n. Sask—and with n. limit tentatively placed at about lat 60° N (Man.–Keewatin boundary); southerly limits not well known and perhaps have changed greatly since Caucasian settlement.

NOTE   A bird banded at Kingsville, Ont. (a logical place for *B. c. interior*), Nov. 4, 1963, and recovered in Umanak Dist. in Greenland, July 11, 1964, has not been satisfactorily allocated to subspecies.

Molt migration   Some prebreeders and nonbreeders molt on lakes within the general breeding range, also on is. in James and in e. Hudson Bay. Others make long flights into Keewatin (w. of Hudson Bay), some to Southampton (and also Coats I.?), and many to n. Ungava, notably to the area between Povungnituk R. and Payne Bay. Those individuals (also very large Canadas of the prairies and intermountain region) that go to n. Keewatin molt within the breeding range of smallish Canadas, *parvipes*; those that go to Southampton molt within the breeding range of diminutive Canadas, *hutchinsii*.

Prebreeders using a particular molting area are spread out considerably in subsequent seasons. Those near ne. Hudson Bay, for example, go s. to destinations spread longitudinally from approximately Wis. to Mass. (but majority to Mississippi drainage). Prebreeders concentrated in the s. perimeter of Ungava Bay evidently fly s. overland, fanning out (Ohio–e. N.Y.), the eventual destination of most of them probably being the Atlantic coastal plain of Md.–N.C. (and afterward, as breeders, probably these birds are widely scattered in interior Ungava). The molting prebreeders in Keewatin undoubtedly represent farthest inland subpopulations that migrate down the Mississippi drainage including, terminally, areas beyond southwestward.

Winter range is inland for the most part; n. limits vary depending on mildness or severity of season (usually n. locally to around latitude of s. Wis. and n. Pa.); w. occasionally to e. Colo.; s. to sheltered Atlantic coastal localities from Long I. (N.Y.) at least to Ga. and also the Gulf Coast and vicinity from the Fla. Panhandle into Texas. At least some of the s. N.Y.–Md. winterers are short-distance migrants—southerly flocks of introduced or restocked birds and their later generations.

H. C. Hanson and Smith (1950) demonstrated that *interior* divides into major subpopulations; from e. to w. these are:

a) S. Atlantic—breeds on s. Baffin I., in Ungava (e. limits unknown), and on is. of se. Hudson Bay and e. James Bay; migrates to and near Atlantic coast from N.J. into N.C. (formerly a very large concentration at L. Mattamuskeet), and a few (included Baffin I. birds) at least formerly reached St. Mark's Refuge in Fla. With changes in agricultural practices, the winter distribution of these geese has altered. For instance, in Md. farmers are growing more corn and they now plough in the spring season; in ne. N.C. the farmers grow as much corn as ever, but have changed from spring to fall ploughing. Therefore, there is less waste grain available for geese in N.C. and they have responded by staying in Md. in greatly increased numbers.

Sizes of the geese evidently differ considerably (smaller northward) in different units within this subpopulation; the specimens measured by Macpherson and McLaren (1959) from northernmost breeding range (Baffin I.) av. even smaller than available averages for nominate *canadensis*.

b) Southeastern—breeds inland from s. coast of James Bay; migrates s. through e. Ont., then se. to winter range inland in the Piedmont area and to some extent the coastal plain (Va., the Carolinas, Ala., and with largest concentration formerly at St. Mark's Refuge in Fla.). Like the preceding subpopulation, these birds now are more northerly in winter distribution because of changes in agricultural practices, and probably they are intermingled more with the so-called S. Atlantic subpopulation. Only about 2,000 Canadas wintered by 1968 at St. Mark's and there were about 2,000 more in scattered flocks in the Tallahassee area.

c) Mississippi Valley—breeds inland from w. coast of James Bay and s. coast of Hudson Bay; winters in Mississippi Valley from latitude of s. Mich. s. to Gulf of Mexico coast. The majority of these geese are concentrated at a few places in winter; in the past they were more scattered, with center of abundance more southerly.

d) Eastern prairie—breeds inland from Hudson Bay in nw. Ont., n. Man., and perhaps w. to n. Sask. (limits unknown); migrates s. mostly through Minn., to winter range extending from points well inland down to the Gulf of Mexico coast in w. La. and westward.

Birds of different units within this subpopulation vary from being essentially like larger birds of the preceding subpopulation in coloration and size (southerly) to smaller, paler, with more slender bills (northwesterly). After the entire subpopulation had been labeled "eastern prairie" because of its migration route, the same route was designated "tallgrass prairie" route of a major segment of *parvipes* and *hutchinsii* (which see).

Introductions and **transplantings** have been numerous (more commonly, however, *moffitti* has been transplanted into the presumed natural range of *interior*). Breeding flocks of *interior* have been established in Ont. and in conterminous U.S. from at least N.Y. (and Vt.?) and a few of those released in Me., s. into Va. and westward perhaps even into the Dakotas. In the early 1970s there were transplantings from N.J. to Me. and to n. and cent. Fla.! The southerly-breeding flocks are quite sedentary. Some introductions abroad apparently have included *interior*, but probably most of those in the present century have been of the larger prairie birds as discussed below under *moffitti*.

moffitti Aldrich—Giant Canada Goose. Largest Canadas (here includes "*maxima*"); geese of the most southerly natural breeding range of the species, and occupying coldest regularly used winter range. At the time of the last glacial maximum, the ancestral stock presumably occurred in various local habitats s. of the ice and, during its recession, presumably at least much of the intermountain environment became usable goose habitat relatively late and the Canadas that occupied it are not as yet differentiated at the subspecies level from the present prairie birds. This is reflected, for instance, in the great disparity among authors as to how much breeding range to claim for so-called "*maxima*" and how much for *moffitti* as defined by previous authors, a very large midsection of the here combined range having been labeled as belonging to one and then to the other. There is considerable evidence that only the local units from opposite sides of the total breeding range, when compared, really show appreciable difference; even this is more n.–s. than e.–w. and is considerably masked by individual variation.

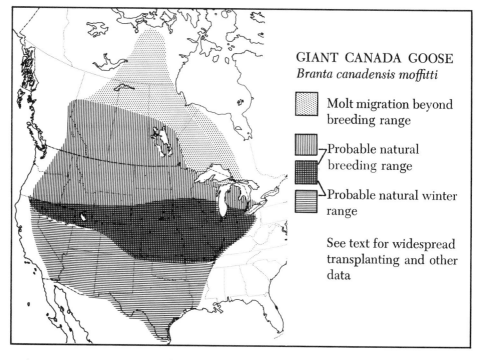

GIANT CANADA GOOSE
Branta canadensis moffitti

Molt migration beyond breeding range

Probable natural breeding range

Probable natural winter range

See text for widespread transplanting and other data

As to very recent events, the prairie units are believed to have been nearly extirpated by the 1920s, but descendants of the survivors (which first were recognized as such in Jan., 1962) have been used very widely in restocking projects.

Aldrich (1946) gave breeding range as extending from interior Cal. eastward to ne. N.D. and cent.-w. Nebr.; Hellmayr and Conover (1948) regarded *moffitti* as a "rather unsatisfactory subspecies"; Delacour (1954) mentioned "completely similar" coloring of prairie and intermountain birds but with latter said to av. smaller. The name *moffitti* has priority over the name *maxima*.

Although, because of inadequate sampling, also local extirpation, the record is incomplete, apparently variation was as follows: an uneven gradient of slight decrease in av. size beginning somewhere on the prairies and continuing westward across the intermountain area; and, at least e. of the continental divide, a greater decrease from s. to n. Also, on the average, paler coloration locally westward. Each unit or "flock" of prairie and intermountain geese that has been studied in any detail has been found to have, as would be expected, some biological uniqueness (such as location and timing of seasonal movements); nevertheless, when considered in relation to the large size of the geese, morphological variation is relatively less than that within some other subspecies of *Branta canadensis* recognized in the present volume.

The subspecies *moffitti* may be defined as: largest, most elongated, Canada Geese; generally rather pale overall coloration (as also are some individuals of *interior*), especially on underparts (and especially ♂ ♂); white of cheeks tends to extend somewhat farther up on side of head (most often in prairie birds) than is usual in the species and sometimes has a small extension posteriorly (a feature less common in *interior* and which occurs even in *parvipes* and *hutchinsii*); white markings on the forehead may be more common in prairie birds (but also occur in many examples of *interior*); a dark longitudinal stripe through the white on chin, incomplete or even complete, is not rare (it is more frequent in intermountain birds and more common to ♂ ♂); quite a few individuals have a sharply defined white collar, sometimes wide, and usually incomplete (interrupted by dark feathering dorsally) at base of black neck.

For excellent monochrome illus. of prairie birds, see figs. 49 and 50 in H. C. Hanson (1965) and for col. fig. of a downy see this volume, opp. p. 242. For a color photo of intermountain downies, see Craighead and Craighead (1957).

Measurements of prairie geese from H.C. Hanson (1965) for captives at Round Lake Waterfowl Station (Minn.) and in parentheses are given the observed range for 2 other series combined (1 from s. Man., the other from birds wintering at Rochester, Minn.), "Adults" 8 ♂: BILL 61–72 mm., av. 65.3 ± 1.4 (range 51–62 in other series); WING 510–566, av. 539.9 ± 6.0 (range 485–547 in other series); TAIL 165–183, av. 170.6 ± 2.9 (range 139–177 in other series); 14 ♀: BILL 55–63 mm., av. 59.8 ± 0.9 (range 51–56 in other series); WING 470–525, av. 500.5 ± 4.0 (range 472–513 in other series); TAIL 145–166, av. 157.7 ± 1.8 (range 136–159 in 1 other series).

Juv. ♂ WING (of 8) 507–537, av. 521.4 ± 3.0 (range 461–520 in other series); TAIL (of 9) 142–165, av. 153.9 ± 2.7 (range 131–152 in 1 other series); 3 ♀ WING 480–520 mm., av. 500 ± 11.6 (range 463–499 in other series); TAIL 137–160, av. 149 ± 6.6 (and in 8 others range was 125–141).

Intermountain birds—museum skins from unstated localities, from tables in H.C. Hanson (1965): "adult and yearling" ♂ BILL (of 14) 50–58 mm., av. 54.6 ± .06; WING (of 13) 486–532, av. 516.6 ± 3.2; TAIL (of 13) 124–165, av. 152.5 ± 3.4. ♀ BILL (of 10) 47–56 mm., av. 51.6 ± .08; WING (of 7) 476–505, av. 490.7 ± 3.8; TAIL (of 6) 134–157, av. 143 ± 3.4.

Apparently the birds Swarth (1913) measured were all from Cal.: ♂ 10 "adult" BILL 47–58 mm.; WING (across chord) 418–527, av. 500.6; TAIL 134–174, av. 156.8; TARSUS 76–98, av. 92.3.

Weight observed range varies greatly. The occasional individuals (all ganders?) that have attained 18–24 lb. have been publicized, but usual fall–early winter wt. of birds in their 2nd year and older is ♂ 9½–14 lb., ♀ 8–13, and first-fall birds approach the latter.

199

The geese weigh about ¼ less during molt than when well nourished in early winter. The following, from H. C. Hanson (1965) perhaps are an indication of the wt. of eastern prairie wild stock of earlier times:

♂ 7 "adult" Dec. 6–8 at Round Lake (Minn.) 4,940–7,484 gm., av. 6,525 ± 337; and 13 Jan. 29–30 at Rochester (Minn.) 4,196–5,415, av. 4,884 ± 98.

♀ 13 "adult" Dec. 6–8 at Round Lake, 4,270–6,435 gm., av. 3,868 ± 101.

♂ 9 "immature" [first fall–winter] Dec. 6–8 at Round Lake, 5,040–7,569 gm., av. 5,963 ± 249, and 20 on Jan. 29–30 at Rochester, 3,430–5,075, av. 4,261 ± 94.

♀ 3 "immature" Dec. 6–8 at Round Lake, 4,760–6,040 gm., av. 5,245 ± 401, and 15 on Jan. 29–30 at Rochester, 3,430–4,337, av. 3,821 ± 81.

Molting "adults" 13 ♂ July 9 at Waubay Nat. Wildlife Reserve, S.D., 3,685–4,905 gm., av. 4,104, and 55 on July 2 at Trimble Wildlife Area, Mo., av. 4,626; 74 ♀ July 2 at Trimble av. 3,830.

The following includes prairie birds, perhaps also intermountain birds, and very likely some *B. c. interior*, weighed in N.W.T. where they had gone to molt: yearlings and older birds lumped together 144 ♂ 6.0–10.1 lb. (2,720–4,580 gm.) and 140 ♀ 5.0–8.5 lb. (2,270–3,860 gm.) (Sterling and Dzubin 1967).

For intermountain birds there is no adequately documented series of any size. For "Western Canada Goose" Kortright (1942) gave: ♂ 7 lb. 5 oz. to 12 lb. 8 oz., av. (of 8) 10 lb. 4 oz.; and ♀ 6 lb. 10 oz. to 9 lb. 8 oz., av. (of 5) 7 lb. 13 oz. These are very close to the data on 9 ♂ and 6 ♀ given by A. L. Nelson and Martin (1953). Two birds taken in Cal. weighed 19 lb. each (J. Aldrich). Moffitt (1931), who listed no specific records, stated many trustworthy hunters had reported birds weighing 16 and 18 lb., even a claim of up to 21 lb. H. C. Hanson (1965) mentioned reports of geese taken in Cal. (local birds or migrants?) that weighed 19, 22, and 24 lb., thus matching even the very exceptional records from the prairies.

Weights of *moffitti* in Wash. and Calif. are very similar; see Yocom (1972) for some details.

Weights of captive-reared young at 11 weeks: 7 ♂ av. 3,275 gm. (about 7 ¼ lb.) and 5 ♀ av. 2,735 gm. (about 6¾ lb.) (Yocom and Harris 1966).

Breeding range of *moffitti*, prior to decimation of birds in the prairie portion of their range (and subsequent restocking) is here defined tentatively as: n. to n.-cent. B.C.; w.-cent. Alta.; and cent. Man.; to include Wis. (possibly part of Mich.) and Ind.; s. to nw. Tenn. and across into Colo.; and w. to include e. half of both Wash. and Ore. and some locations in n. third of Cal. Breeding range has been expanding locally in the Pacific NW; details in Yocom (1962).

Molt migration is not undertaken by some yearlings and other prebreeders and, possibly, any birds of any age from some local units; but it is now well established that many prebreeders and some nonbreeders from the prairies and some distance westward make a long flight northward to the Thelon Game Sanctuary which straddles the MacKenzie–Keewatin boundary; some even continue beyond nearly to the arctic coast. Some easterly birds are thought to have an easterly route from the Great Lakes to s. Hudson Bay, then northwestward, also from s. Man. to the Churchill area (sw. Hudson Bay). For some details of molting habitat, behavior of molting birds, and a listing of various references to molt migration, see Sterling and Dzubin (1967). Very likely there are additional, still undiscovered, molting areas.

A specific example: There is a breeding unit in n. Benton Co. and thereabouts in se. Wash. About 75% of the young in their first winter remain locally and the others move down into Cal. (in either case, presumably remaining with parent birds). In the following spring, many young and a few "adults" (older prebreeders or nonbreeders) migrate past their natal area ne. into Alta. and adjacent parts of Canada—a molt migration —and when still older and as breeders, their seasonal travels tend to be mainly (but there are exceptions) between se. Wash. and n. Cal. The band-recovery data were discussed fully by W. Hanson and Eberhardt (1971).

Winter range Established breeders of southerly breeding units tend to be sedentary; northerly ones bypass them in migration, and some in intermediate localities also move in severe winters. There is a certain amount of diagonal movement, such as birds from parts of Alta. and Mont. migrating to Cal.; another facet of this is a fanning out or crossing over so that winter ranges of intermountain and prairie units overlap. That is, they share certain wintering places. Southerly limits of winter occurrence are mainly within the conterminous U.S., but extend somewhat beyond—for instance, to Gulf of Cal. (Mexico).

Stragglers The following, which are placed under this heading quite arbitrarily, possibly may relate to some such phenomenon as molt migration: Jensen (in Aldrich et al. 1949) included, among places of banding plus recovery, Ore. to S.D. (2 birds) and se. Idaho to n. Nebr. (1 bird). It also may be pertinent to mention that geese from some easterly transplantings that have included prairie birds, and which are migratory at least in colder winters, occur in such seasons even as far as tidewater along the midportion of the U.S. Atlantic coast. A. L. Nelson and Martin (1953) listed a "Common Canada Goose" weighing 22 lb.

Introductions and **transplantings** evidently are very few w. of the continental divide. To the east across the prairies there have been many, within and beyond the presumed natural range (as defined above) of these very large geese. See H. C. Hanson (1965) for data on some of these flocks. Descendants of 43 geese, transplanted in 1939 from Bear R. Refuge in n. Utah eastward to the Necedah Refuge in w.-cent. Wis., migrate from the latter place as far as Mo. and s. Ill. (Samson 1971). H. K. Nelson (1963) stated that prairie stock was the most successful for use in establishing local breeding units in the n.-cent. states.

There are some 20,000 semidomesticated very large Canada Geese in s. Ont. and s. Que. They are raised for food and, formerly, decoys. On the St. Lawrence R. ne. of Montreal at Sorel, there is a very long tradition of raising these birds—a local "goose culture."

Canadas were introduced into the White Mt. area of Ariz. beginning in 1966 and raised young there in 1972.

NOTES The intermountain birds have been studied a great deal, especially in Cal. and Utah. The main earlier papers on them were cited by M. B. Geis (1956); the many more recent ones are scattered in the literature. Papers on the prairie birds were included in the bibliography in H. C. Hanson (1965).

Published reports from hunters of huge geese killed, and a considerable amount of other literature, has tended to result in an overemphasis on the largest individuals, mostly (or entirely?) ganders. This included selection of the largest available bird as the type specimen of "*maxima*." In a population sense, as when viewing live prairie geese of both sexes alongside the same of *interior*, the former are seen in better perspective.

By the late 1960s, attempts were begun to breed selectively the largest individuals from certain captive flocks in hope of developing what might be termed geese of super-giant size.

Introductions abroad Brit. Isles Kear (1966) stated that the feral stock included geese within the wt. range of the very large N. Am. prairie birds and that they also had other characteristics of such birds. In earlier times, when the feral birds were fewer in number, they may have been more sedentary. At the present time, seasonal movements include more or less molt migration (northward). One such movement, from Yorkshire to Invernesshire, was described by Walker (1970). The total number of free-flying Canada Geese in Britain was about 10,500 in 1968 and they were regarded as being too tame for sport shooting (Ogilvie 1969). Over 5,500 had been banded through the year 1969. The birds continue to occupy additional localities.

Iceland This species was erroneously recorded (A.O.U. *Check-list* 1957) as having been introduced. Three individuals have been shot there in recent years; these may have been strays from N. Am. or, more likely, were British birds that had joined with migrant geese of other species that were bound for Iceland. Incidentally, a bird taken in the Faeroes on Nov. 4, 1866, also was believed to have come from England (Salomonsen, in A. S. Jensen et al. 1934).

Norway The very large introduced Canadas remain through winter in the country (almost all of the smaller geese of Eurasian species migrate to warmer winter quarters).

Sweden The geese were introduced in the 1930s and 1940s and appear to be *moffitti* or *interior* (probably the former); they have become established and are extending their breeding range in cent. and n. Sweden. Usually they migrate a short distance to wintering areas within Sweden and to the German North Sea coast, but in a severe winter (1961–62) reached s. France and Switzerland.

Europe Canada Geese, from very small to the largest, are acclimatized as zoo birds. Feral birds from Britain have occurred in France.

New Zealand Canadas have been introduced at various times since 1876; they have become established on South I., but not on North I. (to which they now straggle). According to Stead (in Delacour 1954), some Canadas were imported in 1905 and thrived and multiplied; 10 more were imported in 1920 and again were successful. The actual source of these stocks is not on record. The present birds are, at least preponderantly, very large and are referred to "*maxima*" (Yocom 1970c), included here in *moffitti*. The span for viable eggs in nests is Oct.–Jan. Some of the birds are nearly sedentary, but many have local movements to inland lakes and coastal waters. For further general information, see especially Falla et al. (1966); for data on survival and related matters, from over 14,000 band recoveries, see Imber (1968) and Imber and Williams (1968)

202

parvipes (Cassin)—Lesser Canada Goose.   These birds might be described as either *moffitti* or *interior* telescoped down to rather small size. They vary from pale breasted (*parvipes* narrowly defined) to dusky breasted (some so-called *taverneri* of Alaska). They breed on the continental interior mainland and, to the east, apparently now have complete intergradation with the peripheral-nesting *hutchinsii*. When on the prairies during migration, the *parvipes–hutchinsii* conglomerate uses the same stopover places and individuals can be arranged so as to form an inclusive uninterrupted size gradient (MacInnes 1966). Yet they more or less sort out in winter, the smaller birds (*hutchinsii*) being more southerly. (It is possible that *parvipes–hutchinsii* intergradation is a consequence of enough of the 2 stocks being together for sufficient time for "mixed" pairs to form and, afterward, the goose generally leads the gander back to her natal area.)

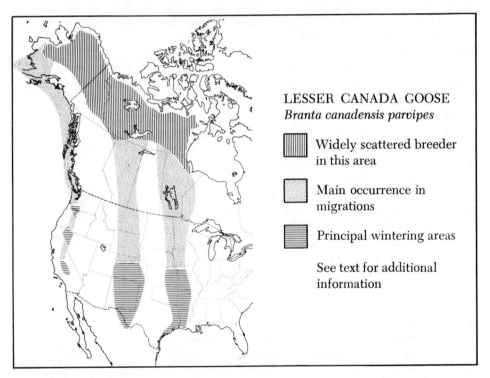

LESSER CANADA GOOSE
Branta canadensis parvipes

Widely scattered breeder in this area

Main occurrence in migrations

Principal wintering areas

See text for additional information

A passable definition of *parvipes* is as follows: a smallish edition of *B. c. interior*; underparts usually palish, but vary to quite dusky in some individuals from interior n. Alaska (these are among the Pacific migrants); bill "normal" in shape, i.e., short but not stubby in appearance, and usually with rounded nail; an incomplete and narrow white collar sometimes present (more often in n. Alaskan birds). Downies of pale-breasted birds are rather muted golden (so far as known); the progeny of a dusky-bellied ♀ were more like downy *minima* in coloring.

Measurements of birds from breeding to wintering localities, 7 ♂ : BILL 38–46 mm., av. 42.; WING (across chord) 413–442, av. 430.9; TAIL 113–145, av. 132.7; TARSUS

74–78, av. 81.7; 2 ♀: BILL 36–45.5, WING (across chord) 410–423, TAIL 123–135, TARSUS 73–82 (Aldrich 1946). This sample is not fully representative even of light-bellied birds.

For migrants in se. Colo., the variation in meas. and wt. in large series of first-fall and older birds of each sex, was shown in a table in Grieb (1970), once again indicating a morphological *parvipes–hutchinsii* gradient.

Dusky birds from arctic Alaska ("*leucopareia*" in A. Bailey 1948); 8 ♂ BILL 34–40 mm., av. 37.1; WING (across chord?) 370–404, av. 390; TARSUS 69–74, av. 72.1; 7 ♀: BILL 34–37 mm., av. 35.1; WING (across chord?) 373–411, av. 388.5; TARSUS 64–75, av. 70.

Weight in summer: at Perry R. (near n. end of Mackenzie–Keewatin boundary) "adults" 3 ♂ 5 lb. 8 oz. to 6 lb. 3 oz., 1 ♀ 3 lb. 11 oz., also a yearling ♀ at 5 lb. 9 oz. (H. C. Hanson et al 1956); 6 in May–June (Alaska plus 2 ♀ from Old Crow in Yukon Terr.). ♂ 2,551 gm., 5 ♀ 1,741–2,250 gm., latter av. 1,825 gm. (Irving 1960).

Breeds in much of interior Alaska (nearly to arctic coast) and on n. Canadian mainland, from tundra evidently to more or less open areas within the forest zone, s. to extreme ne. B.C. and to se. Keewatin.

Migrates presumably over much the same routes spring and fall. Easterly breeders share (with *hutchinsii*) a tallgrass prairie route; see MacInnes (1966) for stopover localities and for separateness of migrant flocks. Most of the westerly Canadian birds use a more westerly (interior) shortgrass prairie route; these birds have been discussed at length by Grieb (1970) and Yeager (1970). The latter route also is used by some Alaska–Yukon Terr. birds; the remainder (includes the great majority of Alaskan birds) have a Pacific route. On the last-mentioned route, thousands of these geese congregate in fall and linger on the Bering Sea side of the Alaskan Pen. in the Izembek–Cold Bay area where they mingle freely with Brant; later they travel via the Pacific Ocean to Puget Sd. and thereafter travel inland.

Molt migration   T. W. Barry reported 25,000 molting geese on deltas of the Kugalik and Smoke rivers (between Anderson and Mackenzie rivers), N.W.T.; Sterling and Dzubin (1967) suspected that these may have been from the *parvipes* stock that breeds along the Mackenzie R. The same authors noted that over 10,000 molting geese were tallied along the arctic coast of Alaska in 1966; they may have come from the Alaskan interior.

Winter range (e. to w.) includes a coastal area of w. La. and part of e. Texas; in the interior, Colo. e. of the Rockies and southward to include parts of New Mex. and w. Texas, to some extent also n. Mexico; and in the Pacific states from s.-cent. Wash. (in large numbers) to interior valleys of Cal. (relatively few). A few have wintered as far n. as Prince William Sd., Alaska.

Straggler to Godhavn in w. Greenland, occasionally to U.S. Atlantic coast from at least N.J. ("*leucopareia*" of Woolfenden 1957) into S.C., to St. Mark's Refuge in Fla. panhandle, and very likely down into w. Mexico.

Boyd (1961b) listed sightings of a number of Canadas, of *parvipes–huchinsii* size, for the British Isles; whether or not they were natural occurrences is unknown.

NOTES   There seems to be no evidence that a pale-breasted Canada Goose has bred or breeds on the Alaska Pen., although this matter was speculated on by Bent (1925) and O. Murie (1959).

Delacour (1951, 1954) stated that *"taverneri"* (here included in *parvipes*) "intergrades" with *minima* in the Wainwright region of Alaska, with *occidentalis* in s. Alaska, and with *parvipes* (as he defined it) in e. Alaska. The first is based on variably dark-breasted June and early July specimens, described by A. Bailey (1948), which are explainable as prebreeding *minima* that had moved northward to molt. The large dark-breasted *occidentalis* is isolated when breeding by terrain unsuited for geese from all other Canadas. And in e. Alaska it would hardly be surprising to find dusky- and pale-breasted birds mated, especially as individuals showing this range of coloring also occur in more or less close association when on winter range.

It is sometimes remarked that the geese of interior arctic Alaska are cliff nesters, implying that this is a distinctive trait, but *leucopareia*—even its surviving remnant —utilizes this sort of terrain.

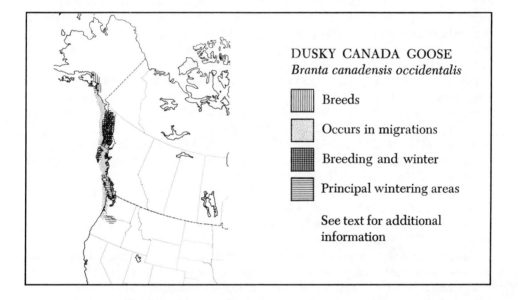

DUSKY CANADA GOOSE
Branta canadensis occidentalis

▦ Breeds

▦ Occurs in migrations

▦ Breeding and winter

▦ Principal wintering areas

See text for additional information

occidentalis (Baird)—Dusky Canada Goose. These fairly large dark geese now occupy a strip of summer habitat that has numerous minor discontinuities plus a major one; that is, it actually consists of what may be termed 2 general areas separated for a distance of about 300 airline mi. by terrain unsuited to breeding geese. All the geese are, at least seasonally, saltwater birds.

The geese of the 2 general areas now are believed to show complete overlap in all morphological characters except perhaps size, the northerly birds av. smaller (clinal effect). The southerly ones have size overlap with smaller examples of pale-breasted *moffitti*. There are 2 major subpopulations (corresponding to the 2 general breeding areas) and there is growing evidence that each is an aggregation of smaller units. The latter phenomenon is apparent, for example, in migratory behavior; in general, from n. to s. in breeding range, there is a trend from birds that make comparatively long migratory flights to short-distance travelers, to essentially sedentary units. There also are differences in timing of movements. There is some overlap in winter range of geese from the 2 general breeding areas.

Although Delacour (1951, 1954) treated the geese of each of the 2 general breeding areas as a subspecific entity, and such measurements of them as he published show no overlap in bill length, the desirability of recognizing 2 subspecies has been questioned by Dickinson (1953) and later authors. Although an understanding of the existence and nature of subpopulations (and smaller units) is especially important from a management viewpoint, there is no adequate justification for applying more than a single subspecific name to all these large dark Canadas.

This description of *occidentalis* includes *"fulva"* of Delacour: generally dark overall but coloring of underparts corresponds to (and varies like) that of *minima*. In definitive feathering, underparts (except for white from vent to tail) vary with individual from deep brownish (toward chocolate) to considerably paler (tawny-chestnut or paler); feather borders on dorsum rather narrow, generally somewhat toward reddish brown; seldom even a partial white collar at base of neck. Again as in *minima*, Juv. birds are somewhat lighter (toward grayish) ventrally.

Downies have upperparts rather brownish olive, face and underparts gray (not yellow), lores and eyelids dusky; that is, they closely resemble downy *minima* in coloring.

Measurements of birds of the northerly (Alaskan) subpopulation, shot in Ore. in fall–early winter. "Adult" ♂ BILL (of 214 birds) 37–51 mm. (46.53 ± 2.74); WING flattened (of 79) 446–510 (478.73 ± 12.57). ♀ BILL (of 199) 40–50 mm. (44.42 ± 2.09); WING flattened (of 61) 408–492 (450.22 ± 15.11). These data are from J. A. Chapman (1970), who also gave meas., by sex, of large series of "immatures." For northerly birds there also are a few meas. in J. Grinnell (1910), footnote in Hellmayr and Conover (1948), in Dickinson (1953), and Delacour (1954).

Southerly birds: 31 ♂ BILL 49–59 mm., WING 440–513; and 17 ♀ BILL 48–59 mm., WING 432–457 (Delacour 1951).

Weight of 1,034 birds of the northerly subpopulation were reported for 4 time periods within the inclusive span Nov. 10–Jan. 6, on winter range in Ore., by J. A. Chapman (1970). There was a gain in wt. in the sexes and age-classes as the season advanced. Lumping all data for the overall span: "adult" 134 ♂ 2,868–4,459 gm. and 98 ♀ 2,584–4,004; "immature" 436 ♂ 1,931–4,658 gm. and 366 ♀ 1,874–3,635.

Northerly birds in late July when thin and growing new flight feathers: "adult" ♀ 8.3 lb., 7 lb., and 3 at 6.5 lb. (Yocom 1963).

Southerly birds weigh up to 13 lb. (Delacour 1954).

Breeds northerly subpopulation—in s. Alaska along coast from vicinity of Bering Glacier on the southeast to Cook Inlet on the west, an airline distance of about 275 mi. Most abundant as breeder in Copper R. delta; for excellent aerial views of this environment, see H. A. Hansen (1961) and J. A. Chapman et al. (1969). Whether the effects on this area of the 1964 earthquake will, in the long run, have a favorable or an adverse effect on this nesting subpopulation is unknown. In Prince William Sd. and on lower

Susitna R. at head of Cook Inlet, only small numbers breed. A very few nest near the confluence of the Bremner with the Copper R., about 50 mi. from the coast, and there are a few scattered pairs about the same distance inland on the Susitna drainage.

The southerly subpopulation breeds in Alaska, from Cross Sd. near Glacier Bay (some 300 airline mi. from closest limits of breeding of the northerly birds just mentioned) through the Alexander Archipelago and on the adjacent mainland coast; also in B.C. (s. limits not adequately reported).

Spring migration occurs throughout April. Moffitt (1937) stated that some of the northerly birds remained in Cal. until early April. Evidently all the birds that are going to breed are back at nesting areas by the first of May.

Molt migration, so far as known, evidently is only a local movement of some of the prebreeders to the periphery of breeding areas and nearby. H. A. Hansen (1962) mentioned a flock, seen in July and believed to be prebreeders, on w. side of Cook Inlet. Some that presumably were prebreeders from the southerly subpopulation have been found n. of breeding range in bays near Yakutat.

Fall migration northerly subpopulation—the majority of the birds begin leaving the Copper R. delta about mid-Sept. and all that are to migrate are gone by end of Oct. They bypass coastal Alaska almost completely. Stopover places are the Queen Charlotte Is., then Vancouver I. where they begin to arrive by early Oct. From the latter place they go directly to Columbia R. Delta (arriving in Oct. and Nov.), then up the Columbia and Willamette rivers to main winter range, a relatively small area in and adjacent to Benton Co., Ore. Some flocks (total 1,000–1,500 birds) are not migratory, remaining through winter among the is. in Prince William Sd. A few migrants remain behind in the Queen Charlottes, also at Vancouver I. A few pass the winter in Columbia R. delta. A few go beyond main winter range to Cal. coastal areas, from Humboldt Bay northward. Four band recoveries from Cal.: 2 in Del Norte Co., 1 from Shasta Co., 1 from San Francisco Bay area.

Southerly subpopulation—62% of band recoveries came from within 100 mi. of Glacier Bay and another 20% within only 50 mi. farther (H. A. Hansen 1962). A few fly directly from Alexander Archipelago to Columbia R. delta, then go inland into Yamhill Co., Ore. Judging from band recoveries (most date after mid-Dec.), they arrive on winter range later than the northerly birds.

Winter range has been mentioned in the 2 preceding paragraphs. In the case of the southerly subpopulation, about $^4/_5$ of the birds remain within their overall breeding range all year.

Straggler to Lahontan Valley, Nev. Also, a large dark-breasted Canada Goose, taken May 27, 1903, in the Anadyr region in ne. Siberia and preserved in the Darwin Museum in Moscow, was listed as *occidentalis* by Dementiev and Gladkov (1952, 1960). A bird banded when a preflight gosling, in the Copper R. delta, Alaska, was recaptured 5 years later at Sand Lake, S. D. (C. D. MacInnes).

NOTES northerly birds—from rough calculations, their total number after the hunting season in the years 1952 through 1960 appears to have fluctuated from as few as 10,000 to a high of 20,000. In fall of 1966, prior to the hunting season, the figure was calculated to be 34,750 (J. A. Chapman et al. 1969). Southerly birds—total number is smaller. See H. A. Hansen (1962) for further details of this and various other topics.

minima Ridgway—Cackling Canada Goose.   Av. smallest of all Canadas, but considerable variation in size for so small a goose; bill stubby, its dorsal profile varying from essentially straight to convex (bulging upward), the nail at end less elongated than in Aleutian birds; color and pattern highly variable; for its size somewhat long-legged and decidedly long-winged. (Probably a great overlap existed in all characteristics, including size, with *leucopareia* when the latter was numerous and had many breeding places.)

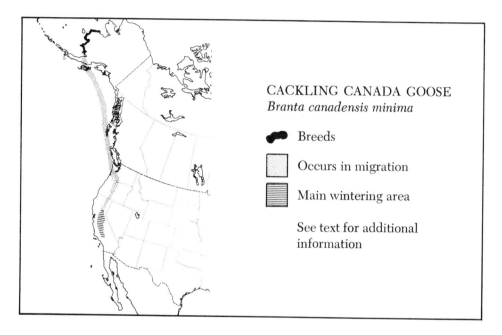

CACKLING CANADA GOOSE
Branta canadensis minima

Breeds

Occurs in migration

Main wintering area

See text for additional
information

Collectively, and assuming that specimens taken away from breeding range are correctly identified as *minima* and do not include small *leucopareia*, they show great individual variation. They demonstrate that, even more than in most Canadas, each color character and structural dimension varies independently. The following is indicative of such variation in color characters:

1 White of cheeks continuous across chin, or interrupted there partially or completely by a black stripe; even the entire chin may be black with white of cheeks reduced in area and having black feathers intermingled. 2 Neck entirely blackish, or with white feathers intermingled, or so many of the latter that the neck is all white in its basal half. 3 At base of neck a white collar, varying from very wide to merely indicated, complete or interrupted dorsally, or absent. 4 Upper breast often darkens (most prominently in paler-breasted individuals) and this is transected at base of neck by a white collar (if present). 5 Underparts commonly rich chocolate (much as in darker *occidentalis* among the large Canadas) but, in definitive feathering, vary with individual to cinnamon, or buffy brownish, or even palish gray (somewhat like *hutchinsii*). 6 Dorsum usually dark grays and rich browns, the feather ends some variant of

tawny-buff, but some individuals vary toward olive or grayed olive with palish feather tips.

The dark birds especially, when in new feathering, have a sheen or bloom, between violet and rose, most evident dorsally.

Birds in Juv. Plumage are somewhat paler ventrally than when older, except for those that continue to be pale breasted, and all have more blended coloring. E. W. Nelson (1887) described the "first plumage" as dull grayish umber-brown, the head and neck almost uniform with rest of body and without trace of white cheek patches. This may fit some dark Juv. *minima*; no trace of white cheek patches is fairly common. (In the Canada Goose, dark-tipped feathers on the cheeks are not limited to the Juv. Plumage, although they are typical of that stage.)

Downies are olive above, whitish below, with dusky line from lores to postocular region (Delacour 1954). See col. pl. facing p. 242. For a color photo, see A. Allen (1951).

Measurements no adequately documented series has been published. Without mention of number of specimens, nor localities, nor sex(es), Delacour (1954) reported: BILL 26–32 mm., WING 330–370, TAIL 100–118, TARSUS 60–70. Swarth (1913) gave meas. of birds (sexes not separated) from winter range in Cal., but it is possible that both Aleutian (*leucopareia*) and mainland (*minima*) specimens were included: BILL (of 65) 26–36 mm., av. 30.8; WING across chord (of 66) 337–421, av. 385.3; TAIL 94–128, av. 111.7; TARSUS 61–81, av. 72.9.

Weight of "adult" *minima* in summer at Hooper Bay, Alaska: 4 ♂ 3 lb. 4 oz. to 4 lb. 2 oz. and 7 ♀ 3 lb. 1 oz. to 3 lb. 3 oz. (Brandt 1943). The ♂ av. 5 oz. heavier than the ♀ (D. L. Spencer et al. 1951). Published wt. in excess of 4½ lb., even for winter birds, probably is exceptional or else pertains to *leucopareia*.

Breeds at present, so far as known, only in coastal Alaska between the mouths of the Kuskokwim and Yukon rivers. Local distribution there was described and mapped by D. L. Spencer et al. (1951). Formerly may have bred farther n. and also farther s. along the coast, but extant information is confusing and unreliable.

Spring migration begins in Feb.–early April (almost all of these geese have left Cal. by mid-April) and they arrive on breeding range from last week of April onward (majority in 2nd and 3rd weeks in May). Spring route apparently is largely the reverse of fall route (described below), but Pacific Ocean portion perhaps is more inshore.

Molt migration No June–early July occurrence in numbers at any distance from breeding range is reported. A few birds, however, have occurred in the Wainwright–Barrow area (see notes under *parvipes*) and several small flocks, presumably of *minima*, were reported by Swarth (1934) as having been seen in very early July on Nunivak I. Conover (1926) wrote that, in late May at Hooper Bay, singles, pairs, and small groups wandered on the tundra breeding range, as if seeking company. This is typical behavior of prebreeding Canadas that have been excluded from breeding territories by their parents, regardless of whether the young continue to remain thereabouts or soon go elsewhere to molt. Very small geese seen June 18 far in the interior on the lower John R. (Bettles area of Alaska) (J. M. Campbell 1969a) might have been *minima*, or possibly *hutchinsii*.

Fall migration is leisurely down the coast to n. shore of base of Alaska Pen. (few occur westward at Izembek–Cold Bay; most of the few Pribilof records are for fall); in early Oct. they fly overland to the Pacific and s. over the ocean (some straggle ashore in Gulf of Alaska and southward) in 2 flights to mouth of Columbia R. (arriving Oct. 15–20 and 25–30). Then they fly e. across the Cascades and on down to Klamath Basin and ne. Cal. where the majority linger until late Nov. before going s. to Sacramento Valley (Cal.). Some move on (some time in Dec.?) to San Joaquin Valley. (Based mainly on U. C. Nelson and Hansen 1959.)

Winter see above paragraph.

Stragglers cannot be inventoried satisfactorily because of likely past confusion with small examples of *leucopareia*, varying application of names, and inadequate recording. A majority of the following probably are acceptable records: n.—to St. Lawrence I., includes specimen (Fay and Cade 1959) and several sightings in spring [any of these geese northerly of breeding areas in late May–early July may indicate molt migration of prebreeders]; e.—to Dawson City in Yukon Terr., specimen (Rand 1946), 1 banded in Cal. and the band recovered in "Northwest Terr." (U. C. Nelson and Hansen 1959), ne. Nev. (includes band recoveries), s. Nev., sightings (Gullion et al. 1959); s.—to Topock, Ariz., wing of hunter-killed bird (A. R. Phillips et al. 1964), and near San Quintin in n. Baja Cal., Mexico (Friedmann et al. 1950); w. infrequently (Berger 1972) to the Hawaiian Is. (Hawaii, Maui, Molokai, Oahu, and Midway)—mostly sightings but includes captures, also Tokyo Bay, Japan, specimen (O. L. Austin, Jr., and Kuroda 1953), Bering I. (Commander Is.), 2 captures (Dementiev and Gladkov 1952), and Attu I. at w. end of Aleutians, specimen (Aldrich 1946). [The Japan, Bering, and Attu records listed here might pertain to *minima*, but the possibility remains that some of the specimens fall within the unknown range of variation of *leucopareia*.]

Bones from an **archaeological site** estimated to be about 2,000 years old, on St. Lawrence I., were assigned to *minima* by Friedmann (1934).

NOTE This little "Cackling Goose" is also commonly called "Brant" by gunners.

leucopareia (Brandt)—Aleutian Canada Goose. Includes *B. hutchinsii asiatica* of Aldrich; the description below is based largely on migrants and especially winterers—presumably from the Aleutians and possibly also from beyond to the westward; very few taken on breeding range are extant. For lack of breeding birds definitely assignable to particular breeding islands (except one), it is now impossible to assess individual variation in color, pattern, or size (probably some overlap in all these characters with *minima*), or to define subpopulations (which surely must have existed on an island chain), or to state whether there were any trends in variation along the Aleutians and beyond to the Kurils. See A. H. Clark (1910) for partial description of 4 birds taken on Aggatu.

Small; underparts moderately dark (but lighter than mantle and variable individually, the upper breast often grading to dark brownish (even blackish) up against (or in absence of) a sharply defined white collar; light feather borders on mantle conspicuous in new feathering; the head, in life, rather squarish in profile (high "forehead"); bill short, tapering to narrow tip and with somewhat pointed nail; white collar (not always present) at base of black neck, variable in width (to relatively very wide), sometimes incomplete dorsally; white from cheek to cheek frequently interrupted by a partial or a complete black stripe along midline of chin; for so small a goose, rather long-legged.

210

On Buldir I. in July, 1963, 47 birds had a distinct white neckband, 9 lacked it, and 8 had breasts so pale that whether a band was present was indeterminable; in several of the breeding pairs observed, only one bird had a white neckband. On these live birds in the wild, the band varied from about ¼ in. to 2 in. wide. (Data from K. W. Kenyon.)

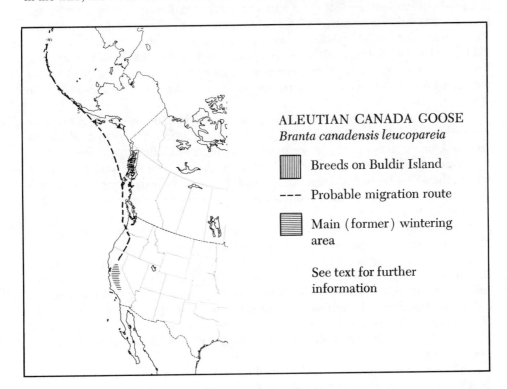

ALEUTIAN CANADA GOOSE
Branta canadensis leucopareia

Breeds on Buldir Island

--- Probable migration route

Main (former) wintering area

See text for further information

Birds in Juv. Plumage are somewhat paler ventrally and have more blended overall coloring. Downies are gray above, whitish below (no yellow), as observed in captive stock.

Measurements, the localities, number of specimens, and sex(es) not stated: BILL 31–36 mm., WING 358–405, TAIL 106–125, TARSUS 66–81 (Delacour 1954). From Bering I. (e. of the Aleutians) there are a few specimens; they have somewhat palish underparts, show considerable size variation for so small a series, and all have wide white collars. There are some discrepancies in the 2 published sets of meas. of them; compare B. "*hutchinsii asiatica*" in Aldrich (1946, WING across chord) and in Delacour (1954, WING flattened?). The biggest bird is a ♀. (From Buldir I., 12 goslings—5 ♂ and 7 ♀—and the numerous progeny they have produced in captivity, are a potential source of mensural and other data on at least one Aleutian subpopulation.)

Weight from Amchitka I. a ♂ June 10, 1952, weighed 1,954 gm. [4 lb. 5 oz.] (Krog 1953) and an "apparently very old" ♀, May 10, 1959, weighed 1,927 gm. [4 lb. 4 oz.] (Kenyon 1961); from Adams Co., Wash., an "imm." ♂ Dec. 12, 1953, weighed 5½ lb. (G. E. Hudson).

211

Breeds in the wild at present, so far as known, only on Buldir I. (outer Aleutians, long. 175°55′ E), some 250–300 birds (half of them prebreeders) in 1963 and no later estimate available.

Formerly bred from Yunaska I. (long. 170°40′ W) or possibly even farther eastward, to westernmost Aleutians (Attu and adjacent islets). On Bering I. (Commander Is.) farther westward, Stejneger (1887) stated that a few Canadas bred; later, Johansen (1934) mentioned former breeding there and that a single specimen was taken as late as 1914. And beyond, Snow (1897) collected eggs in 1892 on Uschischir and Ekarma in n. Kuril Is.; C. J. O. Harrison (1962) gave meas. of an egg taken by Snow as 87.4 × 55.1 mm. [the stated length is 10 mm. more than the av. for Buldir birds, but breadth is the same].

From captive descendants of the goslings obtained in 1963 on Buldir, 75 geese were released on Amchitka I. in March, 1971. They could not be found there that fall, having migrated, or moved out of sight, or possibly having been killed by predators.

Migration   Spring and fall schedules and routes probably are much as in *minima*, at least in the sector from the Alaska Pen. to winter range. There definitely was a movement of *leucopareia* along the Aleutian chain. A few are seen, at least in fall, in the Izembek–Cold Bay area.

Molt migration no information. On July 11, 1963, at the lake on Buldir, there were 120 "adults" on the water, some probably flightless (K. W. Kenyon).

Winter range in former times when abundant: in w. N. Am., from somewhere in B.C. to interior valleys of Cal. (center of abundance apparently n. of that of wintering *minima*) and in Asia to Japan. Where the surviving Buldir birds spend the winter is unknown—possibly with *minima* (judging from a very few probable sightings).

Straggler   Certain few individuals, having characteristics believed to match some Aleutian birds, are known from the Yukon–Kuskokwim delta area (which is where *minima* breeds).

NOTES   The near extinction of the breeding geese of the Aleutians, caused by man directly and by introduced foxes (*Alopex* and *Vulpes*), has been chronicled by Bent (1925), O. Murie (1959), R. D. Jones, Jr. (1963a), and authors they cited. Buldir, having an area of only 6.64 sq. mi., is one of the few Aleutian Is. on which foxes were not introduced. Overshooting on winter range was stressed by J. Grinnell et al. (1918).

The extinct Bering I. birds were named *Branta "hutchinsii asiatica"* by Aldrich (1946), who included the Kurils in probable former range, and with migration probably to Japan. The small extant series has been mentioned above; at most, they represent a slightly palish subpopulation within the subspecies *leucopareia*. Apparently Kuroda (1952) was the first to synonymize *"asiatica"* with *B. c. leucopareia*.

Judging from Turner (1886), this goose occurred in greatest abundance westward beyond Unalaska in the Aleutians. Nevertheless, it migrated in winter chiefly to N. Am., although some went to Japan. In the latter country it occurred regularly and not uncommonly until 1922; see O. L. Austin, Jr., and Kuroda (1953). The last Japanese specimen record is dated Feb. 7, 1929, and the very few alleged sightings subsequent to that date have been questioned.

A few Canada Geese reportedly (Yocom 1970b) migrate to the Kashmir Valley in northernmost India. What subspecies and whether or not they might be escapees is not on record. RSP CDM

FIELD IDENTIFICATION   In most of N. Am., the Canada Goose, in all its varying sizes and shades of coloring, is so well known as hardly to need describing. White cheeks contrasting with blackish of head–neck, and the honking of large birds and the yelping of very small ones, identify it.

Size considerations aside, Canadas and Brant differ in that the latter appear wholly dark from tip of bill at least to lower breast, although there is a small amount of white on side of neck in Brant beyond Juv. stage. Emperor Geese (beyond Juv. stage) have most of head and the rear half of neck white (the white is visible at a distance), the rest of the bird being rather evenly grayed darkish (barring shows at close range). In the Atlantic area, the small Barnacle Goose may be likened to a Canada having white of head expanded over the face and including forehead and a Brant's body (black breast as well as neck).

In general, Canadas by age 2 mo. are much like their parents in size. So long as they retain much Juv. feathering (into fall or sometimes later), however, they can be distinguished as young at close range with the unaided eye, at long range with a telescope. Their coloring is more blended, their dorsal pattern (formed by light ends of feathers) is not evenly arranged, and the cheeks usually are somewhat darkish (not white); older birds have a clear-cut pattern and the dorsal light feather ends are arranged evenly (as barring). In very dark Canadas (large to diminutive sizes), the Juv. birds have grayer, more clouded coloring than older ones.

On short flights (as from resting to feeding areas), Canadas tend to fly low in bunches and broken lines; on longer flights often in larger flocks, strung out in the familiar lines and chevrons. RSP

VOICE   Usual call in the large to largest Canadas is a trumpeted (not bugling) guttural *uh-whongh un-whongh* . . . , the second syllable higher pitched. Loud, resonant, and prolonged by the gander; short staccato honks and yips by the goose (Collias and Jahn 1959); said to be higher pitched in ♂ than ♀. It is increasingly higher pitched, with components uttered more rapidly, in progressively smaller Canadas. From various papers by Moffitt: in the fairly large *occidentalis* the tone is intermediate between that of the very large Cal. birds (*moffitti*) and the decidedly smallish bird of the barrens (*parvipes*); the smallest, or so-called "Cackler" (*minima*), utters a high-pitched yelping *yelk yelk a-lick*, or *lick lick lick*.

When fighting, the breath is exhaled with a hissing sound, bill open, tongue elevated. A gasping, sometimes heard during injury feigning, is of quite similar nature.

In addition to distress calls, also contentment notes of goslings, Collias and Jahn (1959) included the following in a list "not intended to be exhaustive": 1 hiss—in threat or alarm, at short distances; 2 honking—as described above, a long-distance call, used in advertising territorial ownership, in alarm, greeting, maintaining contact during flight, etc.; 3 short-distance call of mate (either sex)—low, short, rather soft grunt *kum kum kum* . . . , sometimes double-noted *wah kum*; 4 short-distance call to goslings (by either parent)—quite like preceding but often faster; **5** special greeting call by gander to mate—rather loud, prolonged, snoring when pair just formed, and in Triumph display, and when mates come together after period of separation. Cowan (1974) determined that the alarm calls of parents with broods are "individually distinctive and could provide a basis for individual recognition of parents" by the goslings. For some further data on voice, see Raveling (1970) and especially Würdinger (1970). (Also see "Reproduction.") RSP

HABITAT Very diverse, over a vast range and in different seasons. Includes a variety of "managed" refuge conditions. A temperate to low-arctic breeder, with the little *B. c. hutchinsii* extending farthest into the arctic. In many ways, the Canada Goose is the N. Am. ecological counterpart of the Bean Goose (*A. fabalis*) of Eurasia.

In spring the geese seek remote areas, free from disturbance, for nesting. In general, they prefer nest sites that command clear views in all directions, and permanent water not far away (the young are led there). In s. part of breeding range marshes are favored, especially those having hardstem bulrush (*Scirpus acutus*) or cattail (*Typha*) with houses and feeding platforms of muskrats (*Ondatra*). Also meadows, gravel bars, islands in inland waters and the sea. They are scattered widely about and in shallow waters in muskeg country and usually near water on tundra. Elevations below 7,000 ft. are sought in Wyo. to avoid snow persisting past mid-April (Patterson and Ballou 1953). Distributional zonation, from the sea inland, of various geese including *B. c. minima* and *parvipes*, are discussed under White-fronted Goose.

Some smallish to very small Canadas go from tundra (summer) to open fields (winter, for feeding). Tiny *minima* goes from wet sedgy tundra (summer) to rather dry inland valleys (winter). Large Atlantic birds (nominate *canadensis*) are preponderantly tidewater geese much of the year, although they are inland breeders. Large dark Pacific coastal Canadas that migrate, i.e., the majority, go from tidewater and vicinity (summer and migrations) to inland fields (winter). At all wintering places, either water and food occur together or else they are within easy aerial commuting distance.

In interior conterminous U.S., under refuge conditions, some of the Canadas in the largest to large size category feed under trees or at margins of ponds having wooded shores. The smaller to smallest ones, of the barrens and tundra, are open country migrants and winterers.

No other species is so profoundly influenced by management. Food (standing crops, winter greens, scattered whole grain), water, and sanctuary provided on state and federal areas have concentrated most continental flights in a few score refuges, near or on which hunting likewise is concentrated. For example, at Horseshoe L. (Ill.), 225 killed/hr. in the early 1940s (Elder 1946b). Some former wintering areas (La.) seemingly were abandoned as a result of the refuge system (Yancey 1954, Lowery 1955). Refuges provide excellent opportunities for live-trapping and many thousands of geese have been banded; these abnormal concentrations also increase the incidence of diseases, some of which are fatal (Herman and Wehr 1954). WHE

DISTRIBUTION This topic has been discussed earlier under 8 trinomial names and mapped for each. In comparing maps, note absence within overall breeding range

214

from some mountain areas, also all of Seward Pen. in Alaska. There are no known stragglers to the Chuckchee Pen. or Wrangel I.

This goose has been expanding its range, as in e. Canadian arctic and by colonizing cent.-w. Greenland; on the other hand, there have been local extinctions at localities from the Atlantic seaboard westward on the continent and to beyond the Aleutians.

Archaeological finds references to the various localities were summarized by Brodkorb (1964a).

Fossil record see Brodkorb (1964a) for references. The species is known from the Pleistocene of Ore., Cal. (various localities, including Santa Rosa I.), Nev. (beds of questionable Pleistocene age), New Mex., Minn. and 3 localities in Fla. To this list add Nebr. (Jehl 1966, Tate and Martin 1969) and Texas (Fedducia 1973). Most records evidently pertain to Canadas of large to very large size. In Fla., the finds at all 3 sites have been assigned to the very small *hutchinsii*, except for additional material from 1 site not assigned subspecifically (see McCoy 1963 and Ligon 1965). As Wetmore (1958) stated, the species has had a wide range for a long period of time. RSP

MIGRATION   As a result of rapid adaptation to newly created refuges and feeding grounds the Canada Goose, more than any other waterfowl species, has "radically altered" its migration routes. Because of the narrowness of routes traveled (and by some other waterfowl also), they are more aptly designated "corridors" than routes. The Canada Goose is in the process of evolving new ones, so that any summation of existing ones probably would be outmoded in a few years. (From Bellrose 1968, which see for many details.) Particular routes (or corridors) and schedules have been mentioned under some subspecific headings earlier in this account, also under activities of prebreeders, etc. The following is general information.

Canadas fly silently or in loud-calling flocks, these being an aggregate of families, in diagonal lines or chevrons containing up to several score birds, seldom hundreds. Usually they fly at a few hundred ft. altitude, much lower in severe weather. Also above range of unaided human vision in fine weather (Trautman 1940). Various mt. ranges are no barrier. For example, the Wasatch Mts. in Utah reach nearly 10,000 ft. and the geese readily migrate over them. (C.S. Williams). Migrants fly at any hour and may arrive on a tail wind. When caught in storm or fog, they have been known to circle many times over city lights or to land on rooftops and wet pavements (F. L. B. 1891, Mershon 1928), and have been struck down in flight by lightning (Cartwright and Lloyd 1933). Reverse migration may occur when migrants overtake a storm (L. Jones 1906).

On migration they have been seen in association with Brant (Broun 1941), Blue and Lesser Snow phases of *Anser caerulescens* (DuMont 1943, T. Barry), and Whitefronts (Parkes 1950), but usually they do not mingle closely with other species.

Migration corridors are unit-specific; that is, banding has revealed definite routes and circumscribed wintering areas for each breeding unit studied.

Spring movements are noted as early as Jan., more often Feb. Rate of advance of the birds was stated to correlate with advance of the 35° isotherm (Lincoln 1935a), but this holds only for the vanguard. The main flights come later. Circling and calling of flocks just prior to departure seems to stimulate others to follow within a few days or weeks.

215

Thus there is great variation in timing of departure but, as the first flight moves on, the time of arrival at a particular locality is much less variable from season to season (W. Cooke 1913b). The total spring migration seems rather long, however, since some birds are slow to be stimulated to travel and so they and their accompanying prebreeders go rather late. Speed of migration accelerates as it progresses, from av. 9 mi./day at 40° N. lat. (cent. Ill.) to 30 mi./day at 62° in N.W.T. (W. Cooke 1906). In their study of *B. c. interior*, H.C. Hanson and Smith (1950) found that, regardless of duration of lingering in conterminous U.S., the final flight over forested Canada apparently often was made without stopping.

In migrating flocks, individuals are seen to shift about so that the lead bird is not always the same one, contrary to the popular notion that an old gander is in charge. Within pairs of mated birds, on the final leg of the journey northward, it is the ♀, as determined by shooting, that leads (H.C. Hanson 1965).

Breeders arrive in N.S. March 3–15 (Tufts 1932); Yorkton, Sask., March 29 (Houston 1949); James Bay April 15–25 (H.C. Hanson and Smith 1950); *minima* at Hooper Bay, Alaska, the last week of April (Lincoln 1926) or first week in May (various authors); *hutchinsii* on Baffin I. May 20–June 7 (Soper 1946), and at Southampton I. June 1 (T. Barry). Additional information was given earlier, under the various subspecies.

Molt migration has been treated briefly earlier in this account, under each subspecific heading for which data exist. Generalities given here, based on the Canada Goose, are believed to apply to most high-latitude *Branta* and *Anser*; see Sterling and Dzubin (1967) for additional details known for *Branta canadensis* and listing of relevant literature.

1 Molt migration follows spring migration in the ordinary sense; that is, the birds migrate to traditional breeding areas and then, immediately or after breeding, fly elsewhere to molt. In small tundra birds studied by MacInnes (1966), however, apparently almost all yearlings had separated from their parents by the time the latter arrived at nesting localities. 2 Prebreeders, nonbreeders, and some failed breeders make such flights, but not all birds in these categories do so. The majority that do are birds approaching 1 year in age. 3 As in various other geese, the Canada trends northward (some ducks may go in any compass direction). The Canadas introduced in England show some predisposition to fly n. to molt (Dennis 1964). 4 These flights are on routes that are unit- or flock-specific (they come from particular breeding places, except possibly some small tundra birds) and some individual geese perform this migration more than once before they become established breeders. 5 Distance traveled to molt may have a more or less inverse correlation with extent to which a particular unit is migratory otherwise. Some southerly units that are nearly sedentary as breeders produce yearlings, etc., that go very great distances to molt; some northerly units that travel far to breed produce yearlings, etc., that evidently go much less (or even perhaps no) distance to molt. In the former category, it may be assumed that the breeders devote their energy budget to breeding, comparatively early in the season, while prebreeders, etc., expend part of the equivalent energy budget in response to a continuing urge to migrate. In the latter category (northerly breeders), all age-classes migrate and the migratory urge is diminished in all by the time the long spring migration is completed, so that subsequent movement by prebreeders and nonbreeders is minimal. 6 Occur-

rence of molting Canadas of one size within the general breeding range of birds of another size has been a major hindrance in the past to understanding distribution and relationships of named populations. 7 Since such molting geese often are distant from where their units breed, this dispersal has considerable bearing on evolution and on survival of their units. For example, birds that depart to molt thus reduce any competition for food in nesting areas. 8 After the molt, the geese are more widespread; some yearlings may return to natal areas and rejoin their parents and the new young.

When flightless in molt, large Canadas can outdistance a man on foot and can maintain high speed over long distances.

Fall   There is various evidence that even sedentary flocks become restless and wary after the molting period.

From their studies of the subspecies *interior*, H. C. Hanson and Smith (1950) found that the earliest flocks travel the greatest distance in the shortest time and reach their wintering grounds before many flocks have left the north country. That is, some geese arrive far s. at concentration points as early as—sometimes earlier than—first arrivals are seen on refuges farther n. First arrivals have been reported for Sept. in such southerly places as Ky., Ga., and Texas. (Compare with *Anser caerulescens*.) South of Canada, peak movements usually occur in early Oct., with other movements into late Nov. at least.

There is a "leapfrogging" phenomenon (apart from differences between flocks of *interior*, just mentioned); southerly birds tend to be sedentary and to move very late and only if forced by weather to do so, while northerly birds start earlier and bypass the southerly ones. Thus, *interior* migrates a full month ahead of migratory flocks of *moffitti* (H. C. Hanson 1965); other examples could be cited.

It has been suggested (MacInnes 1966, Vaught and Kirsch 1966) that prebreeders may remain segregated from breeders and behave differently in autumn migrations. This may pertain to birds in their 2nd autumn, perhaps also some when older.

Winter   Mass movements may occur with each cold spell (W. Cooke 1888).

Homing of birds moved to another migration route was tested by Jack Miner; 25 eastern birds (of unstated ages) liberated in Man. were recovered in e. flights (Miner 1940). Birds of preflight age moved from Utah failed to return later, there being only 2 distant recoveries (C. S. Williams and Kalmbach 1943). Birds (*moffitti*) transplanted 100 mi. when 7–8 weeks old migrated and returned to the release area the following spring (Surrendi 1970). Other comparable instances could be cited. WHE RSP

BANDING STATUS   Latest available figures for the species: total number banded through 1964 was 335,883 and there were 36,894 recoveries through 1961. Most of the banding was done at localities throughout winter range and breeding range in conterminous U.S., also in Que., Ont., Alta., and Alaska (data from Bird Banding Laboratory). The number of papers already published that incorporate information derived from banding is too large to permit listing them here. RSP

REPRODUCTION   The large to largest Canadas, especially *interior* and *moffitti* (which here includes "*maxima*"), have been studied extensively; relatively little is known about some other populations. The number of published sources containing some relevant information is great, however. An additional source was a large MS (1956) by C. S. Williams, later shortened, revised, and published as a useful nontechnical book (C. S. Williams 1967). It should be borne in mind that various sources used here—Balham (1954), Brakhage (1965), Collias and Jahn (1959), Kossack (1950), Wood (1964), part of Elder's work, etc.—were based on birds more or less in captivity.

Age when first breeds in the wild varies with individual and circumstances—in large Canadas, some at 2 years, others when older. Some Canadas in the wild never mate (Balham 1954). A free-flying yearling ♀ *B. c. interior* in Md. laid a clutch of 4 eggs, 3 being fertile (L. Hall and McGilvrey 1971). In "semidomesticated" birds in Mich., Wood (1964) demonstrated that ♂ ♂ at age 2 years appeared to be sexually mature and that most ♀ ♀ examined had open oviducts during their 2nd fall. He pointed out that this condition (in ♀ ♀) is not necessarily proof that eggs have been produced. (New feathering on the abdomen might be a useful criterion, although some prebreeders build nests and preen the down from their bellies.) Ten yearling ♂ ♂ of the largest Canadas "were involved in nesting efforts" of older ♀ ♀ and 3 of these hatched normal goslings (Brakhage 1965). In any event, it is well established (Collias and Jahn 1959, Wood 1964) that crowding of birds in semicaptivity inhibits prebreeders from establishing and maintaining territories, hence from breeding. The same phenomenon occurs in the wild; that is, if suitable habitat in a nesting area is largely preempted by established breeders, fewer prebreeders become breeders. (It is sometimes said that plenty of breeding habitat for geese, as compared with certain ducks, still exists in N. Am.; the geese, however, have their social regulatory mechanisms and do not see it quite that way.)

There are unpublished data, on the "Wilson Hill flock" (Massena, N.Y.), on groups of large to largest Canadas that were approaching age 2 years when released as prebreeders in late March in habitat to their liking; between a third and half of them bred that same year. They responded thus in the absence of any inhibiting elders; then they, in turn, as breeders, established a rigid dominance and the young they produced did not breed at as early an av. age. (Compare with the Trumpeter Swan.)

The geese **arrive** at breeding areas in flocks; that is, aggregates of family units (assuming yearlings have not separated beforehand), also fragments of families that have been broken up by shooting or other causes. Except possibly for a few individuals, those that are to breed already are firmly paired. There is often a considerable "waiting period" between arrival and time the snow melts. When there is bare ground, the birds that had bred formerly reoccupy their territories and previously used nest sites, but some social flocking occurs during feeding periods until incubation is well along.

Pair bond form may be described as **lifelong monogamy** once the birds breed; even as yearlings, however, some individuals form more or less temporary bonds (especially in summer).

At or about the time that breeders show **territoriality**, the gander becomes aggressive toward other individuals (including his own offspring) and drives them away from his mate. In very large Canadas in Mich., about a day of repeated rebuffs by both parents ordinarily was required to convince the young that they no longer were wanted; then prebreeding ♂ ♂ tended to disperse, but ♀ ♀ remained in areas where they were hatched (Sherwood 1967). In a sedentary unit in Mo., "yearlings started loafing in small flocks which often were unisexual" (Brakhage 1965); they were color-marked and

218

of known sex. Yearlings and any other prebreeders thus seldom are allowed on territory and they gather in groups around the periphery of breeding areas for a while before some, or all, move away. While in the vicinity of nesters, they aid in defense of nesters by giving alarm (various authors). Tiny *minima* wander near nesters in small, very tame, flocks (Conover 1926).

As known in Canadas above middle size, at least many of those **prebreeders** that remain near breeders attempt to duplicate parental activities. They engage in pair formation behavior (which includes considerable squabbling), form more or less temporary bonds, "play" with nesting materials, and some even construct nests. Craighead and Craighead (1949) found half as many nests as "territorial" pairs in Wyo.; H. A. Hansen and Oliver (1950) reported 282 nests for 765 pairs of "resident" Canadas in the state of Wash. On the w. side of Hudson Bay at McConnell R., marked yearlings and also failed breeders performed normal nest-building activities during the latter half of June (when successful breeders were advanced in incubation). These pairs returned and nested in the same areas the following spring, indicating they may have chosen their sites the previous year (R. N. Jones).

Mate selection in very large Canadas in Mich. is based (among prebreeders) on experience or acquaintanceship near nesting grounds, but formation of a permanent bond occurs later, on winter range (Sherwood 1967). Yet it also can occur in summer; for many relevant data, see Surrendi (1970). There is a marked tendency for mates to be of similar age, in semicaptive birds (Kossack 1950) and in the wild, since young geese of a particular cohort tend to keep to themselves. In a sedentary flock, pair bonds often were established a year before actual nesting (Brakhage 1965). Probably some measure of experience or acquaintanceship occurs even within molting flocks. As indicated earlier, it may be a general rule that, in mated pairs, the goose is smaller than the gander, i.e., mating is assortative in this respect, not random. This has been demonstrated by MacInnes (1966) in *hutchinsii*. Presumably there is some sort of psychological barrier against siblings forming mated pairs. For polygamous behavior, see Brakhage (1965).

Pair formation behavior has been known ever since Audubon described it rather well over a century ago. Various actions mentioned beyond under territorial defense are used, both ashore and afloat. Sometimes there are fights between ganders for a goose. The winner approaches the goose, his head held low, the neck weaving from side to side and pumping back and forth. When matters have continued to the stage wherein the gander directs a prolonged snoring sound to the goose, the bond is formed (Collias and Jahn 1959); then the pair engages in joint attack against another bird, also the goose will follow the gander into the air. In spring, trio flights are quite often seen—a pair trying to lose a persistent interloper.

Among semicaptives in Ill., Kossack (1950) determined experimentally that, if a bird is separated from its mate, mating with another bird usually takes place the next nesting season; if separated just prior to the nesting season, mating will occur again the same year, even as soon as 16 days. At the Seney Refuge (Mich.): in case of loss of mates, experienced and "acquainted" mature geese, on nesting grounds, can develop a new permanent pair bond in a matter of hours (Sherwood 1967). The same has been observed in the wild (R. N. Jones and Obbard 1970).

The species often is considered to be a semicolonial nester. In fact, the birds usually

219

are dispersed throughout suitable nesting habitat, particularly over the vast boreal and arctic nesting range. Since they are highly selective in choosing nest sites, however, they give the appearance of a colony when habitat is limited in quantity. Since a feeding area with fresh growing grass in the far north (MacInnes and Lieff, in Hine and Schoenfeld 1968) or suitable seeding grasses in Man. (Klopman 1958) is required within short commuting distance of the nest, some seemingly suitable sites may remain unoccupied if there is no food close enough. At least in boreal and far northern regions, the adults may feed very little during incubation, living off reserves until the young hatch. At McConnell R., for example, there is little feed available until late during incubation when green vegetation begins to grow.

Territory of breeders is used for nesting, displays, and some feeding. Kossack stated it is selected by the gander. He also believed the **nest site** is chosen by the gander, but Balham believed it is the goose, since one nested on the same site 5 successive years with 3 different ganders. The goose generally selects it (Collias and Jahn 1959); the goose selects it (Klopman 1962, Brakhage 1965). The goose initiates flights to the future nesting area and "explores" while the gander remains on a nearby "loafing site" (F. W. Martin 1964). At the Seney Refuge in Mich., 2-year-old ♀ ♀ nested or reared their young in areas where they themselves had been goslings (Sherwood 1967). Feeding usually is done nearby, but may be 1–5 mi. away in Utah and N.C. (C. S. Williams and Sooter 1941, Hammond and Mann 1956). If food is plentiful on territory, pairs probably seldom leave it (F. W. Martin 1964).

In Cal., J. S. Dow (1943) found 418 nests spaced 3–150 yds. apart, the distance dependent on the individual gander's aggressiveness; elsewhere Balham found territory size influenced by visibility, availability of firm nest bases, and occurrence of suitable guard sites for ganders. On lake islands in se. Alta. the distribution of nests showed significant deviation from randomness, in the direction of uniform spacing (Vermeer 1970). A density equivalent of 55–66 nests/acre in se. Idaho was reported by G. H. Jensen and Nelson (1948). In Cal., 31 nests were found on half an acre (Naylor 1953). Crowding of nesters, due to various factors, caused fighting and desertion in Alta. (Ewaschuk and Boag 1972), Cal. (Naylor), and Mich. (C. S. Johnson 1947), but not in N.D. (Hammond and Mann 1956). On a barren islet only 30 × 12 ft. in area, in Snake R., Idaho, there were 4 nests (C. S. Williams). In Ore. there were 11 nests on a haystack (Williams).

Among Kossack's semicaptives, territorial defense at first was by both gander and goose, against an intruder of either sex. After incubation began, attack was by the gander, the goose in defense posture on or near the nest. This agrees with Martin's findings on wild birds in Utah. According to Balham, maximum amount of territory is defended at onset of incubation and decreases progressively thereafter; defense, by the gander only, against either sex, ceases when the goslings leave the nest.

Postures during defense: erect neck upstretched, beak repeatedly flipped upwards, a partial rotating of the head (the flipping and rotating display the head pattern), and honking; **Forward**—neck stretched forward, head low, and honking; **bent-neck**—neck in forward-directed S-shaped posture, hissing prior to and during actual attack on ground, or successful attacker even may continue pursuit into the air and honk as he ceases pursuit and circles back to alight near mate; **4 TRIUMPH** (mutual) display—gander alights and approaches mate, neck extended forward, head low, and bill open; he honks and utters a snoring sound while she joins in same posture and utters staccato honks and yips.

Blurton Jones (1960) included some of the above actions in 4 postures, as follows. BENT-NECK the neck doubled back, bill aimed at opponent, a grunting noise. FORWARD head held as far forward as possible, low, sometimes a flicking of closed wings, loud rapid honking. ERECT body tilted up and head held as high as possible, feathers on neck and body raised, trampling of feet, sometimes a hissing noise. HEAD-PUMPING more or less as erect posture, but head rapidly raised and lowered vertically. It is of interest that the neck feathers are raised and vibrated, although they are not modified in shape so as to appear "furrowed" (when not raised) as they are in *Anser*. A rustling of body feathers was mentioned first by Audubon. (Also see under "Habits.")

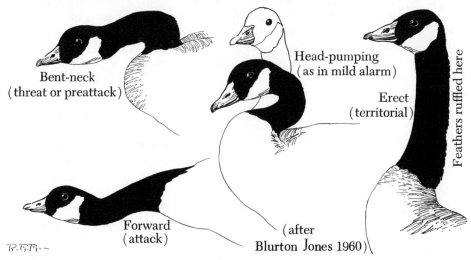

Bent-neck
(threat or preattack)

Head-pumping
(as in mild alarm)

Erect
(territorial)

Feathers ruffled here

Forward
(attack)

(after
Blurton Jones 1960)

As observed in conterminous U.S., sometimes there are more than 2 weeks of guarding territory, during which time the nest site is selected; the goose may make a series of depressions by "wallowing," not by digging or scratching (Kossack 1950, M. Geis 1956). Generally, the site must have unobstructed visibility in all directions, a guard site for the gander (up to a quarter mile away on open terrain), the nest site must be firm and dry, there must be some water not too far away (copulation apparently is more successful when the birds are afloat), and a grazing area within cruising distance (C. Williams). But at Flathead Lake (Mont.), 25% of all island nests were located in woods or under thick scrub (M. Geis 1956).

The site actually is so variable within the species that the nearest to an inclusive statement would be: **usually nests** on drier and slightly elevated spots not far from water. Visibility in all directions, rather than concealment, is a requisite. Sites commonly are near shores, or on muskrat or beaver houses, on gravel bars, islands, rocky ledges, and tops of dykes. Smaller islands seem to be preferred. Many nest in marshes and fields. Forty-six percent of nests studied in Utah were on foundations provided by the activity of muskrats (Williams). Tree nesting has been known from the time of Lewis and Clark in 1804 and Prince of Wied in 1833 in Mo., and cypress stumps still were used there in the 1890s (Widmann 1906). Apparently such elevated sites always were old nests of herons plus those of Ospreys and other hawks. In Mont., 7% of 1,099 goose nests were found in trees, from which the goslings tumbled to the ground (Craighead and Stockstad 1958). Tree nesting is fairly common in B.C. and reported even from Alaska. MacFarlane (1891) found a clutch of 4 (of *parvipes?*) 9 ft. above ground in a crow or hawk nest on the lower Anderson R. in N.W.T. Occasionally a goose selects a brushy stump or a cluster of low scrubby growth, adding a lining. Especially in the Rocky Mt. regions of Colo. and Mont., the geese nest on ledges or cliffs at some distance from water (Bent 1925). They do likewise elsewhere, as in Mo. Aleutian habitat, now mostly unused because of near-extinction of geese there, included talus slopes, steep terrain, and niches in cliffs. (On Buldir I. the remaining geese still nest on more or less heavily vegetated steep talus slopes.) The middle-sized geese of n. Alaskan mainland apparently prefer river bluffs and talus slopes. They select an unused spot or else occupy an old ground nest of a Roughleg or a Raven, adding a lining. Some of the nests are near active ones of Roughlegs and Peregrines (Kessel and Cade 1958). In Alta. they share declivities in cliffs with Prairie Falcons. Elsewhere this species has been reported nesting in or near colonies of the California Gull (J. W. Sugden 1947, other authors), even in contact with the nest of a Ring-billed Gull (Ferry 1910).

Various types of **artificial nest foundations** have been provided, such as boxes, tubs mounted on poles, platforms, and anchored floating rafts. They are accepted readily.

Nest construction is by the goose; the gander, who reportedly gives slight assistance in rare instances, is on guard nearby. Actual building begins 2–3 days before the first egg is laid (Kossack 1950). The nest begins with a bowl scraped in the substrate, then is lined with vegetation from the immediate surroundings. Material is not carried, but may be lifted by stages, the goose standing as far as a meter away and throwing material over her back. Usually, beginning about the time the third egg is laid, some down is added, then more at intervals until incubation begins, and some at any time later until hatching. Much of it may be blown away by the wind. In large light-bellied Canadas, the **nest down** is in large sprays, color grayish brown with light center and tips; any contour feathers intermingled with the down are broad in shape, with squarish ends, and colored a uniform light grayish; see pl. 76A in Witherby (1939). The goose covers her eggs with down and joins the gander in flight to feeding area. A hundred nests of very large Canadas in Utah: depth 1–10 in. (av. 3.9), inside diam. av. 9.4, outside 15–44 (av. 25) (Williams). Bulkier nests are found in such places as marshes where dry plant material is abundant at the site.

Copulation, among semicaptives in Wis., often is seen before, as well as after, selection of a permanent nest site, and ceases when the clutch is completed (Collias and Jahn 1959). Precopulatory display on the water consists of TIPPING or up-ending rapidly, as in bathing, followed by dipping the head and neck slowly and out of phase as mates face each other, then more rapidly and in unison until the goose flattens herself on the water in a receptive posture with neck half extended. The wings are kept folded. The gander mounts, then grasps the neck of the goose; she may be completely submerged during the few sec. of copulation (Balham 1954, Delacour and Mayr 1945). POST COPULATORY DISPLAY begins at once. The gander faces the goose, both hold heads high, bills pointing up and neck feathers ruffled for several sec. before the ♂ settles down and gives a special wheezy call (Balham, Vine 1950). Wing flapping, bathing, and preening occur thereafter on water and on land for up to a half hour. According to Collias and Jahn (1959), often during postcopulatory head-up posture mates rotate so as to face each other, breast to breast; then the gander half raises his folded wings and utters a brief weak snoring call. During the terminal phase the goose begins to bathe and soon also the gander. In a variant, one or both birds rear up on water and flap wings. Then the pair goes ashore and preens. (For added details and variability in copulatory behavior, see Klopman 1962.)

Time of nesting, hence dates for first eggs, is highly variable at any locality, depending on earliness or lateness of season, spells of adverse weather, etc. Kossack's semicaptive birds in Ill. began on Mar. 24 in 1945 and about April 6 in 1944. First eggs in Cal., Feb. 24–Mar. 16; Mont., Mar. 15, with peak 2 weeks earlier at 3,000–4,000 ft. elevation than in Wyo. at 6,500 ft.; in Utah, Idaho, and Ore., peak 3rd week in Mar. to 3rd week in Apr.; Nfld., mid-May; s. Labrador, mid- to late May; James Bay and Belcher Is., late May; cent. Man., April 9–26, av. date being 43 days later than the mean for Cal. (Klopman 1958); at Churchill, Man., on Hudson Bay, late May–early June; *hutchinsii* on Southampton I., June 16–21 (Sutton 1932, T. Barry). References for all except the last are in Klopman (1958) or 1956 MS by C. S. Williams.

The birds introduced in Britain usually begin nesting in early April. Those introduced in New Zealand begin in late Sept. or early Oct.

Clutch size increased slightly with age in a flock in Mo. (Brakhage 1962), but not in a northern study of *hutchinsii* (C. MacInnes). In Utah, 1,384 clutches of 1–10, usually 4–5 (av. 4.8) and Ore. 1,045 av. 4.8 (C. S. Williams); in Cal. 355 av. 5.1 (J. S. Dow 1943); in Wyo. 17 av. 4.6 (Craighead and Craighead 1949); Idaho 364 av. 5.3 (Steel et al. 1957); cent. Man. 40 nests in 1954 av. 5.0 ± 2.5 and 53 in 1955 av. 5.2 ± 2.5 (Klopman 1958); *minima* in Alaska 47 av. 4.7 (D. L. Spencer et al. 1951); *hutchinsii* on Southampton I., 2 clutches of 6, 5 (of 5), 3 (4) (T. Barry) and on se. Victoria I. 5 (of 6), 4 (5), 2 (4), 2 (3) (Parmelee et al. 1967). In Ill. 140 clutches of semicaptive birds 7 (of 2), 17 (3), 23 (4), 39 (5), 36 (6), 15 (7), 2 (8), 1 (11) (Kossack 1950). Many additional data for the largest Canadas were tabulated by H. C. Hanson (1965).

From the above sources, plus more recent (including some unpublished) data, the following generalizations can be made: **1** First nests have been found in Cal. as early as Feb. 24 to March 6 (in different years) and at lat. 61° N on w. side of Hudson Bay as early as May 26 to June 9, depending on year. Other localities fall between these extremes. **2** In Canadas from largest to below middle size, most clutches are of 4–6 eggs (but 2–9 recorded) and av. about 5.2; in the very small *hutchinsii* and *minima*, 3–6 are common (but 1–8 recorded) and the overall av. is about 4.4. **3** There is annual variation in av. clutch size even at southerly localities, and probably the geese at some northerly places are entirely prevented from nesting in unusually adverse seasons.

Egg shape av. nearer subelliptical than elliptical, but some approach oval. Shell **texture** fairly smooth, with some gloss at first, but soon becomes dull and stained. **Color** creamy white.

Egg size *moffitti* in Utah 174 av. 87.2 × 59.1 mm., variation in length was 20 mm. and in width 11 mm. and only 2 eggs in 2,726 were "runts" (Williams); eggs listed as of nominate *canadensis* (in Bent 1925) 84 av. 85.7 × 48.2 mm.; the small *hutchinsii* on Southampton 13 av. 75 × 51.3 mm. (T. Barry); captive *leucopareia*: 158 eggs length 71.4–83.9 mm., mean and standard error 77.4 ± 0.22 and SD 2.80; breadth 50.5–58, mean and SE 54.3 ± 0.12 and SD 1.49 (Stephenson and Smart 1972); and *minima* in Alaska, 40 av. 2.88 × 1.90 in. (Brandt 1943) and 1 egg each from 19 clutches measured length av. 74.66 ± 2.78 mm. and breadth 48.61 ± 2.16 (F. W. Preston). In 1969–72, some 24 mi. se. of Hooper Bay, 3,158 eggs of *minima* (mean and SD): length 74.0 ± 2.94 mm. (extremes 63.3–85.0) and breadth 49.4 ± 1.41 (44.1–53.8) (P. Mickelson). There are extremes, as well as averages, for various series in Bent (1925) and data were tabulated for the largest Canadas and also *B. c. interior* by H. C. Hanson (1965).

Fresh eggs of *moffitti* in Utah av. 5.1 oz.; for the first 22 days an egg loses an av. of 0.89 gm. daily and thereafter a gm. daily (Williams).

Laying Williams found that normally an egg is laid daily, usually before the morning feeding flight. In semicaptives in Ill., in 9 of 27 nests, the 2nd egg was laid the 3rd day and clutches of 4–8 were laid in 6–11 days with some laying at any hour (Kossack 1950). The goose covers the early eggs with debris.

Replacement clutches Various authors state a new nest is built close by and 2nd clutch laid if the first is removed early in incubation. Atwater (1959) proved that a goose will lay a 3rd clutch if robbed twice. Beginning after about a week of incubation, the likelihood of renesting decreases rapidly (Martin). For "continuation nests," "renests," and renesting interval, see especially Brakhage (1965). A goose was shot with fully formed egg Nov. 3 (C. S. Williams 1946). Dropped eggs were found in spring in Ind. (A. W. Butler 1898).

Incubation is by the goose, with gander on his guard site. The nest is kept very clean, but the guard site is fouled by the gander's droppings. Incubation usually begins with laying of last egg (Kossack); the goose does little sitting until clutch completed (Collias and Jahn 1959). As in other Anatidae, no true incubation patch, but a bare area is formed when goose makes very rapid, easily overlooked, nibbling movements in the loosened down and feathers, which are thus removed to line the nest. Incubation is constant in snow, when the goose does not leave to feed (Ray 1912, Balham 1954). In Utah, during early part of incubation, pairs leave and join in flocks to feed in P.M.; later they feed earlier in the day, with much less flocking tendency (Williams). Every 50 min. (Kossack 1950) or less (20–30, Balham), the goose rises from nest, turns, pokes at the eggs to turn them, settles, paddles with feet (to roll and level the eggs), jabs nest rim into shape, pulls in new material. These 5 stereotyped movements always were seen; may also shake body or toy with nesting material (Balham). Ganders have been observed incubating when a ♀ was absent, within a few days of hatching date (G. Sherwood, C. MacInnes). In such cases all normal incubation movements were evident, but paddling and turning on the nest was more frequent than with the ♀. Temperature between eggs immediately after goose left av. 95° F. (Williams); embryos av. 34.8° C. (94.6° F.) (Huggins 1941); [? the cited figures are in error] while Kossack (1947) reported they av. 101.3° F. when breast of the incubating goose was 101.1 and cloaca 105.2–109.2. Embryos of "*maxima*," at 3-day intervals during incubation, were described and illus. by J. A. Cooper and Batt (1972).

Incubation period usually 27–28 days in large to largest Canadas, as determined in

224

several studies; in the diminutive *minima* it was 25 days under a bantam hen (Laidley 1939), or 25–26 (Strutz, in H. C. Hanson 1965). From a study of 25 nests of large Canadas in Ill. it "appears to average 26 days" (Kossack 1950), but he used a shorter time than from laying of last egg to hatching of last in clutches in which all eggs hatch. It av. 26.8 days in se. Alta. (Vermeer 1970). For 8 clutches from semicaptives in Wis. the av. was 28.6 days (Collias and Jahn 1959). For 127 nests in the wild in Cal. it was reported as 28 days by Dow (1943). Worth (1940) reported 29 days. It is lengthened to 31 days in an incubator at 99° F. (Kossack 1947). If the eggs do not hatch, the goose has been known to sit a total of 43 days (Kossack 1950), 49 days (Williams), up to 87 days (J. S. Dow 1943). At least to 56 days, the gander has been known (Brakhage 1965) to maintain territory.

During incubation, on appearance of danger the gander honks and takes wing and the goose lies low on the nest. A flushed gander may alight at a guard site of another gander (Williams). In the wild, only an occasional gander will feign injury at this stage (Williams.)

For approximate hatching dates of various Canadas, add about 6 days (for laying span) plus 28 (for incubation) to any known dates of onset of laying; for *minima* use a 25-day incubation period.

Nesting success The percentage of nests in which one or more eggs hatch is high; see tabulation from various authors in Klopman (1958), also see W. C. Hanson and Browning (1959), H. C. Hanson (1965), and there have been several more recent studies. But severe weather can reduce it greatly. Thus, when there were 21 days of frost in May in Idaho, success was half that of Utah nests (G. H. Jensen and Nelson 1948). Desertion is the cause of most nesting failures, with predation second. Only 2%–3% of 7,086 eggs in Ore. and Utah were believed to be infertile and a small additional number showed embryonic development but did not hatch (Williams).

225

Size of broods at time of departure from the nest usually is relatively large; for example, av. 4.4 goslings in 157 broods in Idaho (Steel et al. 1957). In Utah, lack of predation on 2,599 broods was shown by an av. brood size of 4.87 in May, 4.73 in June (C. S. Williams and Marshall 1938a). (For other intermountain and for prairie units, see many data in table in H. C. Hanson 1965). In southerly populations of the species, evidence indicates that a stated number of breeders produce a fairly constant annual increment of young; there are very few data on northerly ones.

Hatching   Peeping can be heard within the shell 48–60 hrs. prior to the time the first opening in the shell is made, and the span from then to emergence of the gosling requires 8–36 hrs. (Williams). Kossack (1950) found that, among semicaptives in Ill., at first some families may return to spend the night at the nest. The nest then becomes soiled, although parents never defecate on it during incubation (Williams) as do ducks if alarmed. Goslings walk off elevated sites and so tumble down, to be stunned temporarily if they land on a hard surface (Kondla 1973).

Weight of newly hatched goslings: 55 young of the very large prairie birds—mean and standard error 103.3 ± 0.44 gm., SD 3.26, range 80.5–134.8; and for 23 *minima* 67.6 ± 1.17 gm., SD 5.60, range 54.5–73.5 (Smart 1965a).

First **activity of goslings** after they are dry is oiling (Williams). In Utah usually the young are led from the nest on their 1st or 2nd day; they are brooded for the first few days thereafter in marshy tracts, if such are available; then they are led to a rearing area which has open water. Then, if families are in close proximity, the goslings may combine into crèches (rearing groups). As a result, 10–20 goslings of assorted sizes may be under the care of a single pair of breeders (Williams). Up to 68 goslings with a pair in Utah and 44 with 3 breeders in Yellowstone (Williams). In a sedentary flock in Mo. it was not entirely evident how crèches were formed; dominance is a factor sometimes, and also is a factor in defending (maintaining) crèches; both ♂ and ♀ defend; there also may be "escorting" by nonbreeding ♀ ♀ (Brakhage 1965). In Mich., some 2-year-old ♀ ♀ lost, or gave up, their broods to older and more experienced pairs (Sherwood 1967). In *moffitti*, highly aggressive mated ganders may attract preflight young from several families, while less aggressive ones may lose their broods (Raveling). In *hutchinsii*, the goose will brood any young and it is the gander who prevents strange young from thus being brooded; the adoption of "gang broods" is rare (C. MacInnes). Parents that lose their broods behave as failed breeders, i.e., go into molt earlier. Even where there are large concentrations of nesters, however, brood combining by no means invariably occurs (F. Martin 1964); families may join, but the ratio of no. of yg./no. of parents is the same as in a single brood. More common is avoidance of one family by another. Young that have lost their parents are subordinate in the social hierarchy and tend to remain near areas used by family groups. Young of *minima* were reported by Brandt (1943) to form mixed groups with young Emperor Geese. Parents are decidedly quiet when the young are in preflight stage (Moffitt 1931, other authors).

In Mich., Sherwood (1967) reported that, as a result of brood combining, fall combinations (among 8 he listed) range from a family group plus "adopted" young for a total of as many as 21 members in the group down to a breeding pair or single parent without any young. Williams believed that the rearing group may maintain coherence until the following spring. Martin believed that the family group is fully integrated prior to young attaining flight and that it remains intact until the following spring, unless broken by hunting or other loss. The relationship of families to flock was shown by Elder and Elder (1949).

During their first few days out of the nest, the goslings hide in vegetation on approach of danger. Occasionally they stay on land for as long as 3 weeks before going to water (Willett 1919).

When swimming, a parent leads, the goslings follow in single file, and the other parent follows them. Manitoba data: the goose leads during the first 3 weeks, then either parent (Balham). Young may be moved 2–10 mi. to a suitable rearing area (H. Geis 1956), frequently down swift streams (Craighead and Craighead 1949); they may travel several days. Adverse effects of crowding during the rearing stage are shown by data from a Mich. refuge where 15 goslings survived with 286 older birds in large fenced areas; 200 survived in an instance when older birds were reduced to 45.

Both parents may feign injury, call, and flap off across the water, as the goslings dive. The latter may swim as far as 100 ft. while submerged (Weydemeyer and Marsh 1936). The gander may swoop to within a few ft. of a person and lead him away as the goose with young sneaks off through cover (Davison 1925). A paired bird without young distracted an aggressive Mute Swan from a pair with goslings (Tennent 1948). Maximum development of feigning was reported in *hutchinsii*, in which both parents "lay gasping as if at point of death . . . flapped about and trailed off as if wounded . . . [the gander] led me thus fully half a mile" (Sutton 1932).

Growth data in this paragraph refer to *moffitti* as studied by Williams. Seventeen weighed 3.4–7.7 oz. at hatching; they attained 6 lb. in 8 weeks. For 13 goslings, ages in days followed by av. wt. in oz. in parentheses: 1 (3.8), 6 (5.5), 9 (8.4), 16 (15.4), 23 (29.8), 30 (48), 37 (65), 44 (84.6), 51 (93). During the first 2 weeks there are few marked changes in appearance, except coloration becomes dirty gray (faded); at 12 days—some loss of the first down and a stiffening of feathers can be felt in tail region; at 20 days—remiges are evident, tail coverts also; 26 days—blackish tail feathers obvious and breast feathers appearing; 30 days—still appear mainly dirty grayish, the only well-developed feathers being tail and wing coverts; 36 days—white crescent above tail is prominent; 40 days—most of the down gone from neck, which appears blackish; 44 days—cheek patches (white) prominent and contour feathers cover most of body; 56

227

days—the down is gone, feathers still grow, and at a distance the young are not separable from older age-classes.

There are photos of prairie geese at ages 1 day to 10 weeks in H. C. Hanson (1965) and data on more westerly very large Canadas in Yocom and Harris (1965).

In his study of *B. c. interior*, H. C. Hanson (1951a) found that individuals in their 2nd year of life frequently ranked among the largest in size; he concluded that a significant size difference between them and older ones probably does not exist.

Voice Among Kossack's semicaptives in Ill., the young had only gosling calls their first 9 weeks, then a mixture of gosling and mature-bird calls for 3 weeks, thereafter only the latter. They hiss when less than a week old (Collias and Jahn 1959).

Age at first flight in the largest Canadas usually is 8–9 weeks—"appears to fly from 7 to 8 weeks after hatching" (Moffitt 1931), "almost exactly" 2 mo. (Houston 1949), 8 weeks (D. Munro 1960). Mention of "about six weeks" (Craighead and Craighead 1949) is too short and probably an estimate. For a large Canada (*B. c. interior*), H. C. Hanson (1965) estimated the preflight period as approximately 63 days. Tiny *B. c. minima* hatch in 2nd week in July and are flying the 3rd week in Aug. (D. L. Spencer et al. 1951); by Aug. 15 the "six-week-old goslings are testing their flight feathers" (U. C. Nelson and Hansen 1959). This implies some ability to fly perhaps at about age 42 days. Probably 45–50 days is their usual preflight period and it is possible that *hutchinsii* has a longer preflight period than *minima*. Captive-reared Canadas do not fly at as early an age as those in the wild, the additional time evidently varying from about a week in very small birds to as long as 2–3 weeks in the largest ones.

If the geese are not disturbed, probably the young do not fly for several days or even a week after they have attained flight capability. For example, when their parents have become flightless during molt, the young are not easily frightened into leaving them. After the young attain flight (and the parents regain it), the family flies to grazing areas to feed and to river bars and mudflats to get grit and to rest. (Also see "Migration.")

Relations of age-classes through the breeding season, also through the year, were a matter of speculation prior to studies of marked birds in the wild. For comparison, Kossack (1950) reported as follows on semicaptives in Ill. At equivalent of onset of spring migration of wild birds, the flock broke up into small units. Four weeks later breeders were in pairs. In this period of pairs keeping to themselves, there was mild "hazing" of yearlings. By the time of choosing and guarding of territories, serious hazing of yearlings was in progress and the separation of prebreeders from breeders was at its peak. Kossack stated that the same was observed in full-winged birds nesting off the study area. The same pattern evidently holds for the species in general, the apparent exception so far reported being earlier separation of prebreeders from breeders in some *B. c. hutchinsii*.

In large to largest Canadas, successful breeders begin Prebasic molt (of all feathering) when their brood is about 10–15 days old. This is an estimate; the time of onset of this molt undoubtedly varies considerably, depending on whether nesting is early or late, whether the birds have bred before, and other factors. That most parents become flightless just before the young first fly (Moffitt 1931) either is very exceptional or is misinformation. Mates begin their molts within a few days of each other. In large Canadas, assuming parents begin the molt when their brood is 2 weeks old, and assuming the parents are flightless for 5–6 weeks, the latter regain flight shortly before the young attain it. From field observations, however, it is known that the timing of molt in the 2 generations of geese frequently is not this closely synchronized.

Failed breeders depart for molting and resting areas and go into molt earlier than successful breeders. In Mont., however, a goose whose eggs were taken during the laying span renested once and another did so twice; for further details see Atwater (1959). Renesting, if a clutch is lost before incubation is well advanced, is common; see, for example, W. Hanson and Eberhardt's (1971) data on *moffitti*. Prebreeders (yearlings and older birds that have not bred) are the first to become flightless—by late May in Utah and Cal. (See information given earlier on molt migration.) After prebreeders regain flight, some rejoin their parents and siblings on rearing and molting areas (Williams). Thus there is recognition, after a molt and period of separation, between these generations. In Utah in Feb., Martin saw these surviving members of a color-marked family group: parent (♀), birds approaching age 3 years, birds approaching age 2 years, and offspring of the previous summer. The older geese did not show as evident a bond among themselves as was noted among the youngest cohort; however, all birds flew together and remained together for days.

From the information given, it is evident that **age when fully independent** varies; some Canadas are "on their own" seasonally at ages when they are part of a family group during other times of the year. In Mich., Sherwood (1967) found that there were strong ties among broodmates well into their 2nd year, with or without the presence of parents. For much information on interactions during winter, see Raveling (1970). WHE

SURVIVAL Without dissecting the variables, the general pattern in large to largest Canadas may be stated briefly as follows: a breeding unit tends to be a "closed" group, the utilized breeding habitat annually accommodating about the same number of pairs. At the present time, survival (av. life span) varies with hunting pressure, other mortality factors being relatively minor. If hunting losses are heavy, the birds "compensate" by having higher rate of replacement. This evidently fits various subpopulations or units of *moffitti*, *interior*, and nominate *canadensis*. The opposite, low kill and diminished replacement, apparently was the situation in the past in *occidentalis*.

On the above basis, allowable hunting kill is adjustable within limits, but the variables to be reckoned with differ from unit to unit and must be understood. One variable, for example: where hunting is heavy, kill is selective toward the less wary prebreeders—a loss of as many as 60%–70% of these younger birds (H. C. Hanson and Smith 1952). Little is known about subarctic–arctic breeders, but nesting and rearing activities are much more weather-influenced (compare with Brant) than is the case with more southerly nesters. Predation also can be heavy, at least locally. On Southampton I. in 1961, when arctic foxes were abundant, there was a crash in lemming numbers; the foxes then preyed so extensively on nests of *B. c. hutchinsii* (and other waterfowl) as to cause near-failure to produce any young.

For many further data on survival, see especially the following sources and references they contain: H. C. Hanson and Smith (1950), Craighead and Stockstad (1964), H. C. Hanson (1965), R. A. Hunt and Jahn (1966), and Vaught and Kirsch (1966).

The estimated mean annual adult survival rate of Canadas introduced in England was calculated as 0.78 ± 0.03 (Boyd, in Le Cren and Holdgate 1962). For New Zealand data, see Imber and Williams (1968). RSP

HABITS   Generally speaking, the Canada Goose is decidedly terrestrial, primarily a vegetarian, and predominantly a grazer. Some coastal Canadas tend to be more aquatic, except when breeding.

The **fundamental unit** within the flock is the family, which may include several age-classes of young, also "adopted" individuals. Singles seem lost; they call continuously, come to decoys readily, and are easily stalked and shot. Daily feeding flights may be in large loose aggregations, but families maintain identity. On breeding grounds, or when making local flights in winter, the V flight formation seldom is used; they organize into long strings and V's when making long flights (C. S. Williams). There are A.M. and P.M. feeding flights in winter, up to 30 mi. (Glazener 1946), with midday spent at a roost area, bathing and preening there, or often in "one-legged slumber." They normally are day feeders, but if persecuted may feed at night and rest on water. See Raveling (1969a) and Raveling et al. (1972) for many further details. They have been known to perch in trees (R. Williams 1888) and on telegraph poles (Sooter 1943). They may take wing by springing directly into the air from land or water, but on land several preliminary steps usually are taken.

Family integration begins at a very early age; the greeting form of TRIUMPH CEREMONY may be seen in goslings only 3 or 4 days old. Maintenance of the family bond is achieved by frequent Triumph ceremonies, which may be initiated by any member, but it is the gander's behavior which determines the integrity of the family.

Raveling (1970) described clearly the hierarchy that exists in wintering flocks, listing the following postures and activities: **Fleeing** neck erect, its feathers ruffled, and head held high, by a bird when escaping from another. **Submissive** neck curled and bill points down, almost touching the breast, and away from other geese; neck feathers somewhat erected. **Erect** as though alert, but the body usually more erect; the neck may be vertical or tilted away from or toward other nearby geese; neck feathers may be raised, or else sleeked and with body feathers erected. **Head-pumping** a repeated lowering and raising of the head, the neck usually vertical or may be tilted toward another goose as the pumping continues. **Rolling** low intensity—the head is shaken much as in preflight head-tossing, i.e., a vertical lifting of the bill while the neck is erect. Higher intensity—neck and head are waved forward and back and from side to side in an arc-like movement, bill pointing up, the head vigorously shaken laterally. The white cheek patches show conspicuously. There is strident honking. Highest intensity—wings are flicked or shaken. **Bent-neck** head pointed at another goose, the bill often angled slightly downward, neck coiled back in varying degree. **Forward** head and neck thrust forward horizontally and oriented directly at another goose, as if preliminary to attack. **Attack** low intensity—the bird walks toward another, in bent-neck, forward, or inter-mediate posture. Intermediate intensity—the bird runs toward another, often in Bent-neck posture, usually more in Forward posture. High intensity—the bird runs at another with head high or low, neck more or less in sigmoid curve, often with wings somewhat spread.

Large families are dominant over smaller ones, any family over a mated pair, and least dominant are unpaired individuals of the youngest cohort. A defended "family distance" is maintained during feeding (Elder and Elder 1949). It is possible that, in presettlement times, Canada Goose numbers were limited by quantity of available wintering habitat. Under such circumstances, their pattern of family behavior and dominance would have been highly advantageous in insuring survival of the offspring of more successful breeders.

Interspecies tolerance has been noted under extreme crowding in zoos (Jenkins 1944), but is not a marked trait of breeders in the wild. When provoked, Canada Geese have beaten to death a Ring-billed Gull (McCabe and McCabe 1935), a skunk ap-proaching a nest, and have beaten a flightless Bald Eagle that was put in a nest enclo-sure; even when severely crippled and unable to fly, Canadas have knocked down eagles approaching over ice (C. Shanks, G. Arthur). If, during migrations or winter, the geese of an area are put to flight in alarm, the members of a flock, on again alighting, need some time to "sort themselves out," i.e., to get reorganized into their fundamen-tal groupings. When feeding, a sentinel may be posted to "stand watch" as the others move about, picking up food. Formation of permanent pair bonds is, in part, an activity of the winter season.

On fine days in late winter there is a sort of communal display, the geese dipping, diving, and somersaulting on the water with their legs kicking in the air (Lucas 1944); similar behavior also has been observed in spring (Baker 1956, Batty and Cave 1963). In an instance among captives in Dec. in N.Y., it appeared to begin as a sort of progres-sively more exaggerated bathing behavior by an individual until it became somersault-ing; by that time, various scattered nearby individuals were acting similarly; after a while, for no obvious reason, the dozen or so participants all ceased within a couple of minutes (R.S.P.).

Unless forced to take wing hurriedly, the geese commonly show flight intention by waggling their heads both vertically and sideways (as in territorial defense); see Ravel-ing (1969b) for behavior related to flight. In flight, they usually cruise at about 40 mph. In the larger Canadas, 2 wingbeats/sec. = 120/min. cruising. The upward sweep re-quires about ⅜ and the downward ⅝ of the time required for a wingbeat. Top speed probably is about 60 mph and 180 wingbeats/min. These data are from motion picture film (C. Williams). Wingbeats/sec. were reported as 2.6 by Blake (1948). Recorded flight speeds in mph among larger Canadas are 20 (easy cruising) by Cottam et al.

231

(1942), 44½ (Clayton 1897), 45–58 (Rathbun 1934), and 60 (air speed) by M. Cooke (1937). There are a number of reports of flying flocks abruptly changing course on approaching the vicinity of radio and radar facilities. For the aerodynamic advantages of flying in chevron formation, see Lissaman and Sollenberger (1970); there may be some other basis for it, however.

Canadas of any age will hide on land or water by extending the neck and lying motionless. This "playing possum" has been observed frequently. A cripple, on seeing a man or dog, generally assumes this posture.

This goose, a harbinger of seasons, has a niche in native folklore; there seems to be no summary of information on this subject. Interest in this bird as a food source was and is largely in boreal regions; see H. C. Hanson and Currie (1957) for former kill by Indians in the Hudson–James bay area; various authors have described the taking of preflight and flightless molting birds by Eskimos on the Bering Sea coast of Alaska and elsewhere. The Aleuts took many young and domesticated them (Turner 1886). Perhaps this goose was kept occasionally as a penned captive by Indians in presettlement times, but probably could not have survived otherwise in captivity in the presence of native dogs. From the inception of Caucasian settlement, the newcomers fattened these geese for eating in fall—the Michaelmas goose tradition transferred to the New World. In the early 1880s they still were kept commonly in coastal villages in Nfld. (Howley 1884) and the descendants of some decoy flocks still are maintained at scattered localities in N. Am.

No game species more readily loses its fear of man and becomes content in domestic surroundings (Williams). The readiness with which Canada Geese become semidomesticated when given protection possibly may be related to slow development of wariness in young birds: newly hatched ducks are very wild, but young geese are very trusting (H. C. Hanson and Smith 1950). These authors discussed in detail the role of man in conditioning goose behavior at the Jack Miner Sanctuary in Kingsville, Ont. (Also see Vaught and Kirsch 1966.) This tameness is disastrous to geese on opening day of the hunting season where large concentrations are found, such as Horseshoe Lake, Ill., Horicon Marsh, Wis., and Swan Lake, Mo. Hundreds are killed so easily that hunters complain of the lack of sporting quality of the shooting.

A concentration of geese has a decoying effect—even more birds come in. This concentrates them on refuges. Major refuges with big winter feeding programs have altered former migration patterns; they also hold many birds north of their former wintering areas.

When a breeding unit is exterminated, however, the breeding "traditions" are lost with the birds. The area where they bred no longer is breeding range, no matter how suitable it may be. Also, if an area suddenly is rendered unsuitable, evidently ♀ ♀ already established there as breeders seldom will nest anywhere other than at their accustomed sites. A new "tradition" can be established by releasing a few cripples or pinioned birds; as the new breeding unit builds up it frequently attracts many migrants. This aspect of goose "management" is a proven success at widespread localities: B.C., Cal., N.D., Minn., Mich., Ky., Pa., and elsewhere.

At the present time, many small feeding and resting areas have been drained and converted to agriculture. The trend in water storage is toward large impoundments, where these can be created, for irrigation and power. Such places seldom have adequate food, so the geese seek crops on farmland. There they prefer succulent young sprouts or the mature heads of grains. In general, grain growers are tolerant of geese in spring, recognizing that the birds are more apt to aid the crop than ruin it; see, for example, Pirnie (1954). Sometimes, however, they do severe damage to unharvested mature crops. They also swallow lead shot, to their detriment (Trainer and Hunt 1965); for the effects of such poisoning, see Cook and Trainer (1966). (There are other papers on these topics, dating from the early 1930s on.)

Among the larger Canadas, size of food items eaten ranges from small clippings of grass to large tubers of *Scirpus*. Aquatic feeding is incidental, except among coastal flocks. The tip-up method of feeding in water occurs widely, but the birds resort to it mainly when grazing forage is scarce. Although known to dive from the surface, this goose rarely does so. Grit is eaten in all seasons and sometimes considerable soil (especially in winter). In the largest Canadas, usually there are about 10 cc. of sand or gravel in the gizzard; the birds will fly many miles to obtain it (Williams).

There probably were about 1¾ million wild individuals of *Branta canadensis* in N. Am. in late 1970. The species has been studied intensively. Although 252 papers are cited in the present account, this is less than a fifth of those already published that contain significant information on the species. For example, there is a recent symposium devoted to its biology and "management," edited by Hine and Schoenfeld (1968). WHE

FOOD Vegetable—shoots of grasses and sedges, berries, aquatic plants and seeds, and cultivated grains. Insects, crustaceans, and mollusks, perhaps usually when these various items are attached to food plants, and fish occasionally are ingested. (For geese away from breeding range, the data are given for geographical areas, not subspecies.)

ATLANTIC COAST Wigeon grass (*Ruppia maritima*), spike rushes (*Eleocharis*), naiads (*Najas*), glassworts (*Salicornia*), bulrushes (*Scirpus*), salt grasses (*Distichlis*) (A. C. Martin et al. 1951); Me.—rhizomes of eelgrass (*Zostera marina*) and sea lettuce (*Ulva lactuca*) (Norton 1909); lower Hudson valley—buckwheat (*Fagopyrum esculentum*) and unidentified fragments of insects (Foley and Taber 1951); Pa.—leaves of smooth crabgrass (*Digitaria ischaemum*) and trace of seeds of three-square bulrush (*Scirpus americanus*) (Wingard 1952); upper Chesapeake Bay region—principally rushes (*Scirpus americanus, S. olneyi*), salt grass (*Distichlis spicata*), wigeon grass (*Ruppia maritima*) (R. E. Stewart 1962); N.C. (L. Mattamuskeet)—263 gizzards and 31 crops, maize (*Zea mays*), Cyperaceae (chiefly *Scirpus americanus*), rhizomes and roots of spike rush (*Eleocharis* spp.), Gramineae (Yelverton and Quay 1959). S. Atlantic coast—cordgrasses (*Spartina alterniflora, S. patens*), eelgrass, shoalgrass (*Halodule wrightii*) (H. C. Hanson and Griffith 1952).

MISSISSIPPI VALLEY Ohio—sprouted and growing wheat and yearling gizzard shad (*Dorosoma cepedianum*) (Trautman 1940); Mich.—grasses, bulrush (*Scirpus*), and horsetail (*Equisetum*) (W. J. Howard 1934); on a refuge, sugar beets (Ellis and Frye 1965); Wis.—winter and spring, shoots of winter rye (*Secale*), maize on stalk or in shock (Stoddard 1922); Ky.—shoots of wheat and barley (G. Wilson 1929); spike rush (*Eleocharis obtusa*), roots of water cress (*Roripa* [*Radicula*] *sessiliflora*), Italian rye-

233

grass (*Lolium multiflorum*), reed canary grass (*Phalaris arundinacea*) (J. Morse (1950)); Mo.—food from 108 specimens consisted principally of *Echinochloa* 36%, *Polygonum* 10.2%, *Leersia* 10.1%, and *Eleocharis* 8.3% (Korschgen 1955); Ala.—a stomach contained all parts of northern naiad (*Najas flexilis*) and 2 seeds of panic grass (*Panicum*) (A. H. Howell 1924).

GULF COAST   Principally rice (*Oryza sativa*), corn, sorghum grain (*Sorghum vulgare*), watercress (*R. nasturtium-aquaticum*), cordgrasses (*Spartina*), salt grass, glassworts (*Salicornia*), bulrushes (*Scirpus*), Bermuda grass (*Cynodon dactylon*), naiad (*Najas*), berries of matrimony vine (*Lycium*), panic grass, sheep sorrel (*Rumex acetosella*), sea oxeye (*Borrichia*), cranberry (*Lycium berlandieri*), water hyssop (*Bacopa*), bull grass (*Paspalum*) (Glazener 1946).

MOUNTAIN–DESERT   Utah (Bear R. marshes)—mainly sago pondweed (*Potamogeton pectinatus*), bulrush (*Scirpus paludosus*), glasswort (*Salicornia rubra*), salt grass, bromegrass (*Bromus tectorum*), wigeon grass (*Ruppia maritima*), wild barley (*Hordeum gussoneanum*), beard grass (*Polypogon monspeliensis*), sea blite (*Suaeda*), peppergrass (*Lepidium*), alkali grass (*Puccinellia*), saltbush (*Atriplex hastata*), golden dock (*Rumex persicarioides*) (Wetmore 1921, A. C. Martin et al. 1951); Ariz. (Roosevelt L.)—young blades of Bermuda grass (Hargrave 1939); Yellowstone Nat. Park—blades and roots of grasses, also grasshoppers and other insects (Skinner 1928); Nev. (Pyramid L.)—salt grass (*D. stricta*) (R. M. Bond 1940). In the Great Basin area, during the molting and brood-rearing period, food consists mainly of aquatic plants: *Potamogeton pectinatus*, *Ruppia maritima*, *Elodea*, *Ceratophyllum*, *Callitriche*, and *Myriophyllum*; at other times during the breeding season the bird grazes on grasses (mainly *Poa*, also *Hordeum jubatum*, *H. gussoneanum*, *Distichlis*, and *Puccinellia*), *Lepidium perfoliatum*, *Erodium cicutarium*, *Allocarya*, *Plagiobothrys*, *Taraxacum*, *Salicornia*, *Atriplex*, and *Dondia* (*Suaeda*) (C. S. Williams Ms. 1956).

PACIFIC COAST   Nw.—foliage of native grasses and cultivated grains, foliage and seeds of sago pondweed (*P. pectinatus*), seeds, foliage, and roots of aquatic plants (Scheffer and Hotchkiss 1945).

NORTHERN BREEDING GROUNDS   Scant data. *B. c. hutchinsii* feeds on coastal marine plants and their adhering mollusks (Swainson and Richardson 1831, Sutton 1932). *B. c. interior* in interior Ungava feeds on leaves of *Carex aquatilis*, *C. canescens*, *Cochlearia officinalis*, *Achillea millefolium*, *Polygonum viviparum*, *Pedicularis flammea*, *Luzula parviflora* (?), *Stellaria longipes*, *Polystichum*, *Salix*, and *Poa arctica*, stems of *Juncus albescens* and *Equisetum arvense*, inflorescence of *Calamagrostis neglecta* and *Carex vaginata*, and tips of branches of *Vaccinium uliginosum* (Polunin and Eklund 1953). *B. c. parvipes*—in 5 stomachs from Perry R. containing food, reported in H. C. Hanson et al. (1956): 2 contained solely the spikes of *Eriophorum*, a third 35% of this sedge plus 65% *Equisetum*, a fourth contained 90% *Poa* sp., and the fifth 95% unidentified grass. The moss present was believed to be adventitious. In Aug. at Great Bear L., the geese fed on berries of *Empetrum nigrum* (Preble 1908). *B. c. minima*—captured goslings sought the tender blades of grass growing on the housetops of the natives (Turner 1886, E. W. Nelson 1887, Lincoln 1926); in autumn these tiny geese feed on berries of various species of *Vaccinium* and of *Empetrum*. AWS

234

Barnacle Goose

Branta leucopsis (Bechstein)

Smallish goose; in all postdowny stages most of head white or nearly so (sharply delineated from black of rear of crown and nape and this continues to include neck, forepart of mantle, and breast), bill short and slender, wing coverts strongly barred. Might also be likened to a light-bellied Brant having white face, contrasty dorsal barring, and black breast. Tracheal apparatus was mentioned by Eyton (1838). Sexes similar in appearance, ♂ av. slightly larger; length to 28 in., wingspread about 52–56, wt. to over 5 lb. (usually about 4). No subspecies.

DESCRIPTION   One Plumage/cycle, with Basic II regarded as earliest definitive.
▶   ♂ ♀ Def. Basic Plumage (entire feathering), worn from some time in SUMMER to some time the following SUMMER (the intervening molt, of all feathering, occurs earlier in prebreeders and failed breeders than in breeders). **Bill** blackish, **iris** dark brownish, feathering of **head** white or creamy white, with black streak from bill to and around eye, and black begins on crown and extends down back of head. All of neck, breast, and forepart of body black, the feathers grayish basally and, in new feathering, narrowly tipped with ashy buff. More posteriorly, the **mantle** becomes light to medium gray, the feathers with wide heavy black subterminal band and narrow whitish tip, giving conspicuously barred effect. Lower back and rump blackish, but upper coverts near the tail white. **Underparts** (black of breast ends abruptly) largely white, the sides and flanks with light to medium grayish barring. Legs and **feet** black. **Tail** black. **Wing** primaries and secondaries dark gray, grading to black distally; upper coverts barred like mantle (most white is on longest coverts), but barring reduced on primary coverts and alula; under wing coverts light grayish.

Plumage acquired by a molt of all feathering which, in successful breeders, begins well along in July or in early Aug. (that is, early in rearing period). Flight feathers of wing dropped early during molting; duration of flightless period unknown. The ♂ is reported to begin molt earlier than the ♀ (Dementiev and Gladkov 1952); further details unknown.

AT HATCHING   **head** mostly pale yellowish, but a dark line from bill to and around eye, the crown grayish brown. **Upperparts** like crown, with 3 pairs of whitish spots (rear sides, tip of wing, trailing edge of wing). **Underparts** buffy white with brownish band on upper breast. Bill and **feet** dark grayish. For color photo of a downy gosling see Salomonsen (1967a).
▶   ♂ ♀ Juv. Plumage (entire feathering) generally worn in entirety rather briefly in FALL, then succeeded by Basic I (except most of wing retained into following summer). Compared with Def. Basic: scattered blackish feathers in whitish buff of **head** are common, so that the dark line to eye seems to extend beyond to rear of crown. Dark areas of Plumage off-black and without gloss. Barring on **dorsum** less regular and clear-cut, the dark areas narrower. Subterminal bands on greater and median **wing coverts** nearer sepia (not black) and these feathers are narrowly tipped with pale brownish (not white). Brownish tinge on sides and **underparts.** Various feathers (man-

tle, especially scapulars, the underparts, greater and median coverts) shorter and distally narrower; **tail** feathers narrow, with notched ends.

▶ ♂ ♀ Basic I Plumage (all feathering except most of wing) generally begins to replace Juv. in FALL and the molt ordinarily proceeds fairly rapidly. In some individuals, however, the molt is more gradual, or interrupted, or even delayed and then proceeds quite rapidly. This variation in timing, rather than acquisition of another Plumage in spring, accounts for occasional birds found molting when even 10 months old. At least usually, when all the squarish-ended Basic I tail feathers have replaced the notched Juv. ones, the individual has completed Prebasic I molt. All Basic I feathers are quite similar to definitive ones, but they vary with individual bird from being definitive in size and shape to being more Juv.-like (shorter and more roundish ended). The Juv. wing, except for some coverts, is retained and worn with Basic I.

Measurements 6 ♂ (Britain 5, France 1): BILL 29–32 mm., av. 30.5; WING 398–424, av. 415; TAIL 110–135, av. 126; TARSUS 69–80, av. 72; 6 ♀ (Britain 5, Germany 1): BILL 29–33 mm., av. 31; WING 389–419, av. 400; TAIL 115–132, av. 124.5; TARSUS 65–72, av. 68.7 (ETS). These agree well with series in Witherby (1939) who measured wing over the curve. Also see Schiøler (1925) for meas., including flattened WING.

Weight of unsexed birds on winter range, 2½–5 lb., 55 av. 4 lb. (1.8 kg.) (Popham, in Witherby 1939). Breeders in e. Greenland flightless in molt and sexed by cloacal examination: 256 ♂ 3.3–5.3 lb. (1.5–2.4 kg.), 234 ♀ 3.0–4.9 lb. (1.36–2.23 kg.) (Morris and Ogilvie 1962).

Incubator-hatched goslings: 12 on day of hatching weighed 48.4–71.5 gm. (mean and standard error 63.4 ± 1.41) (Smart 1965a).

Hybrids An "apparent" Barnacle × Whitefront hybrid was seen early in 1954 and 1955 at Slimbridge, Glos., England, where 2 similar birds had been seen in Dec. 1939 (Wildfowl Trust, 7th [for 1953–54] and 8th [for 1954–56] *An. Repts.*). In captivity has crossed with Canada Goose and Brant (fertile offspring with both) and with various species of *Anser,* including *A. cygnoides.*

Geographical variation none reported. RSP

FIELD IDENTIFICATION Readily identifiable at a considerable distance. Small goose, all black from bill down to include anterior portion of body, except face and forehead white (not black as in Brant). Barring of the bluish gray back can be seen at much greater distance than the comparatively faint barring on Brant. First-winter Barnacles are identifiable to age-class only at close range.

There is little likelihood of confusing the Barnacle with the rare individual Canada Goose in which the white extends beyond the cheeks to include other parts of the head. RSP

VOICE Chorus of a flock has been likened to the barking of a pack of terriers. When the observer was within a distance of 1 km. of the breeding cliff on Trekroner Mt. in ne. Greenland, the noise from the birds was a "continuous humming, sounding like a distant talk" (Manniche 1910). Individuals utter a monosyllabic bark *gnuh*, sometimes rapidly repeated and varying in pitch. More subdued notes are uttered when feeding. Triumph note differs from that of other geese in being high-pitched and shrill (Heinroth 1911). A "loud complaining" *ark* uttered on breeding grounds (Jourdain, in With-erby 1939); this may be the cackling note of breeders in flight that Jourdain (1922) had mentioned earlier. A hissing noise with beak open and tongue elevated. RSP

HABITAT As a breeder, not so characteristically high-arctic as Brant. Occurs where cliffs and rocky slopes are fairly near lakes, rivers, marshes, the inner reaches of fjords, or even the open sea (but mainly inland). At least in Greenland and Spitzbergen, a few also nest on level ground, sometimes near Brant or Common Eiders. In other seasons near marine shores in marshes, grassy areas, and the like, and on tidal flats. Not frequent inland. RSP

DISTRIBUTION Except for Greenland, only a straggler in our area.

An undoubtedly incomplete listing of localities in N. Am. where this bird has been seen or captured, one or more times, is given below. This surely includes escaped a-viary birds, which cannot be distinguished with certainty from natural occurrences. The earliest record is for 1866 or earlier, the latest included here is for early 1972; most are for fall–early winter. Some of them have been generally accepted; others have fared variously, depending on compiler, the possibility of escapees having been mentioned repeatedly and for over a hundred years. Some recent sightings (especially 1968–70) probably refer to the same individual(s), seen when at different localities. For earlier summaries, see S. F. Baird et al. (1884a), Bent (1925), A.O.U. *Check-list* 5th ed. (1957), Bull (1964) for N.Y., and Godfrey (1966) for Canada.

There are sightings and/or captures from these localities: Mackenzie Dist. (Eskimo report of one killed), Bylot I., Baffin I., n. Labrador, Que. (4 localities, e. James Bay down to C. Tourmente where 2 fall records), N.S. (7 on Nov. 29, 1969), N.B. (May 10, 1972), Ont. (includes 5 at one locality in Oct. 1955), Vt., Mass. (latest—Jan., 1971—was a zoo escapee), N.Y. (inland, also Long I. where specimens from 4 localities), Ohio, N.C. (earliest in 1870, latest in 1972), Tenn., Ala., Okla., and Texas.

In interior w. Canada—in Alta., 4 reported to have been captured, banded, and released in 1930 (they were listed only as total of 4 banded in *Bird Banding Notes* 4 no. 3: 16. 1950).

Alaska—Izembek Lagoon, Sept. 13, 1965, one, closely observed, in a flock of Brant (R. D. Jones, Jr.).

The Barnacle Goose has 3 widely separated breeding areas, the birds from each having a particular migration route and wintering area. See Ploeger (1968) for an attempt to explain origin and history during glaciations on basis of present distribution.

1 During the last glaciation, this goose probably occurred in refugia on w. coasts of Scotland and in Ireland (Johansen 1956). The e. Greenland birds occur there now in winter, from Outer Hebrides s. to nw. Eire and e. to Inner Hebrides. Thus they are scattered; see, for example, localities listed by Boyd and Radford (1958) for Scotland and Cabot (1963) for Ireland. They cross Iceland in migration. A banded individual was found dead near Valencia, Spain (Salomonsen 1959). A list of 69 recoveries of banded individuals (Salomonsen 1967b) included wintering localities in Ireland and w. Scotland, also 22 recoveries from Iceland during migration in May and Sept.–Oct., plus 2 records for w. Norway and 1 in Germany (lat. 53°31′ N, long. 07°06′ E).

2 Spitzbergen birds migrate over the e. Atlantic and cross Scotland to Solway Firth and vicinity.

3 The largest unit nests on the s. island of Novaya Zemlya, with some on nearby Vaigach (where first found nesting in 1957). Their route is westerly and into the White Sea, then overland to the Baltic. Some spend the winter in sw. Baltic area, but most continue on to coastal Germany and Holland. See Kumari (1971) and Ouweneel (1971) for details.

For further general information, see especially Boyd (1961a, 1963). The first paper included map showing migration and distribution of all three breeding units. For Spitzbergen birds, Løvenskiold (1964) gave many data from breeding range, Larsen and Norderhaug (1964) discussed distribution in detail as determined by banding, Norderhaug (1968) added later information, and E. L. Roberts (1966) discussed their movements on Solway Firth. A 1959 map (by S. Uspenskii) of breeding range of the third segment was included in Boyd (1961a); a later one, in S. Uspenskii (1965a), showed fewer breeding colonies. For these same birds, many historical data on estimates of numbers and on changes in wintering localities were summarized by A. Timmermann (1962).

Semiwild Barnacles, reared in Scotland, have migrated to n. Norway (Berry 1951); small numbers nesting on the Lofoten Is. (n. Norway) apparently originated from Scottish escapees.

Stragglers in the Palearctic mostly are omitted here, but it is of interest that there have been occurrences as far scattered as the Kaliningrad region, Franz Josef Land, the Azores, and the delta of the Nile.

The Barnacle Goose is reported from an **archaeological site** each in Ireland, Gibraltar, and Italy, plus 4 on Malta; for full references, see Brodkorb (1964a). RSP

MIGRATION Spring and fall routes presumably are essentially the same for each segment of the total population of the species; the routes were mapped in Boyd

(1961a). Only the Greenland birds, i.e., those of our area, are discussed here, largely from Salomonsen (1950).

Spring Barnacle Geese arrive on the e. Greenland coast from mid-May to early June, in flocks of 15–20 (occasionally over 100); they fly along the coast and then w. into fjords and sounds, and on to their breeding places (mainly inland). **Late summer–fall** Molting flightless breeders with their partly grown preflight goslings move to fjord coasts (where prebreeders, in groups of 10–15, spend the season) and families combine in small groups. In late Aug., when the various age-classes can fly, large flocks assemble in the fjords; then they move to the outer coast and depart, flying at a considerable height. The last ones leave the Scoresby Sd. area about Sept. 8–9. They occur in Iceland in Sept.–Oct. The birds arrive in the Hebrides and beyond (Britain) from mid-Sept. onward. RSP

BANDING STATUS In N. Am., 4 reportedly were banded in Alta., as mentioned previously under "Distribution." Beginning in 1946, the banding of Barnacles has been carried on irregularly in e. Greenland and the numerous "ringing" (banding) recoveries are scattered in over a dozen Danish and British publications. Some of the Spitzbergen birds have been banded, in winter as well as in summer. The number of Barnacles banded in Britain through 1969 was 453 and there were 65 recoveries (*Brit. Birds* 64 145. 1971). There probably has been some banding in other geographical areas. RSP

REPRODUCTION Greenland data primarily from Salomonsen (1950), a few other data from scattered sources.

Age when **first breeds** not recorded (probably 2 years). No details on pair formation (probably on winter range usually); breeders already are paired on arrival at breeding places. For a few data on displays, as observed in captives, see Johnsgard (1965). Migrants go immediately to breeding areas. A **colonial breeder,** up to 100–150 pairs at some Greenland sites, but also smaller groups and even solitary pairs are known. In Greenland they nest on ledges, terraces, and in niches in steep cliffs, usually near water, and facing n., nw., or ne. The largest colonies are in the interior on gigantic mt. walls. There the nests usually are at an elevation of 250–300 m. above valley floors, but are down to 80–100 m. on fjord-facing cliffs, and down to only 30–35 m. on smaller islands. A few nest on level ground (Bird and Bird 1941), as also in Spitzbergen (Løvenskiold 1964). At the latter place their known breeding places are nearer the open sea and the geese build nests on the tops of "stacks" (pillars of rock) as well as cliff ledges. In s. Novaya Zemlya and on Vaigach I. they nest on sea-facing rock cliffs, seldom as low as 50 m. above the water, and the cliffs are shared with 2 species of murre (*Uria*), kittiwakes (*Rissa*), other seabirds, and not infrequently the Peregrine (*Falco peregrinus*) (S. Uspenskii 1965a).

The **nest site,** used year after year, has grayish **nestdown** (darker than that of the Pinkfoot) added, with indistinct whitish centers, and any intermingled feathers are small and pale. The gander commonly has his guard site very close to his incubating mate. For an excellent color photo of a pair of Barnacles on a nesting cliff, see Salomonsen (1967a).

239

Branta leucopsis

Eggs generally are laid toward the end of May and in early June in Greenland. Clutch size 4–6 (2–9 reported). Size of 49 eggs (from Spitzbergen) av. 76.35 × 50.32 mm.; length varied 68.7–82.7 and width 46.4–53.6 (Bent 1925); for a larger series, including eggs from various localities, see Schönwetter (1960). On the average, they are smaller than the eggs of the Pinkfoot and larger than those of Brant. **Incubation** by the goose, **period** (in captivity) 24–25 days. A **replacement clutch** is laid if the first is taken early. Breeders seldom eat during the time of incubation and become very thin.

There have been various and conflicting reports on how the young get down from cliff nests (see Salomonsen 1950). The nearest indication that they are transported in the bills of their parents, by A. Pedersen (see Løvenskiold 1964), is not very convincing. On Novaya Zemlya, S. Uspenskii (1965a) has seen the goose fly down to the sea, then call her goslings, which left the nest and tumbled down the face of the cliff to the sea. He made the point that the downy covering of the young is dense and elastic, a protection against injury during the descent. (Gosling Canada Geese walk off nests high up in trees and survive the fall.)

The **young** are tended by both parents. In Greenland, families stay on lakes for 1–2 weeks, then move to fjord coasts, preferring shores there that have sandy beaches. Families may combine or join with small flocks of molting prebreeders. **Age at first flight** 6–7 weeks (in aviaries).

In 1939 the snow cover remained extraordinarily late in Germania Land (n. Greenland); the Barnacles arrived late, more than a hundred pairs did not breed, and the remaining 30 pairs began as late as June 18 (Pedersen, in Salomonsen 1950). RSP

HABITS Highly gregarious, but not social. They do not usually associate with other geese, but regularly in N. Am. have occurred with Lesser Snows, Canadas and Brant. Relatively unwary. In general habits, much more like the Canada goose than the seagoing Brant. Generally noisy. Feeding birds seem to be engaged continuously in minor quarrels, a goose trait notably developed in this species. They are active at night and often feed after dark.

In Dec., 1959, the total number of Barnacles was "most probably about 30,000"—from Greenland 7,530, Spitzbergen 2,350, and Novaya Zemlya–Vaigach 19,700 (Boyd 1961a). Some overall increase subsequently is indicated by figures in Atkinson-Willes (1963). The Hebridean winterers (from Greenland) increased from about 7,400 in Feb. 1957 to 15,200 in April 1966; at the same time, those in Sutherland and Ireland, protected since 1955 and 1962 respectively, showed less increase (Boyd 1968). The Greenland subpopulation consists of "about" 14,000 individuals (Salomonsen, in Fuller and Kevan 1970).

In a chapter on "bird fish," the folklore about this goose metamorphosing from barnacles was discussed fully by Armstrong (1958); being derived from "fish," the birds could be eaten on Friday and during Lent.

For further information see especially Witherby (1939), A. Timmerman (1962), and E. L. Roberts (1966). RSP

FOOD Largely grasses, sedges, and other plants. Reported use of mollusks and crustaceans requires verification. Captive birds in England in spring ate worms, an

240

"exceptional diet" (Cordeaux, in A. G. Butler 1897). Greenland: in June a stomach contained mainly withered grass, while 2 birds taken Aug. 15 had eaten twigs, leaves, and catkins of arctic willow (*Salix arctica*), grass and various seeds (Manniche 1910). A bird taken there on June 15 contained dry leaves of *Dryas* and leaf buds of *Salix* (Pedersen 1942). Also eaten are leaves and seeds of smartweed (*Polygonum viviparum*) and sorrel (*Oxyria digyna*) (Løppenthin 1932). Stomach of a bird taken Aug. 6 contained: sedge (*Carex*) 40%, grass (probably *Poa*) 35%, and undetermined plant material 25% (Cottam and Knappen 1939). Spitzbergen: stems of grasses and leaves of sorrel (*O. digyna*) (Le Roi, in Koenig 1911). Birds in the U.S.S.R. had eaten *Poa distans, Carex bulbosus, Trifolium repens, Ranunculus* sp. and mollusks (Alpheraky 1905).

Stomachs of 14 specimens taken in England in Jan.–Feb. contained entirely vegetable matter: green grasses (*Schlerochloa maritima, Festuca rubra, Poa*, and unidentified) 93.2%, leaves of other plants (*Bellis perennis, Ranunculus repens, Caltha palustris, Apium nodiflorum*) 4.8%, horsetail (*Equisetum palustre*) 0.4%, moss (*Hypnum cuspidatum*), liverwort (*Lophocolea bidentata*), and fragments of seeds 0.4% (J. W. Campbell 1936).

NOTE   The above does not include all recent information. See, for example, M. Owen and Kerbes (1971) for autumn diet and energy value of certain foods. AWS

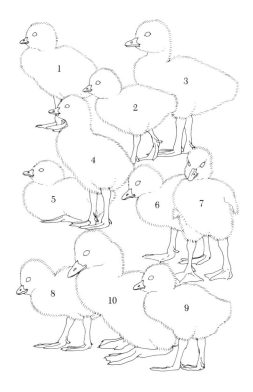

Day-old downies

1 Dark-bellied (Pacific) Brant *(Branta bernicla nigricans)*—from near Hazen Bay, Alaska.

2 Cackling Canada Goose *(Branta canadensis minima)*—from Igiak Bay, Alaska.

3 Giant Canada Goose *(B. c. moffitti)*—from local breeding stock at Delta, Man.

4 and 5 Ross' Goose *(Anser rossii)*—yellow and gray morphs, from Perry River Region, N. W. T.

6 and 7 Lesser Snow/Blue Goose *(Anser c. caerulescens)*—extremes (1 and 5) of 5 categories of downies: golden (Lesser Snow) and darkest (Blue Goose). From captive stock. (For Plumages in color, see plate facing p. 114.)

8 Emperor Goose *(Anser canagicus)*—from delta of the Kuskokwim, Alaska.

9 White-fronted Goose *(Anser albifrons frontalis)*—from Igiak Bay, Alaska.

10 Whistling (nearctic subspecies of Tundra) Swan *(Cygnus columbianus columbianus)*—from vicinity of Hazen Bay, Alaska.

C.H.Nelson

Red-breasted Goose

Branta ruficollis (Pallas)

Evidence of **presumed natural occurrence** may be **open to question.** Records given here point up a recurring problem: when a free-flying waterfowl not wearing a band is taken or seen in the wild, can a definite answer be given as to whether occurrence was natural or whether the bird escaped from captivity?

In our area For a record from Cal., dating from the early 1890s, see J. Grinnell and Miller (1944), who discussed it under the heading "introduced species and those of uncertain occurrence." An im. ♂ was shot Sept. 18, 1960, near Carlsbad, San Diego Co., Cal.; it was reported by L. M. Huey (1961), who discounted the possibility that it might have escaped from captivity. Three seen on April 18, 1962, at Woolwich, Sagadahoc Co., Me., were believed by C. E. Huntington (1962) to be "almost certainly" escapees. Although no thorough search for reports of recent sightings or captures has been made, the following have been noted: in Texas, a single in Kennedy Co. on Dec. 23, 1969; in s. Colorado Co. on Feb. 17 and 26, 1970 (same bird? The localities are about 200 mi. apart); and in Cal., as listed by Wilbur and Yocom (1971), Nov. 1963—1 shot in Los Angeles Co., 1965—others reported shot in San Bernardino Co., 1968—reported shot in Butte Co., and on the 1969 Christmas count—2 at Salton Sea with Lesser Snow Geese.

Comments This handsome little goose, which is popular with aviculturalists, breeds in the w. Siberian tundra and migrates to the s. Caspian region and elsewhere. To the east of breeding range it is not recorded in Yakutia, but Dementiev and Gladkov (1952) recorded it beyond, nearer N. Am., as a straggler to the Chuckchee Pen. Yet Portenko (1972) did not even mention it for that area. It is a straggler (and escapee?) throughout much of Europe, also to Britain (over a dozen presumed natural occurrences), rarely to Iceland (4 occurrences), and a doubtful sighting in ne. Greenland.

For further information, see S. Uspenskii (1965a) for a brief account plus map of breeding range, but especially Krechmar and Leonovich (1967) for general summary of distribution and biology. See Brodkorb (1964a) for records from **archaeological sites.** RSP

FOOTNOTE Apropos the above, among the larger free-flying waterfowl seen in N. Am., and of very dubious origin, are the Bar-headed Goose (*Anser indicus*) and the Egyptian Goose (*Alopochen aegyptiacus*).

Brant

Branta bernicla

Includes Brant or Atlantic Brant and Black or Pacific Brant of Am. authors and subspecies of Brent or Brent Goose of Brit. and some other authors. That is, all Brant (light, intermediate, and black bellied) are included here in a single species.

A small, dark, stocky, short-necked marine goose. The head is dark (to black) and, except for more or less of a white collar (which in Juv. Plumage varies from absent to fairly evident), the dark extends down to include breast and very forepart of mantle; in some dark-bellied birds it also includes much of underparts (but often with some demarcation at lower edge of breast). The longest white upper and under tail coverts extend out to or beyond the tips of the longest tail feathers (but may fall short in worn condition). The trachea was illus. in Schiøler (1925).

Sexes similar in appearance; almost no geographical variation in size; ♂ av. slightly larger; length to about 24 in., wingspread to 45, wt. to almost 5 lb. but usually 2½–3½. Three subspecies are recognized here, 2 with wide ranges in our area, the 3rd extralimital.

DESCRIPTION   One Plumage/cycle, with Basic II regarded as earliest definitive stage. Light-bellied birds (*B. b. hrota*) of e. N. Am. are described here in detail.

▶   ♂ ♀ Def. Basic Plumage (entire feathering), worn from some time in SUMMER to some time the following SUMMER, with intervening molt of all feathering beginning earlier that season in prebreeders than in breeders. **Bill,** entire head, neck (except incomplete collar), forepart of mantle, and most of breast nearly black and this terminates abruptly. **Iris** dark brownish. Well up on each side of neck there is a patch of diagonal white streaks formed by white feather ends (the collar) and a furrowed effect (not always) of the neck feathering, very restricted in area, includes the collar. **Upperparts** rest of mantle including scapulars brownish olive, the feather ends buffy brownish or grayish (obscure or absent after much wear); sides of rump and the long upper tail coverts white, forming a conspicuous V as viewed from above or behind. **Underparts** feathers of lower breast and abdomen with wide light ends, these and the subterminal darker portions arranged as moderately distinct barring, and along upper sides and flanks the broad white ends merge; abdomen lightens posteriorly, to white approximately at the vent, and all posterior feathering is white and extends upwards so as to be continuous with white of rear sides and above tail. **Tail** feathers black. Legs and **feet** black. **Wing** primaries and secondaries very dark; upper coverts mostly a grayed sepia, with margins (widths vary) of grayed brownish, chiefly on middle and greater coverts; general coloration of wing lining and axillars medium brownish gray.

In the ♀ parent, molting of wing quills (after onset of Prebasic molt) occurs about 2 weeks after the brood hatches—the date thus being variable, depending in some measure on when incubation began, which in turn varies depending on the local weather in any season. The time when the ♂ becomes flightless appears to be more consistent. In an early season the ♀ begins first by up to several days, in a tardy season the ♂ first by up to several days.

The flightless period in both sexes lasts only about 3 weeks, so that they are again

244

capable of flight (although they seldom fly) for some days before their young are first on the wing.

AT HATCHING there is considerable individual variation in overall shade and some in pattern. **Head** crown medium grayish with darker grayish center and a line of similar shade from bill to and around eye; nape medium grayish; chin, throat, and foreneck white; bill and eye dark slaty. **Upperparts** light to medium brownish gray, paling on sides of breast, but full shade extends down thighs; in some individuals there is a white bar along trailing edge of wing. **Underparts** broad light grayish band across breast, remainder pale gray to nearly white (the down is grayish brown basally). Feet paler than bill. Downy black-bellied Brant (*nigricans*) are darker overall with obscure head pattern; see col. pl. facing p. 242. Compare with Emperor gosling.

▶   ♂ ♀ Juv. Plumage (entire feathering) grows rapidly and is perfected by age about 42 days, when the birds first attain flight, and is worn briefly thereafter before any noticeable amount of it is succeeded by Basic I. By early winter, however, much (often all) of head–body has been succeeded by Basic I; any still-remaining narrow, tapering Juv. tail feathers usually are dropped in winter, but at least most of the Juv. wing is retained into the following summer.

The Juv. differs from Def. Basic thus: general coloring of **head**–neck–breast toward brownish or sooty (not blackish); side of neck (as is apparent from some time well along in preflight stage) varies with individual, from having fairly conspicuous but less extensive white collar markings, to only a "ghost" of these, or none whatever; **mantle** feathers, including scapulars, have whitish distal margins, somewhat irregularly arranged (not in even barring); **sides of body** also have uneven or blotchy pattern; the tapering **tail** feathers have notched ends (where the natal down broke off), are sooty in color, and vary with individual bird from all being broadly margined white to only a trace of white on outermost pair; **wing** most of the upper coverts have conspicuous white or whitish ends and the secondaries, and sometimes some inner primaries, are narrowly white tipped (white trailing edge in unworn Juv. Plumage), but this wears off.

▶   ♂ ♀ Basic I Plumage (entire feathering, except for retained Juv. wing) acquired through FALL or into winter (molting is protracted in some individuals) and all the new tail feathers quite commonly are not fully grown until into winter. Basic I plus Juv. wing are worn through winter into summer, until age about 1 year, and then the time of onset of molting probably is fairly constant at any particular locality. Some Juv. upper wing coverts are retained longest, a few quite often until after new wing quills have grown and migration has begun.

Basic I resembles later Basics in color and pattern; for example, dorsal feather ends not whitish and are evenly arranged, sides barred, etc. Various feathers are intermediate in shape between the tapering, round-ended Juv. ones and the broad, more squarish-ended feathers of succeeding Basics. Individuals vary; some have more Juv.-like feather shapes, others are more "advanced" and have feathers approaching definitive shape. Although not worn as long as succeeding Basics, this Plumage is notable for bleaching (especially when the birds are on winter range) before it is succeeded by Basic II.

In the wing, loss of Juv. feathering (during Prebasic II molt) beginning in summer occurs as follows. After initial and approximately simultaneous loss of primaries and secondaries (onset of flightless stage), the coverts on both surfaces of the wing are molted in rather irregular sequence, producing a patchy effect—bleached, white-ended Juv. coverts intermixed with incoming unbleached all-dark Basic II coverts. On the upper surface of the wing the last retained (hence conspicuous) Juv. feathers generally are a few middle coverts and the last of these may persist into fall. As long as a bleached, white-tipped Juv. covert remains, it serves to identify a bird as a yearling. For some further details, from study of *nigricans* in Alaska, see S. W. Harris and Shepherd (1965).

NOTE Delacour (1954) stated that individuals having "brown head and neck and mottled white and pale brown upperparts" are not uncommon. These are birds in faded Basic I Plumage.

Measurements 12 ♂ (Great Britain 1, Iceland 1, Mass. 4, N.C. 6): BILL 32–36 mm., av. 34; WING 326–342, av. 335.4; TAIL 94–107, av. 101.6; TARSUS 59–65, av. 61.7; 8 ♀ (Great Britain 1, Iceland 1, Mass. 3, N.C. 3): BILL 30–34 mm., av. 32; WING 319–346, av. 330.3; TAIL 91–105, av. 98.5; TARSUS 56–61, av. 58.4 (ETS).

WING (across chord) 11 ♂ (Ellesmere I., Mass., N.J., N.C.) 278–336 mm., av. 317.2; and 12 ♀ (Greenland, Ellesmere I., Mass., N.Y., N.J., Md., N.C.) 296–338, av. 318.9 (H. Friedmann).

Birds from N. Am. breeding and winter range, Def. Basic WING (flattened) 11 ♂ 341–354 mm., av. 345; and 11 ♀ 310–341, av. 330; and the Juv. WING 4 ♂ 300–331 mm., av. 314, and 6 ♀ 305–317, av. 309 (T. W. Barry). There are also a few comparative meas. in Schiøler (1925).

Weight in N. Am. of "adult" ♂ 18 in spring–summer 1,058.4–1,592.5 gm., av. 1,328.6, and 7 in fall–winter 1,137.8–1,820, av. 1,537.9; and "adult" ♀ 12 in spring–summer 966.9–1,478.8 gm., av. 1,142, and 7 in fall–winter 1,251.2–1,592.5 gm., av. 1,428.7; and young in their first fall–winter 7 ♂ 966.9–1,706.2 gm., av. 1,324, and 2 ♀ 1,380 and 1,422, av. 1,365 (T. W. Barry). For a diagram showing wt. of pre-breeders and breeders, from time of arrival on breeding range until into winter, see Barry (1962).

Birds taken in hunting season: 19 ♂ av. 3.4 lb., max. 4.0, and 14 ♀ av. 2.8, max. 3.9 (A. L. Nelson and Martin 1953).

No data on wt. of downy *hrota*, but see beyond under *nigricans*.

Hybrids 2 taken in the wild have been reported, one with *Anser caerulescens* (Brimley 1927), the other with a small *Branta canadensis* (Ransom 1927). In captivity, fertile crosses with *Branta canadensis* have occurred and the species also has crossed with *Branta leucopsis* and several species of *Anser*.

Geographical variation in the species is practically nil in measurements. Color varies, most strikingly on the venter, from very pale to black. The main problem consists in disposing of the intermediate birds of Eurasia, rather than comparing lightest and darkest ones of N. Am.

Brant of the w. Siberian tundra (L. Taimyr and westward) have only moderately dark bellies (much lighter than breast), reduced white along upper sides, and the white collar is discontinuous at front and rear or only at rear and with the white extending up as parallel diagonal lines. Winter range is in ne. Atlantic waters.

East of the Taimyr Pen., on mainland and is., the birds are very dark bellied, but somewhat variable in this and other respects; the highly variable collar more often is continuous at foreneck and the larger (lower) portion of it typically is an uninterrupted white area. These birds, which either have not been numerous or else are now greatly reduced in numbers, migrate overland to winter quarters along the n. Pacific coast of Asia. (Brant banded in N. Am. have been taken as far westward in summer as the New Siberian Archipelago.)

Light-bellied   Dark-bellied

Not many thousand Black Brant now breed near Alaska in E. Siberia, but units do occur on the Arctic Ocean side (Wrangel I., mainland coasts of Chuckchee Sea) and also on the Bering Sea side (around Anadyr Gulf). Their center of abundance is farther eastward, on the Bering Sea coast of Alaska, and numbers decline in the Canadian arctic. Generally, bill and lower sides match the black breast; the white on upper sides is quite extensive (or at least very conspicuous because of adjoining dark feathering); the collar is variable, but usually is broken only at rear. Many of these birds do not have quite as dark underparts as usually ascribed to "Black" Brant and a slight difference between belly and black breast becomes more evident or accentuated by lightening of the former as the feathering bleaches. These Brant (E. Siberian to w. Canadian arctic) migrate to winter range along the N. Am. Pacific coast. The variation in these birds almost, or perhaps entirely, overlaps that of winterers in ne. Asiatic waters and so together they comprise a single subspecies with divided winter range. (There are insufficient grounds for following Tougarinov (1941), who split off the former, those breeding from L. Taimyr e. to C. Bolshoi Baranov, and named them *orientalis*.)

Specimens of breeding Brant, not arranged in a geographical sequence, yet from various localities across n. Eurasia, can be arranged into a series showing gradual and even transition from less than moderately dark belly to solid black underparts. Specimens also can be sorted in another arrangement, showing extent of variation in some other single character—amount of white on upper sides, details of collar, extent of

247

white in the vent area, etc. (Specimens were examined by the writer in various collections including University Museum, Moscow.) In short, describable external characteristics vary more or less independently of one another on the individual bird; the summation or av. of these differs much more between moderately dark-bellied Eurasian Brant that migrate westward (to Atlantic) and the very dark ones migrating eastward (to Pacific) than between or among breeding units within either, but there is individual variation everywhere.

Again Eurasia. On high-arctic is. remote from the w. mainland (Franz Josef Land, Spitzbergen), the breeding Brant have light bellies; the collar tends to be discontinuous both at front and rear and (usually) is patterned upward with white lines. Brant of this general (but still rather variable) sort also breed in n. Greenland and in the Canadian arctic westward so far as to overlap slightly the summer range of Black Brant. Winter range is divided, easterly birds wintering in the e. Atlantic (and at that season sometimes consorting with wintering moderately dark-bellied w. Siberian Brant), the others having the w. Atlantic (N. Am. e. coast) almost exclusively to themselves.

In the species, darkest downies are the progeny of darkest parents and, apparently within a single brood anywhere, individuals may differ somewhat in color and/or pattern. It is probable that a particular combination of characteristics is manifest in a constant way throughout the life of the individual.

To recapitulate, it would appear that, during the last glacial Brant were of 2 morphs—very pale (Atlantic area) and very dark (n. Pacific–Bering Sea). Subsequently, 1 in colonizing n. Eurasia, an intermediate-colored w. Siberian population has evolved and 2 the latest event in N. Am. consists of lightest and darkest birds extending their ranges so as not only to meet but to overlap slightly. Ploeger (1968) developed this theme at some length, within a framework of too many subspecies. RSP

SUBSPECIES in our area *hrota* (Müller)—Light-bellied or Atlantic Brant. Descr. and meas. given at beginning of this account. The av. of certain rather variable characters follows: small, mostly striated, white patch on each side of neck (interrupted collar); belly light (palish gray or slightly brownish), sharply contrasting anteriorly with black or blackish breast; feathers on sides and flanks have comparatively narrow pale borders. Almost entirely an island breeder and with divided winter range.

nigricans (Lawrence)—Black or Pacific Brant. For definitive stages, the av. of certain rather variable characters follows: small conspicuous white collar, interrupted only at back, and with short upward extensions of white lines from the clear white area; dorsum comparatively dark, bleaching toward brownish (in Basic I even yellowish); underparts and much of sides dark sooty brown to black (continuation of black of head–neck–breast); broad white feather borders on upper sides and flanks. Newly hatched downies (see pl. facing p. 242) have slightly greenish cast in life. The forepart of the head is conspicuously darker than the remainder. Individual variation: of 4 siblings from Banks I., 1 has gray of venter interrupted by a white breast band and 1 has a white throat patch (Manning et al. 1956); of 2 siblings from se. Victoria I., 1 has the band and also the patch (Parmelee et al. 1967).

Predominantly a mainland nester; divided winter range primarily along N. Am. Pacific coast, but westerly units within Siberia go overland to winter quarters along the w. margin of the n. Pacific.

Measurements   12 ♂ (Alaska 7, Cal. 3, Wash. 1, Ore. 1): BILL 31–36 mm., av. 34; WING 325–344, av. 335.5; TAIL 93–100, av. 96.5; TARSUS 57–63, av. 60.8;   8 ♀ (N.W.T. 2, Alaska 4, B.C. 1, Cal. 1): BILL 31–35 mm., av. 33; WING 319–338, and 361, av. 332; TAIL 93–98, av. 96; TARSUS 55–61, av. 58.4 (ETS).

"Adult" birds from Banks I., Franklin Bay, and Alaska: WING (flattened) 12 ♂ 330–352 mm., mean 338.1 ± 1.9; and 6 ♀ 315–329, mean 324.2 (Manning et al. 1956).

Weight of "adults" in B.C. in Feb.–March: 189 ♂ 40–64 oz., av. 51 (1,443 gm.), and 181 ♀ 38–61 oz., av. 45.7 (1,293 gm.) (H. A. Hansen and Nelson 1957).

Wt. when flightless in molt in summer in Yukon–Kuskokwim delta, Alaska: older than yearlings, 11 ♂ 41–60 oz., av. 52, and 17 ♀ 37–54 oz., av. 46; yearlings, 5 ♂ 38–54 oz., av. 47, and 5 ♀ 39–47 oz., av. 43 (D. L. Spencer et al. 1951). Other "adults" in molt at the same locality: 277 ♂ 33–62 oz., av. 44.5 (1,259 gm.), and 285 ♀ 30–57 oz., av. 38 (1,075 gm.) (H. A. Hansen and Nelson 1957). Thus molting ♂ ♂ av. 6.5 oz. less than they do during early stages of spring migration and molting ♀ ♀ av. 7.7 oz. less (ibid.).

Twenty-four incubator-hatched downies weighed 45.1–65.6 gm., the mean and standard error being 54.7 ± 0.96, standard deviation 4.72 (Smart 1965a).

Discussion   The name *Anser nigricans* of Lawrence (1846) is based on individuals taken at Egg Harbor, N.J., in winter range of light-bellied Brant. (Lawrence described and figured a dark ♀; the type—as designated by Hellmayr and Conover (1948)—is a mounted ♂, intermediate in color and now much faded.) These specimens, plus statements of gunners as reported to H. F. Lewis (1937), were the basis on which Delacour and Zimmer (1952) postulated an extinct or nearly extinct subspecies of dark-bellied Brant (for which they retained the name *nigricans*) occurring within the present range of light-bellied Brant in the Canadian arctic (breeding) and on the U.S. Atlantic coast (wintering). Later, a graded series of from light- to dark-bellied birds, mostly those collected by S. D. MacDonald on Prince Patrick I., were discussed and illustrated by Manning et al. (1956); certain of these match Lawrence's specimens from N.J.

Stragglers have long association with, hence opportunity to form a firm pair bond with, birds of the other color type. "Mixed" pairs then migrate to breeding range, where their progeny (and perhaps another 1 or 2 generations) consist of intergrading individuals such as Manning et al. illustrated. There is also the possibility that, in the area of overlap of summer range of the 2 color types, a bird that lost its mate might remate with a bird of the other color type. On Southampton I. in 1956, T. W. Barry saw a dark-bellied ♂ mated to a light-bellied ♀, also another dark-bellied bird and an apparent intergrade in that same local (light-bellied) breeding unit. The logical hypothesis, therefore, is that one of Lawrence's dark birds (the one he figured) is an Atlantic-wintering Black Brant and the other (the writer has examined both) is an intergrade; that is, a dark subspecies of Brant peculiar to e. N. Am. and now extinct or otherwise, has not existed.

Extralimital *bernicla* (Linnaeus)—West Siberian Brant; only moderately dark bellied. The av. of certain variable characters follows: rather small white area on each side of neck, extending upward as parallel white lines; belly medium to considerably darker brownish gray (this extends up to include much of sides), decidedly lighter than breast. Further details in Witherby (1939). Breeds at various localities along n. rim. of w. Siberia from Yamal Pen. e. onto Taimyr Pen. (where there is a major breeding area) and on some is. northward. Migrates westerly, then overland into the Baltic, and thence to winter quarters along portions of coasts of Europe and Britain (where it occurs with *hrota* at times, but generally they keep apart). RSP

FIELD IDENTIFICATION   In N. Am. Brant are near the size of our Black Duck or the Mallard, but very different in proportions. Smaller than our other dark geese (except for darkest small Canadas), with shorter neck and comparatively long wings. The wings appear to be set well back on the body and to be somewhat swept back in flight; the body appears truncated, because it is stout and the dark coloring is concentrated forward. Small dark Canadas do not appear truncated, or particularly short necked, or to have swept-back wings. The Barnacle Goose is more like the Brant, but has white face and longer neck.

   Atlantic (**light-bellied**) Brant: head to breast and the dorsum very dark; in flight, the belly appears pale grayish, silvery, or even white (except in soiled birds). Brant ride high on the water, tail angled up, and showing white rump and pale sides. In good light, the white collar can be seen a fair distance with a telescope. Under favorable conditions, young in their first fall, afloat or ashore, may be identified to age category by irregular pattern of dorsum and wing coverts, general brownish appearance (not black and grays), and some may lack the collar.

   Pacific (**black-bellied**) Brant: dark overall, but especially ventrally, appear almost totally dark except for white around base of tail and some on upper sides. Einarsen (1965) stated that it "would be almost impossible" to distinguish Atlantic and Pacific Brant in flight, but this is not so. (In w. Europe in winter, where the problem is light vs. **intermediate bellied,** hence less difference, Webbe (1958) stated that determination is not easy but is more certain when the birds are ashore and in good light.)

   The rather brownish, blended, and unevenly patterned Juv. Plumage, with white-tipped wing coverts, is readily identifiable under field conditions by a practiced observer using a telescope. Through fall, much of the Juv. is succeeded by Basic I, which has a more clear-cut pattern, darker head–neck–venter, and the diagnostic Juv. wing coverts still are retained. This combination of feathering bleaches very markedly, especially during the time the birds are on winter range, so that, in the following spring and into summer (to age 1 year), the birds are separable afield from other cohorts.

   In mated Brant, the ♀ av. slightly smaller than her mate and, most noticeable on breeding grounds, she appears to be more agile in flight.

   Brant usually are in flocks of 5 to about 75 individuals (a family, or up to 12–15 families combined), which in turn may join others to form much larger assemblies during migration and on winter range. Flock formation: a line of birds abreast, a crescent, or bunches with shifting arrangement. Near nesting areas and occasionally elsewhere, they fly in small flocks in a more or less undulating line (reminiscent of eiders). Except when on long high-altitude migratory flights, usually they fly low over the water.

   A distant line of flying cormorants might be mistaken for Brant, but wings of the latter are swept back and beat slower. Young or ♀ eiders are very different in profile and general behavior. Small dark Canada Geese regularly are referred to as "Brant" by hunters on the Pacific coast. TWB

VOICE   These data, from study of light-bellied (*hrota*) birds, no doubt apply to all Brant. A guttural or uvular *cronk* or *car-r-up* by both sexes, in flight or at rest. In large rafts on wintering ground, a resonant din increased in volume with alarm, or with changes in tide, or as other flocks alight. Babbling can be heard a great distance. Sound from large flock seems higher pitched than individual call, resembling from a distance the din of an excited audience at a sporting event.

Not very loud *cut cut cut cronk* or *cut cut cut* uttered at intervals during flight, an intraflock call, uttered especially by small flocks arriving at breeding grounds.

Drawn-out *crrronk* in mild alarm, most often uttered by singles separated from flock or on nesting territory. Head and neck erect. Uttered once, or frequently repeated, just before flight, sometimes with pumping of head. Fluttering of lower mandible and tongue on *r*'s most easily seen in this call. For more intense alarm, as in territorial defense, occasionally a rising snap on the terminal . . . *nk*, or a double note *tarr-ruk* similar to Canada Goose.

Short explosive *cruk*, an alarm call, uttered once or rapidly given in series, accompanied by horizontal head-and-neck poking and weaving.

Very deep guttural *gurrr*, often drawn out. A growl heard mostly from gander on territory just before attacking an intruding Brant or, more often, when large gull harasses downy goslings. Head and neck held in sigmoid curve, close to ground or water, head pointing slightly upward, bill opened wide, tongue elevated.

Rather subdued *gut*, infrequently uttered, with occasional *cronks*, by ♀ when returning to nest and escorted by ♂ .

An exhaling hiss, as in other geese.

A *peep peep peep* (may be long continued) by downy goslings, often accompanied by head-poking actions similar to those of older birds. Becomes a coarser sound after 2–3 weeks, a hiccup by 4–5 weeks, and a rattling *cronk* by 10 weeks.

In *nigricans*—when about to begin a migratory flight, and the groups and flocks are scattered over the surface of the water, usually in the still of evening, "there is a roar, followed by an excited gabbling for a short while" (Einarsen 1965). The Brant take wing and there is a murmuring as the flocks pass overhead. TWB

HABITAT   **Breeders in summer.**   A great many Brant nest on low and barren terrain which, in a geologic sense, is very recently dry land. They nest from within the subarctic to as far n. as there is any land—n. Ellesmere I., n. Greenland, Spitzbergen Archipelago, Franz Josef Land, and Severnaya Zemlya. They tend to nest far out, away from the ameliorating effects on climate of inland terrain, in outer deltas of rivers, on gravelly and sandy stretches, and on low flats where there are turfy hummocks amidst many puddles and shallows. In Yukon–Kuskokwim delta area of Alaska: near the sea but also well into tidal deltas. Some nest amidst numerous shallow ponds and lakes, even a considerable distance from the sea, on the Alaskan arctic coast, on Banks I., and probably to some extent elsewhere in the high-arctic portion of their range.

They are grazers ashore, on *Carex*, *Puccinellia*, and other turf-forming grasses and sedges, and feed to some extent in shallows and marshy areas. They get grit on shores and beaches.

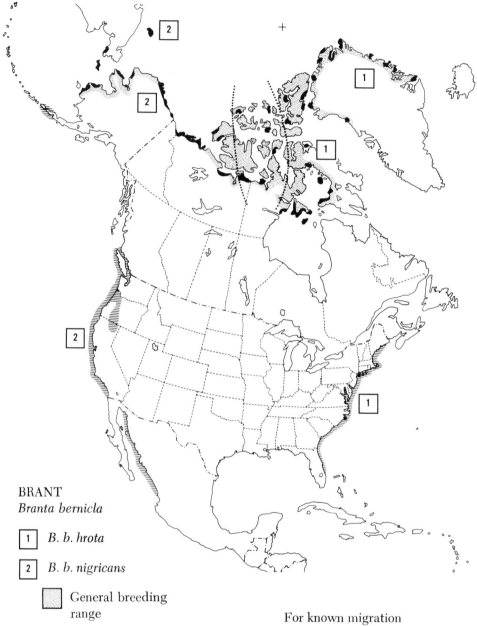

BRANT
Branta bernicla

1 *B. b. hrota*

2 *B. b. nigricans*

General breeding
range

Principal breeding
areas

Enclose area where
intergrades between
subspecies occur in
summer

Winters principally
within these areas

For known migration
corridors, intergrada-
tion, stragglers, and
other data, see text
[There is an addi-
tional subspecies
(*B. b. bernicla*) in
part of the Eurasian
range of the species]

Many **prebreeders** in summer share the same habitat with breeders, others are on tundra lakes; a considerable number are marine and in widely scattered flocks.

In **other seasons,** Brant migrate over land and sea, with relatively few stops on waters and mudflats of large shallow bays, lagoons, and estuaries. In some years, migrants stop on inland waters to some extent, also in fields and on grassy areas, or along beaches. In late winter and spring, some visit salt marshes, islands where sheep have grazed, hayfields, etc. Also see "Migration," "Habits," and the latter portion of the section on "Food." TWB

DISTRIBUTION   (See map.) In discussing distribution in our area, the following are complicating factors.

1   Some prebreeders (joined by failed breeders?) occur in summer and molt at localities away from the general vicinity of where the parents of the former breed; that is, at sea or elsewhere, and some may leave one breeding area and go to (or to the periphery of?) another to molt.

2   Occasional individuals, sometimes small groups or even flocks, remain s. of breeding range through summer. These may be largely prebreeders.

3   There is a question as to which of certain individuals in N. Am. are best listed as *hrota*, which of certain others are properly referred to *nigricans*, and which individuals are best termed intergrades (products of *hrota*–*nigricans* matings). On a graded scale of 1 to 8 inclusive, Manning et al. (1956) arranged specimens, on basis of belly-color, from "extreme pale" *hrota* to "extremely dark" *nigricans*. Then, allowing grades 1–2 to cover presumed normal variation within *hrota*, and 6–8 for the same in *nigricans*, at least the intervening 3–5 may be treated as recognizable intergrades. In summing up various information, this raises a question as to just how a specimen, or a sighting, given as "darker than typical" *hrota*, or with "somewhat lighter" belly than *nigricans*, should be listed. Afield, even a moderately light-bellied bird is notably different alongside dark *nigricans* and the same applies to a darkish-bellied bird in company with pale *hrota*. Decisions are arbitrary. In a biological sense, what is important is mixed occurrence at a time when pair formation could occur.

Below are given first the usual ranges of the subspecies occurring in our area, plus some straggling; then follows a section on "Mixed occurrence and intergrades," which includes overlap—occurrence of one subspecies within the "normal" range of the other, etc. (The latter does not include all relevant information, but gives enough to show an existing pattern.)

hrota—in our area, **breeding range** includes part of n. rim of the Canadian mainland plus various arctic is. from Coats and Southampton to Ellesmere I. and n. Greenland. There is over lap with *nigricans* at Queen Maud Gulf, Melville, and Prince Patrick I.

There is a likelihood that occasional pairs may nest away from usual breeding places, especially among colonial or semicolonial waterfowl such as eiders and Blue/Snow Geese.

A pair with 5 young was seen Aug. 12–Sept. 29 at Kelly Lake in Sudbury Dist. of Ont. (Baillie 1963).

Summer   In late May of 1953, about 2,000 Brant arrived at L. Abitibi and vicinity (Ont.) where they were heavily preyed upon by local Indians; about 1,000 survived and

253

remained (through molt) until Aug., in flocks of 50 or more (W. J. Smith 1957). Occasional Brant occur far s. of the breeding range in summer.

Winter   The light-bellied birds of the w. Atlantic area (the Brant of at least part of n. Canada and Greenland go to the e. Atlantic—n. Ireland mainly) occur almost entirely from Mass. s. into N.C. Exceptionally, some occur as far ne. as Penobscot Bay, Me., and s. into Fla., perhaps very rarely also on the Gulf of Mexico coast.

As a **straggler** inland, may be expected occasionally almost anywhere e. of a line drawn from w. side of Hudson Bay down w. side of L. Michigan and then to Chesapeake Bay. Beyond, in the continental interior, there are records ascribed to *hrota* at least w. into Alta., Idaho, S.D., Nebr., Colo., and Texas. (Pacific coastal and Alaskan occurrences are given below under "Mixed occurrences and intergrades.") Southernmost record is for Barbados in W. Indies.

For **extralimital data** on *hrota* of the Spitzbergen Archipelago and Franz Josef Land, see Norderhaug (1970).

nigricans—in Alaska has 3 major **breeding** areas, 2 on the outer rim of the Yukon–Kuskokwim delta, the other on the arctic coast approximately from Wainwright eastward to include the delta of the Colville. The last includes the C. Halkett region, a focus of summer occurrence of molting birds. In Canada on the nw. Canadian mainland and smaller is. (concentration in Mackenzie delta–Liverpool Bay area) and smaller numbers on the most westerly Canadian arctic islands. In Siberia, Am. Brant "migrate and nest farther west than has been revealed hitherto" (Shevareva 1960), which refers in part to band recoveries subsequently mapped on chart 4 in Einarsen (1965) and discussed beyond.

In **summer** many prebreeders occur on salt water, others on lakes near the sea, and they or others spend time ashore, within the general breeding range. Others occur farther away, at least as far as from coastal B.C. northward to include the Chuckchee Sea (the travels of some of these are discussed beyond). A few hundred usually remain, or move in and out of, Izembek Lagoon. On or close to southerly winter range, Nowak and Monson (1965) reported a few birds inland on Salton Sea in summer of 1963; there have been a number of southerly records subsequently. A few birds usually remain on the Cal. coast.

Occasionally, and sometimes when ability to fly was impaired, Brant have remained behind and bred on winter range—records for Tomales and Humboldt Bays in Cal.; brood of 5 in 1958 on Ore. coast; evidently other such occurrences. Report of a brood at Pavlof Bay at outer end of Alaska Pen.

In **winter,** although some Brant may be found from outer end of the Alaska Pen. southward, at the present time usual winter distribution is from Ore. into Mexico (most are in s. Cal. and farther southward). Largest numbers formerly occurred on the outer (Pacific) coast of Baja Cal., notably in Scammon Lagoon, San Ignacio Lagoon, and Magdalena Bay (the last at lat. 25° N). In late winter (Feb.–March) the birds shifted northward, with notable concentrations in Humboldt Bay, Cal.

Late in 1898 there were great numbers of Brant along the Colo. R., about 40 mi. s. of the U.S.–Mexican boundary (Price 1899). In the winter of 1958–59, a small group of Brant visited the Sinaloan coast of Mexico almost opposite the lower tip of Baja Cal., and in mid-Jan., 1959, a small group occurred as far s. as Acapulco on the Mexican coast

(Einarsen 1965). In 1964, large numbers reportedly wintered at the head of the Gulf of Cal. (Nowak and Monson 1965) and this pattern has continued. Thus there has been a shift from s. Cal. into Mexico; for various information see R. I. Smith and Jensen (1970). Einarsen thought the shift was caused by increased disturbance of the birds at Pacific coastal localities. (Presumably the various spring and summer records of Brant in the Salton Sea area are of birds on the route n. from within the Gulf of Cal.)

When there is open water through winter in Alaska at Izembek Lagoon and Cold Bay, Brant are present in variable numbers up to perhaps 5,000 birds. There is at least 1 winter record of an "adult" bird at Amchitka and frequently single birds in their first winter are found with Emperor Geese at Adak. No significant numbers ever have been found (at any season) in the Aleutians w. of Unimak I. There are winter records for Kodiak, Sanak, Caton, and other is. in the same general vicinity.

Straggler to the Hawaiian Is.—Oahu in 5 different years 1945–69 inclusive, Molokai 1939, Maui in 6 years 1891–1967, Hawaii in 1961 and 1966, and Tern I. in French Frigate Shoal, one captured on Dec. 3, 1970 (Berger 1972). (Stragglers in N. Am. are included under headings below.)

Mixed occurrence and **intergrades** N. Am. Pacific coast light-bellied *hrota* have been reported (in winter range of *nigricans*) as follows: Cal. records for at least 4 counties; Wash. 2 localities; B.C. several localities, including a number of captures, flock of 5 seen, small groups, etc.—see especially A. Brooks (1904), also photo (fig. 1) in Einarsen (1965). Two specimens from Comox, B.C., are "halfway" between *hrota* and *nigricans* (Taverner, in Bent 1925), i.e., are presumed intergrades.

ALASKA (normal range of *nigricans*) in the interior at mi. 123 on Glenn Highway in June, specimen of *hrota* (Gabrielson and Lincoln 1959); Wales June 19, an intergrade (near *hrota*); Icy Cape (s. of Wainwright) Sept. 11, several intergrades killed by natives seen and a specimen saved (A. Bailey 1948).

YUKON TERR. in se. part, 10 light-bellied birds at Frances L. on June 2, 1969.

ALTA. near Jasper, Oct. 18, 1959, bird believed to be an intergrade photographed (Salt 1961).

ATLANTIC COAST (normal range of *hrota*) MASS. For a number of records of *nigricans*, 1883–1950, and of intermediates, see Griscom and Snyder (1955). N.J. Egg Harbor in 1846, ♀ adult, Jan., described (but is not the type specimen) and figured by Lawrence (1846), is *nigricans*; ♂ labelled Juv. (but in definitive feathering), March 18 of same year, an intergrade; a third individual was captured but not acquired by Lawrence; Long Beach, an April 17 record of *nigricans* (in Bent 1925). DEL. Bombay Hook Nov. 1, bird with rather dark underparts (as in nominate *bernicla*) seen (Cutler 1955). VA. Cobbs I. in Sept., specimen in definitive feathering is an intergrade (belly too dark for *hrota*). LA. Cameron, Oct. 21, 1972, black-bellied bird seen (*Am. Birds* 27 71. 1973).

[From at least as early as Lawrence's time down to the present, there have been gunners and fishermen on the Atlantic coast who have claimed to have seen dark-bellied Brant. The same holds for light-bellied ones on the Pacific coast.]

NORTHERN EDGE OF N. AM. MAINLAND AND NORTHWARD includes breeding and molting range of dark-bellied (westerly) and light-bellied birds (easterly to extreme northerly localities), with overlap. ALASKA Colville R. delta, Aug. 27, 1972, white-bellied bird among 200 black-bellied ones (*Am. Birds* **27** 102. 1973); toward e. end of arctic coast at Barter I., "perfectly typical" ♀ *hrota* taken June 30 (Manning et al. 1956); Dist of Mackenzie Franklin Bay July 22, specimen, dark ♀ (suspected intergrade); Coronation Gulf July 21, specimen, ♂ with belly suspiciously light for *nigricans*; Mackenzie–Keewatin boundary Queen Maud Gulf in summer, a "typical" *hrota* seen associating with a pair of Black Brant (H. C. Hanson et al. 1956); e. Keewatin Southampton I. in summer of 1956, dark-bellied ♂ seen mated with a light-bellied ♀, also another dark-bellied bird seen, plus an apparent intergrade, in that same (light-bellied) breeding unit (T. W. Barry); Dist. of Franklin Banks I. (where both light- and dark-bellied Brant occur), 3 specimens too dark-bellied to fit *hrota* and 7 others only dark enough to fit within probable normal range of variation of *nigricans* (Manning et al. 1956); Melville I. specimens of both *hrota* and *nigricans* have been taken (Taverner, in Bent 1925; Manning et al. 1956); Prince Patrick I., in 1949 Handley (1950) saw both light- and dark-bellied Brant, separately; that same year, a ♀ incubating 3 eggs seemed to be "typical Black Brant" while her mate was "a great deal lighter below" and very much resembled *hrota* (MacDonald 1954); and of 15 specimens taken there in 1949 and 1952, at least 5, possibly 7, are intergrades and the remainder include both *hrota* and *nigricans* (many details in Manning et. al. 1956). For Ellesmere I., see below under E. Atlantic area.

Greenland specimen with belly presumably too dark to fit *hrota* included in table in Manning et al. (1956).

E. Atlantic area   A dark-bellied bird (age? sex?), banded in Aug. 1972 on Ellesmere I. at Okse Bay (lat. 77°8′ N. long. 87°53′ W), was recovered in Feb. 1974 at Béhal, Gulf of St. Malo, France. The belly color of the following 2 birds is not recorded, but at least the first comes from an area where *hrota–nigricans* intergrades occur. A preflight ♂ was banded Aug. 5, 1973, on Bathurst I.; it was recovered Oct. 16 of the same year at Lough Neagh, Ulster, N. Ireland. The other (age? sex?), banded in 1972 on Ellesmere I., was recovered later that year, also at Lough Neagh.

addendum   From observations of birds wearing yellow neck collars, it is now known that some Brant from the cent. Canadian high-arctic migrate in fall to sw. Greenland and thence to n. Ireland (principally); in both fall and spring some go via sw. Iceland and across Greenland (Maltby-Prevett et al. 1975 *Bird-Banding* **46** 155–61). Included, as one would expect, are individuals that are intermediate between Light-bellied and Black Brant. Evidently other individuals from the same high-arctic area go westerly and so occur in winter with Black Brant on the N. Am. Pacific coast.

note   A possibility exists that the Del. sighting, listed earlier, pertains to an escaped captive (it might even have been nominate *bernicla*), but that practically all of the other records given above are natural occurrences hardly can be questioned.

bernicla—extralimital (w. Siberia–Europe); for data on it see especially Witherby (1939), Salomonsen (1958), and S. Uspenskii (1960, 1963b, 1965a). For individuals that presumably are intergrades between *hrota* and nominate *bernicla*, on winter range, see Webbe (1958).

The species: Brodkorb (1964a) listed it as **fossil** from the Pleistocene of England (2 or 3 localities), Denmark (5), Italy, Malta (2), Czechoslovakia, Hungary, and in N. Am. in Ore. and Cal. (2). To this list, C. E. Ray et al. (1968) added the marine Pleistocene of

Va. It was reported from **archaeological sites** in Denmark (1 locality), Alaska (1 mainland and 5 island sites), and Fla. RSP

MIGRATION   Brant probably spend more time on the wing than any of our other geese. Their total migrations are long in time and distance, but include large segments covered rapidly, and during winter the birds shift about, depending on tide and on availability of food. For geese, they arrive at breeding areas rather late, all except southernmost nesters making their terminal flights in continuous daylight of the boreal summer. (Inland terrain generally is suitable for various geese, also swans, well ahead of the time when exposed coastal areas of Brant habitat become usable.) There are seasonal differences in portions of their routes and there are some differences between the schedules and places of occurrence of some first-winter birds as compared with breeders.

Brant migrate in flocks of up to at least 200 birds; these may combine into assemblies of 5,000 or more. They are bunched, seldom in line formation, but if in line the ♂ flies ahead of his mate. Usually they fly low over water, along coasts or at sea; overland flights are at higher altitudes. The latter generally follow watercourses or take the shortest distance between 2 water areas.

hrota (w. Atlantic segment, light bellied) **spring** migrants apparently are divided into 2 continental-wintering groups. The first makes rather gradual movement n. along Atlantic coast from wintering areas, with concentrations occurring at Great South Bay on Long I. (N.Y.) and at Monomoy Pt. (Mass.) in March–early April. From there they fly directly overwater to the Bay of Fundy (a few here sometimes in last week in Feb.), then across Isthmus of Chignecto, and gather in Northumberland Strait around Prince Edward I., the Magdalen Is., and mainland. Maximum numbers occur here the first week in May. In late May–early June, these birds fly to n. shore of Gulf of St. Lawrence between Mingan Is. and Seven Is. Most follow the e. coast of Gaspé Pen., crossing w. of Anticosti I. The largest concentration is at Seven Is. (Que.), where they remain briefly. On early June evenings they climb to a great altitude, then depart overland to either Ungava Bay or James Bay (H. F. Lewis 1937, text and maps). The Ungava Bay birds most probably proceed to Baffin and more n. islands.

The second continental group remains in N.J. coastal bays until mid-May, departing

257

on a more direct route overland to James Bay, probably nonstop for most, although some stop on larger lakes and rivers of N.Y., Ont., and Que. in late May. They seem to follow n.-trending watercourses such as Delaware R., Susquehanna R., and Finger Lakes to L. Ontario (a few to e. L. Erie); or Hudson R.–L. Champlain system to St. Lawrence R. They proceed n. over lakes and rivers of e. Ont. and w. Que. (such as Ottawa R. to Timiskaming and Abitibi lakes and James Bay drainage). These later-departing Brant arrive at James Bay in late May–early June, about the time part of the first group arrives from Seven Is. This inland route may account for half of w. Atlantic migrants. Occurrences in the interior are largely after mid-May departure date of this later group. From James Bay the flight continues n. along e. coast of Hudson Bay to Southampton and Baffin is. Fewer birds use the w. Hudson Bay coast. Further movement of *hrota* westward may be along or off the arctic coast rather than over the barrens.

Among 1,500 Brant banded on Southampton I. in 1956, band returns plus sightings of birds that had been marked with neckbands, in the following spring, showed that these birds were among both coastal and inland migrants. Also, they were widely dispersed in late winter, e.g., March 24, neck-banded Brant sighted at Oregon Inlet (N.C.) and Lubec (Me.) 800 mi. apart. Despite the 2 different migration patterns discussed so far, and broad dispersal over wintering grounds, at least 37.5% of banded mature Brant surviving the hunting season returned to nesting areas they had used previously.

Distance between spring stopping places increases as the season progresses. Arrival at breeding areas is consistent in timing—June 8, 1953 and 1956 at Boas R. (Southampton I.) and June 7, 1957, at East Bay across the island—although snow, ice, and water coverage of nest islands varied greatly. Regardless of weather there is continuous daylight. Prebreeders not in family groups arrive about 10 days later (if at all); many remain at sea, some as far s. as lakes within the clay belt around James Bay.

A third group is, in some measure, intermixed with birds from the first group. Presumably, some from the first group going via Ungava Bay continue on to nw. Greenland. Probably the majority of those summering in Greenland, however, are of another group, birds that wintered in Ireland. These fly to Iceland, then west to Angmagssalik Dist. of e. Greenland. From there, a few go up e. coast, but most are believed to cross the icecap to Egedesminde Dist. of w. Greenland, thence go n. to breeding areas. (For some further details about these birds, see Salomonsen 1950, 1958, 1967a.)

Summer There seems to be little information on possible molt migration, on foot or otherwise, of Brant of the e. Canadian arctic. At Southampton I. in 1953 there were large flocks of molting prebreeders "on the margins of the nesting grounds" and their molt began about July 6; and in 1956 and 1957 their ranks were swelled by failed breeders whose flightless period began about a week later than that of prebreeders (Barry 1962). The number of prebreeders in such gatherings does not necessarily reflect closely the number of surviving offspring of local breeders thereabouts; very likely other prebreeders have come there from a distance.

Fall Prebreeders finish molting and are flying again before mid-Aug., heading s. by late Aug. Brant flocks totaling over 500 birds have been reported near Churchill (Man.) by Sept. 1. Family groups combine to form flocks for southward flights in Sept.

258

Migration is mostly along the e. coast of Hudson Bay, fewer birds along the w. coast. Sightings indicate that some may take a direct route down the middle of the bay. They assemble in upper James Bay, also in vicinity of Ft. George, Akimiski I., and Charlton I., where Graham Cooch reported concentrations of up to 10,000 during Oct. 15–20, 1956. At least 10 times that many probably assemble somewhere in the vicinity of Akimiski I., then all depart together. Band returns from Southampton I. Brant fall along virtually a straight line from Boas R. nesting grounds to the N.J. coast. There are returns and/or neckband sightings from: Ft. George, Charlton I., w. Que. near L. Abitibi, L. Ontario, e. L. Erie, Oneida L. in N.Y., Tioga R. (n.-cent. Pa.), Susquehanna R., e. shore of Chesapeake Bay, and N.J. First arrivals: late Sept. These overland routes seem to be spring routes reversed, but are used by many more birds. Local reports indicate the overland route to Gulf of St. Lawrence and on down the Atlantic coast is used by fewer birds than in spring. In 1956 and 1957, southward migration from s. Hudson and James bays was in 3 main flights—Oct. 25, Nov. 3 and 11.

Fall migration from n. Greenland differs in detail from being the reverse of spring routes, as some birds occur in fall in sw. Greenland (Salomonsen 1950).

The character of overland flights varies depending on time of nesting, an early season allowing young to become strong on the wing before departure; flight then is largely nonstop from James Bay to N.J., at high altitudes, except occasionally some of the birds stop at large lakes. Late nesting finds fewer birds in peak condition for migration and family groups and flocks make frequent stops, hence large numbers are seen inland during certain autumns. The inland route seems to have received more use in recent years, reflecting that the Brant population has increased and perhaps that proportionately larger numbers depend less on eelgrass than formerly. It is a high-altitude nonstop flight similar to the overland flight n. from Seven Is. as described by H. F. Lewis (1937).

Brant converge at Barnegat Bay (N.J.) on some spectacular 100,000-bird days in late Oct. (23–25 in 1953, 1955, 1956, 1957). From Barnegat and Great Bay they disperse s. along coastal bays to N.C., depending on weather. Banding returns indicate that some move as far n. as Long I. (N.Y.) later in Dec. to mingle with coastal migrants. Part of the direct flight following the Susquehanna R. continues down the e. shore of Chesapeake Bay to Chincoteague (Va.) and N.C.; this segment is made up largely of young (first-fall) birds. Banding returns indicate a preponderance of birds wintering farthest s. are young.

Winter Shifting about, as just mentioned, is the rule rather than the exception, with some shifting northward in late winter.

nigricans (darkest Brant)—data from various sources, but mainly from R. D. Jones, Jr.

Spring There are some still intact family groups, but most prebreeders and breeders have separated. Movement begins somewhat gradually, in Feb., with a northward shift, first of southerly winterers. The early flocks are comprised almost entirely of mated breeders. As the season advances, the birds tend to concentrate at places along the Pacific coast from n. Cal. into B.C. Some from within the Gulf of Cal. move n. and stop inland at Salton Sea, where they occur in April–early May. Prebreeders (and some breeders) that were southerly winterers probably begin their journey over the Pacific at points as far s. as n. Cal. Some of the northerly birds continue up between the mainland and Vancouver I. and follow along the Alaskan coast; a few stop in the Kodiak area; they arrive at Izembek Bay in late April–early May.

As observed at the outer end of the Alaska Pen., the pattern of spring migration is one of relatively small flocks, flying low over the water, from the ocean into the big bays—Pavlof, Cold, and Morzovhoi. They continue to the innermost reaches and then, climbing to an altitude of about 1,000 ft., cross over to Izembek Lagoon on the Bering Sea side. Arrivals continue from April to very early June. The arriving birds are silent and appear to be fatigued.

Some Brant cross the Alaska Pen. to the eastward, at Chignik Lagoon, but apparently even these are headed for Izembek—flocks are seen flying sw. toward that lagoon while Emperor Geese are migrating in the opposite direction along that same coast.

The earliest arrivals at Izembek are breeders, which are gone by late May; prebreeders straggle in and out, drifting northward (beyond in Bering Sea, past Nome, for example) all summer.

After their stay at Izembek, the birds are traveling in long (and lengthening) daylight; the sun does not set at Barrow, Alaska, between May 10 and Aug. 2.

1 Some have a rather short journey to the Yukon–Kuskokwim delta area, where they begin nesting quite early in May in a "normal" season, 4 to 5 weeks earlier than at some arctic localities.

2 For many others, including birds of the Mackenzie and Anderson deltas, Izembek was only a halfway point in their long travels. The birds fatten there, then the tempo of migration increases, and soon they are traveling in continuous daylight.

Brant follow around the Alaskan perimeter to nesting grounds as far east as Queen Maud Gulf, but some turn off and cross Beaufort Sea to Banks and other arctic islands, including the Ringnes Is. The last groups to leave Izembek presumably are arctic nesters, rather than the early nesters of the Yukon Delta. The former make the long flight from Izembek in about 3–6 days, almost entirely in continuous daylight, and arrival varies only a day or so (about May 25), regardless of season or local weather, at mainland localities in nw. Canada. They settle on seaward places and are quiet for about 1 day; seldom is their habitat ready for occupancy.

Long ago, Richardson (1851) pointed out that Brant headed for the w. Canadian arctic breeding areas avoided circumnavigating Alaska by taking an overland route—up the Yukon valley, across to Peel R., and via the Mackenzie delta. Cade (1955) summarized the older and some recent evidence of inland routes (also see Irving 1960). Just what portion of the arctic birds go via the interior is speculative. Some that go through the interior may, on reaching the arctic coast, turn westward; at Demarcation Pt., May 20 and nearly every day until June 1, 1914, westbound flocks were seen (W. S. Brooks 1915). Some Brant that reach interior Alaska then go n. up river valleys, over the Brooks Range, and on to the Colville delta and probably elsewhere on the Alaskan arctic coast.

As in the W. Atlantic, banding data on Pacific Brant reveal that many young of the year winter farther s. than older birds. Almost all Brant in Wash. and B.C. in Feb. are older birds—370 out of 383 in 1 instance.

260

Many yearlings go n. comparatively late, often to the fringes of nesting areas (though they may not remain there). Others go to shores, beaches, mudflats, and lakes; some spend much time on the sea.

Summer On the w. Canadian arctic mainland there is movement along shores and waterways, by prebreeders while flightless and also by breeders with their young. Prebreeders, captured and marked by T. W. Barry, were recaptured by him 65 mi. away 6 days later.

A useful introduction to the subject of **molt migration** is Pleske's (1928) discussion of Brant of the Siberian tundra. First, breeders return and settle at breeding places; later, any prebreeders that accompanied them, plus others that arrive subsequently, move on northward and molt at places, mostly islands, where Brant also nest (but not in numbers). He mentioned the observations of Baron Toll, who saw Brant flying outward beyond the northernmost islands, a matter taken up again recently by S. Uspenskii.

At hand are recoveries in U.S.S.R. of 15 Brant banded in the years 1949–61, in summer (July 14–Aug. 14) in the Yukon–Kuskokwim delta area. Eleven of these were recorded when banded as "immature," 1 as "juv.," and 2 as "adult ♂ ." They were recovered 1 to 8 years after banding, almost all in June–July. The majority were recovered at places not very distant from Alaska, from Chaun Bay on the Siberian arctic coast down to include Anadyr Gulf in Bering Sea and eastward (see chart 4 in Einarsen 1965). The few from elsewhere include an "immature" recovered 2 years after banding, on Wrangel I., and the 3 most distant from Alaska also were "immature" when banded and were recovered much farther westward, in New Siberian Archipelago (1 on Kotelny 2 years after banding, 2 on New Siberia I. 5 and 6 years after banding). The 2 "adult ♂ " were shot, in late May and in July, 1 and 2 years after they were banded, in the Chaun Bay area.

According to S. Uspenskii (1963b), those Brant that spend the winter in Asiatic (nw. Pacific) waters migrate n. overland to arctic breeding places located from the e. side of Taimyr Pen. eastward to the Kolyma Delta. (For them he uses the name *orientalis* of Tougarinov 1941, which the present author does not recognize.) Their main breeding places are on the mainland, but some nest as far n. as in the New Siberian Archipelago. He has stated that the major molting places of the prebreeders also are in the New Siberian Archipelago.

In several publications, Uspenskii has mentioned his own and other peoples' observations of Brant seen from Bennett, Henrietta, and the DeLong Is. (all n. of the large is. of the New Siberian Archipelago) and from a ship off the Kolyma delta, flying n. beyond these last outposts, or back toward them, in the appropriate season for molt migration. It was believed in former times that Brant went to unexplored land to the north ("Sannikov Land" of the Russians, "Keenan" and/or "Harris Land" of Americans), but these places do not exist, as demonstrated by the arctic flights of Hubert Wilkins, Ben Eilson, and other explorers. Uspenskii has reasoned that the flocks are comprised of prebreeders and that they fly over the polar wastes on what, as viewed on a map, might be termed a curving trajectory which brings them to a point of impact in the Yukon–Kuskokwim delta. (As viewed on a globe, the birds actually would be traveling the shortest distance between the New Siberian Archipelago and the Yukon–Kuskokwim delta). There the birds molt—and some have been banded while flightless—alongside Alaskan breeders. An alternative explanation, that many pre-breeding Brant only migrate as far n. as the Yukon–Kuskokwim delta area (where some are captured and banded), but when older as breeders they migrate beyond to Siberia, makes considerable sense but does not cover all the facts.

In Alaska, E. W. Nelson (1887) was assured by whaling captains that Brant frequently were seen "coming from over the ice to the north of Point Barrow in fall"—strong evidence for the existence of land "beyond the impenetrable icy barrier" to the north. Perhaps the Brant of Wrangel I. (Siberia) or Prince Patrick I. (Canadian arctic) or both places have as the first leg of their fall migration a direct flight more or less toward Bering Strait. Or if such Brant were seen in Aug., then they were prebreeders which had gone to these distant places, molted (early), and were returning. This covers many known facts.

According to S. Uspenskii (1965a), there were 1,000–2,000 pairs of Brant breeding on Wrangel I. in 1964 and at least an additional 10,000 prebreeders molting there. Decades earlier, Pleske (1928) had reported large numbers summering there.

The flocks of Brant still moving n. in Alaskan waters, even as far as Wainwright, in late June, apparently are prebreeders.

To summarize, the known facts fit within the following framework. In yearling (and other?) prebreeders, migration is variable—some do not go as far as nesting areas; a great many do, and molt thereabouts; still others go to breeding areas and, instead of remaining, make an additional long flight (molt migration). A few flocks evidently are moving northward gradually in early summer and molt wherever they happen to be, beginning in late June. Since molt migration tends to be from one area where Brant nest to another such area, a consequence of spring–early summer movement is that, at some northerly localities, the number of molting prebreeders greatly exceeds the number of local breeders and their young, as in New Siberian Archipelago, Wrangel I., and probably C. Halkett in Alaska. Much the same variation and complexity in movement occurs also in another *Branta*, namely *canadensis*.

Fall   The birds travel their spring routes, in reverse direction, except movement is almost entirely coastal and across bays around Alaska (little evidence of any flight in the interior). This allows the arctic nesters to move leisurely, taking advantage of food and shelter in various bays (while the young continue to grow) on the way to Izembek Bay. They arrive there in Oct.—later than those from the Yukon–Kuskokwim delta.

As to the latter, prebreeders are on the move early; by mid-Aug. they are departing from molting areas. Birds from the Yukon Delta and vicinity pass s. to Bristol Bay and on to Izembek Lagoon, the first ones usually arriving about Aug. 25 (earliest record is for Aug. 20). The first arrivals are prebreeders (and probably failed breeders), but flocks of family groups begin arriving soon after. Arrival may continue well into Aug. The birds come in from Bering Sea, flying just over the water. There are 2 lagoons at C. Newenham (s. corner of Kuskokwim Bay) where Brant remain until freeze-up and then head for Izembek Lagoon. During the time the birds are at the latter place, a visible change in them occurs. They are extremely thin on arrival, but by the time they are ready to depart they have a remarkable amount of visceral and subcutaneous fat, reminiscent of the blubber of marine mammals. (At Izembek Lagoon the total crop of eel-grass is of the order of 2.3×10^6 metric tons fresh wt., the largest stand known (McRoy 1970).)

Departure from Izembek Lagoon is spectacular. By about Oct. 23 the birds seem ready to go. Atmospheric pressure patterns that produce favorable winds flowing all the way across the Gulf of Alaska trigger the departure. Most departures have been in Nov., the latest on Nov. 22, 1972. As the time nears, and wind flow becomes favorable at Izembek Lagoon, large flocks go aloft to an estimated 2,000 ft. and somehow test conditions. On the final, favorable, day all the Brant are aloft most of the day, climbing, circling, and dropping back to water. Then, usually at night, all the birds (except a few that remain through winter where there is open water) leave. They are noisy, frequently awakening sleepers. When they can be seen, they always are at high altitudes, probably several thousand feet. Apparently they fly nonstop to Baja Cal., except for a relatively few thousand that appear along the intervening route, for they are not found elsewhere in numbers. A small flock appeared in Drake's Bay (near San Francisco), Cal., 3 days after departure from Izembek Lagoon; it contained 4 birds marked by T. Barry on the Anderson R. delta that summer, 1965.

The above description supersedes earlier reports of departure of flocks from Izembek Lagoon over a considerable period. There is an inward drift to that place, but no outward one; all that are to leave go at one time.

The Brant arrive in the Puget Sd. area, on the Cal. coast, and presumably beyond in Mexico, usually within the span Nov. 5–20, depending on when they leave Izembek Lagoon.

Scattered reports from the Mackenzie basin and as far s. as the Peace R. in Alta. indicate that a very few w. Canadian arctic birds may pass overland to Pacific waters.

The above paragraphs on spring and fall omit almost all continuing flights to and from E. Siberia. Spring routes from Alaska to Siberia are speculative, as also fall routes; see tentative mapping in S. Uspenskii (1963b).

Following are data on 2 Brant of unknown age when banded in Cal. One, banded on March 10, 1953, was recovered on May 6 of the same year on n. side of Anadyr Gulf; the other, banded on March 12, 1953, was recovered 3 years later, on May 25, 1956, at a very distant place, New Siberia I. (easternmost of the main is. of New Siberian Archipelago).

Winter   A northward shift of southerly winterers, beginning in Feb., is mentioned above under Spring. See especially Denson and Murrell (1962) for many data on Brant at Humboldt Bay, Cal.

[The reader who desires information on routes of Brant in the w. Palearctic will find useful diagrams in Salomonsen (1958).] RSP

BANDING STATUS   *B. b. hrota.* As of April 30, 1958, a total of 3,859 had been banded on Southampton I., N.W.T.—2,851 at Boas R., 1,008 at East Bay. Most of the 154 recoveries (as of the same date) were at localities from Long I. (N.Y.) to S.C., others from inland migration routes, and a few in spring and fall along the coast of the Maritimes.

The total number banded in the Nearctic area (includes those mentioned above) was 6,032 through 1964 and there were 533 recoveries through 1961; most of the banding was done in Dist. of Keewatin (data from Bird Banding Laboratory).

There has been no banding of Brant in Greenland.

B. b. nigricans.   Of 8,804 banded in the Yukon Delta, 1949–55 inclusive, the number of recoveries was 767 (as of some time in 1956); of these, 36 were local (within 100 mi. of place of banding). The other recoveries: in Alaska 59, Yukon–N.W.T. 6, U.S.S.R. 8, B.C. 102, Wash. 72, Ore. 10, Cal. 391, Mexico 81, Colo. 1, and Texas 1 (H. A. Hansen and Nelson 1957).

The total was 19,749 banded through 1964 and there were 987 recoveries through 1961; main places of banding: Alaska, Dist. of Mackenzie, and Cal. (data from Bird Banding Laboratory).

Among the Cal. recoveries, 170 were from the Humboldt Bay area (Denson and Murrell 1962).

There has been some banding in the Palearctic region, notably in Spitzbergen. RSP

REPRODUCTION Except where otherwise indicated, the data are for light-bellied birds *(hrota)* in N. Am.

Some Brant **first breed** at age 2 years (in their 3rd calendar year), but usually when a year older.

Pair formation is a result of long association of prebreeders. The sequence of events is about as follows. Most Brant families break up in late fall when the parent birds cease defending the family and discourage the presence of their brood. In *nigricans*, this has been reported on by R. D. Jones and Jones (1966). The young then tend to keep in groups of birds of their own age-class and there seems to be no evidence that they actively engage in pair formation during their first winter. By the time they have returned (as yearlings) to the arctic to molt, their flocks are well organized and are quite independent of other (older) cohorts. Before molting, there are pursuit flights and this activity is renewed again afterward, then interrupted by fall migration, and becomes much more frequent on winter range. The birds fly a zigzag course, dipping and rising, and return to near the takeoff point. By some time in winter a firm bond is established by an unknown percentage of the birds, and after their second spring migration a portion of the birds of this cohort become breeders. In others, the process may be longer or delayed; at least, they become breeders when older.

Families that did not break up in 1st fall are believed to remain intact until the parent birds become territorial in the following year.

There is evidence (Lensink 1968) that colored neckbands, placed as identifying markers on ♀ *nigricans*, inhibited pair formation, as compared with others wearing only metal leg bands.

Pair bond form is **lifelong monogamy.**

It should be noted that, after Prebasic II molt (at age about 12–14 mo.), Brant are "adult" in appearance even though they do not breed for at least another year. This gives an effect of numerous "nonbreeding adults."

Breeding birds **arrive** paired, in flocks seldom exceeding 30 individuals (and some breeders sometimes accompanied by their young of the previous year). At Southampton I., the first arrivals were in midforenoon, later ones (over about a 10-day span) at any hour. Yearlings not with parents are about 10 days behind the others in schedule. Newly arrived flocks gather on the snow, or in runoff pools, or on grassy islets and raised beaches along the coast, and wait for nesting habitat to become clear of

264

snow. There they associate in large feeding flocks with Canadas and Blue/Snows when cleared areas are scarce. Marine algae in digestive tracts indicate that some fly to the floe edge to feed. Runoff pools on the surface of shore ice most frequently are shared with Tundra Swans, Oldsquaws, and King Eiders. As the thaw progresses, Brant flocks subdivide into smaller groups, make reconnoitering flights, and finally the breeders, scattered in pairs, are on nesting habitat. Compared to other geese, they nest comparatively late because their habitat clears later. They nest in what might be termed loose colonies, with many also scattered in the less desirable habitat.

Territory is not well defined or defended until shortly before the first egg is laid. In all territory reconnaissance, the goose precedes the gander, and she determines the location of the territory by selecting the spot where she will nest. Territory is used for mutual display, nesting, and feeding. Its size depends on the amount of area free of snow and water, as well as size of nesting islets. In optimum habitat, strewn with hundreds of islets 1–3 meters in diam. and having a mat of brant grass (*Carex subspathacea*), the av. distance between 66 nests was 33.8 m. In similar areas, but with larger islets, nests were more widely spaced and much of the intervening terrain was undefended common ground. In the Yukon Delta, highest density of *nigricans* nests was 144/sq. mi., within 3–5 mi. of the coast (H. A. Hansen and Nelson 1957).

Perhaps 90% of *hrota* in the author's study areas on Southampton I. were within the distribution of brant grass on low sites within a mile of shore or high tide. The short grass forms a thick mat, in which the birds nest; it also is a major food source for parents and young. Often they nest in flotsammed sea wrack and in kelp strewn by fall storms. Some use low mossy and grassy is. in shallow river deltas and widely scattered islets and shores of tundra pools. They seldom use higher and drier sites inland. Black Brant, especially, are at the mercy of flood tides accompanied by onshore winds.

Both adults participate in **territorial defense** during egg laying, apparently ♂ vs. ♂ and ♀ vs. ♀. There is a mutual Triumph display when intruders are repulsed. The gander assumes the entire defense during incubation, often flying to meet and "escort" intruders through the territory. If an intruding pair, or a group of prebreeders, lands in the territory, the gander rushes at them. A short aerial chase and pulling of flank feathers is more common than ground fighting by biting or by hitting with the "wrist." The gander, often in association with Sabine's Gull, Arctic Tern, or Ruddy Turnstone, chases Herring Gulls and jaegers through the territory. Other species of waterfowl generally are ignored, but a gander repeatedly harassed displaying Oldsquaws and King Eiders. The polar bear is ignored, but Brant flee from man. Pipped eggs and small goslings are defended against any intruder, even man sometimes.

Common ground is frequented by prebreeders and failed breeders. The latter may continue to defend territory (data on 20 marked birds). A gander that lost his mate and her clutch defended territory vigorously and made Triumph displays at the nest site for 10 days before abandoning it.

Copulation is not seen on territory; presumably it occurs when the birds are swimming off the floe edge, also farther s. during the terminal portion of migration. The oviduct of a goose collected 3 hrs. after her arrival on June 7 contained sperm, but the first egg in the colony was not laid until 16 days later.

Although arrival time is constant from year to year, **onset of nesting** is variable, depending on when a suitable amount of habitat is clear. First nests,with span of time after arrival in parentheses, at Southampton I.: June 15, 1953 (7 days); June 20, 1956 (12 days) at Boas R.; June 23, 1957 (16 days) at East Bay. The pubic bones of the goose soften and spread and her abdominal bulge develops 5–7 days after arrival.

Depending on whether free of snow and water coverage, some nest sites (or nearby sites) are used in successive years; of 70 nests checked in 1956, 70% were on new sites, 30% on old ones. A check of banded birds in 1957, covering the identical area studied in 1956, revealed 37.5% of breeders returned to nest in the area.

The first egg is laid in a shallow depression formed by the goose tamping and twisting her body in the turf. Often there is water in the bottom of the depression, and permafrost only a few cm. below. Height of nest above nearest water during laying: av. 18.4 cm. (0–35.5) at Boas R. in 1956 (115 nests); 45 cm. (20.3–91.4) at East Bay in 1957 (33 nests). Distance from water (same nests) 111.6 cm. (30 cm.–6.1 m.) at Boas R. and 4.3 m. (60 cm.–15.2 m.) at East Bay.

Usually the eggs are laid 1/day, in forenoon. Of 158 clutches, 14.6% skipped a day after 1st egg; 22.8% a day after the 2nd; 17.7% after 3rd; 15.5% after 4th; and 36.7% skipped none. In 9 nests, days were skipped twice, usually after 2nd and 4th egg; in 2 nests there were 3 skipped days. In a colony, all laying usually occurs within a 10-day span.

The bowl is formed beforehand, but the **nest** is constructed later, around the eggs. Brant grass is the most common material, pulled from the surrounding turf by the goose while on her eggs, and she forms it into a mound around the perimeter of the bowl. If the site is close to the high-water flotsam line, feathers, sea wrack, kelp, and Brant droppings from the previous season often are gathered as base material. The gray **nest down** most frequently is added beginning with the 2nd egg (in 106 nests: 1st egg, 11%; 2nd, 64%; 3rd egg 25%). The down accumulates until a luxuriant "pillow" is formed; it is very cohesive, adhering in one mass to the nest depression, and highly resistant to wind strewing. The following spring it seldom has blown away and it still retains its cohesive quality. The nest down of *nigricans* is both darker and browner than that of *hrota*.

Nest size depth of depression av. 5.6 cm. (10 nests); diam. of cavity av. 30.5 cm. (29 nests); outer diam. of nest mound av. 45.7 cm. (18 nests). The gander does no building, but remains on territory.

Clutch size probably av. 4.5 eggs, but in 853 nests (in 1953, 1956, 1957) was 3.94— smaller because of predation prior to counting, lateness of seasons, floods, and other factors. There is a definite regression: the later the date of the 1st egg, the smaller the clutch; and, in very backward seasons, laying is inhibited entirely; details in Barry (1962). For *nigricans* in the Yukon Delta, the av. was 3.5 eggs in 116 nests (apparently recorded without regard for losses) and nesting success was 79% on the basis of 123 nests (H. A. Hansen and Nelson 1957).

There is no known renesting after loss of full clutch or young, but the goose will build a 2nd nest nearby and lay the remainder of her clutch if part of it has been laid and destroyed.

Egg shape subelliptical to long elliptical. **Color** creamy white, often tinged pale olive. Av. **size** of 521 eggs on Southampton I. was 72.9 × 47.2 mm. (length varied 65–83 mm., width 44–51). In a clutch, length of the egg decreases with each successive egg: av. for 1st egg 73.8 mm. (128 eggs), 2nd 72.8 (125), 3rd 72.6 (118), 4th 72.5 (99), 5th 71.7 (47); and av. width: 1st egg was 46.9 mm., 2nd 47.4, 3rd 47.4, 4th 47.2, 5th 46.9 (same sample as used for length).

In *nigricans*, one egg each from 20 clutches (Alaska 3, nw. Canada 17) **size** length av. 72.40 mm. ± 3.33, breadth 47.17 ± 1.92, radii of curvature of ends 17.17 ± 0.79 and 12.50 ± 1.58; **shape** elongation 1.54 ± 0.029, bicone −0.030, and asymmetry +0.152 (FWP). In 1969–72, some 24 mi. se. of Hooper Bay, Alaska, 376 eggs (mean and SD): length 70.6 ± 3.38 mm. (extremes 60.3–80.4) and breadth 47.4 ± 1.67 (41.9–51.7) (P. Mickelson). The shell is smooth and quite glossy, **color** varies, mostly light buffs.

Incubation is by the goose, beginning with laying of the last egg, and usually with head and neck resting on the ground. She develops a large incubation patch. The gander stands guard at favored spots in the territory, usually a few meters from the nest, shifting his location because of weather, food, or presence of predators. If the goose leaves the nest to feed, she covers her eggs and they are kept warm by the nest down for a long time. If, in bad weather, the down and nest become soggy, she abandons them. The gander calls the goose from the nest in case of danger and also escorts her from and to the nest to feed (but usually he does not come close to the nest). If the nest is attacked, as by jaegers or a fox, both birds are at the nest and defend it with moaning growls, open bills, thrusting movements, or even by flying up at the attacker. **Incubation period** (laying of last egg to hatching of all) usually 24 days in 130 nests; variation: 22 days (2.3%), 23 (24.6%), 24 (60.0%), 25 (11.5%), and 26 (1.5%).

Loss of eggs and *nonhatching* accounted for 27% of 723 eggs in marked, daily-checked nests as follows: taken by Herring Gulls 14%, abandoned 4%, infertile 3%, taken by jaegers 1%, flooded 1%, cracked and other causes 1%. An additional 3% is for eggs that hatched, but the still wet goslings were abandoned. In a coastal area of brant grass, not broken into islets, an arctic fox took all eggs from 16 nests.

About 48 hrs. (spread 24–60) after the first egg pips, and depending somewhat on weather and clutch size, the nest is vacated. The **goslings** are called by the goose, who stands 5–20 ft. away and utters an alarm note rapidly for 3–5 min.; any young that are unable to walk are abandoned. The gander takes a dominant role as the dry goslings begin to travel. The brood is led immediately to tideflats and pools near the edge of nesting islets, to feed on marine invertebrates, mosquito larvae, brant grass, and small flowers. From pipping onward, both parents are very defensive and will attack anything that approaches. The parents keep the brood between them; the gander leads; the goose, who is weakened and has lost much wt. during incubation, is at the rear of the close formation. The goslings swim as soon as they can walk and they dive well when 2 days old. Predation on them in the study area was largely by Herring Gulls; under certain circumstances in Alaska, jaegers have preyed extensively on *nigricans*. High winds may blow young (up to age 1 week) from the family group, in which case they are drowned or taken by gulls. There is a small defended area around the family, which decreases in size but still exists after feeding flocks are formed and even during early stages of migration.

In the continuous daylight the goslings feed almost constantly, except for brief periods of brooding. Hence they grow very fast, like other arctic geese.

Development Young av. about 43.6 gm. at hatching; at 14 days 315–398 gm. and

267

have pinfeathers in wings and tail; at 32 days about 967 gm., the wings are quite well developed, white barring on secondaries is conspicuous, and body feathers are developing. The primaries grow rapidly during the 4th week and are fully grown by 6 weeks. Head-poking actions and preening begin by age 4–5 days, and ability to keep dry increases from this time. They begin flapping wings and rising on their toes at 10 days. See under "Voice" for its development.

Beginning early during Prebasic molt of parents (before the young can fly), family groups unite to form small flocks. They seek tideflats and water, not distant from nesting areas, for escape. Ashore, breeders can run 100 m. in 16–20 sec. (estimated), especially when not retarded by presence of goslings. Breeders and downy goslings have been driven up to 14 mi. overland and suffered no ill effects.

In *nigricans* in fall at Izembek Lagoon, most families contain 1–4 young; see R. D. Jones, Jr. (1970) for details.

Age at first flight 45–50 days (Barry 1962)—that is, they are on the wing around mid-Aug. in normal seasons. TWB

SURVIVAL In *nigricans*, using the Bellrose and Chase (1950) method of calculation of total mortality, H. A. Hansen and Nelson (1957) arrived at a first-year mortality rate of birds banded as goslings of 45.4%, with av. mortality in later years of about 32.2%. These would include estimates (by 2 different methods) of 26 and 28.6% annual hunting mortality. The data of Hansen and Nelson, as recalculated by Boyd (in Le Cren and Holdgate 1962) gave an estimated mean annual adult survival rate of 0.85 ± 0.05.

There is less information on the following:

B. b. hrota—in N.Am., there is some information in Barry (1956, 1962). For Spitzbergen, Boyd, in the paper cited above, gave estimated mean annual adult survival rate as 0.83 ± 0.08.

B. b. bernicla—for British-wintering birds, using censuses and age ratios (in Boyd 1959a), the estimated mean annual adult survival rate is 0.86 (Boyd, in Le Cren and Holdgate 1962). DSF TWB

HABITS A maritime goose with well-developed salt gland. The following are N. Am. data unless otherwise indicated.

Brant associate with other flocking waterfowl; at Izembek Lagoon in Alaska, for example, with large numbers of smaller Canada Geese (*B. c. parvipes*), also with Emperor Geese. Easterly birds associate with Blue/Snow Geese and Canadas. Young Brant in their first winter and later tend to be in groups preponderantly of their own cohort (hatched the same year). They tend to winter farther s., return n. later, and wander more.

Brant fly at 4.5–6 wingbeats/sec, and ground speed with no wind has been measured at 55–70 mph (several observations in N.J.). The body rises and falls with each wingstroke; the head and foreneck remain stable. In spring in Cal., Brant have been observed "tumbling" in flight, the lead bird suddenly dropping 20–30 ft., followed by the same action at the same spot by each succeeding bird in the flock (Grant 1946). According to R. D. Jones, Jr., at Izembek Lagoon, tumbling is observed commonly in all seasons, being particularly evident when a flock of several hundred goes aloft to test conditions for migrating. Having found them unsatisfactory, the entire flock tumbles back to the Lagoon. A sudden transformation—at one moment, orderly echelons; in the next, the whole bunch comes tumbling out of the sky. Both Brant and Canada Geese also employ this maneuver to evade the stoop of the Gyrfalcon, and probably to evade the Bald Eagle.

Brant swim very well and, although they are not habitual divers, they do dive when closely pursued; one submerged for 3 min. They hide by lying flat on the water or in weeds.

Brant that spend the winter on both sides of the Atlantic were reported to have suffered a serious decline in numbers in the early 1930s, attributed to an eelgrass (*Zostera*) die-off. This favorite, but by no means their exclusive, food almost completely disappeared from all coasts of the Atlantic in 1931–32 (and declined somewhat, at a later time, on the U.S. Pacific coast). Previous Brant fluctuations are known, as reported by J. C. Phillips (1932). That the eelgrass nearly vanished from the Atlantic is a certainty. That Brant went to unusual places to feed also is known. And it is known that some Brant were undernourished. This may have rendered them susceptible to disease, since a few birds found dead were emaciated. That great numbers of Brant died of starvation (Lincoln 1950b) and, as also has been claimed, that the survivors changed their diet in the nick of time before becoming extinct, lack convincing support. Brant are not as specialized feeders as this would imply (see beyond). A decline in Brant numbers in the early 1930s may have been real. It might be rewarding to check any records relating to weather conditions on their breeding range in the late 1920s and early 1930s. (As a result of adverse weather on breeding range in 1961, there was a near-complete failure of light-bellied Brant to produce any young—i.e., that cohort was missing from the population—and nominate *bernicla* suffered in lesser degree; in 1963, flooding of the Yukon Delta caused an almost total nesting failure of a major unit of *nigricans*.) There is also a possibility that the number of Brant wintering in the w. Atlantic prior to disappearance of eelgrass has been overestimated, and a strong probability that such was the case in Europe and Britain.

At least throughout the Canadian arctic and beyond westward to Wrangel I., the summer of 1972 was the most delayed then on record. Only the most southerly-nesting Brant produced any young. The light-bellied *hrota* of the w. Atlantic, in the winter of 1972–73, were estimated at only about 40,000 individuals, down from about 73,000 a year earlier, 150,000 two years earlier, and around 200,000 in the latter part of the 1960s. The summer of 1973 was generally favorable, but that of 1974 was one of failure in much of the arctic (see vol. 3 under "Habits" of King Eider for a listing of adverse seasons).

The light-bellied birds of the e. Atlantic, which have suffered from egging at nesting places (see, for example, Løvenskiold 1964) and from hunting, and the dark-bellied e. Atlantic winterers, reportedly had reached dangerously low numbers in the late 1950s (Salomonsen 1958) and have continued (see figures in Ogilvie and Matthews 1969) to be unsatisfactorily low. By 1950 there was good recovery of eelgrass at most Atlantic localities. The Am. Pacific population of Brant, which shows the expected very decided differences in annual increment, fluctuated around a figure of about 175,000 during the period 1950–65 (table in Einarsen 1965). Figures on their reduced number in winter of 1972–73 are not at hand.

Because Brant fly low, in bunches, a hunter shooting at a particular bird in the flock is likely to hit at least one other. That is, the number hit probably is double the number shot at and many that are hit either are not downed or are not retrieved. The species cannot stand a heavy loss to hunters. On winter range, they would benefit from less disturbance by boats.

Brant are unwary, especially young in their first fall–winter, but a preference for open water saves many from less experienced gunners. This wildfowl is a superb table bird when it has been feeding on eelgrass. As noted in N. J., however, sea lettuce *(Ulva)* imparts an undesirable odor within about a week after the birds arrive.

In winter, Brant gather in huge assemblies, "rafting up" on open water to rest and moving over eelgrass or sea lettuce beds to feed, almost entirely in the daylight hours. Time of feeding is governed by the tide; that is, food is more accessible when the tide is at least partly down. The birds also gather on spits and sandbars, to ingest grit. The winter concentrations shift about, with changing weather or feeding conditions. In late winter or early spring, some visit salt marshes to eat new shoots of salt hay. They have grazed on an athletic field and on an airport at Atlantic City (N. J.), being a nuisance at both places. On their breeding grounds, breeders, at least, spend most of their time on land, grazing grasses or grubbing in moss, at some localities turning over large patches of the latter in search of horsetail *(Equisetum)*. Some prebreeders in summer spend much time on salt water, hence presumably are aquatic feeders during that season.

Einarsen (1965) mentioned that scaups, scoters, and goldeneyes, when getting shellfish from the ocean bottom, often bring fragments of eelgrass and sea lettuce to the surface; Brant have followed the ducks for the purpose of getting these items.

For many interesting details of winter habits of nominate *bernicla* in England, see Ranwell and Downing (1959).

There is much good reading on habits of Brant in Bent (1925); there is a slender volume on Pacific Brant by Einarsen (1965); and Hout (1967) assembled a partial bibliography on the species.

Original information contained in the preceding sections, also beyond, were obtained during work supported by the various agencies listed by Barry (1962). TWB

FOOD *Branta bernicla hrota.* Animal food generally occurs only as traces and usually does not exceed 5%. On the N. Am. Atlantic coast the favorite food is eelgrass, mainly the leaves, but rhizomes taken eagerly when procurable (Norton 1909). When eelgrass is scarce, other marine plants are substituted.

Vegetable Prior to 1932, along N. Am. Atlantic coast, eelgrass *(Zostera marina)* 85% wigeon grass *(Ruppia maritima)* 12%, algae 1%, other plants 2%, and trace of animal matter. After drastic depletion of eelgrass, consumption of it declined to 9% while that of algae *(Ulva, Enteromorpha, Monostroma, Chaetomorpha, Cladophora,* and *Cylindrocopsa)* increased in proportion (Cottam et al. 1944). Principal alga eaten is sea lettuce *(Ulva lactuca)* (J. C. Phillips 1932, R. E. Stewart 1962), a specimen from S.C. having eaten 3 oz. (Chamberlain 1925, Sprunt 1930).

270

Two-thirds of a 13-acre crop of carrots at Port Weller, Ont., was destroyed by a flock of 30 Brant (Sheppard 1949).

Chief food in Grinnell Land (cent. Ellesmere I.): buds of *Saxifraga oppositifolia* (Dresser 1877). In June in Hall Land (nw. Greenland), shoots of *Eriophorum, Ranunculus nivalis*, and *Cerastium alpinum* (H. C. Hart 1880). The stomachs of 4 specimens in spring on Southampton I. contained grass and roots (Sutton 1932). On arriving at Baffin Bay they feed on black lichens (Bent 1925). In autumn in Greenland they feed on berries of *Empetrum nigrum* (Salomonsen 1950).

Data for Britain and Europe pertain to *B. b. bernicla* and *hrota*. Food in s. Britain mainly *Zostera* spp., algae (*Enteromorpha, Ulva*), and *Salicornia*, and to a lesser extent *Aster tripolium, Halimione portulacoides, Spergulia marginata, Armeria maritima, Plantago maritima, Puccinellia maritima, Spartina, Festuca rubra*, and *Triglochin maritima* (Burton 1961, J. W. Campbell 1936, Ranwell and Downing 1959).

At Terschelling (Netherlands) in autumn fed mainly on *Zostera nana*, also on *Salicornia, Puccinellia*, and *Enteromorpha*; in winter on *Enteromorpha*; and in spring on *Salicornia, Puccinellia*, and also frequented the saline areas where *Armeria maritima* and *Festuca rubra* occurred (Bruijns and Tanis 1955). Main food on Jutland, *Zostera* (Salomonsen 1957). On Spitzbergen, algae (*Fucus*), moss, numerous grasses, stems and leaves of *Oxyria digyna*, saxifrages and other unrecognizable phanerogams. Young had fed on Gramineae and *Oxyria* (Le Roi, in Koenig 1911).

Animal Insects, mollusks, crustaceans, and worms. Mussels and frozen quahogs (*Venus (Mercenaria) mercenaria*) recorded from Mass. (Forbush 1925). Ants (Formicidae) found in a N.Y. specimen (Foley and Taber 1951). Stomachs from Spitzbergen contained besides grass and other plant fragments numerous large and small mollusks (Römer and Schaudinn 1900). Crustaceans and mollusks found frequently in Europe. In England, J. W. Campbell (1946) identified the crustaceans *Idotea* and *Gammarus*. One stomach contained over 60 mollusks, of which about 40 were *Hydrobia ulvae*.

Branta bernicla nigricans. (N. Am. data only.) Largely marine plant materials with some algae and small amounts of fish eggs, crustaceans, and mollusks. On Prince Patrick I. (N.W.T.), fed on a plot of lush grass and moss tundra (Handley 1950). Three gizzards from Perry R. (N.W.T.) contained almost entirely *Poa arctica* (H. C. Hanson et al. 1956). Stomach of a bird collected in Sept. on St. Paul I. (Pribilofs), Alaska, contained solely the filamentous alga *Chaetomorpha cannaban* (Preble and McAtee 1923). In winter along N. Am. w. coast feeds at sea on aquatic plants. At Yaquina, Netarts, and Tillamook Bays, Ore., and at Humboldt, Tomales, and San Diego Bays, Cal., largely the leaves of eelgrass (*Zostera marina*) with some roots (S. F. Baird et al. 1884a), W. E. Bryant 1893, Gabrielson and Jewett 1940, J. Grinnell et al. 1918). Moffitt (1932), and various later papers) stated that Brant arrive in Cal. bays shortly after the Nov. spawning of herring (*Clupea pallasii*) and feeds especially on the eelgrass to which the eggs are attached. Also feeds on upland grasses, salt grass, surfgrass (*Phyllospadix*), and algae, particularly sea lettuce (*Ulva lactuca*). The stomachs of 20 birds collected at Tomales Bay in Dec. contained mainly eelgrass with herring eggs. One stomach contained: 6,000 small fish eggs 26%, an amphipod and an isopod 1%, eelgrass 63%, and surfgrass 10%. In spring in Salton Sea they are reported to feed on bulrush, probably

Scirpus robustus which is abundant (Reynolds 1966). In Okla. a lone Brant was feeding with Canada Geese on growing wheat (W. E. Lewis 1925), and Moffitt and Cottam (1941) mentioned Pacific Brant going inland to feed in grain fields. In winter in Alaska eelgrass is consumed almost exclusively (Gabrielson and Lincoln 1959).

The stomachs of 65 birds collected very largely from Ore. to Cal. contained 99% vegetable matter and 1% animal, as follows: eelgrass 76%, surfgrass 12%, sedges and grasses 6%, undetermined plant materials 1%, algae *(Chaetomorpha,* Ulvaceae) 3%, and traces of fish eggs, amphipods, miscellaneous crustaceans, barnacles (Balanidae), hydrozoa, and insects (Cottam et al. 1944). AWS

The above compilation indicates the variety of food eaten. The following, greatly condensed from R. D. Jones, Jr. (in press), is based on some of the same plus other sources, adds new information, and emphasizes feeding habits. The names of subspecies of Brant are omitted.

Preferred food on wintering areas is eelgrass, but Brant migrate northward to areas where it is absent. In their annual cycle, the birds do not stray far from the littoral zone except when migrating, even when they must graze ashore in the absence of eelgrass. Authors have reported that the birds eat both the leaves and rhizomes, even buried rootstalks, but extensive observations at Izembek Bay produced no instance of eating eelgrass rhizomes. Nor were they observed "puddling" there, but it has occurred elsewhere, on mudflats devoid of eelgrass. Brant have been seen in Britain, "pattering" on mud with their feet to bring up lugworms *(Arencola marina)* which were eaten. In Denmark, "trampling" to secure eelgrass rhizomes. At Izembek Lagoon the eelgrass supply is, in terms of waterfowl needs, unlimited (which may preclude a need for the rhizomes) and it is so dense as to produce a tenacious mat that may discourage attempts to uproot the plants.

The feeding pattern of Brant changes through autumn at Izembek Lagoon. When the birds arrive, the eelgrass leaves are attached to buried rhizomes and, at low tide in daylight, the birds pull the leaves loose. They do not dive for them. They up-end in shallow water and also walk about, grazing, when the tide is down. As the season advances, the leaves are sloughed off the plants and float and there is a change toward high diurnal tides and low water at night. The detached leaves, in mats and windrows, are blown ashore. Thus they are available when afloat and when stranded. (Among *Zostera* species, *marina* produces much drift in autumn.)

In stomachs from the e. coast of N. Am. and dating prior to the depletion of eelgrass, it was their main food, with some wigeon grass *(Ruppia)* and a few minor items. In post-1932 stomachs, there is a small amount of *Zostera,* an increase in *Ruppia,* 50% was green algae, 14% other algae, etc. (*Zostera* and *Ruppia* are quite similar in appearance and occupy the same environmental niche.) The birds were emaciated, suggesting low palatability and nutritive value of their diet. More animal food was taken. Brant accompanied diving ducks, snatching eelgrass and wigeon grass loosened by them. They also followed oyster dredges that pulled up eelgrass and other plants. Flocks grazed on *Spartina* and *Distichlis spicata* on salt flats.

Consumption of animal food by Brant appears to be random, except when preferred foods are absent. Eating fish eggs, Nereid worms, and an instance of eating small gastropods are known. At Izembek Lagoon, considerable animal matter must be ingested incidentally; in spring the eelgrass leaves are encrusted with diatoms.

272

The depletion of Atlantic eelgrass was not duplicated on the Pacific coast. Stomach analyses show much *Zostera*, also rockgrass (*Phyllospadix*) which is not an Atlantic plant.

In Europe, of 3 *Zostera* species—*marina*, *nana*, and *angustifolia*—only the first 2 are important to Brant. The first produces a larger standing stock and, where available, is the main winter food. Where the birds subsist on *nana*, there is a later shift to other foods, especially green algae. In the Netherlands, *Z. nana* is the main autumn food, but they also eat *Enteromorpha*, *Salicornia*, and *Puccinellia*. Later, when the other plants are gone, *Enteromorpha* mainly. In spring, *Salicornia* and *Puccinellia* at the water's edge and, on salt meadows, *Armeria maritima* and *Festuca rubra*. In Britain, the shift is to *Enteromorpha* and *Ulva*, with visits to salt meadows at high tide. The birds there also change local feeding areas from winter to winter. In Denmark, extensive meadows of *Z. nana* developed in a lagoon near the w. coast of Jutland in the 1960s. The Brant had foraged ashore. With expansion of *nana* plus appearance of *Z. maritima* in 1966, the birds do not come ashore in autumn but do in spring.

Under certain conditions at Izembek Lagoon, massive concentrations of Brant and Emperor Geese form; one or both species then feed on *Honckenya peploides*, which is similar to *Salicornia* in succulence.

When Brant go n. they become grazers. At Southampton I., early in the season, they feed on tender grass shoots under the edges of kelp drift. Later, almost exclusively on short grass growing in their nesting habitat. At Anderson R. delta, at first they feed in runoff channels on fragments of *Potamogeton filiformis* probed out of bottom ice by Tundra Swans. Later, they bring their young to the *Potamogeton* beds and their feeding schedule is governed by periodic tidal exposure of fronds and seed heads. The young readily eat insects and aquatic invertebrates.

Brant nest in a zone near the edge of high tide. On Southampton and in the Anderson delta, the plant association is *Carex subspathacea* and *Puccinellia phryganoides*. In the Yukon Delta, *Carex rariflora* and *Puccinellia phryganoides*; dense stands of *Elymus arenarius mollis* are avoided. The 2 sedges and the grass are alike in growth form. None fruits extensively and all require occasional immersion in seawater.

In the Yukon Delta, the lakes and ponds are unproductive. The Brant graze heavily on *Carex*, beginning at the edges of mudflats and tidal ponds and working back from these. Frequently the plants are grazed to the ground and there is a preference for those already grazed (tender new growth presumably is sought). Where nesting density is high, the entire area may be heavily grazed, which contributes to erosion. Although *Potentilla pacifica* and *Stellaria* may be abundant nearby, they are scarce on Brant "meadows," hence presumably are eaten. Later, when young and older Brant are flying, they go to lagoons where there is eelgrass. RDJ

NOTE H. F. Lewis (1931) recorded many interesting data on eelgrass (*Zostera marina*); he included an account of commercial gathering of this plant, at Isle Verte, Que. (for use in upholstering furniture and for insulating buildings), and in Denmark. See R. C. Phillips's (1964) bibliography on this plant, supplemented by McRoy and Phillips (1968). RSP

Ruddy Sheld-Duck

Tadorna ferruginea (Pallas)

Usual range extends, discontinuously, from Spain and n. Africa to Korea. In 1892 there was a remarkable flight, which J. C. Phillips (1923a) believed originated in s. Russia. Without giving all details here of this westward flight, which included many flocks, it is of interest that the species was noted successively in Denmark, Britain, Iceland (in July: 3 shot from flock of 20, 1 from flock of 4), and **in our area** 2 captures that summer in high latitudes in w. Greenland: near Ritenbenk (70° N) and near Augpilagtok (73° N). These data are from Schiøler (1925), as G. Timmermann (1949) gave wrong year for occurrence in Iceland. The 1931 A. O. U. *Check-list* included occurrence both in N. J. and N. C.; the 1957 edition gave only the former—a capture in Nov., 1916, at Barnegat Bay (G. B. Grinnell 1919)—even though J. C. Phillips (1923a) was inclined to wonder whether it may have been an escaped aviary bird. Similar doubt, and at times certainty, applies to other sightings and captures; latest noted was a bird taken Oct. 8, 1951, at Block I. (R. I.) and now in the school museum on that island.

For further information, the reader is referred to Delacour (1954) for col. pl.; to Dementiev and Gladkov (1952) and Bannerman (1957) for general accounts; and to Vielliard (1970) for distribution (with maps), migration, habitat, and habits. Brodkorb (1964a) listed records of occurrence as fossil and from Precolumbian sites. RSP

Common Sheld-Duck

Tadorna tadorna (Linnaeus)

No certain record of natural occurrence. A young ♀ whose "perfect condition indicated that the bird had not been in captivity, at least since the molt" (!) was shot Oct. 5, 1921, near mouth of the Essex R., Mass. (Forbush 1922). On the basis of this report the species has been accredited to our area ever since. Other reports also exist, perhaps more readily explainable on the basis that this common aviary bird occasionally has escaped from captivity. The nearest entirely satisfactory records of this Eurasian species are for a few occurrences in the Faeroes and 7 in the months Oct.–Feb. on the sw. coast of Iceland.

For further information see Delacour (1954) for brief account plus map and col. pl.; Witherby (1939) and Dementiev and Gladkov (1952) for general accounts; Eltringham and Boyd (1963) for molt migration; Hori (1964) and Young (1970) for reproduction, social habits, and relevant literature; Olney (1965) for food and feeding habits; and Brodkorb (1964a) for records of Pleistocene occurrence and in Precolumbian sites. RSP

Mallard

Anas platyrhynchos

Common or Green-headed Mallard of some authors. Fairly large duck, familiar over vast area because of occurrence of domesticated strains, self-tamed unconfined wild birds, and truly wild stock. Sexes strikingly different most of the year (Alt. Plumage), the drake having greenish head, white collar, reddish chestnut breast, and recurved central tail feathers. The duck in all Plumages has a broken (rather streaky) pattern of browns, buffs, and some white; in Alt. Plumage (plus Basic wing), pure ♀ stock may be characterized as having: outer rectrices predominantly white, scapulars with wide buffy edges and 3 buffy bars, flank feathers with wide light edges and wide dark subterminal zone, secondary wing coverts with broad white subterminal bar and dark tip, under tail coverts predominantly white, and breast feathers predominantly near-white with brownish spots or crescent, all illus. in Johnsgard (1961a). Both sexes have wide white bar along trailing edge and another along leading edge of blue speculum. The sexes are nearly alike in Juv. Plumage; ♂ Basics are quite ♀-like in head pattern.

The drake's tracheal bulla was described by Latham and Romsey (1798) and various subsequent authors. It is "large, left-sided, and connects directly with the left bronchus, . . . This tracheal bulb is already indicated in embryos ten days old, and in both sexes. But in females it begins to retrogress after the twenty-seventh day, till it finally disappears" (J. C. Phillips 1923b, citing Gadow 1890). Very fine illus. of the bulla are figs. 99 and 109 in Schiøler (1925). For experimental work on hormones vs. the bulla during embryonic life, see L. B. Lewis and Domm (1948), E. Wolff (1951), and sources they cited.

The Mallard usually is about 24 in. long (21–28), wingspread about 35 (31–40)—the figures in parentheses include individual and geographical variation (largest are Greenland Mallards); ♂ av. larger than ♀; usual wt. 2½–3 lb., heavier in Greenland. There is a very wide ranging (circumboreal) subspecies plus another which occurs in part of w. Greenland, i.e., both are in our area. The Common Mallard is not regarded here as conspecific with related (and relatively nondimorphic) members of the "Mallard group."

DESCRIPTION *A. p. platyrhynchos* 2 Plumages/cycle in both sexes. Basic I is limited in amount of feathering and is worn briefly–so far as known. Although Alt. I (acquired in 1st fall) is essentially like later Alts., the definitive cycle begins with the succeeding Plumages (Basic II and Alt. II) and their molting.

Recent descriptive work on the Mallard has resulted in only minor improvement on the work of Schiøler (1925) and the account in Witherby (1939). For feather distribution and, for the wing, number and arrangement of the various categories of feathers, see Humphrey and Clark (1961). Certain details of feathering and of timing of molts were reported by Carney and Geis (1960). For interrelations of gonad cycle and molt in sexually mature birds of both sexes, see O. W. Johnson (1961); for discussion of factors affecting molting and feather pigmentation of all ages, see discussion in Oring (1968). By far the best col. pls. are Larsen's (in Schiøler 1925). Treatment below is abbreviated somewhat, emphasizing features regarded as diagnostic of species (or subspecies), Plumage, sex, or age.

▶ ♂ Def. Alt Plumage (all feathering except, in wing, only a few innermost feathers) acquired during FALL and retained into following SUMMER. **Bill** almost entirely yellow with greenish cast; **head** and most of neck predominantly dark metallic green (toward ultramarine-violet in reflected sunlight); **iris** chestnut (darker than ♀); on lower neck a white collar, generally incomplete at nape; **upperparts** down midportion of back mixed coloring and fine dark markings, total effect cinnamon to near black; scapulars mostly appear light grayish (vermiculated dark on light); rump and upper tail coverts black with cobalt-ultramarine gloss; **underparts** breast (after any narrow white feather margins are lost by abrasion) appears uniform chestnut to reddish chestnut, usually ending abruptly in a transverse line; sides and belly to vent appear rather light grayish (individual variation in amount of dark vermiculations on white base); under tail coverts black; **tail** 4 central feathers black with emerald sheen and frequently so recurved as to form a complete circle, next pair smoke gray and each next outer pair lighter (especially lateral vane), the several outer pairs varying from having much white to being all white. In the **wing** the new innermost secondaries ("tertials") are grayish, broad, long, and taper to a fine point; their coverts also are grayish. Legs and **feet** vary from muted to a rather vivid scarlet-orange.

♀ Def. Alt.   ♂ Def. Alt.

In the summer molting period, about at the time when the drake has acquired Basic head–body feathering, there is nearly simultaneous loss of Basic flight feathers of wings and then the tail. In truly wild stock, within the span during which the new wing feathers are growing (3–4 weeks), the new Alt. head–body begins to replace the corresponding portion of the briefly-worn Basic and the Alt. body down grows. Usually the last Alt. feathers to grow fully are the innermost secondaries, their coverts, and the recurved central tail feathers. The drake is flightless approximately 25 days and regains flight before the new wing feathers are fully grown. Drakes acquire Alt. II (as yearlings) earlier than they acquire succeeding Alts.; this is indicated by yearlings commonly becoming flightless early in June, a few even in late May; some drakes of older age-classes become flightless well along in June, but most in July, and a few of these do not regain flight until Aug. 10 or thereabouts.

▶   ♂ Def. Basic Plumage (entire feathering), head–body–tail worn not more than a few weeks in SUMMER, the wing (except some innermost feathers) retained nearly a year. Not as nearly like ♀ Def. Basic as commonly stated, there being many distinguishing features—solid dark crown, darker dorsum, slight upturn to central tail feathers, etc. For excellent col. illus. see 2 upper figs. on pl. 29 in Schiøler (1925), also col. photo in A. A. Allen (1951).

Drakes in
Def. Basic

R. M. Tjengel –

Bill almost entirely muted yellowish olive, usually lacking dark blotches; crown very dark with obvious greenish sheen; a dark streak (generally wide) through eye; rest of **head–neck** brownish, streaked dark (no white collar); **underparts** much of mantle nearly uniform and dark (fuscous), some feathers having inconspicuous lighter margins; scapulars plain; **underparts** breast usually blotched or spotted irregularly, brownish or even reddish brown, the feathers with large dark centers; sides and flanks (at one extreme of individual variation) quite even tawny-fuscous and occasionally vermiculated creamy, to scalloped effect (fuscous feathers with brownish or muted buffy margins); breast feathers have 3 color zones—lighter, darker, and even lighter at the shaft, the variation in the zoning illus. by J. C. Phillips (1915); belly **1** as ♀ , **2** more heavily streaked or spotted, or **3** ranging from smoke gray to more brownish, often somewhat vermiculated dark, and with no to many sizable dark spots; under tail coverts usually as ♀ but spots, when present, larger and generally more numerous. **Tail** the 4 central feathers straight or with slight upturn distally, sepia with light buffy edges, the others as in Alt. Plumage.

Wing primaries predominantly medium fuscous-gray; most secondaries have outer webs metallic greenish to ultramarine-violet (the speculum) and some are black subterminally with broad white tips (form white bar at trailing edge of speculum), innermost secondaries deep brownish (not grayish) grading toward olive brown on inner webs; upper wing coverts and the alula medium fuscous-gray, sometimes with overall

277

reddish cast (no light edging on at least the 4 distal primary coverts), except greater secondary coverts are white subterminally and black at tips, the white bar thus formed along leading edge of speculum almost always ends at proximal edge of metallic area; axillars and most of wing lining white, proximal coverts vermiculated dark.

This Plumage is acquired by a molt of all feathering which usually begins in breeders about the 2nd or 3rd week in June, but even as early as late May in some unmated yearlings. Basic head–body is acquired first, by 2–3 weeks of molting; after that, the old wing feathers and any remaining tail feathers are dropped and the flightless period follows (see above under Def. Alt.). Then, while the Basic wing is growing, the rather briefly worn remainder of that Plumage begins to be succeeded by incoming Alt. (head–body plus part of tail, finally innermost wing feathers and central pairs of tail feathers). Over a period of 7 weeks or longer molting is more or less continuous—into Basic and soon after (except for most of wing) out of it. In semicaptive and feral birds the schedule tends to be different: the drake acquires entire Basic, i.e., can fly, and then remains in this Plumage for a number of weeks before any Alt. begins to appear.

▶ ♀ Def. Alt. Plumage (all feathering except, in wing, only a few innermost feathers), acquired in FALL and retained until SPRING. Much of **bill** between cinnamon and orange (but individuals vary to brownish olive) and usually with conspicuous fuscous or blackish blotches having a focus at midsection of upper mandible. **Head** crown blackish brown (but not as dark as in ♂ Def. Basic) and finely streaked, the feathers having narrow buffy edges; sides of head and much of neck generally buffy with fine dark streaks; dark line from near side base of bill through eye; chin and upper foreneck light buffy (sometimes nearly white), usually unmarked; iris rufous-tawny (lighter than ♂). **Upperparts** feathers toward blackish brown, with buffy markings including bars and wide edges; **underparts** breast variably buffy whitish with dark markings (each feather with spot or subterminal crescent which is fuscous) arranged more or less in rows; along sides and flanks the feathers have alternating (from edges inward) narrow buffy and broad dusky zones, giving a somewhat scalloped effect when feathering is new; remainder of belly to vent appears nearly white; under tail coverts same with darker centers or spots and whitish margins (hence area appears white in new feathering). **Tail** central feathers predominantly sepia, the others having alternating zones of warm buff and sepia, but laterally the buff pales to white (much white in outer feathers). In the wing the innermost secondaries ("tertials") have brownish edges and light buffy markings. Legs and **feet** usually orange.

As in at least a great many species of ducks, molting of the ♀ Mallard differs from that of the ♂ in one major respect; in the former, all of the feathering except much of the wing molts into Basic in late winter or early spring (prior to the nesting season) and the molting of most of the wing is "offset" until about the time the ♀'s brood attains flight. (In the drake, beginning in summer, the head–body–tail molt overlaps or is followed immediately by wing molt.) The duck probably is flightless about 22–27 days, generally beginning some time in Aug. and, within the span during which the new Basic wing quills are growing, the head–body–tail begin molting back into Alt. This molting generally extends until well along in FALL. The ventral body down acquired when molting back into Alt. is pale (grayish) and shorter than the Basic down acquired in spring.

▶ ♀ Def. Basic Plumage (entire feathering), head, body, tail, and innermost wing feathers acquired in SPRING and retained into late SUMMER or FALL, remainder of wing acquired beginning in very late SUMMER or early FALL and retained until late SUMMER of following year. Differs from Def. Alt. in having crown and mantle (including scapular area) darker, more muted, any buffy feather edges narrower (usually absent from mantle). **Wing** upper coverts toward brown, the greater secondary coverts with broad white subterminal bar, the middle and lesser ones almost always with broad lighter edges; little or no light edging on primary coverts; white bar at leading edge of speculum often extends proximally beyond the metallic area, but not onto innermost secondaries; the most proximal of the light under wing coverts have dark barring.

The molting into and out of Basic is included in discussion at end of above section on Alt. The Basic includes the nest down, acquired in spring, which is longer, coarser, and much darker (Bowles 1917, Broley 1950) than the Alt. down.

AT HATCHING   See col. pl. facing p. 370. There are at least 2 kinds of variation on continental N. Am.: **1** geographical (darker overall on Kenai Pen. than on Canadian prairies) and **2** from mixing with game farm stock (increased variation in pattern and coloring). In "pure" stock the eye stripe is narrow but usually complete; yellows are palish, especially on venter; legs and feet are yellower than in Black and Mottled Duck (they are muted orange in the Mexican Duck). A Mallard duckling having widened or sculptured eye stripe and conspicuous cheek stripe probably is not of "pure" stock.

▶   ♂ Juv. Plumage (entire feathering) fully grown at age about 55–65 days (soon after flight is attained), then molted beginning in late SUMMER or early FALL, except most of wing retained through WINTER into following SUMMER. **Bill** usually a blend of pale olive and yellowish, sometimes with very dark patch on upper mandible; narrow dark streaking on sides of face and on neck; **underparts** appear to have simple bicolored pattern with dark streaks comparatively narrow and bordered brownish; tail feathers narrow, tapering, pointed, in worn condition with shafts extending slightly beyond vanes, color largely smoke grayish (seldom any white) with some buffy markings; legs and feet usually grayed tawny. **Wing** the several more distal primary coverts have slight to conspicuous light edging on inner web (individuals vary); middle and lesser coverts small, narrow, edged (seldom conspicuously) with light brownish which may wear off; innermost secondaries shorter than in succeeding Plumages and with less brownish suffusion.

For some details of development of Juv. Plumage in captive stock, see N. Am. data in Southwick (1953a) and European data in Veselovsky (1953).

According to Schneider (1965), under field conditions, the interval from the time the first Juv. feathers are seen until the bird appears fully feathered is 27 days in N. D., but only 15 (? error for 25) at Tetlin, Alaska.

The notched Juv. **tail** feathers may be lacking beginning at any time after about the first of Sept. (depends on date of hatching of the individual). The narrow, rounded, innermost secondaries generally disappear some time within the span mid-Oct. to late Nov. and, contemporaneously, there is loss of some of their longest overlying coverts.

▶   ♀ Juv. Plumage (entire feathering) much as ♂ but some differences. **Bill** blended dusky olive and yellowish, dark blotches on upper mandible not invariably present; some feathers of **back** and rump very dark and not always barred buffy; legs and **feet** sometimes quite yellowish; little or no light edging on most upper **wing** coverts and it varies from conspicuous to absent (but usually present) on greater primary coverts; innermost secondaries shorter, browner, than in ♂ of corresponding age. For some further information see references cited above under ♂ Juv.

Timing of loss of the Juv. **tail** apparently is about as in the drake. In the wing, however, the innermost Juv. secondaries and their overlying coverts usually are retained much longer, often into spring.

▶ ♂ Basic I Plumage is fragmentary and fleeting. The production of new feathering, including acquisition of Juv. through acquisition of Alt. I consists of 3 molts that are so little interrupted as to be an essentially continuous process. When the Juv. Plumage is fully developed, the next-incoming feathers are the limited Basic I, consisting of: **1** dark brownish or blackish and also some dark-tipped buffy feathers, on forward **cheeks, chin,** and sides of **throat; 2** at least a few pale-margined very dark feathers in forward **mantle** and **scapular region; 3** brownish feathers with round blackish spots on the **breast;** and **4** palish feathers coarsely vermiculated dark brownish on upper **sides** and **flanks.** Some individuals show less Basic I than just listed; in others perhaps this Plumage is more extensive, especially on underparts. A fine example of fullest development of this Plumage is shown in the 2 left-hand figs. on pl. 32 in Schiøler (1925). The Basic I feathers, except perhaps in late-hatched birds, usually are lost in OCT. or by early NOV. and are succeeded by the green head, grayish flanks, etc., of the incoming Alt. I.

▶ ♂ Alt. I Plumage (all feathering except, in wing, only a few innermost feathers), acquired beginning at age about 65–75 days and continuing through FALL; retained through WINTER into early SUMMER. Differs quantitatively from later Alts. as follows: many feathers narrower and not as broadly rounded at end; reddish chestnut feathers of breast quite commonly have more pronounced white edges (soon lost by abrasion); occasionally some dark spotting on breast and even belly (might be lingering traces of Basic I, or a characteristic of Alt. I, or both); central 2 pairs of tail feathers vary with individual from slightly to (rarely) fully recurved; innermost elongated secondaries somewhat shorter and narrower.

This Plumage usually is acquired fully by some time in NOV.; the scapulars often appear late and the last feathers to develop fully are the innermost secondaries and the central tail feathers. In some individuals either there is a lag or pause in the molt so that these elements of tail–wing are not acquired until some time in WINTER. An occasional individual also retains some Juv. feathering on lower back into or even through WINTER but, when it is long retained, generally it is lost before the full molt in summer begins.

Drakes in Alt. I are, of course, recognizable when in hand because they still retain most of the Juv. wing, previously described.

▶ ♀ Basic I Plumage (extent of inclusive feathering variable). Not sufficiently different from other ♀ Plumages to be readily recognized. Usually well along in AUG. or in SEPT., in birds that are not late hatched, among the Juv. feathers there begin to appear some new feathers on **head, neck, breast,** anterior **mantle,** and in **scapular region.** Most of these have their dark portions heavily pigmented (darker) and are distally wider than their Juv. precursors. Apparently they are retained a rather short time, but possibly longer than ♂ Basic I. The 2 ♀ ♀ shown on pl. 33 in Schiøler (1925) appear to have molted entirely into Basic I (except presumably most of wing) and to have retained it until late Jan., past the time when most young ♀ ♀ are in Alt. I.

280

▶ ♀ Alt. I Plumage (head–body, possibly tail in some individuals); acquired as in ♂ Alt. I (see above) and retained into late WINTER or SPRING. The pale (buffy) feather edgings on **crown** and dorsum generally are wider and the **scapulars** tend to have narrower markings than in later Alts. Practically all of the wing is retained Juv. feathering (described above).

▶ ♀ Basic II Plumage (entire feathering), most of it acquired in spring before age 1 year, most of the wing not until at least late summer at age over 1 year. The last Plumage with which the Juv. wing is worn.

NOTES Tougarinov (1941) illustrated a supposed sex difference in feathers of underside of bend of Juv. wing (♀ plain, ♂ barred); however, these feathers may be barred or vermiculated in either sex.

There is more variation in ♂ Basics, especially in amount of dark pigmentation, than most authors state or imply. Once a drake is "physiologically mature," variation in any year probably reflects such factors as nutrition and presence or absence of stress while molting. There seems to be no proof of any trend or change correlated with advancing age. In Alt. Plumage the same applies to such details as width of dark vermiculations on sides and flanks.

Both in the wild and in captivity, instances are known of ♀ ♀, presumably as a result of atrophy or some other ovarian malfunction, assuming ♂ feathering. For descriptions and illus. of wild-taken examples, see J. M. Harrison (1968) and Kuroda (1960).

Black spotting on lower breast of the drake has been described (J. G. Harrison 1949, J. M. Harrison and Harrison 1963b) as an "unusual variant" occurring throughout the range of *A. p. platyrhynochos*, being increasingly common in Iceland, and constant in *A. p. conboschas* in Greenland. Such spotting occurs in Basic I (it is most prevalent in fall in younger drakes that still retain some ventral Basic feathering), possibly in some birds in Alt. I, and definitely in some drakes in later Basics. The writer has not seen a good example of such spotting in continental N. Am. drakes in full Def. Alt.; it occurs, but is not constant, in such birds from Greenland.

For growth and regression of the Bursa of Fabricius, see Ward and Middleton (1971).

Measurements of birds from conterminous U.S. and Canada 12 ♂: BILL 47–59 mm., av. 55.3; WING 273–300, av. 286; TAIL 82–92, av. 86.7; TARSUS 45–53, av. 47.7; 12 ♀: BILL 48–57 mm., av. 53.6; WING 256–278, av. 272; TAIL 82–91, av. 86.4; TARSUS 41–48, av. 44.6 (ETS). Combined series from N. Am. and Eurasia 85 ♂: BILL 41.9–59.9 mm., av. 55.4; WING (across chord) 257–294, av. 277.5; TARSUS 41.2–51.1, av. 44.8; 74 ♀: BILL 43.2–55.5 mm., av. 51.5, WING (across chord) 239–282, av. 259; TARSUS 40.1–48.6, av. 43.2 (H. Friedmann). For British series, the WING meas. over the curve, see Witherby (1939).

Weight of fall birds in Ill. ♂ 631 "adult" av. 1,240 gm. (2.8 lb.) and 730 "juvenile" (= 1st fall) 1,170 (2.6 lb.); ♀ 402 "adult" 1,080 gm. (2.4 lb.), 671 "juvenile" 1,030 (2.3 lb.) (Bellrose and Hawkins 1947). See the same source for a graph showing frequency distribution of wts. by sexes and age-class; in the opinion of the authors, "most Mallards weighing over three pounds are from, or related to, barnyard birds." In the span Nov. 1–Jan. 15 in Ark., 3,425 birds with age-classes not indicated, ♂ av. 2.8 lb. and ♀ 2.4 (T. W. Wright 1960). For 3,936 ♂ (ages and localities not stated) av. was 2.7 lb., max. 4.0, and 3,169 ♀ av. 2.3 lb., max. 3.6 (A. L. Nelson and Martin 1953). When starved, a Mallard can lose an av. of up to 44% of total wt. and recover satisfactorily (Jordan 1953). For foreign data on wt. cycle around the year, see Folk et al. (1966). For comparison of wts. from New Zealand and N. Am., see Balham (1952).

Hybrids   Mallard (*A. p. platyrhynchos*) and North American Black (*A. rubripes*) cross to a limited extent, perhaps mainly as a result of overlap of their present winter ranges (where pair formation usually occurs); they interbreed as a consequence of pen-reared stock (Mallards, not all identical with pure wild stock) being released in Black Duck environment, also in some places where one of the species greatly out-numbers the other, and in captivity. It is interesting to note that the retrieved hunting kill estimates for 1964 and 1965, in a recent *Waterfowl Status Report* (H. A. Hansen and Hudgins 1966) included these categories: Mallard, Domestic Mallard, Black Duck, and Black × Mallard—including 100 of the last category for 1964 in the ad-ministrative unit known as "Pacific Flyway" (where the Black occurs as a very small minority). Mallard × Black hybrids were included in pen-reared stock liberated by the Pa. Game Commission (Grimm 1952).

With changes in land use and an increase until recently in number of Mallards, in the last few decades this bird has made "enormous inroads" into what formerly was Black Duck environment, the reverse being true to a very limited extent in the Great Lakes region (Johnsgard 1961b). The major zone of overlap of these species in winter has moved eastward approximately 300 mi. in the last half century and the total area of overlap has increased (Johnsgard 1967). There is, however, preferential or assortative mating (of birds with their own kind) so that obvious hybrids rarely comprise more than 2% of the combined numbers occurring in a particular area; see Johnsgard (1967) for details. Many birds, ♀ ♀ especially, that are shot and are of mixed parentage may not be recognized as hybrids. At the present time, in U.S. Atlantic seaboard states and nearby, about 1 in 20 Mallards shot in fall shows some "Black Duck characteristics" or other variant from the usual concept of "pure" Mallard.

Boyer (1959) believed that Mallards, released in the Maritimes, where at least some of them crossed with Blacks, would be absorbed into Black Duck stock. In Maine, ac-cording to Coulter (1954), the Mallard is increasing; it hybridizes with the Black. In the Toronto region they frequently cross (Goodwin 1956).

Hybrids with the Mexican Duck (*A. diazi*) have been reported to be locally common in New Mex., but to what extent presumed "Mallard characters" are inherent in "pure" Mexican Ducks remains to be discovered. As to wild Mallard × Mottled Duck (*A. fulvigula*), apparently natural hybrids either are infrequent or else seldom re-ported.

Cockrum (1952) compiled a list of published sources on reported wild crosses in N. Am. of Mallard with Black Duck, Gadwall (*Anas strepera*), Pintail (*A. acuta*), Cinnamon Teal (*A. cyanoptera*), Greenwing (*A. crecca carolinensis*), Baldpate (*A. americana*), and Canvasback (*Aythya valisineria*). The list includes "Brewer's" or "Bemaculated" Duck (Mallard × Gadwall), painted by Audubon. There are several observations of ♂ North American Wood Ducks (*Aix sponsa*) consorting as paired with ♀ Mallards, but no hybrids are known. There are 2 reported instances of trios consist-ing of a ♂ Greenwing consorting with a pair of mated Mallards (Nellis et al. 1970). Ramsay (1961) described differences (from parent stock) in sequence and nature of dis-

282

plays observed in captive ♂ hybrids of Mallard × American Black Duck, Mottled Duck, and Pintail. The displays and calls of the F2 Mallard–Pintail ♂ hybrids were reported on at length by Sharpe and Johnsgard (1966). See Gray (1958) for a long list, compiled on a worldwide basis, of natural and captive hybrids with the Mallard. Beer (1968) figured the tracheal bullae of captive ♂ crosses with *Anas poecilorhyncha* and *Netta rufina*.

A drake Mallard × Wigeon (*Anas penelope*) natural hybrid, taken alive in winter when in Alt. Plumage, was kept in captivity and molted into Basic in summer; it was more Mallard-like when in Alt. and more Wigeon-like when in Basic (Kuroda and Kuroda 1960, photos and text).

In parts of New Zealand the introduced Mallard, which is replacing the native Gray Duck (*Anas superciliosa*) in some localities, crosses readily with the latter; see Sage (1958) and especially Falla et al. (1966) for descriptions of birds of mixed ancestry. The Black Duck of Australia (same species as Gray Duck of New Zealand) is crossing with introduced Mallards (Frith 1967). For descriptions and illus. of captive crosses of Mallard × Australian Black Duck, see J. C. Phillips (1915).

The so-called Marianas Mallard (*Anas "oustaleti"*) of certain Micronesian islands has 2 patterns, one predominantly Mallard-like, the other much like the Spotbill (*Anas poecilorhyncha*), and were believed by Yamashina (1948) to be genetically unstable hybrid stock. Basic and Alt. Plumages of both types of individuals are known.

Especially as drakes (of 2 of the 4 N. Am. members of the "Mallard group") and ducks (of 3 of them) are quite similar, the writing of comparative descriptions that (hopefully) are diagnostic and also include variation is very complicated. The handling of other topics about each, however, is rendered easier by not "lumping" these birds. With separate treatment, it follows that the progeny of mixed pairs are referred to as hybrids, not as intergrades.

Geographical variation The nearly panboreal *A.p. platyrhynchos* is an aggregate of subpopulations, with interchange of birds hindering subspeciation. Eurasian birds av. slightly smaller than those of N. Am. (Hartert 1920a, J. C. Phillips 1923b). Coloration of the upper mandible of the ♀ varies, the majority in N. Am. have a dark "saddle" on muted orange-yellow background; in most Eurasian birds the dark usually extends to the feathering and the background is more grayish (tinged buffy or pinkish). Greenland birds (*A. p. conboschas*) more nearly resemble continental N. Am. birds in bill characters. Aside from the Greenland birds, Schiøler (1925) recognized 3 subspecies, an untenable splitting: 1 typical, 2 large northern, of the White Sea region, and 3 Icelandic. In Eurasia, from Britain to Kamchatka, and based on winter occurrence and analysis of banding data, Shevareva (1968) defined 9 subpopulations within nominate *platyrhynchos*.

The Greenland birds differ in molting and in attainment of breeding age. At least in the ♀, year-old individuals still retain many 1st-winter (Alt. I) feathers (Schiøler 1925). Both sexes have "deferred maturity," i.e., in their inclement surroundings apparently they do not breed until approaching age 2 years (Salomonsen 1972).

Individual variation in wild stock in N. Am. is difficult to assess separately from influences of hybridism, geographical variation (if it exists), and mating of wild birds with domesticated strains and mongrels. Some variation, especially in the drake, has been mentioned earlier in descriptions of Plumages. Partial albinism, such as white areas on chin, upper breast, or belly (or a combination of these areas) occurs occasionally in drakes, but total albinism is rare. Some drakes have more or less buffy brown areas that "normally" are dark-colored. A palish buff (not domestic) mutant occurs rarely in both sexes. Occasional ♀ ♀ are much darker than average, with blue of speculum obscure or even absent. Drakes occasionally show melanism in various degrees to overall nearly black, sometimes with much white on neck or breast.

Domestication dates from at least centuries B.C. in China, se. Asia, and the Mediterranean basin. All domestic ducks except Muscovies—from all-white to blackish green and also in various patterns, shapes, and sizes—are derived from the Mallard. These may be strikingly different mutant strains, selectively bred, or nearer typically Mallard-like domestic strains, or a result of their interbreeding. See Jull (1930) and Delacour (1964) for brief accounts of domestication, description of various strains, and col. illus.

Mallards formerly were kept in **captivity** in N. Am. as "call ducks" (for decoy purposes) and certain of these stocks are still maintained. Perhaps as a result of inbreeding or from mixing of strains, some of the pen-reared stock which has been produced and released in the wild in great quantity is atypical of the wild Mallard. In a common type the drake is darker ventrally with amount of chestnut on the breast more or less reduced. Semi-domesticated game farm Mallards have a longer breeding season, higher egg production, higher fertility, and heavier weight than those hatched from eggs of wild Mallards (Prince et al. 1970). But they also have serious disadvantages (see beyond under "Survival").

In various city parks and other sanctuaries, usually where winters are not severe and where food is provided, there are **feral** or **semi-domesticated** flocks. It is common at such places for people to turn loose ducklings or older birds, of various strains and mongrels, that had been kept temporarily as pets. The result of such mixing is highly variable stock, a common type of drake being dark with much white on lower neck or breast and ducks that are quite pale overall. Such local flocks attract migrant and wintering wild Mallards and may have some influence on the genetic makeup of wild stock. RSP

SUBSPECIES *A. p. platyrhynchos* Linnaeus—description and meas. given above; smaller; breast color in ♂ Alt. Plumage tends to end in a transverse line (occasional British specimens are said to have it more like Greenland birds and it is somewhat variable in Icelandic stock); at least part of belly of ♀ usually plain; very large geographical range; mostly migratory. Icelandic birds, at least most of which have only local seasonal movements, are included here.

A. p. conboschas Brehm—the ancestral stock may have arrived in Greenland during a warm interglacial period (Johansen 1956); the present Greenland Mallard is large; it has only local seasonal movements (possibly it has straggled to Ungava); a saltwater bird much of the year, with large nasal glands and correspondingly more narrowed interorbital bony area than even Icelandic birds (see pls. 37–38 in Schiøler 1925); the extent to which large size of the gland is genetically or phenotypically determined has not been investigated (Schmidt-Nielsen and Kim 1964); ♂ in Alt. Plumage has upperparts more gray, vermiculations on sides and flanks tend to be rather coarse, and red-dish chestnut area of breast often has blackish spotting in its lower portion and the area usually tapers in a mid-ventral direction; ♀ decidedly gray in general tone, with dark markings extending over more of underparts. Said to have "deferred maturity" and young ♀ ♀ to have delayed molting (see earlier under geographical variation). **Measurements** 12 ♂ : BILL 48–57 mm., av. 52.6; WING 279–305, av. 293.6; TAIL 87–99, av. 92; TARSUS 45–49, av. 47; 8 ♀ : BILL 45–54 mm., av. 50; WING 260–293, av. 276.5; TAIL 82–93, av. 88.5; TARSUS 44–49, av. 46 (ETS). In close agreement with these figures are data on 69 ♂ and 41 ♀ given by Schiøler (1925). RSP

FIELD IDENTIFICATION   In *Handbook* area. Among dabbling ducks, the Mallard and its close relatives (Mexican, Mottled, and Black ducks) have heaviest body for their length of wing. The wings are, however, unusually broad, thereby giving an appearance of large-winged ducks. As a result of their breadth, the wings appear to be farther back on the body than in most ducks. In flight the neck has a slight crook, the axis of the head being above that of the body. Wingbeats are slower and flight not as rapid as in most dabbling ducks.

Mallards fly in lines and various U and V formations, with individuals spaced nearly wing to wing. Where this species is abundant, assemblies are exceedingly large, frequently numbering hundreds and even thousands of birds, especially in flights to grain, corn, or rice fields.

Drakes in Alt. Plumage (most of the year) have much gray in the body and the dark greenish head is separated from reddish chestnut breast by a nearly complete white neck ring. The V of white tail feathers shows prominently against the black tail coverts and rump, especially when the drake springs into the air. In a drake flying nearby, the iridescent ultramarine speculum, broadly bordered white on both trailing and leading edges, is conspicuous. Viewed from above, as when waterfowl censusing from an aircraft, the gray scapulars and white tail feathers outline the diamond-shaped black rump and upper tail coverts. Although ♂ Shoveler and Common and Red-breasted Mergansers also have dark greenish heads, the large amount of white elsewhere on these birds distinguishes them from the Mallard.

The ♀ has much straw-brownish coloring, variably marked darker, and somewhat resembles ♀ Gadwall and Shoveler. All 3 have yellowish or somewhat orange bills, and both Mallard and Shoveler have palish tails, but only the Mallard has ultramarine speculum conspicuously bordered white on both trailing and leading edges.

Juv. Mallards rather closely resemble the ♀ ; mature drakes when in Basic body feathering (part of summer into fall) are intermediate, having no white collar, dark crowns, and darker upperparts than ♀ ♀ . Drakes usually have lost the Basic body feathering and are back into the green-headed Alt. Plumage by Oct.—earlier than is usual in our other dabbling ducks except the close relatives of the Mallard and also the Wood Duck. In years of extensive late nesting, a moderate proportion of young drakes may have only traces of Alt. feathering even in late Nov.

Compare with Mexican, Mottled, and Black ducks. Also see preceding sections on hybrids, domestication, etc. The commonest hybrids are Mallard × Black. Among first-generation crosses with species not as closely related, drake Mallard × Pintail is reported most often, its pattern of mixed characteristics being striking and obvious. In protected areas, such as city parks and sanctuaries, one may expect to find birds of mixed (and often speculative) parentage and showing various degrees of hybridism; wild or some domesticated derivative of Mallard parent stock often is included. FCB

VOICE   *A. p. platyrhynchos.* To many people the Mallard's quack is symbolic of all duck calls. It is the ♀ that is heard calling vociferously in autumn, a time when most ducks generally are silent. The well-known quack is a loud, repeated *raehb* pitched on F#2. When alarmed, she utters it more loudly and shrilly, separately rather than in series. When feeding, a soft *tuck a tuck,* repeated in a continuing roll.

Drake utters soft lisping *pshup* or *tseep* in response to ♀'s quacking; for such a weak call, it carries surprisingly well. The drake's quack is a reedy *raehb* pitched on F#4 (if drawn-out, has warning function) and a soft sibilant *ur-r-r-r* uttered with closed bill.

A 2-syllabled *raehb-raehb* by ♂ and ♀, and with chin-raising, is a sort of palaver (analogous to Triumph ceremony of geese and sheld-ducks) when mates again are together (ashore or afloat) after separation. Intensity varies.

Ducklings have 1-syllabled whistling *peep,* varying from subdued "conversational" use (to maintain contact) to shrill in alarm (as when deserted).

Below, under "Reproduction" for the ♀ also see: Inciting, Gesture of repulsion, Decrescendo call, copulatory behavior (includes quacking), and territory (persistent quacking); and for the ♂: Grunt-whistle, Head-up-tail-up, Down-up, "gasping," and Preen-behind-the-wing (nonvocal mechanical sound).

[Postscript. For an elaborate study of the voice of the Mallard, see Abraham 1974 *Condor* 76 401-420.] FCB

HABITAT   *A. p. platyrhynchos* in *Handbook* area—primarily small shallow waters, except that it rests on large rivers, lakes, and reservoirs if plentiful food is nearby.

During breeding season, occurs in greatest abundance on potholes in the great plains of Dakota, Man., Sask., and Alta.; next most abundant on potholes, ponds, and lakes of Canadian parklands. Lowest breeding density on lakes and marshes of coniferous forest, except high density in Peace R. delta. The various photos in Anderson and Henny (1972) are an excellent visual introduction to various Mallard breeding habitats.

In migration and winter, most abundant in Mississippi drainage. In lower Mississippi drainage, most winter n. of coastal marshes in overflow river-swamps or on reservoirs and lakes adjacent to corn and rice fields; farther w., in winter on playa lakes of Tex. panhandle, feeding in sorghum fields; in Pacific area, greatest concentration in Sacramento Valley, Cal., where it feeds in rice and barley fields; e. of Mississippi drainage, most abundant in old rice field area of S.C.

Occurs on brackish and sheltered marine waters rather sparingly, almost entirely outside breeding season.

The Greenland subspecies (*conboschas*) nests about inland lakes and waterways and also on fjord-islands, but is an exclusively coastal saltwater inhabitant while fresh waters are frozen. FCB

DISTRIBUTION   (See map.) On a worldwide basis, for summary of older literature, see J. C. Phillips (1923b); for a recent concise summary of range, see the 1957 A.O.U. *Check-list.*

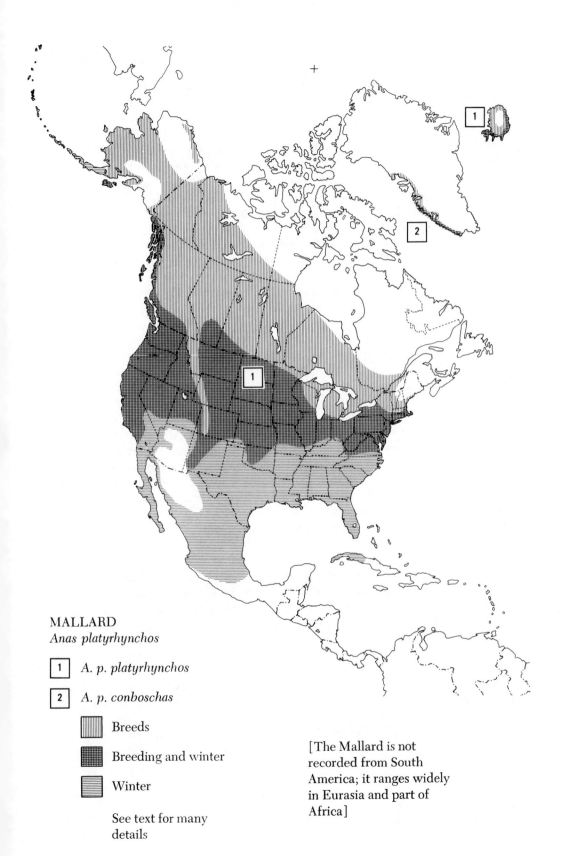

MALLARD
Anas platyrhynchos

1   *A. p. platyrhynchos*

2   *A. p. conboschas*

Breeds

Breeding and winter

Winter

See text for many
details

[The Mallard is not
recorded from South
America; it ranges widely
in Eurasia and part of
Africa]

Before proceeding with the green-headed species, it is important to discuss the distribution and relationships of the 4 members of the so-called Mallard group in N. Am. It is the writer's belief that ancestral Mallard stock entered N. Am. from Eurasia long ago, before it had become sexually dimorphic. In subsequent times of maximum glaciation, this stock was isolated (as though on islands) in 1 what is presently nw. Mexico and thereabouts, 2 in the se. U.S., and 3 in the cool maritime region of e. Canada and thereabouts. Each of these populations evolved, in its particular niche, to the species level, while remaining essentially nondimorphic sexually. Meanwhile, Mallard stock in Eurasia became highly dimorphic sexually—the green-headed Mallard—and, subsequently, this stock invaded N. Am. and also became established. More recently, the green-headed Mallard reached Greenland, where its main evolution has been toward larger size plus adaptations to saltwater environment seasonally. The most recent relevant major event in N. Am. has been alteration of the environment as a result of Caucasian settlement. This, coupled with climatic variations, has affected continuities and discontinuities of distribution, a notable example being modification of "barriers" between the Mallard and the Black Duck (which see). Within the present hypothesis, it is relatively easy to comprehend why each species in the group has special characteristics and habitat requirements and why there are discontinuities in distribution. It also eliminates a dubious notion that all 4 once were sexually dimorphic, then 3 of them "lost" this condition; in fact, there is nothing to indicate they ever had it.

A. p. platyrhynchos **Continental N. and Cent. Am.** Extent of total range in N. Am. has increased considerably over many decades, eastward to the Atlantic coast in all seasons, accompanied or followed by an extension of eastern breeding range northward and, to some extent, southward. Apparently there has also been an increase elsewhere northward in breeding range. Further changes may be expected. The situation is complicated by such factors as partially domesticated birds reverting to the wild state, transplantings and/or liberations of pen-reared stock within and beyond the limits of natural breeding occurrence, and the feeding of birds in winter to maintain them at places where they might not survive otherwise.

Foley et al. (1961) stated that no wild stock was definitely known to breed in N.Y. in 1934 and that present breeding stock is believed to be derived from released birds. Boyer (1966) referred to the status of the wild Mallard as "uncertain" in the New Brunswick–Nova Scotia border region; residents at Sackville (N.B.) kept free-flying birds, also a total of 223 hand-reared Mallards was released in 1953–55 at 2 localities. There was varied duck-nesting habitat in former times in the Central Valley of Cal. and more than a half dozen species used it commonly; now that the environment has been altered by man, the Mallard is dominant and perhaps only 2 other duck species nest there regularly.

Now a local breeder at least as far n. as Me. (see above for Maritimes) and farther s. in e. N. Am. than formerly. In n. Canada, breeding range extends via the Mackenzie drainage nearly to the arctic coast. In Alaska, breeding on the arctic slope is very local and possibly irregular. (Drake Mallards, occurring in summer–early fall in n. areas in both hemispheres, presumably flew northward to molt.) Locally plentiful on unfrozen waters in interior Alaska in winter. At C. Prince of Wales, on the Bering Strait coast of Alaska, many Mallard bones were found in oldest dated to most recent of archaeological sites excavated (Friedmann 1941). Along s. edge of N. Am. range: in Fla. widespread in winter in small flocks, but probably not regular in s. part; in Ariz., transient, winterer, and scattered breeder. South of Mexico: reported from Nicaragua, Costa Rica, and Panama (1 record).

Peripheral localities, for the most part of birds presumably from N. Am., are listed clockwise around the continent. Nfld.—1 Jan., 1 March, and several fall records. Bermuda—irregular but frequent. Dry Tortugas—1 record. Bahamas and Greater Antilles—casual on 4 is. and rare in Cuba; no satisfactory records for Jamaica, Hispaniola, and Lesser Antilles (J. Bond 1961a) and no records for continental S. Am. In the Pacific and near the mainland—breeds on Vancouver I., the Queen Charlottes, and various other is., including Kodiak; Breeds on some of the Aleutian Is. and is sometimes locally plentiful during winter (but evidently is not as much a saltwater bird as is the Greenland Mallard); breeds in Commander Is. In Bering Sea—breeds on the Pribilofs; a record (not breeding) for St. Lawrence I.; a drake taken in Cresta Bay on s. side of Chuckchee Pen. North of continental Canada—occurs occasionally on Victoria I.

Remote from N. Am.—straggler to the main Hawaiian group (where there also are domesticated birds) and to Midway; seen in late fall on Christmas I. (Line Is. in cent. Pacific); occurs and probably breeds on Canton I. (Phoenix group); seen on Kwajalein (Marshall Is.). The Mallard may straggle widely in the Pacific, either from the Nearctic or Palearctic regions. The birds of the Marianas are mentioned earlier under hybrids.

Eurasia There are various useful distribution maps, such as in Voous (1967) for breeding range. In Iceland the Mallard is widely scattered in lowlands when nesting and there seems to be no conclusive evidence (as from banding) that any of them migrate elsewhere. In the Faeroes, where few nest, Salomonsen (in A. S. Jensen et al. 1934) thought that those irregularly present in winter came from Iceland or possibly Scandinavia. On the Eurasian continent there have been noticeable changes in distribution in the present century, such as some increase northward in breeding and in winter range. Records of stragglers within and from Palearctic range are not summarized here.

Introduced at the following places remote from natural range:

E. Falkland (Falkland Is.)—introduced in 1930s and small numbers reportedly still breed there (Cawkell and Hamilton 1961).

Australia—introduced from England; now common in parks and gardens in some cities and towns and occasionally encountered in the wild; occurs both purebred and as hybrid × A. superciliosa (Frith 1967).

New Zealand—first introduced in 1867 (pair from Australia), others from England in 1893 and 1904 and their progeny were liberated each year; still later introductions included stock mainly from N. Am. Common on both main is. (now constitutes most of shooters' bags) and Stewart I.; occurs in Chatham Is.; straggler to Macquarie I. Hybridizes with A. superciliosa. Older sources of information were listed by G. R. Williams (1964); also see B. L. Sage (1958), Falla et al. (1966), and Frith (1967).

A. p. conboschas—resident in w. Greenland (n. limits in Upernavik Dist.) and, on e. coast, breeds at Lindenow Fjord and in Angmagssalik Dist., possibly elsewhere, and reported seen in Scoresby Sd. region. There are more reports of occurrence of Mallards in the Ungava Pen. than there are satisfactory records for subspecies and locality. A fall bird from Okak was recorded by B. Hantzsch as *conboschas;* a fall bird from Nachvak is atypical of either subspecies; see Todd (1963).

For the species, records of occurrence as **fossil** of Pleistocene age and also from **archaeological sites** were summarized on a worldwide basis by Brodkorb (1946a). The list includes occurrence as fossil in 6 states (13 localities) in conterminous U.S., also in Cuba, and from archaeological sites in 6 states (11 localities) in conterminous U.S. (Alaska accidentally omitted). Additional fossil records already have been reported.

From a large number of fossil bones of Pleistocene age, from near Binagada in Azerbaijan, Serebrovsky (1941) described *A. p. paleoboschas* as a somewhat larger bird than the present *A. p. platyrhynchos.* RSP

MIGRATION   *A. p. platyrhynchos* in N. Am. No comprehensive study exists, but some indication of general pattern may be deduced from the following:

If Alta. is divided about equally down the middle, most birds w. of that line migrate to points w. of the Rockies; most of those e. of it travel more or less se., toward the lower Mississippi drainage and Gulf Coast, but part of these veer more easterly toward the Atlantic coast. A vast number of them do not go the full distance; they remain for the winter in interior localities. There are various migration "corridors" in N. Am., such as: along the nw. Pacific coast, diagonally westward from the interior, the various heavily utilized corridors down the interior, the more diagonal ones from the interior toward the Atlantic seaboard, and an Atlantic coastal strip; see Bellrose (1968) for "corridors" in conterminous U.S. e. of the Rockies and numbers of birds occurring in these and at wintering areas.

Spring   Departure from wintering areas begins in late Feb. or early March. Migrants usually arrive as far n. as the Canadian border about the 3rd week in March. Beyond, dates vary more with season, the birds arriving with the beginning of the spring thaw. Most are on breeding areas in the prairie provinces about mid-April and are at northerly breeding limits beginning in the same month.

Summer   First to travel, some beginning in late May, are drakes. Although some drakes may remain in the general vicinity of their incubating mates, the usual pattern is for them to leave their mates and to form small groups. These wander at first; then they merge in concentrations, some of very large size, at a marsh, shallow lake, quiet stretch of river, or a flooded area, and generally remain there through their flightless period. Thus, in summer and early fall, there are unisexual flocks of drakes. The Mallard and Pintail are the earliest of our shoal-water ducks to begin this pattern of movement, with some Mallards having as long as a month between taking leave of their mates and beginning of flightlessness. Some drakes travel a considerable distance. Females whose nesting was disrupted join drakes at molting places, so that the pattern of unisexual ♂ flocks is discontinued.

The young travel after they attain flight. Members of a brood may scatter, individuals going in any compass direction, in some instances as far as several hundred miles. Later, by the time they are ready to migrate, they have joined older birds and accompany the latter. As a consequence, members of a brood may be widely scattered in winter and, once they occupy a particular wintering area, each tends to return to that particular area in subsequent autumns (Martinson and Hawkins 1968).

Most of the ♀ ♀ that have been successful in producing a brood molt near where they nested; they join the drakes elsewhere later, on staging areas, preceding fall departure.

Fall Shifting about occurs, with no clear-cut differentiation between gathering and lingering at choice feeding areas and onset of migration. That is, individuals become ready to migrate at different times so that, at a given marsh, numbers may increase and/or decrease throughout a period as long as 6–8 weeks. In the Peace–Athabaska delta, Soper (1951) reported that the large number of summering Mallards is augmented by arrival of more birds in Sept.–early Oct. At C. Tatnam (Man.) on s. shore of Hudson Bay, this species becomes fairly plentiful on coastal barrens in autumn (Manning 1952). The reason for a sizable massed northward flight from N.D. into Man. on Oct. 10, 1948, was not readily apparent but perhaps was influenced by hunting pressure (Mann 1950). Although that instance was exceptional, some "reverse" movement occurs every year in late Sept.–early Oct.

Migration in northerly areas extends from about mid-Sept. until the last waters at feeding places are iced over; in s. U.S. there is perhaps no true migratory movement after Dec. 15. Generalizing rather broadly: most migration in the prairie provinces and in similar latitudes occurs over a long span from late Sept. into Nov.; in n. third of conterminous U.S., mid-Oct. through Nov.; and farther s., mid-Oct. into Dec. For a detailed report, based on band-recovery data, of movement of Mallards from Canada down the Mississippi to the Gulf Coast, see Bellrose and Crompton (1970). The reader is referred to Bellrose (1957) for description of a very large, spectacular, and rapid migratory movement, which was recorded all the way from w.-cent. Canada to the Gulf of Mexico. It was predominantly of Mallards; the dates were Oct. 31–Nov. 3, 1955; the cause was low-pressure areas in Canada resulting in a southward flow of a mass of continental arctic air.

Winter There is some local shifting of birds as waters freeze or thaw, or its levels change, or new food supplies become available.

NOTE An "adult" drake, banded Sept. 26, 1958, in Sask., was killed July 2, 1959, near Egvekinot, in Kresta Bay on s. side of the Chuckchee Pen. (Dzubin 1962).

POSTSCRIPT Since the above section was completed, 3 lengthy papers have appeared: A. D. Geis (1971), using banding and hunting-kill data to relate breeding to wintering areas; D. R. Anderson and Henny (1972), using band-recovery data to discuss distribution and migration from breeding areas; and Bellrose (1972), defining and discussing Mallard migration corridors from s. Canada southward.

A. p. conboschas—the Greenland birds have local seasonal movements between salt water and inland nesting places. RSP

BANDING STATUS The total number of *A. p. platyrhynchos* banded throughout the Holarctic must be well in excess of two million birds. In Canada and U.S.: 1,501,047 banded through 1964, with 216,734 recoveries through 1966, and places of banding were scattered from breeding to winter range (data from Bird Banding Laboratory). By the end of 1969 there were over 350,000 recoveries. There has been very extensive use of band-recovery data in many publications.

A. p. conboschas—in Greenland in 1946–65 a total of 534 were banded and there were 54 recoveries through 1965 (Salomonsen 1966). RSP

REPRODUCTION   N. Am. data on nominate *platyrhynchos*, supplemented by information from European studies.

When migrating to breeding grounds, Mallards fly in compact flocks of a few to about 200 birds, generally 10–15. They arrive during the night or early morning, less commonly through the day. Seasonally resident birds arrive first; subsequent flights contain those bound for more northerly breeding areas (Sowls 1955). As in Russian findings of Larionov (1956), probably the interval between arrival and nesting is progressively shorter northward.

The Mallard has the nearest to a balanced sex ratio among our common game ducks. Tallies of some 53,000 birds showed regional variations in drakes from 50.3 to 55.9% (Bellrose et al. 1961). In Man., during April of 1947 and 1949, drakes composed 52.5 and 53.9%. There have been a few local studies, in N. Am. in winter or early spring, showing an even greater local preponderance of drakes. By the early 1970s the sex ratio of prairie Mallards was changing markedly; there was increasing mortality of ♀ ♀ due to decreasing amount of nesting cover and an increase in predators (notably the red fox). A study of thousands of birds in the Netherlands showed that the ratio varied through the seasons, from 106 ♂:100 ♀ just prior to breeding season to an unknown figure exceeding 114:100 in Nov. (Eygenraam 1957).

First breed at age 1 year. (Sexual maturity in ♀ and ♂ by age 7 mo., possibly earlier in the ♀, has been reported in captives that hatched in England in Nov. (Kear 1961), but this must be exceptional.) Unmated drakes, or "surplus" ones from unbalanced sex ratio, may extend fertility by mating with ♀ ♀ that renest after their mates of earlier in the season have departed.

Events (displays, etc.) that are an integral part of the breeding cycle begin at least as early as the preceding autumn; that is, remote in time and place from where migrant Mallards nest.

Displays are treated tersely here, based primarily on studies in Europe by Lorenz (1941, 1958) and N. Am. studies of Ramsay (1956) and Dzubin (1957). Those interested in further refinement or exhaustive detail also will consult especially the European studies of Geyr von Schweppenburg (1959, 1961), Raitasuo (1964), Weidmann (1956), and Weidmann and Darley (1971), also sources cited by these authors.

Sexual reactions and calls of the female   INCITING duck turns toward mate or prospective mate, swims after him and, at the same time, partially turns her head away toward another ♂ (or makes this ritualized movement in absence of other ♂). No pronounced chin lifting. Her call may be described as *gueggege ggeggeggeggegge*, irregular in length and accenting. Sometimes she makes short dashes toward the drake. The same call is used in flight when Inciting her mate against a following drake. Inciting occurs as a primary stimulus to elicit sexual display of ♂ ♂; there is no real nodding, only rapid swimming with head forward near water. After pairs are formed, a ♂ usually responds to mate's Inciting by alternately threatening the indicated bird and uttering the *raehb raehb* call repeatedly toward his ♀.

GESTURE OF REPULSION   If mate is absent and ♀ is pursued in flight by drakes, she flies with upper mandible bent as far upward as possible, feathers of head and back greatly ruffled, head drawn deeply into neck, and utters series of sharp hiccoughlike *gaeck* calls. (When the pair bond is waning, the flight of pursuing drakes may include her mate.)

DECRESCENDO CALL   Generally about 6 syllables *quaegeageageageag*, accent on second and diminishing thereafter. Uttered by unmated ♀♀, also by those with firm pair bond when the drake is absent from the ♀. Sight of mate in flight is strongest releasing stimulus for this call, but unmated ♀ may respond even to other birds than ducks.

NOD-SWIM   a powerful stimulus for ♂ displays (see #7 under ♂).

HEAD-PUMPING   See copulatory behavior.

Sexual reactions and calls of the drake   DRINKING   When ♂ meets ♀ on water, either one gets out of the way of the other or both drink. (Two birds that eat and drink close together have no "bad" intentions toward each other.) Done in social situations, also by mates, etc.

PREEN-BEHIND-THE-WING   After Drinking by drake in presence of duck he is wooing, ♂ frequently raises a wing slightly (as though to preen) and moves tip of his bill quickly along underside, producing a rattling *Rrr* sound. Although most frequently used toward a prospective mate, it also occurs in various circumstances when there is motivational conflict.

Lorenz (1958) listed the following 10 behavioral components which "belong to the common genetic heritage of surface-feeding ducks" as exemplified by the **drake** Mallard:

1   INITIAL BILL-SHAKE   Quick flipping up of the bill; functionally introductory to the major displays.

2   HEAD-FLICK   Drake rears up, the bill attaining steep upward angle and head flicked (rotated slightly).

3   TAIL-SHAKE   Lateral shaking, the drake in "normal" resting position on water. Obligatory sequence: 3-2-3.

4   GRUNT-WHISTLE   Drake thrusts bill into water and then rears upward; the shaking bill is pulled upward along breast; then as the head is lifted while the body settles back on water, there is a loud sharp whistle followed by a deep grunt. A frequent low-intensity display. Obligatory sequence: 1-4-3.

5   HEAD-UP-TAIL-UP   Drake moves head backward and upward, tail erected toward vertical and spread, so that bird has short high posture. Bill pointed toward ♀ as drake utters single burp (sharp whistle). Higher intensity than #4 and not linked to it.

6   TURNING-TOWARD-THE-♀   Drake raises head and turns it so as to present full-face view toward ♀.

7   NOD-SWIM   Both ♂ and ♀ stretch out head and neck so that chins graze water and (with no actual nodding in the Mallard) each bird makes a short circular dash around the other. Linked to #5 in ♂; independent of other behavior in ♀.

8   TURNING-THE-BACK-OF-THE-HEAD   Head lifted high and turned so that nape is directed toward ♀ (toward whom he has just been pointing bilmay be either unpaired duck or his mate. Obligatory sequence: 5-6-7-8. Drake Mallards also "lead" Inciting ♀♀ by means of #8 (Johnsgard 1960) and this combination apparently is important in pair formation.

9   BRIDLING   Drake flings head far back without lifting it high.

10   DOWN-UP   Drake thrusts bill in water and jerks head up without lifting breast, which is kept low in water. A tiny jet of water is lifted by the bill. When head held highest, a whistle uttered and this is followed by a nasal *raehb raehb*. A high-intensity

293

display. Used as sexual display toward ♀, also appeasement toward another ♂; many drakes often perform at same time.

"Gasping" Individual drakes, with no particular movement, but at same instant when nearby ones utter the whistle, make a peculiar hoarse sound; likened to *chachacha* while breathing out, then in, then out.

Copulatory behavior Mutual HEAD-PUMPING Pair face each other, with extreme position of vertical head movement (as ♂ very high, ♀ low), then jerking movements of the head, more rapidly downward than upward. May continue several min.,

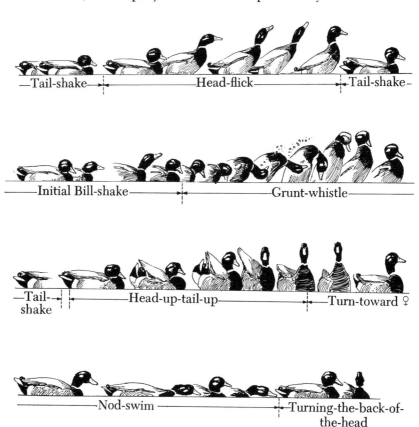

—Tail-shake— · ————————Head-flick———————— ·—Tail-shake-

————Initial Bill-shake———— · ————Grunt-whistle————

—Tail-· · ————Head-up-tail-up———— · —Turn-toward ♀
shake

————————Nod-swim———————— ·—Turning-the-back-of-
the-head

R.R.R. Bridling   Down-up
(after Lorenz 1958)

then ♀ extends neck, lowers body in water, and is mounted by ♂. After treading, drake does Bridling movement (#9); if he still is grasping nape feathers of ♀, her head also is pulled backward. Then he Nod-swims (#7) and Turns-the-back-of-the-head (#8) to-

Precopulatory behavior

ward her. Postcopulatory call a lisping *tseep* by ♂, a quacking by ♂. Copulation occurs without relation to displays or to pair formation, but not within a social group. Some copulatory behavior occurs in autumn even though ♂ is not fertile until spring (Höhn 1947); for details of the ♂ gonad cycle, see O. W. Johnson (1966) and papers he cited.

The **occurrence of displays** may be divided roughly into 3 phases, having their particular functions, prior to occupation of a breeding place.

Social phase   The drake seeks the presence of others of the same species. They swim together in groups of 5–15, closely, some individuals even momentarily in contact. The head feathers are raised as much as possible (head then appears black, without green iridescence), the neck is withdrawn in a manner to conceal the white collar, various "under" feathering is ruffled so that the drake swims high in the water, and the back feathering is held smooth. Then a drake may make a Bill-shake (#1) in incipient fashion, repeating this several times in progressively more elaborate fashion until, in the final shake, he is tilted up diagonally forward and nearly out of the water. On reaching this degree of display intensity, one of these patterns follows: #1-4-3, #10 or #5. Then all the drakes may thus perform for a time at each other.

♂ Postcopulatory
Nod-swim

Sooner or later the group is joined by 1 or more ♀ ♀ which swim among the drakes. A drake may merely stay on course or either he or she may swim around another bird. The next event consists of the birds making an initial Bill-shake (#1). Soon the ♀ is Inciting or Nod-swimming (or both) which may stimulate several to as many as 10 drakes, who respond with various displays and **pursuit.** This may continue as they go back and forth on the water, the ♀ continuing to Nod-swim or Incite and, when closely

group palaver

pursued, she takes wing and the drakes follow. The group turns and wheels erratically, towering high and scooting low. All the drakes may give up the chase, return to water, and quiet down, or a drake may overtake the ♀ and sail on set wings; or the ♀ may be forced down to water where her pursuer forceably attempts to copulate with her. (Persistent assaults on a ♀ may result in her death by drowning.) Such activity is observed in Ill. as early as mid-Jan., but is most frequent through Feb. In March it is observed less frequently in Mallards than in Pintails and Baldpates.

The initial stages of this phase function to bring ♂ ♂ of the species together and to exclude other species, i.e., hinder hybridization. The whole phase is a complex aggregate of activity and differs from species to species. The function of later stages is to enable individuals of the sexes to become "acquainted." The social phase is manifest from fall through spring, most actively on sunny mornings in winter; that is, it continues until all pairing is accomplished or the birds depart on migration. On cold or windy winter days when the birds do not display, they may return to "rafting"; then various species—Mallards, Blacks, Pintails, and others—may be closely intermingled.

Pair formation   As members of the sexes become "acquainted," display is directed by 1 individual toward another. The ♀ swims more or less alongside and directs her Inciting toward a particular drake. The latter may respond negatively and even bite the duck, who then turns her attention toward another drake. Often, however, the ♀ returns to the same drake and persists, possibly even as long as several weeks if necessary, until the drake responds by Drinking and Preening-behind-the-wing (in that order). The former indicates "friendliness" and it may be done mutually; the latter, in this context, also is friendly. Although there may be periods of seeming disinterest after this stage is reached, a degree of attachment does exist and the duck and drake swim together more and more from then on. By the time the drake follows,

296

or pursues, the duck, the pair bond is established. After that there is much mutual Head-pumping, Inciting by the ♀ (to cause the drake to attack some other drake) and, if the partners are separated even briefly, their noisy palaver on being reunited has much in common with the Triumph ceremony of geese. Members of a pair go through their daily routine together and the drake tends to threaten or repel any approaching Mallard. Paired birds do not engage in social play with others. Most of the activities involved in pair formation occur not only afloat but also ashore or on ice.

The ♀'s behavior "harmonizes" the drake as a sexual partner and is responsible for pair formation, which the drake develops. Thus this phase functions to form a bond that endures at least until a breeding place is established and a fertile clutch is being laid. It has been suggested that ♀ ♀ attempt to select, i.e., are more attracted to, mates having wider white collars and certain other characteristics of adornment.

Pair formation begins in Nov. in Ill. and a quarter of the population is paired by late Dec. Near Amarillo, Texas, most of 10,000 observed in late Jan. were paired (Hochbaum 1944); in Cal. 75% are paired in Feb. and 95% by the end of March (Earl 1950); in Mont. there is some pairing the last week of Nov. and by mid-Dec. most are paired (Girard 1941); in S.D. 72% were paired April 16 and 100% April 23 (Murdy 1953).

Pursuit flights and attempts to assault the ♀, which have been described previously, continue during and after the time pairs are being formed.

Pair bond maintenance Since the bond may be formed in fall or any time later (probably not until winter in the youngest cohort), its duration varies greatly from pair to pair. The pair keeps apart from others and the drake, especially, repels any intruding Mallard of either sex. In addition to the functionally introductory Initial bill-shake (#1), displays commonly seen include at least the latter half of those listed previously for the drake. Behavior in this phase may assist in synchronizing the reproductive cycles of mates. The pair is together during migration.

Few ♀ ♀ arrive on breeding grounds unmated. Therefore, pursuit flights by ♂ ♂ that occur there are directed at certain ♀ ♀ already paired. On occasion, a ♀ may be pressed into flight by ardent attention from unmated drakes; on other occasions the ♀ gives her Inciting call, which suggests that in these instances the pair bond is tenuous. In Man. and Sask., the latter sort of pursuit flight is observed most commonly April 1–May 10.

NOTES Various behavioral components of both sexes are ambivalent or even polyvalent, motivated one way in one context and sometimes quite the opposite in another. Examples: see Preen-behind-the-wing and Down-up, described earlier.

Since behavioral activities are parts of a continuum, a fragment can be misunderstood when taken out of context. Example: a ♀ Mallard is seen flying behind (rather than "typically" ahead of) a group of drakes. Perhaps it is a mated ♀ who was forced into flight and, pursued by these same drakes, is joined by her mate. The sexual pursuit drive waned, or possibly was thwarted by her mate interposing himself between the ♀ and her pursuers. The flight continued, the ♀ now keeping station some distance behind so as to maintain a spatial relationship with her mate.

Probably it is not necessary for a Mallard to have a social-play phase prior to pair formation, nor need the latter be prolonged or followed by a lengthy period of bond

297

maintenance. Almost all aspects of the reproductive cycle are variable and, to a considerable extent, can be "adjusted" to circumstances.

Various behavioral studies of the Mallard are based on free-flying birds that are as much feral as they are truly wild, in parks and sanctuaries where they are fed and where their numbers seasonally may reach a saturation level. In some of these situations, it is quite likely that some pairs have essentially no disruption of pair bond around the year; the duck and drake may maintain at least visual contact daily in the rearing period and throughout molting. It is common in feral and semitame stock to see a drake in Sept., still wearing Basic head–body–tail or portions of it, in close company with a ♀ and behaving as though paired. Even in wild stock, especially of less migratory individuals, it is likely that many pairs form (or re-form) before social display ordinarily begins in fall.

Territory in the Mallard and other ducks has been defined by Dzubin (1955) and Sowls (1955) as the defended portion of the home range from which a drake attacks another pair, or a male or female, of his own species. Attack may be launched from a drake's waiting area (his "activity center," Dzubin 1969) or from wherever he or he and his mate feed. Home range is defined as the total area in which the pair is most active during the breeding season (Dzubin). Early in the nesting season, territory and home range more or less coincide but, as the season advances, progressively less area is defended than is utilized (Dzubin). Viewing the total reproductive cycle, which extends for a period of months and overlaps consecutive calendar years, it appears that the drake is concerned primarily with defense of his mate; his attack is a movable phenomenon, occurring wherever the birds happen to be so long as their sexual bond is maintained, and topography, even in the nesting season, is secondary.

A few days after arrival on breeding grounds, pairs separate from other migrants. They lose gregariousness (have aversion for alighting or feeding with other Mallards) and their movements become limited to small water areas or a segment of a large one embracing about 2 sq. mi. Several days after pairs are thus established, ♀ ♀ first utter a loud, montonous *qua*, repeated rapidly for many min. with intermittent pauses. This call, termed Persistent quacking, occurs on the Canadian prairies April 10–May 15. It functions in the spacing of pairs over the breeding ground. Persistent quacking of the ♀ is contemporaneous with drake's aerial pursuit of other pairs. European studies have shown that an intruding ♀ is pursued with intent (which may be successful) of sexual assault by a drake having territory; the ♀'s dread of this functions to keep the birds dispersed; see discussion by Tinbergen (1957).

The ♀ searches for a **nest site** 5–10 days after first uttering her Persistent quacking call. In warm spring seasons, laying starts 4–5 days after the first ♀ is noted in nesting cover. The drake accompanies his mate in search of a nest site, also on daily trips there later for egg-laying, usually early in morning (Soals 1955). The site usually is located within ½ mi. of water, but sometimes as far as 1½ mi. away in grasslands. Occasionally this duck nests in marsh vegetation. On upland, in snowberry (*Symphoricarpos*) clumps, willow (*Salix*) and aspen (*Populus*) groves, among weeds and grasses along roadsides, in pastures, and in wheat and barley stubble fields. A great many atypical sites are recorded—amid woody sprout growth and on stumps, on limbs and in hollows in trees, in an old Magpie nest, on understructure of a bridge, in box on a barn roof, etc.

298

See J. C. Phillips (1923b). In a very wet season, Mallards nested up off the ground in pollarded willows in Holland (Lippins 1937), a habit which has continued there; frequent utilization of the hollowed tops of stubs, cavities in trees, etc., in flooded timberland in N.Y. was discussed fully by Cowardin et al. (1967). They readily accepted nest baskets in Iowa (R. A. Bishop and Barratt 1970) and in the city of Uppsala, Sweden.

Some ♀♀ return to nest in same areas used preceding year(s); it is doubtful if all do even under favorable conditions. Drought on breeding grounds results in Mallards moving considerable distances from one year to the next. Drakes show less homing to breeding grounds than ♀♀.

The drake typically has 3 **areas of activity**. 1 Primary waiting area—small pond or segment of large water area from which he launches most pursuits. However, on the Canadian prairies, waiting areas overlap between pairs in crowded situations. The drake spends the largest part of the day waiting for his mate. The ♀ joins the drake at this site until the pair bond is terminated. 2 Feeding area—includes 1–5 water areas, as far as 2 mi. from waiting area. Drake may launch pursuit from any of these waters. 3 Secondary waiting area—slightly utilized by drake waiting for mate and from which intruding pairs are pursued.

The drake defends his mate and, in the process, an area around her having invisible boundaries that vary with individual, with nesting density, and through the span of time that he is present. His aerial pursuit of other pairs is termed Three-bird flight. Drake of "home" pair takes flight and pursues mated pairs and ♀♀ attempting to fly or land nearby. With intrusion of mated pair, home drake directs his attack at the ♀; he pursues her about 200 yds. in prenesting period and even a half mi. during early part of incubation period. Drake of pursued ♀ follows some 50 ft. behind attacking drake. After the chase, pursuing drake returns to his waiting site and the pair that intruded alights elsewhere. Three-bird flights among Mallards are most common in late April and early May, but occur until July.

Spacing mechanisms and their relation to survival of young have been studied on Canadian parkland and grassland by Dzubin (1969). There are many variables; the subject may be outlined as follows.

Mallards space themselves in any habitat that they utilize. They (also Baldpates and Gadwalls) show the greatest intolerance toward other pairs of their own species. Yet there is a "cluster" problem, the bulk of the birds showing preference for certain water areas. Early in the season, Mallard pairs occupy small, shallow ponds (these are ice-free earliest) and later other pairs occupy larger, deeper, ponds (which thaw later). The ♀ nests nearby and prefers fairly high vegetative cover. Late comers seek the same places, ♀♀ attempting to settle into nesting cover, but the "resident" drake interferes. Pursuit by the drake is directed mainly toward ♀♀ and the number of hostile and sexual chases increases with increase in number of "prospecting" birds. As a result of such pursuits, and of avoidance of occupied areas, pairs disperse to other locations that are less than optimal habitat. Nesting cover may be poor or distant from water, ponds may be few and shallow ones become dry; such factors vary with yearly differences in climate.

On parkland, with intermediate density of nesters, spacing mechanisms operate when increasing pair density results in more interactions of pairs, forcing a portion of them into suboptimal pond areas where production of young is reduced. In grassland habitat, with comparatively high density of pairs on reduced number of ponds, a high number of pair interactions forces some ♀ ♀ to nest great distances from water (to escape pursuit of drakes) and the increased distance from water results in lower survival of ducklings in their trek to water. With low and intermediate densities, the dispersal of nests probably serves to lessen predation; with high densities, there is an effect of overdispersion into poor habitat ("lethal brood areas") which has negative effects on survival of young. High density in poor habitat or in time of drought may result in immigration to forested habitat which, in turn, is not optimal for the Mallard.

Mallards probably are in an optimal situation when each pair has a total of at least several acres of land plus water. Much the highest density so far reported from Canadian parkland was at Lousana, Alta., in 1958—93 pairs/sq. mi. or .61/acre and the number of ♀ ♀ that produced broods approached 50% (Dzubin). As in some other *Anas* species, there are extremely high densities reported from islands where, presumably, there is adequate nearby water area to accommodate the seasonal needs of drakes. There were an estimated 78 and 60 nests in 2 years in preferred habitat on part of a 9-acre island in a lake in se. S.D. (Drewien and Frederickson 1970); 268 nests on a 105-acre island in Loch Leven, Scotland (Boyd and Campbell 1967); 23 nests in 1 year and 29 in another on a 5.7-acre island in L. Champlain, Vt. (Coulter and Miller 1968).

The Mallard is widespread as a breeder and difficult to study where nesting is not concentrated, although scattered nesters contribute very heavily to the total population. In Czechoslovakia, Havlin (1968) found that nesting begins earlier and clutches are larger along streams (which open earlier) than at ponds (which thaw later). This relationship of time of nesting and size of clutch to time of thaw probably is a general rule in the species.

The duck accumulates some nest material at her site, then sits on this and rotates while kicking, until a **nest bowl** is formed. As laying, and then incubation progress, the duck continues to pick material within reach while she is sitting and passes it over her shoulder. No material is carried to the site (Heinroth 1911, Sowls 1955). The dark **nest down** (see "Description") on her underparts becomes so loosened that it falls into the nest during regular preening movements; this begins to accumulate in the nest bowl some time during laying and continues into the incubation period.

One **egg** each from 20 clutches (4 Minn., 4 Sask., 2 Utah, 2 N.D., 2 Pa., and 1 each from Man., Wash., Cal., Ore., S.D., and Ohio) **size** length 58.12 ± 1.92 mm., breadth 41.69 ± 1.03, radii of curvature of ends 15.98 ± 0.96 and 12.50 ± 1.08; **shape** usually near subelliptical, elongation 1.39 ± 0.42, bicone −0.042, asymmetry +0.117 (FWP). **Color** creamy to a greenish buff; gloss increases during incubation. Eggs normally are laid at rate of 1/day.

Clutch size usually 7–10 eggs. The following are averages from various published and other sources; presumably all are for first clutches: Cal.—av. 8.9 (494 clutches), Utah—8.6 (185), Mont.—7.1 (257), Alta.—8.2 (138), Sask.—8.3 (855) and 9.0 (190). The differences probably are less than could be observed at any one of the localities during a series of seasons having marked weather variations.

First clutches generally are completed by about April 10 in s. part of U.S. breeding range, from late April to early May in n. conterminous U.S., by about mid-May on the

Canadian prairies, and about June 1 at upper fringe of breeding range. In much of the breeding range, first clutches are completed throughout a span of at least a month, overlapping another long span during which replacement clutches are laid; that is, viable eggs may be found in conterminous U.S. from very early April until at least late July. It is probably safe to generalize that, where Mallard and Black Duck both nest, various peaks (of completion of clutch, hatching, etc.) are a week later in the former species.

Termination of pair bond generally occurs early in (often at the very beginning of) incubation. Details of how this comes about ar not fully known; just what transpires may vary in content, timing, and sequence. The drake maintains his waiting areas and the duck, as laying progresses, shows diminishing interest in associating with him. The drake's hostility toward other drakes wanes; he wanders more, and several ♂ ♂ may feed and loaf together. Either the duck begins to react in a hostile manner toward her mate, with Gesture of repulsion described earlier, or else, if an intruding ♀ or Mallard pair enter the area, the "home" ♀ is pursued by the "home" drake just as he pursues the others. At any rate, by the time the drakes are in groups, they chase off-duty ♀ ♀ in flight and attempt sexual assault. Some drakes leave the flight; others join in, so that 3 to 20 or even more are in pursuit. Such group chases begin about the 2nd week in May and continue into July, when the last drakes depart to molt.

It seems probable that physiological events leading up to the drake's molting are influenced temporarily by some such prior "external" event as nest building or laying behavior of his mate. The drake's "internal" mechanism probably can be slowed (inhibited) briefly by continuance of the sexual bond, but the drake's schedule is not very flexible. Some pattern such as this may determine when the drake leaves. Unmated drakes begin molting early; failed breeders molt early; later-nesting (or renesting) ♀ ♀ lose their mates early. Some drakes give an impression of remaining a long time, even to or past hatching; in such instances, evidently the season was early and the ♀ succeeded in her first nesting attempt. Thus the normal time for the drake to depart came comparatively late in the ♀'s cycle. Captured wild birds, exposed to artificial lighting in mid-Dec., developed sexual activity first and later began to molt (Walton 1937).

Some ♀ ♀ that cease attempting to nest join concentrations of molting drakes. Sometimes, if the nest is destroyed before the pair bond is dissolved, the pair joins postbreeding groups (consisting mostly of drakes at first); how long the bond persists thereafter is unknown (Oring 1964).

For discussion of various kinds of chasing and listing of relevant literature, see McKinney (1965a.)

Incubation, by the ♀, begins with laying of the last egg of the clutch. According to Prince et al. (1969), there is a positive correlation between order of laying and of hatching: in wild-taken eggs placed in an incubator, the first eggs laid were the first to hatch. For details of the routine of the ♀ on the nest, see McKinney (1953). She leaves twice daily, in early morning and late afternoon, for 1–2 hrs. each time. She joins the drake if he still is maintaining a waiting area, and they feed together, preen, etc. **Incubation period** usually 27–28 days in the wild; published statements include: 23–29, usually 26 days (Bent 1923); av. 28–28½ days in 100 cases (Dersheid 1938); about 28 days but varying 2–3 days either way (Girard 1941); 25½–26 days (Heinroth 1911) in feral birds; usually 26 days but, according to some writers, if the eggs are placed under a hen they hatch about 2 days sooner (J. C. Phillips 1923b); 22–24 days in an incubator (Hochbaum 1944). A method of determining how long the eggs have been incubated was described and illus. by H. C. Hanson (1954); for graphs of embryonic growth vs. incubation in days, see Prince et al. (1968). The eggs hatch within a span of a few hrs. The shells are not removed from the nest. The duck has been known to sit on nonviable eggs for as long as 49 days.

"Observer interference" According to Balát (1969), nesting Mallards will tolerate considerable activity nearby. One flushing from the eggs, however, establishes fear; the next flushing occurs before the nest is approached closely and may result in abandonment. Females differ and so does their behavior through laying and incubation. Yet it is hard to escape a feeling that the Mallard (or almost any waterfowl) does poorly where studied assiduously and much better where let alone.

Hatching success varies considerably. For example, some eggs hatched in 42.8% of 1,961 nests (studies at a number of localities combined); from an av. of 8 eggs in successful nests an av. of 6.9 hatched. In nest baskets in Iowa, the av. clutch was 9.9 eggs in 205 successful nests (total of 2,033 eggs) and 1,743 (86%) hatched (R. A. Bishop and Barratt 1970). Within 12 hrs. after hatching, the ducklings are ready to leave and they follow the duck overland for a distance varying from a few ft. to 1½ mi. to reach water. Brood mortality some years on the plains amounts to 70% during the trek from nest to water (A. Dzubin).

Replacement clutches av. smaller (see European data below). In Vt., first clutches of 24 marked ♀♀ contained 7–15 eggs, av. 10.3, and replacement clutches of 15 of these same birds contained 7–14, av. 9.6 (Coulter and Miller 1968). In captive ♀♀, fertility of eggs laid during 1st week of isolation from drakes was 64%, 2nd week, 37%, 3rd week 3% and, for corresponding periods, hatchability declined 73%, 64%, and to zero (Elder and Weller 1954). If a duck is going to renest in the wild, generally she does so within 5–15 days after loss of a clutch. Renesting probably is more the rule than the exception; see, for example, Keith's (1961) data for se. Alta. In Sweden, Bjärvall (1969) reported 2 instances of ♀♀ laying second clutches after successfully hatching first ones.

For comparison of nesting studies (Idaho., Cal., England), see Ogilvie (1964). His English data (Slimbridge, Glos.) include: normal time of onset of laying is mid-Feb. in a mild winter (as in 1963–64), but 3 weeks later in severe winters (the 2 preceding ones); first clutches av. 12.6 eggs, replacement clutches av. 9.9; usually a day is skipped during laying of the first 7 eggs; av. incubation in 51 clutches was 27.6 days (24–32); 88.7% of 180 nests were successful; and 82.4% of the eggs hatched.

Hatching, voice of the duck and her ducklings while still in the nest, and departure, have been described by Bjärvall (1968). The **ducklings** generally feed beginning shortly after they reach water. From British studies, Kear (1965) noted that undoubtedly they can survive in the wild if they do not feed during their first 48 hrs. The duck uses her distraction display in defense of the brood. Young that hatched in a box on a barn roof tumbled to the ground on vocal signal from the duck (Lincoln 1929). Very exceptionally a family may return to the nest; also, occasionally (both in feral and wild birds) a drake is seen in company with a ♀ and brood. There is an innate tendency for a

♀ with brood to move from a rearing area, especially if in any way disturbed, and when they go overland they do not orient toward another pond.

Generally the duck remains with her brood until they are near flying age, but 42% of dabbling duck broods of feathered young have been reported to be unaccompanied by a parent (C. D. Evans et al. 1952). It would seem that the ♀ may stay with early-hatched young, but deserts them if late-hatched (as in renestings). Unattended broods remain as a unit until they are able to fly (Chura 1961) and, shortly before reaching that stage, young Mallards have completed their shift from mainly animal to mainly plant foods. For daily activity of preflight young in Utah, see Chura (1963). Preflight broods are highly mobile; 2 broods moved 3 and 3½ mi. in 2 days (A. Dzubin); 2 moved 0.48 mi. in 38 days and no brood occupied the same pothole more than 20 days (C. D. Evans et al. 1952).

Weight of ducklings in gm.: 29 (1 day), 66 (1 week), 148 (2 weeks), 288 (3 weeks), 388 (4 weeks), 453 (5 weeks), 683 (6 weeks) (Southwick 1953a). Twenty that were incubator hatched, then weighed before they had fed: 34.6 ± 0.49 gm. (mean and SE), 2.18 (SD), 31.2–38.4 gm. (range)—from Smart (1965a) who also gave wt. of F_2 and F_3 Mallard–Pintail crosses. Kear (1965) gave wt. of ducklings from 2 days pre- to 14 days posthatching; she noted that birth wt. doubles in a week and quadruples in 2 weeks. For growth curves, see Veselovsky (1953).

Density effects are noted throughout the nesting–rearing periods. For example, when a number of ♀♀ nest in close proximity, they are harassed more when off duty, the drakes may not correctly identify their own mates, drakes may alight at waiting areas of other drakes, and so on. During rearing, broods need space. If, for example, a duck is forced away from her brood by one or more drakes, any of her ducklings that swim in the vicinity of another duck with brood commonly is attacked and frequently killed by the other duck. Such killing is a common sight where Mallards are numerous in parks and sanctuaries.

Age at first flight varies, even among members of a brood. Wild Mallards reach flying age at 52–60 days (Gollop and Marshall 1954), captive-reared ones at 49–60 days

(Hochbaum 1944). The longer preflight birds are held before release in the wild, the later they fly; N.Y. stock released at age 3 weeks flew in 9–10 weeks, but if held 4 weeks longer they flew in 10–11 weeks (Foley et al. 1951). In stock from Man., 77% of a sample attained flight during or before the 9th week, but only 42% of N.Y. stock flew that soon (Foley et al. 1961).

Wild Mallards normally are **single-brooded.** Rarely there may be a second brood in the wild (Benson and Foley 1962), but apparently not if the first is reared. Semidomesticated Mallards occasionally are double-brooded. FCB AD

SURVIVAL *A. p. platyrhynchos.* Recoveries of 8,019 ♂ banded as young in Ill., 1939–44, indicated an annual survival rate of 45% the first year and 58% each subsequent year; in 8,628 ♀, age when banded not recorded, the data indicated an annual survival rate of 53% (Bellrose and Chase 1950). Small numbers banded as young in several regions of N. Am. showed a survival rate of 32% the first year and 50% each subsequent year (Hickey 1952). Recoveries of Mallards banded in 4 areas in Colo. showed an annual survival rate of 61–70% (R. A. Ryder 1955). From a survey of existing information, Boyd (in Le Cren and Holdgate 1962) concluded, contrary to some N. Am. authors, that the Mallard is not capable of sustaining itself when adult losses exceed a rate of about 55%; see his paper for discussion.

A British sample of 271 young had a first-year mortality rate of 88%; a sample of 305 adults had mean mortality rate of about 65% (Höhn 1948). In New Zealand the introduced Mallard has an av. mortality rate of 55.8% as compared with 70.3% for the native *A. superciliosa* (Balham and Miers 1959).

Recent studies in N. Am. and in Denmark have revealed that young captive-reared individuals, when released in the wild, lack wariness, have low survival, and high vulnerability to shooting; see, for example, Schladweiler and Tester (1972).

Although a wild Mallard in N. Am. has survived to age at least 24 years, very few individuals live 5 years. Av. life expectancy of ♂ ♂ banded in Ill. is 1.56 years, ♀ ♀ 1.38 (F. C. Bellrose). DSF

HABITS *A. p. platyrhynchos* in N. Am. Since, as in waterfowl generally, activities relating to the breeding cycle occur practically throughout the year, much of the information given in previous sections applies equally here.

Drakes start moving to larger lakes and to extensive marshes for molting in late May. Some ♀ ♀ (failed breeders) join the drakes there, but a great many molt in marshes and at waters near their nesting places. Numbers of Mallards steadily increase through summer at molting places until, by late Aug., thousands are associated together. They generally are silent when molting and they tend to feed at any time in daylight rather than having an inactive period during the middle of the day.

Flocks of Mallards start feeding in unharvested wheat and barley fields in early Aug.; later they feed in stubble fields until they depart on fall migration. As they move s. in migration they feed in wheat stubble in the Dakotas and w. Nebr. and in fields where corn has been harvested in the midwest. Their daily feeding flights generally occur in daylight near sunrise and sunset, but they fly any time of day when it is cold and cloudy. There are flights to rice stubble in Ark., La., and Cal., where multitudes of the birds are present through winter. In the panhandle of Oklahoma and Texas, Mallards feed extensively in sorghum fields. Field feeding is most common in fall and winter, less so in spring.

The birds mass by tens of thousands on extensive sheets of water, flying ¼ to 30 mi. to grainfields. They also feed in shallow water, tipping up for aquatic plant seeds in marshes and for acorns in flooded swamps. They are capable of diving for food, but rarely do so.

Flocks vary in size from about 20 to 200 birds, composed of both sexes and mixed age-groups. The Mallard is gregarious, except for a short time in the nesting–rearing season, and also social, the Black Duck being the most common associate e. of the Mississippi and the Pintail in the west.

A certain amount of raising and lowering the head, and turning it laterally, usually precedes taking flight. If startled, a Mallard "jumps" nearly straight from the water. A dozen or more authors have published flight speeds—air speeds of 26–60 mph, probably not over 50 except when pursued (C. H. Blake). From radio telemetry data, it appears that respiration is synchronized with wingbeat (2 beats: 1 respiration), there being about 192 wingbeats/min.; for further details see Lord et al. (1962).

Mallards follow the same migration corridors from year to year (with some shifting by individuals), hence there is a tendency to form more or less overlapping subpopulations. Wintering areas vary with food supplies and water levels. Snow cover on food may force them farther southward; flooding of southern river swamps results in movements there for distances up to several hundred mi. In recent years, more and more Mallards have lagged behind in fall migration to feed in corn and wheat fields. Dams on the Missouri R. in S.D. have resulted in late buildups to over a million birds which have reduced the numbers in the lower Mississippi area.

Age-group ratios of Mallards in the Mississippi drainage show marked oscillation in yearly production of young. The proportion of young was low in 1940, 1945, 1950, and

1954; it was high in 1939, 1943, 1948, and 1951. Some of these lows in production of young were related to drought on the plains, but others occurred despite favorable water conditions. Breeders are known to shift n. and also e. to parklands when drought affects the plains. From winter censusing, the continental population apparently has averaged about 7,400,000 Mallards annually during the past 2 decades; that is, not quite double the number of our next most numerous duck, the Pintail. In summers, 1955–73, the number of Mallards on main breeding areas surveyed annually has av. 8,796,000; additional thousands nest elsewhere. Mallard numbers have been declining, however, in the prairie provinces, their prime nesting area. There has been loss of breeding places, drought, increased predation on the prairies, and possibly an excessive hunting kill.

Over 30,000 Mallards were reared and released in N.Y. in 1934–52 inclusive; The total number released only in the states on and near the U.S. Atlantic coast in the last 3 decades probably was at least 50,000 birds annually, a most conservative figure (in Md. in a recent year, about 55,000 were released!). In the past 30 years, states in the vicinity of the Great Lakes have released in excess of 400,000 Mallards. Over 40 years ago, J. C. Phillips (1928) was of the opinion that stocking had not affected the natural population much, but that same statement could not be made today.

Of the 10 species of birds in N. Am. having the largest number of published references of some significance, 4 are gamebirds and 2 of these are waterfowl, the Canada Goose and Mallard. No monograph on the latter exists, nor is there room here even to mention much that is recorded about this species. FCB

FOOD *A. p. platyrhynchos*—mostly N. Am. data. Stems and seeds of aquatic plants, cultivated grains, mast, aquatic insects, mollusks, tadpoles, frogs, small fish, and fish eggs. Examination of 1,578 stomachs from 22 states and 2 Canadian provinces, mainly from La. and Ark., showed about 90% vegetable material and 10% animal (McAtee 1918).

Vegetable Sedges: seeds or other parts of bulrushes (*Scirpus*), *Fimbryistylis*, chufa (*Cyperus*), and saw grass (*Cladium*), 21.6% grasses: wild rice (*Zizania aquatica*), wild millet (*Echinochloa crusgalli*), switch- and crabgrasses (*Panicum*), rice cutgrass (*Homalocenchrus* (*Leersia*)), giant cutgrass (*Zizaniopsis*), rice, oats, corn, barley, wheat, and buckwheat, 13.4%; seeds of smartweeds, particularly *Polygonum sagittatum* and *P. hydropiper*, 9.9%; pondweeds (*Potamogeton*, especially *P. pectinatus*), wigeon grass (*Ruppia maritima*), northern naiad (*Najas flexilis*), and eelgrass (*Zostera marina*), 8.2%; duckweeds (*Lemnaceae*) and coontail (*Ceratoihslum demersum*), 12%; wild celery (*Vallisneria spiralis*) and seeds of frogbit (*Limnobium spongia*), 4.3%; seeds of trees and shrubs: water elm (*Planera aquatica*), hackberry (*Celtis*), acorns (*Quercus*), buttonbush (*Cephalanthus occidentalis*), 8.22%; miscellaneous seeds, e.g., hickory nuts (*Carya*), and other parts of plants, 8.9% (McAtee 1918).

Principal foods of 85 specimens from upper Chesapeake Bay were seeds of *Ruppia maritima*, *Potamogeton perfoliatus*, *Polygonum* spp., *Scirpus* spp., *Sparganium americanum*, *Peltandra virginica*, *Zea mays*, and beech and oak mast (R. E. Stewart 1962). The 306 specimens collected in Minn. in the fall of 1940 showed mainly the seeds of *Zizania aquatica* (35.5%), *Potamogeton strictifolius* (22.8%), and *Sparganium chlorocarpum* (11.1%) (Stoudt 1944). The Ill. birds, numbering 2,825, had consumed predominantly *Zea mays* 47.37%, *Leersia oryzoides* 12.83%, and *Polygonum* spp. 7.12% (H. G. Anderson 1959). The principal foods in the 1,467 gizzards from Mo. were *Zea mays* 26%, *Polygonum* spp. 19.9%, *Echinochoa* spp. 15.4%, and *Quercus* 8.2% (Korschgen 1955). Rawls (1958) examined 798 gizzards from Reelfoot Lake. Among a large number of plant species utilized, the chief ones were maize 11.37%, acorns 8.72%, and seeds of buttonbush 6.85% and smartweeds 6.83%. In La. the crops of 215 birds contained chiefly the seeds of wild millets (*Echinochloa crusgalli, E. walteri*), panicum (*Panicum dichotomiflorum*), and paspalum (*Paspalum plicatulum*) (Junca et al. 1962).

In w. Mont. the food preferences in order were pondweeds (*Potamogeton pectinatus, P. foliosus, P. pusillus*), smartweed (*Polygonum amphibium*), wigeon grass (*Ruppia maritima*), muskgrass (*Chara*), duckweeds (*Lemna minor, L. trisulca*), and waterweed (*Elodea canadensis*) (Girard 1941). At Bear. R., Utah, ducklings consumed animal life (terrestrial and aquatic insects) at first and shifted over to vegetable (mainly seeds of *Scirpus, Zannichellia*, and *Potamogeton*) as they neared flying age; for full details see Chura (1961). In Man. the daily consumption of wheat was 114 cc. [7 oz.] (Bossenmaier and Marshall 1958).

The vegetable food in w. Europe consists mainly of the vegetative parts or seeds of *Ranunculus, Callitriche, Ceratophyllum, Lemna, Galium, Suaeda, Carex, Persicaria, Polygonum*, and *Zostera*; acorns, fruit of *Rubus*, and cultivated grains (Witherby 1939). On arrival in spring at lakes of the Barabinsk steppes (w. Siberia), principal foods are the seeds of *Atriplex, Salicornia* and *Suaeda*, and wheat in the fields. When warm weather begins, the diet is 60–97% animal. On the Barabinsk steppes (lat. 55° N, long. 78° E) the stomachs contained 65.6% animal food. In order of importance: chironomid larvae, mollusks, and aquatic beetles. *Donacia*, eaten in both adult and larval stages, was important here and in other regions. The birds appear in summer in the lake region of N. Kazakhstan (cent. Asia), where they consume Orthoptera while at the same time in the s. part of the Kazakh S.S.R., *Ceratophyllum* and *Lemna* are important foods. In the Volga delta, when the birds are flightless during molt, food is almost exclusively vegetable (*Ceratophyllum, Lemna, Nymphaeaceae, Potamogeton*, and *Butomus*) and on the Barabinsk steppes Cruciferae, *Vallisineria spiralis*, waterlilies, and the tender shoots of reeds. Food in winter is largely seeds of *Sagittaria* and *Myriophyllum*; on the steppes principally seeds of *Salsola*, and at the lakes seeds of *Ruppia, Panicum, Sparganium, Scirpus*, and *Polygonum*. Ducklings consume 83.4% animal matter (taken from plants at the level of water) consisting mainly of dragonfly larvae 35%, crustaceans 15%, and mollusks 8%. Vegetable food becomes predominant at the end of Aug. (Dementiev and Gladkov 1952).

Animal Insects: water beetles (Haliplidae, Dytiscidae, Hydrophilidae and Gyrinidae), land beetles (Carabidae and Chrysomelidae), aquatic bugs (Corixidae, Notenectidae, Nepidae, Belostomatidae, Naucoridae, Veliidae, and Gerridae), nymphs of dragonflies (Odonata), flies (Diptera), especially the larvae of mosquitoes (*Culex*), ants (Hymenoptera), and larvae of mayflies (Ephemerida), stoneflies (Plecoptera), and caddis flies (Trichoptera) 2.67%; crustaceans: water fleas (Copepoda), sand fleas (Amphipoda), sow bugs (Isopoda), freshwater shrimps and crayfishes (Decapoda)

307

0.35%; mollusks: principally freshwater snails (Gastropoda) and small bivalves (Pelecypoda) 5.73% (McAtee 1918). Snails, *Amicola* spp. and *Gyraulus* spp., were eaten on the lower Hudson R. (Foley and Taber 1951). Stated to eat barnacles in Cal. (W. E. Bryant 1893) and in Alaska in winter (A. Bailey 1927). A univalve (*Littorina atkana*) formed 75% of the stomach contents of 2 specimens taken in Nov. in the Pribilof Is. (Preble and McAtee 1923). Miscellaneous animal matter: fishes, fish eggs, marine worms, earthworms, water mites (*Hydrocarina*), leeches (Hirudinea), spiders (Arachnoidea), and freshwater bryozoans 0.72%. Curculionidae, Acarina, and Pisces reported from Ill. (H.G. Anderson 1959).

For rate of **passage of food through the digestive tract** (it can be surprisingly rapid), see Malone (1965). Captive Mallards, perhaps after having overeaten, have been observed to regurgitate or vomit food; in the wild, they may thus disperse aquatic organisms that would not remain viable after passage through their entire digestive tracts (Malone 1966).

A. p. conboschas—little information. Presumably the food is largely **vegetable** in summer since the Greenland Mallard frequents the heads of fjords, streams, and especially shallow lakes with dense vegetation on their banks. The stomach of a "juvenile" contained 80 seeds, mostly crowberry (*Empetrum*). An adult had eaten a diving beetle (*Colymbetes dolabratus*). In winter it feeds in the littoral zone and the diet is almost entirely **animal:** mollusks (*Margarita helicina, Modiolaria discors, Macoma calcarea*) and a few amphipods. Many starve to death. (Based on Longstaff 1932 and Salomonsen 1950). AWS

Mexican Duck

Anas diazi Ridgway

Both ♂ and ♀ resemble ♀ Mallard in general appearance but have darker, richer, browns (especially breast) and av. slightly smaller in size. No black at side base of bill in purebred drakes. Bar at leading and another at trailing edge of speculum white or, in both sexes, former varies to indistinct (brownish or dusky); 3 lateral pairs of tail feathers have little or no white (predominantly brownish, edge pinkish tan). (For affinities and evolution, see under "distribution" of the Mallard.) Tracheal apparatus of drake presumably as Mallard, but undescribed. Usual wt. 30–38 oz. (♂ av. larger than ♀). The Mexican Duck is not regarded here as a subspecies of *A. platyrhynchos*, but instead as a species in which there is considerable individual (but no proven geographical) variation.

DESCRIPTION   Not much information; by inference, Plumages and their sequence as Mallard, but molts may differ somewhat in timing. The following is limited mainly to features believed to be diagnostic, in purebred stock, of age, sex, or to distinguish from ♀ Mallard.

▶   ♂ Def. Alt. Plumage (all feathering except, in wing, only a few innermost feathers) worn from LATE SUMMER or EARLY FALL around the year into following SUMMER. **Bill** olive-yellow, no black spot at side base in over 150 individuals examined (W. S. Huey), the nail black. **Iris** dark brownish. Feathers of **mantle** have internal, complete (not interrupted distally), brownish U-shaped markings; on the longer scapulars they are elongated and V-shaped. **Underparts**, especially breast, rich reddish brown in general tone in fresh feathering, the feathers with large dark areas in centers which tend to be aligned (streaked effect); under tail coverts show considerable dark color terminally. **Tail** darkish laterally, perhaps paling to near white in some individuals. Legs and **feet** deep orange. Wing almost entirely retained Basic feathering (see below).

▶   ♂ Def. Basic Plumage (entire feathering), worn for some time in SUMMER or into EARLY FALL, except most of wing retained into following summer. **Mantle** (including scapular) feathers have reduced internal markings and more buffy edging than in Def. Alt.; **wing** somewhat darker in general than ♀ Mallard's, the speculum more toward green (not violet).

▶   ♀ Def. Alt. Plumage (all feathering except, in wing, only a few innermost feathers) LATE SUMMER or FALL into LATE WINTER or EARLY SPRING. **Bill** usually more olive-green than in ♂, with only traces of orange at base and usually none or few dark markings on upper mandible. In **overall feathering**, the browns not as richly rufescent as in ♂. Differs from ♀ Mallard, and as described by W. S. Huey (1961), thus: rump feathers lack light subterminal bar (usually present in Mallard), upper tail coverts not patterned along quill and with border narrower and darker, under tail coverts dark brown with light brownish edging. Legs and feet muted orange. Two (of about 50) individuals had black and brown barring on outer web of certain "tertials" (11th–13th secondaries), presumably individual variation.

▶   ♀ Def. Basic Plumage (entire feathering), head–body–tail and innermost feathers of wing generally acquired in LATE WINTER or EARLY SPRING, the remainder (most) of

309

the wing much later (well along in SUMMER or in FALL); then the Basic is succeeded by Alt., except most of the wing is retained nearly a year. In general, somewhat more neutral-colored, a rather "washed-out" appearance as compared with Def. Alt. **Various feathers** have rather broadly rounded ends (especially breast, scapulars, and on flanks) and paler margins; internal markings are reduced. **Wing** has speculum vivid green to bluish (as ♂) and usually the light bar at leading edge of speculum is suffused with some variant of tawny.

AT HATCHING   Among Black Duck and allies, palest overall, with largest dorsal spots; eye stripe typically thin and incomplete; legs and feet muted orange. (Compare with Mallard, Black, and Mottled Duck.)

▶   ♂ ♀ Juv. Plumage (entire feathering) more streaked than older stages, since any light edges of feathers are wholly lateral; scapulars shorter, more rounded; all feathering softer than in older stages. Juv. ♀ described by W. S. Huey (1961) had more finely marked pattern, especially breast, than ♀ Mallard.

Other Predefinitive stages—no useful information. A fair photograph of a 5-month-old ♀ in Lindsey (1946).

Measurements of specimens from New Mex., Mexico, and a ♂ from Nebr.—10 ♂: BILL 52–55 mm., av. 54; WING 289–295, av. 284.5; TAIL 89–97, av. 92.2; TARSUS 42–50, av. 46;   11 ♀ BILL 49–55 mm., av. 52; WING 158–270, av. 266.6; TAIL 85–97, av. 90; TARSUS 43–48, av. 45.5 (ETS). For other meas. (wing across chord), by sex and for northern and southern localities, see Aldrich and Baer (1970).

Weight few data; maximum recorded only slightly exceeds av. for ♂ Mallard. Twelve from New Mex. weighed 2.2–2.8 lb. (A. Leopold 1921). A. S. Leopold (1959) stated that drakes weigh 960–1,060 gm. (34.4–38 oz.) and ♀ 815–990 (29–35.4 oz.).

Hybrids in the wild × Mallard are found at least in n. part of the range and would occur wherever such birds may travel.

Geographical variation is not proved, but there is considerable individual variation. For a time it was believed that northerly birds differed from more southerly ones, then considered to be separate populations (and named as subspecies) in that the former allegedly differed in having wavy barring on mantle and a tendency toward darker, more mottled, breast. Pitelka (1948), however, demonstrated that these are invalid criteria. Hellmayr and Conover (1948) regarded alleged differences as individual variation, or due to age or season, not locality. From examination of additional material, the present writer concurs, as did Aldrich and Baer (1970). Presumed color differences in some New Mex. ♀ ♀ can be accounted for by hybridization with Mallard. The northerly and southerly birds are not isolated from each other, since at least many of the former probably spend the winter (season of pair formation) within the range of the latter. RSP

FIELD IDENTIFICATION   "The local names 'Black Duck' and 'Black Mallard,' applied to it by most of the few sportsmen who distinguish it at all, express generic recognition but specific confusion" (Lindsey 1946). Both ♂ and ♀ are much like ♀ Mallard, except darker, with more richly colored body, light bar at leading edge of speculum generally clouded with brownish so as not to be readily apparent, and with no or very little white in tail. (Most Black Ducks have a white bar only at trailing edge and, in the Mottled Duck, even that sometimes is absent.) Hybrids with Mallard have blending inheritance of characters. RSP

VOICE   As Mallard so far as known. RSP

HABITAT   Watercourses and adjacent marshy areas, the dominant herbaceous vegetation usually being cattail (*Typha*), three-square (*Scirpus*), and *Phragmites*. Also irrigated fields of grain and rice. Nests in drier situations where there are tall grasses not distant from water. RSP

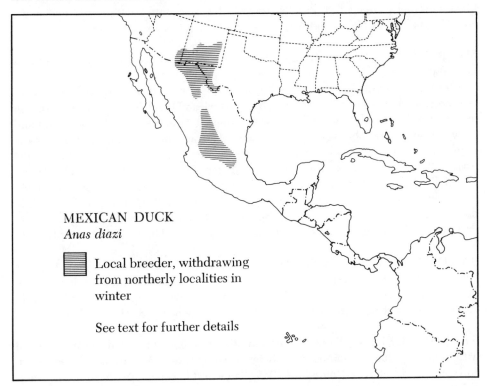

MEXICAN DUCK
Anas diazi

Local breeder, withdrawing
from northerly localities in
winter

See text for further details

DISTRIBUTION   (See map). This is a Mexican species primarily, found at such wetlands and water areas as are scattered in a generally arid environment. It bred at a few such localities in sw. U.S., in the Rio Grande watershed in New Mex. and Texas and the Gila watershed in sw. New Mex. (Lindsey 1946). Recent occurrence, including breeding, in Texas was reported by Ohlendorf and Patton (1971). It may have ceased to breed some time ago at Bosque del Apache Refuge, s. of San Antonio, New Mex. Levy (1964) thought that perhaps the only place in the U.S. where it could be sought with any assurance of finding it was San Simon Cienega, or marsh, astride the s. Ariz.–New Mex. boundary. However, some other places of recent known occurrence in the U.S. were listed by C. A. Davis (1972) and still others by Tomlinson et al. (1973), extending the known breeding range. Such extension may be recent, a result of destruction of

311

historical marsh habitat and the creation of scattered temporary marsh habitat by the pumping of underground water in irrigated farming communities. Yet the number of purebred birds occurring in the U.S. in the early 1970s most likely cannot exceed a few score.

A few recorded sightings may be questionable, because of possibility of confusion with the ♀ Mallard. Furthermore, although mated Mallard–Mexican Duck pairs might migrate considerable distances, specimen or other records of the latter at places distant from usual range should be considered in terms of their possibly pertaining to variant Mallards, or Mallard–Mexican Duck hybrids, in addition to being purebred Mexican Ducks. Accepted locality records for stragglers, based on specimens, are: Cherry Co. in Nebr. and Adams and Sedgwick Co. in Colo. RSP

MIGRATION   The birds are not strictly sedentary; some evidence of migration is as follows.

After hunting in the Rio Grande Valley for many years and keeping records of ducks seen and killed, A. Leopold (1921) noted that Mexican Ducks "pass southward early in the [hunting] season." Lindsey (1946) stated that, at Albuquerque, during winter and early spring, hybrids between Mallards and Mexican Ducks usually outnumber the pure Mexican form, since "few of the latter winter this far north." At Bosque del Apache Refuge, New Mex., there were about 75 nesting pairs each of Mexican Ducks and Mallards; in weekly censuses 1949–50, maximum numbers (20) of Mexican Ducks were seen in May–June, dropping to 3 in late Aug., and in the period Jan. 5–March 24 their numbers ranged 0–10; in comparison, there were 75 –125 Mallards in May–June, dropping to 25 during July, and maximum of 4,600 in early Jan. (R. J. Fleetwood). RSP

BANDING STATUS   In New Mex., 136 birds had been banded through the year 1964 (data from Bird Banding Laboratory). Of 40 birds banded 1959–61 inclusive by the New Mex. Div. of Game and Fish, there were 4 recoveries up to mid-1964; 3 within 60 mi. of place of banding, 1 from Chihuahua, Mexico (W. S. Huey). RSP

REPRODUCTION   The following activities have been observed and are identical with those of Mallard: Inciting, Nod-swim, Turning-the-back-of-the-head, Down-up, and copulatory behavior (Johnsgard 1965). They **first breed** at age 1 year (C. A. Davis 1972).

Almost the only other available data, from which the following are taken, are Lindsey's (1946) for New Mex. **Nests**, lined with vegetation and down, have been found in grassy and sedgy areas. Earliest egg date was April 30 for a clutch of 9, incubated about 2 weeks. Other records (include replacement clutches?): May 15 (5 eggs), May 16 (6), May 21 (2 clutches of 8), June 17 (5), and June 25 (2). More recently, Aldrich and Baer (1970) provided a few data from Mexico, including a clutch of 4 eggs on July 8, 1958, and a brood of 8 downies as late as Aug. 3, 1957. Nesting plus renesting appears to be spread over a long span of time, as in the Mottled Duck. **Egg size** 23 from New Mex. av. 56.8 × 41.2 mm. and 73 from Mexico av. 55.2 × 41.0; **color** white faintly tinged greenish. The few observations in New Mex. indicate that this duck deserts readily if the nest is disturbed; a ♀ whose nest was approached flew up with an egg in

312

her bill. At a nest found April 30 in New Mex., with eggs then advanced in incubation, the drake still was in attendance on May 4. Recorded broods are of 8, 7, 6, 4, and 3 ducklings. Recently, at San Simon Cienega, in 6 broods there was an av. of 5.7 young that survived to flight age; the young prefer dense vegetative cover, then move to open water when they can fly (C. A. Davis 1972). RSP

SURVIVAL   No information.

HABITS   Outside the breeding season, usually in small flocks or groups on small bodies of water. Although it crosses readily with the Mallard, the 2 species have very little breeding contact, perhaps almost entirely in the U.S. portion of the Mexican Duck's range. In Mexico, according to A. S. Leopold (1959), this duck is relatively more wary than other ducks during the period of normal winter hunting. He also emphasized that its marsh habitat in the central uplands of Mexico is shrinking rapidly from water diversion and drainage, the loss being slightly compensated by creation of artificial lakes and impoundments. Levy (1964) pointed out that almost all of this duck's preferred habitat in New Mex. and Ariz. is now gone. Loss of habitat throughout the range of the species was discussed at length by Aldrich and Baer (1970) and C. A. Davis (1972). Johnsgard (1961a) estimated the total "adult" population as probably less than 20,000 in Mexico and probably not over 100 in New Mex. In the early 1960s, the peak number of these birds in New Mex. was estimated at 150, varying downward some years to 100, possibly even fewer (W. S. Huey). The total population of the species in the late 1960s has been estimated at as few as 10,000 individuals, a figure that probably is much too high.

For further information see: Aldrich and Baer (1970), Bent (1923), W. S. Huey and Travis (1961), Jahn (1963), Johnsgard (1961a), A. S. Leopold (1959), Levy (1964), Lindsey (1946), and J. C. Phillips (1923b). RSP

FOOD   Feeding habits are like those of the Mallard, but there is little specific information. Green shoots of alfalfa and cattail, roots of grass, seeds of weeds and grasses, and freshwater mollusks (Bent 1923). In Mexico, stubbles are gleaned for wheat, rice, and corn (A. S. Leopold 1959). AWS

313

Mottled Duck

Anas fulvigula Ridgway

Dusky Duck or, in part, Florida Duck of some authors. Sexes superficially alike and quite similar to Black Duck, but general coloring not quite as dark (though darker than ♀ Mallard); size slightly smaller than Mallard. White bar only at trailing edge of speculum (and often obscure or lacking, especially in Fla. birds); lightest tail feathers (several lateral pairs) some shade of gray. Differences from Black Duck are matters of degree: in Alt. Plumage, body feathers have broader and av. paler edges; chin, throat, and cheeks some variant of pinkish buff and these areas vary in individuals from having much fine streaking to few streaks to none; ♀ has fewer spots or blotches on upper mandible. (For affinities and evolution, see "Distribution" of the Mallard.) Tracheal apparatus undescribed, but presumably as in Mallard.

Length to 24 in., wingspread to 36, usual wt. 32 –38 oz. (♂ av. larger and heavier than ♀). The Mottled Duck is regarded here as a species, not as a subspecies of *A. platyrhynchos*, apparently having slight geographical variation in color characteristics.

DESCRIPTION Fragmentary data, due to lack of opportunity to examine adequate material, but enough has been seen to demonstrate that Plumages and their sequence are homologous with those of Mallard and Black Duck. There seems to be great variation in times of molting.

▶ ♂ Def. Alt. Plumage (all feathering except, in wing, only a few innermost feathers), generally acquired in LATE SUMMER or FALL and retained into the following EARLY SUMMER. **Bill** vivid yellow or toward orange (fall–winter) with black nail and small amount of black at side base. **General coloring** of feathers as stated above. Various feathers are more tapering, browner, and with narrower palish margins and internal markings than in Basic; innermost secondaries tapering and quite pointed, very dark brownish but grade to even darker on outer web, and rather narrowly edged tan on both webs. Within the dark area of a breast feather, typically there is a buffy brown U-shaped mark; the breast is quite dark overall, with mottled or spotted effect. Legs and **feet,** including webs, some variant of orange. In birds after their 2nd summer, almost all of the wing is retained Basic.

▶ ♂ Def. Basic Plumage (entire feathering), head–body–tail generally acquired by some time in SUMMER, the wing last, and retained into FALL; then head–body–tail are succeeded by Alt., but all of the Basic wing except some innermost feathers are retained nearly a year. **Bill**, legs, and **feet** muted orange–yellow. **Feathering** has more scalloped pattern than in Alt., especially the venter, the feathers with wide buffy to pale tan margins (individual variation) and wide and very dark adjoining internal zone. Feathers of mantle, including scapulars, and on flanks, have conspicuously more rounded ends than in Alt. Innermost secondaries rounded and quite broadly edged pale tan. **Wing** speculum cobalt-ultramarine or ultramarine-violet, the white band at trailing edge often reduced or absent; wing lining frequently all white (more often than in *A. rubripes*) or with under primary coverts entirely or basally gray and/or with scattered dark feathers with pale edges near leading edge.

NOTES Judging from museum skins, there is great variation in the time drakes acquire Def. Basic head–body–tail, some getting it even as early as midwinter, some at least as late as the warmest part of summer.

In both sexes the Basic wing is molted from the outer feathers inward and, in a captured wild bird, the **flightless period** lasted "approximately 4 weeks"; details in T. W. Johnson (1973).

▶ ♀ Def. Alt. Plumage (all feathering except, in wing, only a few innermost feathers), generally acquired well along in SUMMER or in FALL, and retained until late WINTER. **Bill** muted orange-yellow with dark olive spots or blotches on upper mandible, concentrated at the middle. The venter appears lighter and more definitely streaked than in the ♂, because of wider buffy or tan lateral margins on the feathers. Innermost secondaries ("tertials") blackish brown (plain), comparatively pointed, and very narrowly edged whitish buff to pale tan; some individuals have blackish and brownish barring on outer web of 11th–13th secondaries. Legs and feet some variant of orange. Most of wing, from 2nd summer onward, is retained Basic feathering

▶ ♀ Def. Basic Plumage (entire feathering), head–body–tail acquired generally during LATE WINTER or very EARLY SPRING, the wing well along in SUMMER or in EARLY FALL; then head–body–tail and innermost feathers of wing are succeeded by Alt., while the remainder of the Basic wing is retained nearly a year.

Head any dark markings on cheeks are more like spots than streaks. On the **venter**, the dark feathers with light edging are arranged in a more definitely streaked pattern than in Alt. Internal markings of **body feathers** are reduced or absent. Innermost secondaries have rounded ends, are fuscous, with internal pale markings (buffy to buffy brown) and are broadly edged whitish buff on outer web and more brownish on inner. **Wing** essentially as ♂ Def. Basic, the white border at trailing edge of speculum perhaps more often lacking.

AT HATCHING Overall coloring is intermediate between that of the dark Black Duck and paler Mexican Duck, about on a par with the mallard; the eye stripe is complete but thinner than in the Black Duck; legs and feet are dark. (Compare with Mallard, Mexican Duck, and Black Duck.)

▶ ♂ ♀ Juv. Plumage (entire feathering), paler than Black Duck; by age 6–7 weeks the bill of ♂ uniformly light, of ♀ largely dark, the nail dark in both sexes. Venter of ♀ more streaky than ♂.

Other predefinitive stages—little useful information other than that, by late fall, spring-hatched birds are quite similar in general appearance to older age-classes. The shorter Juv. wing, with narrow coverts and innermost secondaries, and muted speculum, is worn for about a year. Bill and feet are decidedly more muted in coloring in birds at estimated age of 6–7 mo. as compared with older age-classes. Since hatching occurs over a period of months, the dating of events in terms of elapsed time posthatching (such as attainment of flight, times of molting) are more or less correspondingly variable.

Measurements of Fla. birds, 21 ♂: BILL 51.1–57.8 mm., av. 54.6; WING (across chord) 237–264, av. 252, TARSUS 42–49.1, av. 45.9; 9 ♀: BILL 49.1–52.1 mm., av. 50.4; WING (across chord) 222–245, av. 234; TARSUS 41.5–45.3 (H. Friedmann).

"Adults" from La. and Texas; 13 ♂: BILL 50.1–63.1 mm., av. 54.9, WING (across chord) 248–264, av. 256, TARSUS 43.1–48.2, av. 45.5; 9 ♀: BILL 47.8–54.9 mm., av.

315

51.7; WING (across chord) 229–253, av. 239; TARSUS 38.1–46.2, av. 42.5 (H. Friedmann).

Another series, wing flattened; 6 ♂ from La.: BILL 53–58 mm., av. 56; WING 255–268, av. 261; TAIL 85–90, av. 88; TARSUS 42–46, av. 45; 8 ♀ (Texas 5, La. 3): BILL 51–60 mm., av. 54.4; WING 239–268, av. 248; TAIL 80–90, av. 85; TARSUS 44–47, av. 45 (ETS).

Weight of "adults" from Fla.: 30 ♂ av. 1,030 ± 107.2 gm. (av. 37 oz.), max. 1,280 (45.5 oz.); 11 ♀ av. 968 ± 76 (34.5 oz.), max. 1,131.8 (40.4 oz.) (Beckwith and Hosford 1957).

Wt. of 22 newly hatched ducklings was 27.5–34.6 gm., mean and standard error being 30.7 ± 0.42 and SD 1.97 (Smart 1965a).

Hybrids in the wild with the Black Duck apparently are few in number, but with the Mallard evidently are more frequent. If kept in captivity with Mallards and Blacks, the Mottled Duck "will indiscriminately mate with the former, but very seldom with the latter" (Delacour 1956). (Also see discussion of hybrids under Mallard and Black Duck.)

Geographical variation evidently is rather slight, the Fla. birds tending to have plainer heads and to be less migratory. Possibly because of some facet of habitat preference, the Mottled Duck is scarce or absent locally from the Fla. panhandle westward nearly to La.—that is, more or less of a gap or hiatus exists in the overall range. Birds e. and w. of the gap were named differently long ago, and were regarded as acceptable subspecies. The existence of the names, plus the gap, probably accounts for acceptance of 2 subspecies by Peters (1931), a state of affairs continued in the 1957 A.O.U. *Check-list*. On the other hand, J. C. Phillips (1923b), who examined a "very large series" of specimens, recognized that individual variation was greater and geographical variation less than previously believed, hence recognition of subspecies was unwarranted. Hellmayr and Conover (1948) concluded similarly. RSP

FIELD IDENTIFICATION   Nearly size of Mallard; dark brownish, except decidedly lighter head and neck. Under favorable conditions one may note that in fall–winter the drake has a yellow bill, the ♀'s being muted orange-yellow with olive markings (in the Black Duck usually it is nearer olive). Although Black Ducks are present seasonally in some parts of the Mottled Duck's range (compare maps), within the usual range of the latter similar-appearing individuals associating in pairs probably are of this species. (Sexes differ greatly in the Mallard.) This characteristic is helpful mainly from about Feb. to June or July. Unlike the ♀ Mallard, the Mottled Duck has an essentially plain head and no white on tail. FCB

VOICE   Like Mallard's, so far as known. FCB

HABITAT   Shallow waters and adjacent land. In Fla.—mainly fresh waters, but also coastal waters, marshes, and in fields; nests on man-made is. in Indian R. estuary. La.—fresh and brackish waters and marshes of coastal parishes; Texas—mainly coastal tier of counties, on fresh and brackish water and adjoining terrain such as marshes, ungrazed fields, and rice stubble. In Mexico—coastal marshes, ponds, and adjoining terrain. In Texas and Mexico occurs on coastal islands having suitable marshes, ponds, etc. RSP

DISTRIBUTION (See map.) In peninsular Fla. this duck apparently has expanded its range n. and w. in recent years, but within its overall range in the state there has been loss of habitat because of drainage, manipulation of water levels, real estate development, and other influences. "The heart" of the range in the state "should presently be considered to be the vicinity of Hendry, Lee, Charlotte and Glade counties" (Chamberlain, Jr., 1960). There is a sight report for Key Largo.

For the Fla. panhandle and Ala. there are various records, the earlier ones having been mapped by Johnsgard (1961).

In Miss. there was a sizable number of these ducks in Hancock Co. in the summer of 1960 (L. E. Williams 1961).

In cent. Kans. (Barton Co.), Mottled Ducks bred in 1963 on the Cheyenne Bottoms Wildlife Refuge; whether or not these birds are migratory is not yet known (McHenry 1968).

At least in Texas, in the postbreeding period, some individuals occur inland beyond the usual range of the species in the state.

In Mexico, breeds in coastal Tamaulipas from the Rio Grande delta s. at least to Tampico; in winter its range extends farther s. along the Gulf Coast to the Alvarado marshes in Veracruz (A. S. Leopold 1959).

Records of **stragglers,** based on specimens taken, include: Kans.—Woodson Co.; Okla.—Washita Co.; Colo.—near Loveland, also 8 mi. e. of Ft. Collins.

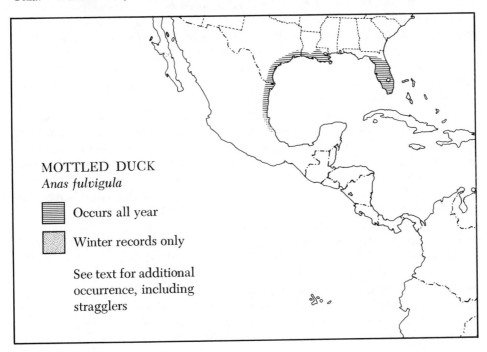

MOTTLED DUCK
Anas fulvigula

Occurs all year

Winter records only

See text for additional
occurrence, including
stragglers

Recorded as **fossil,** from the Pleistocene, at several Fla. localities; also from an **archaeological site** in that state; for full citations, see Brodkorb (1964a). Regarding identity of fossil remains from a Fla. site, Ligon (1965) wrote, "I was unable to separate elements of *Anas platyrhynchos, rubripes,* and *fulvigula,* . . ." RSP

MIGRATION   So far as known, not migratory in peninsular Fla., the few banding returns indicating local seasonal dispersal only. In La., numbers are much reduced during early winter, many birds evidently having migrated w. and then s. along the Gulf Coast; their number has increased again in La. by March. Occurs all year in Texas, but in markedly fewer numbers in winter, indicating migration. In Mexico, the number present is greater in winter, indicating presence of migrants; also, the species occurs farther s. in Mexico in that season. RSP

BANDING STATUS   Total number banded was 1,751 through the year 1964 and total number of recoveries was 103 through 1961; they were banded in Fla., La., and Texas (data from Bird Banding Laboratory). RSP

REPRODUCTION   The following activities have been observed and are identical with those of the Mallard: Inciting, Grunt-whistle, Head-up-tail-up, Nod-swim, Turning-the-back-of-the-head, Down-up, copulatory behavior, and pursuit flights (trio-flying).

The data given below are based on studies in the interior of Fla. in the L. Okeechobee region (Beckwith and Hosford 1957), the Indian R. estuary of e. coastal Fla. (Stieglitz and Wilson 1968), and coastal counties of Texas (Singleton 1953).

Pair formation occurs in winter and the birds are at nesting localities beginning in late Feb. or early March. For the species as a whole, **nesting** is exceptional in Feb., frequent in March, with peak during April, and later (mostly replacement) clutches are laid thereafter until into July or Aug. In Texas, the nest usually is within 1,000 ft. of permanent or semipermanent water, on a ridge above tide in coastal marshes, on ungrazed grassy areas inland, or even in rice stubble with little or no concealment. In Indian R. estuary in Fla., on "spoil" islands (man-made, from dredging channels) .05–6.1 acres in size, commonly in *Paspalum vaginatum* which grows about 15–24 in. high, or near a change or break in cover such as a bare area or abrupt bank. In this locality, 88 nests were 6–79 (mostly 10–40) ft., av. 27.8 ft. from water. The islands, which will become unsuited to the ducks because of vegetational succession and erosion, are little used except for nesting; perhaps there is a lack of suitable loafing sites thereabouts, since the drakes go to water impoundments on Merritt I.

The duck lines a shallow depression with dry vegetation, obtained at the site. In the Indian R. estuary, first **eggs** in 43 nests in 1966 were laid March 6–June 25 (midpoint March 29) and in 63 nests in 1967, first eggs Feb. 11–July 17 (midpoint April 3). The peak of nest building was March 1–April 15. Clutch initiation declined in May and probably consisted of renesting attempts from then on. The duck covers the early eggs with vegetation before leaving the nest; after the 5th or 6th egg, the nest down is deposited over a period of time and is intermingled with plant materials. In nest maintenance, the rim may be built up several in. by the time of hatching.

318

Eggs are laid at a rate of 1 per 24 hrs. In Texas, size of 108 **clutches** was 7–14 eggs, av. 10.4. In Indian R. estuary, 5–13 eggs in 78 clutches, with av. 10.1 before May 1 and 8.9 afterward, i.e., late (presumed replacement) clutches are an egg smaller. The duck deserts readily if disturbed during laying or early in incubation, but some are close sitters later on. In Fla. some ♀ ♀ could be touched while on the eggs; occasionally a ♀ defecated on the clutch when flushed from it. The duck probably leaves twice daily. There are several records (from Texas) of 3 attempts by the same bird to renest; predation by dogs, raccoons, snakes, Boat-tailed Grackles, and man, result in repeated attempts to produce a brood which, in turn, is preyed upon by turtles, alligators, large fish, and so on. One ♀ built 5 nests (she deserted the first 4) and laid 34 eggs: March 23—nest + 6 eggs; March 27—n. + 3; April 1—n + 5 (+ 1 the next day); April 12—n + 8, later 10, which hatched May 31.

One **egg** each from 20 clutches (Fla. 16, Texas 4) **size** length 56.74 ± 1.71 mm., breadth 43.19 ± 1.63, radii of curvature of ends 17.31 ± 1.14 and 13.97 ± 1.02, **shape** between elliptical and subelliptical, elongation 1.30 ± 0.038, bicone −0.049, asymmetry +0.102 (FWP). For Fla., Bent (1923) reported 52 eggs av. 57 × 44.3 mm., for La.–Texas 75 av. 54.9 × 40.5 mm. From Fla., 10 eggs from 2 (probably replacement) clutches av. 55.2 × 40.6 mm., largest 60 × 45, smallest 51 × 38. Shell smooth; **color** pale buff, sometimes greenish, occasionally pale tan. **Incubation period** in the wild 25–27 days (both Fla. and Texas data); clutch of 9 under a domestic hen hatched in 24 days; 2 clutches in an incubator required 26 days. In the Indian R. estuary, the hatching peak was the last half of April in 1966 and first half of May in 1967. In this area, 78 clutches contained 739 eggs; there were 612 eggs in successful nests and 573 (93.6%) of these hatched; that is, an av. of 9 ducklings in successful nests. See both Singleton (1953) and Stieglitz and Wilson (1968) for egg losses and predation.

At about the normal hatching time, in last half of April or into May, the drake departs (in Texas, apparently to the coast), and the duck tends the brood.

In Texas, at 8 weeks posthatching, 17 surviving broods av. 6.1 ducklings.

In penned young, sides and breast are partly feathered at age 4 weeks; breast, belly, sides, and back at 5 weeks; all except wings fully feathered at 6 weeks; wings almost fully developed at 8 weeks; and 10-week-old young hardly are distinguishable in flight from mature birds.

In the wild in Fla. the ducklings are very terrestrial, presumably to avoid aquatic predators which occur in abundance (LaHart and Cornwell 1971).

Age at first flight in the wild estimated as 54–60 days. RSP

SURVIVAL   The only information is for preflight birds in Fla., the few data indicating a greater decrease through this period in brood size than in other members of the Mallard group; see LaHart and Cornwell (1971) for details. RSP

HABITS   A marsh duck primarily. The following figures mostly are from Johnsgard's summary. Fla. numbers in the period 1948–55 varied from 17,000 to 30,000 and later, in the 1950s, because of hunting pressure and loss of habitat, probably dropped below 10,000. In Texas in 1947–52, the av. was over 7,000 in Oct. (max. 23,000 in 1947), decreasing to an av. minimum of 1,000–2,000 Nov. through Feb.; estimated summer numbers in 26,000 sq. mi. in 1952 was 18,500 in March and 31,000 in Aug. Evidently rather few breed in Mexico, though some thousands of migrants winter there. In fall of 1966 there were an estimated 50,000 Mottled Ducks in Fla., with a hunting kill of 14,900 (Stieglitz and Wilson 1968). Recent Jan. inventories for conterminous U.S.: 72,100 in 1968, 81,200 in 1969, and 66,000 in 1970. RSP

FOOD Stomachs collected from Fla. to Texas gave about 60% plant and 40% animal; while in the vicinity of L. Okeechobee (Fla.) the food consisted of 87% plant and 13% animal matter. Seeds of grasses and sedges, and stems, leaves, and rootstalks of aquatic plants form the most important items. The animal food consists mainly of mollusks, insects, crustaceans, and fish.

Vegetable Throughout its range, based on 48 stomachs, mainly Gramineae, followed by smartweeds *(Polygonum* spp.) 9.5%, seeds, and tubers of sedges (Cyperaceae) 6.5%, seeds of waterlilies (Nymphaeaceae) and coontail *(Ceratophyllum demersum)* 3%. Seeds of buttonbush *(Cephalanthus occidentalis)* and of bayberry *(Myrica* spp.) were of some importance (McAtee 1918, A. C. Martin et al. 1951).

The examination of 144 stomachs from L. Okeechobee showed that the important foods in spring were panicum *(Panicum* sp.), ragweed *(Ambrosia elatior)*, fringeleaf paspalum *(Paspalum ciliatifolium)*, bristle grass *(Setaria geniculata)*, choisy *(Jacquemontia sp.)* and smartweed *(Persicaria (Polygonum) punctata)*; and in fall redtop panicum, smartweed, carpet grass *(Axonopus furcatus)*, *Centella repanda*, and paspalums *(P. ciliatifolium, P. dissectum)* (Beckwith and Hosford 1957).

Along the La. coast, wild millet *(Echinochloa crus-galli)*, panic grass *(Panicum)*, foxtail *(Chaetochloa)*, and cultivated rice *(Oryza sativa)*, chufa *(Cyperus esculentus)*, Fimbrystylis, bulrush *(Scirpus)*, nut rush *(Scleria)*, beak rush *(Rynchospora)*, saw grass *(Cladium effusum)*, and spike rush *(Eleocharis)*; pickerelweed *(Pontederia cordata)*, naiad *(Najas)*, duckweed *(Lemna)*, banana waterlily *(Nymphaea flava)*, and smartweed *(Polygonum)*. In fall and winter chiefly seeds of feather grass *(Leptochloa fascicularis)*, panic grass *(P. dichotomiflorum)*, and wild millets *(E. crus-galli, E. walteri)* (McIlhenny 1943).

Animal Largely mollusks (Gastropoda), some snails being an inch in diameter, larvae of caddis flies (Trichoptera), nymphs of dragonflies (Odonata) larvae of flies (Diptera), water bugs (Belostomatidae), and water beetles (Hydrophilidae, Dytiscidae, Haliplidae), crayfish (Crustacea), and fishes (McAtee 1918). At L. Okeechobee insects formed 18.3% of the diet in spring, 38.7% in summer, and were minor the remainder of the year (Beckwith and Hosford 1957). Two Fla. birds contained shells of *Truncatella subcylindrica* and *Odostomia impressa* (F. C. Baker 1980). AWS

Recently Stieglitz (1972) reported on contents of 85 gizzards from 2 Fla. counties, the localities including glades and brackish marsh habitats. **Plant** materials consisted mainly of *Naias, Rhynchospora, Polygonum, Diplanthera, Cladium,* and *Chara;* the most important **animal** foods were gastropods, pelecypods, and insects (including larvae). See his paper for food species and their production as related to various habitats. RSP

American Black Duck

Anas rubripes Brewster

Sexes superficially similar (there are some differences in head profile, feather markings, etc.); size as Mallard. Definitive stages: bill yellowish to greenish olive (varying with sex and season) with dark nail; most of head and neck (down to include where the collar occurs in the drake Mallard) light to medium brownish or grayed buff with fine markings (usually dark streaking); dark crown and nape, not sharply delineated; dark stripe through eye variable in length and clarity (sometimes obscure, or may even merge with crown); body some variant of dark fuscous brownish, the feathers having buffy brownish margins that are most conspicuous on upper sides and flanks; legs and feet in the brownish–fleshy–scarlet range (vary with age, sex, and season); no barring on 11th–13th secondaries ("tertials"); bluish purple speculum with, commonly, a narrow white bar at trailing edge only (but, in some individuals, obscure or lacking even on that edge); upper wing coverts patterned like dorsum, the lining of the wing light (mostly white). Juv. Plumage more streaked, especially ventrally. The Black Duck's tracheal apparatus has been described by various authors, including Audubon; the drake's bulla is similar to that of Mallard (J. C. Phillips 1923b).

Length 22–26 in., wingspread 33–37, ♂ av. larger within these spans; in their 2nd year and older, drakes weigh 2½–3¼ lb., ♀ 2¼–2¾. The Black Duck is regarded here as a species, not as a subspecies of *A. platyrhynchos*, having some clinal size variation.

DESCRIPTION Two Plumages/cycle in both sexes. All Plumages known in the Mallard are present and occur in the same sequence (are homologous) in the Black and they are described in the same order under each of these species in this volume. In any Plumage, in either sex of Black, the most noticeable individual variation, which is considerable, consists of relative amount of dark internal area vs. width of the light (buffy brownish) edging on the feathers. For internal (concealed) markings and other characteristics of feathers on side of breast, see text fig. The definitive Plumages of the drake are clearly dimorphic, in Basic being plain internally (in material examined, except sometimes a curved mark in late-incoming feathers of Basic I) and in Alt. having an inverted U- or a lyre-shaped mark. In the ♀, Basic feathers evidently always are plain within the dark area, but Alts. vary with individual from internally plain to indefinitely marked to clearly marked with an inverted V (or may have this on middle of breast but not laterally). The scapulars of the various Plumages of both sexes were figured by Palmer (in Farner and King 1972: chap. 2). (Also see discussion of variation and hybridism at end of this section.)

▶ ♂ Def. Alt. Plumage (all feathering except, in wing, only a few innermost feathers) acquired SUMMER–EARLY FALL and worn through WINTER into following early SUMMER. **Bill** yellowish, grading toward olive basally, frequently with a small amount of black at side base, and black nail. **Iris** deep brownish (much darker than ♀). **Head** crown and upper nape vary with individual from solid dark to narrowly streaked light, often with considerable iridescent greenish feathering; generally a dark stripe through eye (which also may be greenish); remainder of head and most of the neck variable, buffy brownish to more grayish, generally with abundant irregular fine dark streaking. **Upperparts** the dark feathers generally have no light internal markings but have nar-

321

row light edging (scaled effect in new feathering); occasionally a tapering, pointed, scapular has a buffy line within the outer (wider) vane. **Underparts** most feathers have broadly rounded (toward squarish) ends, their light margins often widest across the end, and a poorly defined light V (its point aimed distally) astride the shaft. Feathers on upper sides of breast, anterior to folded wing, are variable both as to presence or absence and to shape of internal light marking; typically, many are U-shaped in the drake. Flank feathers long, tapering, with light borders, and internally plain (dark) in some birds and with buffy line within 1 or both vanes in others. **Tail** feathers dark, any paler

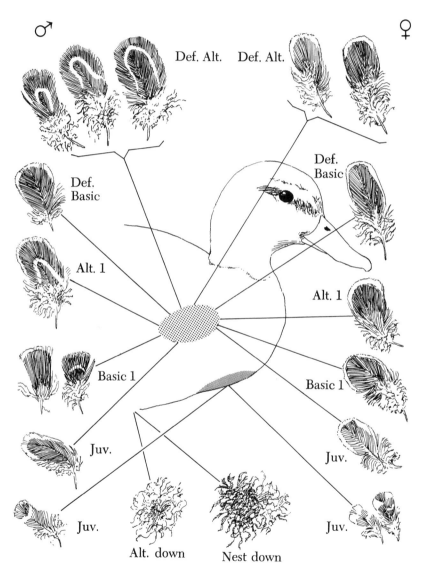

322

edging being mostly on outer vane and width varies depending on individual. Legs and feet vary from somewhat brownish red toward vivid coral red, the webs black. **Wing** is retained Basic (described below) except: tapering, innermost secondaries ("tertials") are plain, dark, with narrow light edge on outer vane, and their greater coverts also are bicolored.

This is a comparatively dark Plumage, especially anterior body, which contrasts greatly with head–neck. In new feathering, much of the ventral surface tends to be beautifully scalloped rich brown on very dark. With wear, various feather margins become frayed or lost, so that the body becomes more uniformly dark-colored.

This Plumage is acquired as in the Mallard; that is, some time well along in summer or in early fall after the Basic head–body feathering is present and the wing quills are dropped, the bird molts again (while the new Basic wing also is growing) into Alt. head–body–tail. Sometimes the tail is renewed gradually, a few Basic feathers being retained until well along in fall or even later.

NOTES   A few Black Ducks of both sexes have buffy tan or even rusty chin, throat, and feather margins on venter; this is ferrous staining.

The variation in Def. Alt. apparently is geographical to an unknown extent. One might define an ultratypical drake as having no internal markings on feathers of anterior dorsum, lyre-shaped markings on feathers of forward sides, and flank feathers ummarked internally and with comparatively narrow pale borders. In ♀ Def. Alt., such an individual has feathers on forward sides that are plain internally, but those on middle of breast have an inverted light V (not U- or lyre-shaped).

▶   ♂ Def. Basic Plumage (entire feathering) worn a few weeks at most, beginning in SUMMER, the wing (except for some innermost feathers) retained until following summer. Characterized by broadly rounded feather ends and this accentuated by the even width of the tan borders, especially on venter and sides; the various feathers are plain (unmarked) internally. **Bill** mostly muted olive. **Head** face and much of neck quite ♀-like, the dark markings on pale base not in streaked arrangement. **Upperparts** feathers plain dark with narrow pale borders, the scapulars comparatively short and rounded (not tapering at end). **Underparts** feathers without gloss and with fairly even brownish buff margins (scaled effect) and without internal U-shaped marking (or such are faintly indicated); feathers of sides and flanks smallish, terminally rounded (not tapering), with fairly even brownish buff margins, very marked scaly effect. Legs and feet usually between muted scarlet-orange and tawny, webs black.

Wing much of upper surface resembles dorsum in color and pattern; coverts broad, with rounded ends; greater primary coverts plain dark, rarely with very narrow pale edging terminally on broader vane (it soon wears off); most other coverts margined buffy brown; greater secondary coverts bordering the speculum have black ends, forming a bar or stripe at leading edge of ultramarine-violet speculum, and sometimes there is more or less of a thin or poorly defined white line forward of this black stripe; the secondaries of the speculum have broad black ends, then vary with individual bird from white at very tip (forming broad black and narrow white stripes at trailing edge) to ends solid black; the 2 other (lateral) borders of the speculum are black; the iridescent area of the speculum usually extends distally on the wing to include all secondaries except the outermost one; the innermost secondaries are shorter, more rounded, than

323

in Alt. plumage; in the wing lining, many greater coverts are light gray, the others white, except that some sooty-fuscous coverts with whitish margins generally are present beyond the bend of the wing; axillars white.

The Basic head–body–tail are acquired in SUMMER, usually beginning some time in June or very early July; the flightless period (duration unknown, probably as Mallard) comes later, generally beginning before the end of July; and beginning in Aug. or early Sept. (while the new Basic wing is growing) the head–body–tail and innermost feathers of wing molt back into Alt. Even after the new Alt. is acquired, quite often some old Basic coverts still are retained along the leading edge of the wing; often they are present (in both sexes) into fall or even early winter.

▶ ♀ Def. Alt. Plumage (all feathering except, in wing, only a few innermost feathers) acquired in FALL (later than in ♂) and worn until LATE WINTER or SPRING. **Bill** some variant of olive, usually with dark markings that merge into a black patch on midsection of upper mandible, nail blackish. **Iris** medium brownish (lighter than ♂). Compared with ♂ Def. Alt.: **head** generally more light streaking on crown; no greenish in crown or nape; dark stripe through eye often better defined; much of face–neck more heavily marked (dark on light) with less streaky arrangement of markings. **Body** overall shade of coloring av. somewhat lighter, because buffy brown feather margins av. wider; scapulars dark, plain except for very narrow light margins, tapering but terminally rounded; central breast feathers buffy terminally and along their sides and, within the dark portion, in some individuals, a well-defined V-shaped pale marking, but other individuals have this vaguely indicated or merely have the feather grading to only slightly less dark basally; regardless of ventral feathering, the V-marking occurs on feathers of upper side just anterior to folded wing. Flank feathers without internal marking (at least in specimens examined) and grade to less dark basally. **Legs and feet** muted fleshy orange, webs black. **Wing** is retained Basic (described below) except: the long innermost secondaries which have pale outer webs or at least pale edging, and the longest overlying coverts which have a subterminal blackish zone, then pale (usually light brownish) edging.

NOTE Compared with the drake, the lateral light feather margins possibly are somewhat wider, hence the duck, after the feather ends are much worn, tends to appear somewhat more streaky than the drake. In new feathering, the breast does not appear darker than the belly, as it often does in the drake.

▶ ♀ Def. Basic Plumage (entire feathering) worn from LATE WINTER or SPRING to LATE SUMMER or EARLY FALL, the wing (except for a few innermost feathers) retained until following late summer. This Plumage has a "washed-out" appearance, the **head–neck** toward whitish buff and marked with shorter streaks than in Alt.; feather edges on **sides** and **venter** palish, contrasting more with the plain dark internal areas. The **bill** generally becomes dark bluish or greenish olive with very dark saddle, also typically a small dark area at side base, and black nail. Many feathers are shorter, with more broadly rounded ends, than in Alt. Plumage. Scapulars essentially as in ♂ Def. Basic; innermost secondaries somewhat rounded distally and without pale edging; and their greater coverts nearly plain; all breast feathers lack internal V-shaped light marking. **Legs and feet** more or less brownish yellow or very grayed orange. **Wing** essentially as described for ♂ Def. Basic except: iridescent area usually does not extend onto the 2 (or sometimes 3) most distal secondaries.

324

This feathering, especially on underparts, becomes very worn and ragged as the season advances. Broken feathers are common. The duck and her brood part company, usually about the time when the latter become able to fly. Soon the old Basic wing quills drop and the flightless period begins. Then the head–body–tail molt back into Alt. beginning during the span when the Basic wing is growing (and thus is "offset" from the rest of the same Basic feather generation).

AT HATCHING   Compared with the Mallard (which see), the eye stripe is heavier, complete, and black; there is an obscure auricular spot (no cheek stripe); yellows are toward orange, but the venter is a "dirty" neutral color; legs and feet dark. (Also compare with Mottled and Mexican Duck.)

▶   ♂ Juv. Plumage (entire feathering), fully developed when or soon after flight attained, then most of it replaced in LATE SUMMER–EARLY FALL, except almost all of wing retained through winter into following summer.

Head–body feathering develops rapidly and covers the bird well at a time when wing quills show hardly any growth. Some time in the preflight stage the **bill** is dark greenish olive; some time after flight is attained it pales to almost entirely greenish. **Iris** dark. **Head** crown nearly solid dark (though not as dark as in later Plumages); face and neck av. more brownish than in later Plumages and have very fine dark streaking. Most body feathers comparatively narrow and with rounded (not squarish) ends. **Upperparts** the fuscous feathers have pale (brownish buff) margins that are, usually, interrupted at end of the feather and thus produce a streaked effect. Scapulars somewhat tapering, then rounded at end, with poorly defined buffy brown border around terminal third of the feathers. **Underparts** dark central zone in the feathers fairly broad, the lateral (light) margins correspondingly narrow—total effect of rather broken heavy darkish streaking with reduced warm buffy brown. **Tail** feathers pointed, with notched ends. Legs and **feet** in preflight stage dusky with black webs, but gradually become pale fleshy (except webs). **Wing** (compared with Basic wing): innermost secondaries short and narrow; greater coverts over the secondaries have less clearly delineated dark tips (may be brown, apparently never any white); smaller coverts narrow with rather angular (not rounded) ends; at least several of the outermost primary coverts have their wider vane light edged; wing lining mostly white; axillars white.

Early-hatched young are losing the notched Juv. tail feathers by very early Sept. and others lose them some time thereafter until very late fall, occasionally later.

▶   ♀ Juv. Plumage (entire feathering), timing, etc., as ♂, except most of wing is retained even longer, well into or through the duck's first brood period.

Principal differences from ♂ Juv.: **crown** generally has much fine light streaking; **upperparts** pale feather margins are more toward whitish, av. wider, and taper to side end of feather; **underparts** the median dark portion of each feather is comparatively narrow and often broken by a broad transverse bar (or portions of one), toward whitish buff like the lateral and broad terminal margins, total effect very broken dark streaking on whitish buff background. **Wing** as in ♂.

▶   ♂ Basic I Plumage (fragmentary), fleeting, generally present briefly some time in FALL, then succeeded by Alt. I. Includes some feathering on head, neck, more or less of breast, and occasionally is more extensive (scattered feathers on mantle, sides, and flanks). The Basic I feathers are very dark internally, with rich brown margins, and are much more broadly rounded distally than the antecedent Juv. feathers. Occasionally late-incoming Basic I feathers show an Alt. character, an internal pale curved mark. All Basic I feathers appear to be loosely attached and readily fall out. The tail feathers which succeed the notched Juv. ones (from early Sept. onward) may be assignable to Basic I rather than the Plumage described next.

▶ ♂ Alt. I Plumage (all feathering except, in wing, only a few innermost feathers), acquired by a molt in FALL during which the Alt. replaces most of the Juv. and all of the fragmentary Basic I, then is worn through WINTER into SUMMER. **Bill** becomes light greenish yellow, generally with a small amount of black at side base, and blackish nail. **Crown** variable, often solid dark, in some with greenish sheen (less than in later Alts.), and in some narrowly streaked light. Feathering, in general, like later Alts. except various feathers not as wide, the long scapulars tapering but still not pointed at end. On **upperparts** the light feather margins often are not continuous across the ends of the feathers. **Underparts** seem to be more variable than in later Alts.; that is, the dark portion of breast feathers varies from rather straight sided and extending to end of the feather (so that the lateral lighter areas are wide and separated—streaked effect) to dark portion enclosed (light margin encircles end of feather—scaled effect). The breast feathers have, within the dark area, a sharply defined pale inverted U or a somewhat lyre-shaped marking. Legs and **feet** become orange-salmon, with black webs. Sometimes some faded, tapering, notched Juv. tail feathers remain into winter, rarely longer. In the **wing,** in fall (late Sept.–late Nov.), the Juv. innermost secondaries are succeeded by elongated, pointed, Alt. I feathers and during this molting there generally also is replacement of some of the innermost greater coverts. The remainder of the wing is retained Juv. feathering.

▶ ♀ Basic I Plumage (evidently more extensive than in ♂) perhaps present longer than in ♂ in FALL; may include considerable of head and body and most or all of tail. **Head** and neck rather evenly colored (quite different from Juv.) and with clearly defined dark markings; the feathers on **body** are dark (especially toward ends), broadly rounded, plain internally (on venter, very different from Juv.), and margined some variant of brownish buff. This Plumage succeeds the Juv. quite rapidly, beginning at estimated age of 8–9 weeks; before all of it is acquired, part of it already may be in the process of being succeeded by Alt. I.

▶ ♀ Alt. I Plumage (all feathering except, in wing, only a few innermost feathers), acquired in FALL (late Sept. to late Nov.) and retained until LATE WINTER or EARLY SPRING. **Bill** becomes greenish yellow, heavily marked black; **iris** lighter than ♂. Differs from ♂ Alt. I thus: **head** no green sheen on crown; av. more light streaking on crown; pale portion of head–neck tends to be more heavily streaked dark; on **dorsum** the feather margins tend to be more toward grayish buff than brownish buff; in some individuals on forward sides in the (concealed) dark portion of the feathers there is an inverted pale V-mark; the **venter** appears slightly more streaked than is common to drakes of approximately the same age. Legs and **feet** generally a muted flesh color (seldom much orange or salmon), joints dark, webs blackish. The molting extends onto the wing so as to include some new pointed innermost secondaries and some of the overlying greater coverts. The remainder of the wing is retained Juv. feathering.

Measurements of a series of specimens from all parts of range, 12 ♂: BILL 51–60 mm., av. 56.2; WING 259–296, av. 284.7; TAIL 90–99, av. 94; TARSUS 44–51, av.

47.2; 12 ♀: BILL 47–54 mm., av. 50.4; WING 259–274, av. 265.7; TAIL 81–90 (+ one at 96), av. 87.6; TARSUS 40–46, av. 43.3 (ETS). Another series, WING meas. across chord: 27 ♂ 259–292 mm., av. 274.7 and 17 ♀ 249–267 mm., av. 260.6 (H. Friedmann).

Weight of fall birds in Mass.: ♂ 376 "adult" 2 lb.–3 lb. 14 oz. (0.9–1.8 kg.), av. 3 lb. 1 oz. (1.4 kg.) and 564 "juvenile" (1st fall) 1 lb. 12 oz.–3 lb. 7 oz. (0.8–1.5 kg.), av. 2 lb. 10 oz. (1.2 kg.); ♀ 176 "adult" 2 lb.–3 lb. 4 oz. (0.9–1.5 kg.), av. 2 lb. 8 oz. (1.1 kg.) and 540 "juvenile" 1 lb. 10 oz.–3 lb. 4 oz. (0.7–1.5 kg.), av. 2 lb. 6 oz. (1.0 kg.) (G. F. Pushee Jr.).

For a much smaller fall series from New Bruns. and Que. with maximum wt. of ♂ at 4 lb., see B. S. Wright (1954). Some 3,000 other fall wts. are on record, by sex but a few also by age-class. Example: 366 ♂ av. 2.7 lb., max. 3.8 and 297 ♀ av. 2.4, max. 3.3 (A. L. Nelson and Martin 1953).

Twenty-five newly hatched young weighed 27.3–37.2 gm., the mean and standard error being 31.3 ± 0.47 and SD 2.36 (Smart 1965a).

Variation (individual, geographical) and **hybridism.** For decades after Brewster (1902) described subspecies in the Black Duck, there was controversy over whether to adopt his viewpoint. The matter has been decided, so to speak, pro and con at different times.

Feathering—the Plumages and molts of the Black are homologous with those of the Mallard. In the Black, occurrence and extent of individual variation in characteristics of feathering has been underestimated.

Soft-part coloration—varies greatly with age, sex, and season (Shortt 1943) and geographical variation in this coloring is inconsequential.

Size—age for age and sex for sex, northerly birds are larger. This was shown to a slight extent in Brewster's 1902 paper. Judging from specimens handled (but not measured) by the writer, an av. size difference between breeding birds say from Md. and from northerly portions of Que. apparently is greater than would be suspected from reading Brewster's paper. Blacks from southerly breeding range and northward to include N.Y., New Eng., and at least part of the Maritimes are comparatively small; somewhere northward beyond the trend is to larger size. Fall flights southward, after about Oct. 20, on the Atlantic coast and in the interior, are of larger birds, a matter well understood by gunners and by certain waterfowl banders. Large birds taken beginning in early Nov. in N.Y. and New Eng. are in full Alt. Plumage and drakes especially tend to have any light streaking on the crown comparatively wide, and dark markings on face and neck tend to be large (occasionally nearer spotting than streaking), on a light background, so that head–neck contrasts more with the body than in southerly birds.

Hybridism—an unsolved problem has to do with whether certain commonly occurring Mallard-like characteristics occur in "pure" Black Duck stock or whether they reflect some degree of secondary contact (recent hybridism) with the Mallard. Examples: few to many iridescent greenish feathers in dark of head (crown, eye stripe, upper nape) of drake in Alt. Plumage; bronzy green sheen on dorsum, especially rump, of drake in new Alt. Plumage; more or less of a thin white line at leading edge of speculum; some bending up of central tail feathers, again in ♂ Alt. Plumage. At least the first 2 probably are inherent ("latent," J. C. Phillips 1912) Mallard characters in

327

pure Black Duck stock; that is, probably they occurred widely in Blacks in former times when the 2 species had essentially separate ranges. All of them, however, occur in F_1 crosses with Mallard. Variations in ♀ Blacks are not as readily singled out as Mallard-like. (Also see under Mallard for current extensive overlap in geographical ranges of the 2 species and for limited hybridization.)

It is exceedingly unusual for a Black Duck of breeding age from the latitude of New Eng. to have the face and neck plain or with very few dark markings; down the Atlantic coast, however, such plainness, which is a common condition in the Mottled Duck (*A. fulvigula*), occurs occasionally. This characteristic may be inherent in more southerly Black Duck stock, or indicate limited hybridizing with *fulvigula*, or perhaps occurs in either circumstance.

To recapitulate, the Black has considerable individual variation in characters of feathering, some geographical variation in these, some clinal variation in size (larger northward), and the effects of limited crossing with Mallard and perhaps Mottled Duck are somewhat obscured by imprecise knowledge of the full extent of variation in "pure" Black Ducks. For further information the reader is referred to J. C. Phillips (1912), but especially his later paper on experimental crossing of Mallards and Blacks (J. C. Phillips 1915), and to Johnsgard (1961a). RSP

FIELD IDENTIFICATION   Size and general shape of Mallard. On water, uniformly dark body and wings with lighter neck and head, but no well-defined markings. In flight, silvery wing lining contrasts with dark of rest of wings and body. Flight characteristics as Mallard. Near-vertical ascent from water or land, as other dabblers.

Sexes differ somewhat in proportions, more in color of soft parts. Fully mature ♂ is larger, more thickset, than ♀; head more puffy, neck thicker; bill (except late summer) yellow vs. olive with dusky mottling in ♀. First-fall birds are somewhat smaller, slimmer, than older birds of corresponding sex, and have underparts streaky rather than scaly. Their feet are more brownish, not the vivid reddish of older birds. A drake in first fall lacks the puffy head and neck of older age-classes and the bill is more greenish and mottled. Such young drakes usually are larger, longer necked, and with less mottled bill than ♀♀ of corresponding age, but the sexes are not easily distinguishable by external criteria. After Dec., birds of the year are not separable in the field from older age-classes; that is, they develop the characteristics of full maturity and the sexes, rather than ages, become more easily distinguishable.

The most common hybrids are with the Mallard; see earlier discussion in this account, also data under Mallard.

The sexes and all ages of Black Duck are darker than the Mottled and Mexican Ducks and ♀ Mallard. Compare with these. In the Black, ashore or afloat, if any white shows at all in the wing it is the narrow trailing border of the speculum. The head of the Black Duck is less chunky, the neck longer and slimmer, than scoters. JAH

VOICE   Evidently very similar to that of the better-known Mallard. Voice of ♀ about 1 tone lower than Mallard, on E_2; a series of quacks sometimes begins with prolonged sound *kwa-a-a-k*, followed by shorter ones grading down in pitch; voice of drake about as Mallard (A. A. Saunders). Some vocalizing is mentioned in context under "Reproduction." RSP

HABITAT At different places and seasons found on fresh, brackish, and salt water, from confined woodland pools to broad bays and around offshore ocean ledges; in swamps and marshes of every sort from flooded closed-canopy hardwoods to open coastal meadows; on brooks, ponds, lakes and rivers whether bordered by city parks or wilderness; on tidal flats along the coast; less frequently in upland grain stubble, and in the north on berry barrens. On the whole, makes greater use of wooded habitat than other *Anas* species.

Breeding habitats and nest sites are so diverse that the presence of water, no matter how restricted, is virtually the only characteristic in common. Even the relationship of the site to water varies widely: many nests are in tussocks of grass or clumps of bushes in marsh or swamp, surrounded by water; many others on sloping shores or banks not far from the water's edge, under cover of grasses, herbs, briers, bushes, small conifers, or brush piles; some on grassy or woodland hillsides from 100 yds. to a mile or more from water, with no obvious reason for choice of sites; a few in tops of rotted stumps, in cavities and crotches of large willows and maples near or over water (for tree nesting see especially Cowardin et al. 1967), and in abandoned nests of other large birds. Examples: cordgrass marshes of St. Lawrence estuary and middle Atlantic coast, typically nests on high places in patches of last year's dead grass; New Eng., nests on offshore is. that are mostly rocky, about natural cranberry bogs in coastal sand dunes, on small salt-marsh is., in and about freshwater cattail and *Sparganium* marshes and brushy bogs, along woodland brooks, in thicket of low blueberry bushes under tall white pines 1,300 ft. from nearest water; Maritime Provinces, in diked hay meadows along the coast, in and about freshwater marshes and bogs, in overgrown pastures, under young spruce trees on wooded hillsides overlooking marshes and streams, and in river valleys subject to extensive spring flooding, rather frequently in large cavities of old trees; in the coniferous forest zone in Ont. and much of Que., on islets, islands, and peninsulas in beaver flowages, natural ponds, and lakes.

Breeding densities, even in favorable habitat, are very much lower than for other dabbling ducks. Gross (1945) recorded 8 nests or broods from a coastal island containing only "a few acres," but this is atypical because of probable radial arrangement of territories. Islands in freshwater lakes sometimes have relatively high densities of Blacks (also Mallards). Mendall (1949a) described an increase of nesting pairs on a 70-acre managed marsh from 6 before improvement to 12 afterward. B. S. Wright (1954) estimated 1 pair to 39 acres for optimum natural range in New Bruns. in a single year; estimates for cordgrass meadow in s. N.J. and in Md. are comparable. For areas of considerable extent, particularly if terrain and habitat types are varied, higher densities are unlikely and the av. is very much lower. See R. E. Stewart (1958) for estimates based on major habitat types.

Spring and **fall** migration habitats are too diverse to warrant listing; the species may appear on or near any water, in numbers roughly proportional to available food supply and lack of disturbance.

Winter habitat is more restricted than at other seasons. In general, most of the population is compressed into relatively narrow strips along Atlantic coast and larger river valleys of e.-cent. interior, south of ice line. Primary requirements at this season are food, correlated largely with open water, and partial freedom from disturbance. In area of principal concentration (Atlantic coast from N.J. to N.C.), preferred habitat is chiefly brackish marshes bordering bays and estuaries, but includes freshwater marshes, swamps, rivers and creeks, old ricefields, reservoirs, impoundments, and smaller ponds and pools. In Mississippi and Ohio valleys, similar diversity of freshwater types is occupied, with more extensive use, locally, of stubble fields and flooded woodland. A third division of winter range, n. Atlantic coast from Cape Cod to Nfld., represents a major adaptation by the Black Ducks wintering there. Essentially maritime, its habitability depends on strong tidal fluctuations to maintain open water in cold weather; food is gleaned from bare flats and exposed shell banks and ledges at low tide, from surface of salt meadows, and from floating beds of kelp and rockweeds at high tide. For Me., also see F. E. Hartman (1963).

Wintering density of Blacks tends to be highest in ne. maritime habitat, median in middle Atlantic brackish habitat, lowest in freshwater habitat of interior; these densities are correlated with total food supplies available during most severe part of winter. JAH

DISTRIBUTION (See map.) During later glaciations, before ancestral "Mallard stock" became appreciably dimorphic sexually, a portion of it was isolated in essentially maritime environment in ne. N. Am. It continued to evolve into the present Black Duck and, in more recent warmer times, has expanded its range. This hypothesis is adequate to explain why both the physical characteristics and some facets of the life cycle of the Black differ from those of the Mallard. (The latter, after becoming dimorphic in the Palearctic, entered N. Am. with the waning of the ice; it is an interior and more open-country bird.)

It is probable that, a century ago, the breeding area of the Black did not extend westward much beyond L. Erie and cent. Ont. Areas where this duck has occurred as a regular breeder inland, especially in the conterminous U.S., continue to become bet-

330

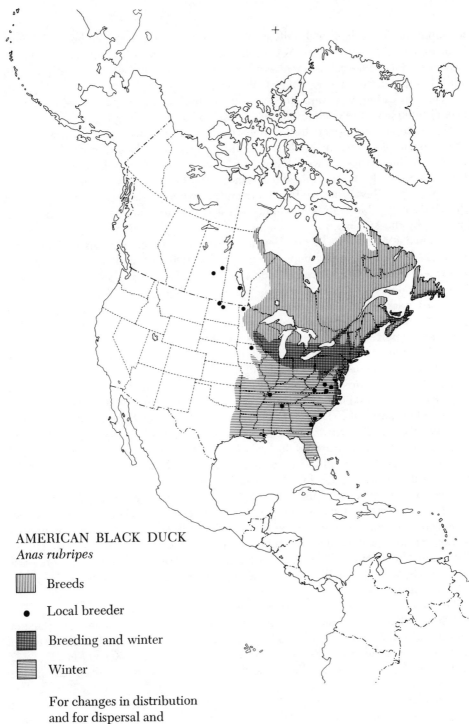

AMERICAN BLACK DUCK
Anas rubripes

||| Breeds

• Local breeder

▓ Breeding and winter

|| Winter

For changes in distribution
and for dispersal and
stragglers, see text

ter suited to the Mallard (naturally-occurring and introduced stock) through change from woodland to agriculture. Yet the Black continues to adjust to change. The w. movement includes establishment as a breeder in Minn. perhaps as recently as 1910 and it has spread through parts of w. Ont. during the past 3–4 decades. Thus the Black has been spreading westward, to some extent into Mallard country, even when its overall numbers were declining in its "usual" range.

There are various aspects to the Mallard–Black interrelationship, however. In e. Ont. and part of s. Que. the Mallard (and Blue-winged Teal) have increased manyfold; Blacks, in some places, have "islands" of breeding habitat which are encircled by breeding Mallards. An example of this is in the clay belt area of extreme e. Ont., n. of L. Nipissing, at New Liskeard. In n. Ont. (and elsewhere?) the Black has been vacating the Hudson Bay lowlands and is now almost completely succeeded, as a breeding species, by the Mallard.

Summer   Many of the records beyond authenticated breeding range evidently are for drakes (singles, small groups, even flocks) that have left their mates and gone elsewhere to molt. Ont.—breeds in decreasing numbers in the James and s. Hudson Bay areas. Man.—breeds in at least the se. part of the province, also near the Hudson Bay coast. Sask.—apparently now a regular breeder in small numbers in se. part of the province. Alta.—first breeding record was for vicinity of Hanna, in June 1963 (Leitch 1964) and reported to breed near Kelsey (Godfrey 1966).

The black nests on and near tidewater marshes and on coastal is. from N.C. northward to include James Bay and much of the Ungava Pen.

This duck has occurred in summer (see Godfrey 1966) in distant areas such as n. Alta. and Districts of Mackenzie (at least to Thelon R.), Keewatin (n. to Chesterfield Inlet), and Franklin (3 coll. at C. Dorset, Baffin I.). (See below for stragglers in other seasons.)

In sw. Hudson Bay, in vicinity of Fox Is. (near Churchill, Man.), about a thousand were reported seen in scattered flocks on June 7, 1932 (Taverner and Sutton 1934). If they were correctly identified, i.e., were not scoters or ♀ eiders, this would seem to be a remarkable concentration for a Hudson Bay locality and so early in the season.

Fall   The postbreeding dispersal that began in summer continues into early fall. The Black then is found, for example, on the barrens near the s. Hudson and James Bay coasts and beyond tree line in interior n. Ungava. It is "common" during the hunting season at some places in Man. and there are many reports of occurrence "each fall" for Sask. and Alta. (Leitch 1964). In the Atlantic coastal area, from n. Labrador down at least into New Eng., the Black occurs during this season at many is. besides those on which it nests.

Bermuda—regular autumn migrant, sometimes lingering into winter.

Winter   For distribution, numbers (which were declining), and relative population density, see R. E. Stewart (1958) and Johnsgard (1961b). Recorded in this season at Cartwright, Labrador (Godfrey 1966). Sizable numbers (over 2,000 on Feb. 18, 1972) in inner St. Lawrence on shoreline on both sides of Saguenay R. mouth. Uncommon in s. Fla.

Straggler   In conterminous U.S., w. of a line drawn from N.D. down through Texas, the Black has been recorded reliably in every state except Ariz. and New Mex. It might be debated whether all records for Pacific coastal states are for naturally occurring (rather than escaped captive) birds, also whether some in interior states perhaps might be misidentified Mexican or Mottled Ducks. Compare, for example, accounts of all 3 species in Bailey and Niedrach (1965).

Alaska—a single (with Mallards) each of 3 midwinters 1969–71, in Glacier Bay, and one photographed at College on May 5, 1972.

Puerto Rico—taken once.

England—1 record.

Ireland—3 records (includes ♀ captured).

Azores—one shot on Terceira, Nov. 28, 1968.

Recorded as **fossil** from the Pleistocene of a number of localities in Fla. and one in Ga., all listed by Wetmore (1967), and from several **archaeological sites** each in Fla. and Ill.: see Brodkorb (1964a) for localities and references. (The problem of identifying bones of the "Mallard group" to species is mentioned under Mottled Duck.) RSP

MIGRATION   The Black Duck is somewhat less migratory than various other North American ducks because large numbers winter as far north as open water and food are available. Northern interior populations make longest migrations, tending to pass through and beyond areas occupied by more sedentary populations of conterminous U.S. breeding range. Migration apparently is accomplished at night; except for strictly local flights, there are few observations of daytime movement overhead; departure on migration during the day is very rarely seen or at least recognized as such, and arrival is evidenced only occasionally by the precipitous descent of flocks from high in air soon after first daylight, or by the presence of "new" birds in a marsh where there were none the day before. So far as known, migrant flocks are small—rarely over 30, more commonly in the 12–20 range.

Banding operations indicate rather complex patterns of migration, with recoveries from any station covering an arc of 30–120 degrees and departures often following two or more distinctly different routes; for example, about half the Blacks banded in the 1920s at Lake Scugog, Ont., went s.-se. toward Chesapeake Bay, the remainder sw. toward w. L. Erie and the Ohio–Mississippi drainage. Nevertheless, a basic picture of migration may be drawn in terms of the "flight corridors" outlined by Bellrose (1968). From Atlantic coastal waters westward, and using his estimate of number of Blacks using each, there are 5 recognizable corridors, as follows: 1 Northeastern coastal, from Nfld. and the Maritimes southward to N.J. and (irregularly) N.C. (about 150,000, of which a large part winter north of N.J.); 2 South Atlantic coastal, from w. Que. and e. Ont. via Champlain–Hudson valley (20,000), Delaware and Susquehanna valleys (135,000) to N.J., Del., Chesapeake Bay, and the Carolinas; 3 from e. Ont. sw. across west end of L. Erie to confluence Wabash and Ohio Rivers (thus crossing several other corridors at nearly right angles) and s. to eastern Ark. (35,000); 4 from nw. Que. and n. Ont., through e. and w. Mich., thence dividing, with one contingent to coastal S.C. and Ga. (20,000), another to Ohio and Tennessee river valleys (perhaps 30,000), and remainder to the middle Mississippi drainage in Ill., Mo., w. Tenn. and Ark. (100,000); 5 from w. Ont. s. across Wisc. and e. Minn. into the Mississippi drainage (25,000). (The figures given are relative and do not add up to the total population. Of these corridors, the Northeastern and South Atlantic are best defined by reason of the lead-line effect of the coast; to the west the corridor concept implies little more than several axes of movement with innumerable overlaps and crossings from one to another, yet it proves useful in visualizing the underlying pattern.

The complexities of Black Duck migration stem, in part at least, from the somewhat discontinuous nature of breeding range. The Black is the Mallard-like duck of the forested northeastern quadrant of the continent, but in contrast to the Mallard itself in the more homogeneous habitat of the prairie states and provinces, can occupy in the nesting season only relatively small parts of its range, i.e., the scattered bogs, streams and marshes which lie partly or wholly isolated in a matrix of wooded upland. As a result, the total population tends to be made up of many regional subpopulations, each having its particular areas of residence and lines of travel. This fact and the general hardiness and adaptability of the Black Duck have their effect on seasonal movements.

Summer   Drakes leave their incubating mates and gather in groups of considerable size to molt; unmated drakes gather with them. This movement, which is first evident in late May and early June, is to favorable places—lake, estuary, or marsh—not only within the nesting range but beyond its n. and nw. limits, as n. coastal Labrador, head of Ungava Bay, James Bay, s. Hudson Bay, and n. Man. Toward end of rearing season, ♀ ♀ leave young birds and retire to molting areas; when their wings are grown they join gathered groups within the nesting range but rarely to the north of it. As young of the season reach flying stage they disperse at random from place of hatching but probably at first as broods of siblings. This movement continues through latter part of summer until all young birds are on the wing and gathered into the loose all-age ♂ + ♀ aggregations which precede southern migration. There is banding evidence to suggest that even some of the young from the Middle Atlantic nesting areas disperse up the coast during the summer. The end effect of summer movements, particularly in the early fall gatherings of Canada and the border states, is a very considerable mixing of birds from different subpopulations, and the subsequent sorting out of these may well produce some of the puzzling crosscurrents which turn up in southward migration.

Fall   In general terms, the Black Duck is indifferent to cold if food supplies are ample but sensitive to the rapid reduction in availability of food when ice forms. Accordingly, Blacks do not "anticipate" freezing weather as do Blue-winged Teal and Pintails, but are moved by its actual arrival. Again in general terms, isotherms characteristically bulge southward in autumn over the interiors of N. Hemisphere land masses, fresh waters freeze sooner than salt, and shallow quiet waters before deep; it follows that the onset of fall is earliest in the interior parts of Black Duck range and lags in the coastal portions. Migration is under way in the n. interior in the first few days of Sept. and proceeds southward and outward in broad fan shape, its flanks toward and along the Labrador and James Bay coasts, its wide center more rapidly through interior Quebec. By Sept. 20 the James Bay contingents are departing overland to the south and thereafter take on the characteristics of the interior subpopulations to the east, thus extending the front of the fan to cover the whole width of Ontario. In contrary fashion, as birds from extreme e. Que. reach the Gulf of St. Lawrence many of them merge with the maritime population eastward. By early Oct. numbers are building rapidly along the general line from New Bruns.–St. Lawrence valley–upper peninsula of Mich., and now a man-made factor comes into play: the gun pressures which in recent decades have certainly affected the timing of migration, if not sometimes its direction. As a shooting season opens, Blacks adapt to it by leaving small marshes, concentrating on larger bodies of water during the day, feeding more at night, and if still much disturbed, passing on southward into a zone where hunting has not yet begun. A third factor also makes itself felt before Oct. is ended: the progressive exhaustion of a number of favored foods, chiefly the seeds of aquatic and semiaquatic plants. The order of priority among these three factors—food depletion, shooting, and closure by ice —varies from place to place and time to time, but in some combination they supply the major incentives to movement. Under their influence the front of migration shifts steadily southward through Nov., following the corridors already described, and reaches its farthest limits on the Gulf Coast before Jan. There is a high degree of homing to winter quarters.

Fall—maritime. The foregoing account of fall migration is generally applicable to the whole interior range of the Black Duck and to its coastal range from N.J. southward, but must be modified to cover the ne. maritime range, where strong ocean tides are the basis of a radically different environmental situation. These tides, rising and falling twice a day, have a range of 3–6 ft. in the sounds on the s. New Eng. coast, 9–14 ft. on outer shores from Cape Cod north, and 20 ft. or more in the Bay of Fundy. Their most direct effect on Black Ducks is to provide an abundance of animal food (see under "Food"), but additionally the salinity of the water and the strong currents induced by the constant ebb and flow retard the formation of solid ice until temperatures approach Fahrenheit zero. In consequence, the maritime population (which may be roughly defined as the nesting Blacks of the eastern Maritimes, Nfld., and Labrador e. of the George and Natashquan Rivers) gathers at n. coastal points early in the fall as the back country freezes up, but thereafter moves s. at a more leisurely rate, and winters several hundred miles farther north, than comparable numbers of interior birds. Major arrivals of n. birds on the s. New Eng. coast are delayed until very late Oct. or early Nov., continue through latter month, and taper off in early Dec.

Winter The migratory urge is largely spent by Dec. 10, and there is so little movement during the winter that if food becomes depleted or inaccessible under the ice in some n. localities, Blacks starve rather than shift ground. For the s. there are records of movement in late Dec. and Jan. but whether they indicate terminal fall migration or the beginning of spring migration is debatable.

Spring Even more than in fall, open water is the key to spring migration. Movement begins at the first break in winter weather, by middle or late Feb. as far n. as Mass., and thereafter the nesting birds of any given locality will arrive with the first breaking of ice. Routes of travel are essentially the reverse of fall routes, subject to minor variations in the relative timing of ice-out. Far-northern breeders tend to linger on wintering grounds after local birds have eggs or even broods, but appear to know when their own territories will open. Migration is completed in U.S. by mid-April, in s. interior Canada by late April, and to the n. limits of nesting range before the end of May.

Older ♀ ♀ return to where they nested a previous year; whether yearling ♀ ♀ tend to return to the area where they hatched remains unknown.

Whether Blacks at the s. end of their breeding range, in N.C., are migratory or whether they remain in the general vicinity is not known.

There is much published information on migration of this species, based on band-recovery data. The papers by the principal authors (Addy, Bellrose, Geis, Hagar, Hickey, Lemieux) and by others are listed at ends of contributions to a symposium (Atlantic Waterfowl Council 1968) and in A.D. Geis et al. (1971). To these should be added Bellrose and Crompton (1970) for the Mississippi drainage. JAH

BANDING STATUS   The total number banded was 362,966 through 1964 and the total number of recoveries was 47,958 through 1966; the birds were banded at localities throughout winter range, also summer range n. to about lat. 51° (data from Bird Banding Laboratory). On a map in Addy (1953) are shown places of banding, probably through the year 1952. The places in Canada and U.S. where 100 or more Blacks (the numbers are given) were banded, prior to 1961, were listed in a table, and in another table the number of recoveries by province and state, in A.D. Geis et al. (1971). As indicated in the preceding paragraph, there has been very extensive analysis of Black Duck banding data. RSP.

REPRODUCTION   Both sexes are ready to **breed** as yearlings, but because of unbalanced sex ratio many young ♂ ♂ are not actually mated until 2nd or later years. As in *Anas* generally, events related to reproduction occur throughout most of the year, social and other displays beginning on completion of molting in fall. These are Mallard-like, but some aspects are not yet clearly understood. In general, group displays are very similar in the 2 species, perhaps identical; pair formation activities and territorial behavior of the Black apparently are simpler. The differences may not be real but might rather reflect difficulties of observation: sexes of the Black are less readily distinguished, the nature of the habitat limits visibility, and the birds are more secretive. Alternatively, lower nesting densities, resulting in minimum intraspecific contact, may tend to simplify territorial behavior. Trautman (1940, 1947) has given the best connected account of displays and related behavior in wild Blacks. For technical analysis of display, see Heinroth (1911), Lorenz (1941), Weidmann (1956), and Johnsgard (1960).

Basic elements of **display** are given here in approximate order of appearance; the terminology is Trautman's followed in brackets by that of Lorenz as used under Mallard in this volume: BACK-AND-FORTH movement of head [Inciting] sideways along breast and flank, done by ♀ and accompanied by continuous somewhat irregularly accented calling. RAPID SWIMMING [Nod-swim] with frequent changes and reversals of direction, head in normal position or head and neck outstretched along surface of water. Diving and noisy splashing, with half-open wings. HEAD-BOBBING [Down-up], in which the head is raised and lowered rapidly and jerkily, with bill held horizontal when neck is fully extended, but the tip submerged against the breast when neck is retracted and then often flipped upward, throwing up or outward small jets of water. TAILSTAND [Grunt-whistle] in which the body is raised to vertical position, with or without wing flapping, and the neck and head, starting from bowed position with bill touching chest, are stretched straight upward smoothly and rather quickly, then returned to bowed position. BUMPING by ♂ against side of ♀, accompanied by picking at feathers of her neck, back, or rump. FLIGHT DISPLAY in which ♀ leaves water, ♂ follows and overtakes her, passes above and in front of her, stretches his neck downward, spreads tail widely, and displays white of his under wings. PURSUIT FLIGHT in which ♂ chases

336

♀ over water or land, high or low, displaying above and before her, nipping at her back and tail with his bill, and presently attempting to force her down on water of his territory.

Calls associated with displays are noisy quacking by ♀, more often in climactic stages; reedy grunting and a clear whistling call by ♂ almost throughout.

Copulation takes place on water. The ♀ indicates willingness by swimming with head and neck outstretched and body partly submerged, ♂ pursues with outstretched neck, ♀ sinks lower until only crown of head and dorsal ridge of bill are above water, ♂ usually seizes feathers at back of her head in his bill, swims over her, and coitus is quickly effected. The ♀ emerges, shakes herself vigorously, either or both birds bob their heads, twitch their tails from side to side, flap their wings, and preen; the ♂ may give whistling call.

Of the several elements of display, the Pursuit flight with noisy quacking is wholly confined to the nesting season and territory, and bumping by the ♂ usually is preliminary to attempted union; the others are practiced generally over a long period of time from early fall to late spring, but with wide individual, daily, and seasonal variations of intensity. The early phase of display, both by solitary pairs and pairs within groups, begins as soon in Aug. as the first old birds are through molting and young are strong on wing. It increases by degrees as more birds finish molting, reaches a mild subclimax in late autumn, is less evident during midwinter when weather is severe, resumes toward end of winter, and quickly builds to climax, at least with respect to frequency, in late Feb.–early March. During fall and winter it is largely confined to quiet sunny days; in late winter and spring it may continue even when snow is falling.

Interpretation of display in flocks is difficult; at times many or most of a group of birds may be involved, but in different degree. Close analysis indicates that the several forms of display correspond to progressive levels of intensity, one following another as events lead to forming the pair bond. This rarely is evident under ordinary circumstances, however, because particular birds in a group can only be distinguished momentarily; the impression usually given is that various displays go on at the same time, without much order. In fall groups, display probably is initiated by 2 birds already in an early stage of pairing, whose actions excite other members so that additional ♂♂ pursue the ♀ briefly, or other pairs begin displaying. But frequently a pair withdraws to the edge of its group before beginning display, and in any case usually arrives there, leaving the remainder of the flock apparently indifferent. Later in the cycle, all members of a group may engage in display at one time, but often, it seems, more in spirit of play than serious purpose; the birds swim rapidly, weaving in and out, feint with outstretched head and neck, splash and dive to avoid mock attacks of others, bob their heads, and the drakes, in an abbreviated form of flight display [it has been termed Leading display], leave the water with drooping bodies and legs, fly a few feet, plump back with a splash, and plane across the surface before sinking to normal swimming depth. [The drake appears to compete for the leading place in the display group; compare with Shoveler, in which the drake tries to induce a ♀ to follow him, hence the ♂ may swim and flutter in any or various directions.] Winter and spring groups run strongly to drakes under a year old, which may be determining factor in this type of social display.

A firm **pair bond** may be formed at any time between Aug. and early spring; in terms

337

of regional subpopulations it is a cumulative process. Some birds appear to be paired almost as soon (after molting) as display begins; a few banding recoveries suggest re-pairing of former mates immediately upon regaining flight. Two Blacks, banded at the same time in 1942 were bagged together 6 years later. Early pairs soon reach the stage of copulation, although their gonads are functionally inactive. The percentage of mated pairs in a regional subpopulation increases steadily during autumn, but evidence indi-cates that only birds old enough to have already bred at least once are involved until late Nov. Young ♀ ♀, on basis of primary and secondary sex characters, mature 6–12 weeks ahead of young ♂ ♂ and, by Dec., are appearing among mated pairs (Stotts 1958a). Young ♂ ♂ reach sexual maturity in midwinter; although they have been dis-playing since early fall, they are less persistent than older age-classes of drakes and rarely reach the point of attempted copulation before Jan. By inference, it is the matur-ing young ♂ ♂ which cause the marked increase of display in late winter, at a time when older mated pairs already are withdrawing from wintering flocks.

Although some aspects of display and pair formation need further study, several im-portant points in the foregoing outline are reasonably certain. For example, there is little doubt that the bulk of potential pairs are already formed by early winter, leaving surplus young drakes (from unbalanced sex ratio) to compete for few remaining ♀ ♀ and to carry on modified form of display mostly in groups during late winter and spring. There is some indication from banding, however, that a substantial number of older drakes, in unisexual groups, tend not to migrate as far in fall as ♀ ♀ and young birds; many of these birds, presumably, would have to wait until ♀ ♀ moved n. in late winter–early spring before they could engage in pair formation activities. In form, pair bond is at least **seasonal monogamy,** and quite often may be **sustained monogamy** partly masked by high mortality rate. Many old birds are paired for minimum of 8–9 months of year, which provides the basis for social organization.

Home range, as defined by Sowls (1955), is occupied before March 1 in s. coastal portions of breeding range, and on first appearance of open water northward. Mated pairs which have wintered nearby apparently select ranges in course of daily food and exercise flights and gradually spend more and more time on them. Pairs that have win-tered s. of their nesting grounds arrive in vicinity of where the ♀ will nest with first break in weather; the birds wait in loose groups at the nearest place where food is avail-able, then select and occupy (or reoccupy) individual ranges at earliest opportunity. Thus, resident pairs characteristically are on station before the migration of northern nesters has passed, or wintering flocks in the vicinity have wholly dispersed. Scattered banding records and bits of circumstantial evidence indicate that migrational homing is a major behavioral trait of ♀ ♀ and that older ♀ ♀ arrive and nest several weeks earlier than first-year birds.

Territoriality in the Black Duck is difficult to appraise because home ranges are large, often noncontiguous, and in most cases are heavily vegetated. Trautman's (1947) data, for a pair having territory relatively free of these limitations, supply the basic pattern. The territory covered 6 acres of water in the corner of a small bay adjacent to a rocky island in L. Erie; it included a large emergent rock used by the drake as a loafing station, and a feeding area along the shore; in most years it was bordered on one side by another Black Duck territory. On first arrival, the already mated pair remained to-

338

gether on territory except at dawn and dusk, when both left together to feed on grassy upland. Later on the ♀, accompanied by the drake or alone, left the territory at other times of day to hunt a nesting site in a field of orchard grass; when the ♂ went, he alighted with the ♀ near the prospective site, but stood guard on a slight eminence, his body almost vertical and neck stretched to upward limit, while she investigated clumps of grass. At intervals she raised her head and neck high to look over the situation, or to see if ♂ on guard; if he noticed her, he sometimes head-bobbed, or flapped his wings, whereupon she resumed her search with head down. When alarmed, or when having finished hunting for a nest site, the ♀ arose on wing, followed at once by ♂ who fell into usual position behind her, and both returned to his territory.

Within a short time, as egg-laying began, the ♀ showed increasing reluctance to accept ♂'s company and began to elude him, sometimes by slipping ashore on foot and hiding while he was occupied in feeding or preening, more often by flying toward open lake and circling back to vicinity of nest without again crossing his territory. He usually noticed her departure within a few seconds and pursued, but turned back when he had gone a few hundred yds. beyond the boundary of his territory. After an unaccompanied absence, the ♀ returned by flying into territory; the ♂ rose on wing as soon as he noticed her approach, flew to meet her, took position behind her, and the 2 birds alighted together. If, for any reason, the ♀ failed to alight, the ♂ passed over and beyond her in a burst of speed, gained position immediately in front and a little to one side, forced her to circle gradually until again headed toward territory, when he resumed his customary place behind her, and both alighted. Occasionally, when leaving or entering territory, the ♀ flew over an adjacent territory, from which the occupying ♂ rose in pursuit; the ♀ then began to quack loudly, her mate rose at once, interposed himself as soon as possible between her and pursuing ♂, and appeared to chase her back into his territory. No other form of territorial defense was noted.

Observers in other parts of breeding range have noted enough variations from the foregoing account to indicate great flexibility in territorial requirements. When the nest is located in a marsh, the drake's loafing station and the feeding area for both members of the pair can be close by and the pattern is recognizably similar to Mallard and some other dabbling ducks. At the other extreme, when the nest is in a dry pasture or a woodland some distance from water, the need for conventional territory is greatly diminished and ♂'s behavior is correspondingly modified. Boyer (in MS) reported a case in point: in New Bruns. he saw a ♂ alight, in late afternoon, in a corner of an upland field about a mile from nearest water, and on investigation the observer flushed a ♀ from a clutch of 10 eggs a short distance away. Both birds circled the area, calling repeatedly. This ♂ clearly did not wait for an evening appearance of the off-duty ♀ on his water territory, but waited instead on dry land near her nest. Defense of territory is equally flexible, as circumstances require; ♂ may defend against unattached drakes, he may defend against other mated pairs or feed amicably with them on common ground, or may even shift his loafing and feeding ground at frequent intervals as water levels or other conditions change, so that any sort of defense is reduced to a minimum.

From time of arrival in the nesting area, the drake is very attentive; he follows the ♀ constantly when she is with him, and rapid swimming, chasing, and head-bobbing occupy considerable periods of time. Flight displays increase and soon are elaborated into prolonged pursuit flights; both birds are more vociferous, the ♀ quacking loudly and persistently (compare with Mallard). Copulation is frequent. As egg-laying begins, the ♀ absents herself increasingly until finally she appears only at morning and evening dusk. The waiting drake shows considerable excitement prior to her arrival, swimming back and forth and frequently grunting. The ♀, on arrival, alights near the ♂ and nearly always drinks. The ♂, greatly excited, bobs, grunts, swims toward her, bumps her in the side, raises himself vertically in the water, and flaps wings (compare with noisy palaver when members of a Mallard pair reunite). The ♀ soon begins to quack; both birds spring into the air in a pursuit flight which may last 15–25 min. Until the clutch is completed, flights tend to be over water, climaxed by copulation when the ♂ finally forces the ♀ down. As incubation begins, flights are even longer, more elaborate, and more frequently over land, now high, now low, and take on the character of exercise flights for the ♀. Toward end of incubation, the ♀ begins to elude the ♂ and to take her exercise flight over land without showing herself to him. He becomes increasingly inattentive; by hatching time usually he has departed. (Based on Trautman 1947.)

Johnsgard (1960) found no qualitative difference between ♂ Mallard and ♂ Black Duck displays; quantitative differences were: 1 Blacks have a distinctly lower threshold of display response and 2 apparently a somewhat more specific response.

The reader is referred to B. S. Wright (1954) for a summary of earlier studies of Black Duck reproduction. Also, to supplement the preceding paragraphs, 3 recent studies—in Md. by Stotts and Davis (1960), at Ile aux Pommes, Que., by Reed (1964, and in Atlantic Waterfowl Council 1968) and in n. New Eng. (Me. and Vt.) by Coulter and Miller (1968)—are drawn on here. Although the environments differ considerably, those parts of the studies that are comparable are in close agreement.

For general environment of **nest sites,** see "Habitat." Local requirements are 1 concealing cover, 2 some kind of substrate (ground litter), and 3 a location near a break or change in plant cover (Coulter and Miller). Beginning as early as 3–4 days before laying, the ♀ prepares a nest basin, then some plant materials from around it are added over a span of time; the down from the ♀ accumulates in the nest usually beginning after several eggs are present and continuing into incubation. The **nest down** is large and very dark; any intermingled feathers (Basic Plumage) are large, dark, without noticeable internal gradation in shade, and generally have a light area along the sides (Broley 1950). A formerly used site is a definite stimulus and is reused quite often, or the ♀ may nest fairly near her previous site. For tree nesting in N.Y., see Cowardin et al. (1967); for nesting on duck blinds in Chesapeake Bay, see Stotts (1958b).

The **laying season** in Que. in 1963–67 began April 14 to 24 (depending on year) and the last clutches were started in 2nd and 3rd week in June; over half the clutches were started by about May 6. In Md. the season varied, beginning in different years on dates ranging from March 9 to 27, ending June 14–July 4 (and ending later if started later), and with number of clutches started reaching a peak within about April 18–30 in different years. In 1959 and 1960 at Pea. I. (N.C.), at s. limit of breeding, the peak of hatch was in the first half of June, indicating that many clutches were completed before mid-May (Parnell and Quay 1965).

In Que. in 1963–67, 209 clutches contained 5–17 eggs (mostly 7–11), with mean of 9.28 and SD 1.70 (essentially same mean as for clutches in Md.). Mean **clutch size** varied from 9.8 in 1964 to 8.4 in 1965. Lumping the data for all years, clutch size decreased

340

from 11.1 (39 clutches April 12–25) to 7.4 (12 clutches June 7–20). In Md. the decline through the season was from a mean of 10.9 (17 clutches March 15–28) to 7.5 (17 clutches June 7–20). In Me. and Vt., regardless of date, year (1938–64), or locality, 620 clutches contained 4–15 eggs (8–11 in 82% of nests) and mean size was 9.5 ± 0.063. Apparently a Black Duck does not often lay in another's nest, though this is suspected for some large clutches.

Older ♀ ♀ lay larger clutches than ♀ ♀ laying for the first time, the difference averaging about 1 egg less between 1- and 5-year-olds, and the av. decrease between the primary clutch of the season and 1st renesting by the same ♀ also is about 1 egg (Stotts and Davis 1960). That is, as figures given above indicate, **replacement clutches** are smaller than first clutches.

Egg shape, color, and shell texture as Mallard. One egg each from 20 clutches (from localities throughout most of breeding range) **size** length 58.97 ± 1.52 mm., breadth 42.54 ± 1.12, radii of curvature of ends 16.71 ± 1.20 and 13.20 ± 1.00; **shape** elongation 1.38 ± 0.053, bicone −0.028, asymmetry +0.114 (FWP).

Incubation period in Que. in 10 clutches av. 29.3 (27–33) days, with mode 27; in 51 nests in Md. it was 23–33 with av. 26.2 (air temperature is warmer than in Que.) and mode 25, and 13 clutches in incubator at 99°F. av. 25.6 (22–30). All viable eggs in a clutch usually hatch in a few hrs., but hatching occasionally was prolonged in the Que. study. The young are led to water. At Ile aux Pommes, Que., this often occurred after dark and ♀ ♀ led their broods 3½ mi. over open water to the mainland.

Hatching success apparently varies from year to year everywhere. In Que. in 1963–67, it varied in different years from 51.4% to 83.3%; the percentage of ♀ ♀ that hatched eggs was 63.8 and they produced 221 ducklings, or 5.34 ducklings/♀ . In 106 nesting attempts, 14 were believed to have been abandoned due to observer interference; of the remainder, 32 (34.8%) hatched at least 1 duckling, 13 (14.1%) were deserted for various reasons other than observer interference, and 47 (51.1%) were destroyed by crows or gulls. It was estimated that these 106 nests were the work of 53 ♀ ♀ and that each produced an av. of 5.23 ducklings that season. Of 574 clutches in Md., 218 (38%) were successful, 66 (11.5%) were abandoned for various reasons other than observer interference, 287 (50%) were destroyed by crows, mammals, and other known and unknown agents, and only 3 clutches (0.5%) had all eggs infertile or addled. An additional 132 clutches were abandoned due to observer interference and 25 more met an unknown fate. Overall nesting success for 340 clutches in Me., mostly from marshes, 1938–64: some eggs hatched in 55% of them (it varied 36–79% with year); and on is. in L. Champlain, Vt., 1951–55, in 231 clutches success ranged annually 67–84% (much higher than in Me. marsh habitat).

In Md., examination of 336 eggs disclosed that 1 (0.3%) was infertile and 7 (2.1%) had developed only slightly.

Also in the Md. study, calculations suggest that about 510 ducklings were produced by 100 ♀ ♀ and mortality of ducklings from hatching to flying age was estimated at a rather low 9.2%.

From various studies it is evident that **renesting** is nearer the rule than the exception in the Black Duck; it occurs regularly if the first clutch is lost, occasionally even if the ♀ loses a very young brood. In n. New Eng., 2 ♀ ♀ laid 3 clutches each during a single season. From various studies of both Black and Mallard it is also safe to generalize that,

341

in areas where both breed, the peak of hatching in the Black is about a week earlier.

The **brood** is tended by the ♀. Young Blacks attain flight, usually, in their 8th week, and about that time the ♀ departs to molt her flight feathers. The brood stays together a few days longer, then tends to amalgamate with other young, thus forming small flocks. These roam, seeking suitable feeding areas, and perhaps often occur at the same places as older drakes that already have molted and are again on the wing.

For **growth rate** of captives through their first 8 weeks of life, under experimental conditions optimum for growth and development, see Penney and Bailey (1970). JAH RSP

SURVIVAL   Analysis of a sample of 939 recoveries of birds banded in Ill. at various ages indicated an annual mortality rate of about 50% (Bellrose and Chase 1950, Farner 1955). Study of banding recoveries at 4 stations in Que., 1947–55, indicated a mortality rate at Baie Johan Beetz of 52.6% (based on 3,327 individuals); for Ile Plate, Laprairie, and Peribonca it was 59.7% (1,574 individuals) (Lemieux and Moisan 1959) and these 3 stations had a kill rate so high as to appear atypical. Also see important discussion of "production" in Stotts and Davis (1960).

Survival and losses, including hunting kill, were reported on at length by A. D. Geis et al. (1971), based on band-recovery data through Jan. 15, 1961, plus aerial censuses, questionnaires, and a sample of wings of birds taken in hunting season. It is important to bear in mind that there was a drastic decline in the number of Black Ducks during most of the period covered by this study. The following are among the findings.

The ♂ and ♀ are equally likely to be shot in their first fall and 1.5 times more likely to be shot than birds of older age-classes. Between 1946 and 1960, the av. first-year mortality rate was about 0.65. Based on winter bandings, "adult" ♂ ♂ had an av. mortality rate of about 0.38 in that same period and in "adult" ♀ ♀ (based on less representative samples) it was about 0.47. The av. annual mortality rate, including all years of life, of birds banded as "immatures," was estimated as 0.552, suggesting that an increment of 1.2 young per adult was needed to maintain a stable population.

Although hunting mortality in young Blacks is additive to natural mortality in a significant portion of deaths, this replacement is much less in "adults." As hunting mortality increases, so does total mortality. The rate at which Black Ducks died was 4–5 times greater during the hunting season than during the remainder of the year.

It was estimated that for every 100 Blacks bagged, an additional 38 were killed and not retrieved. The hunting kill (about 30% in Canada, 70% in U.S.), including crippling loss, during the period 1952–60 av. about 1,025,000 annually. (The retrieved hunting kill in N. Am. 1952–60 av. about 691,700 birds.) The population declined greatly, probably due to high rate of kill, long hunting season, and liberal bag limits. Failure of the population to recover, even with more restrictions, apparently was due to a high kill rate.

It was estimated that, in "adults," there was a ratio of 1.2 ♂ per ♀. RSP

HABITS   The Black mingles with other waterfowl, but habitat preferences and a tendency to keep with its own kind apparently reduce the extent of close association even with the Mallard. It is more hardy than the latter. It is largely a bird of the boreal

342

forest zone in summer and much of the population occurs in marine habitat in winter. In the latter season there is appreciable sex segregation of mature birds, groups of drakes predominating in more exposed situations. It seldom travels in very large flocks. Usually it flies at 2–2.7 wingbeats/sec., but up to 5/sec. have been recorded (C. H. Blake). Recorded flight speeds vary from 26 and 30 to 55 mph, the last figure determined electronically by Lanyon (1962). The Black can dive to a depth of 10 ft., but cannot stay down; hence it can get corn thrown into that depth of water but cannot tear

R. M. Mengel –

mussels (*Mytilus*) loose. The Black is not shy where protected and fed, but is considered the wariest of shoal-water ducks where hunted.

The Black is an important game species, first among wildfowl in the northeast. In different parts of its overall range there is variation in relative amount of fluctuation in its numbers. Averaging these, the extent to which the total population has fluctuated, based on Jan. inventories, is indicated by figures (which serve as an index and may include only a third of the birds) for certain years (from R. E. Stewart 1958): 1952— 518,000, 1955—804,000, and 1956—670,000. The number of Blacks gradually increased about 1948–55, then declined until at least 1967 to perhaps only half as many birds as in peak years of the early 1950s, and has remained depressed. The total breeding population in 1968 was estimated to be about 850,000, with the increment of young increasing this to about 1,800,000 before the fall hunting season. About ⅔ or ¾ of these are in Canada at the beginning of the fall period.

The Black eats more, and more varied, protein food (small animal life) than, for example, the Mallard; this may result in a higher intake of long-residual pesticides which, in turn, occur widely in Black Ducks and their eggs. These may influence over-all numbers (see, for example, Benson 1966), but their effects remain unknown.

For further information on habits, the reader is referred to general accounts in Bent (1923) and J. C. Phillips (1923b), for summer activities to A. A. Saunders (1926), and for general treatment to B. S. Wright's (1954) volume. RSP

FOOD Varies so widely in different habitats as to limit the usefulness of conventional tables of composite diet. In general, a typical regional diet includes a few foods taken as staples, in significant quantity, and a wide range of less important items taken incidentally. Plant foods normally predominate in fresh- and brackish-water habitats, animal foods in maritime habitat. Principal determinant of diet at a given place and time is easy availability of 1 or more staples, in water sufficiently deep to float birds while feeding.

Fresh-water foods include a wide variety of seeds and grains, some leafy and fibrous materials in moderate amount, a few tubers, nuts and fruits, and a minor proportion (usually less than 20%) of small animal forms. Seeds which appear most frequently in stomach analyses are pondweeds (*Potamogeton, Najas, Zannichellia*) smartweeds (*Polygonum*), sedges (*Carex*), spike rushes (*Eleocharis*), wild rice (*Zizania*), wild celery (*Vallisneria*), rice cutgrass (*Leersia*), wild millets (*Echinochloa*), burreeds (*Sparganium*), cow lily (*Nuphar*), watershield (*Brasenia*), and pickerelweed (*Pontederia*). Corn and buckwheat are gleaned occasionally from stubble fields, particularly around rain pools. Leaves and stems of pondweeds and wild celery usually are taken with their seeds, and muskgrass (*Chara*), coontail (*Ceratophyllum*), and duckweeds (*Spirodela, Lemna*) are eaten whole. Tubers of arrowheads (*Sagittaria*) are staple wherever available, and to a lesser extent the tubers and rootstalks of several bulrushes (*Scirpus*), pondweeds and wild celery, and axil-borne bulblets of a loosestrife (*Lysimachia terrestris*). Acorns occasionally assume some importance in flooded bottomlands, and in Canada blueberries (*Vaccinium*) and crowberries (*Empetrum*) are regularly eaten on upland barrens in late summer and the latter in early spring. Insects, snails, crustaceans, and small fish make up animal portion of diet, usually in such diversity that inclusion appears to be incidental; exceptionally they assume local importance, for example, gizzard shad (*Dorosoma*) in Ohio (Trautman 1940).

Brackish-water foods (Atlantic coast from Conn. south) are less diversified than freshwater foods, but essentially similar. Commonest staples, found in nearly every stomach: seeds, stems, and rootstalks of wigeon grass (*Ruppia*) and sago pondweed (*Potamogeton pectinatus*). Other seeds used in quantity, at least locally: bulrushes (*Scirpus*), cordgrasses (*Spartina*), saw grass (*Cladium*), water hemp (*Acnida*), arrow grass (*Triglochin*), eelgrass (*Zostera*), and from upper limits of tide where salinity is very low, burreeds, smartweeds, and wild millets. Animal foods cover a wide range of mollusks, insects, crustaceans, and small fish, almost never in quantity.

Foods from maritime habitat (Atlantic coast, e. Long I. to Labrador) reverse balance of foregoing diets: main dependence during 6–8 months of year on animal forms. Commonest staple, found in nearly every stomach: blue mussel (*Mytilus*). Other items, staple at different times and places: small clams (*Mya, Macoma*), saltwater snails (*Melampus, Littorina, Nassa*), various scuds and isopods (*Gammarus, Orchestia,*

344

Idothea, Cyathura), several shrimps and shrimplike forms (*Crago, Palaemonetes, Corophium*), small crabs (*Carcinides, Neopanope*), marine worms (chiefly *Nereis*) and minnows (chiefly *Fundulus*). Examples of animal foods eaten in quantity for short periods only: in early fall a grasshopper common on salt marshes (*Melanoplus femurrubrum*), in late winter a scale insect of thatch grass (*Chionaspis spartinae*), which then, killed by the cold, floats free of grass and washes up into windrows on each rising tide, and in spring, spawn of herring (*Clupeidae*). Of seeds utilized in maritime habitat, a few (*Spartina alterniflora, Ruppia, Triglochin, Acnida*) are eaten in quantity early in fall but are soon consumed, lose palatability (*Spartina*), or become unavailable. A wide variety of other seeds (for example, *Myrica, Rhus, Rubus, Ilex, Prunus, Vitis, Nyssa*) turn up in specimen stomachs, but only as trace items. The tender lower stems and rootstalks of wigeon grass (*Ruppia*), sago pondweed (*P. pectinatus*) and eelgrass (*Zostera*), together with tubers of sago, are eaten along with their seeds whenever available, but do not bulk large after early fall. Several marine algae (chiefly *Ulva*) also appear in specimen stomachs, but rarely in quantity.

Downy young feed themselves from the beginning; first diet runs strongly to miscellaneous insects found in or on the water, which the ducklings are extraordinarily quick in catching. At 3 weeks, proportion of plant foods begins to increase and, when half grown, diet approximates that of old birds in same habitat (see Mendall 1949).

Amount of food taken at one time varies widely, but often is large. The stomach itself holds 15 cc. at most, usually less, but gullet, filled to upper end, will take upwards of 100 cc. additional. Several factors influence volume of different foods in samples: i.e., scattered seeds are gathered more slowly than seeds in heads, or collected into pockets of water; soft-bodied animals (*Nereis*) and thin-shelled bivalves (small clams and mussels) are digested much more rapidly than seeds which require grinding in gizzard; buried foods (*Mya, Nereis*) are dug out of mud more slowly than surface foods (*Mytilus, Melampus*) so that speed of digestion more nearly approaches rate of ingestion. A blue mussel (*Mytilus edulis*) passes through the digestive tract in 30–40 min. (Grandy 1972). Following examples illustrate maximum amounts of typical foods found in stomach and gullet of single birds: 40 cc. (several hundred) seeds of wild rice; 21 cc. *Lemna* plants; 86 cc. thatch grass seeds (6 cc. in stomach, 80 cc. in gullet); 34 cc. arrow grass seeds; 78 cc. (2,400 grains) buckwheat (Mendall 1949b); 80 cc. (456) tubers of arrowhead (Mendall 1949b); 90 cc. (more than 8,000 individuals, very small) blue mussel; 16 cc. *Mya* clam; 114 cc. (more than 2,700) *Melampus* snails (10 cc. in stomach, remainder in gullet); 80 cc. *Gammarus* scud; 30 cc. (70 whole, plus fragments) of minnow (*Fundulus*); and 69 cc. of thatch grass scale, *Chionaspis spartinae* (9 cc. in stomach, 60 cc. in gullet).

The above is based on approximately 1,550 specimen stomachs, including 400 in Fish and Wildlife Service collection, 59 reported by B. S. Wright (1954) from e. Canada, 600 reported by Mendall (1949b) from Me., 300 from Mass. (files, Mass. Div. Fisheries and Game), and 133 reported by Pirnie (1935) from Mich. By habitat, representation is roughly 800 freshwater, 450 brackish water, 300 maritime. JAH

[Additional information: on 138 gizzards in fall–winter from Penobscot Bay (Me.) estuarine environment, see F. E. Hartman (1963); for 22 from Currituck Sd. (N.C.), see Quay and Critcher (1965); and for fall foods of 32 from inland S.C., see McGilvrey (1966c). RSP]

Spot-billed Duck

Anas poecilorhyncha

Size of larger examples of Mallard, but appears somewhat longer necked; seasonal and sexual differences in feathering in the Spotbill are not strikingly different, being about on a par with the N. Am. Black Duck. Bill at least bicolored, terminal third yellow, basal portion very dark (with red spot on each side of top of base in 2 of the 3 subspecies); from head down onto breast light (buffy, pale tawny, etc.) with very dark crown, hindneck, and broad stripe from bill to eye and diminishing in postocular area; body appears dark, except breast and sides may appear rather light because of width of light (buffy, pale tawny, etc.) feather margins; legs and feet some variant of orange; wing dark, except elongated innermost secondaries have at least exposed portions white, and metallic speculum usually bordered white at leading and trailing edges. Drake's tracheal bulla said to be identical in shape with that of Mallard (Johnsgard 1965).

RECORD   Well out in the Aleutian Chain, at Adak, 3 ducks arrived on April 10, 1970, fed with Mallards, were carefully studied, and eventually one was identified as a Spotbill (*Aud. Field Notes* **24** 634. 1970). This species was seen there on various dates through April 18, 1971 (*Am. Birds* **25** 785. 1971).

REMARKS   Of the 3 subspecies, the one presumably most likely to reach our area is *A. p. zonorhyncha* (Swinhoe) of e. Asia. It lacks red spots at base of bill, has a blue (not green) speculum, and 2 elongated innermost secondaries are white on outer webs only (which shows when the birds are afloat or flying). This subspecies is said to have crossed in the wild with the Mallard; in captivity the Spot bill has crossed with many species, as listed by Gray (1958). For further details about the species, see Dementiev and Gladkov (1952) and Delacour (1956, text and col. pl.). RSP

Green-winged Teal

Anas crecca

Eurasian plus Aleutian birds have been called Teal, Common Teal, and European Teal; continental N. Am. birds formerly were regarded as a separate species, called Green-winged Teal. (Teals from various parts of S. Am., which are also green winged, differ greatly from the Holarctic bird in other respects; they all were referred to *A. flavirostris* by Delacour (1956) and may be called Speckled or Yellow-billed Teal.)

Our smallest dabbling duck. Green speculum; no large light area or patch on upper surface of wing. The feathering at top base of bill typically extends forward in a point on the midline, but sometimes is very truncated, or occasionally elongated nearly to above the nostrils. Sexes highly dimorphic in Alt. Plumage: ♂ head appears oversized (a tuft or "mane" at nape) and is rufous-chestnut with a large tear-shaped green area (surrounds eye) on the side; most of mantle and sides of body rather dark (light, vermiculated black); a cream-colored patch bordered black at side base of tail (as in ♂ Falcated Teal); ♀ head darkest on crown–nape plus a usually clearly defined darkish stripe through eye; dorsum quite dark, grayed or a buffy brown, the feather edging much paler; chin and much of underparts very light (often white), plain or with small dark markings on venter. The Juv. and Basic Plumages of the drake are more or less ♀-like.

Yellowish or rusty coloring, most evident on ventral feathering, is ferrous staining.

The tracheal apparatus of the drake *A. c. crecca* was described by J. C. Phillips (1923b) as "merely a miniature reproduction of that of the Mallard"; beginning in 1838 it has been illus. many times, probably best in Schiøler (1925), also satisfactorily by Lorenz and Wall (1960).

Birds of continental N. Am.: ♂ length 14¾–15½ in., wingspread to 26, usual wt. 11–14 oz., ♀ length 14¼–15 in., wingspread to 25, wt. usually 9–12 oz. First-fall birds are smaller.

Because of qualitative differences of Alt.-Plumaged drakes, quantitative differences in Basic wing of ♀ ♀, and perhaps still unknown quantitative or other differences in displays, the Eurasian–Aleutian and the continental N. Am. populations may be regarded as nearly semispecies, i.e., differentiated but below the species level. Also, within the former there is a size difference, the Aleutian birds averaging largest. Because such differences as are known are rather minor, the Greenwing is treated here as a single species (as by Hartert 1920a) comprised of 3 subspecies (as in Delacour 1956), of which 2 breed in our area and the third (Eurasian) occurs as a straggler, sometimes evidently mating with local birds.

DESCRIPTION   *A. crecca carolinensis.* Two Plumages/cycle in both sexes. Basic I is limited and fleeting in the drake, but is an extensive early-fall Plumage in the duck. There is much individual variation in timing of early molts, probably correlated with variation in hatching dates. In the definitive cycle, the drake often acquires entire Basic (including wing) and wears it for some time, i.e., is capable flight for a considerable period before the head–body–tail molt back into Alt.

▶   ♂ Def. Alt. Plumage (all feathering, excepting all but innermost feathers of

347

wing) worn from LATE SUMMER or, usually, some time beginning in FALL through WINTER into SUMMER. **Bill** nearly black, lightening somewhat in spring; **iris** dark brownish. **Head** rufous-chestnut with large tear-shaped iridescent green area on side that tapers toward upper nape, where there is a "mane" that varies from black to (occasionally) cobalt-ultramarine; on the chin a patch, variable in size and shape, usually black but occasionally dark gray-brown. In some individuals the green area, especially its anterior and adjoining part of bottom margin, are bordered by a cream-colored line; sometimes this has an extension from side of forehead diagonally down and then parallel to side base of bill. Most of **upperparts** off-white (very pale gray or creamy), finely to sometimes coarsely vermiculated black; rump varies from plain to vermiculated; a black band along outer web of most scapulars, collectively forming a longitudinal bar. **Underparts** breast varies with individual from rich tawny-buff to pale pinkish cinnamon, spotted (usually somewhat sparingly, but sometimes heavily) dusky to black (these become conspicuous with wear); sides like upperparts, with a transverse (i.e., vertical in the swimming bird) broad white bar or crescent (very rarely lacking?) just forward of bend of folded wing; belly white; vent to tail black, enclosing a triangular light buffy or creamy patch (it bleaches to whitish) on each side; **tail** medium gray or darker, the feathers pointed; legs and **feet** usually a grayed flesh color, webs nearly black.

In the **wing** the elongated innermost secondaries and their greater coverts are plain gray, or occasionally with buffy distal edges, except the most distal one (adjoining the speculum) has a sharply defined black band along its outer edge; remainder of wing is retained Basic feathering (described below).

This Plumage is acquired within the span of late summer to early winter—in any individual, largely within a portion of this time, and generally by some time in Oct. The last of the scapulars and some flank feathers develop late, even in early winter.

▶ ♂ Def. Basic Plumage (entire feathering), acquired beginning in SUMMER and retained for some time after the new wing has grown, hence generally worn into FALL and then succeeded by Alt. (except most of the wing, acquired after a flightless period and within this span, is retained nearly a year).

Differs from ♀ definitive stages thus: **head** dark stripe through eye absent or seldom clearly indicated; **upperparts** more uniformly dark, the feathers having lighter (but not strikingly contrasting) margins and generally those on anterior mantle have a straight transverse narrow light line through the dark area which adjoins the pale margin; scapulars dark bordered light or, in some individuals, have internal buffy bars or markings; **underparts** more coarsely marked, with fewer spots or blotches on breast on (usually) more neutral-colored background. Differs from ♂ Juv. in having underparts spotted (not streaked) and various feathers, most evident on dorsum, are broader and with rather squarish ends. Legs and **feet** variably darkish to lead-colored or olive greenish, webs much darker. **Tail** feathers dark, narrowly edged pale, and broader distally than in ♂ Def. Alt.

Wing innermost secondaries brownish olive (not gray), often with pale edge distally on outer web; the outermost, or even several, of these secondaries have 3 longitudinal zones of coloring: blackish (exposed outer web), next a smoke gray or pale grayed olive stripe, and remainder brownish olive. Speculum metallic green, occasionally bronzy

348

or even partly violet as viewed under certain lighting conditions, the feathers (distal ones especially) sometimes tipped pale buffy or whitish; greater secondary coverts dark brownish with broad buffy to buffy brownish ends, forming a bar along leading edge of speculum and usually the bar is deeper colored distally. The other coverts generally are pale brownish, occasionally somewhat pale edged, though such edging usually is confined (when present) to the greater primary coverts; primaries sepia. Most of wing lining white, the under primary coverts light gray and occasionally with white ends; the feathers along leading edge gray-brown with white margins; axillars white, rarely with small blackish internal markings distally.

The drake's Basic is acquired by a molt of all feathering which generally begins quite early in summer and is completed in July; in the final phase of this molt, the tail and the wing quills are dropped (the latter almost simultaneously) and then there is a flightless period (about 21 days?) while the new Basic wing grows. The drake then is entirely in Basic and is capable of flight for an unknown period of time (probably individually variable, perhaps to as long as 5–6 weeks) before head–body–tail–innermost feathers of wing begin to be replaced by Alt. in fall.

▶ ♀ Def. Alt. Plumage (all feathering, excepting all but innermost feathers of wing), acquired in LATE SUMMER–FALL (bulk of it usually by some time in Sept.) and retained until within the span late Feb.–late April (usually EARLY MARCH).

A gray Plumage. **Bill** upper mandible a muted greenish or a grayish, often more or less blotched darker, often with a hint of yellow laterally, the very edges and tip black. **Iris** dark brownish. **Head** crown and stripe through eye (generally interrupted in front of eye) dusky to blackish with fine lighter markings, sides of head generally pale grayish buff streaked dusky, quite often with unmarked circular white area at side base of bill (such as is typical of the ♀ Baikal Teal); chin and upper throat white. **Upperparts** dusky brownish feathers broadly edged and boldly marked muted buff or sometimes grayish or even partly white (varies with individual); **underparts** breast usually toward buff, spotted dusky; feathers of sides and flanks dusky with broad, nearly white margins; belly white, occasionally with sharply defined small dark markings; **tail** feathers slender, pointed, dusky with light edging, and plain internally. Legs and **feet** usually a grayed flesh color, webs dusky. **Wing** innermost secondaries taper distally to a point and are brownish olive with buffy (usually) or whitish exposed edge, the one next to the speculum has a brownish (not black) stripe along its outer web that merges with coloring of the remainder of the feather; remainder of wing is retained Basic feathering (see below).

NOTE   Drake-feathered ♀ ♀ have been taken occasionally; for a color illus. of *A. c. crecca* see upper right fig. on pl. 17 in Schiøler (1925). Various ♀ "intersexes" have been described by Kuroda (1937), Ali (1943), and J. M. Harrison (1968).

▶ ♀ Def. Basic Plumage (entire feathering); all except most of the wing is acquired in SPRING generally in first half of March, and retained until well along in summer; then the duck becomes flightless (simultaneous loss of wing quills is the "offset" terminal phase of the Prebasic molt that occurred in spring) and, during a flightless period, the new Basic wing grows. Apparently the molt out of Basic head–body, etc., begins in successful breeders not later than soon after the duck regains flight in FALL. Most of the Basic wing is retained nearly a year.

A buffy or brownish Plumage. **Bill** upper mandible usually a dusky olive greenish, without spots, and graying laterally, then some yellow or palish orange-yellow close to the edges. **Head** crown and nape, plus often an indistinct stripe back from the eye, streaked blackish and buffy and the latter predominates on rest of head and the neck (very exceptionally the crown is blackish green); **upperparts** more dusky than in Def. Alt., the light markings (feather edgings, barring, crescents, etc.) vary with individual from a muted buff toward pinkish tan; **underparts** breast feathers with crescentic fuscous or blackish markings and rather buffy tips; sides and flanks various buffs or off-white with large fuscous or sepia zones astride the feather shafts; lower breast and much of belly white or nearly white, quite often with somewhat indistinct spots or small dusky blotches, but some individuals have all of underparts heavily marked (almost streaked) dusky brownish. Legs and **feet** as ♂ Def. Basic. **Tail** feathers comparatively wide distally (tips blunt), color brownish sepia, with 2–3 narrow buffy bars in their wider web, markings of same in the narrower web, and buffy edging.

Wing much as ♂ Def. Basic, but these are some differences: innermost secondaries comparatively short, distally broad, and blackish (but fade toward olive brownish) with creamy buff indentations and edges, and the ends of the overlying coverts are buffy but they become progressively more brownish buff outward along the wing over the bases of the secondaries; the median upper coverts are more brownish than in the drake, usually with light buffy edges but sometimes plain; greater primary coverts typically plain dark, occasionally slightly pale edged; wing lining mostly white; axillars usually all white, rarely with a small amount of dark distally.

NOTE   According to Witherby (1939), in *A. c. crecca* there are "two types of breeding plumage, one darker and plainer, one lighter and barred." In *A. crecca carolinensis* there is a gradient of considerable individual variation in Basic ("breeding") feathering, but the only way to get "two types" would be to compare grayer Alt. (fall–winter) with the usually brownish Basic (spring–summer). According to Kuroda (1937), Alt. is a "gray type" and Basic a "reddish-brown type."

AT HATCHING   See col. pl. facing p. 370 for subsp. *carolinensis*. Much smaller and trimmer than Mallard; where the latter is yellowish, the former is more toward cinnamon; there is a broad cheek stripe; legs and feet dark. Aleutian birds (*A. c. nimia*) are similar. The pattern of an Icelandic duckling (*A. c. crecca*) was illus. in monochrome by Sutton (1961).

▶   ♂ Juv. Plumage (entire feathering), perfected soon after flight is attained and then some individuals begin a gradual molting (belly unmarked white by early Sept.), but many retain the entire Juv. feathering for up to several weeks before any molting is evident; the Juv. wing, except for a few innermost feathers, is retained into the following summer.

A blended, buffy tan, quite ♀-like Plumage. **Bill** olive greenish or slaty, sometimes with dusky or yellowish areas (usually laterally); **iris** grayed brownish. **Head** markings comparatively diffuse, brownish on pale base; chin–throat off-white and varies with individual from finely marked dark to plain; **upperparts** the feathers are brownish fuscous with buffy brown margins; **underparts** breast heavily streaked brownish fuscous on buffy tan; the feathers on sides with dark internal and wide lateral buffy tan zones (broadly streaked effect); lower breast to vent usually a pale buff with small, poorly defined, dark markings, the same general patterns extending to under tail coverts; the narrow **tail** feathers are toward sepia, margined buff, and have notched ends. Legs and **feet** usually lead-colored, webs much darker.

Wing innermost secondaries comparatively short, narrow, and gray edged buffy (as are their overlying coverts); the secondary adjoining the speculum has a very dark border on the outer web; speculum more muted (less iridescent greenish, sometimes toward cinnamon distally) than the later Basic wing; upper wing coverts comparatively narrow (not broadly rounded), the ends of the greater secondary coverts nearly white and form a conspicuous bar (unlike the later, Basic, wing, sometimes these coverts have some light markings, even a transverse white bar, in addition to their light ends); greater primary coverts conspicuously white edged; much of wing lining white, the greater under primary coverts gray, axillars white (rarely with some gray spotting).

▶ ♀ Juv. Plumage (entire feathering), acquired as ♂ and, typically, all of it (except most of wing) is molted fairly soon, often (in early-hatched birds?) in Aug.

Like the drake, a brownish Plumage with rather diffuse markings. **Bill** and **iris** as ♂ Juv. **Underparts** breast buffy tan, heavily marked dusky brownish; lower breast to vent rather coarsely spotted or with somewhat streaky wide dusky brownish markings throughout; on the sides the streaking is more toward dusky tan on buff; the notched tail feathers sometimes are retained well into fall. Legs and **feet** as ♂ Juv. In the **wing** the elongated innermost secondaries have broad buffy edges and darkest color in outer web of outermost of these is dusky brownish; greater wing coverts have white ends, sometimes also some additional white markings in the dark portion; middle and smaller upper wing coverts variable, usually plain, sometimes light edged; green area of speculum sometimes reduced (only on outer webs of a few feathers).

▶ ♂ Basic I Plumage (typically consists only of some feathering on head–neck, breast, mantle, and sides). The feathers of this quite striking Plumage often grow in EARLY SEPT. and they drop out generally by the time considerable Alt. I head–body feathering has appeared in OCT. On the **cheeks** they are blackish, or some also dark brownish; on upper **neck** they are very coarsely marked black; any in the **mantle** are white with coarse irregular black lines; on lower **side of breast** they are barred black on white; and on the **sides** they are white or pale buffy tan with irregular heavy black barring. For a col. illus. of a drake showing Basic I on mantle, sides, and lower side of breast, see center fig. on pl. 17 in Schiøler (1925).

NOTE Basic I may, exceptionally, include practically all of the feathering (except most of Juv. wing). Schiøler (1925, upper rt. fig. on pl. 14) illustrated in color a young drake *A. c. crecca* in a gray Plumage. Part of the sides are heavily barred black (there are also some Juv. feathers on the sides); the venter is white, very faintly spotted gray anteriorly; and the tail feathers are new, without notched ends.

▶ ♂ Alt. I Plumage (all feathering, excepting all but innermost feathers of wing), acquired in FALL, often from late Sept. well into Oct., with the last incoming feathers (long scapulars) not fully grown until in Nov. Some, presumably late-hatched individuals, do not have complete Alt. I until some time in Jan. This Plumage is worn through WINTER and SPRING into SUMMER.

This Plumage appears to be the same as later Alts. and is as individually variable in small details. Examples: the black area on chin is variable in size; the ventral spotting

351

may end on upper breast or even may extend down over the belly. The tail feathers are dark internally with narrow, very light, edging.

▶ ♀ Basic I Plumage (all feathering, excepting all but innermost feathers of wing). Depending on date of hatching, this Plumage begins to succeed the Juv. in AUG. or SEPT., possibly even later sometimes; unlike the drake's, it is an extensive Plumage and is common in SEPT.

Grayer than Juv. Plumage; **bill** usually medium grayish with some yellowish laterally. The various markings (such as fine ones on **head**–neck) narrow and sharply defined; chin white; **upperparts** a slightly brownish dark gray, the feathers with sharply defined pale margins; **underparts** breast to vent unmarked white, or, rarely, with fine dark markings; sides have broad fuscous streaking on white or off-white; under tail coverts white with sharply defined, more or less oval, very dark markings (largest on longest feathers). Quite often some, or even all, of the notched Juv. tail feathers are retained until after the entire Basic I head–body is fully grown; then the barred, buffy-edged Basic I tail feathers grow.

▶ ♀ Alt. I Plumage replaces all of Basic I, generally in LATE SEPT. and in OCT. or, in late-hatched birds, may still be growing in Nov. or even Dec.; it is retained until SPRING (usually late March–early April). A decidedly gray Plumage, generally with unmarked white belly and abdomen; most of the Juv. wing is retained and worn with it. The first Plumage in which the innermost secondaries taper to a point.

▶ ♀ Basic II Plumage (entire feathering), head–body–tail–innermost feathers of wing acquired in SPRING, before the nesting season. The first Plumage in which the ♀ nests. Molting resumes, beginning late in or after the rearing period, with loss of Juv. wing and then the "offset" Basic II wing grows.

NOTE   In *A. c. crecca*, evidently some yearling ♀ ♀ nest late, hence have delayed wing molt, and so join with migrants and reach winter range before becoming flightless. In Japan, such flightless individuals usually are found in Oct., actual dates being Oct. 8–Nov. 12 (Kuroda 1937). Since drakes are free of reproductive duties earlier, they can begin wing molt earlier, and never have been found flightless on winter range.

Aberrant coloring   In both nominate *crecca* and *carolinensis*, occasionally a drake has some white on the lower neck, even a partial or complete collar; ♀ ♀ occasionally are pale overall, toward buff or variably gray (to nearly white).

Measurements of *A. crecca carolinensis* birds from breeding and winter range; 12 ♂: BILL 36–40 mm., av. 38.2; WING 180–193, av. 186.3; TAIL 66–73, av. 69.5, TARSUS 30–34, av. 31.7;   11 ♀: BILL 35–38 mm., av. 36.5; WING 173–187, av. 179; TAIL 61–70, av. 66.7; TARSUS 30–32, av. 30.8 (ETS).

In this series the wing is meas. over the curve (not flattened): 12 ♂ BILL 34–37, WING 179–191, TAIL 65–73, TARSUS 27–30; 12 ♀ BILL 33–36 mm., WING 172–183 (Witherby 1939).

For meas. of 7 drake *carolinensis* taken Jan.–March in Japan, see Kuroda (1961b).

The flattened WING of the drake in N. Am. usually meas. 180 mm. or longer, of the ♀ 179 or shorter (Carney 1964).

In each sex the Juv. wing undoubtedly is shorter than the Basic wing, as it is in *A. c. crecca* (see below).

352

Weight in fall in Ill. (in lb. plus standard error): ♂ 21 "adult" 0.86 ± .01 (390 gm.), 38 "juvenile" 0.82 ± .01 (372 gm.); ♀ 10 "adult" 0.78 ± .02 (354 gm.), 38 "juvenile" 0.74 ± .02 (336 gm.) (Bellrose and Hawkins 1947).

Wt. of fall birds, age-classes not separated: 194 ♂ av. 0.8 lb. (about 364 gm.), max. 1 lb. (454 gm); 81 ♀ av. 0.7 lb. (about 318 gm.), max. 0.9 lb. (409 gm.) (A. L. Nelson and Martin 1953).

From the Brooks Range in Alaska: 6 ♂, May 24–June 26, weighed 293–379 gm., av. 332; 3 ♀, May 20, 29, weighed 265–334, av. 343 (Irving 1960).

Three incubator-hatched ducklings, before they had fed, weighed 16–16.5 gm. (Smart 1965a).

Hybrids For the species, Gray (1958) listed many crosses, most of them having occurred in captivity. In the wild this teal presumably has crossed with at least 5 species of *Anas,* probably most often with the Pintail (*A. acuta*). Two wild-taken drakes in N. Am. were a cross each with Mallard (Stone 1903) and Pintail (T. Howell 1959). Occasional, somewhat unusually patterned drakes (for example, having more or less of a white collar) possibly have a hybrid in their lineage. If there are any wild-taken ♀ hybrids, even of the first generation, evidently they have not been recognized as such.

Two drakes, one a Mallard and the other a Greenwing, observed in May in Sask., appeared to have established a close bond with the same ♀ Mallard (Nero 1959).

In the past, when the Am. Greenwing was regarded as a different species ("*carolinensis*") from the Eurasian (and Aleutian) birds, the progeny of matings between them were listed as hybrids; they should be regarded as intergrades and are discussed below at the end of "Subspecies."

Geographical variation continental populations of N. Am. and Eurasia (including Iceland and Britain) consist of birds of about the same av. size; the Aleutian derivative of the Eurasian stock, however, consists of birds that av. decidedly larger. There seems to be no evidence of a gradient or cline of increasing size eastward in Eurasia. Furthermore, continental birds on both sides of Bering Sea are migratory, but the Aleutian birds are not. Eurasian–Aleutian drakes in Alt. Plumage have both clear-cut and quantitative differences in pattern from continental N. Am. Greenwings, mentioned below. In both sexes of continental N. Am. birds the light bar along forward edge of the speculum is more heavily pigmented, especially its distal portion, in a higher percentage of individuals than in Eurasian–Aleutian birds; all ♀ Greenwings are very similar in coloring otherwise. RSP

SUBSPECIES The first 2 listed are similar in almost all respects except for av. size, while the third (described above in detail) differs from the others in pattern and/or coloring, chiefly in ♂ Alt. Plumage. Certain intergrades between the subspecies are mentioned at the end of this section.

crecca Linnaeus—Eurasian Greenwing. Breeds from Iceland across Eurasia to Koryakland, the Commander Is., and the Pribilofs; straggles widely, including to continental N. Am. (where evidently it mates with local stock). Drake in Alt. Plumage: generally a conspicuous white line separates the green area from the rufous chestnut on side of head and usually a whitish buffy extension down to side of chin near bill; mantle and sides generally coarsely vermiculated black (the markings are, in fact, so coarse that they can hardly be called vermiculations); part of each of the long scapulars is white (collectively forming a longitudinal white stripe above folded wing. In both sexes and in both Juv. and Basic wing, the bar within the wing along leading edge of the speculum is "almost always very pale buff, or pure white," especially the distal half (J. C. Phillips 1923b); this is particularly true of ♀ ♀, but there are exceptions (Kuroda 1937).

Measurements   Specimens from Britain and across Eurasia, 12 ♂: BILL 36–40 mm., av. 37.7; WING 178–193, av. 184; TAIL 65–71, av. 68; TARSUS 30–33, av. 31.2;   and 11 ♀: BILL 34–37 mm., av. 35.7; WING 171–187, av. 180; TAIL 62–68, av. 65; TARSUS 29–33, av. 31.2 (ETS).

Birds taken in Denmark (mostly migrants), "adults," 114 ♂: BILL 33.5–40 mm., av. 37; WING 165–193, av. 181; TAIL 36–42, av. 39.5; TARSUS 28–34, av. 31;   51 ♀: BILL 32–38 mm., av. 35; WING 166–180, av. 174; TAIL 35–43.5, av. 39; TARSUS 29–32, av. 30 (Schiøler 1925). As would be expected, the Juv. wing is shorter: 75 ♂ 169–188 mm., av. 179; 51 ♀ 162–180, av. 170.5 (Schiøler). The same author also gave meas. of nominate *crecca* from Greenland, Iceland, Scandinavia, Japan, and Sakhalin I.

Migrants in Honshu, Japan: adult ♂ BILL 34.5–38 mm. in 359 birds, but 28 exceptional ones extend the range to 33–41 mm.; WING 180–185 mm. in 357 birds, but 30 exceptional ones extend this to 165–194; adult ♀ BILL 33.5–36 mm. in 463 examples, but 18 exceptional ones extend the range to 30.5–40 mm., WING 165–175 in 457 birds,

354

but 14 others extend this to 160–185. First-fall birds (with Juv. wing): BILL 34–38 mm. in 68 birds, but 5 exceptional ones extend this to 33–40.5, WING 175–180 in 71 birds, but 2 others extend this to 168.5–183; ♀ BILL 33.5–35 in 61 birds and 8 others extend the range to 160–183. These figures are from Kuroda (1937), who stated that they are in close agreement with those in Hartert (1920a).

For various other series, WING across chord, see Friedmann (1948); for small series, WING meas. over the curve, see Witherby (1939).

Weight (exceptional examples omitted) in fall in Honshu, Japan: mature ♂ 320–360 gm., ♀ 285–330; first-fall ♂ 280–320 and ♀ 275–310. The birds gain much wt. in winter and are heaviest just before spring migration. They can "attain astonishing wts. of as much as twice the normal wt. of the species. This is owing to an accumulation of fat and there is no great difference in the amount of flesh" (Kuroda 1937, transl.).

For many data on wt., by sex and season, also see Bauer and Glutz von Blotzheim (1968).

nimia Friedmann—Aleutian Greenwing. The Aleutian Is. from Akutan westward; not migratory; no certain records of occurrence elsewhere. Size av. larger than nominate *crecca*, which it otherwise closely resembles (thus it also is larger than *carolinensis*).

Measurements 13 ♂: BILL 33.2–37.4 mm., av. 35.8; WING (across chord) 182–204, av. 193.1; 3 ♀: BILL 34.2–36.1 mm., av. 35.1; WING (chord) 185–189, av. 186.7 (Friedmann 1948).

Four ♂ (Kiska and Little Kiska I.): BILL 35–38 mm., av. 36.5; WING (flattened) 194–203, av. 196.5; TAIL 66–71, av. 68; TARSUS 31–34, av. 33; 2 ♀ (Little Kiska, Atka) BILL 34–35 mm.; WING 185–190; TAIL 64–66, TARSUS 32–33 (ETS).

In drakes, the nail on the bill av. larger (especially longer) than in the 2 other subspecies; *nimia* (17 ♂) width 3.1–4.2 mm., av. 3.6, length 7.0–8.3, av. 7.5; a series of nominate *crecca* width 3.0–4.0 mm., av. 3.3, length 6.0–7.1, av. 6.6; series of *carolinensis* width 2.5–3.5, av. 3.0, length 6.1–7.4, av. 6.6; the ♀ ♀ of all 3 subspecies do not reflect this size difference, except length of nail av. slightly longer in *nimia* (R. Laybourne).

Weight of "adults" June 2–5, from Amchitka: 15 ♀ 310–440 gm., av. 392 (14 oz.); 4 ♀ 338–418, av. 378 (13½ oz.) (E. L. Schiller).

carolinensis Gmelin—American Greenwing. Much of N. Am., straggling elsewhere. Migratory. Detailed descr. and meas. were given at the beginning of this account. Drake in Alt. Plumage: white lines on sides of head reduced or even absent; fine (occasionally rather coarse) black vermiculations on mantle and sides; breast usually more deeply and richly colored than in nominate *crecca*; no white areas on scapulars; a white bar or crescent (as in ♂ A. *formosa*) on side anterior to bend of folded wing. In both sexes and all ages, the wing bar at leading edge of the speculum usually is richer in color (brownish buff), particularly the distal half (J. C. Phillips 1923b, Schiøler 1925); in ♀ ♀, probably 9 out of 10 specimens can be identified to subspecies by this character (Phillips).

Intergradation As a prelude to discussing this topic, a recapitulation of some background information is appropriate. Drake Greenwings in Alt. Plumage differ, most obviously as follows: 1 A. *c. crecca* (also *nima*)—white scapular stripe present, heavy black lines on mantle and sides, no white bar down side of breast; and **2** *A. crecca carolinensis*—no unmarked white in scapulars, fine vermiculations on mantle and sides, conspicuous white bar down side of breast. Mature drakes of nominate *crecca* and *carolinensis* usually have molted into somewhat ♀-like Basic Plumage by late July or some time in Aug. and, so long as they remain in Basic, they cannot be distinguished under field conditions. (In hand, the light bar within the wing is a helpful character.) Drakes commonly do not molt back into Alt. head–body until well along in fall. During this period of molting, the feathering on side of breast (with or without a white bar) typically is fully developed for a considerable time (up to several weeks?) before the long scapulars grow. These scapulars are the last of the incoming Alt. feathers and often they are not fully grown until very late Nov. or sometimes as late as in Jan. For specimen data on timing of their presence in *A. c. crecca*, see Bull (1964). Thus the period when all characteristics of drake body feathering that are useful afield in distinguishing *crecca* (and possibly *nimia*) from *carolinensis*, or in recognizing individuals having mixed characteristics, extends only from about Dec. into the following summer.

Stragglers, wanderers, and any escaped individuals of whatever origin, undoubtedly associate readily with any Greenwings they encounter regardless of the characteristics of their respective feathering. It "is not a very rare sight in early spring on Hempstead Reservoir [Long I., N.Y.] to see drakes of both the European [nominate *crecca*] and Green-winged [*carolinensis*] performing before the same duck" (Cruickshank 1936). In addition to such scattered chance opportunities for forming "mixed" pairs, it is of interest that both nominate *crecca* and *carolinensis* occur regularly in the Pribilofs (Hanna 1920, later authors). To round out the picture, at least drakes of the highly migratory *carolinensis* have occurred (usually in winter–spring) sparingly throughout the Aleutian chain, at times in company with the local *A. c. nimia*. Furthermore, since *A. c. crecca* breeds in the Commander Is. and has been taken several times in the Pribilofs, some migrants may reach the Aleutians, where they would be indistinguishable in life from the local birds (*A. c. nimia*). Near the end of the Alaska Pen., at Cold Bay, on May 21, 1965, 2 drakes—one *carolinensis* and the other presumably *nimia*—were displaying to a ♀ teal (R. D. Jones, Jr.). In summary, the resident Aleutian birds are visited, at least seasonally, by migratory *carolinensis* and possibly also nominate *crecca*.

At Hempstead Reservoir (mentioned above) in early March, 1936, a drake was seen that had both the scapular stripe of nominate *crecca* and the lateral bar of *carolinensis* (Cruickshank 1936). Near Reading, Pa., March 1, 1939, a drake had black and white in the scapulars, also a white lateral bar; a typical ♂ nominate *crecca* was present and useful for comparison (Poole 1940). There are skins of 4 drakes (descriptions are in MS) that show intergradation, including pattern of scapulars: one each from St. Lawrence I., the Pribilofs, Ft. McMurray in Alta., and Nebr. (R. Laybourne). Yet another was seen in Butte Co., Cal., on Dec. 13, 1969 (*Aud. Field Notes* **24** 534. 1970). Several were reported seen, in B.C. and Cal., in the winter of 1971–72 (*Am. Birds* **25** 572, 645, 650. 1972). At a waterfowl decoy in Chiba Prefecture, Japan, a drake was taken alive on March 3, 1961, and Kuroda (1961a) included a photo of it with his published description; the bird had a light scapular stripe, a narrow white lateral bar, and there were fine vermiculations on the body.

It would be most desirable to assemble an adequate series of captive-reared inter-grades, of both sexes and of known parentage, for comparison with wild-taken sus-pected examples. RSP

FIELD IDENTIFICATION   In N. Am. Smallest of our native dabbling ducks. In flight, because of comparatively short neck, the wings appear farther forward on the body than is usual for a dabbling duck. Even so, the Greenwing has a well-balanced appearance. On taking flight, the birds form in compact bunches which may twist and turn, dashing high and low like sandpipers. When not nesting, Greenwings prefer to be in groups or flocks (to well over a hundred birds) and, at some localities, these come together in vast assemblies.

The drake Am. Greenwing, from late fall into the following summer, has the rufous-chestnut of head interrupted by a large green area on the sides and these colors seldom are separated by more than a narrow white line; no white shows in the scapulars; there is a broad white transverse bar or crescent (vertical in the swimming bird) on side in front of wing; there is a cream-colored patch, bordered black, at side base of tail. The other drake Plumages are rather difficult to describe satisfactorily, being more or less gray or drab and darkish, with (after the streaked Juv. stage) usually a white belly. Any green in the speculum is not visible very far or in overcast weather. Lack of any visible white (except belly) or vivid coloring in a bunch of small fast-flying ducks would indi-cate this species. (Our other teals have a sizable pale area on the wing; the larger Gad-wall has some white.) At a distance Greenwings appear gray with dark heads. Their seemingly effortless towering, then swooping flight, in tight bunches, is more useful in identification. The drake utters his *krick* call, the duck her thin *quack*.

Drake Eurasian Greenwings, plus the identical-appearing Aleutian Greenwing, are separable when in Alt. Plumage (about Dec. into the following summer) from drakes of the continental N. Am. subspecies; in the former there are white areas in the long scapulars which combine to form a longitudinal stripe, the green on side of head usu-ally is well set off by a white border, and there is no white bar on forward side of body. There are some problems in identifying drakes to subspecies, depending on stage of molting, which were discussed in the section on Plumages. The main point is that drakes in fall that lack a white bar on forward sides presumably are Eurasian (or Aleu-tian) Greenwings, regardless of whether they lack the white scapular line and soon will acquire it, or whether they already have it.

The Juv. ♂, older ♂♂ in Basic Plumages, and ♀♀ in all ages and seasons, are not known to be distinguishable afield from continental N. Am. Greenwings. The pale bar at forward edge of the speculum does not show adequately in the folded wing, nor is its paleness an invariably dependable criterion (some continental N. Am. birds are cor-respondingly pale).

Some characteristics of drakes of "mixed" (Eurasian, or, possibly Aleutian, plus con-tinental N. Am.) parentage, having mixed or intermediate characteristics, were men-tioned at the end of the preceding section. RSP

VOICE   As known in *A. crecca carolinensis*. The common call of the drake, heard most often in winter–spring, is a high, shrill, almost trilled, whistle that somewhat re-sembles the spring call of the tree frog, *Hyla versicolor*. This "krick" sound is uttered singly, often in doublets, also in series. The series are heard constantly from groups of drakes during the social phase of display. Sometimes they utter a mixture of harsh and whistled sounds. They have a variety of calls, generally 3- or 5-syllabled, as *ti tiu te* or *te tiu tu tete*; there is no movement of the body, nor does the bill appear to open, when they are uttered (McKinney 1965b). Below, under "Reproduction," note calls mentioned under the following displays of the drake: Burp, Grunt-whistle, Head-up-tail-up, Bill-up, Down-up, and Bridling.

As carefully noted among captive birds, the voice of the drake is "hoarser and not so clear-cut" in autumn as in spring (Warren, in J. C. Phillips 1923b). Phillips mentioned a "scraping, creaking, snipelike call heard in early autumn," which may come from young drakes.

The quack of the ♀, compared to the Mallard, is thinner and higher pitched (as it is in some other species). Also see below for calls associated with these displays of the duck: Inciting, Preen-behind-the-wing, Decrescendo and Loud repeated quacks. RSP

HABITAT In N. Am. *A. crecca carolinensis*—for **nesting,** prefers a mixture of grassy or sedgy terrain plus brush or scattered trees, usually not distant from water; in northerly localities, away from forest, areas of herbaceous growth plus patches of low or dwarf birch alder or willow, generally near water. In summer–fall also on any waters where suitable food is available. In **migration,** shallow inland and brackish coastal waters, preferably with much floating and emergent vegetation; also visits grainfields. In **winter,** brackish tidal marshes, creeks, estuarine areas, shallow fresh waters inland, and rice fields. When visiting remote oceanic is., generally found on fresh or brackish ponds. In substance, it occupies much the same niche as the Mallard, but eats smaller food items.

A. crecca nimia—in the treeless Aleutians, as noted on Amchitka by Kenyon (1961), in warmer months prefers freshwater ponds and lakes and nests in grassy areas thereabouts, spending comparatively little time feeding or resting on marine beaches. In colder months, common on marine beaches, at low tide feeding in pools and in shallow waters among exposed reefs. RSP

DISTRIBUTION (See map.) Where Greenwings of one subspecies are reported as occurring in the usual range of another, almost all records are based on drakes in Alt. Plumage. (The exceptions are certain specimen records from Greenland and 2 banded individuals that were recovered.) Am. birds are treated first in this and the next section.

Both nominate *crecca* and *A. crecca carolinensis* have been imported into each other's range by aviculturalists and the possibility exists that some captives may have escaped into the wild.

A. crecca carolinensis—main areas of **breeding** extend from the prairies in conterminous U.S. northwestward to or near the arctic coast in w. Mackenzie Dist. and Yukon Terr., and various areas in Alaska s. of the arctic slope. Lesser concentrations occur from Cal. n. in Pacific coastal states and mainland B.C. (also breeds locally on Vancouver I.), s. Ont.–Que., n. Ont. and adjacent Que. (coasts and is. of James Bay), and some breed in extreme n. Que. (vicinity of Ungava Bay); breeds in Labrador and suspected of breeding in small numbers throughout interior Ungava; breeds in Nfld. The s. and se. limits of breeding have changed over the years, with a cessation in some areas during or as a result of the era of unrestricted wildfowling, and some reoccupation. Some changes in the last several decades may have been influenced by the creation of various waterfowl refuges. For older records of breeding distribution, see J. C. Phillips (1923b); recent southerly limits were given in the 1957 A.O.U. *Check-list*. Also see Bull (1964). For map of relative density of breeding birds in N. Am., see Moisan (1966).

The N. Am. Greenwing nests on the Alaska Pen. and possibly also on certain is. of the Aleutian chain; Unalaska is a good possibility (see Cahn 1947), also Unimak. Drakes, at least, have been recorded in one season or another all the way to the end of the chain, generally in company with local birds (*A. c. nimia*).

Other **peripheral occurrences** of *carolinensis* on the continent and nearby: Pribilofs (breeds); St. Matthew I.; St. Lawrence I. (occurs and probably breeds); mainland Alaska—several occurrences on arctic coast, Umiat on arctic slope (breeding record), and Sheenjek Valley in ne. interior (breeding record); Herschel I. in Yukon Terr. (breeding record). Other northernmost places where it has been found, from w. to e.—Victoria I., Jenny Lind I., Repulse Bay on the mainland, and C. Dorset on s. Baffin I.. W. Greenland—at least a dozen records. Bermuda—regular fall–winter. In W. Indian region apparently most numerous in Cuba, but scattered records eastward to include various of the Windward Is.

Winter range   Northern limit varies depending on mildness or severity of season. In the Aleutians this subspecies was found at Dutch Harbor on Unalaska I. in every month except Aug. (Cahn 1947); Gabrielson and Lincoln (1959) possibly made an overstatement in reporting it as wintering "more or less commonly" in se. Alaska and in the Aleutians w. to Unalaska, but it is a hardy bird. In interior Alaska there were 8 at Paxson on Feb. 22, 1972 (*Am. Birds* **26** 642, 1972). On the Atlantic side, highest winter count in Nfld. was 168 birds in late 1963.

Southerly limits—there are few birds in parts of Mexico, but large concentrations on the Pacific side (Sinaloa, Nayarit, Jalisco) and Atlantic side (n. Veracruz). Plentiful in parts of Cuba, Nicaragua, e. Colombia, and n. Venezuela. Reported from Tobago.

Occurrences at places remote from usual range include Brit. Isles (not over 5 records to 1939, reported annually by the 1960s, maximum of 7 records in a year, generally reported in the span Oct. into May); one banded in N.B. on Aug. 22, 1970, was shot at St. Mary's in Scilly Isles, Jan. 2, 1971. EUROPEAN MAINLAND (Finland 1, Sweden 1, Netherlands 4, Belgium 2) and AFRICA (drake taken in Morocco, near Casablanca, April 13, 1959). PACIFIC AREA main Hawaiian group (apparently now regular visitant, judging from Berger 1972, and see below under nominate *crecca*), Midway (various records, not to subspecies—Clapp and Woodward 1968—but *carolinensis* seems probable), and Layson (not identified to subspecies); Marshall Is. (taken on Jaluit); Japan (11 plus an intergrade presumably between nominate *crecca* and *carolinensis* taken in the period 1916–61 inclusive).

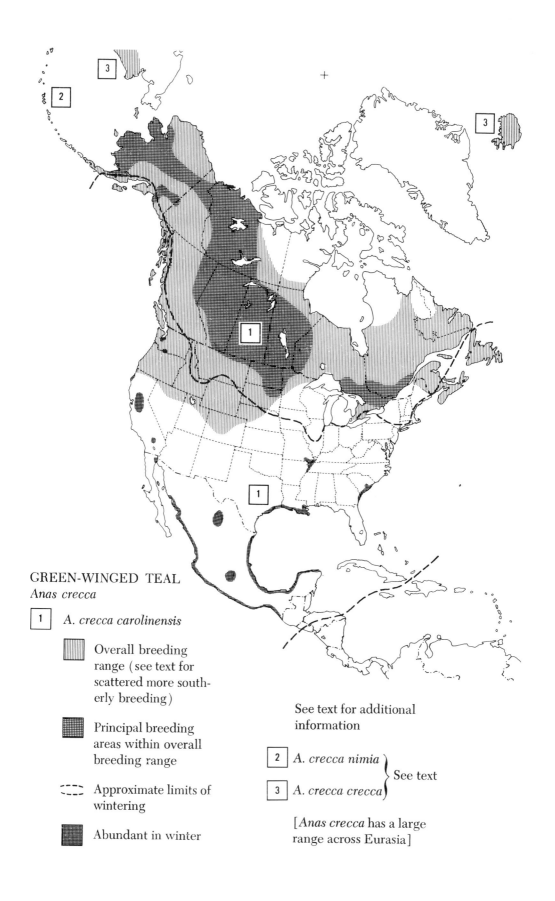

GREEN-WINGED TEAL
Anas crecca

1   *A. crecca carolinensis*

▥   Overall breeding range (see text for scattered more southerly breeding)

▦   Principal breeding areas within overall breeding range

- - -   Approximate limits of wintering

▨   Abundant in winter

See text for additional information

2   *A. crecca nimia* ⎫
              ⎬ See text
3   *A. crecca crecca* ⎭

[*Anas crecca* has a large range across Eurasia]

In the New World this species has been recorded as **fossil** from the Pleistocene of Ore., Cal., Nev., Ariz., New Mex., Kans., and Texas, and 7 Fla. localities; and from **archaeological sites** in Ariz., Iowa, and Ill.; see Brodkorb (1964a) for details.

A. c. nimia—in the Aleutians, locally common in suitable habitat in **all seasons** (O. Murie 1959, Gabrielson and Lincoln 1959). Center of abundance seems to be well out in the chain, from Adak to Amchitka inclusive (R. D. Jones, Jr.). This subspecies was stated to be "resident (apparently)" by Friedmann (1948), but there is at least some seasonal dispersal. On the mainland, near the outer end of the Alaska Pen. at Cold Bay, a drake *nimia* was taken on Jan. 29, 1952 (Univ. Alaska coll. no. 502). There are various sightings, presumably of *nimia*, at Cold Bay. For example, 8 birds on Jan. 24, 1967, also one of the 2 drakes displaying to a ♀ teal on May 21, 1965 (R. D. Jones, Jr.). (The subject of occurrence also of highly migratory subspecies in the Aleutians was discussed earlier under "Intergradation.")

A. c. crecca—vast **breeding** range: Iceland (common; mostly migratory, mainly to Brit. Isles), Spitzbergen (1 record), Faeroes, Brit. Isles, across the Eurasian mainland to occasional nester at Chaun Bay at w. edge of Chuckchee Pen., and to the north on s. Novaya Zemlya; and various Pacific Is.: portions of Japan, also Sakhalin I., and the Commanders; in Bering Sea possibly the Pribilofs. In **winter** s. to tropical Africa, India, se. Asia, and the Phillippines.

For **Greenland** many records from 1823 onward, including both coasts but majority on sw. coast from Julianehaab to Godthaab (may be an annual visitor; possibly breeds). A bird banded when young at Myvatn, Iceland, July 31, 1933, was killed at Frederiksdal, Nanortalik Dist., Greenland, in early May, 1934 (M. Cooke 1945). Another young bird, banded at Myvatn on July 4, 1954, also was taken at Frederiksdal, Nov. 15, 1954 (Salomonsen 1967a).

Continental N. Am. and nearby Specimen records begin at least as long ago as 1854. For listing of all CANADIAN records, see Godfrey (1966). A ♀ banded in England on Nov. 9, 1952, was shot less than a month later, on Dec. 5, in Fogo Dist., Nfld. There are records (of drakes, at times in company with *A. crecca carolinensis*) for at least the following places: ATLANTIC COASTAL AREA Labrador, Nfld., N.S., N.B., Me., Mass., Conn., N.Y. (now seen most winters on Long I., maximum of 6 at 1 locality in April, 1937, and Dec., 1938), N.J., Md., Pa., Va., N.C., S.C., and Fla.; INLAND Ohio and Nev.; PACIFIC COASTAL AREA B.C., Wash., Ore. (at least 3), and Cal. (at least 4); BERING SEA Pribilofs (3 taken on St. Paul I. where identified by Friedmann 1948). This listing undoubtedly is incomplete.

There seem to have been more occurrences (or better reporting?) in e. N. Am. in the 1930s and 1940s than earlier or until very recently (compare with occurrence of Wigeon, *A. penelope*).

Elsewhere This is a partial listing of places outside usual range where Eurasian Greenwings have occurred: NORTHWARD Bear I., Spitzbergen (occurrences plus above-mentioned breeding), and Chuckchee Pen. (known only as a visitant eastward beyond Chaun Bay; ATLANTIC AREA Canaries, Madeira, Azores; PACIFIC Hawaii (drake seen on Oahu, Jan. –March, 1970, see Berger 1972) and known from the Marianas (uncommon winterer in Micronesia).

For a long list of Palearctic records as **fossil** and from **archaeological sites**, see Brodkorb (1964a). RSP

MIGRATION *A. crecca carolinensis.* In broad outline, the migratory pattern approximates that of some other waterfowl that have a large breeding range in N. Am. Most of the northeasterly birds (Ungava Pen.; Maritimes) travel to and via an Atlantic coastal corridor; there is a large wintering concentration in se. S.C. Birds of a vast area in the continental interior (U.S.–Canadian prairies, beyond northward, plus much of interior Alaska s. of the arctic slope) go down through the interior, the preponderance of easterly ones to wintering areas around the Gulf Coast (and some as far as n. S. Am.?); many of the more westerly (and northwesterly) ones turn quite abruptly westward, cross over the Continental Divide, and move on southward (large wintering concentrations in interior Cal., for example), many even to Mexico. The birds of a broad zone adjoining the Bering Sea coast of Alaska, and those of localities around southward to include se. Alaska and B.C. west of the Continental Divide, have their main wintering area in the Puget Sd. region. This last aggregate is a rather distinct subpopulation, even more so than the Ungava–Maritime birds.

As noted in w. Europe by Lebret (1947), there also is some "leapfrogging" in N. Am., ♀♀ going farther than ♂♂ and so predominating at more southerly wintering areas. Drakes are in excess in winter at mid-Atlantic, Gulf Coast, and Cal. localities. At some northerly areas (Ore., Wash., B.C.), however, the sex ratio in winter is approximately even.

Spring Greenwings generally travel in compact bunches, or these join into flocks of up to about a hundred individuals, usually bunched, occasionally strung out. Departure from southerly wintering areas begins early, generally by late Feb. In conterminous U.S., also part of B.C. and se. Alaska, the bulk of movement occurs in March, but it extends well into April in upper interior Canada and Alaska. In normal seasons, breeders have arrived at coldest portions of breeding range in the 2nd week in May.

Since winterers at more southerly places are preponderantly ♀♀, it seems likely that early migratory movement is such as to result in a more nearly even sex ratio at places en route. In temperate latitudes, at least, the birds pass through in a number of waves, the early ones containing mated pairs and some unmated drakes. The waves may represent movement from different wintering areas, the schedule of any particular wave being influenced by weather, age and sex composition of flocks, total distance to be covered, etc. As waves reach various breeding areas, pairs drop out and are nesting even before the last wave of the season reaches or passes through that area. The entire pattern is complex and few details are known.

Summer Drakes take leave of their mates (usually during incubation); some gather in small groups and go into flightless stage of molting locally. Others also form in aggregations, then have a **molt migration**. This seems to be a movement in the general direction of subsequent fall migration. On June 26, 1946, there were 125,000 waterfowl on the marsh at Whitewater Lake, Man. (Sowls 1955), a large percentage being Greenwings. Not all were unattached drakes, there also being pairs presumably of failed-breeders. Large numbers of Greenwings also go to Delta Marsh, in the same province; many must come a considerable distance, since the total number molting is far greater than the number that breed thereabouts. As the season advances, drakes of early-nesting pairs are joined by those of later nesters, also by failed-breeding ♀♀. Many of the drakes have new wing quills and are flying again, in groups, early in Aug. Other

Greenwings, depending on timing of their flightless period, are again on the wing later—failed-breeding ♀ ♀, successful ♀ ♀, and young of the year. Four flightless ♀ ♀, live-trapped in se. Mo. on Sept. 25 (Rogers 1967), presumably had flown a long distance southerly away from breeding range prior to dropping their wing quills (also see earlier under ♀ Basic II Plumage for similar occurrences in Japan). The whole pattern for summer into fall, with its many variables, allows for formation of unisexual and bisexual groups, for groups to amalgamate, for young birds to form aggregations or to join with those of different age-classes that will migrate to various wintering areas, and so on. Compared with some larger waterfowl, Greenwings are very mobile for a relatively long time prior to migration.

Fall Some segregation of sexes, such as parties containing only mature drakes, reflects the above-mentioned differences in timing of molt. The main time of passage of Greenwings in s. Canada and conterminous U.S. is Oct.–Nov. The birds are gone from the Canadian prairies by early Nov. and, by about the middle of the month, several hundred thousand are present in the marshes along the La. coast. At northern localities a few birds linger very late, until driven out by freeze-up. At southerly localities, migration continues well into Dec. In Fla. they seldom arrive until Dec.; also, there is migration in that month in coastal Texas, in Mexico, and beyond—13,000 wintering Greenwings in Nicaragua in 1951, 5,000 in Cuba in 1954, 40,000 in Colombia and Venezuela in 1960 (Moisan et al. 1967). A differential in timing of molt is not an adequate explanation for a preponderance of ♀ ♀ at southerly wintering areas.

The reader is referred to the following papers for further information: J. Munro (1949c) for B.C., Moisan (1966) for Labrador to Gulf of Mexico, Moisan et al. (1967) for overall coverage, and Bellrose (1968) for numbers of Greenwings using certain migration corridors. The above account is based mainly on these papers.

NOTE In addition to making long flights away from usual range, individuals shift about within it. Examples: one banded Sept. 26, 1940, in Tulare Co., Cal., was shot June 10, 1943, at Henley Harbor, Strait of Belle Isle, Labrador; one banded Aug. 16, 1946, in Penobscot Co., Me., was found Oct. 5 of the same year in Winnebago Co., Wis. (Low, in Aldrich 1949).

A. crecca nimia—only rather local movements are known.

A. c. crecca—data are scattered and in various languages; for w. Europe, see Lebret (1947) and W. J. Wolff (1966); for U.S.S.R. see Riabov (1960). RSP

BANDING STATUS For continental N. Am., total number banded was 148,956 through 1964 and total number of recoveries was 9,195 through 1966; main places of banding were Cal., Sask., Ore., B.C., Alta., Wash., and Que. (data from Bird Banding Laboratory). For further information on banding localities, etc., and various data based on band recoveries, see Moisan et al. (1967).

In the Aleutians, 325 Greenwings were banded through 1964, with no recoveries through 1966.

Abroad a great many teal have been banded. In Britain, for example, over 50,000 had been banded and over 9,000 recovered through the year 1969. RSP

REPRODUCTION *A. crecca carolinensis*. Although displays have been described (McKinney 1965b and literature he cited), no comprehensive study of breeding biology has been published for any subspecies.

Both sexes **first breed** as yearlings.

Most Greenwings arrive already paired on breeding grounds; also there are pursuit flights over breeding areas consisting of a ♀ (unmated?, or without firm pair bond?) and 5–12 drakes.

Pair formation occurs earlier, on winter range, also during spring migration, and to some extent after arrival. It seems likely that early formed pairs are of birds old enough to have bred previously and that spring pairing is an activity primarily of prebreeders. On winter range in La., at the Rockefeller refuge, virtually all Greenwings were paired in Mid-March (McKinney 1965b) and in e. Wash. most ♀ ♀ were paired by then (Johnsgard 1955), but in s. Man. some Greenwings still were unpaired on arrival in mid-April. The social display phase (group activity), with many ♂ ♂ performing around a ♀, is notably conspicuous and animated in the Greenwing. Much of this activity is on the water, but groups come ashore sometimes; wherever they are, frequently they take wing in rapid pursuit flight, the drakes following the movements of the ♀. Such flights are shorter in duration than in other *Anas* species; groups may fly for only a minute or two, then alight at or near their point of departure.

Displays are similar to those of nominate *crecca*, described by Lorenz (1941). Most postures have homologues (and some are essentially identical) with those of the Mallard, but all movements of the Greenwing are faster. Displays are listed below for each sex in the same sequence (plus an addition under ♀) and with same terminology as in McKinney's (1965b) study of captive and wild birds; boldface numbers match those of homologous activity of the Mallard, as described earlier in this volume.

Sexual reactions and calls of the duck INCITING sideways head movements, as ♀ quacks (as in Mallard); usually indicates that the pair bond is formed. Shakes occur during social phase, on water, and perhaps should be regarded as displays. HEAD-UP-TAIL-UP the ♀ responds to preliminary Shaking, Grunt-whistle, and Head-up-tail-up of drake by also performing Head-up-tail-up; Lorenz (in Ramsay 1956) never noted ♀ to thus display in nominate *crecca* or other ducks. NOD-SWIM as in ♂ (see below), during social display. PREEN-BEHIND-WING seen once, within this sequence: Decrescendo call, Preen-behind-wing and, as mate approached, she Incited when beside him. DECRESCENDO usually 4–7 distinct notes, the first longer and higher pitched. (Usually distinguishable from that of the Bluewing by its squeaky quality.) Given by captives in Man. as late as in May. LOUD, REPEATED QUACKS heard in March in La. from mated ♀ of flying pair; and in late May–early June in Man. from ♀ ♀ on the ground. (Compare with various activities of ♀ Mallard.)

Sexual reactions and calls of the drake BURP head raised vertically as a loud liquid *tliu* is uttered; crown feathers are raised, the "mane" on nape is conspicuous and, as the call is given, the feathers on back and wings are vibrated momentarily (as though shuddering). Often repeated several times. Sometimes done by drake when his mate is some distance away. **4** GRUNT-WHISTLE done broadside, and not very close, to ♀. Preceded by 1–2 rapid Head-shakes. Drake rears up, with head bent forward in arc; at peak of movement the bill is shaken very rapidly in water, causing a fine stream of droplets to be thrown in air on side toward ♀. Accompanying sound is a single, loud,

364

liquid *tliu,* followed by quiet "grunting." Fast, quiet, cheeping noises (as in Bill-up described below) have been heard during the initial Head-shake. Usually the Grunt-whistle is followed by Head-flick plus simultaneous 3 TAIL-SHAKE, then frequently also by HEAD-UP-TAIL-UP and TURN-TOWARD-THE-♀. 5 Head-up-tail-up and 6 Turn-toward-the-♀ almost invariably are linked. In the former, light areas at side base of tail are prominently displayed; a single clear whistle is uttered, not as loud as in Grunt-whistle. BILL-UP ("Chin-lifting"—Lorenz) head drawn into "shoulders," bill pointed up at an angle, and chittering notes uttered. (A series of very rapid lateral Head-shakes may be performed during Bill-up.) Associated with overt hostility between drakes; the speed and pitch of chittering increases until the sound is altered to a series of very rapid whistles and distance between 2 drakes decreases. 10 DOWN-UP often precedes and is followed by Bill-up, the combination occurring especially when hostile ♀ ♀ approach one another closely. Accompanied by series of 3 rapid whistles. 7 NOD-SWIM the head is merely moved forward and back, with varying degrees of intensity, as the bird swims. Often done by drake in a group when trying to maneuver into a favorable position to perform a display oriented toward a ♀. 8 TURN-BACK-OF-HEAD done independently or sometimes follows 4-5-6. 9 BRIDLING done ashore, the drake broadside to ♀, who may be swimming. Common linkage 1-3-9 and, at same time, ♂ pushes his head backward slightly, the chest protruding forward, and while in this posture he utters a single whistle. SHAKE on land or water; ♂ broadside to ♀; like normal comfort move-

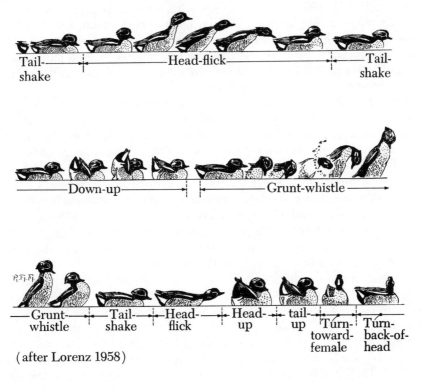

Tail-shake ———|——————Head-flick——————|—— Tail-shake

——————Down-up——————|———— Grunt-whistle ————→

——Grunt-whistle —|— Tail-shake —|—Head-flick —|— Head-up —|— tail-up —|— Turn-toward-female —|— Turn-back-of-head

(after Lorenz 1958)

ment, or the same slightly exaggerated. **1** HEAD-SHAKE rapid, lateral, independent or linked to certain other displays. **2** HEAD-FLICK rapid, with a rotary component, independent or with Grunt-whistle or Wing-flap. BILL-DIP not rigidly linked to other displays, but several times noted in association with Preening. DRINK drake swims, or stands at edge of water, broadside to ♀; sometimes immediately preceded or followed by any one of several other displays. PREENING 3 ritualized movements—dorsally, on belly (only on land), and behind wing—the ♂ with body lateral to ♀. WING-FLAP not strikingly different from normal comfort movement; done with lateral orientation to ♀. JUMP-FLIGHT done during social display phase; consists of flights a few yds. in length; not as obviously ritualized as corresponding activities described by Lebret (1958a) for Mallard and Shoveler. MULTISYLLABLED WHISTLES see "Voice." PRECOPULATORY PUMPING vertical movements of head, as seen in many *Anas;* may be done by both members of pair and not be followed by mounting.

Copulatory behavior little information; pattern probably similar to Mallard. Preceded by Precopulatory pumping by both sexes. In nominate *crecca,* postcopulatory display consists of a single Bridling movement (Wall 1963).

There is scant information on size of area utilized by breeding pairs. There are flying trios (J. Munro 1949c), as in the Mallard. Also, during laying, mated drakes have been seen "loafing" together.

Nest sites in the Cariboo parklands of B.C. were in grasses, sedge meadows, on dry hillsides with aspen or brush, also in open woods adjacent to ponds or sloughs (J. Munro 1949c). In mixed prairie habitat in s. Alta., most nests were in *Juncus balticus* on low ground near sloughs, or occasionally on dry prairie (Keith 1961). In N.D., 30 nests were in grass–herb mixtures, grasses, and sweet clover (M. Hammond). The nest usually is within 200 ft. of water. Pairs are thinly distributed in many parts of breeding range and J. Munro (1949c) reported very great fluctuation from year to year in numbers occurring on the large area he studied.

The **nest bowl** is shallow, contains some bits of dry vegetation, and usually is well concealed by surrounding vegetation which often forms a canopy. The **nest down,** in bulk, appears to be about half dark, half white, the latter being the diffuse white centers; the individual sprays are small and without white tips; any intermingled feathers are small and have light shafts, are some shade of gray, and some have very broad and others very narrow white to pale buff margins; see Broley (1950) for illus. This material is added beginning after several eggs have been laid and continuing into incubation.

Laying begins about mid-May in N.D. (M. Hammond), normally the third week in May in s. Alta. (Keith 1961), and late May–early June in coldest parts of range. Time of onset of laying varies depending on weather conditions. Drakes usually leave their mates well along in the laying period, nearly always by the time incubation begins, but in *A. c. crecca* it is reported that drakes occasionally are seen with duck and brood.

Clutch size Gem, Alta., 18 clutches: 1 (of 6 eggs), 3 (7), 4 (8), 4 (9), 5 (10), 1 (11), av. 8.67 (Keith 1961); at Lower Souris refuge, N.D., 28 clutches: 5 (6), 3 (7), 5 (8), 9 (9), 3 (10), 3 (11), av. 8.39 (M. Hammond).

One **egg** each from 20 clutches (2 w. Canada, 1 Mackenzie delta, 13 Utah, 1 S.D., 2 Magdalen Is.) **size** length av. 45.87 ± 1.43 mm., breadth 33.76 ± 1.1, radii of curvature of ends 13.97 ± 0.61 and 10.70 ± 0.80; **shape** usually between elliptical and short subelliptical, elongation 1.36 ± 0.05, bicone −0.005, asymmetry +0.132 (FWP). For other series, see especially Bent (1923). The shell is smooth, with little gloss; **color** whitish cream to pale olive buff.

Later clutches tend to be smaller (J. Munro 1949c, Keith 1961); they probably include **replacement clutches,** perhaps also first clutches of late-laying yearlings.

Incubation by the ♀, **period** usually about 21 days, but 20–23 in the wild reported (various authors), 23–24 in captivity. As in most ducks, the incubating ♀ covers the clutch before leaving to feed and rest; when disturbed by the approach of someone, usually she sits tight, finally flushing at a distance of 1–12 ft. (M. Hammond). One flushed at 20–30 yds., continuously quacking as she flew away (J. Munro 1949c).

Hatching success at Gem, Alta., 23.8% of 21 nests were successful, hatching an av. of 8 eggs (Keith 1961); at Lower Souris, one or more eggs hatched in 76.7% of 30 nests and the av. number of eggs that hatched was 7.3 (M. Hammond). The peak of hatching usually is between mid-June and mid-July in much of breeding range. In B.C., earliest date for downy young was June 20, latest Aug. 10 (J. Munro 1949c). The duck, in distraction display on land or water, beats her open wings as she retreats, sometimes makes short flights and, on land, may run rapidly; she utters harsh grating quacks almost continuously when an intruder is near her brood. J. Munro (1949c) reported several ♀♀ performing distraction displays together; this, he thought, had no survival value when man was the intruder but might be effective against the coyote (*Canis latrans*).

Brood size av. 6.2 ducklings (48 broods in July; 17 in Aug. gave same figure) (Munro); 7.0 in 25 broods (Hawkins and Cooch, in Crissey 1949); av. varied 4.1 (16 broods) to 8.2 (8 broods) for various localities and seasons in Alaska (U. C. Nelson et al. in Farley 1955).

Age at first flight probably about 35 days in the wild.

A. crecca nimia—data from Kenyon (1961) for Amchitka I.: pair formation occurs in March and, by May 9, pairs were scattered among small ponds and lakes; the nesting period is prolonged; earliest date for newly hatched brood was June 12, latest was July 31; by late Aug. the Greenwings were in flocks on lakes.

A. c. crecca—at the Lapland Reserve in subarctic U.S.S.R., a teal (studied by means of an electrical recording device) began incubating on the day after the last (tenth) egg was laid; she av. 2.55 absences daily (daylight lasts long in the subarctic) and av. time away was 84 min.; the eggs were turned on the av. of once/hr.; the period from start of incubation to start of hatching was 23.8 days; all eggs hatched in a span of 41 hrs. and the duck and brood left on last day of hatching span (Semenov-Tian-Shanskii and Bragin 1969). For a graph showing increase in wt. of 3 captive young, see Veselovsky (1953). He reported that contour feathers were visible at age 16 days and flight feathers of wing at 20 days, i.e., earlier than in other *Anas* and *Aythya* that he studied; the captive young attained flight at age 36 days. RSP

SURVIVAL *A. crecca carolinensis*. So many variables must be reckoned with that no brief statistic explains much of anything satisfactorily. The av. annual mortality rate in the period 1946–61 was 63%, being 70% for "immatures" and 50% for "adults" (Moisan et al. 1967). The mortality rate, especially of "adults," was related directly to rate of hunting kill. See text and tables in Moisan et al. for many further details.

Based on data from Utah, the estimated mean annual adult survival rate is 0.52 ± 0.02 (Boyd, in le Cren and Holdgate 1962).

A. c. crecca—for data on British-wintering birds, see Boyd (1957, and in Le Cren and Holdgate 1962). RSP

HABITS *A. crecca carolinensis.* For a waterfowl species that is relatively plentiful in N. Am., the impression gained from published accounts is that a good deal of fundamental information remains unknown. The dominant social unit consists of a small group or a family and these perhaps are more sensitive to slight environmental differences and more given to shifting about in their travels than are units of larger *Anas*.

Greenwings are not shy and are easily hunted. Where not molested, they loaf a good deal, ashore or afloat, in daytime; they are very active, flying about, the drakes whistling, early and late in the day and on clear nights. They feed a good deal at night. Like the Bluewing, they stand or rest on mudbanks, stumps, etc., and sometimes perch on low limbs of dead trees. Their flight speed has been overestimated repeatedly, rarely being over 50 mph, as pointed out by J. C. Phillips (1923b). When various kinds of ducks forage in the same area, their local flights are slow and leisurely; Greenwings, however, do not slow down and, as a consequence, give an impression of great speed as they overtake and rapidly outdistance flying Mallards and Black Ducks. Common associates of the Greenwing include Mallards, Blacks, Bluewings, Pintails, and Shovelers.

For the period 1946–61, the annual av. continental N. Am. population prior to the hunting season was estimated at between 7 and 10 million birds and the mean annual hunting kill in the U.S.–Canada was 1 million (Moisan et al. 1967). The continental (included Mexico) winter survey of Jan., 1966, yielded a figure of 1,456,900 birds censused (H. A. Hansen and Hudgins 1966), the Greenwing being outnumbered (among species censused) by the Baldpate, Pintail, and Mallard. The figure for Jan. 1970 was about 1,787,000, with over 175,000 then wintering in Mexico.

For additional information on habits, the reader is referred especially to the accounts of "European Teal" and "American Green-winged Teal" by J. C. Phillips (1923b). RSP

FOOD *A. crecca carolinensis.* Largely vegetable, such as seeds of pondweeds, bulrushes, other sedges, and grasses, waste grain, berries, wild grapes, and mast; also insects, crustaceans, and mollusks. The contents of the stomachs of 653 specimens examined in the Biological Survey showed 90.67% vegetable and 9.33% animal matter (Mabbott 1920). [But in Aug.–March in France, animal food was 20 times more abundant in crops than in gizzards (Tamisier 1971).]

Vegetable Sedges: bulrushes (*Scirpus*, chiefly *S. americanus* and *S. paludosus*), and other sedges (*Carex, Cyperus, Eleocharis, Fimbristylis, Rynchospora* and *Cladium*) 38.82%; pondweeds: true pondweeds (*Potamogeton*), wigeon grass (*Ruppia maritima*), eelgrass (*Zostera marina*), and najas (*Najas*) 11.52%; grasses: panic grasses (*Panicum*), wild millet (*Echinochloa*), wild rice (*Zizania*), cutgrass (*Zizaniopsis*), yellow foxtail (*Chaetochloa glauca*), and *Monanthochloe littoralis* 11.0%; smartweeds (*Polygonum*) 5.25%; algae (*Chara*) 4.63%, duckweeds (Lemnaceae) 1.9%, water milfoil (Haloragidaceae) 1.11%; and miscellaneous plants 16.44% (Mabbott 1920).

Spring food in Me. consisted of 94% vegetable and 6% animal matter. The vegetable food: *Carex* spp. 63.4%, *Polygonum* 8.2%, *Sparganium* spp. 6.4%, *Potamogeton* spp. 7.2%, and miscellaneous 8.7% (Coulter 1955). The 12 stomachs from the upper St. Lawrence contained vegetable matter only: undetermined 53.4%, *Bidens* sp. 28.9%, *Scirpus* sp. 8.9%, *Sparganium americanum* 4.4%, and miscellaneous 4.4% (Kutz et al. 1948). The 5 stomachs from the lower Hudson contained: *Echinochloa crusgalli* 55%, *Leersia oryzoides* 20.5%, *Potamogeton pusillus* 8%, *Lemna* sp. 5%, unidentified 7.5%, and miscellaneous 4% (Foley and Taber 1951). The principal foods in 47 specimens from the upper Chesapeake region were *Scirpus olneyi*, *Ruppia maritima*, *Cladium mariscoides*, *Polygonum* spp., *Scirpus validus*, and *S. fluviatilis* (R. E. Stewart 1962).

The 393 gizzards from Ill. contained 85% vegetable and 15% animal matter. The vegetable food: *Cyperus* spp. 41%, *Echinochloa* 10.1%, *Eragrostis hypnoides* 4.9%, and miscellaneous 29% (H. G. Anderson 1959). The principal foods in 318 gizzards from Mo. were seeds of smartweeds (*Polygonum* spp.) and millets (*Echinochloa* spp.) (Korschgen 1955). The 84 gizzards from Reelfoot Lake, Tenn., contained chiefly Lemnaceae, *Potamogeton* spp., *Cephalanthus occidentalis*, and *Decodon verticillatus* (Rawls 1958).

Two specimens from the Pribilof Is, had eaten seeds and foliage of crowfoot (*Ranunculus trichophyllum*) and a pondweed (*Potamogeton filiformis*) (Preble and McAtee 1923).

Animal Larvae and pupae of midges (Chironomidae), crane flies (Tipulidae), soldier flies (Stratiomyiidae), and ephydrids (Ephydridae) 2.07%; beetles (Coleoptera), bugs (Hemiptera), caddis flies (Phryganoidea), and miscellaneous insects 2.5%; mollusks, particularly snails of the genera *Physa*, *Neritina*, and *Planorbis* 3.59%; crustaceans, mainly ostracods and amphipods 0.92%; spiders and mites (Arachnida), centipedes (Myriapoda), and miscellaneous items 0.25% (Mabbott 1920). Me. birds had consumed 5% earthworms (Coulter 1955). Specimens from upper Chesapeake region: Amphipoda (mainly Gammaridae), Gastropoda (*Bittium varium*, *Littoridinops* sp.), Isopoda (*Chiridotea coeca*), and Chironomidae and Diptera larvae. The birds at Reelfoot Lake contained insects 7.44%, crustaceans 0.95%, and snails 0.48%. The taking of fish (*Dorosoma cepedianum*) at Buckeye Lake, Ohio, was considered abnormal by Trautman (1940). In feeding on dead salmon, maggots (fly larvae) are probably consumed mainly (Blanchan 1898). In early fall in the Skeena R. region of B.C., the Greenwings shot from time to time invariably contained eggs of the humpbacked salmon (*Oncorhynchus gorbuscha*) (Swarth 1924).

NOTE These are not included above: late spring to early fall food in se. Alta. (Keith 1961); data on 140 teals (2 species lumped) in s. La. (Glasgow and Bardwell 1965); 17 Greenwings from N.C. (Quay and Crichter 1965); 32 from S.C. (McGilvrey 1966c), and 16 from Lubbock Co., Texas (Rollo and Bolen 1969).

A. crecca nimia—no specific information; feeds at tidal pools and sheltered marine waters in winter.

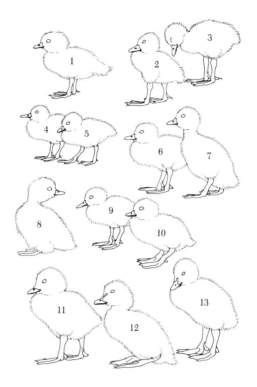

Day-old downies

1 North American Wood Duck *(Aix sponsa)*—from Vergennes, Vt. (For heads of both sexes in all Plumages, in color, see vol. 3, plate facing p. 120.)

2 Fulvous Whistling Duck *(Dendrocygna bicolor)*—from Lafayette, La. This is the usual color; there is also a silvery-gray variant or morph.

3 Red-billed Whistling Duck *(D. autumnalis)*—from Mathis, Texas. In dozing posture.

4 Cinnamon Teal *(Anas cyanoptera septentrionalium)*—from Bear River Migratory Bird Refuge, Brigham City, Utah.

5 American Green-winged Teal *(Anas crecca carolinensis)*—from Delta, Man.

6 Mallard *(Anas p. platyrhynchos)*—from Strathmore, Alta.

7 Gadwall *(Anas strepera)*—from Delta, Man.

8 Baldpate *(Anas americana)*—from Delta, Man.

9 Northern Shoveler *(Anas clypeata)*—from Delta, Man.

10 Northern Pintail *(Anas acuta)*—from Delta, Man.

11 Spectacled Eider *(Somateria fischeri)*—from near Hazen Bay, Alaska.

12 Western Atlantic subspecies of Common Eider *(Somateria mollissima dresseri)*—from Ile aux Pommes, Que. (For some Plumages in color, see vol. 3, plate facing p. 376.)

13 King Eider *(Somateria spectabilis)*—hatched in captivity, the ♂ parent from Iceland. ♀ from Greenland.

A. c. crecca—the stomachs of 5 birds taken in N. Am. contained 19.8% **vegetable** matter consisting of algae, grasses and sedges (*Panicum, Scirpus,* and *Carex*), crowberry (*Empetrum*), and mare's tail (*Hippurus*) (Cottam and Knappen 1939). Seeds, tentatively identified as swamp buttercup (*Ranunculus septentrionalis*), were found in a bird taken in March in Mass. (G. H. MacKay 1890a). **Animal** This amounted to 80.2%. Gastropods formed 85% in stomach of a bird taken in Va. Four Alaskan and 1 Va. specimen had eaten: crustaceans 60%, gastropods 17.2%, insects (largely midges, Chironomidae) 2.6%, and miscellaneous 0.4% (Cottam and Knappen 1939). AWS

The food and feeding habits of nominate *crecca* in its more usual range have been treated at length by Olney (1963a), and for Aug.–March in the Camargue, France, by Tamisier (1971). RSP

Baikal Teal

Anas formosa Georgi

Spectacled Teal. Unique head pattern in Alt. Plumage (see text figs.): ♂ clear-cut, complicated pattern of black, green, buffs, and white, the cheeks being buff, bisected by a black stripe down from the eye; ♀ has noticeable to conspicuous usually round whitish area ("spectacle") at side base of bill, the head otherwise rather like that of the Greenwing. The drake has a rudimentary tracheal bulla, shaped like that of the Greenwing; it was illus. by Eyton (1838). The Baikal Teal is somewhat larger than the Greenwing, drakes averaging over 1 lb. in wt., ♀♀ perhaps about 14 oz. No subspecies.

DESCRIPTION   Two Plumages/cycle in both sexes. In definitive (2nd and later) cycles, the drake is not in full Alt. until late in fall; after that, pale feather edgings or tips wear off so that the head pattern, which at first was partly concealed, becomes sharply defined in early winter. The ♀ molts out of Alt. (head–body–tail) in spring, hence her 2 body molts are spaced months apart as in the Greenwing. There is not much information on predefinitive stages. The following is limited to a few diagnostic features.

▶   ♂ Def. Alt. Plumage (all feathering except, in wing, only a few innermost feathers), acquired through FALL and worn into following SUMMER, about July. **Bill** leadcolored, **iris** dark brownish; **head** as described above and illustrated; **upperparts** upper back appears medium gray, most of remainder has feathers olive brownish with tawny or rusty margins; several scapulars much elongated, tapering, downcurved, one web white, the other orange-cinnamon grading to black toward shaft; **underparts** breast tawny-buff or the same with violet cast, with dark spots, and a white bar down side of breast near bend of folded wing, sides finely vermiculated (appear medium to dark gray), a white bar down side of rump, vent to tail black; **tail** olive brownish; legs and **feet** dingy yellowish with darker webs; most of wing is retained Basic feathering.

▶   ♂ Def. Basic Plumage (entire feathering), acquired in SUMMER (molt includes flightless period) and, except for most of wing, soon succeeded by the next Alt. through LATE SUMMER–FALL. Quite like ♀ as described next below. Whitish spot at side base of bill. Differs from ♀ thus: body feathering has more sharply defined pattern, richer coloring, the feather margins wider and more tawny; a few scapulars elongated somewhat and colored various browns (one edge rusty color); belly usually whitish; **wing** most upper coverts brownish olive, but greater secondary coverts broadly terminated orange-cinnamon (this forms bar at leading edge of speculum), the speculum bronzy green and black, these feathers being broadly tipped white (form bar at trailing edge).

▶   ♀ Def. Alt. Plumage (all feathering except, in wing, only a few innermost feathers), acquired in LATE SUMMER–FALL and retained until LATE WINTER or SPRING. **Bill** muted medium greenish, **iris** dark brownish, **head** as described in opening paragraph (also see text fig.). According to J. M. Harrison (1958), about 15% of ♀ ♀ show (extent of development said to vary with individual) a dark line from gape along sides of chin, broadening and angling upward a short distance on lower rear of cheek. **Upperparts** feathers brownish olive with brownish buff margins that are narrower than in ♂ Def. Basic. In many individuals (Alt., Basic, or both?) feathers of mantle and upper back have pale buffy crossbars. Some scapulars elongated (about as in ♂ Def. Basic), dark olive-brown to fuscous, broadly margined light tawny-buff. **Underparts** belly less whitish (more suffused buffy) than ♂ Def. Basic. Body down pale brownish (Hartert 1920a). Most of wing is retained Basic feathering.

▶ ♀ Def. Basic Plumage (entire feathering), the head–body–tail acquired through SPRING, most of the wing not until well along in SUMMER or FALL, by which time head–body–tail is molting back into Alt. Few details at hand. A browner, more blended, coloring than in Alt., the white spot on face sometimes obscure. The **nest down** is deep brown, almost black (Hartert 1920). **Wing** light tips of greater secondary coverts paler and much narrower than in the ♂ Basic wing, speculum more muted, paler, with much narrower white bar at trailing edge.

AT HATCHING quite like the Greenwing, but light areas of head vivid yellowish and no dark cheek stripe.

▶ Predefinitive stages—largely unknown. Juv.—no light spot adjoining side base of bill. The ♂ said to be otherwise quite like "adult" ♀, also mantle feathers said to have light barring (J. C. Phillips 1923b), but some museum specimens labeled ♀ also have them; ♀ said by Phillips to be like "adult" ♀ but to have lower abdomen spotted or streaked brown. An "immature" ♂ taken Dec. 20 and partly described by Hatter (1960) had no white on elongated scapulars (they were rusty and pale tan), light patches on side of head margined gray, black on side rear of neck and (to lesser extent) midfacial stripe had whitish tan feather margins, black feathers of crown and forehead margined rusty. This is Alt. I, which was described by Isakov (in Dementiev and Gladkov 1952) as brown backed and with or without any barring or vermiculations on mantle.

Measurements of birds from breeding and winter range, 12 ♂: BILL 38–40 mm., av. 38.7; WING 203–225, av. 211; TAIL 74–87, av 77.6; TARSUS 36–39, av. 37;   12 ♀: BILL 36–38 mm., av. 37; WING 201–214, av. 206.5; TAIL 74–83, av. 78; TARSUS 33–38, av. 35.7 (ETS).

Series of "adults" from China, Japan, and Korea, 11 ♂: BILL 34.1–37.1, av. 35.9, WING (across chord) 198–223, av. 212;   10 ♀ BILL 33.2–37.4 mm., av. 35.8; WING 193–213, av. 201 (H. Friedmann).

Weight 500–600 gm. (Dementiev and Gladkov 1952).

Wild **hybrids** with Pintail (*Anas acuta*), Greenwing (*A. c. crecca*), and Wigeon (*A. penelope*) have been reported, also crosses in captivity with at least 4 additional species of *Anas* and with *Netta rufina*. Most of the references to these crosses are in Gray (1958). The *formosa–crecca* hybrids are said to be fertile. RSP

FIELD IDENTIFICATION   In our area. The drake, most of the year, is readily identifiable by his bizarre head pattern; the ♀, from fall at least into spring, might be likened to a ♀ Greenwing with a sizable round whitish spot (better defined than in our other *Anas* that have it) close to the side base of bill. Young birds, and older ones in certain stages and seasons, may not be readily distinguished from Greenwings except under very favorable conditions of observation. (Except for specimens taken in the Pribilofs, all Am. records are for drakes in Alt. Plumage.) RSP

VOICE   Russian vernacular names are "gurgler" and "bubbling teal." The common call of the drake, especially in winter–spring, is an extraordinarily unducklike, far-carrying, disyllabic *wut wot, ruk ruk*, etc. (variably transliterated and the 2 syllables have a subtle difference), followed by more slowly uttered series of *wot* notes if the bird is alarmed and also in certain displays. The quack of the ♀ is rather weak. For a few further details of vocabulary, such as Decrescendo call, see Johnsgard (1965). RSP

HABITAT   Breeds within the forest zone in fairly dry situations having low vegetation (grasses, sedges, brush) not distant from ponds and watercourses, and northward beyond in grassy and willow areas even to the lower reaches and deltas of certain Siberian rivers. Migrates along inland watercourses, also over the sea to Japan. Winters on all sorts of shallow fresh waters and on rather sheltered marine waters within daily commuting distance of fields or flooded areas having suitable forage. RSP

DISTRIBUTION   This teal breeds in E. Siberia and winters mainly in China and Japan. It has straggled to our area, where it also is a common aviary bird. Some authors have suggested that it possibly may breed occasionally in Alaska.

Alaska   Wainwright, Sept. 2, 1921, ♂ taken; King I., May 23 and 25, 1931, 2 ♂ taken; St. Lawrence I., July 23, 1937, pair taken; Wales, June 8, 1942, pair collected, and June 22, 1944, ♂ collected; C. Sabine, May 28, 1959, pair seen; St. Paul (Pribilof group), in 1961, 4 seen (1 shot) on Sept. 9, 2 shot Sept. 21, and 1 shot Oct. 8. Original references through 1959 were included in Maher (1960); the Pribilof records were reported by Sladen (1966).

Elsewhere in N. Am.   N.C., Currituck Co., Swan I., Dec. 9, 1912, ♂ shot; Cal., near Brentwood, Dec. 13, 1931, specimen; Ohio, Delaware Co., Scotio R., April 1933, 1 seen; B.C., Ladner, Dec. 20, 1957, young ♂ collected. The original sources were listed by Sykes (1961), who cited published opinions that the Cal. and Ohio records were based on birds that had escaped from captivity. It may occur (usually as an escapee?) almost anywhere; for example, a drake seen in 2 different recent years in the Cape May area of N.J.

Asia   The trend in records has been to extend the known breeding range of this teal; for example, down to latitude of s. end of L. Baikal. It breeds in the drainages of the great northward-flowing Siberian rivers, in some—Yana, Indigirka, and Lena—clear to their mouths. It nests in Koryakland, Kamchatka, and in the w. part of the Chuckchee Pen., but is only a straggler farther east (nearer Alaska). It has straggled beyond the arctic coast to Great Lyhakov I. (New Siberian Archipelago) and Wrangel I. It is a straggler to the Commander Is. On the mainland it has straggled (or bred?) w. to cent. Asia and there are a number of records for localities across the top of the Indian subcontinent and beyond, Burma to W. Pakistan.

374

Some summer records around the periphery of the breeding range evidently are for drakes that have taken leave of their mates, but have not traveled very far, to molt.

Europe This teal has been reported as occurring in Italy, various parts of cent. Europe, the Brit. Isles (6 records 1920–70, all of uncertain provenance), and it even was alleged to have bred at Mývatn in Iceland in 1837, after there supposedly was an invasion of these birds into Europe in 1836 during which 5 examples were taken on the Saone R. in e. France. The following is based on J. C. Phillips (1923b). The Baikal Teal bred in the London zoo in the years 1840–43 inclusive, possibly even earlier on an estate in England. Then it was absent for a time, then introduced again in 1867, and it bred in captivity in Holland in 1872 and 1873. Until about 1910 it was scarce in dealers' shops, but beginning about 1911 it became one of the commonest imported waterfowl in Europe. In 1914 so many were brought to San Francisco that they could not be disposed of. Since they seldom breed in captivity, the aviary supply is maintained by further importations. Not all such stock has been properly pinioned and some of the birds have, after molting, escaped. Delacour (1956) regarded all European records as pertaining to escapees.

It is evident that this teal has some tendency to wander, also a natural inclination to escape from confinement when physically able to do so. It may be concluded, therefore, that which records are or are not based on natural occurrence can be argued endlessly. RSP

MIGRATION Winterers in Japan arrive from late Sept. into Nov. and most depart by the end of March; their route both seasons is via Korea (O. L. Austin, Jr., and Kuroda 1953). Mainland data: see Isakov (in Dementiev and Gladkov 1952) for cursory overall coverage and Skryabin (1968) for the Baikal region. In summer the drakes, on taking leave of their mates, usually molt in groups and at places not very far from where their mates are incubating or are rearing young. RSP

REPRODUCTION This duck may display while ashore, as well as afloat. For a few data on **displays** of captives, see Johnsgard (1965). The **nest** is in a dry situation, **laying** occurs from late April to early July, and the **eggs** resemble those of the Greenwing (av. about 48.5 × 34.5 mm.). The **incubation period** has been given as 28 days, but probably is 24 (Delacour 1956). RSP

HABITS Not much useful information. Migrates in flocks containing a few birds or even several scores and these combine at some places to form huge wintering concentrations. RSP

FOOD In winter, feeds in ricefields in Japan (Seebohm 1892). Birds collected along the Pacific coast of Asia had eaten seeds which appeared to be from *Papaver, Seteria italica,* and *Panicum miliaeceum.* Soybeans (*Soya*) are important. During spring flight in vicinity of Khabarovsk they search for acorns as distant as 700–800 meters from water, as many as 24 having been found in a bird. A drake shot in Aug. on the Anadyr R. had eaten seeds of *Carex.* Plankton was found in a ♀ collected in July at Ingora L. on the upper Angara R. (Summarized from Dementiev and Gladkov 1952.) AWS

Falcated Teal

Anas falcata Georgi

Also called Falcated Duck. Rather small for a duck, but large for a teal; about size of Gadwall, with which it has many similarities. Drake in Alt. Plumage has foreshortened body profile and the head appears oversized because of pendant crest or "mane" which rests on back; long decurved inner flight feathers of wing (they are longer than the primaries) extend back and down alongside the tail which is largely hidden by long coverts. The ♀ is rather Gadwall-like, but has small mane, generally brownish coloration with dark markings (includes crescents on breast and sides), whitish chin and abdomen with indistinct markings, legs and feet dark (no yellowish), inner secondaries white only on edges. For description and illus. of the drake's tracheal bulla, see Lorenz and Wall (1960). This teal is about 17–18½ in. long, usual wt. of ♂ about 1 lb. 10 oz., ♀ 1 lb. 7 oz. No subspecies.

DESCRIPTION   Two Plumages/cycle in both sexes; timing of molts in ♀ still largely unknown, also most details of predefinitive stages of both sexes. The following is limited mainly to features diagnostic of species, sex, and Plumage.

▶   ♂ Def. Alt. Plumage (all feathering except, in wing, evidently only the inner elongated feathers), acquired in LATE SUMMER–FALL and worn into following SUMMER. **Bill** nearly black; **iris** dark brownish; much of side of **head** from front of eye back to include most of pendant crest or mane greenish bronze; top and front of head (except white spot above bill), upper cheeks, and top of mane violet-magenta to coppery red; chin to breast white, intersected by a narrow black collar that has a greenish sheen. Head has hoary cast in fall, but feather ends wear off to reveal full iridescence and vividness of coloring by early winter. Most of **mantle** feathers pale gray with pale edges, the outer ones black; rump grayish; longest upper tail coverts black and they almost entirely conceal the medium grayish tail. **Underparts** breast feathers white with black crescentic bands (scaled effect), sides heavily vermiculated pale grayish and blackish, abdomen light buffy or whitish and usually with wavy dark (to black) markings; as in Green-winged Teal, a creamy buff patch partly or entirely bordered black on sides of rump. Legs and **feet** some variant of lead-color, webs darker. **Wing** has inner secondaries ("tertials") very greatly elongated, sickle-shaped, narrow, blackish blue, with narrow white edges and shafts; remainder is retained Basic feathering.

▶   ♂ Def. Basic Plumage (entire feathering, worn for a few weeks or less in SUM-

376

MER–EARLY FALL, except most of wing retained nearly a year). Very like ♀ (described below) but with finer markings; much reduced, but slightly iridescent, mane at rear of head; **body feathering** quite like ♀ Gadwall—dark brownish markings on various buffs and browns, chin and abdomen nearly white with dark markings; **wing** upper coverts medium gray with white ends (ends of the longer ones form bar adjoining leading edge of speculum); primaries grayish brown; the innermost secondaries are plain-colored, not much curved, and only as long as 4th primary; speculum black and grayed greenish with narrow white trailing edge; wing lining mostly white, the under primary coverts evenly pale gray, axillars white.

▶ ♀ Def. Alt. Plumage (all feathering except, in wing, evidently only the inner secondaries), acquired in LATE SUMMER–FALL and worn at least until LATE WINTER (no spring specimens examined). Superficially like ♀ Gadwall. **Bill** has upper mandible dark gray, more or less freckled black, lower mandible black. **Iris** as ♂. **Head** has rudimentary mane without greenish sheen; **mantle** feathers have pale cinnamon to buff edges and median V-shaped marks; rump feathers and upper tail coverts banded with fulvous; **underparts** feathers of upper breast have dark crescentic bands on tawny base and pattern continues along sides; abdomen pale to whitish with indistinct dark markings. Legs and **feet** as ♂. In the wing the innermost secondaries are only slightly curved; remainder of wing is retained Basic feathering.

▶ ♀ Def. Basic Plumage (all feathering); whether head–body, etc. is acquired in spring or not until early summer is unknown; the wing is acquired in late summer or fall and (except for innermost feathers) is retained nearly a year. An early summer specimen, apparently in Basic Plumage, had dorsum, breast, sides, and flanks betwen fuscous and olive, most feathers quite broadly margined muted buffy. In the wing the upper coverts are a grayed brownish, the greater ones more prominently edged white, forming white bar at leading edge of speculum; speculum dark greenish and black; innermost secondaries plain and nearly straight; wing lining and axillars as ♂.

AT HATCHING rather like Wigeon (*A. penelope*) but with larger bill, sides of head reddish (color vanishes as ducklings grow), line through eye not well defined, and no spot over the ear. (Young of *A. penelope* often have reddish on head and have no facial stripes; S. Quintin, in J. C. Phillips 1923b).

Predefinitive stages not well known. Juv. ♂ and ♀ said to resemble ♀, except no "mane," darker crown, more blended pattern, darker dorsum, muted coloring in speculum. Said to molt into Alt. I on winter range. Young ♂ in Jan. was very nearly "adult," except no long innermost secondaries (St. Quintin 1917). Also see Isakov (in Dementiev and Gladkov 1952).

Measurements of birds from Manchuria, Japan, and China, 12 ♂: BILL 39–48 mm., av. 42.8; WING 244–268, av. 253; TAIL 70–80, av. 73.5; TARSUS 37–44, av. 39.8; 9 ♀ BILL 36–40 mm., av. 38.8; WING 226–236, av. 231; TAIL 68–76, av. 71.3; TARSUS 36–40, av. 37.7 (ETS).

WING (across chord): 13 ♂ 240–259 mm., av. 248; and 4 ♀ 226–239, av. 231 (H. Friedmann).

Weight of ♂ about 750 gm., ♀ 640–660 (Dementiev and Gladkov 1952).

Presumed wild **hybrids** with Gadwall, Wigeon (*A. penelope*), and Ruddy Sheldduck [!] have been reported; at least most others included in Gray's (1958) list occurred

377

in captivity. The tracheal bulla of a captive-reared cross with the Baldpate (*A. americana*) was figured by Beer (1968). SDR

FIELD IDENTIFICATION   The drake in Alt. Plumage (most of the year) is unlike any other waterfowl, having crested greenish bronze head and very long sickle-shaped tertials. The ♀ closely resembles the ♀ Gadwall, but legs and feet are dark (no yellowish coloring), the inner secondaries blackish with white edges only (not all white). SDR

VOICE   Drake has a curlewlike chuckle as well as a low teallike whistle; ♀ quacks like Gadwall. For further information, see especially Lorenz and Wall (1960). SDR

HABITAT   In breeding season, at ponds, small lakes, and quiet stretches of rivers, having either open or wooded shores; in Japan in winter, seldom far from salt water (O. L. Austin, Jr., and Kuroda 1953), but farther s. it occurs on various interior waters and rice paddies (Dementiev and Gladkov 1952). SDR

DISTRIBUTION   An e. Asian species that nests within the forest zone and migrates to Japan, e. China, and nearby.
   Straggler to our area   ALASKA Pribilofs—St. George I., April 8, 1917, ♂ collected (Hanna 1920); St. Paul, June 3, 1962, ♂ seen (Sladen 1966). Attu—May 23–24, 1945, pair seen (R. Wilson 1948). Adak—in 1970, ♀ captured Oct. 15, ♂ and 5 ♀ seen Nov. 7, and ♀ seen Nov. 29; in 1971 a single seen Feb. 9 (probably repeat of a bird seen earlier); in 1972 two ♂ and a ♀ June 4–9, a ♂ collected June 9, and remaining pair seen June 13–15. COMMANDER Is. rare straggler. OTHER PLACES B.C., near Vernon, ♂ seen April 15, 1932 (A. Brooks 1942); Cal., near San Francisco, 1 seen on dates from April 5 to May 20 or 21, 1953 (Hedgpeth 1954). Whether these last 2 were natural occurrences might be debatable.
   Elsewhere, in addition to its range in far eastern Asia, this bird has straggled to localities from Burma westward to the head of the Persian Gulf. There are records for Sweden, Czechoslovakia (several), and Austria (in 1839); the validity of at least some of these is very doubtful. RSP

MIGRATION   Spring migration extends from late Feb. into May and fall migration from early Sept. into early Nov. In Bengal, said to be common in cold winters, and these s. limits of winter range said to be reached chiefly by ♀ ♀ (Finn, cited in Dementiev and Gladkov 1952). RSP

REPRODUCTION   **Displays** are quite like those of the Gadwall. The drake's HEAD-UP-TAIL-UP display shows his crest, elongated secondaries, and creamy patch at side of rump very prominently. He has a short, rather rapid GRUNT-WHISTLE, the final whistle being thinner, more teallike than Gadwall's. As in that species, the order of grunt and whistle are reverse of Mallard's. See Lorenz and Wall (1960) for displays and voice compared with closely related species, notably the Greenwing, Gadwall, and Wigeon (*A. penelope*). Usually **nests** in May–June, the site being dry and well con-

378

cealed in rank vegetation. **Eggs** 6–9, **size** of 21 av. 56.2 × 39.65, **color** creamy white. **Incubation period** in an aviary was 25 or 26 days (T. Jones 1951). For rather scant information, see J. C. Phillips (1923b), T. Jones (1951), and Dementiev and Gladkov (1952). SDR

HABITS In Japan. Anything but teallike; in winter and migrations, on saltwater bays, dives with facility and acts more like a scaup; also comes inland to feed in paddies and lakes (O. L. Austin, Jr., 1949). RSP

FOOD Very little information. Stomachs of birds taken on their arrival in se. Siberia in April contained nothing but quartz sand and a few shoots of plants (Radde 1863). Two birds taken in the Commander Is. had eaten grass and the leaves of plants (Stejneger 1885). The stomach of a bird taken on St. George I. (Pribilofs) was about half filled with sea lettuce (*Ulva lacuca*) (Preble and McAtee 1923). AWS

Gadwall

Anas strepera Linnaeus

Smaller (av. several in. shorter) and trimmer than Mallard. Bill rather narrow, straight-sided (edges nearly parallel), rather thin in lateral profile; frontal feathering extends in a point to nearly over the nostrils, which are high up and near the base; nail abruptly downcurved; lamellae clearly visible; at least sides of bill more or less orange or yellowish (except usually all bluish part of the year in drakes of breeding age); legs and feet more or less yellowish or some variant of orange; wing has some distal secondaries partly black and some nearer the body partly white, the latter forming a conspicuous white patch that extends from trailing edge of the wing inward (at least the white reduced or perhaps even absent in some Juv. ♀ ♀). The drake most of the year (Alt. Plumage) has much gray dorsally and on sides (coarse to fine black markings on white), the breast more coarsely marked black; in most other Plumages the Gadwall is largely rather muted brown with abdomen predominantly white. The drake's tracheal apparatus has been described and figured many times; for figs., see pl. 248 in Heinroth and Heinroth (1928) and Lorenz and Wall (1960).

Length 18–23 in., wingspread 30–35 (♂ av. larger within these spans), wt. of ♂ usually about 2 lb., ♀ about 1¾.

As treated here, no subspecies.

DESCRIPTION Two Plumages/cycle in both sexes, with Basic I fragmentary and fleeting. Emphasis here is on features diagnostic of Plumage and/or sex and on individual variation. See Oring (1968) for description of molts and for further details regarding Plumages, including illus. of various feathers.

▶ ♂ Def. Alt. Plumage (all feathering, excepting all but innermost feathers of wing), acquired beginning in SUMMER and completed in FALL or even later (probably in Sept. in N.C., but not until early Nov. in latitude of s. Canada); last feathers to grow are the tail and long scapulars, which often are not fully grown until EARLY WINTER. Then this Plumage is worn through winter and spring into SUMMER. A predominantly dark grayish, black, and white Plumage.

Bill slaty bluish, or with mere trace of muted orange on sides; **iris** medium brownish; **head** varies with individual, from whitish to buffy tan ground color, with fine dusky streaks and bars, grading to nearly black feathers having grayish or brownish markings on crown (these are elongated), nape, and line extending back from eye; a few individuals have a broken or even a complete white collar on lower neck (example: pl. 43 in Schiøler 1925); **upperparts** upper back and some scapulars vermiculated, or finely barred or scalloped (like breast) black and white and, apparently, the darker the feathering on breast and sides, the farther back this dorsal pattern extends; other scapulars medium brownish or gray with tan to buffy edges; remainder of back very dark with fine light markings; rump and upper tail coverts black; **underparts** feathers of breast usually have crescentic markings of black (broadly) and white or somewhat buffy (narrowly), but individuals vary greatly in relative amounts of black and white and even in shape of markings (occasional birds have an almost blotched or freckled pattern); sides and flanks marked black and white (appear quite dark); lower breast, belly, and vent area usually white, but sometimes finely vermiculated or even more or less spotted or barred some shade of gray or dusky brownish; most under tail coverts appear black (are finely to rather coarsely vermiculated black); **tail** grayed brownish, outer feathers paler, sometimes edged buff; legs and **feet** vivid to muted orange, webs dusky; **wing** innermost secondaries elongated, tapering at ends, pearly gray and paling distally, their greater coverts part black and part gray; remainder is retained Basic feathering. A few Basic body feathers sometimes also are retained for a considerable time and worn with this Plumage.

NOTES   A drake in full Alt. has a pronounced dense mane on crown and nape, which gives the head a decidedly enlarged appearance.

The drake's long scapulars and some feathers on the rump sometimes are not fully grown until Jan.

The long, very tapering, innermost secondaries reach to within an inch of the tips of the folded wings and are pearly gray, paler distally, and their ends fade to white.

▶   ♂ Def. Basic Plumage (entire feathering); the head–body feathering is acquired rapidly, in JUNE–JULY (even earlier in southerly birds?); the tail comes in quite gradually, the flight feathers of wing last (preceded by flightless period of about 25 days) and, by the time these are growing, the Basic head–body–tail already is being succeeded by the next incoming Alt. in LATE SUMMER–FALL. This is a brownish Plumage.

Sides of **bill** usually show considerable orange or yellowish; **head** and neck generally more coarsely marked than in Alt. and with crown not as solidly colored or as dark; **upperparts** feathers of upper back more coarsely marked (barred) than typical of Alt., with wide blackish brown and narrow light (usually buffy tan) markings; rest of back and most of rump mainly olive-brown; **underparts** breast varies greatly, general effect usually very broken pattern with coarsely and irregularly scalloped (crescentic) dark markings on feathers and these alternate with narrow tan areas (white basal ones concealed), but many drakes have much freckling or coarse blotching; sides and flanks variable, feathers usually broadly barred some shade of fuscous and much more narrowly pale tan, but sometimes have more V-shaped dark areas; lower breast to vent white,

381

occasionally with few to many dark spots; under tail coverts bicolored, white or whitish with dark spots or large subterminal markings; **tail** grayed brownish; **wing** primaries mainly brownish gray, paling on inner webs; several outer secondaries show much black and have white tips and several inner ones (usually 3) are predominantly white; most greater coverts are black; many middle coverts black, or chestnut with black ends, or entirely chestnut; lesser coverts vermiculated (appear grayish brown), but sometimes have cream-colored spots or margins; elongated innermost secondaries shorter, with broader ends, than in Alt. Plumage; wing lining mostly or entirely white. The upper surface of the wing, as just described, has more boldly contrasting pattern than in ♀ Juv. or Basic and than nearly all ♂ Juv. individuals.

NOTE Occasional individuals of either sex and in any season are more or less cream-colored or more or less white.

▶ ♀ Def. Alt. Plumage (all feathering, excepting all but innermost feathers of wing), mostly acquired in EARLY FALL, the tail and elongated innermost secondaries by early winter (often sooner), and retained through winter into SPRING. **Bill** dusky with muted orange-yellow sides on which there are small dark spots that fade during fall; **iris** medium brownish; **head** crown, nape, and broad line through eye mainly very dark brownish, remainder of head and most of neck buffy tan with fine short dark streaking (chin and throat usually darker than in Def. Basic); **upperparts** feathers blackish brown with clear-cut buffy tan borders which become narrower from wear; **underparts** breast and sides much as back, but with lighter feather margins which wear off (breast then appears almost solid dark); belly to vent usually plain white, sometimes spotted brownish; large dark blotches on white under tail coverts; **tail** grayish brown, more or less marked whitish or pale buffy; legs and **feet** more yellowish than in ♂. Body down medium gray, grading through pale gray to white basally. **Wing** innermost secondaries ("tertials") olive-brownish, irregularly barred and at least terminally edged buffy; their greater coverts same, broadly tipped white; remainder is retained Basic feathering.

▶ ♀ Def. Basic Plumage (entire feathering); head, body, innermost secondaries and a few overlying coverts, and the tail acquired in SPRING and, usually in late summer the old Basic wing is molted (with flightless period of about 25 days) and the new Basic wing grows in FALL; contemporaneously with renewal of wing, all the rest of this Basic is being molted and the ♀ is returning to Alt. head–body, etc. In general, in Def. Basic, chin and throat are buffier and head–body feathering is more broadly edged buff than in Alt. or Juv. Plumages.

Bill dusky with muted orange or yellow sides, with or without a few small dark spots, until early stages of incubation; then the vividness of coloring and amount of spotting increase slowly in late stages of incubation and rapidly after the eggs hatch (spotting heaviest late July through Sept.). Most of **head** and neck have fine dark streaking; **underparts** breast and sides streaky (not scalloped); lower breast to vent whitish, frequently heavily streaked or spotted dark (these markings grayer than when present in Def. Alt.), and this is independent of the ragged condition ventrally that results from any loss of feathers by the nesting ♀; under tail coverts longitudinally streaked darkish; markings on tail feathers more often buffy or creamy than in Def. Alt.; **wing** differs from ♂ Def. Basic thus: innermost secondaries olive-brown with obscure creamy tips; outer web of middle secondaries grayish with black margins; greater coverts not black (but very dark) over less wing area, outer ones grayish brown tipped white, inner with olive-brown inner webs; median coverts lack chestnut in some individuals (and apparently never as much present as in ♂); and less coverts variable—plain or edged buffy, or with both buffy internal markings and edging.

NOTE Evidently ♀ ♀ occasionally migrate southward prior to becoming flightless (see "Migration").

AT HATCHING See col. pl. facing p. 370. Most obvious differences from Mallard are the paler dorsal patches and all light areas very pale—"washed out." Legs and feet partly yellowish, partly grayish. The yellowish tinge on light head–body areas begins to fade within a day or two and fading continues 8–9 days. Also, as the duckling increases in size, the 1st nestling down (prepennae) is spread over more surface area, the shafts and barbs of many get broken, and the 2nd nestling down (preplumulae) grows. The duckling then is gray and remains so until the Juv. feathers (pennae) are evident during 3rd week.

▶ ♂ Juv. Plumage (entire feathering), almost fully developed by age 56 days, when fragments of it begin to be replaced by Basic I, and more beginning at about 10 weeks by Alt. I, but the Juv. wing (except for a few innermost feathers) is retained through winter into the following summer. This schedule may be delayed (i.e., much Juv. feathering retained into winter) if the bird is hatched very late, inadequately nourished, diseased, or kept captive in unfavorable quarters. The Juv. Plumage is characterized by narrow body feathers, protruding shafts on tail feathers (where the natal down broke off), and muted coloring of wing.

Bill gray with yellowish edges; **iris** dark brownish; **head** crown and nape dark, remainder pale buffy, streaked dark (least on chin), and usually an indistinct darkish line through eye. **Upperparts** back and scapular feathers very dark, edged buff, and sometimes with buffy internal transverse or V-shaped bars; rump and tail coverts very dark, some feathers edged buff. **Underparts** upper breast feathers sepia, tipped and irregularly marked with buff, cream, or white; remainder of breast and the belly white to buff, the feathers usually spotted or streaked dark, or both (and least on belly), sometimes approaching the double spotting found in some Juv. ♀ ♀. **Tail** feathers sepia, usually edged buff. Legs and **feet** muted yellowish. **Wing** primaries grayed brownish, paler on inner webs; distal secondaries also grayed brownish, tipped white; adjoining ones with black outer webs and tipped white; the next inner (short) ones white with pearly gray outer webs, the innermost ("tertials") medium grayish brown and usually tipped buff; greater primary coverts gray-brown, the proximal 3 sometimes with much white on inner webs; some greater secondary coverts partly black, the distal ones grayish and some tipped chestnut and more or less bordered blackish on outer webs, the inner ones tipped buff on inner webs, the longer median coverts mostly black or chestnut tipped black, the next series forward and some distal ones of lower series chestnut, smaller coverts mostly gray-brown flecked or marked cream (bolder than on Basic wing). Lesser and median coverts of many Juv. ♂ ♂ have distinct cross bars of buff that are absent later (from Basic wing). Most of wing lining and the axillars pearly gray.

▶ ♀ Juv. Plumage (entire feathering), timing of development as in ♂ and also succeeded at corresponding ages by Basic 1 and Alt. I; last traces of Juv. body feathering (on rump, the long innermost secondaries, and a few other feathers) sometimes are retained into spring; all of remainder of Juv. wing is retained through winter, spring, and into late summer or early fall (i.e., longer than in ♂). Soft-part colors as ♂, except bill may or may not have a few brown spots. Wing has less blackish, white, and chestnut (in some individuals little or no chestnut or white).

In Juv. Plumage the ♀ usually can be distinguished from the ♂ by generally smaller size, less barring on upper back and scapulars, lighter lower back and rump, frequently more buff in tail, and almost always by more muted coloring of wing (usually with no chestnut on middle coverts). In the ♂ the body down is distally gray, grading to white basally, and in the ♀ it is white to pearly gray.

▶ ♂ Basic I Plumage (typically limited to part each of breast, sides, and lateral portions of upper back); replaces corresponding Juv. feathers. The Basic I feathers are first noticeable in FALL at age 65–80 days (and in some they continue to appear for several weeks, say into early Nov.) and usually these feathers drop out by MID-DEC. (or earlier in early-hatched individuals). **Breast** feathers blackish brown, edged buff, crossed distally by a comparatively wide buffy tan crescentic stripe or with a V- or U-shaped mark, and more basally by paler (to white) transverse stripes; on the **sides** the scattered feathers have wide dark brown and narrow tan transverse bands; on lateral areas of **anterior dorsum** the feathers are gray-brown, striped and barred variously with tan. This fleeting Plumage is shown well in center right fig. on pl. 42 in Schiøler (1925), of a bird taken Nov. 30 in Greenland that still was retaining Basic I after having acquired much Alt. I.

NOTE   A drake, taken Sept. 15 in Alta., had all of lower half of breast in Basic I, also scattered feathers on mantle including some short scapulars, and a few coarsely barred feathers (among Juv. ones) along sides.

▶ ♂ Alt. I Plumage (entire feathering, sometimes excepting some feathers of lower back, rump, and a few scattered elsewhere on the body, and, in the wing, only the innermost secondaries and their greater coverts); this Plumage begins to show at age 70–80 days, i.e., beginning from about MID-SEPT. into NOV. (depending on date of hatching) and continues to grow for at least a month; the tail may come in quite early, but commonly both it and the innermost secondaries are not fully grown until into winter. (The gray Alt. I body down is through the skin at about age 65 days, prior to appearance of contour feathers.) It is retained into SUMMER.

This Plumage is essentially like Alt. II (definitive), but sometimes does not include quite as much feathering. The lower breast and belly are more often spotted and less often vermiculated than in succeeding Alts. By some time in winter, soft parts attain full coloring. Worn with this Plumage: any retained Juv. feathering on lower back and rump, and most of wing.

▶ ♀ Basic I Plumage (extent of feathering as in ♂), timing as ♂; the relatively few Basic I feathers have as much variation as corresponding feathers of the next incoming Plumage (Alt. I). That the ♀ grows these Basic I feathers, and in the same areas and at the same time as ♂, and timing of their loss is as in ♂, was amply demonstrated by examination of both flesh side and feather side of skins of known-age birds by Oring (1966, 1968).

▶ ♀ Alt. I Plumage (includes head, most of body, and tail, but only a few innermost feathers of wing), the bulk of this acquired through FALL, as in ♂, and worn into SPRING. The molt by which this is acquired may either slow down or be interrupted, so that the Juv. innermost secondaries and their coverts are not replaced by corresponding Alt. I feathers until spring. The new innermost secondaries (compared with their predecessors) have more rounded ends, more extensive buff edges, and occasionally are marked or barred buff. Alt. I can be distinguished from later Alts. by presence also of any retained Juv. on lower back, rump, plus most of wing.

NOTE   There is mention of "two types of males" in Witherby (1939). Actually, however, general coloring of head–neck of the Alt.-Plumaged drake ranges from decidedly grayish (uncommonly) to variants of grayed buff (majority of individuals) to almost rusty tan (rarely). Such variation exists both in N. Am. and Eurasia.

Measurements of definitive-feathered birds, 12 ♂ (9 from conterminous U.S., 3 Alta.): BILL 41–50 mm., av. 45.6; WING 262–281, av. 271.7; TAIL 80–92, av. 86.3; TARSUS 40–43, av. 41.5;   10 ♀ (6 conterminous U.S., 4 Canada): BILL 40–43 mm., av. 41.8; WING 246–268, av. 255; TAIL 81–91, av. 85.8; TARSUS 37–43, av. 40 (ETS). For meas. that include WING across chord, see J. C. Phillips (1923b); for another series, WING meas. over curve, see Witherby (1939).

Weight (converted to metric) in fall in Ill.: "adults" 16 ♂ av. 990 gm. and 14 ♀ av. 849; "immatures" 68 ♂ av. 908 and 66 ♀ av. 808 (Bellrose and Hawkins 1947). Birds of unstated (and undoubtedly various) age-classes: 122 ♂ 709–1,134 gm., av. 907 (Kortright 1942) and 104 ranged to 1,077 with av. 907 (A. L. Nelson and Martin 1953); 101 ♀ 595–1,021 gm., av. 822 (Kortright) and 89 ranged to 1,361, av. 680 (Nelson and Martin).

From study of 82 wild Gadwalls (47 ♂ and 35 ♀) taken in s. Man., Oring (1966) reported as follows: ♂♂ gained wt. rapidly after taking leave of their mates (in summer); then wt. remained relatively constant until final stages of wing molt, at which time they lost about 75 gm.; ♀♀ lost much wt. during incubation, but regained it rapidly while rearing broods; then they probably lost wt. while growing new wing feathers (but data were inadequate to demonstrate this). For a few further details, for both sexes, see Oring (1969). According to A. Leopold (1921), Gadwalls in the Rio Grande Valley increase steadily in wt. throughout Nov.–Jan. inclusive.

For wt. of ducklings, see below under "Reproduction."

Hybrids or presumed ones in the wild with Mallard, Pintail, Shoveler, Wigeon, and Baldpate were mentioned by J. C. Phillips (1923b); a longer list, which included crosses that occurred in captivity, was given by Gray (1958). At Netherby, England, a hybrid Gadwall–Mallard stock became well established in feral condition (Delacour 1956).

Geographical variation in the species—apparently none. The writer has examined series from N. Am., Greenland, Iceland, Europe, and U.S.S.R. and all show much individual variation.

Two individuals, fully grown but only of teal size, and differing in other respects (more lamellae in bill, somewhat different soft-part colors, etc.) from the Gadwall as described above, were taken in 1874 on Washington I. (in Line Is., sw. Pacific) and described under the specific name *couesi* by Streets (1876). The writer, who has examined these specimens, recognizes that whether they are listed as another species

385

or as a subspecies of *strepera* can be decided arbitrarily either way, sees no advantage in the latter alternative. See Greenway (1958) for details of later attempts to find this diminutive Gadwall, which is extinct. RSP

FIELD IDENTIFICATION   Smaller than Mallard, which it somewhat resembles in conformation when on water, and with which it is commonly confused by hunters. Visible white patch extending in from trailing edge of wing is diagnostic; in addition, ♂ has gray flanks and blackish rear end, ♀ usually has orange in bill and is smallish in size. Floats higher than species of the Mallard group; ashore, frequently stands with retracted head, giving bulky appearance that belies true slimness. On wing appears to be most slender of our ducks aside from Pintail and possibly some teal. Long neck, trim body, relatively long pointed wings, and comparatively large wedge-shaped tail—the last especially evident when bird flies overhead. Travel in small compact flocks, direct, without convolutions characteristic of Baldpate.

Drake (except possibly for some individuals in Juv. Plumage) has more or less chestnut and black in wing plus the conspicuous white patch mentioned above; most of year (Alt. Plumage) the drake's dark grayish body is contrasted with lighter (usually grayed buff) head and, at a distance on water, appears remotely like the Black Duck. Closer inspection, however, reveals a different head profile (steeper forehead) and black feathering around base of tail which contrasts with lighter back and flanks. White belly is quite prominent in flight. Drake in summer–early fall (Basic Plumage) quite closely resembles ♀.

The ♀ is grayish brown without any pronounced diagnostic features (white wing patch concealed) when on water. Often at least a hint of yellow or orange in bill. In the air, white patch at trailing edge of wing and whitish belly are differences from ♀ Mallard. (The Baldpate and Wigeon have white patch in forepart of wing.)

Juv. birds are quite ♀-like, but show less white ventrally. FCB

VOICE   Published descriptions are at variance, possibly indicating that described calls vary, or that more calls exist than have been identified accurately, or even some confusion with whistling of the Pintail and Baldpate.

Burp display (accompanying calls are drake's most common vocalizations) requires a lifting of the head and stretching of the windpipe. At first there is a nasal, exhaled, *geee* sound; then, when the neck is fully stretched, a *raeaeb* sound. (Latter is homologous to the whistle in the Pintail's Burp and to the *raeaeb* call of the Mallard which it resembles—Lorenz 1941, Wall 1963.)

In breeding season, drakes have a regular call, given singly or in series, presumably the "softly-breathed" note of Lorenz (1941), certainly the "deep reed-like note" of Wetmore (1920) and the 1- to 3-syllabled "mating call" that Wall (1963) stated may be preceded by the *geee* sound used in Burp display (a combination presently known only for this species). In sexual pursuit flights it is often repeated 4–5 times. A reed-like note is especially noticeable when the drake circles the nest site just after his mate has gone to her nest; it has a recognition function.

Grunt-whistle—a far-carrying whistle is followed in smooth transition by the grunt; that is, a whistle-grunt (sequence reverse of Mallard). Wüst (1960) stated that drakes sometimes continue uttering this call after taking flight, the neck then in an "S" posture and breast protruding.

Mutual chin-lifting—drake grunts on 1st and 3rd movements and whistles on 2nd; the calls and actions of ♂ and ♀ are synchronized.

In Head-up-tail-up—a loud quack.

Decrescendo call—rarely heard; higher pitched and has fewer syllables than in Mallard.

The quack of the ♀ is higher pitched and more nasal than the Mallard's. It may be uttered in series, diminishing in pitch and loudness. When on water after being flushed from her nest, the ♀ calls repeatedly, also early in nesting season as the pair circles over nesting cover (latter may be the "going away call" of Lorenz). In alarm, her voice becomes higher pitched, the quacks uttered singly or in series. At times she calls repeatedly before taking wing, which alerts her mate. In group chases, she utters a rapidly repeated harsh call, with Inciting actions or with Gesture of repulsion; Wüst (1960) described this "chatter."

The ducklings have the same calls as Mallard. MCH

HABITAT   In N. Am. **Breeds** on prairies—most numerous dabbler in some areas; in parklands—not numerous except in Alta.; w. plateaus, slopes, mt. valleys, parks, etc. (upland areas of grassland and brush, often with a history of grazing abuse and with scant water except in impoundments)—fairly common; larger marshy areas (irrespective of nature of surrounding terrain) have high densities, notably at Lower Souris, Bear R., Tule and Klamath Refuges; coastal marshes, mainly with cordgrass—probably can only be rated plentiful very locally at one or two Atlantic seaboard localities; forested areas—absent or rare, but common to locally numerous within the forest zone in deltas, marshes, and on is. in some lakes.

In **migrations,** in spring anywhere that food is available, hence more often on very shallow waters than in fall when aquatic vegetation has attained a summer's growth in less shallow waters.

In **winter** on any open water (fresh, alkaline, or brackish preferred to salt) with or near adequate food. Lakes with wooded shores are not avoided. Saltwater bays are used by some Gadwalls for resting. La.—mainly coastal marshes, but go elsewhere if drought or salt tides temporarily damage the marshes. Fla.—brackish marshes, some also on interior waters. Cal.—interior marshes and waters, coastal lagoons and bays. Texas—mainly coastal marshes of the panhandle. Atlantic coast—fresh to saline waters and marshes, from N.Y. southward. Mexico—interior lakes, marshes, and impoundments, lagunas (freshwater areas separated from the sea by a ridge), areas of mangrove swamp (especially where they give way to open marsh, savanna, prairie, or cultivated land), largest concentrations in vicinity of mouths of freshwater streams. (Mexican coastal habitats occur on Atlantic coast from Tamaulipas s. and on Pacific from Sinaloa southward.)

Some factors in habitat selection   In breeding season generally avoids woods or thick brush and waters with such borders. Intensive agriculture and heavy grazing by livestock over much of breeding range are factors that reduce relative numbers of this waterfowl. In some areas, nesting is concentrated in few and smaller cover patches and

387

here predation is heavy. Land-use practices, such as haying and summer fallow, are destructive during nesting. In overgrazed pastures, the cover available in buckbrush patches is more acceptable to the Gadwall than most other ducks. Alfalfa is a choice cover, but nests are destroyed during harvest. Nesting islands surrounded by open water are preferred to those within areas of emergent aquatic plants. The area used by a breeding pair often includes a broad stretch of open water as well as small potholes. Alkaline and brackish waters are used more by the Gadwall and Shoveler than by other dabblers during breeding season and fall. Throughout Alta., alkaline waters are favored over fresh, perhaps because they have fairly stable water levels and an abundance of submerged aquatics.

In coastal marshes there is a preference for edges of areas of *Spartina patens* and *S. alterniflora*. For description of environment at Atlantic coastal breeding places, see Parnell and Quay (1965). Broods do not remain long on small waters; they prefer those of moderate to large size, having submerged aquatics for food and deep channels for escape (by diving). Similar conditions are sought for molting and thousands of Gadwalls assemble at certain favored localities.

The Gadwall thus is shown to be far more a bird of open, often brackish or alkaline, waters than stated in the standard waterfowl treatises. This generalization, based on field observations, aligns with results from experimental work on the salt gland by Cooch (1964). (In this section, the author's data were combined with those of other workers, especially J. Gates and H. Duebbert, plus a survey of published information.) MCH

DISTRIBUTION (See map.) Older data for the entire Holarctic range of the species were summarized by J. C. Phillips (1923b); there is concise later coverage in the 1957 A.O.U. *Check-list*.

The Gadwall's breeding range has expanded n. in recent decades—in e. Canada in the inner St. Lawrence drainage (possibly even to James Bay vicinity), probably to some extent in w. Canada, almost certainly within Alaska, also across Eurasia, and within Iceland. Limits of northerly breeding are at lower latitudes near the N. Am. Atlantic seaboard (cooled by Labrador–w. Greenland currents) than in Iceland–Europe (warmed by Gulf Stream). Recent acquisition of breeding range locally down in the U.S. Atlantic seaboard may be explained as occupation of favorable habitat, especially on wildlife refuges, contemporaneous with increase (which became evident at least as early as 1938) in number of Gadwalls wintering in coastal Carolinas and Ga. In this century there has been an abandonment of some southerly breeding places in the continental interior.

The Gadwall is capable of extensive overseas travel; for example, it migrates from Iceland to Ireland (Atlantic); it also reaches Hawaii and Midway (cent. Pacific) and Marshall Is. (sw. Pacific).

Breeding Formerly bred in New Mex. and Ariz., but apparently not at present. Bred in Iowa long ago. Nested in 2 localities in Kans. in 1963. Local breeder in interior B.C. In addition to where it is definitely known to breed in Man. and Ont., it occurs elsewhere in summer; the same holds for areas beyond known breeding range westward across Canada and in parts of Alaska. The Gadwell definitely breeds on the Alaska

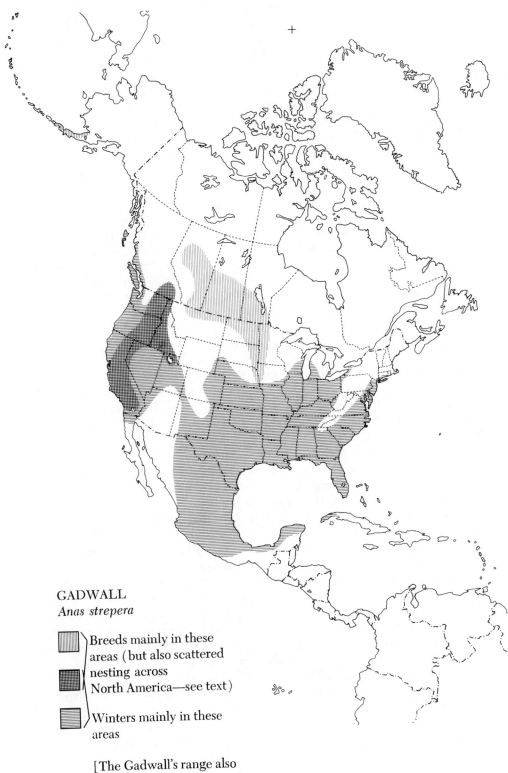

GADWALL
Anas strepera

Breeds mainly in these areas (but also scattered nesting across North America—see text)

Winters mainly in these areas

[The Gadwall's range also includes much of Eurasia]

Pen., probably at least elsewhere not far from the n. edge of the Gulf of Alaska and definitely in the interior (has bred at Wonder Lake in Mt. McKinley Nat. Park); the pattern appears to be that of scattered nesting and then, in late summer–fall, the birds gather at places where they are more easily observed as at Copper R. flats (where some also may breed). An 1861 alleged sighting of a half-grown Gadwall on Anticosti I. (Que.) is questionable. Has become established as a local breeder on Long I. (N.Y.), at Egg I. (N.J.), Bombay Hook (Del.), in Somerset Co. (Md.), and at Pea and Bodie Is. on "outer banks" of ne. N.C.

The Gadwall breeds in the Brit. Isles and also locally in parts of Europe, including Scandinavia. It now breeds and occurs in summer farther n. in Eurasia than indicated in earlier texts.

Winter There were 9 Gadwalls one season at Adak (cent. Aleutians); more recently, 25–30 wintered at Unalaska in the e. Aleutians. There are winter records for Kodiak and Afognak is. in n. Gulf of Alaska. Northern limits across the N. Am. mainland vary depending on weather. Up the U.S. Atlantic seaboard it occurs in some numbers n. to Long I. (N.Y.) and very sparingly in s. New Eng. Occurs throughout peninsular Fla., but numbers in cent. and s. Fla. have fluctuated greatly—estimated 23,000 in 1955 and only 3,000 in 1958. There are large concentrations in interior Cal., se. Ark., at places along the Gulf Coast from Ala.–La. around toward the Yucatan Pen. Distribution in Mexico is mostly near coasts (mainly e. coast), being spotty in the interior. Occurs in small numbers in w. Cuba.

(In the Palearctic region, as in the Nearctic, certain southernmost specimen records of occurrence are old and, although they have been construed by some later authors as indicating regular wintering at these places of capture, this is not supported by recent field work. In Africa s. of the Sahara, there are a few records for the Sudan and 1 for L. Chad.)

Straggler on the N. Am. mainland to s. Hudson Bay (Churchill, Man.) and in Alaska almost to the Arctic coast near Prudhoe Bay; in Bering Sea to the Pribilofs (St. Paul I.); in the Pacific to Hawaii (Molokai, Oahu, French Frigate Shoal) and Midway; and in the Atlantic area to Greenland, Bermuda, and Jamaica.

Erroneously reported (1957 A.O.U. *Check-list*) as breeding in the Commander Is., where it is a rare visitor.

Liberated birds, from releases in 1957 and 1965, resulted in the Gadwall becoming established as a breeder at Great Meadows Ponds near Concord, Mass. (Borden and Hochbaum 1966). Preflight young from Delta, Man., were released in the Chassahowitzka Refuge in Fla. in late Aug., 1968 (Cornwell 1969). Also from liberations, local breeding stocks were established in England at Norfolk (Thorburn 1926) and in Suffolk and in Kinross in Scotland (Witherby 1939). In a recent work on wildfowl in Great Britain, Atkinson-Willes (1963) wrote: "Present status somewhat confused: probably a resident, summer visitor, winter visitor and passage-migrant."

Recorded as **fossil** from the Pleistocene of N. Am. in Cal. and Fla. and reported from **archaeological** sites in Iowa and Fla. There also are Pleistocene records for Italy, Czechoslovakia, and Azerbaijan. For references to all these, see Brodkorb (1964a). RSP

MIGRATION   (In N. Am.) There is rather scant information, especially for spring, and almost none on any season for some parts of range.

Gadwalls from much of the n. prairie area go (e. of the Rockies) southward to some inland U.S. localities, Fla., the Gulf Coast from Ala. around toward Yucatan, and interior Mexico; much smaller numbers go se. to the Carolinas plus some to Fla.; and those of the w. U.S.–Canadian intermountain areas and vicinity go to Pacific coastal states, mainly Cal., and some continue on to w. Mexico. There is a very small flight on the Atlantic coast.

Bellrose (1968) mapped various migration "corridors" in the U.S. e. of the Rockies. His figures included: 665,000 Gadwalls travel in 5 corridors over the plains and Missouri–Mississippi drainage; 7,000 use a Mobile Bay (Ala.) corridor; 2,000 use a corridor from n.cent. Ill. to coastal N.C.; and 40,000 go from the interior to S.C. (The figures, which omit Pacific coastal states, etc., include less than ⅔ of the av. total number migrating in fall in N. Am.

Spring   Migrates rather late, about the same time as the Blue-winged Teal and Baldpate. In n. Gulf Coastal area and similar latitudes, there is some movement in the last few days of Feb. (later some years?), with bulk of departures in first third of March, and last birds leave in early April. In Cal. first departures may av. somewhat later, beginning in early March, than from Gulf Coast, and they all occur within a shorter period. In n. U.S., from Great Lakes to the Rockies, Gadwalls begin arriving in mid-March (very few up to a week earlier) in most seasons, but bulk of flight usually occurs in first ⅔ of April. There, and in prairie provinces, the flight is not over until mid-May. In parts of Alaska, migration perhaps does not end until June. On U.S. Atlantic coast, migrants may be expected, on av., by March 15 in Md., the 20th on Long I. (N.Y.), and about 1–2 days later in s. New Eng.

Molt migration   When drakes leave their mates (usually during incubation), they may go in any compass direction (lateral movements are common), sometimes considerable distances, to favored molting places; these are shared with Baldpates, Pintails, etc. This movement begins about June 10 in N.D. and a few days later at Delta (Man.). At Lower Souris Refuge (N.D.), there are loose flocks of several hundred Gadwalls by early July and often several thousand birds in Aug. Drakes first become flightless there July 5–10, are at peak numbers through Aug., and late molters regain flight in early Sept. A total of 30,000–40,000 (including ♀♀) molted on Lower Souris Refuge in 1954. The best-known locality to see many molting Gadwalls in ne. N. Am. is Montezuma Marshes in cent. N.Y. The time of molt of ♀♀ is more variable; many become flightless while tending their preflight young, hence are scattered over breeding range. At Lower Souris, early dates for flightless ♀♀ are Aug. 2 and 5, with peak in late Aug.–early Sept. One was flightless Oct. 10 at Delta. Chabreck (1966) found 2–3 dozen ♀♀ flightless in La. in Oct.; this appears to be an exceptional instance in which the birds migrated prior to their wing molt (compare with ♀ Greenwing).

Fall   When flight is regained (and the young attain it), there is a certain amount of dispersal; some birds also soon migrate. Summering Gadwalls at Delta (Man.) were leaving by mid-Sept. and were rare there by the end of the month (Oring 1966). Some Gadwalls reach La. the first week in Sept., and more by the end of the month.

In Sept.-Oct., migrants occur in flocks which prefer open water over submerged vegetation. They are restless on windy days, the downwind birds making short flights to the upwind side of the flock. Concentrations of over 100,000 occur at some favored places, as at Bear R. Refuge (Utah) and Valentine Refuge (Nebr.). Departures continue through Oct. (thousands already on winter range in latter half of the month) and into Nov. in n. and cent. prairie states. There was a single flock of 80,000 as early as Oct. 17 near Venice (La.). Probably, depending on weather, last arrivals do not reach southerly winter range until the first few days of Dec.

At Pea and Bodie is. (ne. N.C.), southernmost Atlantic coastal breeding place, whether the local-breeding Gadwalls migrate or whether they remain in the general vicinity is not reported.

Winter Flocks vary in size from large to small and there is some local shifting about to obtain food. MCH

BANDING STATUS The total number banded in N. Am. was 27,554 through 1964 and there were 3,735 recoveries through 1966; the birds were banded at localities throughout much of breeding range, very few on winter range. (Data from Bird Banding Laboratory.) RSP

REPRODUCTION (This section is based on data gathered 1936–57 at Lower Souris National Wildlife Refuge (N.D.), supplemented by information from manuscripts by M. Hammond and H. Duebbert, by additional information from many persons but especially Duebbert and John Gates, and various published information. European studies of Geyr von Schweppenburg (1961), Lebret (1951, 1955), Lorenz (1941), Wall (1963), Weidmann (1956), Wüst (1960), and Balát and Folk (1968), have been consulted to some extent but have not been fully utilized.

Commonly, both ♂ and ♀ **first breed** at age 1 year, but some not until older. A few, primarily yearling ♂ ♂, in the wild are believed never to engage in display activities and are the first to form in groups and to molt their remiges (Oring 1966). **Pair formation** occurs as in the Mallard (Weidmann 1956), but perhaps may require a longer period of association between prospective mates. Temporary attachments of gradually increasing duration are seen Sept. 11–Oct. 15 in N.D. At first, the ♀ takes the initiative. Pairs having stable bonds were noted among winterers in Dec. in Cal. (F. Kozlik). In La., 40% are paired in mid-Jan. (R. Chabreck). At Chincoteague Refuge (Va.), about 20% of 600 individuals were paired by the end of Jan. and, by March 5, nearly all of the 100 then present were paired (J. Valentine Jr.). There is much pairing activity during spring migration. Early arrivals at Ogden Bay (Utah) consist of unpaired migrants on the larger water areas and scattered pairs on the smaller ones. In the Dakotas, most April–May arrivals already are paired; extra ♂ ♂ among early migrants accompanied paired or unpaired ♀ ♀; later ones associated with pairs. Most Gadwalls are paired when they arrive at Delta (Man.), but yearling drakes still are trying to get mates (Oring 1966).

In the following paragraphs displays are not numbered as in the account of the Mallard, but most display names are identical.

Displays on water GRUNT-WHISTLE Very like Mallard in actions, but vocalizing

392

differs (see "Voice"); near its beginning, after the bill tip is placed in water, it is raised to one side, flinging up some droplets; it is always followed by tail-shake, head-flick, tail-shake (as in Mallard). This low-intensity display is common Sept. 11–Oct. 15 in N.D. and in Oct. in Utah, also again in early spring, but winter frequency is unknown. It appears to be supplanted gradually in early spring by "courting flights" and these evolve into "pursuit flights" on breeding grounds (Lebret 1951). HEAD-UP-TAIL-UP very different from Mallard. The drake gives a loud quacklike call (not a whistle), points his bill toward ♀, then immediately TURNS-THE-BACK-OF-THE-HEAD toward her with NOD-SWIMMING. The BURP display (with call) is the ♂'s most common sexual reaction; it lacks the Mallard's down-up movement entirely, contrary to Lorenz (1941) (also see "Voice"). The ♀ never Nod-swims and her INCITING differs from Mallard; it is likened to Chin-lifting and, in addition to over-the-shoulder Inciting action, her chatterlike Inciting call accompanies almost any aggressive move she makes. CHIN-LIFTING is distinctive in the Gadwall (and Baldpate). The ♀ lifts her chin between Inciting movements and the ♂ responds with 3 Chin-lifts, the 1st and 3rd in unison with ♀ and 2nd as she Incites (Lorenz 1941). It is a mated-pair reaction, but either mate may do it independently. It may be akin to the Triumph ceremony of geese and is most commonly seen when pairs are in conflict or an unmated ♀ annoys a pair (Lorenz).

Aerial activity COURTING FLIGHTS (mating flights of Wüst 1960) occur when the birds are not normally at full sexual development; occasionally in fall–winter in the Netherlands (Lebret 1951); they begin about the first of March in Cal. (F. Kozlik), but are occasional all year. They are regularly tied in with swim displays. Variation: flight of unmated ♀ and drakes (usual), pair and extra ♂ ♂ (common), 2 or more pairs (occasional through nesting), pair with pair of Shovelers (summer, once at Lower Souris). This activity has been described by Trautman (1940) and reported to be similar to that of Mallard by Lebret (1951) and Dzubin (1957). THREE-BIRD CHASE typically is a reaction of ♂ having mate close by. He flies 200 yds. or less, following the intruding pair, and returns to his departure point. His mate sometimes follows him.

There is much anomalous aerial behavior when nesting density is high; it starts during prenesting and is prevalent into the early part of laying period.

So-called sexual pursuits or harassing flights are common beginning before drakes separate from their mates and occur afterwards even when drakes are molting body feathering. They are initiated when an intruding ♂ closely approaches a ♀, or when a pair or ♀ flies within view of extra drakes or ♂ ♂ that have separated from their mates. Readiness to pursue any ♀ in sight and to copulate increases from late in the laying period through incubation. A Three-bird chase may evolve into sexual pursuit if additional drakes join in. Early in the breeding cycle ♀ ♀ appear to participate more or less willingly or even occasionally initiate such flights. Where nesting density is high, during prenesting and nesting, group flights of 12–15 pairs with both sexes calling have been observed. Harassing flights or chases (♀ tries to avoid ♂) appear not to be as aggressive as in the Mallard and Pintail, although a "repulsion" posture and call occur and ♀ infrequently dives into cover to escape. For **renesting**, the usual pair formation behavior is omitted and a combination of the last 2 types of flights just mentioned, or variants of them, insure fertile eggs.

Copulation occurs occasionally after "courting flights," rarely after Three-bird chases, and frequently after the last 2 types of flights described in the above paragraph. Probably copulation is irregular in mated pairs before arrival on nesting areas; it is most frequent right after occupation of nesting habitat, declines during the latter part of egg-laying, and ceases soon after incubation begins. Normally it is preceded by head pumping; as in the Mallard, this is initiated by the drake and is done by both sexes. Wetmore (1920) reported the ♂ head pumping, with gentle biting of ♀ and shoving her gently on one side and then the other. The drake gives an exaggerated Burp display (with call) as he dismounts from the ♀, then points his bill toward her briefly (J. Gates). Then the pair engages in displacement activities—bathing, wing flapping, and preening.

Pair bond form usually is **single-brood monogamy,** but sometimes the bond is weak and the ♀ changes partners even more than once during a single nesting cycle. There is a possible tendency toward polygamy where there is a high nesting density on islands; ♂ ♂ accompanied ♀ ♀ to nests late in incubation but their exact relationship remains unknown. (But note beyond that sometimes the drake is with the ♀ and her young brood.) Drakes are promiscuous after pair bond severance, sometimes earlier. Early dissolution of the bond is fostered by late nesting, high breeding densities which provide more opportunities to chase ♀ ♀, and possibly other factors. The bond is maintained by constant companionship until nesting is begun; the ♀ even threatens other Gadwalls at times. With onset of nesting, the ♂ calls and flies over the site and the ♀ and spends time at his waiting site or at places they both use. The ♀ does not seek the ♂ when she leaves her nest; he must seek her and when he ceases to appear or to remain nearby regularly the bond is terminated. As in the Mallard, some birds behave as pairs on molting areas, hence perhaps some mates are reunited there. This could result in the bond being continuously maintained (or else renewed) for more than one breeding season.

If the drake's defended area is adequate in size, his defense is as aggressive as that of any species of duck (S. W. Harris 1954). But Gadwalls have a tendency toward colonial breeding (Duebbert 1966a). Where there is a relatively high nesting density on an island, the ♂ sometimes used feet and bill during aerial attack. Drakes even chased ♀ Mallards quite often. Under high-density conditions, both Gates and Duebbert found ♂ ♂ with ♀ ♀ later into incubation than did R. Benson and Hammond with "normal" densities on the mainland. On the other hand, when the birds were crowded, the former observers noted indications of weak pair bonds, a tendency to promiscuity, and apparent confusion of drakes trying to identify their mates. Even the temporary absence of drakes may have led to pair recombinations. There was an island **density** as high as 200 nests/acre at Lower Souris (Henry 1948). There are other known instances of nests a few ft. apart, even inches apart, also 25 nests in a 15 × 40 yd. area. Where nesting density is high, however, a chronological spacing of nesting by the various ♀ ♀ may allow the aggression peak of one ♂ to subside before that of another develops (Oring 1966). Territorialism (in the classical sense) probably is of minor importance in regulating relative numbers (which are low) in most of breeding range. There are about 2–6 pairs/sq. mi. in much of the Dakotas and prairie provinces; in pothole areas there, 8–10 pairs/sq. mi. (60–80 acres/pair), but individual territories often overlap. Highest recorded marsh shoreline density at Lower Souris was 300–500 ft. between pairs.

At Delta (Man.) the peak of arrival of breeders occurred 23 days prior to av. date for first egg and in Utah it was 28 days (Oring 1966). At Lower Souris the span of territory establishment to nesting av. 16 days for 15 marked ♀ ♀; this period is devoted to nest-site selection, Three-bird chases, etc. Extra (unmated) drakes seem to become more active then, moving from pair to pair; a drake is more often found with another drake than earlier (Hochbaum 1944, Hammond). Some marked ♀ ♀ have been found in the same area in successive years, using the same nest sites in some instances.

Onset of nesting begins with search flights by the ♀ accompanied by her mate, to find (or become reoriented to) a suitable site. There is frequent circling. The general location perhaps is chosen from the air, but the ♀ on the ground selects the actual site. Then she digs one to several nest bowls. Most ♀ ♀ dig bowl and lay the first egg the same morning, whether or not they also make excavations earlier.

The **nest site** usually is well drained, but occasionally is a damp spot or even on matted floating vegetation. Favored places include transition in habitat—water to land, a break or opening in cover, a patch or clump within a uniform stand of vegetation—or near a mound or stone or some other landmark. The nest usually is within 50 yds. of water and within 10 ft. of a landmark (Oring 1966). In se. Alta., av. distance from water of 63 nests was 123 ± 40 ft. (Keith 1961). There is a strong preference for dense low herbaceous vegetation, but taller grasses are nearly as acceptable. Usually new vegetation already is 8–15 in. high when the first egg is layed. Various exceptional sites have been reported, including (A. Brooks 1934) a Crow's nest in a tree. They nest rarely in grain stubble unless other herbaceous cover grows there. Some use ricefields in Cal., if near a marsh. Unhayed grasslands are strongly preferred to hayed areas. They prefer taller cover than most ducks, which provides more shade for this comparatively late nester. Thus the nest usually is concealed about as is usual for Baldpate and Shoveler, better than Mallard and Pintail, and poorer than teals and scaups. The waiting site of the drake generally is on bare shoreline or some object such as a log or rock. The feeding area of a nesting pair usually is within ¼ mi. of the drake's waiting site and, after termination of bond, the ♀ usually feeds and rests in a small area closer to the nest.

The **nest** is made of vegetation, gathered at the site by the ♀; a small amount is first added when the 2nd or 3rd egg is present; after the 5th egg, the nest normally is well covered when the ♀ leaves; but most material is added toward end of the laying period. In a stereotyped manner she places material over her shoulder, very rarely in front. To escape rising water, a ♀ has been known to pile much material on the nest, then get the eggs up through this accumulation (W. Anderson 1956). In accumulating nest down from her belly, the duck uses preening and picking motions. Writers have indicated that the down for first nests apparently becomes detached and is rubbed or falls out in preening. In renesting, probably it is plucked (L. Keith). The **nest down** has dark centers and relatively inconspicuous white tips (they are conspicuous in the Baldpate); the intermingled breast feathers have the dark area of the feather darkest in the center (Broley 1950).

Egg dates and clutch size Analysis of data from scattered localities showed fair correlation with J. R. Baker's (1938) proposition that egg seasons are delayed some 20 or 30 days for 10° increase in latitude, but climate and elevation probably mask the pattern. In some years, first nesting in N.C. (36°), Utah (41°), and Waubay, S.D. (45°) were on

395

about the same date as at Lower Souris, N.D. (49°). Nesting in se. Wash. (46°) is earlier than expected. On the Atlantic seaboard, it is a late nester on Long I., N.Y. (Sedwitz 1958, and others); compared with Black Duck and Blue-winged Teal it is late at Pea I., N.C., with hatching peak spread over the last 3 weeks of June in 1959 and 1960 (Parnell and Quay 1965). Where the nesting season is long, as in Utah, first clutches are earlier and so there is more time for renesting after predation (Oring 1966). Island nesters in N.D. had a shorter overall nesting period than those on the mainland (Duebbert 1966a).

Early in the season (mostly **initial clutches**) Lower Souris, May 16–31, 13 clutches of 8–12 eggs (av. 10.6); Ogden Bay, Utah, May 1–15, 12 of 11–12 eggs (av. 11.3), and May 16–31, 35 of 9–14, (av. 11); at Delta, Man. (Sowls 1955), May 15–June 15, 17 av. 10.5 and (Oring 1966) 26 initial clutches there contained 8–14 eggs (av. 10.6). In Oring's sample, clutches were initiated (1st egg) May 22–June 4. Midseason clutches, which include more **renesting**: N.D., June 1–15. 103 clutches of 6–12 (av. 10), and June 16–30, 42 of 5–12 (av. 9.2). Late in season, with many renestings: N.D., July 1–15, 23 of 7–11 (av. 8.6); Ogden Bay, July 1–15, 9 of 6–9, (Av. 8.1), and July 16–31, 3 of 6–7 (av. 6.3); Delta, after June 25, 10 av. 9.5. In 55 clutches in se. Alta., clutch size av. 9.8 in those initiated before June 16, 9.9 June 16–30, and 8.8 after June 30, the overall figure being 9.4 ± 0.4 (Keith 1961). There are Canadian and Cal. averages for the entire season that are as high as those given above for early in the season. Nine captives at Delta, Man., laid smaller clutches (5–11, av. 8.7 eggs) than those in the wild (Oring 1969).

Joint layings On islands, clutches usually are larger—2 or more ♀ ♀ lay in the same nest—and often there is little renesting. At Kazan Lake (Sask.) 38 nests had 5–16 eggs; Tule–Klamath (Cal.), 344 nests av. 11 (A. W. Miller and Collins 1954); Lower Souris, an av. of 10.5 in 355 nests and (excluding clutches of 6 or fewer) range of 7–21 with 10 as highest frequency. Joint laying may be assumed when there are more than 12 eggs. Gadwall nests in areas studied have had deposited in them (in decreasing order of frequency) eggs of Redhead, Mallard, Lesser Scaup, and Pintail. Gadwalls lay in each others' nests, rarely (if ever) in nests of other ducks. In 1956–61 inclusive, on islands in the U.S.S.R. Black Sea Reserve, 50 of 2,052 Gadwall nests contained eggs of the Shellduck (*Tadorna tadorna*), 24 contained eggs of the Red-breasted Merganser, and 10 contained eggs of both of these species; see Ardamatskaya (1965) for further details. In Czechoslovakia, mixed clutches included eggs of *Netta rufina, Anas platyrhynchos, A. clypeata, Aythya ferina,* and *Phasianus colchicus* (Balát and Folk 1968).

Measurements One **egg** each from 19 clutches in N. Am. size length 54.73 ± 1.9 mm., breadth 38.76 ± 0.73, radii of curvature of ends 14.81 ± 1.01 and 11.26 ± 1.02; **shape** usually between elliptical and subelliptical, elongation 1.40 ± 0.058, bicone -0.050, asymmetry $+0.129$ (FWP). For other series, see standard works such as Bent (1923) and Schönwetter (1961). The shell is smooth, glossy, **color** when fresh slightly off-white (cream or buff). Occurrence of blood spots on shells comes with the peak of down deposition or a little afterward (M. C. Nelson). Fresh eggs usually weigh 43–45 gm. At Lower Souris there were 3 dwarf and 2 giant eggs in a sample of 5,990. Eggs usually are laid early in the morning at a rate of 1/day, but a day sometimes is skipped toward end of laying period.

Renesting occurs in the same territory if the habitat remains suitable, as observed in marked birds (Sowls 1955, Gates). In se. Alta., an estimated 82% of ♀ ♀ that had their first nests destroyed attempted renesting (Keith 1961). The number of eggs decreases in successive replacement clutches, as observed by Gates in marked birds: 11–10–9–6, 11–8–7, 11–8–6, 10–8–6, and in single renestings. There is about as much nest down with replacment clutches.

Behavior during incubation The ♀ approaches her nest in flight, followed by her mate (if they are still paired); they may circle in that vicinity, then she alights sometimes 100 or more ft. from the nest. After a watchful period she makes 1–2 short flights, alternating with watchful periods, then walks the last few ft. to the eggs. Interference by drakes alters this pattern. She uses both bill and feet to uncover the eggs. Her behavior on the nest is essentially as known for the Mallard, but she changes position more often. Her absences from the nest are longer than reported for most other dabblers. Absent ♀ ♀ do not respond to an approaching storm, but often return a few min. after heavy rain begins. Nor are pipped eggs a strong brooding stimulus, as she leaves them for her usual rest period.

Cessation of sexual activity of drakes is marked by their assembling in small groups. At Lower Souris this began in very late June or a little later, 2–4 weeks after many ♀ ♀ first began incubating. In the very retarded spring of 1950 there was late nesting and the flocking of drakes began earlier in relation to the nesting cycle.

Incubation period 25–26 days in N.D., but 24 days was noted most frequently in Utah. At L. Miquelon (Alta.) the period in 10 clutches was 22–27 days, av. 25.1 (Vermeer 1968). Artificially incubated eggs hatched in 23–24 days (J. C. Phillips 1923b); normal hatching in the wild has occurred after as long as 29 days. For variation in reported incubation periods in the wild, also Gadwall eggs under domestic fowl, and in a hatchery incubator, see Oring (1969).

In fair weather the **brood** departs soon after the ducklings are dry. At this stage in the breeding cycle, some brood mothers can be picked up; they peck and beat their captor's hands with their wings. Distraction display is less frequent than in other dabblers and seems less intense than in some of them. Weak broken-wing behavior, noted from the 11th day of incubation, is more intense when the brood is on the water. When escape cover is lacking and the ♀ "believes" her brood is unseen, she may "hide" motionless with neck stretched along the surface of the water, as is done by geese (J. Gates).

Hatching success varies much with locality and in the same area in different years; predation, agricultural practices, and inclement weather are major influences. Many studies are subject to an unknown degree of observer bias; that is, the presence and activities of the observer reduces success as compared to what it would be if nests were not visited. Tabulation (omitted here) of data for N.D., Idaho, Utah, and Cal. showed mean clutch size varied 9.4–11.7; percentage of nests in which 1 or more eggs hatched ("successful nests") varied from 39 to 90; and av. number of eggs hatched in successful nests ranged from 7.4 to possibly 10.9. See Duebbert (1966a) for detailed data for N.D. and comparison with other studies. In some areas the California Gull (*Larus californicus*) preys heavily on poorly concealed nests. At Miquelon L. (Alta.), of 29 clutches, eggs hatched in 26 and 3 were deserted, but no young survived to attain flight, mostly because of predation by the California Gull (Vermeer 1968).

Where nests are well concealed (which is typical), they are more vulnerable to crow

397

(Corvus) predation than are nests of other duck species in the same general area (Kalmbach 1937), so the actions of the ♀ Gadwall presumably reveal to the crow the whereabouts of the nest.

Eggs classed as infertile, and dead embryos, account for the main egg loss in success-ful nests, 4.4–7.6% of total number of eggs in most studies. The desertion rate is slightly lower at mainland nests (island studies omitted) than in other dabblers nesting there, probably from fewer flushings as ♀ ♀ are absent longer to rest and feed. About 50% of nests are deserted if disturbed before the 5th egg is laid.

In absence of Crow predation, the Gadwall often is the most successful nesting dab-bler because: it nests comparatively late, when the rate of predation on any single prey species is lower; it is less inclined to concentrate nests near water, except in special cases; it is less subject to early-season losses from ploughing and burning (but losses in alfalfa and hay fields may be heavy); it uses island habitat extensively and losses there are slight; and the ♀ spends less time on eggs, as noted above. For various data on nest losses, hatching success, and brood size in se. Alta., see Keith (1961).

Development of young The ducklings weigh 20–26 gm. at hatching (Hammond); 7 hatched in an incubator weighed 19.2–26.2 gm., with mean of 23.8 (Smart 1965a). They can run the day they hatch. In captive birds the down covering is succeeded by feathers as follows: 17 days—ensheathed innermost secondaries are first visible; 3 weeks—some birds are completely covered ventrally with feathers and remiges are plainly visible; 3½ weeks—greater wing coverts and axillars visible; 4 weeks—well covered with Juv. Plumage, principal wing feathers all visible; during 5th week—many body feathers and the rectrices become clear of sheaths and there is a surge in wing growth; 6 weeks—Juv. rectrices, scapulars, and side feathers fully grown and the body down of Alt. I Plumage is apparent along the midventral line (Oring 1966).

Both sexes have full-sized culmens and tarsi by about age 5 weeks and rapid wt. gain ceases by 7 or 8 weeks (Oring 1966). For a growth curve (wt./age) of 3 captives and some details of their development, see Veselovsky (1953); for a curve based on more birds that were studied longer, see Oring (1966).

Broods of 2 marked ♀ ♀ could just rise from the water at ages 46 and 49 days; these and other data indicate that **age at first flight** in the wild is about 48–52 days (Ham-mond). The captives in Veselovsky's study flew at 59 days, and in Oring's study most of them first flew at between 50 and 56 days. Late-hatched young fly at an earlier age than early-hatched young (Oring 1966).

Mothers with broods usually do not travel more than a small fraction of a mile from the nest, but do not hesitate to go overland to water. They also have been observed to leave nests on islands and to swim about ⅖ mi. to the mainland. The broods prefer open-water areas and, when disturbed, they gather into a flock; that is, their behavior is more like that of diving ducks than of other dabblers, since the latter prefer shorelines and spend more time being brooded on dry sites. Some physical characteris-tic must reduce wetting of the feathers of young Gadwalls.

A marked ♀ left her brood at 48 days. Often, however, broods are temporarily or permanently motherless earlier. Counts of motherless broods at Lower Souris: 1.3% of 75 broods of downies, 11% of 120 partly feathered broods, 53% of 34 feathered ones. The duck stays longer with early-season broods. At Ogden Bay, drakes associated with about ⅓ of early-hatched broods during their downy stage (J. Gates). Lone ♀ ♀ or small groups of ♀ ♀ are attracted to, but seldom are successful in appropriating, broods; the mother repulses with threat and attack. Broods that also contain either Lesser Scaup or Redhead have been noted, but hostility between the mothers (if both were present) was apparent. Redheads hatched from eggs laid in Gadwell nests are accepted by, and they accept, the foster parent. Congregations of adults at molting areas are avoided by small young, but older young may join them.

When broods are numerous, there is frequent **mixing,** scattering, and recombining of young of all ages. Groups of 13–35 small downies comprised 34 (4%) of 841 "broods" observed at Lower Souris in 1946–57. Older young in various reported samples represent more first nestings, which may av. larger (without any combining) than renestings; 2 samples of the latter av. 6.8 young (Lower Souris) and 8.2 (Ogden Bay). Thus various factors must be reckoned with in trying to obtain reliable data of any sort that is related to true brood size. Only when Gadwalls are dispersed so that brood mixing is unlikely, and when renesting is at a minimum (or a reliable correction factor is applied), are the data satisfactory. MCH

SURVIVAL (Note comments above regarding true brood size.) At Tule and Klamath Refuges, most brood mortality occurs during the first week after hatching and later losses are negligible: av. of 10.5 young hatched in 344 nests, with av. down to 6.8 at age 1 week (326 broods), to 6.5 at 2 weeks (227 broods), and the loss in a total of 1,064 broods inventoried continued small in succeeding weeks; see A. W. Miller and Collins (1954) for details. At Pea and Bodie is. (N.C.), small downies av. 6.85/brood (70 broods), large downies 5.68 (45 broods), and feathered but flightless young av. 3.68 (16 broods) (Parnell and Quay 1965). During the first 3 days after hatching there is a trek to water and adjustment to feeding, drinking, being brooded, and imprinting. Smaller losses than at Tule–Klamath have been noted at Ogden Bay and Lower Souris. From study of available data, published and otherwise, it appears that the av. probability of survival through the downy stage is 0.84 and to flying age (say 50 days) is 0.72. In 2,440 postdowny young, banded by various agencies, the sex ratio was 110:100 (1,418♂:1,284♀). This is essentially the same as the spring (prenesting) ratio in N.D., 112:100; for this regional stock there does not appear to be selective mortality for either sex from preflight stage to the following spring. No useful survival data based on banding are currently available. MCH

HABITS N. Am. data. The Gadwall associates readily with other species sharing similar habitat—notably the Baldpate, Pintail, Shoveler, Green-winged Teal, N. Am. Coot, and some diving ducks. At times, however, small assemblies to many thousands occur with little or no mixing. It is not as prone to close flocking and is less gregarious than the Mallard and Pintail. Where undisturbed, the birds make local flights in small temporary groups of up to 6 birds; in longer movements and on migration, usually they are in flocks of less than 25, but at times to over 50. Migrants fly in oblique lines, rarely in wedges.

Wingbeat is more rapid than that of some larger ducks, and with a low whistling sound. Usual speeds, however, are believed to be slower than in the Pintail or Mallard,

399

about as the Shoveler. Recorded flight speeds (ground speed) vary from 29 to 40–50 mph, 55 when pressed.

Gadwalls feed on shallowly submerged and on floating material usually, and more often out in open water than our other dabblers. The incidence of shot found in gizzards is low. The birds dive well for food when necessary. Feeding flights occur when food is scarce at resting areas in spring; they also occur in the hunting season and then may be mostly at night. They regularly spend both day and night on the water. This species occasionally is reported foraging in grain stubble, very rarely in woods for acorns. The use of vegetative parts of submerged aquatic plants (see "Food") in fresh, alkaline, and brackish waters is almost unique, at least among N. Am. ducks. As noted in La., Utah, Mexico, and elsewhere, for example, a favorite food is wigeon grass (*Ruppia*), a plant of brackish and saline waters.

Gadwalls, both numerically and relative to other ducks, declined throughout the interior range in the period of settlement of the prairies. Various agricultural practices reduce the amount of preferred habitat and disrupt nesting; control of fires has permitted more woody growth to become established around water areas. The number of Gadwalls in the 1960s (usually over a million wintering birds) and proportion in the duck population fluctuate even to the extent of decreasing by ⅓ or ½ within a year or so. The number shot (averaging about 375,000) show variations of similar amplitude. The ultimate causes of short-term fluctuations are believed to be weather (affects nesting success) and hunting (affects survival). There is evidence of heavy to moderate overhunting of this duck in interior and Gulf states. The Gadwall comprises half the total hunters' bags in some La. marshes. (Based on published sources plus original data mainly from J. Gates, H. Duebbert, and the author). MCH

FOOD   Mainly leaves and stems, rather than seeds, of grasses, sedges, pondweeds and other aquatic plants; insects, mollusks, crustaceans, amphibians, and fish. Examination in the Biological Survey of 362 stomachs taken from Sept. to March showed 97.85% vegetable and 2.15% animal matter (Mabbott 1920). Food of young taken in July comprised 67.54% animal and 32.46% vegetable matter.

Vegetable   Pondweeds: (*Potamogeton*), wigeon grass (*Ruppia maritima*), bushy najas (*Najas flexilis*), eelgrass (*Zostera marina*) 42.33%; sedges, mainly seeds: bulrushes (*Scirpus americanus, S. paludosus,* and *S. robustus*), saw grass (*Cladium effusum*); and chufas (*Cyperus*) 19.91% algae (*Chara*) 10.41%; coontail (*Ceratophyllum demersum*) 7.82%; grasses (*Panicum repens, Poa, Distichlis spicata, Hordeum pusillum, Syntherisma sanguinale, Echinochloa crus-galli, Zizaniopsis miliacea, Homalocenchrus oryzoides, Spartina, Panicularia,* and *Monanthochlöe*) 7.59%; cultivated grains 1.31%; arrowhead (*Sagittaria platyphylla*) 3.25%; miscellaneous vegetable items 5.23% (Mabbott 1920). Examination of 24 gullets and gizzards from the upper Chesapeake region showed the principal foods to be the leaves, stems, rootstalks, and seeds of wigeon grass, eelgrass, muskgrass (*Chara* sp.), rootstalks of salt grass (*Distichlis spicata*), seeds of bulrush (*Scirpus olneyi*) and saltwater cordgrass (*Spartina alterniflora*); also a few fishes (R. E. Stewart 1962). Two specimens taken in Fla. had eaten 1,100 and 1,200 seeds respectively of a white water lily (A. H. Howell 1932).

400

The food in 98 fall specimens in Ill. showed 97.2% vegetable and 2.8% animal matter. In order of importance: coontail 71.85%, algae 7.41%, smartweeds (*Polygonum* spp.) 3.37% (H. G. Anderson 1959). In Mo., 47 fall specimens revealed millets (*Echinochloa* spp.), 30%, smartweeds, 23.4%, and panic grasses (*Panicum* spp.) 10.5% (Korschgen 1955). Gadwalls (195 specimens) at Reelfoot Lake, Tenn., had eaten principally naiad (*Najas guadalupensis*), fanwort (*Cabomba occidentalis*), and duckweed (Lemnaceae). The food consisted of 95.7% vegetable, and 4.3% animal matter (Rawls 1958). The 199 stomachs from n. Utah contained the vegetation of *Potamogeton pectinatus* 27.2%, vegetation of *Ruppia maritima* 16.7%, seeds of *Distichlis stricta* 10.8%, seeds of *Scirpus acutus* 8.1%, and vegetation of *Zannichellia palustris* 7.8% (Gates 1957).

In England grasses, buds, leaves, roots and seeds of *Potamogeton*, *Glyceria*, *Carex*, *Scirpus*, and some grain, especially oats (in Witherby 1939). Foliage and sprouts mainly of aquatic plants in Russia. At the mouth of the Mologa during the spring flight they feed on *Elodea* while at the Rybinsk Reservoir the food is 99.5–99.9% vegetable at all seasons. *Lemna* is important in May, *Sparganium* in June–Aug., and *Potamogeton* in Oct. Animal food, predacious diving beetles (Dytiscidae) and caddis flies (Trichoptera), a very minor item. During March–April in the delta of the Volga plants form 88.4% of the food: *Vallisneria* 25.3%, *Ceratophyllum* 16.3%, filamentous algae 15.6%, seeds of *Arabis* and *Polygonum* 11.3%, and insects (Dytiscidae) 0.3%.

Locustidae, particularly *Calliptamus italicus*, are of the highest importance in n. Kazakhstan. They are taken on the water and on the steppe 1.5 to 2 km. from the lakes. Even nestlings weighing 26–150 gm. had grasshoppers in their stomachs. When wheat, buckwheat, in places rice, and especially millet ripen they feed all day in the fields. Favored food in autumn, tubers of *Potamogeton* and bulbs of *Sagittaria*. During low water they are dug from the ground, fairly large pits being formed. There is a shortage of green food during the latter half of winter in the Lenkoran–Mugan area on the Caspian Sea, and seeds of Gramineae, *Ruppia*, *Potamogeton*, and *Scirpus* form 81.4% of the food. (Summarized from Dementiev and Gladkov 1952.)

Animal   (In addition to items mentioned above.) Mollusks, chiefly a snail (*Neritina virginea*) 1.6%, insects (Phryganoidea, Diptera, Hemiptera, Coleoptera, Odonata) 0.39%, Crustacea 0.08%, miscellaneous 0.08% (Mabbott 1920). Insects formed 3.7% of the food at Reelfoot Lake. The only animal food mentioned from the upper Chesapeake was fish. Stomachs of 2 specimens taken at Buckeye Lake, Ohio, each contained 4 gizzard shad (*Dorosoma cepedianum*) (Trautman 1940).

Orthoptera and other insects are eaten in winter on the meadows of n. India (Dementiev and Gladkov 1952).

In se. Alta., Gadwalls of preflight age ate chiefly surface invertebrates during their first few days. These were gradually replaced by aquatic invertebrates and plants until, by 3 weeks of age, Gadwalls were essentially herbivorous. The preflight diet was 10% animal—entirely invertebrates—the most important being chironomid larvae and adults, aquatic beetles, cladocerans, and corixids. *Potamogeton pusillus* foliage was 34%, Cladophoraceae 19%, *Beckmannia* seeds 10%, and *Lemna minor* 7% of the preflight diet. (Condensed from L. G. Sugden 1973.) AWS RSP

Wigeon; Eurasian Wigeon

Anas penelope Linnaeus

Although main distribution is across entire Eurasia, this species has been listed as "European" Wigeon by many authors; and many use "American" Wigeon rather than Baldpate (which is equally acceptable) for the Nearctic counterpart.

Smaller than Mallard, somewhat larger and stouter than Gadwall. Except in certain definitive Plumages, differs so little from the Baldpate as to render specific identification of some individuals difficult or perhaps impossible. Bill rather different from Gadwall's, being stouter, with dorsal profile slightly but evenly concave, nail larger, and few or no lamellae visible; feathering terminates in an almost even line around base of upper mandible (essentially no forward projection on top); bill color mostly bluish to slaty in older ♂ ♂ , variants of slaty in ♀ ♀ and in younger birds of both sexes, Axillars largely mottled and/or clouded gray, i.e., are not almost or entirely white. Legs and feet bluish to slaty. The drake's Basic wing (which succeeds the Juv.) has a large white patch on the coverts, i.e., extends to near leading edge of wing; in the ♀ the Basic wing has this area largely grayish, although greater coverts are at least very pale distally on outer web; and in both sexes in Def. Alt. Plumage the outer (exposed) web of an inner secondary is white, and this adjoins proximal edge of the speculum (which is deep blue-green and black in ♂ Basic but rather clouded and less colored in ♀).

The drake's tracheal bulla has been described and figured many times, from 1798 onward; it is a "transversely oblong bony dilatation, bulging out on the left side in a rounded form, and an inch in its greatest diameter" (MacGillivray 1852); perhaps the best illus., showing it in 2 positions, are in Schiøler (1925). There are more recent illus. in Beer (1968) and Lorenz and Wall (1960). (Also see under Baldpate.)

Length ♂ to about 20 in., ♀ to 19; wingspread to about 32 in.; usual wt. of ♂ about 1¾ lb., ♀ to about 1½.

No subspecies. The 3 wigeon species form a very distinct group within the genus *Anas; penelope* and *americana* may be regarded as comprising a superspecies, somewhat apart from *sibilatrix* of s. S. Am.

DESCRIPTION   Two Plumages/cycle in both sexes. Practically every collection of Wigeon specimens contains individuals that do not fit published descriptions. There are various reasons. **1** Authors have consistently omitted the Juv. Plumage and, instead, have labeled a later one (usually Basic I head–body) as Juv. **2** The full number of head–body molts of the ♀ in her first year has not been recognized; the resulting Plumages are rather similar. Some of the reported variation in ♀ ♀ thus actually is a difference between Plumages—more blended and muted (Basic) or clearer-cut and toward rusty or gray (Alt.). That is, especially the early Plumages of the ♀ are sufficiently alike to have been mistaken for variation within one Plumage rather than products of different periods of molting. **3** In both sexes, in the definitive cycle, the molts are later than is usual in N. Hemisphere *Anas*. Rather commonly, when a new generation of feathers is developing, it seems as though the physiological mechanism controlling shape, pattern, and color of feathers is in a state of change between regulating one Plumage and the next. Within a single span of molting of various tracts, some new feathers may re-

402

semble those of the "outgoing" Plumage, or "outgoing" and "incoming" may be represented on different areas of the same feather (illus.: pl. 29 in Millais 1902), and later feathers may be typical of the "incoming" Plumage. There are also cases in which feathers or entire tracts are not typical of any particular Plumage. (Possibly the condition relates in some way to an evolutionary process of either increase or decrease of sexual dimorphism.) **4** It is comparatively common for ♀♀ to acquire more or less "drake" feathering.

Obviously it is impossible to describe an infinite range of minor variation; the following descriptions, although incomplete, emphasize features regarded as diagnostic of Plumage and/or sex.

▶ ♂ Def. Alt. Plumage (head–body, tail, and a few innermost feathers of wing), mostly acquired in FALL (last half of Aug. through Sept.), with some feathers still appearing in Oct., even to late Nov., and some tail feathers sometimes not until early winter. This Plumage is retained through winter, spring, and into SUMMER (usually late June or early July).

Bill medium bluish, the end (including nail) black; **iris** dark brownish. **Head** forehead and crown light buffy or pale cinnamon (bleaches to white); nape chestnut, the somewhat elongated feathers barred black distally and tipped green (iridescent); most of remainder of head–neck some variant of rusty (reddish brown), the feathers with black tips that wear off quickly; chin highly variable, from spotted effect (black feather ends) to (commonly) a black patch, to (rarely) lower cheeks plus chin and anterior third of neck down to breast black. **Upperparts** mantle, including scapulars, vary with individual from finely to rather coarsely vermiculated dark gray on white; rump finely vermiculated same; the center upper tail coverts mostly white, lateral ones black. **Underparts** most of breast between magenta and rose ("wine-colored"), the feathers with narrow white edges that wear off; sides and flanks vermiculated like mantle; lower breast to vent, including sides of rump, white, sharply delineated from black under-tail area. Legs and **feet** bluish gray, sometimes tinged yellowish, webs dusky. **Tail** central pair of feathers elongated, tapering to point, usually darker than the others (blackish gray) and without narrow pale edging that is present on lateral pairs. **Wing** innermost secondaries narrow, tapering, but very tips rounded; inner web medium gray, outer black, latter bordered white and the shafts white; the feather next to speculum has inner web gray, outer white evenly bordered black and the terminal margin white; the longest coverts overlying the innermost secondaries are pointed and gray, usually with some vermiculation at ends. Remainder of wing is retained Basic feathering (described below).

▶ ♂ Def. Basic Plumage (entire feathering), usually acquired beginning in LATE JUNE—first the head–body, then tail, and up to several weeks later (commonly in late July, occasionally even in late Sept.) the wings are molted (flightless period follows) and, as the Basic wing of this feather generation grows, the head–body is losing the corresponding Basic and molting back into Alt. (beginning in LATE AUG. or EARLY SEPT.).

Much reddish brown on dorsum and sides; vent to tail area has broken pattern of white and very dark; central tail feathers not elongated; innermost secondaries wide (not tapering).

Bill slaty. **Head** light area of forehead–crown usually more coarsely marked dark (spots, bars) than ♀ Def. Alt.; chin and much of neck brownish cinnamon, narrowly streaked black; **upperparts** mantle has great individual variation, the feathers usually blackish brown with broad edges and some internal markings that may be light cinnamon, or a buffy, or gray, but feathers in center of mantle vary from barred, to less barred, to coarsely vermiculated black on white, depending on individual; the longer scapulars usually are nearly black, with cinnamon-brownish edges and internal markings, and some have white ends; rump feathers gray-brown, tipped much paler; **underparts** upper breast and sides cinnamon-brownish or even a rich rusty color, any darker interior portions of the feathers largely concealed, the flank feathers sometimes coarsely vermiculated dark; lower breast to beyond vent white, under tail coverts have wide white edging and transverse barring, the other internal transverse heavy markings being very dark; **tail** grayed brownish, the feathers very narrowly edged white distally, the central pair hardly longer than adjoining pair and wider distally than in Def. Alt.

Wing primaries and their coverts sepia; secondaries sepia, tipped white, and all except 2 outermost have basal half of outer web white, distal half black with greenish sheen (the speculum); the adjoining secondary at inner edge has most of outer web white with or without very narrow black edge, and the innermost secondaries are somewhat rounded, brownish black, nearer black on outer web, and outer webs very narrowly margined white; most greater coverts have outer web white, inner gray-brown, and broad black end, but innermost ones are all gray-brown with thin pale edge; median coverts white; smaller coverts gray edged pale buff or white; **axillars** and under wing coverts very pale (to white), dotted and clouded grayish.

▶ ♀ Def. Alt. Plumage (all feathering except, in wing, only a few innermost feathers), acquired mostly through FALL (principally in Oct.) quite often into early winter, the central tail feathers usually before midwinter; this Plumage is retained into following SPRING.

Forehead and forecrown usually paler than rear of crown; usually much brownish or tan on head, neck, mantle, breast, and sides; white of underparts extends posteriorly beyond vent; central tail feathers noticeably elongated. Much individual variation, for example, on dorsum: feathers plain or with internal markings, and grayish- to reddish brown (toward rusty); dark grayish to fuscous feathers with narrow brownish to whitish barring and edging probably commonest; an extreme is plain (fewer, usually incomplete, bars) and gray, the mantle feathers dark internally and with gray edges that are very little lighter.

Bill dark grayish to somewhat blue-gray; **iris** dark brownish. **Head,** neck, breast, and sides between rusty and buff (but paling to white on chin) and the feathers have broad but poorly defined pale margins; **mantle** as described above; long scapulars taper distally, are dark, with paler bars and edges; **underparts** feathers of breast and sides have broad and poorly defined pale margins; lower breast to beyond vent white; the longer under tail coverts have blackish internal areas. **Tail** central pair of feathers protrude beyond the adjoining pairs and are tapering and pointed, usually a grayed brownish. **Legs** and **feet** medium grayish with any bluish faintly indicated, webs dusky. **Wing** innermost secondaries blackish brown edged pinkish tan mostly on outer web; the feather next to speculum has outer web black, then a gray stripe, then white stripe along outer edge; the longest overlying coverts are dark brownish edged white; remainder of wing is retained Basic (described below).

NOTES   It would seem that variation toward red-brown coloring, with some transverse barring on hindneck and mantle, is toward ♂ characteristics. Occasionally a ♀ is very brown headed, darkest on chin.

Females largely in drake feathering are shown in color on pl. 17 in Millais (1902) and pl. 60 in Schiøler (1925).

▶   ♀ Def. Basic Plumage (entire feathering), head–body, tail, and innermost feathers of wing acquired in SPRING (much molting in April) and worn into FALL; then, after flightless period, while the Basic wing is growing, the rest of the feathering is molting out of Basic and back into Alt.—usually beginning about late Aug., rarely still flightless in Oct., but some molting may continue into Nov. or even Dec. The nest down grows during the spring molting.

Much of head (including forecrown) evenly quite dark; pattern on mantle usually rather scalloped (broadly rounded dark feathers with lighter margins); usually all feathers beyond vent partly dark (fuscous with white edging); central tail feathers not elongated.

Head and neck some variant of pinkish buff (it fades quickly to pale grayish), coarsely marked blackish brown; chin–throat paler (to plain buff); **upperparts** mantle feathers medium brownish or darker, margined whitish or buff, and some anterior ones commonly barred pinkish buff; the long scapulars are shorter, more rounded, than in Alt., blackish brown, and broadly margined lighter brownish to pinkish buff (depending on individual); rump medium brownish, grading to pinkish cinnamon laterally and feathers edged white; **underparts** upper breast, sides, and flanks medium brownish, the feathers paling to whitish margins; lower breast and belly white, shading in vent area to dusky; the shorter under tail coverts white with dark markings, the longest ones dark brownish edged and barred whitish buff; **tail** much as ♂ Def. Basic, the feathers sometimes marked buff, the central pair (not as long or tapering as in Alt.) deep brownish gray edged white.

Wing primaries and their coverts as ♂ Def. Basic; 4 outer secondaries deep brownish gray tipped white, most of the others have outer web blackish tipped white (the

405

speculum), usually with some greenish sheen; the secondary at inner edge of speculum has much of its outer web white, and the innermost ones are very dark brownish with pale (whitish to tan) edging on outer web; the greater coverts are very dark, both webs tipped whitish (broadest on outer); in some individuals a broad blackish terminal zone on outer web, with or without a narrow internal whitish border; median and lesser coverts brown to a clear dark gray, broadly edged white; under wing coverts gray or brownish, marked or edged white; **axillars** as in ♂ Def. Basic.

NOTES   Commonly in the ♀ Def. Basic wing, all the median and lesser coverts have clear-cut white terminal margins. Millais (1902) apparently was referring to this when he stated that nearly all "old" ♀♀ show a tendency toward "old" ♂ feathering by having a "much lighter and sometimes nearly white shoulder."

The ♀♀ that are rusty in Alt. are brown in Basic and those that are more toward gray in Alt. are toward gray-brown in Basic.

AT HATCHING—**bill** mostly slaty; **iris** very dark; **head** crown and nape blackish brown, remainder and down to breast cinnamon, without dark line through eye, but a fragment of one underneath the eye and generally a darkish auricular patch present; **dorsum** and upper surface of wing approximately as crown; light patches (on back near base of wing, side of rump, part of trailing edge of wing) poorly defined, more or less tan or toward cinnamon; **underparts** some variant of cinnamon-buff; legs and **feet** dark, toward slaty.

▶   ♂ Juv. Plumage (entire feathering) fully developed at age about 45 days and soon afterward the head–body molt into Basic I; the Juv. tail generally is retained into winter and the wing (except for a few innermost feathers) into the following late summer.

Brownish and blended pattern; internal dark areas of feathers on dorsum plain (no barring or other markings); lower breast to tail not plain white since, at least along lower sides plus vent area to tail, the feathers have a dusky internal area giving effect of dusky spots to blotches on white (some individuals have center of abdomen unmarked).

Bill toward slaty; **iris** dark brownish; **head**–neck buffy brownish or darker, heavily streaked blackish brown; **upperparts** feathers of forward mantle toward blackish brown with buffy brown borders, the scapulars (which are narrow and tapering) also dark internally, but margined tawny-rufous; feathers of rump to tail dusky edged whitish gray; **underparts** feathers of breast and sides toward rusty and margined buffy tan; rest of underparts white marked dusky or same with middle of venter plain; **tail** feathers narrow, tapering, rather dusky but paling at edges, and with notched ends; legs and **feet** grayish with yellowish cast.

Wing differs from Basic wing thus: speculum area varies from outer webs of secondaries bordered black with greenish sheen to reduced blackish and near-absence of green; innermost secondaries short, rounded, and olive brownish paling at exposed edge; greater coverts grayish brown, or outer web white and inner grayish, with very dark ends, and with or without a subterminal buffy or whitish bar, or even the feathers grayish brown with broad white ends; median coverts also vary, ashy brown with dark shafts and grayish ends, or white irregularly marked ashy brown (i.e., not broad white ends as in ♀ Basic wing); smaller coverts ashy brown with narrow white edging (which wears off).

406

NOTE The Juv. Plumage is well shown on col. pl. 113 and on monochrome pl. 245 (both sexes) in Heinroth and Heinroth (1928).

▶ ♀ Juv. Plumage (entire feathering), timing, etc., presumably as ♂, tail generally retained into winter, almost all of wing into following late summer.

Feathering as ♂ Juv.; a few specimens sexed as ♀ were more finely and densely marked ventrally than others sexed as ♂, but perhaps this is individual variation.

Wing as ♀ Def. Basic except: speculum not as dark, or even sepia, and more or less clouded light grayish; innermost secondaries short, rounded, and nearly unicolor; greater coverts ashy brown with whitish tips (or tips freckled or more or less black); median coverts olive brown with whitish, grayish, or buffy ends, or even almost as broadly tipped white as in ♀ Def. Basic; the smaller coverts as in ♂ Juv. All Juv. coverts in both sexes are narrower than Basic.

▶ ♂ Basic I Plumage (all feathering except, in wing, only a few innermost feathers), head–body and innermost secondaries and a few long overlying coverts apparently acquired rather rapidly beginning not long after flight first attained and worn through FALL into WINTER; the Basic I tail generally succeeds the Juv. in winter; most of the Juv. wing is retained.

A dark Plumage; feathers of upper **mantle** internally blackish, transversely barred buffy tan or whitish; the scapulars deep rusty with very broad internal dark barring; breast, sides, and flanks muted brownish, the feathers more or less barred dusky brownish; **underparts** feathers of upper breast usually have some internal dark areas; lower breast to vent white, sometimes conspicuously spotted (not streaked) very dark; vent to tail area has very large dusky blotches; **wing** innermost secondaries olive-brownish, the outer webs very dark with greenish sheen (usually) and narrowly edged buffy or white.

NOTES This Plumage varies a great deal. Some individuals have head–neck dark brownish mottled or finely streaked blackish; some have pale (to whitish) forecrown and the black markings extend into this light area; occasional specimens have all the white area on venter spotted dusky or blackish. Generally, by some time in Nov., drakes in Basic I also have a few scattered gray (Alt. I) feathers on flanks and dorsum. The Basic I tail generally is acquired late and then retained into the March period of molting during which head–body go from Basic I into Alt. I.

On occasional individuals, some ventral spotting still is present after head–neck and dorsum have molted extensively out of Basic I into Alt. I.

▶ ♂ Alt. I Plumage (all feathering except, in wing, only a few innermost feathers), usually acquired by rather protracted molt which begins any time within the span LATE OCT. to MIDWINTER and usually is completed (with new long tail feathers) before the end of MARCH. Aside from growing a few gray feathers on mantle and flanks, some individuals acquire very little Alt. I until about Feb., then the molt is essentially completed by very early April. This Plumage is retained into EARLY SUMMER.

As Def. Alt., including innermost secondaries, and as individually variable. The new central tail feathers are elongated and pointed. Most of the Juv. wing is retained.

▶ ♂ Basic II Plumage (entire feathering), head–body, then tail, generally acquired LATE JUNE through JULY (at age 1 year), well before the worn and faded Juv. wing is molted (then a flightless period while the Basic II wing is growing) in EARLY FALL. This is the last Plumage with which the Juv. wing is worn. Feathering as in later Basics.

407

NOTES   Many drakes are in full Basic II head–body–tail for a considerable time before molting the Juv. wing, even well into Sept.(♂♂ in unisexual flocks).

Millais (1902) stated that molting of the wing quills, in Aug. or Sept., occurs "alternately or in small patches," so that "young" ♂♂ do not become incapable of flight like "old" ♂♂. He was correct about timing, but apparently wrong otherwise.

▶   ♀ Basic I Plumage (all feathering except, in wing, only a few innermost feathers), acquired as in ♂, i.e., rapidly succeeds Juv., but not retained as long. A FALL Plumage.

Variable; generally paler overall than Juv.; clear-cut, rather than blended, pattern. **Head** coarsely spotted black on some variant of gray-buff or palish tan; **upperparts** mantle feathers have widely spaced narrow light and dark transverse barring; scapulars usually with internal light tan markings; rump feathers very dark, quite evenly margined white; **underparts** breast and sides muted brownish; lower breast to vent white, occasionally with some well-defined blackish spots; on vent to tail the white feathers typically with roundish dark internal markings, but on some markings are V-shaped. **Wing** innermost secondaries essentially as in ♂ Basic I in material examined.

NOTE   On some individuals the feathers of forward sides are indistinctly barred tan and dark brown, or this also may continue across breast, while the feathers of anterior mantle have a very fine salt-and-pepper pattern (appear more gray than brown). As in the ♂, the Basic I tail generally succeeds the Juv. tail late, then is retained into spring. Occasionally, part of the Juv. tail is retained until spring or later.

▶   ♀ Alt. I Plumage (all feathering except, in wing, only a few innermost feathers), usually succeeds Basic I in FEB., but sometimes beginning considerably earlier and occasionally later; retained well into SPRING.

Forehead to nape typically lighter than sides of head (in the antecedent Basic I the head tends to be uniformly colored). The earliest Plumage in which any ♀♀ have richly colored breast and sides, typically vinaceous, sometimes palish, or suffused brown, the feathers commonly with whitish margins (which wear off). New feathers on rump are nearly black with sharply defined white margins and few or no light (brown) internal markings. White of venter extends to include most of under-tail area. Thus this Plumage is essentially as Def. Alt., including innermost secondaries. Often there is only partial renewal of the tail (new pointed central feathers), the others being retained Basic I. Most of the wing is retained Juv. feathering.

NOTE   As in many waterfowl, the predefinitive molts of the ♀ Wigeon vary with individual from rapid and complete to slow or even interrupted and possibly incomplete, some feathering of one Plumage that "normally" is molted being, instead, retained and worn after much of the next Plumage is acquired.

▶   ♀ Basic II Plumage (entire feathering), head–body acquired in SPRING (usually late, in April–May), the nest down well along during this period of molting; the Basic II wing is acquired much later, in LATE SUMMER or EARLY FALL when the rest of Basic II is being succeeded by Alt. II.

As later Basics. The earliest nesting Plumage. The last one with which the Juv. wing is worn, i.e., summer ♀♀ having any remaining Juv. wing coverts are in Basic II.

Measurements   12 ♂ (3 N. Am., 9 Eurasia): BILL 34–38 mm., av. 35.6; WING 250–269, av. 258.5; TAIL 94–108, av. 100.5; TARSUS 38–43, av. 39.9;   10 ♀ (from

Eurasia): BILL 34–38 mm., av. 35.3; WING 235–260, av. 246.3; TAIL 82–90, av. 85.5; TARSUS 35–42, av. 38.7 (ETS).

From Denmark: 76 ♂ over a year old BILL 31.5–39.5 mm., av. 36, WING 239–273, av. 260; and 61 in 1st fall–winter: BILL 31–38 mm., av. 34.6, WING 242–261, av. 251.6; 48 ♀ over a year old BILL 31–36.5 mm., av. 33.5, WING 231–255, av. 242.4, and 45 in 1st fall–winter: BILL 30.5–38 mm., av. 33, WING 231–250, av. 239 (Schiøler 1925). Adequate series from Iceland, also measured by Schiøler, are essentially like the Danish birds.

For other series, WING meas. over the curve, see Witherby (1939).

Weight of birds taken in Denmark: 42 ♂ over a year old 610–1,073 gm., av. 819, and 23 in 1st fall–winter 555–888, av. 706; and 24 ♀ over a year old 552–962 gm., av. 724, and 20 in 1st fall–winter 576–811, av. 632.5 (Schiøler 1925).

Hybrids taken in the wild in N. Am. consist of 2 ♂ presumed Wigeon–Baldpate crosses, from Fla. and Va.; for full discussion see Watson (1970) and Hubbard (1971). In Eurasia, wild crosses with various *Anas* (Mallard, Greenwing, Baikal Teal, Falcated Teal, Gadwall, Garganey, and Pintail) have been reported, also allegedly the Black Scoter (*Melanitta nigra*). Apparently crosses occur most often with the Pintail. In captivity has crossed with additional *Anas* species plus these genera: Wood Duck (*Aix*). Red-crested Pochard (*Netta*), and Tufted Duck (*Aythya*). For some further details and full references, see Gray (1958). Both Alt. and Basic Plumages of a presumed Mallard–Wigeon drake, taken wild and then kept in captivity, were described and illus. by Kuroda and Kuroda (1960).

A drake cross in captivity of Wigeon (*A. penelope*) of Eurasia with Chiloë Wigeon (*A. sibilatrix*) of S. Am. strikingly resembled the Baldpate (*A. americana*) of N. Am. (Shore–Bailey 1918). This cross has been occurring among captives in St. James's Park, London, and the drake hybrids are, in most characters, very like *A. americana* (J. M. Harrison and Harrison 1968, text and photos)—so much so as to make misidentification in the field of any escaped full-winged birds "a real possibility."

For descr. and illus. of tracheal bullae of ♂ crosses of *A. penelope* with *A. acuta, clypeata*, and *sibilatrix*, see Beer (1968).

Geographical variation none reported. Some birds from Iceland and from the w. U.S.S.R. evidently winter together in Britain or Europe; in spring, some of the former presumably accompany the latter back to the U.S.S.R., i.e., Icelandic-banded individuals have been recovered in the U.S.S.R. (Donker 1959). RSP

FIELD IDENTIFICATION In N. Am. Most similar to the Baldpate, but also might be confused with the Gadwall. Medium-sized duck, typically out on open water where it rides high; mixes readily with shoal-water and diving ducks. Tends to associate with Baldpates.

The drake most of the year has a darkish (brown, not gray) head with very pale forehead and crown, much of the body lighter (grayish), a white patch in folded wing, and rear of venter black (as in Baldpate and Gadwall). In flight, the white wing patch is large and extends from the leading edge well back, as in Baldpate (but in the Gadwall it extends from the trailing edge inward). When in Basic (mid-to late summer), the drake's head, neck, and dorsum are a muted brown. The ♀, season for season, might

409

be described as like the ♀ Baldpate but generally more brownish; the head, from fall to spring, and when seen in good light, has a rusty cast; it is more muted from spring to fall.

Females, young of both sexes, and even mature drakes in Basic, are so little different from homologous stages of the Baldpate as to render field identification uncertain. The likelihood of seeing the dusky axillars (the Baldpate's are white) is rather remote.

The drake has a louder, somewhat more abbreviated, call than the ♂ Baldpate; typically it is 2-syllabled. The ♀'s voice is somewhat harsher. Compare "Voice" of the 2 species.

Wigeon rise steeply from the water and fly swiftly, in decidedly compact bunches. RSP

VOICE   The usual call of the drake a whistled *whew* or *whee-oo* (accent on the 2nd syllable), is typically louder, and more far carrying, than the more mellow and often trisyllabic call of the ♂ Baldpate. The ♀, when Inciting, has what might be described as a rolling growl, repeated over and over; when uttered in alarm, it is more grating and harsh. A few other calls, seldom heard, have been reported for this species. RSP

HABITAT   Quite like the Baldpate, with which it commonly associates in N. Am., except more of an open-country bird (of barrens, tundra, and moorland) when nesting and more of a coastal (rather than inland) bird in winter. RSP

DISTRIBUTION   (See map.) Hasbrouck (1944a) examined 596 records of occurrence in N. Am. plus Greenland. See his paper for localities, seasons, and maps; there has not been much useful later information.

The Wigeon **breeds** from Iceland eastward across Eurasia to the Pacific Ocean. It is a fairly boreal nester, quite like the Pintail. For a satisfactory map, see Voous (1963). There is, as yet, no proven N. Am. breeding record. A young bird from Ft. Rae, Mackenzie Dist., reported as of this species by Hasbrouck, was misidentified; this already had been pointed out by Preble (1908). "Has bred in Greenland" (Jourdain, in Witherby 1939) is possible but not proven. The Wigeon long has been **suspected of nesting** in N. Am., notably (E. W. Nelson 1887) in the Aleutians where it now occurs in pairs and small groups. Not known to breed in the Commander Is.

Limits of occurrence in our area, all seasons combined: on the Bering–Pacific side, from the Seward Pen. and St. Lawrence I. southward to extreme n. Baja Cal. (Mexico); on the Atlantic side, from cent. w. Greenland down to e.-cent. Fla., the Gulf of Mexico coast of Texas and La., and Barbuda in the Lesser Antilles.

In winter, on the Pacific side n. to Adak in the cent. Aleutians; in the interior, northward to about the latitude of n. Ind., but probably varies depending on seasonal limits of open water; on the Atlantic side, n. to sw. Me.

Main places recorded   Bering Sea localities and the Alaskan mainland interior to Fairbanks; Pacific localities from s. third of B.C. down to Mexico; in the interior (in spring) in the s. Great Lakes drainage and cent. Mississippi drainage; and the Atlantic coastal area from sw. Me. to Ga. or upper Fla. Yet it may be expected almost anywhere, in interior Alaska, in s. Canada plus the Ungava Pen., and throughout the conterminous U.S., but rarest in the westerly interior.

410

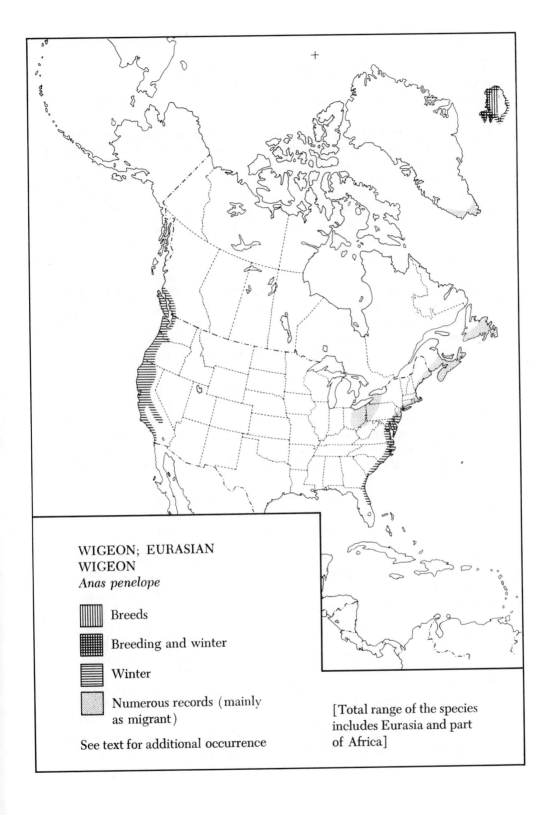

WIGEON; EURASIAN
WIGEON
Anas penelope

Breeds

Breeding and winter

Winter

Numerous records (mainly
as migrant)

See text for additional occurrence

[Total range of the species
includes Eurasia and part
of Africa]

In e. N. Am. the Wigeon appears to have been relatively scarce in the previous century and apparently most numerous in the second quarter of the present century; in Pacific–Alaskan localities, evidently becoming more frequent at the present time (but also better reporting).

In Iceland, this species is a common nester in lowland areas; a great many migrate to the Brit. Isles and some reach continental Europe and even e. N. Am.; some thousands remain in Iceland through the winter.

The Wigeon is a widespread **straggler,** having occurred at such northerly places as Spitzbergen, Bear I., and Novaya Zemlya, and southward in the Atlantic to the Azores, Madeira, and Canary Is.; in the cent. Pacific to the Hawaiian group (Hawaii, Oahu, Midway, Kure Atoll); in the far w. Pacific s. to Borneo and Celebes.

There are a few records of occurrence as **fossil** in the Pleistocene of the Palearctic; see Brodkorb (1964a). RSP

MIGRATION Many Wigeons make long crossings over land and water. In Eurasia, a great many birds from the far interior make more or less diagonal flights to winter quarters on the sides of the continent, a migratory pattern intermediate between that of sea ducks and shoal-water species. Most of the birds go to Eurasian winter range but a few to N. Am., from ne. Asia to Pacific N. Am. and from Iceland to Atlantic N. Am.

In N. Am. **spring** migration is largely in March–April, but extends well into May at least in Alaska; fall migration, in conterminous U.S., is mainly from late Sept. into Dec. It remains unknown whether Pacific–Bering travelers all have destinations in far e. Asia or whether some remain through summer in N. Am. It would appear from Hasbrouck (1944a) that many Atlantic coastal birds in conterminous U.S. shift westward, inland (to the s. Great Lakes and cent. Mississippi drainage), then disappear to Iceland or possibly to somewhere in nw. N. Am.

Band recoveries Birds banded in Iceland have been recovered in our area in Nfld., P.E.I., N.S., Mass., Md., and N.C. (Donker 1959). Two, banded as ducklings in Iceland, were recovered in the same year in Nfld., as was another on the nearby island of St. Pierre (Tuck 1971). All these recoveries were in the span Sept.–Dec. inclusive. (Some Icelandic Wigeons go to our area, some remain through winter in Iceland, and still others reach Britain, Europe, and even beyond to the southward.)

For further N. Am. data, the best source still is Hasbrouck (1944a); for the area from Iceland to w. U.S.S.R., see Donker (1959). RSP

BANDING STATUS To and including 1964 a total of 60 birds, banded in Alta., Ore., Ala., and Ohio, were reported as *A. penelope* (Bird Banding Laboratory). RSP

REPRODUCTION Since there is no record of nesting in N. Am., a few Palearctic data are given here. Both sexes **first breed** when approaching age 1 year. **Pair formation** occurs in winter–early spring; see Lorenz (1941) and Johnsgard (1965) for displays. The **nest** usually is in an open area among heaths, grasses, or low woody vegetation, typically within a few yds. of water but sometimes distant from it. The **nest down** is dark with indistinct light centers and lighter (not white) tips; included feathers are white or with the middle gray (Witherby 1939). **Eggs—length** av. about 55.5 mm., **breadth** 38.3; **color** creamy buff, much like those of the Gadwall. **Clutch size** 7–11, 9 commonest; see especially Bengtson's (1971c) data on 629 Icelandic clutches in 1961–70 inclusive. **Incubation period** 22 days (Heinroth 1910). The young **attain flight** in 6 weeks (Heinroth). RSP

SURVIVAL   From published British and Icelandic recoveries, estimated mean annual adult survival rate was calculated as 0.53 ± 0.04 by Boyd (in Le Cren and Holdgate 1962). RSP

HABITS   Much like the Baldpate, allowing for small differences in preferred habitat in different seasons. For good accounts in English see especially Millais (1902), J. C. Phillips (1923b), and Tucker (in Witherby 1939). RSP

FOOD   Examination of 22 stomachs from N. Am., largely from the Atlantic coast, showed 100% vegetable matter (Cottam and Knappen 1939). Bulk of food consists of succulent parts of pondweeds.

   Vegetable   Algae (*Chara* and *Enteromorpha*), 8%; stems and foliage of pondweeds (Najadaceae): true pondweeds (*Potamogeton pectinatus*, largely), 49.8%, wigeon grass (*Ruppia maritima*) 9.6%, eelgrass (*Zostera marina*) 5%, and other Najadaceae, 7.7%; seeds of grasses and sedges 2.2%, and bulrush (*Scirpus robustus*) 5.7%; miscellaneous and unidentified 12.2%. Grass eaten extensively in Great Britain in spring (Millais 1902). At a salt marsh in Somerset, England, they feed on *Puccinellia maritima/ Agrostis stolonifera* sward in preference to *Festuca rubra* sward (Cadwallader et al. 1972).

   In Europe in winter, chiefly eelgrass. Other plants consumed: *Glyceria, Potamogeton, Polygonum, Ranunculus, Tridolium, Carex, Hippuris, Lemna* and *Enteromorpha*.

   Animal   In Europe: mollusks, shrimps, earthworms, small fish and frogs, insects and their larvae. Occasionally feeds largely on cockles (*Cardium edule*) (Millais 1902). A bird taken in France contained a bug (Hemiptera), a spider, and the following genera of beetles (Coleoptera): *Carabus, Nebria, Harpalus, Hister, Dermestes, Agriotes, Onthophagus*, and *Sitona* (Madon 1935). AWS

413

Baldpate; American Wigeon

Anas americana Gmelin

Like Wigeon (*A. penelope*) in many respects—see diagnosis of that species—but differs as follows: bill av. slightly longer; axillars white, seldom with any gray vermiculations (if present, they are light and only on feather ends). Drake in Def. Alt. Plumage (most of year) differs from *penelope* in same Plumage most obviously as follows: forehead and crown white; much of remainder of head and the neck heavily marked black; a fairly large area, extending from just below level of eye up to white of crown and posteriorly to nape, dark iridescent green; chin–throat usually like cheeks, but vary to black; the back brownish (not grayish) in general tone; "wine color" of breast extends along sides and flanks; and in the wing the feather (secondary) adjoining the proximal border of the speculum has part of exposed web gray (but it bleaches). In Def. Basic wing, any green iridescence generally is limited to a portion of the speculum.

The ♀ in Def. Alt. (late fall to spring), compared to same Plumage of *penelope*, sometimes has forehead–crown appreciably paler than adjoining areas (thus mirroring the drake's "bald" pate); the head typically has whitish to pale buff ground-color (not toward tan). In her Basic wing, the greater coverts have white (not off-white or darker) outer webs and very wide black (not narrow blackish) ends.

Some comparisons of other Plumages are included in descriptions below; there are cases in which specific identification is difficult, unless the bird is in hand and its axillars examined.

The tracheal bullae of drakes of the 3 members of the wigeon group are similar in general conformation, but differ much in size; smallest, i.e., teal-sized (*americana*), twice as large in volume (*penelope*), and volume again doubled (*sibilatrix*). The bulla of the Baldpate was described and figured over a hundred years ago; for a recent useful illus., showing bullae of all 3 wigeons to same scale, see Beer (1968).

The drake usually is about 19–22 in. long, ♀ 18–20, wingspread ♂ to 35 in., ♀ to 33, usual wt. of ♂ about 1¾ lb., ♀ about 1½.

No subspecies.

414

DESCRIPTION Two Plumages/cycle in both sexes. Compare with the better-known Eurasian bird (*penelope*), since sequence and timing are similar, but individual variation in color and markings is considerably less in *americana*, judging from material examined. The early Plumages are not well represented in museum collections.

▶ ♂ Def. Alt. Plumage (all feathering except, in wing, only a few innermost feathers), acquired through FALL or into early WINTER and retained into following SUMMER.

Bill as in *penelope*, except has some black also at very base; **iris** as in *penelope*. **Head** forehead and crown white or pale buff (fades to white), sometimes with black markings; nape feathers (somewhat elongated, as in all wigeons) usually have much black; the large greenish patch beginning around the eye generally tapers to an end at nape (merges with black), but sometimes also includes considerable part of upper hind-neck; remainder of head–neck nearly white (toward buff, but bleaches) heavily spotted black with transition from spots to short bars down the neck; chin or chin–throat sometimes black; **upperparts** mantle, including scapulars, toward buffy tan ground color, finely vermiculated black; rump gray (off-white and vermiculated black); longest, tapering, upper tail coverts black narrowly edged white on inner web; **underparts** breast, sides, and flanks between rose and magenta ("wine color"), the longer feathers of sides and flanks nearer tan and vermiculated black; remainder of underparts white except vent to tail black. Legs and **feet** bluish gray, webs darker. **Tail** feathers usually medium to darkish gray, but middle pair (which tend to be longer than in *penelope*) vary from medium gray to nearly black; the other pairs have outer margins edged whitish.

In the **wing** the conspicuous elongated, tapering, innermost secondaries have inner webs medium gray-brown, sometimes vermiculated light distally, shafts white, outer webs black and narrowly edged light gray (there are 4 of these feathers, the 3 proximal much longer and more tapering than the one next to speculum). Retained Basic feathering includes all of the wing except these innermost secondaries and their longest overlying (evenly dark) coverts. The short Basic central tail feathers occasionally are retained well into winter; that is, the long tapering Alt. ones come in late.

NOTES Occasionally the drake has white of forehead–crown extending down onto upper cheek.

Although chin–throat usually are somewhat spotted or streaked black (like cheeks), occasionally they are heavily spotted or even solid black, in which case sides of head are more heavily spotted black and there is more black on nape adjoining the green feathers and even black all around the eye.

Heavy ferrous staining is quite common (also in the ♀); this discoloration is not limited to head–neck and underparts, but sometimes includes dorsum.

▶ ♂ Def. Basic Plumage (entire feathering), head–body and then tail acquired in SUMMER, usually beginning in late June; in late July or early Aug. (occasionally later) the wing quills are molted (then a flightless period lasting probably about 21 days) and, as the Basic wing grows in FALL, the head–body of that generation of feathers is being succeeded by Alt. As in *A. penelope*, all or part of the Basic tail sometimes is retained until very late fall or even into winter.

In molting from Alt. to Basic, the drake goes from patterned head (white, green, etc.) to rather evenly colored (palish with small markings), vermiculated to rather plain mantle, and from solid black to patterned under-tail area. Further details: **head** buffy tan to grayish (less brown than in *A. penelope*), heavily marked (including crown) with black (rear of crown sometimes almost solid black); body more or less resembles ♀ *americana* at same season, but browns of **upperparts** darker and richer and the white wing patch is diagnostic of ♂. Mantle feathers brownish black with wide tan edges and usually some internal barrings of tan; longer scapulars variable, usually very dark and generally with wide tan margins and some indication of internal tan barring, but sometimes there are areas of fine dark vermiculations on pale grayish (hence about the same range of variation as in *A. penelope*); rump mostly grayish, the lateral feathers barred alternately blackish and buffy; **underparts** breast and forward sides a variant of tan, generally with poorly defined wide dark barring which usually is lacking from tan feathers farther posteriorly along sides and on flanks; belly white; under tail coverts widely and irregularly marked whitish and more or less blackish. **Tail** feathers very dark, with white on outer webs of at least 3 outer pairs; central pair wider and shorter than in Alt., but they do extend beyond adjoining pair.

   Wing speculum black, the forward third with green iridescence and the very ends of the feathers white; the secondary adjoining inner edge of speculum has outer web gray (not white), but it becomes faded and frayed; the other inner secondaries are shorter, less pointed, than in Alt., with both webs very dark. Greater coverts over the speculum have outer webs white, inner medium gray, and both webs have wide black ends (black bar along forward edge of speculum); median coverts predominantly white; smaller coverts a slightly brownish medium gray (they fade). **Axillars** white, occasionally speckled pale grayish at tips and bases only. Wing lining partly white but zone bordering leading edge and the primary coverts largely grays.

   NOTE   The axillars fall out well before onset of flightless period and the new ones are full-sized when the new Basic wing quills still are short.

▶   ♀ Def. Alt. Plumage (all feathering except most of wing), acquired through FALL, or from fall into winter (quite commonly), the tail last; usually retained well into SPRING.

   Bill and **iris** as in *A. penelope*. **Head**–neck forehead and crown blackish mottled white, remainder typically off-white (toward buffy) and heavily spotted blackish brown; **upperparts** feathers mostly dark fuscous internally with widely spaced narrow tan stripes, and buffy tan borders; the longer scapulars tapering, dark fuscous (some have narrow transverse brown barring) with tan borders or ends; rump dark, the feathers edged whitish; lateral upper tail coverts variable, usually blackish with widely spaced whitish bars; **underparts** breast pinkish tan, the feathers usually with wide but indistinct internal fuscous barring, giving effect of coarse broken pattern; sides pinkish tan; flanks same, the feathers generally with very distinct wide darkish barring; at side base of tail the feathers blackish with widely spaced narrow whitish bars; belly white; on under-tail area the pattern on feathers alternates very dark (wide) and white (narrow), being mainly transverse markings. **Tail** feathers dark gray-brown edged white, but some individuals have several lateral pairs indistinctly marked pale tan. Legs and **feet** as in *A. penelope*. **Wing** innermost secondaries tapering, rounded at very tip, and very dark in color, outer webs velvety black narrowly margined whitish buff, except

416

much of exposed web of feather adjoining speculum is white; longer coverts overlying these inner feathers all dark except narrow white margin on exposed portion; remainder of wing is retained Basic (described below).

NOTE   This Plumage fades a great deal, especially dorsum and breast, and various lighter feather margins wear off completely.

▶   ♀ Def. Basic Plumage (entire feathering), head–body acquired in SPRING (mainly April), the tail in late spring or early summer, and the wing (after flightless period) not until late summer or in FALL and at the time when the same generation of head–body feathering is being succeeded by Alt. Most of the Basic wing is retained nearly a year.

Comparatively dark and blended coloring. **Head**–neck a variant of tan, heavily marked black (heaviest on rear of cheeks and on nape). **Upperparts** mantle, including scapulars, brownish fuscous, the feathers plain internally or with hint of a tan marking; the longer scapulars dark fuscous grading distally to medium brownish and sometimes with faint indication of tan barring; rump feathers dark, sometimes with transverse white barring; **underparts** breast, sides, and flanks rather muted warm brownish, mostly with indistinct wide tan barring (especially sides); at side base of tail the blackish feathers have fairly wide and usually curved (rather than narrow and transverse) internal whitish bars; belly white, occasionally with darkish markings laterally, commonly with same posteriorly; feathers of under-tail area white with wide clear-cut internal black markings; tail feathers gray-brown with paler edges, the lateral pairs with indistinct dullish tan areas. Wing much as in *A. penelope*; speculum velvety black but becoming vivid iridescent green in anterior inner corner (the ♀ Juv. wing lacks this green); the overlying greater coverts have wide black ends that form a clear-cut wing bar, then are white (forming another bar) and, basally, the distal or outer web is off-white; middle coverts centrally light, marked (more or less barred) brownish, and narrowly edged white; lesser coverts variably gray-brown (generally quite grayish); innermost secondaries have rounded ends and dark outer webs edged white, except exposed web of feather next to speculum is white or evenly pale gray; feathers of wing lining brownish edged white or with some all white; **axillars** as in ♂.

AT HATCHING   See col. pl. facing p. 370. No well defined facial striping; sides of head dark browns; palish eye ring. Small ducklings of both *americana* and *penelope* (and probably *sibilatrix*, but none examined) appear to be, among *Anas* species, comparatively large headed. Eight day-old young were described by Southwick (1953a), who also described changes in appearance to age 5 weeks.

▶   ♂ Juv. Plumage (entire feathering), grows until shortly after flight is attained, then head–body are molted quite rapidly; the Juv. tail generally is worn at least until well into fall, often into winter, sometimes into spring; most of the Juv. wing is retained well into summer. Juv. feathers appear within 3 weeks posthatching, on flank and scapular areas; during 6th week the down disappears from head and patches remain only on rump and wings. The Juv. Plumage is then "complete" and flight will be attained within 2 weeks thereafter (Southwick 1953b).

Bill toward slaty, **iris** dark brownish. **Head**–neck generally less brownish (more toward grayish) than in *A. penelope*; **upperparts** rather somber, the feathers very dark, plain internally, and bordered brown (richest coloring is margins of scapulars); rump

417

streaked dusky and pale grayish; **underparts** much of breast, sides, and flanks a muted buffy brown, the feathers paler at ends; on side of breast the feathers have broad zones, somewhat blended, and in this sequence from tip inward: buffy brown, sepia, buffy, and medium grayish; lower breast to vent whitish, mostly (sometimes entirely) with coarse and somewhat diffuse dusky streaking; under-tail area patterned similarly; **tail** feathers narrow, tapering, their ends notched, middle feathers not elongated, and all are toward dusky but paling at exposed edges; legs and **feet** grayish, webs darker.

Wing differs from ♂ Basic wing most obviously as follows: all coverts narrow (not with broad and evenly rounded ends); greater coverts over the secondaries variably palish gray-brown, with basal portion of distal (outer) webs white; middle coverts may vary (sometimes even on the individual) from off-white to quite dark and paler centrally, and sometimes margined pale; there is little green in the speculum; on underside of wing many of the coverts generally are a palish gray-brown or same edged white (if some are palish gray flecked darker, either individuals vary or perhaps, if any Juv. coverts are lost, they are succeeded by such flecked ones).

▶ ♀ Juv. Plumage (entire feathering), timing, etc., presumably as ♂, except the wing retained until later in the following year.

As ♂ Juv., blended pattern, light area on **venter** streaked darkish. **Wing** differs somewhat from ♂ Juv.—bases of outer webs of greater coverts over the secondaries off-white or a palish gray-brown and the row of longest overlying middle coverts are variable (all darkish, or same with somewhat paler centers, or some distal ones have palish edges); most under wing coverts typically are toward brownish and margined white.

▶ ♂ Basic I Plumage (all feathering except, in wing, only a few innermost feathers), the head–body generally goes from Juv. to Basic I quite rapidly, probably beginning about age 7 weeks; the Basic I tail comes in late, at any time from about Nov. to well into winter. A FALL Plumage.

A dark Plumage. **Head**–neck heavily marked with sharply defined black markings on off-white, the forecrown varying with individual from dark to somewhat paler than rear of crown; **upperparts** the feathers a variant of fuscous or dusky with one very sharply defined exposed narrow transverse pale buffy tan bar and a concealed one which also is very narrow and often incomplete; the long scapulars vary, plain internally or with widely spaced and incomplete whitish buff crossbars, and palish edges; **underparts** breast, sides, and flanks a variant of pinkish tan, the feathers with more or less well-defined wide darkish crossbars (on upper sides of breast the tan and fuscous bars are very clear-cut, rather than poorly defined as in Juv.); lower breast to vent white (or rarely with some black spots); at side base of tail and on under-tail area the feathers alternate from margins inward with zones of white and fuscous (sharply defined); the pointed **tail** feathers (central ones not elongated) are very dark with exposed margins narrowly whitish; **wing** inner feathers much as ♂ Def. Basic, remainder being retained Juv.

NOTE   As in *A. penelope,* a few scattered Alt. I feathers quite often appear early, on dorsum and sides or flanks, even weeks before there is any other obvious molting out of Basic I head–body.

418

▶ ♂ Alt. I Plumage (all feathering except most of wing), head–body generally acquire much of this feathering beginning in early WINTER, i.e., Dec. onward, and the Alt. tail (central feathers elongated) generally grows after midwinter. This Plumage is retained into SUMMER (usually late June or into July).

Essentially as ♂ Def. Alt., being the earliest Plumage with white and green head pattern, vermiculated mantle, elongated and pointed innermost secondaries, wine-colored breast, vermiculated sides and flanks, and vent to tail black; in the wing the longest inner secondary (next to innermost) has outer web velvety black with gray margin; most of wing is retained Juv.

▶ ♀ Basic I Plumage (all feathering except most of wing), timing, etc., apparently as ♂.

A dark Plumage with sharply defined markings. **Head**–neck heavily marked black on off-white, upper part of head preponderantly black; **upperparts** mantle feathers rounded, blackish, some margined gray and some tan (even on same individual), and scapulars much the same usually with hint of internal tan markings; the longest scapulars nearly black and distally margined white; rump feathers very dark, quite evenly margined white (scalloped pattern); **underparts** breast rather blotchy tan and toward dusky (feathers have wide terminal tan ends and alternating wide transverse dusky and tan bars); sides and flanks muted tan, the feathers with more or less obscure darker barring; feathers at side base of tail and on under-tail area as ♂ Basic I; **wing** innermost feathers as in ♀ Def. Basic, the remainder being retained Juv. Most good examples of ♀ Basic I head–body were taken in OCT., before the new dark tail feathers had appeared.

▶ ♀ Alt. I Plumage (all feathering except most of wing), generally acquired in early WINTER and retained well into SPRING.

Essentially as ♀ Def. Alt. and with similar individual variation—forehead and forecrown vary from being as dark as sides of head to decidedly lighter; number and width of transverse tan bars on feathers of anterior dorsum, including scapulars, varies; obscure to distinct darkish bars on tan flank feathers; etc. Most of the wing is retained Juv. feathering.

▶ ♀ Basic II Plumage (entire feathering), the head–body acquired beginning in SPRING, the tail coming in late, and the wing not until weeks later, usually beginning in late summer; most of this Plumage is retained into FALL.

A good example, advanced in molting from Alt. I to Basic II (Mont., May 16): **head**–neck heavily marked black on off-white, the black greatly preponderant on upper half of head; **upperparts** incoming Basic feathers blackish brown bordered tan with fragments (usually on one web) of tan bars, but some feathers plain internally; a new upper scapular is plain blackish internally, bordered buffy tan, and with end broadly rounded; **underparts** breast irregularly somewhat barred, the feathers palish tan with wide internal darkish transverse zones; on the flanks the feathers have alternating broad bars of palish tan and medium fuscous; lower breast to vent white; feathers at lower side base of tail fuscous or darker, margined whitish buff, and with fairly broad and curved pale buffy internal bars. This individual still retained a worn and faded Basic I tail. **Wing** innermost feathers as in ♀ Def. Basic; the remainder are Juv.

419

feathers, which are retained into LATE SUMMER or FALL; after wing molt (with flight-less period), the Basic II wing grows.

Measurements of birds taken fall–spring inclusive, 12 ♂ (arctic Alaska to Cal. and Kans.): BILL 35–39 mm., av. 37.4; WING 256–275, av. 264; TAIL 98–123, av. 111; TAR-SUS 37–43, av. 39.7; and 12 ♀ (arctic Alaska to Ariz. and N.C.): BILL 35–40 mm., av. 36; WING 236–256, av. 246; TAIL (of 11) 81–92, av. 88; TARSUS 37–40, av. 37.2 (ETS).

Weight in Ill. in fall, av. in lb. plus standard error: "adults" 19 ♂ 1.78 ± .05 and 16 ♀ 1.66 ± .05; "juveniles" (first fall) 82 ♂ 1.72 ± .03 and 92 ♀ 1.58 ± .02 (Bellrose and Hawkins 1947).

Age-classes not distinguished: 264 ♂ av. 1.7 lb., max. 2.5, and 108 ♀ av. 1.5 lb. max. 1.9 (A. L. Nelson and Martin 1953).

For 33 wts., Nov.–Jan. inclusive, from Rio Grande Valley, New Mex., see A. Leopold (1921).

Wt. of 33 flightless drakes in Aug. in ne. Alaska, max. 1 lb. 12 oz. (794 gm.), min. 1 lb. 4 oz. (567 gm.), mean 1 lb. 7.76 oz. (674 gm.), (Yocom 1970a); they had been confined (without food?) for up to several days.

Hybrids 2 ♂ presumed Wigeon–Baldpate crosses, from Fla. and Va., were dis-cussed at length by Watson (1970) and Hubbard (1971). There were sightings of appar-ent Mallard–Baldpate hybrids in 1971 on March 3 near Gradyville, Pa. (*Am. Birds* **25**, 559 and photo. 1971) and at Stevensville, Mont., April 3 and 7 (*Am. Birds* **25** 772. 1971.) Fig. 4 in C. G. Sibley (1957) illustrates "the extent of natural and captive hy-bridization" of 9 Nearctic *Anas* species, showing the Baldpate to have crossed in the wild with Mallard and Green-winged Teal. Gray (1958) compiled a list of wild and cap-tive crosses of *A. americana* with 10 *Anas* species (presumed crosses with Mallard fre-quently have been reported), also *Aythya* (3 species), *Cairina*, and *Netta*.

Hybrid ♂ *A. penelope* × *A. sibilatrix* closely resemble *A. americana*; see discussion under Wigeon (*A. penelope*.)

Geographical variation none reported. RSP

FIELD IDENTIFICATION   Medium-sized duck. Frequently associates with other species on open water. Has high profile when afloat, not low like, for example, the Gadwall. When tipping for food, leaves only the rear end above water and the pure white of the drake's posterior underparts contrast sharply with the black under-tail area. Rises perpendicularly from the water, with a rattle of wings, and flies swiftly and erratically in irregularly shaped small compact groups or flocks. The large white area, extending forward to leading edge of the wing, is a distinguishing feature of flying drakes; this wing patch also is very light in the ♀. The patchy pattern of the drake's head, with white cap, and the white of lower side of rump are visible at considerable distances on birds in flight as well as alighted.

The main field problem is to distinguish Baldpate from Eurasian Wigeon; sometimes they occur together and direct comparisons can be made. The drake Baldpate appears dark bodied with light head and the Wigeon appears the reverse. The drake Baldpate's common call usually consists of 2 or 3 syllables, all much alike, while the Wigeon gen-erally has the terminal syllable much prolonged. The ♀ Baldpate is, in general, grayer than the ♀ Wigeon (latter often appears quite reddish tan); head–neck of ♀ Baldpate are paler than the body, from fall into spring, and underparts show more white than ♀ Wigeon. Various younger stages of the 2 species, as well as older birds in Basic Plumage in late summer, may not be distinguishable under field conditions; compare the descriptions of their Plumages.

Gadwalls are dark headed, without white on sides of rump, and the white wing patch extends to trailing (not leading) edge of wing.

Escaped hybrid Eurasian × South American Wigeon may be mistaken for the Baldpate, a matter perhaps of importance in field identification in Britain and Europe. LGS

VOICE   Drake usually utters a trisyllabic unmusical call, the syllables repeated in quick succession and with accent on 2nd; generally this call is weaker than that of Eurasian Wigeon. It may be reduced to 2 syllables, especially when flying in pursuit of ♀ ♀ during pair-formation activities, when it is heard constantly. Baldpates also are vocal while swimming or feeding. The drake's voice has been described as a lisping, throaty whistle (Bowles, in Bent 1923), and as a shrill yet mellow whistle (Nordhoff 1902). Griscom (1920) described another call, apparently uttered rarely, as *ti-ew-whew* with pronounced burr and with accent on middle syllable. McClanahan (1942) described the call of a drake, while flying from a brood it was attending, as *ti-chuck-tick*.

The ♀ in flight utters a soft call-note, repeated numerous times in quick succession. It is identical with alarm note she gives when concerned for safety of her young (J. Munro 1949a). Southwick (1953b) described it as a guttural *qurr qurr* and Wetmore (1920) as *qua-awk qua-awk*. Griscom (1920) stated that the ♀ also utters a loud cry described as *kaow kaow*. Even when rearing her brood, the ♀ is a noisy bird (Beard 1964). LGS

HABITAT   In N. Am. breeding birds favor marshes having waterways with more or less exposed shorelines (Hochbaum 1944). Baldpates are not associated commonly with small temporary water areas as are Mallards and Pintails. Larger inland marshes, with extensive open-water areas, and lakes are preferred during the annual wing molt. Broods frequent open water more than do other pond-duck species except the Gadwall. Marsh edges and sloughs are used for autumn feeding (Hochbaum 1944).

On the coast in winter the birds may remain on the littoral zone of the sea exclusively, or rest on sheltered bays and feed on inland fields, or even spend much time ashore inland until fresh waters thaw (J. Munro 1949a). In R.I., Baldpates used inland fresh water until it froze, then moved to salt water (Lynch 1939). In B.C. a few may winter on larger unfrozen lakes and rivers; in these circumstances, usually they feed in deep water in company with diving ducks and coots *(Fulica)* and are largely dependent on them for food (see "Habits"). LGS

DISTRIBUTION   (See map.) Breeds mainly from the prairies westward and thence n. to include the Mackenzie delta and interior Alaska. Winters on N. Am. seaboard areas, to some extent also in interior. Relatively little overlap of breeding and winter ranges. There have been both losses and gains in extent of breeding range. In e. N. Am., beginning about 1950 and continuing, there has been a great increase in the number of Baldpates, with scattered nesting records. Straggles widely.

Breeding   In Alaska occurs widely, including n. to Umiat and to Anaktuvuk Pass and probably other localities, and westward nearly to the Bering Sea coast in various places. Canadian distribution, as mapped, is from Godfrey (1966); the e. breeding localities are recent discoveries. As it has increased in numbers, it has tended to linger later in s. part of breeding range in the east. In conterminous U.S., limits of usual breeding are approximately as mapped. The Baldpate also has nested at places s. of usual range; for full summary of older records, see J. C. Phillips (1923b); these are some records of more recent vintage: n. Ariz. (latest record is 1929), nw. Pa. (Pymatuning, 1936–38); N.Y. (Montezuma Marsh—records begin in 1959, Massena—3 broods in 1960, Long I.—broods at 2 localities in 1961), and Vt. (Addison Co., 1962). (Recent published Kans. records actually pertain to the Gadwall).

Summer   Some occur beyond breeding range; seen on arctic slope of Alaska on tundra waters (where they probably molt), in nw. Canada from Anderson R. w. to mouth of the Mackenzie. There have been a few occurrences beyond on Banks I. Occasionally recorded s. of breeding range; for example, a record each for Va. and N.C.

Molting localities   There is little explicit information. The peak number was 5,000 at Swan L. (w. of L. Winnipegosis) in sw. Man. on Aug. 21, 1970 (R. D. Bergman 1973).

Regular migrant in Hawaiian Is., including various records for Midway Atoll and Laysan I.

Winter   In w. Gulf of Alaska, common at Kodiak and Afognak is. and occasional on s. side of Alaska Pen.; a ♂ and 2 ♀ wintered at Adak I. (cent. Aleutians) in 1970–71, also singles at Adak and Unalaska in winter of 1972–73; in B.C. in numbers (including some on open water inland), very large numbers in n. Cal. and farther s. in the state at Humboldt Bay (where there are many hundreds of acres of eelgrass) it is the most abundant winterer, and there are others at various localities southward on the Pacific seaboard to Costa Rica (a few beyond; see below); in N. Am. interior has wintered n. into Utah, Colo., Ill., Wis., and s. Ont. On Atlantic seaboard, a record for N.S., winters occasionally in s. New Eng., and increases to rather common in Chesapeake Bay and locally plentiful farther southward. There are wintering concentrations in Fla., large numbers to the west in n. Gulf Coast areas (major wintering area), and evidently in diminishing numbers around the sw. Gulf Coast. There are records for Bermuda, Barbados, Cuba, Hispaniola, Jamaica, Puerto Rico, St. Thomas, St. Croix, St. Kitts, St. Lucia, Nevis, Antigua, Grenada, Tobago, and Trinidad; also Aruba, Curaçao, and Bonaire. (This list probably is incomplete.)

In extreme se. Cent. Am., irregularly in fair numbers in Canal Zone (records include bird banded as duckling in Sask., July 27, 1956, taken in Dec., 1957); and on S. Am. mainland, in Venezuela (L. Maracaibo, band recovery) and Colombia (Cauca Valley and E. Andes, Oct.–April occurrences).

Occasional or **accidental** in CANADIAN ARCTIC on Banks I. In the BERING–PACIFIC Pribilofs—specimens, sightings; cent. Aleutians (Adak)—sightings; Commander Is. (Bering I.)—♀ found dead, May 1, 1883; and Japan (Honshu)—6 records 1908–34.

ATLANTIC AREA   Bermuda—all seasons except summer; N. Shore of Gulf of St.

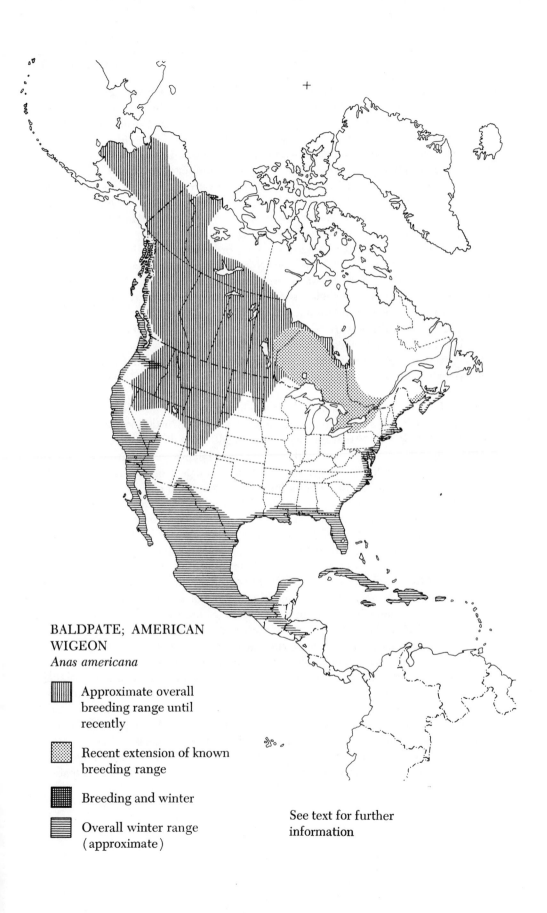

BALDPATE; AMERICAN
WIGEON
Anas americana

Approximate overall
breeding range until
recently

Recent extension of known
breeding range

Breeding and winter

Overall winter range
(approximate)

See text for further
information

Lawrence—various old reports, mostly doubtful; Nfld.—no acceptable record (L. Tuck) and none for Ungava; Greenland (Julianehaab Dist.)—June 1, 1898; Iceland— (alleged nesting in 1899 is not an acceptable record) according to Gardarsson (1969), 15 occurrences 1898–1968, with 11 for May–Aug. and 4 for Nov.–Jan.; the list includes ♂ *americana* paired to either *penelope* or *americana* and an additional such pair was seen by S-A. Bengtson between Mývatn and Husavik in summer of 1973; Brit. Isles—some 30 records (one of a flock of 13 in Ireland, Oct. 1968) to end of 1968 and many since then; most records for Britain and Europe are for fall–spring; a ♀ flightless when banded at Grand Lake, N.B., Aug. 6, 1966, shot in Scotland (Shetland) Oct. 7 of same year; young ♂, also banded at Grand Lake, Aug. 29, 1968, recovered Oct. 10 of same year in Co. Kerry, Ireland; Azores—3 records; France; Holland; Germany (Wurttemberg)—spring of 1960; and nw. Norway—late spring, 1967.

Reported as **fossil** from the Pleistocene of Ore., Cal. (2 localities), Nev., New Mex., Okla., and Fla.; from **archaeological sites** in Iowa and Ill.; full references in Brodkorb (1964a). Pre-Columbian bones from L. Valencia, Venezuela (1957 A.O.U. *Check-list*).

NOTES   In Ont. there were no nesting records before 1934, but the species had been found nesting at 10 localities by 1960 (Baillie 1969).

Gardarsson (1969) suggested that *americana* reaches Iceland attached or paired to *penelope* when the latter is on its return journey from N. Am. in spring. RSP

MIGRATION   Perhaps mainly a diurnal migrant, though known to travel at night, at least during fall. Commonly in small compact flocks (5–15 birds) in spring (Saunders, in Bent 1923, J. Munro 1949a) and larger ones in fall. They fly at no great height (Bent 1923). Frequently they associate with Pintails and Mallards. There are reports of the sex ratio being heavy to ♂♂ early in, and even near the peak of, spring migration; the surplus may consist mainly of prebreeding birds under a year old. In older age-classes most of the birds are paired by some time in Feb., the month when many begin departure from wintering localities, and paired birds are among the first to migrate.

ROUTES   There is little useful recent information. The older literature (Lincoln 1935b; A. G. Smith, in Aldrich 1949) did not allow for extensive segregation of sexes (a result of molt migration of drakes) nor any differences among age-classes (which, except by extensive banding, would be difficult to recognize). The following statements are tentative. Spring migrants from s.-cent. states travel n. via the plains to breeding areas of cent. n. states and e. prairie provinces. Some evidently continue nw. to N.W.T. and Alaska. The route(s) of Pacific coast winterers which nest on the prairies is not clear. Apparently there is some spring migration n. through cent. Wash. and interior B.C. and an early flight n. along the coast to at least Vancouver I.

The main fall flight through Pacific states and intermountain areas was described by Lincoln (1935b) as being from prairie provinces across nw. Mont. and n. Idaho, along Snake and Columbia r. valleys, thence sw. across cent. Ore. to interior valleys of Calif. Also a heavy flight down through cent. U.S. to Gulf of Mexico. Some pass the winter as far n. as w. Gulf of Alaska, for example, around Kodiak and Afognak s. A small portion of Alaska–Yukon birds may migrate through B.C. w. of the continental divide. Most breeding birds in n. Utah go westward to the coast. The recent increase in Baldpates in the Maritimes and vicinity is reflected in C. O. Bartlett's (1960) notes on increase in numbers migrating through N.S. since 1956.

Spring migration from wintering areas starts in Feb. and most birds reach breeding grounds before mid-May, many by late April. Analysis of arrival dates of inland migrants indicates some acceleration as the season advances. From southern wintering grounds to n. tier of states, the rate is roughly 4 days per degree of latitude; beyond, it increases to as much as double that rate. Inland arrival dates in Utah, Idaho, Ore., Wash., and s. B.C. av. 2–3 weeks earlier than those e. of the continental divide. Various recently published dates of Baldpate arrival are, in general, in agreement with those of Bent (1923). There is considerable year-to-year variation. The 15-year av. for Delta, Man., is April 15 (Hochbaum 1955); a 5-year av. for arctic coastal Yukon Terr. is May 24 (Porsild 1943, T. W. Barry).

Molt migration Like the Pintail, drake Baldpates may fly a long distance to a suitable area of marshland with broad expanses of open water, where they spend the flightless period. This results in large concentrations at places where few pairs nest and the birds that go there are mostly drakes plus some failed-breeding ♀ ♀ . The majority of successfully breeding ♀ ♀ pass the flightless period at the locality where they had their brood. The drake leaves the duck early during incubation, perhaps generally within the first week, hence molt migration begins fairly early in June. Examples of places where there are heavy concentrations of molting Baldpates include: Camas Refuge in se. Idaho, Bear R. Refuge in n. Utah, Delta and other marshes in s. Man., various marshes close to s. shore of L. Erie, Montezuma Refuge in cent. N.Y., and Wilson Hill area near Massena, N.Y. (close to St. Lawrence R.). The drakes leave these molting places beginning some time in Aug., but many linger well into Sept. or even Oct.

Fall Migration is quite variable, since there seem to be regional units of birds, and is spread over a considerable time; the main flights are later than, for example, those of the Blue-winged Teal and Pintail but earlier than Mallard. In conterminous U.S., early migrants are traveling from some time in Aug. to early Sept., major flights occur in Oct.–Nov., and diminished movement continues to late Dec. in at least some years. Bellrose and Sieh (1960) described heavy flights through Ill. on Oct. 25, 1957, and Nov. 8, 1956. In freshwater and brackish marshes in Fla. and westward near the Gulf Coast, some birds arrive by mid-Sept., there are heavy flights in late Oct.–early Nov., and evidently some birds continue to arrive thereafter until peak numbers are reached in late Dec.; then numbers are fairly stable until a decrease begins in the 2nd week in Feb. or later. LGS

BANDING STATUS The total number banded was 117,153 through the year 1964 and the number of recoveries was 12,605 through 1966; main places of banding were Cal., Ore., Sask., and Alta. (data from Bird Banding Laboratory). No extensive analysis of recoveries has been made. RSP

REPRODUCTION Not much information. Important sources are J. Munro (1949a, 1949b), Keith (1961), Sowls (1955), and Soutière et al. (1972). In general, probably like the better-known *A. penelope* but, for example, few displays have been reported for *americana* up to the present.

A captive drake displayed in Nov. of the year it hatched (Hochbaum 1944). Both sexes **first breed** as yearlings (J. Munro 1949a).

Pair formation activity occurs occasionally during very late fall and, at times, is frequent on winter range beginning in Jan.; the majority of older birds are mated by some time in Feb., prior to spring migration. Many of those that are not paired by early spring probably hatched the previous year.

Displays of the duck, so far as known, are similar to those of *A. penelope*, the INCITING call being essentially the same, the DECRESCENDO CALL consisting of 1–3 syllables (Johnsgard 1965).

Known for the drake: INTRODUCTORY SHAKE, PREEN-BEHIND-THE-WING, and TURN-THE-BACK-OF-THE-HEAD. While on the water the drake utters his comparatively weak whistling notes, at times his neck extended and head low, bill wide open, and ends of the folded wings elevated so that the tips are pointed up at about a 45° angle, and he swims rapidly behind or alongside the duck (C. W. Townsend 1916). This posture, which is common to and typical of all 3 members of the Wigeon group, has been illus. frequently.

Aerial activity Displaying groups include 5–14 ♂ and, in SHORT FLIGHT (also called Jump flight), a drake flies from one side of the group to the other, apparently to get positioned ahead of a ♀ (Soutière et al. 1972). There also are the usual longer pursuit flights, of 2 or more ♂ and a ♀, as described by Sowls (1955). The birds fly swiftly and erratically. The drakes dart ahead, setting their wings in a decurved position and throwing their heads up (Wetmore 1920). The duck, in full flight, sometimes turns her head back to point bill at one or another of the pursuing drakes (Hochbaum 1944), an attempt to repulse an unwanted suitor. Many of the flights are more or less circular and the birds alight near their takeoff point.

Apparent **copulation** was described by L. M. Bartlett and Atwell (1955). The drake swam up behind the duck, while HEAD-PUMPING vertically, and quickly mounted, forcing the duck entirely under water. Her head reappeared 2 or 3 times during the brief period that the drake stayed mounted. Hambleton (1949) saw a drake drop into a group consisting of 2 ♀ and a ♂ on the water. The drake started to chase one of the ducks. Both flew, the ♂ behind. He caught the duck's tail feathers in his bill and held on; both birds dropped into the water, the ♂ on top and still holding the ♀'s tail. The ♀ sank into the water until only her head showed and they then copulated. Three instances in paired birds on winter range in Texas: there was precopulatory Head-pumping by both sexes, then the ♂ mounted; in 2 of the instances, after treading, the ♂ assumed an erect posture and swam away from the ♀; because the birds were at a distance, any vocalizing was not heard (Soutière et al. 1972).

Baldpates tend to be spaced out, a single pair to a marsh-bordered pond. In B.C., drakes did not seem to use regularly or defend a particular loafing area (J. Munro 1949a), but defense was observed in e. Wash. (Johnsgard 1955) and in s. Alta. (Dzubin 1955). In 2 parkland areas (in Sask. and Man.), breeding pairs showed great intolerance of other Baldpate pairs; pairs regularly interfere with successful utilization of desirable areas by other pairs and the period when drakes show greatest intolerance is the last ²/₃

426

of May (Dzubin 1969). At Delta, Man., breeding pairs, although few, occupied only small areas (Hochbaum 1944).

Pair bond form is **seasonal monogamy**, i.e., evidently for production of a single fertile clutch, and the drake departs early, perhaps usually within less than a week after incubation begins.

Among our puddle ducks, a decidedly **late nester**. Although observations are lacking, the ♀ presumably selects the **nest site**. Typically it is well concealed, ashore or on an island or islet. The cover used by 21 ♀ at Gem, Alta., was 81% *Juncus* community (predominantly *J. balticus*), 14% mixed prairie (mainly grasses), and 5% weeds (Keith 1961). Away from grassland, tree, brush, herbaceous, and sedge cover are used (various authors). At Astotin L., Alta., the Baldpate nests in the surrounding shrub and tree areas, often in heavy woods at some distance from water (Soper 1951). Av. distance from water of 23 nests near Gem, Alta., was 72 ± 31 ft. (Keith 1961). In the Yukon, nests were located among spruce trees a half mile from water (Bent 1923).

The **nest,** in a dry place, generally contains bits of dry grass, weed stems, and down. The **nest down** has light centers and very conspicuous white tips (they are inconspicuous in the Gadwall) and any intermingled breast feathers have their dark area mottled (it is darkest in center in the Gadwall); see illus. in Broley (1950). If not frightened, the duck covers the eggs before leaving them.

Egg dates   The mean date of initiation of the first half of successful clutches for a 5-year period at Gem, Alta., was May 11 (Keith 1961). The majority of ♀ ♀ in Cariboo Parklands, B.C., either were laying or incubating by first week in June (J. Munro 1949a).

Clutch size of 20 complete clutches at Gem. Alta.: (with 5 eggs), 2 (6), 3(8) 6(9), 6 (10), and 2 (11); of these, 5 (with 9 eggs), 5 (10), and 2 (11) most probably were first clutches (L. B. Keith, letter). Sixteen clutches at Lousana, Alta.: 1 (with 3 eggs), 1 (4), 1 (5), 1 (6), 4 (7), 3 (9), 1 (10), and 1 (11) (A. G. Smith, letter).

One **egg** each from 20 clutches from widespread conterminous U.S. and Canadian localities **size** length av. 54.96 ± 2.48 mm., breadth 38.42 ± 1.38, radii of curvature of ends 13.97 ± 1.26 and 11.26 ± 0.94; **shape** between eliptical and subelliptical, elongation 1.42 ± 0.065, bicone–0.061, and asymmetry +0.101 (FWP). For other series, very close to these in size, see Bent (1923) and Witherby (1924). The shell is smooth, rather thin, and somewhat glossy, **color** creamy white, varying from deep cream to nearly white.

There seems to be no information on time of day the eggs are laid, or rate of deposition. There are records of parasitism of Baldpate nests by White-winged Scoter and Lesser Scaup (Bent 1923) and Shoveler (Job, cited in Weller 1959). There are no data on clutches definitely known to be replacement clutches.

Incubation by ♀ only (Bent 1923), the **period** for one clutch in an incubator being 23 days (Hochbaum 1944). A duck sat 46 days on a clutch that did not hatch (Sowls 1955).

Hatching success of 25 nests with completed clutches at Gem, Alta., over a 5-year period was 20%; skunks destroyed 60% of the nests (Keith 1961). Of 18 nests at Lousana, Alta., 38.9% were successful (A. G. Smith, letter). At Lower Souris, N.D., success of 20 nests in 1936 was 58% and of 43 in 1937 was 72.5% (Kalmbach 1938). It would appear that nest losses are high but this may be partly compensated for by the large

427

clutches the Baldpate lays. **Brood size** av. between 6 and 7 in a very large number counted at various Alaskan localities in the early 1950s (U.C. Nelson et al., in Farley 1955).

Average weight in grams of 8 young from artificially incubated eggs taken in the wild: 24 ± 1.3 gm. (1 day), 54 ± 6.2 (1 week), 139 ± 20.0 (2 weeks), 259 ± 33.9 (3 weeks), 382 ± 20.9 (4 weeks), 433 ± 37.8 (5 weeks, av. of 5 birds) (Southwick 1953a).

Although most drakes fly elsewhere to molt long before incubation ends, there are various reports of broods attended by both a duck and drake, but without information as to whether such cases are a continuance of the usual pair bond. McClanahan (1942), for example, observed drakes with 4 broods on June 12, 1941, near Horizon, Sask. The duck generally is associated closely with the brood until the young are well along in their preflight stage, and sometimes (J. Munro 1949a) until they can fly. At times, several ♀ ♀ with broods may join forces (Munro). For some details of ♀ behavior when with brood, see Bent (1923) and J. Munro (1949a, 1949b).

At the Seney Refuge in n. Mich., young Baldpates generally moved rather slowly through the marsh, dabbling and surface-feeding "with characteristic thoroughness." They fed vigorously and made considerable noise as their bills sucked in water. Sometimes they jumped for insects, or skittered along the surface in pursuit of food. When about half-grown (age 4 weeks or more), they began tipping for food. (Summarized from Beard 1964.)

Dissolution of the family bond apparently varies depending on circumstances. Thus, if the ♀ does not remain and molt on the rearing area, her departure may occur before the brood can fly. Presumably, the later a brood hatches the earlier it is deserted. On the other hand, if she remains and becomes flightless, in all probability the young have left before she is again on the wing. And again presumably, she is more likely to remain if the water area or marsh is extensive rather than small.

Age at first flight of captive-reared young was 45–63 days (Hochbaum 1944). In ducks in general there is a considerable difference in this period, even in the same brood (Hochbaum). LGS

HABITS Not much definite information. Small groups, especially, give an appearance of flying quite rapidly, but there seems to be no recorded flight speeds over about 30 mph. Flocks combine to form assemblies, sometimes containing at least several thousand birds, at favored places on winter range, along migration corridors, and when molting.

Both the Baldpate and the Wigeon spend much time ashore, grazing; they are the most terrestrial of our *Anas* species.

In summer in subarctic nw. Canada, Baldpates feed in quiet stretches of water, where there are dense growths of aquatic plants, notably *Potamogeton filiformis*.

Postbreeding drakes form gatherings of various sizes and associate with other ducks, both shoal-water and diving species, and Coots (*Fulica americana*). J. Munro (1949a) reported them associating with Tundra Swans. Such flocking usually is evident by about mid-June and most drakes have become flightless by very early Aug. (remaining so for about 3 weeks). Among our dabbling ducks, the Baldpate is unique in preferring to stay well out on open water at this time, in company with diving species. Yet they do not dive if pursued (J. Munro 1949a), as diving ducks do.

In winter and later Baldpates continue their association out on open water with diving ducks, coots, swans and, among geese, at least Brant. They are parasitic, a habit most prevalent on wintering areas, actually robbing their associates of food—as when pilfering wild celery brought to the surface by Canvasbacks, or eelgrass brought up by Brant. They also get plant material that has been dislodged by the feeding activities of ducks, swans, etc. According to J. Munro (1949a), young Baldpates begin "poaching" soon after they hatch, but Sugden did not observe this behavior during a 5-year study in s. Alta. Munro suggested that there is a relationship between the Baldpate's association with diving ducks and its unique preference for open water.

On the Pacific seaboard and inland areas, the Baldpate has developed a fondness for truck crops, notably lettuce and spinach. Being thus a grazer on succulent plants, it prefers areas of quite high rainfall or irrigated land as part of its winter habitat. J. Munro's (1949a) statement is probably still correct that although Baldpates do local damage to cultivated plants their value to sport and as food more than compensates for such loss.

In the hunting season Baldpates frequently feed at night and leave their feeding fields and marshes at daybreak to rest on sheltered areas of the sea or on larger inland waters. They are fairly tame during the nesting season, but become shy when hunted. Hochbaum (1955) stated that Baldpates hatched in captivity from wild eggs never become as tame as Mallards; he termed this "heritable wildness."

In the late 1960s the winter population of this species was roughly 1¾ to 2 million birds. LGS

FOOD In 229 stomachs, largely vegetable (93%), pondweeds, grasses, algae, sedges, wild celery, and other aquatic plants; animal matter (7%) consists mainly of snails plus a few insects (Mabbott 1920).

Vegetable Stems and foliage of pondweeds (*Najadaceae*): true pondweeds (*Potamogeton*), wigeon grass (*Ruppia maritima*), eelgrass (*Zostera marina*), bushy pondweed (*Najas flexilis*), horned pondweed (*Zannichellia palustris*), 42.8%; grasses (Gramineae): panic grass (*Panicum*), wild rice (*Zizania aquatica*), salt grass (*Distichlis spicata*), barley (*Hordeum pusillum*), and cultivated rice (*Oryza sativa*), 13.9%; algae (*Chara*) 7.7%; seeds of sedges (Cyperaceae): three-square (*Scirpus americanus*), prairie bulrush (*S. palustris*), river bulrush (*S. fluviatilis*), spike rush (*Eleocharis*), chufa (*Cyperus*), saw grass (*Cladium*), *Carex*, and *Fimbristylis*, 7.4%; frogbits (Hydrocharitaceae) wild celery (*Vallisneria spiralis*), and waterweed (*Philotria canadensis*), 5.8%; water milfoils (*Myriophyllum* and *Hippuris vulgaris*), 3.5%; duckweed (*Lemna*), 2.2%; smartweeds (*Polygonum*), 1.5%; miscellaneous plants, 8.5% (Mabbott 1920).

At Wenham Lake, Mass., entirely vegetable: *Potamogeton*, *Vallisneria*, and seeds of *Sparganium*, *Brasenia*, and *Polygonum* (J. Phillips 1911). Gullets and gizzards of 157 birds from upper Chesapeake region showed principally vegetation and rootstalks of pondweeds (*Potamogeton perfoliatus*, *P. pectinatus*), eelgrass, wigeon grass, muskgrass (*Chara* spp.), waterweed (*Elodea canadensis*), buds and leaves of wild celery, and seeds of wild rice (R. E. Stewart 1962).

In Ill., 160 birds had consumed 93.66% plant and 6.34% animal matter. Chief foods were coontail (*Ceratophyllum demersum*) 69.9% and pondweeds (*Potamogeton* spp.) 7.8% (Anderson 1959). Thirty specimens from Mo. showed corn (*Zea mays*) 39%, wild millets (*Echinochloa* spp.) and Japanese millet (*E. frumentacea*) 15.7%, and rice cut grass (*Leersia oryzoides*) 12.5% (Korschgen 1955). The 41 gizzards from Reelfoot Lake, Tenn., contained 94% vegetable and 6% animal matter. The plants consisted mainly of naiad (*Najas guadalupensis*) 23.05%, buttonbush (*Cephalanthus occidentalis*) 10.73%, duckweed (Lemnaceae) 7.44%, and algae 6.83% (Rawls 1958).

A bird taken on the Columbia R. had eaten 2,800 seeds of love grass (*Eralrostis hypnoides*), 1,200 seeds of panic grass, and 750 seeds of spike rush (Gabrielson and Jewett 1940). In Cal., consumes a large amount of young grass blades (J. Grinnell et al. 1918). Also see above under "Habits."

For fall food of 40 birds in S.C., see McGilvrey (1966c).

Animal Mollusks, chiefly snails (Gastropoda) 6.3% and insects (Hydrophilidae, Dytiscidae, Scarabaeidae, Chrysomelidae, Rynchophora, Dermestidae, larvae and pupae of Diptera) 0.4% (Mabbott 1920). Birds from upper Chesapeake had eaten a few mollusks (*Macoma balthica*, *Bithium varium*), while those at Reelfoot Lake had consumed 4.51% insects and 1.22% snails.

Food of preflight young L. G. Sugden (1973) analyzed esophagus–proventriculus samples from 129 young Baldpates collected in s. Alta. The diet contained 11% animal and 89% plant food. At first, Baldpates ate predominantly animal food, chiefly invertebrates captured near the water surface, but by age 3 weeks they were eating less animal food. Diptera adults, principally chironomids, were the most important invertebrates and made up 4% of the preflight diet. *Potamogeton pusillus* foliage, Cladophoraceae, *Cares lanuginosa*, and *Lemna minor* contributed 47%, 18%, 9% and 4%, respectively, to the preflight diet.

In **summer** near Great Slave L., N.W.T., nearly a third (by volume) of the food in 10 adult birds was animal matter; it was about ²/₃ in 16 smaller young, but dropped to an av. of 12% in 2 older preflight and 9 flying young. The animal food was aquatic insects and a few other small invertebrates; the plant food was filamentous algae, mosses, horsetails, pondweeds, bladderworts, and unidentified foliage, seeds, and fruits; further details in Bartonek (1972). AWS

430

White-cheeked Pintail

Anas bahamensis

Other names include Bahama Duck or Bahama Pintail (although the Bahamas are only a fragment of its range); those in the Galapagos have been called Galapagos Pintail.

Smallish slender duck, of large teal size. Sexes differ somewhat. All postdowny stages: cap and nape dark; sides of head and the foreneck white; tail some variant of tan (even buffy), rather long, wedge-shaped, the central feathers slightly to greatly elongated depending on Plumage and sex (longest in ♂ Def. Alt.). From an early age onward, the bill has considerable bluish color distally, scarlet proximally, and black along top; iris scarlet. Wing of both sexes in all flying ages: along leading edge of green speculum a creamy bar and, at trailing edge, a narrow black bar and then a very wide creamy buff terminal bar. The drake's tracheal apparatus apparently has not been described. Length 14–19 in. (♂ av. larger within this span), wt. about 1½ lb. Three subspecies, 1 in our area.

DESCRIPTION *A. b. bahamensis.* Two Plumages/cycle in both sexes, although authors have implied or stated only one. This species has all of the Plumages of *A. acuta,* but lack of adequate series of specimens precludes full coverage here.

▶ ♂ Def. Alt. Plumage (all feathering except most of wing), worn MOST OF YEAR (ex-

♂ Def. Alt.

cept for part of summer or fall). In addition to details given above: **iris** quite reddish; **head** cap and nape dark brownish, the former generally streaked blackish; **upperparts** feathers dusky brownish or darker, with sharply defined and rather narrow margins of tawny-rufous to tawny-buff (individual variation); on the anterior dorsum the feathers also have 2 internal pale transverse stripes or bars (width varies), which sometimes coalesce at the shaft; **underparts** vary with individual from quite rich to palish tawny-rufous or a buff with reddish cast, with variable number of roundish dusky spots that are larger on sides and flanks (and generally fewer in number on the breast than in ♀ Def. Alt.); in the wedge-shaped **tail** the central pair of feathers is considerably longer than the others; legs and **feet** bluish gray, webs nearly black. **Wing** innermost secondaries elongated, somewhat tapering, rounded at very ends, and rather pale with black median stripe; remainder of wing is retained Basic.

▶ ♂ Def. Basic Plumage (entire feathering), most of it worn probably a few weeks in SUMMER or into FALL, but most of the wing nearly a year. Very similar to Alt., but more blended pattern and more muted coloring. On the anterior dorsum the pale feather margins are not as sharply defined as in Alt. and, internally, either there is a small pale mark across the shaft or else most of the feather is plain (dusky). The diagnostic features of the speculum area of the wing were described in the opening paragraph under this species.

▶ ♀ Def. Alt. Plumage (all feathering except most of wing), SUMMER or FALL to LATE WINTER or possibly later. Much like ♂ Def. Alt., but paler overall, with fewer spots on breast and generally more on venter, and shorter tail. The pale-margined feathers on anterior dorsum typically have, within the internal dark portion, a single, somewhat curved, transverse pale brownish or buffy bar.

▶ ♀ Def. Basic Plumage (all feathering), head–body–tail acquired well along in WINTER or later and retained well into SUMMER or later, most of the wing acquired in the later span and then retained nearly a year. More muted and darker overall than ♀ Def. Alt., the buffy or brownish buffy feather margins not as clearly defined, and evidently more or larger dusky spots on underparts. On the anterior dorsum the feathers have buffy brown margins (which fade) and there is no pale marking within the internal dark portion.

AT HATCHING quite like Northern Pintail (*A. acuta*), but light areas are mostly a rich yellowish.

▶ ♂ ♀ Juv. Plumage (entire feathering) rather blended and all coloring appears "washed out," the ventral spotting rather obscure.

▶ ♂ ♀ Basic I Plumage—no satisfactory material examined; the greatest number of spots (which are small) apparently occurs on the venter in a predefinitive stage, probably Basic I.

▶ ♂ ♀ Alt. I—like later counterparts, but with most of Juv. wing retained.

NOTES The side base of upper mandible is "said sometimes to be light yellow" (Wetmore and Swales 1931), but whether this may occur at some particular age or may be individual or some other kind of variation is unknown. It is characteristic of another pintail, *A. georgica*.

A very pale dilutant has occurred among captives in Europe (Delacour 1956).

Measurements 10 ♂ (5 Bahamas, 5 St. Croix in Virgin Is.): BILL 43–46 mm., av. 44.7; WING 200–217, av. 211; TAIL 79–108, av. 97; TARSUS 38–43, av. 40; 7 ♀ (2 Bahamas, 1 Haiti, 4 St. Croix): BILL 40–45 mm., av. 42.6; WING 185–203, av. 197; TAIL 80–95, av. 85; TARSUS 35–40, av. 37 (ETS).

For additional meas., also with WING flattened, see Delacour (1956); for WING across chord, see Bangs (1918).

A **hybrid** (*A. b. rubrirostris?*) × Yellow-billed Pintail (*A. georgica*) was taken in Argentina (J. C. Phillips 1923b). In confinement this species has produced fertile crosses with *A. georgica, flavirostris,* and *platyrhynchos,* and also has crossed with other *Anas* species and the Brazilian Teal (*Amazonetta brasiliensis*). See Gray (1958) for list of crosses and relevant literature.

Geographical variation in the species is relatively slight. Birds of the Caribbean area are smaller, less vividly colored, than those s. of the Equator in S. Am.; the Galapagos birds are smallest, palest, and their head pattern is not sharply delineated. RSP

SUBSPECIES **In our area** *bahamensis* Linnaeus—description and meas. given above; size intermediate; sedentary; mostly islands and coastal mainland.

Extralimital *rubrirostris* Vieillot—largest; southerly; coastal and inland range in S. Am.; those well s. said to be migratory to some extent; for meas. with WING across chord see Bangs (1918), and for WING flattened see Delacour (1956).

galapagensis (Ridgeway)—smallest size; small island range; dark of cap and nape blend into white of sides of face and the foreneck; general coloration rather "washed out" compared with both above-listed subspecies; for meas., WING across chord see Bangs (1918), and for WING flattened see Delacour (1956). RSP

FIELD IDENTIFICATION of the species. Of large teal size but slender in shape; dark cap and conspicuous white cheeks and foreneck; most of body rather tan in general coloration with more dark intermingled dorsally than ventrally; at rest or in flight shows light buffy tan tail and adjoining feathers, much lighter than back. Singles, pairs, flocks (usually small). RSP

VOICE Of the species. The usual call of the drake is squeaky or wheezy and not very loud; the ♀ has a high-pitched quack. Full vocabulary is quite extensive; see "Reproduction" for calls used in displays. RSP

HABITAT Shallow fresh and brackish waters and their vicinities, but said to feed also in fields some distance from water. RSP

DISTRIBUTION (See map.) Older records in U.S.: Fla. (March 1912); Va. (Dec. 1937, in a flock of Northern Pintails); and Wis. (Sept. 1929). In the 1960s there were at least 15 acceptable reports of occurrence (sightings, at least 2 captures), Dec.–April inclusive, in s. Fla. Most of these were in late winter–spring and it is suspected that this species associates with wintering Blue-winged Teal and migrates n. with them. A ♀ was shot at Chincoteague, Va., Nov. 14, 1966. There have been several sightings in Ala.

Because the White-cheeked Pintail is common in aviaries, where it breeds quite readily, there is no way of knowing whether some U.S. occurrences pertain to escapees. (And, hopefully, this species will not be introduced deliberately in Fla. with the idea that it might become a gamebird there.)

This duck reportedly is absent from some apparently suitable islands not distant from others where it occurs. Status in Jamaica not well known. Occurs in Trinidad, Aruba, Curaçao (breeds), and Bonaire. Occurs in n. Colombia, but no breeding records found. There are at least 6 specimen records for mainland Venezuela (where it may occur regularly) and one for Margarita I. There are very few records of occurrence in Guyana. There seem to be no breeding records for Surinam, Fr. Guiana, or lower Amazonia (Brazil), but the species evidently occurs all year.

433

A. b. rubrirostris—breeds in Ecuador. Known Peruvian occurrences (none for breeding) are scattered through the seasons. Postbreeding dispersal or some other seasonal movement may account for occurrence in considerable portion of recorded range. Recorded once from the Falklands.

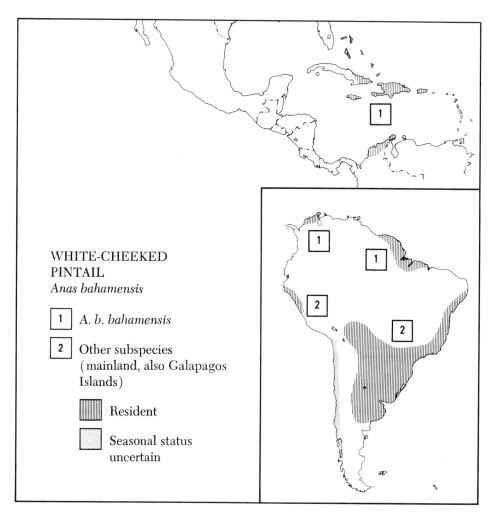

WHITE-CHEEKED
PINTAIL
Anas bahamensis

1   *A. b. bahamensis*

2   Other subspecies
(mainland, also Galapagos
Islands)

  Resident

  Seasonal status
uncertain

A. b. galapagensis—Galapagos Archipelago, evidently excepting Narborough and outlying n. islands. RSP

MIGRATION   See preceding section. Said to "appear to migrate to some degree" in s. part of range of the species (Delacour 1956). RSP

REPRODUCTION   Scant information on the species. **Breeding season** in W. Indies said to be late spring (J. C. Phillips 1923b); near S. Am., in Curaçao (Lesser Antilles), eggs April 25, May 25, early July, and ducklings April 25 and Oct. 23 (Voous 1957); the southerly subspecies *rubrirostris* nests in austral spring (Oct.–Nov.) according to Delacour (1956), but April nesting and (probably replacement) clutches in June in Ecuador (Marchant 1960); the season is Feb.–Sept. (and possibly all year) in the Galapagos subspecies (Levêque 1964).

Displays of captives (*rubrirostris?*) were described by Lorenz (1941). There was no active swimming about. **Displays of the duck** include INCITING as Northern Pintail, but vocal utterance higher pitched, less creaky (has more rolling *rrr* sounds). DECRE-SCENDO call harsh, of several syllables. GASPING a sharp *chaechaechae* when stimulated by social display of ♂ ♂. GESTURE OF REPULSION as Northern Pintail. PREEN-BEHIND-THE-WING a sexual display toward ♂ ♂.

Displays of the drake include INTRODUCTORY SHAKE of drakes when close together; at full intensity can "lift" a drake right out of the water; followed by exaggerated HEAD-UP-TAIL-UP breast submerged, bill against throat, both wing tips to one side, tail cocked forward over head showing ruffled under tail coverts, and bird utters soft *i-hieh i-hieh i-hieh* (middle *i-hieh* replaced by whistle in high-intensity display). [Lorenz (1941) described the Head-up-tail-up, which he later (Lorenz 1958) called the Down-up; Johnsgard (1965) believed the display is the latter quickly followed by the former and then a turning of the bill toward the ♀; the drake utters the call described above, into which a double-noted whistle is inserted.] BURP the drake calls *hiiihiii* to a particular ♀ (his bill pointed toward her), after returning to normal posture from moderate Shaking. TURNING-THE-BACK-OF-THE-HEAD (toward ♀) occurs after Burping, as well as when Leading an Inciting ♀. BRIDLING as Mallard. PREEN-BEHIND-THE-WING not common. [Grunt-whistle not reported in this species.]

Copulation precopulatory HEAD-PUMPING as in Mallard; postcopulatory BRIDLING as in Mallard, but not followed by Burp and no Nod-swim reported.

So far as known, this duck nests on the ground in or near thick vegetation and not far from water. A hearsay report (in J. C. Phillips 1923b) of nesting just above tide limit in low mangroves. The **nest down** is sooty brown with conspicuous white basal spots (Voous 1957). **Eggs** (of *A. b. rubrirostris?*) **size** length 55–59 mm. and breadth 37–39 (Phillips), but in Ecuador a clutch of 11 av. 51.6 × 37.1 mm. (Marchant 1960); **shape** long oval to long subelliptical; **color** pale olive brownish, but fades to buffy. A clutch of 11 *A. b. bahamensis* from Curaçao av. 49.9 × 36.3 mm. (Voous 1957). **Clutch size** 6–10 eggs (Delacour 1956), but 2 containing 11 mentioned here. Incubation by ♀ with ♂ remaining in vicinity. **Incubation period** of captives (*rubrirostris?*) 25–26 days (Phillips). In Ecuador, Marchant observed broods of 3–12 ducklings up to about a week old accompanied by 2 adults; larger groups of older ducklings seemed to be amalgamations of remnants of 2 or more broods tended by 1 adult. Broods seen in the Galapagos were tended by a single adult (Phillips). Age at first flight unknown. RSP

HABITS of the species. Little information. A surface feeder, but young also dive. Numbers have been seriously reduced on some islands in the Caribbean area by shooting and by predation on nests by introduced mammals. In southern S. Am. the White-cheeked Pintail commonly associates with the Yellow-billed (*A. georgica*). In the Galapagos the White-cheeked is remarkably tame, like other wildlife there. RSP

435

FOOD   *A. b. bahamensis.* Largely vegetable. Stomachs of 8 adults taken in Puerto Rico contained seeds of wigeon grass (*Ruppia maritima*) 16.25% and foliage and antheridia of algae (*Chara*) 83.75% (Wetmore 1916). It was assumed to eat numerous corixids on a pond in Haiti (R. M. Bond 1934).

The food of 2 downy young consisted of the seeds of foxtail grass (*Chaetochloa*), wild millet (*Echinochloa crus-galli*), and panic grass (*Panicum*) 94%, miscellaneous seeds 2.5%, and animal matter consisted of water boatman (*Corixa*), water creeper (*Pelocoris*), and young snails 3.5%. AWS

Northern Pintail

Anas acuta Linnaeus

Also called Common Pintail or simply Pintail. Medium-sized duck; slender, relatively long-necked, the tail wedge-shaped with central pair of feathers elongated in Alt. Plumages. Bill longish with sides nearly parallel; in lateral view it appears rather thin in distal $2/3$ with top and bottom margins nearly parallel, but profile of basal top margin ascends quite steeply. Sexes differ slightly in Juv., more in Basic, and greatly in Alt. Plumages. Def. Alt. Plumage: ♂ (most of year) head mostly plain brownish, sides and part of dorsum vermiculated black on white, venter mostly white, central tail feathers greatly elongated; ♀ (fall–spring) head pale gray-buff or whitish streaked dark, dorsum and sides have coarse broken pattern, belly whitish, central tail feathers considerably elongated. Basic wing (all year): ♂ has speculum mostly purplish bronze (but occasionally brownish), in ♀ purplish to brownish (or same with hint of green), and in both sexes a light bar at leading edge and white one at trailing edge. Bill, legs, and feet largely bluish or lead-colored. (See below for other Plumages.)

The drake's tracheal apparatus has been described and illustrated many times, beginning in 1798. The bulla, which is left-sided, is somewhat smaller and nearer spherical than in the Mallard; best illus. are figs. 39 and 46 (and also see fig. 81) in Schiøler (1925).

Length ♂ 24–29 in., ♀ 20–24; wingspread ♂ to 37, ♀ to 35; wt. of ♂ usually 1¾–2¼ lb., ♀ 1½–2 lb.

The Holarctic bird is treated here as a species without subspecies (the S. Hemisphere oceanic birds, of Kerguelen and Crozet, are regarded as another species, *A. eatoni*).

DESCRIPTION   Two Plumages/cycle in both sexes. Authors have failed to recognize that the Juv. Plumage is succeeded early and rapidly, in both sexes, by a second ventrally streaked Plumage (Basic I) that includes all of feathering except most of the wing. Millais (1902) recognized the change, but believed it occurred through actual change in color and pattern of the grown Juv. feathers! He was quoted by Bent (1923). The "juvenile" in Witherby (1939) is a composite of Juv. and Basic I characters of head–body (plus Juv. wing). In the "adult" (definitive) cycle in Witherby, the description labeled ♀ "eclipse" is actually the gray Alt., acquired in fall and worn into spring, while that labeled ♀ "summer" is the more brownish Basic. Both sexes have Alt. head–body–tail in winter (time of pair formation); the ♀, however, molts back into most of the Basic (i.e., homologous with ♂'s Basic or "eclipse") in spring, before nesting—the usual pattern in N. Hemisphere species of ducks.

Characteristics of the Pintail include: **1** acquisition, in fairly rapid succession, of 3 extensive Plumages; **2** the 2nd (Basic I) is very extensive, rather than a mere trace as in the Mallard: **3** as in the Gadwall, for example, at top base of wing there are some concealed (except when wing fully spread) axillarlike feathers (much elongated innermost median coverts?) which are included in each molt of the body and are most highly developed in ♂ Def. Alt.; **4** there is considerable individual variation in details of pattern and general coloration in most or all Plumages, including pattern of Basic wing lining and axillars; and **5** there is variation in order of molt of (also within) different parts of the individual. The molt into Basic I sometimes extends out to include a considerable number of upper wing coverts.

Full description would require at least 30 printed pages. The following is schematic, omitting some features and emphasizing those that are diagnostic of sex, age, and Plumage, with mention of some individual variation, based on specimens examined from many parts of the range of the species.

♂ Def. Basic   ♂ Def. Alt.

▶ ♂ Def. Alt. Plumage (all feathering except, in wing, only the innermost secondaries and their coverts), largely acquired in LATE SUMMER–FALL, the long pointed scapulars often not fully grown until winter. This Plumage is retained into the following SUMMER, into June.

Bill varies from vivid blue to lead-colored, with black stripe along top (includes nail) and some also along cutting edges; **iris** dark brownish. Almost all of **head** medium to dark brownish (new feathers have small buffy tips which soon wear off) with purplish sheen laterally, and penetrated up side of nape by narrow extension of white of foreneck; nape black. **Upperparts** mantle vermiculated black on white (appears medium grayish); the longer, narrow, tapering and pointed scapulars are black edged buffy tan to white; some shorter outer scapulars black (form a patch above folded wing); rump grayish, the feathers often with creamy markings; central upper tail coverts gray with black shafts and buff edges, lateral ones have outer webs black. **Underparts** foreneck to vent white; sides vermiculated (as mantle); side of rump has creamy tan patch (soon bleaches to whitish); vent to tail black, except longest under tail coverts bordered white. **Tail** central pair of feathers very narrow and very long (to about 8½ in. or 22 cm.), tapering, slightly upcurled, and black; next pair has black outer web and succeeding pairs have diminishing amount of blackish and grayish, the outer pair nearly or all white on outer web. Legs and **feet** medium bluish gray, joints darker, webs black.

In the **wing** the innermost secondaries ("tertials") are long, tapering, and pointed, with part of inner web medium gray, then a black zone astride the shaft, then paler gray. The one next to the speculum has most of outer web velvety black, the light end of that web being wide and pale tan to white. The remainder of the wing is retained Basic feathering. The axillar-shaped feathers at top base of wing are dark gray-brown without edging, i.e., darker than most of the upper cover area.

438

▶   ♂ Def. Basic Plumage (entire feathering), acquired in SUMMER, usually beginning in early June, the head–body well developed by early July usually, and soon afterward (commonly in 2nd week in July) the wing and any remaining tail feathers are dropped; then, beginning before or not long after the new wing quills are fully grown (flightless period closely estimated at 27–30 days), the head–body begin losing Basic and acquiring Alt. Thus the Basic head–body–tail are worn for a few weeks at most, but nearly all of the wing is retained into following summer.

Rather brownish overall; obvious characteristics include: head ♀-like, but more finely streaked dark or even plain brownish; neck and breast brownish with dark markings; coarse barring on flanks; belly varies from nearly plain (off-white) to same variably marked to finely marked dusky throughout; central tail feathers only slightly longer than adjoining pair.

Head and neck usually medium brownish (varies from buffy tan to cinnamon), generally with fine dark streaks (not coarse as in ♀ definitive Plumages) but varies to entirely unmarked. **Upperparts** mantle feathers have broad dark barring or coarse lines or heavy vermiculations alternating with narrower brownish to grayish to nearly white zones, the light feather edges narrow (not broad and buffy tan as ♀); the shorter scapulars are darker than upper back, with pale edges and buff tips; longer ones broad, rounded, very dark (to black) with light gray edges and buff tips (if upper back has the light feather areas decidedly brown, this also includes the scapular edges); upper tail coverts very dark, irregularly barred and edged (usually buff). **Underparts** highly variable as to amount of spotting or other markings; upper breast irregularly marked dark on brownish; feathers of sides and flanks dark brownish with broad somewhat U-shaped buffy to whitish zones and broad pale edges (some feathers vary toward coarsely vermiculated white on dark); lower breast and belly nearly white, usually many of the feathers with brownish spots; rear of abdomen (including vent area) off-white, with dusky brownish markings (barring, spotting, or coarse vermiculations). **Tail** central pair of feathers wider and much shorter than in Def. Alt., and brown; next pair edged buff, and others are (unlike Alt.) more toward buff than gray; all feathers broader distally than in Def. Alt.

Wing innermost secondaries broad, their ends somewhat rounded; they are medium gray with a very dark middle zone that is not sharply defined, and are narrowly margined white distally; the one next to the speculum has the light middle stripe gray (not white as in Alt.); secondaries of speculum have outer webs at least partly metallic bronzy greenish to coppery (occasionally plain brownish) with wide subterminal black zone and white ends; those beyond the speculum are sepia with broad white ends (may be suffused tan); most greater coverts gray tinged slightly brownish, with broad subterminal tawny zone and narrow whitish distal margins; most median and the lesser coverts medium gray tinged slightly brownish, sometimes with obscure paler edging (it wears off) and light fleckling. Primaries and their coverts toward sepia, the former paler on inner webs. Wing lining variable, usually various grays (darker toward leading edge) and little white; axillars white, usually with at least gray mottling along shafts, or mottled or distinctly patterned gray throughout, rarely all white. The axillarlike feathers on the body at top base of wing are shorter than in Alt. and the same color as adjoining coverts.

439

NOTES   Briefly, during the molt out of Basic head–body, when the incoming Alt. Plumage has appeared on head and upper neck, the drake bears a considerable resemblance to individuals within the range of normal variation of Alt.-Plumaged drake of the Kerguelen race of *Anas eatoni*. Compare figs. on pl. 14 in Delacour (1956).

Rarely, a drake in Def. Basic has many small roundish dark spots on the pale venter, quite different from the elongated dark markings of Basic I.

▶   ♀ Def. Alt. Plumage (all feathering except, in wing, only the innermost secondaries and some overlying feathers), acquired in LATE SUMMER or into FALL (later than ♂ Def. Alt.), the last feathers still growing even as late as early winter.

Compared to ♀ Def. Basic, this Plumage is grayer overall, although individuals vary from quite grayish toward buffy tan (latter fades considerably).

Bill slaty blue and black as in ♂; **iris** dark brownish. **Head** crown tan to cinnamon, heavily and broadly streaked blackish; remainder of head and the neck nearer buffy (paling to whitish chin and throat), finely streaked blackish brown. **Upperparts** most of the feathers have wide U-shaped zones of blackish brown alternating with narrower ones of gray, buff, or tan, with margins of same; longest scapulars very dark, usually with at least a few clear-cut internal light markings and also pale margins (widest on outer edge); on rump, as compared to mantle, the dark feather markings are more attenuated, the light zones paler. **Underparts** feathers of upper breast buffy to tan with broad internal dark zone, the general effect being a somewhat broken pattern; lower breast and belly usually all white, sometimes with a few dusky spots (not many spots overall as is common in ♀ Def. Basic); feathers of sides have alternating broad U-shaped zones of sepia and buff (margins are latter); under-tail pattern white streaked dusky. **Legs and feet** blue-gray or near a neutral color, webs slightly darker. **Tail** feathers pointed, the central pair considerably longer (20–25 mm.) than next pair and nearly all black or with traverse whitish barring; the other pairs also are dark, with buff or whitish internal markings and edges. **Wing** the several innermost secondaries toward sepia, the exposed web with partial bars and margin of buffy tan; the one next to speculum patterned and colored much as in ♂ Def. Basic. Remainder of wing is retained Basic feathering. The axillarlike feathers at top base of wing are shorter than in ♂ Def. Alt., brownish sepia, margined buffy tan at least on outer web and tip.

NOTE   Females are said to occur that have underparts more or less heavily spotted sepia (in Witherby 1939); this is the character of Basic and not Alt. Plumage.

▶   ♂ Def. Basic Plumage (entire feathering), head–body and usually all of tail acquired during SPRING, almost all of wing much later (after nesting); then the Basic head–body–tail is succeeded by Alt. during a span that begins in LATE SUMMER or in FALL. Thus this is a spring to early fall Plumage, except that the late-acquired wing is retained into the following late summer or later.

Typically browner overall than Def. Alt., the dorsal feathers and flank feathers with more broadly rounded ends, the underparts varying with individual from plain to spotted to somewhat streaked.

Head and neck buffy brownish to tan, paling nearly to white on chin, and with more diffuse dark brownish streaking than in Def. Alt. **Upperparts** exposed feathers of mantle blackish brown with internal markings and wide margins that are tan, rust-colored, or even cinnamon; longer scapulars comparatively short, mostly blackish, margined tan or browner but lateral margin paler (nearly white). **Underparts** breast quite brownish with broken pattern of dark markings; belly to tail whitish, plain or with dusky spots or (mainly beyond vent) streaks. **Tail** central pair of feathers broader and shorter than in Def. Alt.; all tail feathers dusky brown, barred and broadly margined buffy tan.

Wing the several innermost secondaries have somewhat rounded ends and are very dark, margined white, and with internal white areas; the one next to speculum brownish gray, with whitish gray internal zone (alongside shaft, on outer web) and wide white margin, widest distally on outer web; the secondaries forming the speculum usually have much of the outer web brownish, but in some it is gray-brown, and in still others partly bronzy or greenish; the same web is narrowly black subterminally (not widely black as ♂) with broad white end (but not as broad as in ♂) on both webs; most greater coverts vary with individual from a medium gray-brown to a somewhat lighter gray with margins of corresponding color (they fade toward off-white); median and lesser coverts are broadly rounded, gray-brown, margined buffy tan (it fades and ends also wear off) or nearer white; the longest median coverts typically also have a pale area (part of an incomplete transverse bar) on each web well back from the end; primaries and their upper coverts as ♂; wing lining various grays, darker toward leading edge, most feathers (except primary coverts) usually with rather broad pale margins; axillars white, broadly marked or barred medium grayish.

For excellent color illust. of ♀ ♀ molting in spring from gray Def. Alt. to brownish Def. Basic, see cent. and especially lower left fig. on pl. 23 in Schiøler (1925).

AT HATCHING See col. pl. facing p. 370. Neutral coloring—grays, white, with tinge of brown but no yellow. Facial markings not as dark as Mallard. Pattern becomes less distinct, the darker areas lighter, as the duckling grows.

▶ ♂ Juv. Plumage (entire feathering), grows rapidly. The feathers begin to appear (scapulars, flanks, rectrices) by age 3 weeks; at 30 days the bird is predominantly feathered; at 5 weeks the speculum is becoming visible; at 40 days the mantle feathers are grown enough to show the light transverse barring (unlike longitudinal markings in ♀), and within a very few days the bird can fly (Southwick 1953a). Flight is attained, on the average, at about 42 days; within perhaps a week thereafter, while some of the Juv. feathers still are growing on the dorsum, some of those on head, neck and underparts already are beginning to be succeeded by incoming Basic I.

This Plumage is quite buffy, with part of underparts broadly streaked dark (but center of underparts typically unmarked); dark markings not as dark and less sharply defined than in the next incoming Plumage (Basic I). **Bill** quite dark, with indication of blackish stripe along top. **Head** finely streaked dark on buff or buffy tan and this streaking becomes progressively broader on neck, upper breast, and forward sides; **upperparts** mantle feathers brownish sepia with rather narrow buffy tan barring and edging; the longer scapulars taper somewhat, have rounded ends, and are dark internally with narrow whitish buff edging; **underparts** belly whitish buff, plain or with very few dark streaks; ground color deeper and streaking abundant and broader on abdomen to tail; feathers along upper sides are tapering, with broad dark internal V-shaped marking next to the broad whitish buff edging. **Tail** feathers sepia, barred, streaked, and edged creamy buff. Legs and **feet** olive-gray or dusky, webs usually about the same, rarely lighter.

441

Wing innermost secondaries ("tertials") plain gray-brown, distally margined pale buffy; the one next to speculum has additionally a wide black zone within outer web; those of speculum dark grayish, on outer web darker and with greenish or bronzy purple sheen, plus wide subterminal black zone and sharply defined broad, nearly white, end on both webs; distal secondaries gray-brown tipped buffy tan to white; greater coverts narrow, medium gray-brown, with cinnamon ends (widest on outer web); the other upper coverts also gray-brown, faintly edged paler (the former fades, the edging wears off); primaries and their coverts about as in Basic. Wing lining various grays, with narrow (compared to ♀ Basic) pale feather margins; white axillars have some light gray, mostly along shaft, but seldom the indistinct gray barring common to ♀ Basic.

▶ ♀ Juv. Plumage (entire feathering), timing of development as ♂. The less colored speculum than ♂'s apparent at age 5 weeks or soon after, the longitudinal striping of mantle feathers (not transverse barring as in ♂) noticeable at age 40 days, i.e., the sexes distinguishable.

As ♂, but differs in above-mentioned features. Also, usually, more and broader streaking ventrally. **Wing** quite like ♀ Def. Basic, but differences include: innermost secondaries lack internal buffy markings (but sometimes have whitish ones) and are narrowly edged white at tip only; greater coverts adjoining speculum have narrow whitish edge on exposed web, a wider zone largely of same across end of both webs, and a more or less distinct palish bar across the brownish sepia inner portion of each feather; the longer middle coverts also margined whitish (mostly on end) and with a pale notch on each side well back from the end.

▶ ♂ Basic I Plumage (all feathering except, in wing, only several innermost secondaries and a variable number of upper coverts), generally is rapidly succeeding the Juv. feathering by estimated age 60 days. Therefore, depending on date of hatching, this Plumage is well developed in AUG., or in SEPT., or sometimes later, and it in turn is being succeeded by Alt. I within a short (but unknown) time after it is well developed.

Head–neck and all of underparts are streaked very light on light (no plain or nearly unmarked belly as in Juv.). The streaking is sharply defined, not somewhat diffuse as in Juv., and varies with individual from very narrow to variable width to (rarely) so wide throughout as to be the predominating color.

Head buffy tan (deeper tan on crown), paling to buffy on chin–throat, with wide dark streaking on crown, fine narrow streaking on sides, and few (rarely no) streaks on chin–throat. **Upperparts** feathers of mantle have very dark exposed portions with narrow whitish transverse markings and some similar edging; some of the feathers grade into a basal pattern of coarse white vermiculations on medium gray, while late-incoming feathers have this pattern throughout (forecasting the next incoming Alt. I generation); longer scapulars are wide distally, then taper slightly and the ends are nearly round; these feathers are largely medium grayish or darker (with few, often no, internal markings) and with sharply defined whitish margins that are much wider distally; the longest scapular usually is rather pointed; on the rump the dark feathers have narrow whitish transverse markings. All of **underparts** whitish to somewhat buff, heavily marked (elongated spots) or streaked (very narrowly to broadly) dusky or darker, the streaking heaviest from vent to tail. **Tail** central pair of feathers a few mm. longer than adjoining pair, very dark, with very few (sometimes no) whitish buff internal markings

442

and narrow edging; the outer tail feathers not as dark, with wider light edging, and vary with individual from internally plain or with 1 to 3 irregular transverse bars; the outermost pair is comparatively light on both webs. **Wing** the 3 innermost secondaries are nearly equal in length, narrowly margined white distally, and sometimes with a few fragments of narrow whitish cross barring; the secondary next to speculum has the internal zone grayish; there are some new, broader upper coverts; remainder of wing is retained Juv. feathering. The axillarlike feathers at top base of wing are rather broad, tapering somewhat distally, and plain.

For excellent illus. of this Plumage, see the 2 left-hand figs. on pl. 40 in Millais (1902a) and all large figs. on pl. 25 in Schiøler (1925).

NOTE   When banding about 2,000 Pintails, Cooch (1952) found 4 "immature" birds (a ♂ was mentioned specifically) in which the legs and feet were not pigmented; their feathering "showed no albinistic features."

▶   ♂ Alt. I Plumage (all feathering except, in wing, only some innermost secondaries and coverts), largely acquired beginning in or during OCT. by many individuals, but occasionally earlier and quite often later; the long scapulars and the black-margined innermost secondaries often are not fully grown until very late fall or early winter; the last of the new tail feathers also commonly are late in growing. Thus many individuals are not in "high" Plumage until some time in winter. This Plumage is retained into the following SUMMER.

This is the first Plumage in which the head is brown (unicolor), the dorsum and sides finely vermiculated (appear gray), scapulars narrow and tapering, foreneck to vent white, vent to tail black, and central tail feathers conspicuously elongated.

As ♂ Def. At., including soft-part colors, except: underparts apparently more variable, sometimes being sparingly mottled dusky (more heavily on abdomen), or even with fine transverse wavy dark lines giving gray appearance to abdomen and rear sides; scapulars and central tail feathers perhaps not as elongated and the scapulars often with outer (as well as inner) margin quite gray.

▶   ♀ Basic I Plumage (all feathering except, in wing, only a few innermost feathers), timing presumably as ♂, i.e., a FALL Plumage.

As ♂ Basic I, but differs in such details as: exposed portions of feathers of upper mantle have a fairly wide internal light bar and wide, rather conspicuous, palish edging; longest scapular usually plain dark internally with sharply defined narrow white margin limited mainly to outer web. For excellent illus., see the 2 left-hand figs. on pl. 41 in Millais (1902a) and the 2 right-hand figs. on pl. 26 in Schiøler (1925).

▶   ♀ Alt. I Plumage (all feathering except, in wing, only a few innermost feathers) acquired, depending on date of hatching, in FALL or sometimes even as late as early WINTER, and retained into SPRING.

Quite gray overall appearance. As ♀ Def. Alt. so far as known. Some Basic I lateral tail feathers commonly are retained into winter and most of the Juv. wing is retained throughout and also worn with the next-incoming (Basic II) Plumage. The change in the young ♀ from the ventrally-streaked Basic I to Alt. I (much of belly typically white, long scapulars tapering, central tail feathers elongated) is shown on pl. 41 in Millais (1902a).

NOTE   Occasionally a bird of either sex, in Juv. or a later Plumage, has much feathering rust-colored (like ferrous staining on white geese) or a more muted brownish. Good examples are illus. in color on pls. 23 and 24 in Schiøler (1925).

Measurements of mature birds from N. Am. summer to winter range; 12 ♂ : BILL 45–54 mm., av. 52; WING 262–283, av. 273; TAIL 162–223, av. 187; TARSUS 43–47, av. 45.2; and 12 ♀: BILL 44–49 mm., av. 47; WING 244–265, av, 254.5; TAIL 88–112, av. 101; TARSUS 38–45, av. 42 (ETS).

"Adults" from New and Old Worlds, 82 ♂: BILL 46.2–56.2 mm., av. 51.2; WING (across chord) 235–278, av. 263.1; TAIL 144–204, av. 168.4; and 57 ♀: BILL 43.4–52.1 mm., av. 47.5; WING (across chord) 220–262, av. 245.4 (H. Friedmann).

Flattened WING of "adult" ♂ 23 from New World 257–290 mm., av. 271.9, and 30 from Old 259–266, av. 269 (Parkes 1953).

For British series, WING meas. over the curve, see Witherby (1939).

The following (from Schiøler 1925) shows the difference between the "adult" (Basic) and the shorter 1st fall (Juv.) WING, almost all birds taken in Denmark: ♂ 71 "adult" 256–281 mm., av. 272.5, and 40 1st-fall 251–273, av. 259; ♀ 24 "adult" 240–255 mm., av. 246.5, and 32 1st-fall 230–255, av. 243.

Weight in fall of mature birds in Ill.: 232 ♂ av. 2.28 ± .02 lb. (av. 36.5 oz. or 1,035 gm.) and 60 ♀ av. 1.96 ± .03 lb. (av. 31.4 oz. or 986 gm.) (Bellrose and Hawkins 1947). In N. Am. in fall, age-classes not separated, 937 ♂ av. 2.2 lb. (999 gm.), max. 3.4 (1,444 gm.), and 498 ♀ av. 1.8 lb. (817 gm.), max. 2.4 lb. (1,090 gm.) (A. L. Nelson and Martin 1953).

In Denmark in fall: 40 mature ♂ weighed 746–1,111 gm., av. 928, and 32 in 1st fall 710–1,096, av. 882; and 17 mature ♀ weighed 601–845 gm., av. 762, and 15 in 1st fall 665–913, av. 710 (Schiøler 1925).

Pintails probably are near minimum wt. when flightless in molt. Flightless drakes, taken in July in Sask.: 69 alive av. 31.4 ± .05 oz. (av. 895 gm.) and 116 dead 40–55 hrs. av. 30.1 ± .05 oz. (av. 858 gm.) (Keith and Stanislawski 1960). These authors also summarized various N. Am. wt. data not included here.

Spring wt.—in March in the Charyn lowlands in Kazakhstan (Soviet central Asia), Gavrin (1964) weighed large series each year 1955–60 inclusive. For ♂ ♂ the lowest av. was 816 gm. (153 birds) in 1960 and highest was 862 gm. (146 birds) in 1956; for ♀ ♀ the lowest av. was 706 gm. (13 birds) in 1958 and the highest was 775 (47 birds) in 1956.

In N. Am., on day of hatching, 19 ducklings weighed 19.5–32.3 gm., the mean and standard error being 25.5 ± 1.09 gm. (Smart 1965a). Also in N. Am., for wt. of known-age captives at intervals to age 7 weeks, see Southwick (1953a).

Hybrids or presumed hybrids in the wild in our area consist of several with Mallard (*Anas platyrhynchos*) and 1 with Redhead (*Aythya americana*) (references in Cockrum 1952) and 1 with the Greenwing (*Anas crecca*) (T. Howell 1959). In parks and zoos, Mallard–Pintail crosses occur quite commonly and such of these as are free flying are not necessarily restricted to these places.

In the Old World by the late 1950s the Pintail was reported as having crossed with at least 5 species of *Anas* in addition to those mentioned above, 2 of *Aythya*, and *Somateria mollissima!* Evidently the commonest natural crosses are with Mallard, Greenwing, and Wigeon. For a worldwide list of wild plus captive crosses, various mention of their known or probable fertility, and the extensive relevant literature, see Gray (1958).

444

The following matters are of interest. Five ♂ crosses of *Anas acuta* × *A. crecca* have a facial pattern much resembling that of the Baikal Teal, *A. formosa* (J. M. and J. G. Harrison 1971). The tracheal bullae both of parent stock and crosses of *Anas acuta* with *A. penelope* and *A. sibilatrix* were illus. by Beer (1968). The displays and voices of Mallard–Pintail hybrids have been described, as mentioned under Mallard.

Geographical variation in the species (as treated in this volume) is now regarded as probably slight or nonexistent; the N. Am. birds are not larger, nor do ♂ ♂ have longer tails, than Eurasian ones. For discussion see Tougarinov (1941), Hellmayr and Conover (1948), Parkes (1953), and note intercontinental travels of Pintails mentioned beyond under "Migration." Portenko (1972) attempted to reopen the subspecies question without sufficient evidence. RSP

FIELD IDENTIFICATION In N. Am. Both sexes, and omitting the drake's elongated central tail feathers, are nearly as long as the Mallard, but with long slender neck, slender tapered body, and narrow pointed tail. Because the tail is long, the wings appear to be centered on the body, rather than farther back; they are long, pointed, and relatively narrow, giving a "swept back" appearance in flight—which is swift, elegant, and with rapid wingbeats that extend over a greater arc than, for example, in the Mallard. Flying flocks have a wavy appearance and, within groups, individuals are closely spaced. White trailing edge to inner part of wing. Bill dark.

The trim drake is unmistakable, both as to species and sex, from about mid-Oct. through winter into June: dark head, upperparts and sides a clean gray, upper foreneck to vent white, central tail feathers very long and narrow. An alert flock of drakes, with necks upthrust, resembles a flotilla of toy sailboats. In summer–early fall, more like the ♀ but darker, with tendency toward barring on dorsum and especially upper sides. The ♀ all year is delicate and slender, with narrow pointed tail, grayish to gray-brown dorsum, inconspicuous speculum, white in wing only at trailing edge, and dark bill (no orange or yellowish). Some other ducks, such as ♀ Gadwall, may appear somewhat grayish but are not as slender.

Younger stages more like ♀, but ♂ in 1st fall begins to acquire dark head, gray back, white neck and underparts.

Hardly to be confused with the comparatively thickset Oldsquaw, even though both are long tailed. FCB

VOICE The drake is silent part of the year, but in winter and spring his musical whistled *whee* fills the air wherever Pintails are plentiful. Sometimes it is softer, lower pitched, melodious, and commonly doubled; the note is somewhat like the *krick* of the Greenwing, and longer, flatter, than note of Baldpate.

The ♀ in any season infrequently utters a low *keck* or variants from more of a quack (quite like ♀ Mallard) to a rolling growl. A rolling call, similar to that of the Lesser Scaup, may be common to both sexes (Bent 1923). Others have described a rolling call as reminiscent of that of Wigeon (*Anas penelope*). Actually, depending on the situation, the ♀ has a considerable repertoire of recognizable variants of her rather simple calls. Some of the vocalization of each sex is mentioned in context of described displays. Also, toward end of the section on "Reproduction," voices of ducklings and age when they change to "adult" calls are mentioned. FCB

445

HABITAT   In N. Am. **Breeding season** Typically in open country having many scattered small bodies of water (some may become dry later on). Grasslands, barrens, dry tundra. Dry meadows near watercourses. Farmland with small waters and, for nesting, last year's grain stubble (only Pintail and Mallard commonly nest there). At Delta, Man., mainly in *Scholochloa*, bluegrass*(Poa)*, and cordgrass*(Spartina)*. In B.C., some within scattered patches of aspen and of lodgepole pine. In Utah, mainly in salt grass *(Distichlis)*, bulrush*(Scirpus)*, and willow*(Salix)*. Some nest where there is interspersion of drier habitat within large marshes. Generally avoids timbered or extensive brushy areas. Drakes need bare water margins or mudbanks. If, because of favorable weather and other factors, an area becomes suitable Pintail breeding habitat, the birds occupy it readily; on the other hand, certain areas are abandoned during drought. **Migrations** Primarily shallow waters—fresh, brackish, salt—sheltered from wind, and preferably with mud or sandbars. May be expected occasionally in any sheltered marine environment (unless islands there have ponds or lakes), as some make long flights over salt water. **Winter** Freshwater and brackish coastal marshes, shallow lagoons, mudflats of river courses, sheltered marine waters. A great many fly to grain, flooded rice, and corn fields to feed. LKS

DISTRIBUTION   (See map.) NEW WORLD **Breeds** in n. Bering Sea on St. Lawrence I. (several hundred pairs, not very successfully) and probably occasionally at other Bering Sea localities. In the Aleutians, introduced foxes probably prevent more regular nesting on various is. (O. Murie 1959); broods seen on Amchitka (Kenyon 1961). Beyond, in the Commanders, the most numerous nesting shoal-water duck (Johansen 1961). On mainland Alaska, occurs on the arctic slope as migrant and scattered nester, but evidently more numerous when molting in summer. Pintails (mostly drakes that have scattered to molt) occur n. beyond usual breeding range; there are records for Banks I., sw. Victoria I. (occurs regularly), Adelaide Pen., Southampton I. (where it also has bred), n. Ungava, and Baffin I. (several localities). Beyond to the north a pair nested in 1966 at Hazen Camp (lat. 82° N) on Ellesmere I. In w. Greenland, bred in Disko Bay area (on Disko I. and the mainland), 1947–52.

Quite likely an occasional pair nests in interior Ungava in area left blank on map; presumably nests occasionally in Nfld. It is increasing as a breeder in ne. N. Am. Its occurrence and increase as a nester in the Maritimes, from the 1940s onward, is well documented; see, for example, Boyer (1966).

Like many of our ducks, has nested at scattered localities s. of general breeding range, to s. Cal., n. Ariz., New Mex. (formerly not breeding, later a numerous breeder at L. Burford—W. S. Huey and Travis 1961), Iowa, cent. Ill., Washington, D.C., and elsewhere.

Pintails are sensitive to water levels; some of the shallow ponds and potholes in nesting areas are dry by late summer even in years of av. rainfall. The first birds to leave, in June, are drakes, bound for more permanent and larger waters where they molt. They go in any compass direction—a great many northward. During a series of dry seasons, 1958–68, as the number of water areas on the prairies decreased, many Pintails (both sexes) moved n. of the prairies and parklands; as the proportion occurring northward increased, the index of annual production of young on the prairies declined (R. I. Smith 1970).

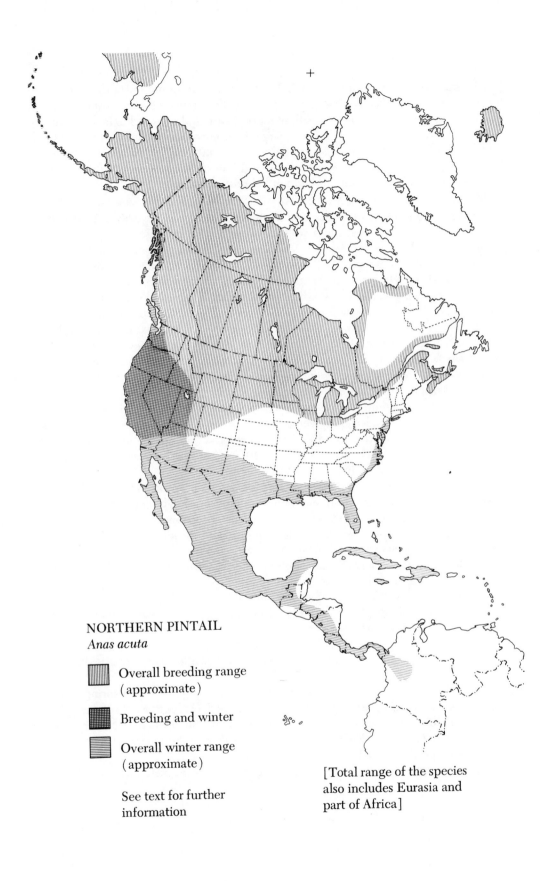

NORTHERN PINTAIL
Anas acuta

Overall breeding range
(approximate)

Breeding and winter

Overall winter range
(approximate)

See text for further
information

[Total range of the species
also includes Eurasia and
part of Africa]

Migrations In the Aleutians, probably commonest in spring and fall, also in Bering Strait region (a very considerable number cross the Strait). More widespread and in much larger numbers, at least in fall, in most of Ont. and eastward to include parts of Ungava, the Maritimes, and ne. New Eng. Has occurred in Greenland in Jan., April, May–June, and Sept.–Oct.; records up the w. coast into the Upernavik Dist., a few on the e. coast, including 1 at Scoresby Sd. and 1 in northeast Greenland. This is the shoal-water duck most likely to be found almost anywhere.

Winter Locally plentiful in the Aleutians, may be found in sheltered unfrozen waters around the Gulf of Alaska, and winters in numbers in se. Alaska. In the continental interior, occasional birds well n. of main winter range, especially in mild seasons. On the Atlantic side, very few occurrences in the Maritimes and not in any numbers until s. of New Eng. Bermuda—scarce and irregular. W. Indian area—in numbers on some larger is. and may occur on any of the others. Cent. Am.—lack of records from some coastal areas indicates either lack of habitat or of reporting. S. Am.: Colombia—Oct. to April; n. Venezuela—3 records; Surinam—1 record.

Pacific oceanic Hawaiian Is.—regular winterer on main is. and records also for Laysan I. and Midway Atoll; drake banded Feb. 26, 1954, on Oahu was recovered May 29, 1960, at an e. U.S.S.R. locality. Widely scattered occurrence (see "Migration") indicates very extensive wandering or possibly some still unknown winter quarters.

Old World Scattered **breeder** in Iceland; about 20 recoveries of Icelandic birds from w. Europe, mainly during migrations. Has nested in Spitzbergen. Across Eurasia has nested at scattered localities well away from main breeding range, as in w. Europe to s. Spain and scattered southward in Asia (as in Turkestan). Breeds on Sakhalin I., the Kurils, and Commanders (as mentioned earlier). Molting birds occur n. of general breeding range, as on Bely I., n. of Yamal Pen.

Widespread on unfrozen fresh and brackish waters in **winter.** Visitor to Wrangel I. In Africa, on n. rim of the continent (largest numbers in Egypt); perhaps occasional at Sahara oases; a few near the Gulf of Guinea coast; probably rare elsewhere s. of the Sahara. May occur on waters throughout the Indian subcontinent; Ali (1953) did not include it for Tranancore and Cochin. May occur almost anywhere in se. Asia, but no records from wide areas. May only winter in n. part of the Philippines. More than one Bornean record, but none recent.

Recorded as **fossil,** of Pleistocene age, in the Nearctic region in Ore., Cal., Nev., New Mex. (3 localities), Kans., and Fla. (4 localities); in the Palearctic in Ireland, England, Monaco, Switzerland, Germany, Hungary, and Azerbaijan. From **archaeological sites** in the Nearctic in Iowa, Ill. (3 localities), and Fla. References to all these are listed by Brodkorb (1964a), plus H. Howard (1971) for New Mex. RSP

MIGRATION Nearctic data primarily. Migration begins early in spring and very early in fall continuing into winter. Small groups and flocks, or these closely associated; often with Mallards. A complex pattern of movements. Somewhere in N. Am. Pintails are traveling every month of the year, probably with least shifting about in latter half of July, perhaps also early Feb.

Routes Information is tentative, from scattered sources including Low (in Aldrich

448

1949); breeding subpopulations from w. to e. are discussed; parts of various routes are not definitely known.

Pintails have been seen crossing Bering Strait (A. Bailey 1930). "In general," Pintails summering in ne. Siberia from the cent. and upper Kolyma and the Magadan area (near Kresta Gulf within Anadyr Gulf) to the Chuckchee Pen. spend the winter in N. Am.; the birds arrive in Siberia beginning in May and an adult ♂ was back in Cal. on Aug. 28; birds taken in Siberia had been banded in Sask., Man., Cal., Wash., Idaho, N.D., and 1 on the Texas Gulf Coast near Aransas (Shevareva 1960). To June 12, 1961, there were recoveries from the U.S.S.R. of 121 Pintails banded in N. Am. (Dzubin 1962). The subject was discussed further by Henny (1973), with map of recovery localities in e. Asia. From his paper: in 1954–70 a total of 230 N. Am.-banded Pintails were recovered in e. Asia; 84% of recoveries were in spring–summer, mostly from lowland valleys near mouths of large rivers; autumn and winter recoveries generally were from locations farther s. in the U.S.S.R., also in Japan and 1 in Korea; and birds banded

"anywhere on N. Am. may be recovered in Asia, although the opportunity increases as the banding locations shift from east to west." He mapped 1 fall–winter and 2 spring–summer recoveries in the far interior of the U.S.S.R.

Many Alaskan Pintails winter in Cal. and some probably go beyond to Mexico. Many (others?) in spring apparently reach interior, and even Bering Sea coastal Alaska via the continental interior (through Canada) and return via the interior; this probably includes most of those that go to Siberia. The Puget Sd. region is a major wintering area; whence the birds come is not reported. Inland, w. of the Mississippi in conterminous U.S., presumably many Pintails use approximately the same route up and down the interior, but large numbers go se. to the Gulf Coast (abundant winterer in La., large numbers in Fla.). It seems that Pintails are not plentiful in n. interior Mexico, but occur in large numbers westward, southward, and eastward. Substantial numbers have a rather complicated itinerary—from interior nesting areas and molting places s. via the prairie provinces, then to Mont., then westerly into Ore. and Cal., and s. into Mexico; they cross eastward to the Gulf of Mexico coast (arrive Nov.–Jan.) and go n. in spring up the interior (main part of the Mississippi drainage w. to the Rockies) to breeding areas.

449

Many Ore. birds go to Cal., but others (via the route just mentioned) reach the Gulf of Mexico coast; the same applies to Utah birds. Where those summering in Cal. go is not well reported; some are believed to reach the Gulf of Mexico coast in Oct.–Nov., but their return route seems to be unknown.

The whole movement is very prolonged. By mid-Sept. there already are tens of thousands of Pintails in w. Mexico, but in Jan. still a great many in Cal. that apparently go to Mexico afterwards and, eventually, up through the continental interior. If they spend much time in Cal., it would almost seem as though the "spring migration" were at first southward, then eastward, and then northward.

Some birds from the prairies and parklands go e. and se. toward or to the Atlantic seaboard; a sizable flight reaches the Maritimes in the latter half of Oct.; e. of the Mississippi in conterminous U.S. this diagonal movement is to destinations from N.J. southward, including the W. Indies. See Bellrose (1968) for some migration "corridors" in the e. U.S. Some local birds of the Maritimes and Que. (and many more that come there from the westward) go down the Atlantic seaboard; part of the local birds travel westward via the St. Lawrence and Great Lakes, with banding recoveries as far w. as Wis., Minn., and even Alta., before they move on to winter quarters.

In La. in recent years there have been good crops of natural foods, such as wild millet (*Echinochloa*), which has resulted in large numbers of Pintails wintering there.

In s. Fla. small numbers arrive in Oct., there are large numbers by about mid-Nov., probably peak numbers in Jan.–early Feb., and a great many depart in 2nd and 3rd week in Feb.

Dates   Because of unusual (and some unknown) routes, long early summer flights of drakes in any compass direction, some movement later on by postbreeding ♀ ♀, and the explosive movement of young prior to their fall travels southward, it is hard to establish meaningful dates for most areas and seasons.

SPRING movement n. begins in Feb. and the vanguard, in the interior, reaches the states bordering Canada late that month in most years. Usually they arrive about April 5 at Delta, Man. Many reach the vicinity of northerly breeding areas up to several weeks before conditions on breeding areas become suitable for nesting. As with other waterfowl, there is early movement along the Pacific seaboard.

SUMMER   There are widely scattered small groups of molting drakes (many are flightless by the 2nd week in July) on larger waters scattered among the potholes and ponds of the breeding range. The majority, however, have a more extensive molt migration, some birds going hundreds of miles, and gather in thousands and tens, perhaps hundreds, of thousands at certain localities. Most notable are the Bear R. marshes in n. Utah and the Tule–Klamath basin in Ore.–Cal.; other places include the Camas Reserve in n. Idaho; some other waters in nw. conterminous U.S.; in Canada, L. Winnipeg and some other lakes in that region, other lakes scattered in w. Canada (as Pel Lake in Sask.), and apparently some waters nw. to include interior Alaska. Drakes prior to wing molt may fly in any compass direction—many southward to Bear R. and Tule–Klamath, many northward toward or to the tundra.

LATE SUMMER–FALL   Beginning about Aug. 1, drakes have new flight feathers and so are again on the wing; movement southward, from early Aug. until well into Sept., is mainly of unisexual flocks (drakes). The ♀ ♀, most of which are well scattered when

450

flightless and molting, again are on the wing about a month later than drakes. Thus various later migrant flocks are preponderantly of ♀♀. Soon after the young attain flight, a great many of them disperse widely (up to several hundred miles) and evidently join others of their own age or older. A young ♂ banded Aug. 29, 1969, in Glen Co., Cal., was shot Oct. 11, 1969, on the Stikine flats n. of Wrangel, Alaska; the bird had gone 1,600 mi. in a northerly direction in not over 43 days (Baysinger 1971). Some Oct. flocks evidently consist almost entirely of young of the year.

Even allowing for overlapping schedules of birds of the different categories, from widely scattered localities, and with movement in all compass directions, there still is a great deal of segregation by sex and age from late summer to the beginning of winter. Then, in Dec.–Jan., mixing is general and pair-formation activities begin.

Interesting records (some with incomplete data). ATLANTIC AREA Young bird banded Aug. 9, 1948, at Hamilton Inlet, Labrador, shot Sept. 15 of same year in Devon, England (Low, in Aldrich 1949). Young ♂ last retrapped Sept. 16, 1951, at Hamilton Inlet, shot Sept. 25 of same year in Hampshire, England (Cooch 1952). Young ♂ banded June 30, 1930, in n. Iceland, shot May 1, 1932, near Bradore Bay, Que. (H. F. Lewis 1933). One banded Dec. 15, 1962, near Reykjavik, Iceland, recovered April 17, 1963, at Frederiksdal, Nanortalik Dist., Greenland (Salomonsen 1967a).

Icelandic Pintails winter mainly in the Palearctic area (recoveries in Brit. Isles and Europe, including n. Mediterranean), but quite likely some reach the N. Am. Atlantic area (see above). Salomonsen (1967a) thought that most Greenland occurrences, including those of breeders in the Disko Bay area, were from N. Am. On the other hand, Maher and Nettleship (1968) suggested the possibility that the pair found nesting at lat. 82° N on Ellesmere I. was of European stock.

N. AM.–EURASIA A Pintail banded at Bitter Lake Refuge, New Mex., in 1967, 2 years later was live-trapped, examined, and released at the Shimaha Duck Refuge in Japan. A young ♂ banded in Cal. on Sept. 20, 1961, was recovered in Japan in s. Honshu on Jan. 25, 1968. A Pintail banded Jan. 17, 1967, at Salton Sea Refuge in s. Cal. was recovered on June 3 of the same year in the Anadyr region, U.S.S.R. Another, banded Sept. 8, 1964, at San Luis Lake in cent. s. Colo., was recovered May 18, 1968, also in Anadyr.

An "adult" drake, banded in the "nesting season" in "Canada," was taken within a year, also in the "nesting season," far to the west in the upper (northern) Kolyma basin in Yakutia (Vorobev 1963). Pintails banded in N. Am. have traveled distances up to at least 2,000 mi. w. of the N. Am. mainland into Asia (it is, of course, possible that some, after their mates were nesting in E. Siberia, flew farther westward to molt). (See earlier in this section for more on N. Am.–e. Asia.)

PACIFIC OCEANIC On Midway Atoll at least 6–12 birds seen and a ♀ killed on Nov. 12, 1958 (Frings and Frings 1960); flocks of up to 20 fairly frequent on Sand I. in winter, 2 separate flights of more than 30 birds in Dec., 1961, and on Eastern I. a pair seen Nov. 30, 1963 (H. I. Fisher 1965). Main Hawaiian group—100 to 300 or more, even 1,000 on a single pond, on a census day at Christmas time (Cooper and Lysaght 1956); 50 banded in 1935 at San Francisco, Cal., then shipped to Hawaii and released (probably about March 15, 1935), and at least 1 returned to Cal., where it was shot at Los Banos on Dec. 4, 1936 (M. T. Cooke 1945). Palmyra I. (Line group, cent. Pacific)—

flock of very exhausted birds landed Nov. 15, 1942, including a ♂ banded the previous Aug. 15 in Utah (Lincoln 1943). Christmas I. (Line group) —hundreds 2nd week in Nov., 1953; at same time hundreds not far away at Fanning I. (and Pintails observed there in other years); a few stayed at Christmas I. until Jan.–Feb., but "most of them passed on" (Cooper and Lysaght 1956). At this locality in 1958, began arriving in late Sept. and, except for a break in Dec., present until late Feb.; arrived so tired a bather could pick them from the water (Gallagher 1960). Line group (sw. Pacific)—Jarvis I., specimen, 1939, and Washington I., bird recovered Dec. 13, 1956, that had been banded in state of Wash., U.S., as recently as Oct. 16 of the same year. Phoenix group (cent. Pacific)—records for the Marshall, Mariana, and Palau Is.

EURASIA   There is a considerable literature on migration and many scattered reports of band recoveries. A useful brief general account is that of Shevareva (1965). RSP

BANDING STATUS   In N. Am. the total number banded through 1964 was 697,159 and the number of recoveries and returns through 1966 was 66,634; the banding was done mostly at scattered localities within main breeding range and, in winter, mainly in Cal. and La. (data from Bird Banding Laboratory). The number banded each year for 1954–70 inclusive was listed by Henny (1973), the total for this period being 686,383; he also gave an annual "recovery rate index." There are no comprehensive published papers based on recovery data. An incomplete list of bandings in Eurasia includes: in U.S.S.R. a total of 57,120 banded through 1959; in Brit. Isles a total of 2,035 through 1969 and 286 recoveries. Published recoveries are scattered widely in the Palearctic literature. RSP

REPRODUCTION   N. Am. data. Both sexes **first breed** at age 1 year. **Pair formation activity** begins on winter range and many spring migrants are paired. In La., drakes begin whistling about mid-Jan., but the birds are not conspicuously paired (as are Mallards) when they leave the marshes on migration. The sexes migrate together, with a surplus of drakes, and there is much display wherever Pintails congregate. Pair formation displays continue to occur after arrival, into the period when the ground becomes warm, gregariousness wanes, and the already-mated ♀ ♀ are scattered and nesting.

This duck is not a social nester, yet there definitely are concentrations in or within optimum habitat.

Displays of the Pintail abroad were described by Lorenz (1941) and in N. Am. in wild birds and in context with seasonal activities by R. I. Smith (1968). Both should be read, for text and illus.; the latter is condensed here, with minor additions from other sources.

Group activity   Displays leading to pair formation occur on land, water, and during flight. In a display situation there may be several drakes, or only one, and a ♀. When only one drake, the birds engage in various actions such as ritualized PREENING (in various forms), DRINKING, INTRODUCTORY SHAKE, feeding, and so on. The drake begins CHIN-LIFTING and BURPING. In the latter the head is raised slowly, the bill moved down against foreneck, and then there is a lowering of the head while a *whee* whistle is uttered with rising inflection. The 2 displays often are linked and may occur repeatedly in a brief time. When thus displaying, the closer the drake to the duck, the more his body is oriented in a manner suggesting preparation to mount her. The whistle attracts other Pintails, which then engage in pair formation activities.

When several ♂♂ are competing the ♀ selects one, usually the one that has established a relationship with her prior to the approach of the others. Otherwise, the ♀ selects a ♂ "within a matter of minutes or even seconds" and then an intruding drake must win the duck's favor by replacing the one she had selected. At this stage the ♀ has a single display, INCITING. As she moves or follows the preferred drake, she orients her head and neck movements (these are rhythmic) toward other ♂♂ that approach her, while almost continuously uttering *kuk-kuk-kuk* (may be prolonged). This call attracts drakes. The entire performance apparently serves to attract and to space individuals.

If the preferred ♂ is forced from his position, the ♀ may take wing. Prior to this, she assumes an alert position, upon which signal the group becomes synchronized for **aerial activity**. The resulting type of flight occurs in Jan.–Feb., is most frequent in March–April, and seems to be more prevalent in the Pintail than in the Mallard. There is a constant shifting of relative position of the flying drakes; the ♀ assumes special postures (illus. by Smith) and she utters *kuk* calls.

The ♀ has a HEAD-UP posture when in flight which seems to have no counterpart when she is on land or water. With neck stretched, she raises the horizontal axis of her head above that of the body, and is silent. This occurs more commonly later, during nesting.

During the group phase, the common displays of the preferred drake are CHIN-LIFTING, BURPING, and TURNING-THE-BACK-OF-THE-HEAD (all these also have aerial forms); the ♀ responds (when alighted) to the last-mentioned by following and Inciting.

Among the competing drakes, the GRUNT-WHISTLE (as in Mallard) and HEAD-UP-TAIL-UP (while facing the ♀) are frequent. Both have a vocal component. The former is performed at a greater distance from the ♀ than is the Burp and with lateral orientation of the drake to the duck not as pronounced.

NOD-SWIMMING (see #7 under Mallard) is abbreviated in form and given only occasionally by ♂ Pintails.

Copulation occurs on the water. There is no head-pumping by the ♀; she assumes the PRONE position and the drake gives a display called PRECOPULATORY PUMPING—head raised and lowered rhythmically and repeatedly. As the ♂ mounts, he grasps the feathers of the ♀'s nape with his bill. After copulation, as the drake prepares to dismount, he performs a BRIDLING display (#9 under Mallard) in which, as the head is drawn upward and backward, he utters his whistle.

Promiscuity In the case of a pursuit flight, if there is promiscuous copulation with a pursuing drake, other drakes then occasionally will mount and copulate. The duck's mate generally is at the edge of the group in alert posture. There are no preceding, nor following, displays; the group disperses, the mated pair frequently being the last to leave.

Soon after groups and pairs of Pintails are present at nesting areas, exploratory or **prospecting flights,** instigated by the ♀, occur in morning and evening. A pair takes wing, leaves the flock, circles over surrounding habitat, and returns to the flock; others may join in, so that several birds of each sex thus may be engaged in a kind of social aerial display. In due course the ♀, accompanied by her mate, spends much time in low flight and on the ground, examining grassy areas, brushy patches, stubble fields, and so on; finally she selects the site for a nest.

Pursuit flights occur if a mated ♀ approaches a strange ♂. She flies up and he follows, then usually her mate also. There are variants. Such flights may be very brief, a few hundred yds., with the mate regaining his position beside the ♀. The pair, or all 3, may return to the takeoff point, but occasionally do not. This activity may be repeated over and over.

Long flights, as seen in Alaska, were described by E. W. Nelson (1887). The pair flies to a great altitude, the ♀ in the lead, then they descend at about a 45° angle with meteorlike swiftness, on stiff, slightly decurved, wings. The noise of air through the wings can be heard before the birds come into view—at first a murmur, then a hiss, then a roar. When the birds are close to ground or water, they level off, wings rigid and feet thrust forward, and land after 100–300 yds. of nearly horizontal glide.

J. Munro (1944) stated that pursuit flights start suddenly. The ♂ pursues the ♀ on water and they take wing, the ♀ turning and twisting, the ♂ close behind. One or more extra ♂♂ may join in, or a small group of them sometimes fly in pursuit of several ♀♀. (Also see J. C. Phillips (1923b) for some further details and variants.) R. I. Smith (1968) noted that the ♂ may try to touch the flank or breast of his flying mate, and she responds by rising upward and changing course; then he passes beyond her, returns, and tries again.

The flying ♀ may assume the Head up position-(raised horizontal axis), also 2 other positions (figured by Smith) in which the head is drawn back. The pursuit flight may end on the ground, with the male(s) continuing their pursuit and trying to copulate. The ♀ may avoid them or submit (see above description of copulation).

As observed in mated marked ♀♀ at Delta, Man., in 1959, the ♀ is involved in aerial pursuits from about 12 days before laying of 1st egg until the clutch is complete; drake activity reached a peak about 10 days before ♀♀ began incubating (Smith). Unmated drakes, however, were less inclined to pursuit activity and more inclined to engage in pair formation displays.

There is all gradation between pursuit behavior and harassment of ♀♀ whose nests have been destroyed. There is frequent harassment of "broody" ♀♀ (that are incubating or are attending broods) and only such ♀♀ give the Gesture of repulsion (as in Mallard) while uttering a characteristic harsh *kak kak kak* (indefinite series). Harassed ♀♀, in response to a human approaching a brood, vary in their vocalization from harsh to soft.

Broody ♀♀ in flight have a posture apparently associated with harassment, the head–neck angled downward, in form, signal, and motivation probably the opposite of Head-up.

Smith took the eggs of 6 marked ♀♀, at known time from 4 to 20 days after beginning of incubation. The interval between nest robbing and initiation of a **replacement clutch** varied from 6 to 10 days in 4 cases. A ♀ whose eggs were taken on 20th day of incubation did not begin incubating a 2nd clutch until 20 days later; another that had incubated 20 days was ready to lay 13 days later, at which time she was killed, evidently by drakes. Five of the ♀♀ retained their original mates and the 6th got a new one the day her eggs were taken. The group phase of display activity did not necessarily recur before the laying of another clutch.

It may be noted that, in spring on the Canadian prairies, there are more unpaired Pintails than other species of waterfowl. Among paired birds, Pintail drakes seem highly mobile and least attached to their **waiting sites** or "activity centers." A drake will seek a ♀ to chase, or other drakes to loaf or feed with, while his mate is at the nest. If a drake approaches or is approached by a pair, he may or may not pursue the ♀, depending on her reaction, but in either case is rarely prevented from doing so by the ♀'s mate. Thus there is relatively little overt aggression and so a relatively large number of individuals can utilize a preferred pond. Not only is there considerable promiscuity, but also considerable flexibility in distribution and spacing of nests.

Nests usually are located in open dry areas of short vegetation (it becomes taller) and quite often farther from water than is typical of other prairie ducks, occasionally ½ mi. away. In se. Alta., av. distance from water of 97 Pintail nests was 164 ± 59 ft. (Keith 1961). The duck uses a natural depression or makes one. The **nest down,** which is added beginning within the laying span, appears, in bulk, quite dark grayish to a drab brownish (variation from nest to nest) with small and inconspicuous whitish centers (illus.: Broley 1950; also see Brandt 1943). Intermingled feathers generally are small and plain darkish with light margins. (On the prairies, the most similar nest lining is that of the Shoveler.) By the time the eggs are half incubated the nest is a fairly deep and well-formed bowl, with dry vegetation intermingled with the down and feathers.

Some **laying dates.** In Utah they begin laying in first week in May, reach a peak in June, and end in mid-Aug. (C. S. Williams and Marshall 1938c). Beginning dates for 227 clutches at Delta, Man.: April (45 clutches), May (124), June (47), and July (1). There is variation, probably everywhere, between years in time of egg-laying. In New Bruns., eggs April 26–June 18 (Boyer1966). At Hooper Bay, Alaska, earliest egg May 20, peak number of fresh eggs June 4–8 (Brandt 1943); it was not an early season. **Clutch size** In n. Cal., 41 successful nests av. 9.2 eggs in 1952 and 196 av. 7.9 in 1957 (Rienecker and Anderson 1960). Forty complete first clutches at Delta, Man.; 10 eggs (12 nests), 9 (16), 8 (12). An av. of 9.3 eggs in 9 nests in New Bruns. (Boyer 1966).

One **egg** each from 20 clutches (9 Cal., 2 Alaska, 3 Man., 1 James Bay, 1 Sask., 1 Utah) **size** length av. 53.74 ± 1.23 mm., breadth av. 37.88 ± 1.17, radii of curvature of ends 14.38 ± 0.098 and 10.70 ± 0.82; **shape** between elliptical and subelliptical, elongation 1.42 ± 0.044, bicone −0.06, asymmetry +0.138 (FWP). Shell smooth, **color** somewhat greenish yellow or varying toward grayish. In s. Man., white eggs have been found (M. Milonski). Usually eggs are laid at rate of 1/day.

Pintails **renest** readily (see above) after loss of 1st clutch, but replacement clutches usually are smaller. They renest immediately if the 1st clutch is destroyed when incomplete, i.e., continue laying elsewhere. For data on success in renesting in s. Man., see Sowls (1955) and Milonski (1958). In se. Alta., clutch size av. 7.2 ± 0.4 before May 15 and 6.2 ± 0.6 after May 31; details in Keith (1961).

The ♀ begins incubating when the clutch is completed; **incubation period** usually 23 days in the wild, but a spread of 21–25 (Hochbaum 1944); 21–22 in incubator. In s. Man., when nests were moved to prevent their loss to agricultural operations, the period varied 21–27 days (M. Milonski). The surrounding vegetation grows and, if there is sufficient amount, the duck pulls it in over her and forms more or less of a canopy.

As laying terminates and the ♀ becomes occupied with incubating, drakes seek each other's company more often and spend increasing amounts of time together. Some time, perhaps generally well along during incubation of 1st clutch, the ♂'s occupation of a waiting site or "activity center" terminates, but small groups of drakes may remain in the general vicinity for up to perhaps 2 more weeks before departing to molt their flight feathers. Before leaving, they already have molted much or even all of head–body feathering.

Highest **nesting success** is reported from n. Cal. In 41 nests in 1952, with total of 376 eggs, 92.3% of the eggs hatched, 5.1% had dead embryos, and 1.9% were infertile (A. W. Miller and Collins 1954). In 1957 in 196 nests there were 1,556 eggs, of which 90.6% hatched, 4.4% had dead embryos, and 3.7% were infertile (Rienecker and Anderson 1960). In Utah, 82% of 796 eggs hatched (C. S. Williams and Marshall 1938c). At Lower Souris, N.D., in 1936 and 1937, hatching success (% of nests in which 1 or more eggs hatched) was 63% and 68% (Kalmbach 1938). At Delta, Man., 23% of 34 nests hatched (Sowls 1948). On a study area of Man. farmland only 6% of 132 nests hatched successfully in 1956 and 25% of 130 nests in 1957; details in Milonski (1958).

Brood size   At Delta, Man.: 12 ducklings (1 brood), 11 (2), 10 (5), 9 (4), 8 (6), 7 (12), 6 (15), 5 (9), 4 (2), 3 (7); av. of 63 broods was 6.6. Bue et al. (1952) in S.D. reported 38 broods in 1950 av. 5.2 young at 1 week and 5.0 at flying age; and 40 broods in 1951 av. 4.4 at 1 week and 3.5 at flying age. In Alta., Sask., and Man. in late July of 1935 plus 1938–42 inclusive, a total of 55,763 Pintail broods attended by ♀ ♀ were counted; the yearly av. varied from 4.9 to 6.37 young/brood (Cartwright 1944) and the combined av. was 6 young/brood. In n. Cal., brood size at hatching av. 8.5 young, 1 week 6.5 (26 broods), 2 weeks 7.5 (12 broods), 3 weeks 5.0 (5 broods), 4 weeks 5.0 (5), 5 weeks 6.3 (4), 6 weeks 6.5 (2), 7 weeks 4.8 (9), 8 weeks 6.0 (8), and 9 weeks 5.3 (2) (A. W. Miller and Collins 1954). (There are other published data on hatching success, brood size, and so on, but the above will suffice.)

The **young** follow the mother from the nest, generally a few hrs. after hatching. See Southwick (1953a) for some details of growth of captives. **Age at first flight** of captives 38–52 days (Hochbaum 1944), 7 weeks (Southwick), 5 ♂ av. 45.8 days and 5 ♀ av. 40.8 (Oring 1964). Periods of inactivity are much shorter in continuous daylight of northerly part of breeding range and, according to Irving (1960), young may attain flight 4 or 5 days sooner there. Presumably, at least with early-hatched broods, young and mother do not part company until about the time the latter can fly. J. Munro (1944) suggested that some brood members may remain together during at least part of autumn migration.

From R. I. Smith (1968): young ♂ ♂ from age 7 to 16 weeks have vocalizing slightly modified from calls when they were downies. The *peep* of the duckling becomes *whee* or *kwee* (singly and in series). At 18–20 weeks the whistle develops (in addition to the *whee*) and this coincides with beginning of sexual behavior oriented toward ♀ ♀. Young ♀ ♀ at age 7 weeks are "capable of sounds that have the tonal quality of adult calls." The *peep* becomes *kuk* (singly or in series; corresponds to *whee* of ♂). in addition, ♀ ♀ utter a rapid sequence of highly pitched *ke ke ke ke ke* notes—a squeal, not heard from sexually mature ♀♀. Smith also described and illustrated postures associated with these calls.

There is a tendency for Pintails to return in another year to the area where they hatched (Brakhage 1953, Sowls 1955). LKS

SURVIVAL   There seems to be no N. Am. data, but it is probable that Pintails that survive to attain flight have an av. life span of less than 3 years. Boyd (in Le Cren and Holdgate 1962) recalculated some older Russian data: estimated mean adult annual survival rate 0.52 ± 0.01. RSP

HABITS   Quite wary. The Pintail has considerably narrower environmental preferences than the Mallard, with which it commonly associates. It also readily associates with other dabblers, especially the Baldpate and Blue-winged Teal. There is a surplus of drake Pintails; Evenden (1952), for example, found a ratio of 136♂ :100♀ for Oct.– May, in Ore. and Cal. primarily.

Pintails prefer to feed in very shallow water, at the surface or by up-ending, and they rarely submerge entirely. In agricultural areas, during migrations, there are morning and evening flights (often with Mallards) to grain fields to feed. Generally speaking, they are more active at these times of day, but they also feed at night. They prefer to rest on fairly exposed places, at the water's edge on mud or sand and, when molting and flightless, become very secretive and hide in heavy stands of emergent aquatic vegetation.

Recorded flight speeds are 49 to about 52 mph; when pursued, about 65 mph.

In the late 1960s, judging from available censuses, the total number of wintering Pintails in N. Am. was of the order of 3½ to 4½ million birds.

For further information on habits, see especially J. C. Phillips (1923b). LKS

FOOD   Largely seeds of pondweeds, sedges, grasses, and smartweeds; also mollusks, crustaceans, and insects. Examination of the stomach contents of 790 Pintails collected in conterminous U.S., Alaska, and Canada showed 87.15% vegetable and 12.85% animal matter (Mabbott 1920).

Vegetable   Seeds of wigeon grass (*Ruppia maritima*), eelgrass (*Zostera marina*), and pondweeds (*Potamogeton, Zannichellia,* and *Najas*) 28%; sedges: bulrushes (*Scirpus*), saw grass (*Cladium effusum*), spike rush (*Eleocharis*), chufa (*Chufa*), beak rush (*Rhynchospora*), and the genera *Frimbrystilis* and *Carex* 21.8%; grasses: switch grass (*Panicum*), wild millet (*Echinochloa*), wild rice (*Zizania*), cut-grass (*Chaetochloa*), cultivated rice and other grains 9.6%; smartweeds (*Polygonum*) and docks (*Rumex*) 4.7%; arrow grass (*Triglochin maritima*) 4.5%; algae (*Chara*) 3.4%; arrowhead (*Sagittaria*) and water plantain 2.85%; miscellaneous plants 9.6% (Mabbott 1920).

The 61 stomachs from the lower Hudson River contained 34.8% of pondweed (*Najas minor*) and 61.8% of unidentified plant matter (Foley and Taber 1951). On the upper Chesapeake the important foods, based on percentage of occurrence, were the grasses, *Zea mays, Digiteria* spp., *Alopecurus* spp., *Panicum dichotomiflorum, Spartina* sp., German millet (*Setaria italica*), three-square bulrush (*Scirpus olneyi*), wigeon grass (*Ruppia maritima*), twig rush (*Cladium mariscoides*), and clasping-leaved pondweed (*Potamogeton perfoliatus*) (R. E. Stewart 1962).

The 881 gizzards examined by H. G. Anderson (1959) in Ill. showed 97% plant and 3% animal matter. In order of importance were wild millet (*Echinochloa* spp.) 20.71%, rice cut-grass (*Leersia oryzoides*) 16.36%, corn 15.70%, and sedges (*Cyperus* spp.) 14.54%. Millets and smartweeds formed 78.1% of the fall food of 148 specimens in Mo. (Korschgen 1955). The food in 126 stomachs from Reelfoot Lake contained 94.3% vegetable and 5.7% animal matter. In order of importance were *Najas guadalupensis* 11.15%, *Potamogeton* spp. 10.16%, Lemnaceae 9.84%, *Taxodium distichum* 7.74% (Rawls 1958). Pintails wintering on the Laguna Madre in Texas consumed a submergent spermatophyte, shoalgrass (*Diplanthera wrightii*), this being 88% by volume of diet (McMahan 1970).

In Alaska, stated to feed on the roots of *Equisetum* (Dall and Bannister 1867), the tender shoots of grasses and sedges (Turner 1886), and seeds of grasses (J. Grinnell 1900). The 4 birds collected during the flightless period in the Perry R. region, Canada contained seeds of *Potamogeton filiformis, Hippuris* sp., *Carex,* achenes scales and other parts of *Eriophorum* and *Ranunculus,* and an undetermined grass. The contents of one stomach consisted of 90% moss (H. C. Hanson et al. 1956). The contents of the proventriculus and gizzard from 122 flightless birds from Pel Lake, Sask., consisted of 57.1% by volume of vegetable and 42.9% animal matter. The vegetable matter comprised alkali bulrush (*Scirpus paludosus*) 32.4%, sago pondweed (*Potamogeton pectinatus*) 14.5%, and hardstem bulrush (*S. acutus*) 9.5% (Keith and Stanislawski 1960).

458

In w. Europe the food is chiefly *Cochleria, Potamogeton, Carex, Polygonium, Rumex, Fillularia, Glyceria* (in Witherby 1939), and occasionally oats (Naumann 1905b). A bird in Britain had eaten its fill of acorns (Newstead 1908).

A comprehensive treatment of the food in the Soviet Union, where it varies greatly in time and place, is given in Dementiev and Gladkov (1952). On the floodplain of the Mologa R. the birds on arrival feed on the green parts of plants only, *Lemna, Elodea,* and Gramineae. After the opening of spring in April, larvae of midges form the principal food. At the Rybinsk Reservoir the food was 60% animal: caddis-fly larvae (*Phryganea grandis*) 30%, and midge larvae (Chironomidae) 10%. Green parts of plants and coontail (*Ceratophyllum*) were important. Few seeds eaten. In the Volga Delta during the spring flight, the vegetable food consisted mainly of *Vallisneria*, along with *Potamogeton* and green algae 41.5%, and seeds of *Vallisneria, Potamogeton, Scirpus* and others 40.6%. The seeds of *Sparganium* and *Potamogeton* served as gravel. Some mollusks, including the snail *Theodoxus*, were taken when obtaining the rhizomes of *Vallisneria.* Cereal grains were gleaned from the fields.

Consumption of animal food at the Rybinsk Reservoir in May–June increases to 70.5%, larvae of midges forming 30% and mollusks 15%. In July–August mollusks, especially *Planorbis*, increase. The food of adults in the floodplain of the Mologa in summer is 70% animal—insects 40% and mollusks 30%. The animal food (80%) of the young consisted of mollusks 20%, larvae of Odonata 20% and midges 15%, and small crustaceans (Copepoda, Phyllopoda, and Ostracoda) 15%.

During the molting period in the Volga Delta animal food decreases to 1.7%. The chief foods are *Najas marina* with its seeds, and *Vallisneria*. On the Taiga and steppes of Siberia they feed on berries. On the Iamala in spring on the residual berries of *Empetrum nigrum*, and in summer on the fruits of *Vaccinium vitis-idaea* and *V. myrtillus*. When the Orthoptera develop *en masse*, these insects are captured both on the water and on dry land.

Animal food (68%) predominates during the fall flight at Rybinsk Reservoir and consists mainly of the larvae of midges and caddis flies. At the same time the food in the Volga Delta is 53.4% vegetable. The birds wintering on the northeast shore of the Caspian Sea consume mollusks and seaweeds. On the wintering grounds in the province of Azerbaijan the food consists of the seeds of *Ruppia, Scirpus* spp., *Polygonum* spp., and halophytic plants (74.5% by weight), and the green parts of plants (23.7%).

Animal Mollusks, mainly univalves (Gastropoda) 5.8%; crustaceans: crabs (*Hexapanopeus angustifrons*), crayfishes, and shrimps 3.8%; aquatic bugs and beetles, larvae of flies (Diptera), and larvae and nymphs of dragonflies (Anisoptera), caddis flies (Phryganoidea) and damselflies (Zygoptera) 2.9%; miscellaneous, including fishes and frogs 0.4% (Mabbott 1920). Stomachs of 15 Fla. specimens contained shells of a mollusk (*Truncatella subcylindrica*) (F. C. Baker 1889). At Fort Franklin, Mackenzie Dist., fed on the abundant small mollusk, *Lymnaea palustris* (Preble 1908). Due to the absence of suitable vegetation on the Pribilof Is., the food is almost entirely animal: larvae of midges (Chironomidae), caddis flies (Trichoptera), and blowflies (Calliphoridae) (Preble and McAtee 1923). In the upper Chesapeake region, Gastropoda (*Melampus bidentatus, Bittium varium*), Pelecypoda (*Volsella demissa, Pisidium atlan-*

ticum), Isopoda (*Cyathura* sp.), and nymphs of Libelluloidea; in Illinois, Gastropoda, Pelecypoda, Hemiptera, and Diptera: and at Pel Lake, Sask., mainly the egg cases of water fleas (*Daphnia* sp.). The stomach of a downy young in Alaska was packed with mosquito larvae (R. D. Hamilton 1950).

In a 5-year study in s. Alta., L. G. Sugden (1973) found that the food of young Pintails was predominantly surface invertebrates, later replaced by aquatic forms. In the preflight stage, they ate 67% animal food—gastropods 36%, insects 26%, and cladocerans 4%. The dominant insect order was Diptera 18%, chiefly chironomid larvae. Vegetable—seeds of Gramineae 19% and Cyperaceae 8%. As the birds grew, they did more bottom feeding (rather than subsurface feeding as by Baldpates and Gadwalls), mostly in water less than 12 in. deep. AWS

The following have not been summarized: Currituck Sd., N.C.—winter food of 19 birds (Quay and Crichter 1965); S.C.—fall food of 34 birds (McGilvrey 1966c); s. La.—winter food in crops of 65 individuals (Glasgow and Bardwell 1965). Very large numbers of Pintails are present in winter in s. La.; in the area where the last-mentioned study was made, grasses were far more important than sedges in the diet of this waterfowl. RSP

Garganey

Anas querquedula Linnaeus

Also called Garganey Teal. Size of Blue-winged and Cinnamon Teals and with equally striking sexual dimorphism. The smaller feathers of the wing (lesser and middle coverts) are gray or bluish gray, seldom a clear blue as in Blue-winged and Cinnamon Teals; speculum uniformly green with wide white border at leading and at trailing edges. Bill dark. Drake most of year (Alt. Plumage) has dark head with curved white area extending from above eye back along side of crown and nape; anterior end of body dark, the sides and venter light (belly white) and sharply defined from the breast; the elongated tapering scapulars are nearly black with white central stripe. In both sexes, the legs and feet are more or less slaty, not yellowish. Head–body of ♀ resemble those of ♀ Bluewing, except for slightly paler (hence more obvious) buffy brownish or paler (depending on Plumage) feather margins, and sides of head tend to be somewhat more distinctly patterned.

The drake's tracheal apparatus has been described and illustrated many times, from 1798 onward; the bulla is unlike that of related species. For concise description, see J. C. Phillips (1923b); probably the best illus., showing the bulla in 2 views, is in Schiøler (1925).

No subspecies. RSP

DISTRIBUTION **Straggler to our area.** ALASKA Adak. I.—May 29, 1970, ♂ seen in company of Common Eiders and White-winged Scoters (*Aud. Field Notes* **24** 634. 1970); and May 20, 1971, one seen (*Am. Birds* **25** 785. 1971)—the latter said to be the 3rd Aleutian sighting. CANADA Alta.—Two Hills, June 24–26, 1961, seen; Man.—near St. Ambroise, May 23, 1971, ♂ (photo *Am. Birds* **25** 759. 1971). CONTERMINOUS U.S. N.C.—near C. Hatteras lighthouse, March 25, 30, and 31, 1957, ♂ seen (*Aud. Field Notes* **11** 334. 1957). W. Indies Barbados—specimen, date not given by J. Bond (1965).

As with various waterfowl that are of infrequent occurrence in N. Am. outside captivity, there is the recurring question as to whether or not some reports (but certainly not from the Aleutians!) may possibly pertain to escaped individuals.

This species has straggled to the Commander Is. (Tougarinov 1941, Johansen 1961).

In the Hawaiian Is.: sighting on Hawaii in Feb. and March, 1961; Oahu on March 23, 1967 and March 3, 1968; and at Midway 2 collected on Sand I., Sept. 17, 1963 (references in Berger 1972).

It would appear that the Garganey, which breeds all across the Palearctic, from Iceland to Kamchatka, has a tendency to straggle considerable distances. Not many Palearctic Anatidae are regular migrants to Africa s. of the Sahara, but the Garganey is one of these, as discussed by Moreau (1967).

For occurrence as **fossil** in the Pleistocene, also from **archaeological sites,** see Brodkorb (1964a). RSP

OTHER TOPICS Because of the similarity of the ♀ to ♀ Blue-winged and Cinnamon Teals, there is rather little likelihood that ♀ ♀ will be identified afield in N. Am.

461

In many ways, the Garganey is the Palearctic counterpart of the Bluewing of the Nearctic. In habits, however, it is somewhat more like the Northern Shoveler (*Anas clypeata*). Tamaisier (1971) stated that, in the Camargue in s. France, the Garganey exploits the same feeding habitat as the Greenwing (*Anas crecca*), but that its times of abundance are before and after the big winter concentrations of teal, which reduces competition. The drake Garganey in spring is said to utter a "peculiar low crackling sound" (Witherby 1939). Plumage sequence is the same as in other *Anas* and, as in Northern Shoveler, Basic I is retained for a comparatively long time during 1st fall. Beer (1968) figured the tracheae of some interesting captive ♂ hybrids with *Anas strepera, A. cyanoptera,* and *Aythya fuligula.* There is an extensive literature on this species. Witherby (1939) still is very useful, aside from serious errors in "Description"; also Dementiev and Gladkov (1952). RSP

462

Blue-winged Teal

Anas discors Linnaeus

A small, rather trim, member of the genus *Anas;* large pale bluish patch on wing (the lesser and middle coverts); speculum green (but little or no green in ♀), this area bordered anteriorly with wide, and posteriorly with narrow, white margin. Definitive-feathered drake most of the year (Alt. Plumage): sides of head bluish to purplish slaty, a large white crescent on forward side of face (between bill and eye), feathers of upperparts sepia or dullish olive marked with buff or tan, sides and underparts typically some variant of pinkish cinnamon with many black spots. Other stages (♂ ♀) beyond the streaky Juv. Plumage: crown dark, often a whitish area at side base of bill; much of rest of head–neck streaked dark on whitish or buff with chin–throat plain; breast and sides some variant of pale buff to pale cinnamon with clear to indistinct dark subterminal and other feather markings; abdomen white or whitish, in some Plumages blotched or spotted dusky.

The Bluewing is not always separable from the Cinnamon Teal. In general, the bill of the Bluewing av. shorter (♂ about 42 mm., ♀ about 40) and does not appear to be swollen distally and there is very little, often no, reddish cast to the feathering.

The drake's tracheal bulla is much smaller than that of the Cinnamon Teal. It "faces to the left and front, is roughly spherical in shape, but more expanded toward the left, smooth and hard, and measures 15 mm. or less in its largest diameter" (J. C. Phillips 1923b).

Length 14–16¼ in., wingspread 22–25 (♂ av. larger within these spans); usual wt. about 12–14 oz. No subspecies.

DESCRIPTION   Two Plumages/cycle. The Juv. ♂ and ♀ have underparts heavily streaked. Then Basic I is the Plumage of early to late fall; it is variable (plain to blotchy venter, for example), early- and late-hatched birds differing. Both sexes molt into Alt. I in late fall to early winter (some ♂ ♂ acquire it rapidly in Jan.); then the ♂ retains Alt. I (head–body–tail) into summer, but the ♀ molts into the head–body–tail portion of Basic II in spring. The early Plumages are superficially similar and, being somewhat variable, may be confused. It also must be noted that the timing of early molts, which tend to occur at fairly definite intervals posthatching, thus vary with individual because of variation in hatching dates. It appears that the energy demands of migrating in fall tend to reduce or halt molting, i.e., there is an interrupted Prebasic I molt, longer retention of Basic I Plumage (if acquired early), or interrupted Prealt. I molt. In the definitive cycle the drake wears Basic for a comparatively long time and generally has not acquired much of the succeeding Alt. until about Oct. and it may not be fully developed until Dec. or even later. In both sexes, the last Def. Alt. feathers to grow are the long scapulars. Castrated ♂ ♂ regenerate Alt. feathering; ovariectomized ♀ ♀ tend to acquire ♂ Alt. feather characteristics (Greij 1973).

▶   ♂ Def. Alt. Plumage (all feathering, excepting all innermost feathers of wing), largely acquired well along in FALL, the long scapulars not fully grown until Dec. or even Jan.; this Plumage is retained through WINTER into JUNE, when the Prebasic molt (first on head–body) begins. Traces of the white facial crescent often remain visible until the molt into Basic is advanced and it reappears gradually during the molt back into Alt.

Bill deep slaty (nearly black), **iris** very dark brown; **head** crown, forehead, chin, and feathers bordering white facial crescent black; the white crescent between bill and eye sometimes has an extension, a white line, along side of crown (also see note below) and sometimes there is more or less white across chin; remainder of head and neck bluish slaty with violet-magenta sheen; **upperparts** mantle feathers toward sepia or grayed olive with sharply defined internal irregular (includes many U-shaped) markings that are pale pinkish cinnamon or sometimes nearly white; the long scapulars are narrow, taper to a point, and are black with greenish sheen but also have a median tapering pinkish buff stripe; the outer web of some outer scapulars is a variant of pale bluish; lower back and much of rump largely fuscous. **Underparts** breast and most of belly usually some variant of pinkish cinnamon or tawny buff with many conspicuous round black spots or (less commonly) transverse barring; abdomen, sides, and flanks more toward brownish red, the pattern changing (on some individuals) from spots to narrow transverse bars on abdomen and (on most individuals) to wide and conspicuous bars on flanks; posteriorly, on side base of rump, a more or less triangular white patch; vent to tail black; **tail** feathers olive brownish or darker with narrow pale edging; legs and **feet** yellowish or muted orange, webs dusky.

Wing innermost secondaries sepia with greenish olive gloss, their outer webs velvety blackish with greenish sheen and shafts are whitish; innermost greater coverts comparatively broad, with rounded ends, and sepia tinged a muted greenish; their outer webs are more or less pale bluish toward tip. Remainder of wing is retained Basic feathering.

NOTES   Much of the underparts of the drake vary with individual from pinkish buff to a deep brownish red such as is typical of the drake Cinnamon Teal; the coloring of feather markings and margins on the dorsum reflect in a general way the depth of coloring of the underparts of the individual. Apparently independent of individual variation in general coloring, the black spotting on underparts varies from sparse to dense and the size of the spots also varies with the individual. Some drakes vary from spotted toward transverse barring and others are entirely barred from lower breast to vent, but the sides remain spotted.

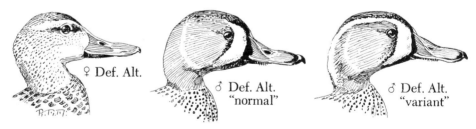

♀ Def. Alt.   ♂ Def. Alt. "normal"   ♂ Def. Alt. "variant"

Kennard (1919) described, as a subspecies, a variant of ♂ Def. Alt. Plumage in which the facial crescent not only continues as a white line along side of crown but also continues down the nape (where it joins with the one from the other side, there forming a white patch). Such individuals have been reported from La. westward into Ariz., also

464

occasionally farther northward. S. C. Arthur (1920) described a captive drake that had such characteristics in 2 Alt. Plumages, then had only the "normal" crescent in the next Alt.

▶ ♂ Def. Basic Plumage (entire feathering); the head–body–tail are acquired over a span which usually begins quite early in JUNE in breeders and extends well into JULY; in the latter month the old wing quills are dropped and the new Basic wing grows. The av. flightless period of 8 captive drakes was 21 days (Oring 1964). Flying drakes in full Basic are most common in the first half of Aug. (specimens seen are dated July 20–Aug. 28). In FALL the Basic head–body–tail and innermost feathers of wing begin to be succeeded by Def. Alt., with last traces of the old Basic sometimes remaining into Nov. After they are lost, the drake is back in Alt., except almost all of the Basic wing is retained until well into the following summer.

Rather ♀-like. Typically the belly and abdomen are white, more or less blotched dark, and the feathers on forward mantle have no internal markings. **Head** forehead and sides pale pinkish buff or almost white, streaked dark; a fairly distinct darkish stripe on side of head through eye; crown and upper nape blackish; chin and upper throat unmarked whitish; **upperparts** mantle olive brownish, the feathers broadly rounded, edged medium to buffy brownish or grayish, generally without internal markings (but sometimes a very few); scapulars rather short, with broadly rounded ends and broad deep buffy margins; lower back and rump mostly dark grayed olive. **Underparts** feathers of breast and sides buffy brownish, on latter with wide pale buffy edging; abdomen whitish, the feathers with subterminal dusky spots that show through overlapping feathers (indistinct blotching or even barring); under tail coverts whitish with large subterminal (and additional) dark areas; **tail** feathers fairly wide distally, then pointed, and dusky olive with pale edging.

Wing innermost secondaries greenish black on outer web, sometimes with very narrow pale edging, generally tan at very tip (which is rounded); the overlying greater coverts dark or same with blue on outer webs; most of the lesser and median coverts light turquoise-cobalt (bluish patch extends to leading edge of wing); greater upper coverts over speculum have white ends (forming a white bar), but sometimes have a few concealed dark spots on inner web; speculum vivid iridescent green, its trailing edge narrowly bordered white; primaries and their upper coverts olive-brownish to sepia; in the wing lining the coverts along leading edge are dark (sometimes with distinct bluish sheen), tipped and edged white, the remainder and the axillars white.

NOTE   Although molting into Def. Basic generally is not evident until some time in June, occasionally a drake shows traces of incoming Basic on head–body even as early as April.

▶ ♀ Def. Alt. Plumage (all feathering, excepting all but innermost feathers of wing), acquired in LATE SUMMER–FALL and retained until SPRING (usually April).

Comparatively grayish, with white belly; feathers of anterior dorsum vary with individual from plain darkish to dark with internal U- or V-shaped markings astride the shafts. **Bill** mostly bluish slaty, the edges of both mandibles toward yellowish flesh color; in fall the many blackish spots and patches (the latter may even coalesce) on upper mandible, which had faded or some even had disappeared earlier (beginning in spring), again become prominent and remain so through winter (C. W. Dane 1968).

465

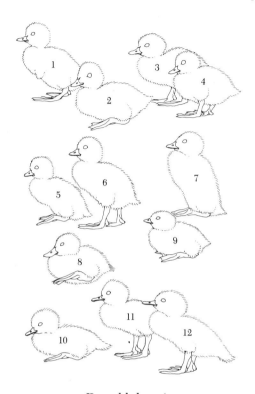

Day-old downies

1 Lesser Scaup *(Aythya affinis)*—from Strathmore, Alta.
2 Canvasback *(Aythya valisineria)*—from Minnedosa, Man.
3 Redhead *(Aythya americana)*—from Minnedosa, Man.
4 Ring-necked Duck *(Aythya collaris)*—from Guelph, Ont.
5 Bufflehead *(Bucephala albeola)*—from Strathmore, Alta.
6 Common Goldeneye *(Bucephala clangula americana)*—from Delta, Man.
7 White-winged Scoter *(Melanitta fusca deglandi)*—from Miquelon Lake, Alta.
8 Ruddy Duck *(Oxyura jamaicensis rubida)*—from Delta, Man. (For heads of Ruddies in various Plumages, in color, see vol. 3, plate facing p. 504.)
9 Oldsquaw *(Clangula hyemalis)*—from Churchill, Man. Note the breast-band, which is lacking in the downy Harlequin *(Histrionicus)*. (For definitive Plumages of the Oldsquaw, in color, see vol. 3, plate facing p. 248.)
10 Hooded Merganser *(Mergus cucullatus)*—from Vergennes, Vt.
11 Red-breasted Merganser *(Mergus s. serrator)*—from Lake Manitoba, Man. In some individuals the white stripe from below eye to bill is uninterrupted and there is little or no white above the eye.
12 Common Merganser *(Mergus merganser americanus)*—from Lake Manitoba, Man.

CHNelson

Iris dark gray-brown. **Head** forehead, crown, nape, and stripe through eye largely dusky, the feathers more or less edged buff (wider edging on crown than in ♂ Def. Basic); remainder of head and the neck some variant of whitish or pale buff, finely streaked dark except for unmarked chin–throat and, usually, a circular area at side base of bill also is white or nearly so. **Upperparts** mantle feathers brownish sepia or nearer neutral, with light buff or even whitish margins and narrow to no internal light markings; the long scapulars are distinctly rounded, brownish fuscous, and have sharply defined margins that are whitish or palish buff. **Underparts** the breast feathers are distally whitish with a broad darkish internal marking; belly the same or nearer white, occasionally with buffy pink cast (it fades); feathers of sides and flanks toward sepia with buffy to tan margins and broad dusky internal markings; vent to tail whitish and the exposed internal markings of the feathers tend toward oval shape. The ventral body down is pale. **Tail** feathers pointed, grayed or olive-brownish, edged nearly white. Legs and **feet** muted yellow, webs dusky. **Wing** innermost secondaries sepia, tinged olive-green, and narrowly edged creamy on outer web; the overlying greater coverts are blackish edged tan. Remainder of the wing is retained Basic, described below.

▶ ♀ Def. Basic Plumage (entire feathering), the head–body–tail acquired in SPRING (usually April), but sometimes the tail is acquired gradually or later. This is the Plumage worn during nesting. Afterward, the flight feathers of wing drop simultaneously. Then, while the new Basic quills grow (there is a flightless period of about 21 days), the bird also is molting out of Basic head–body–tail and innermost feathers of wing back into Alt. This process frequently continues well into FALL. Def. Basic thus is a spring–SUMMER Plumage, except most of the wing is retained nearly a year.

This Plumage generally has a palish buff cast, much of underparts are irregularly streaked dark, and feathers of dorsum have pale internal markings. **Bill** the dark spots and blotches on upper mandible fade as the Basic head–body feathering grows. **Head**–neck, compared with Def. Alt., more toward buff and the dark streaking on face is more broken. **Upperparts** feathers have broader and more buffy margins and their internal markings are separate on each web (do not meet at the shaft); the scapulars taper somewhat (but some are very broad and distally squarish) and generally have very narrow pale margins. **Underparts** belly blotched dark (not plain white) and becomes more blotchy with wear (the internal dark markings of the feathers generally are bilobed in shape); an unmarked white or whitish area at side base of rump is most evident in the ♀ in this Plumage; under tail coverts have more streaky pattern than in Alt.; the ventral body down is dark tipped. **Tail** feathers have broader ends than in Alt. and broader light edging plus wide irregular internal whitish barring.

Wing much like ♂ Basic in general pattern, but distal greater coverts (which are white in ♂) are broadly barred dark and narrowly barred white; innermost secondaries have both vanes about the same dark brownish; they are widely margined nearly white, and they taper but their very ends are rounded; their overlying greater coverts are evenly dark or have some whitish edging. The outer webs of most secondries are sepia tinged greenish, seldom iridescent (speculum more muted in coloring than ♂); the greater coverts over the secondaries have rounded edges, the very tips white, and each feather has an internal V-shaped whitish mark (bottom of V at the shaft and pointed toward distal end of feather); the large pale patch extending to forward edge of

467

wing (middle and lesser coverts) is not as clear bluish as in ♂, often having a slaty tinge; wing lining and axillars as ♂, except not as dark areas in feathers along leading edge of wing.

AT HATCHING   Eye stripe usually complete; cheeks usually plain; vivid yellows on light areas; legs and feet orange-yellow and browns. Bill not slightly spatulate, as it is in downy Cinnamon Teal.

▶   ♂ Juv. Plumage (entire feathering), begins to show by age 2 weeks; scapulars, flank feathers, and rectrices are visible at 3 weeks; cheeks and secondaries at 4 weeks; at 5 weeks some young still are predominantly downy, while others appear to be completely feathered; these data from known-age captives (Southwick 1953a). The last of the down vanishes from head and rump at age about 6 weeks (Bennett 1938). In conterminous U.S., most young are flying by mid-Aug.

The Juv. is the only drake Plumage having the venter entirely streaked. Light parts of **head**–neck are more or less toward buff (not gray); sides of the head and foreneck finely streaked (compare with Basic I). **Upperparts** the feathers fuscous, edged buffy tan, almost always without internal light markings; the longer scapulars taper somewhat, have rounded ends, and are dusky edged brownish buff; **underparts** breast streaked moderately dark on buffy brown, abdomen mottled and streaked dusky on whitish; **tail** feathers narrow, with notched ends (where the down broke off); **wing** innermost secondaries sepia edged buffy tan, their overlying coverts narrow, rather pointed, usually with light brown edging that extends around the ends of the feathers; the greater coverts over the speculum have exposed portions of the feathers white, generally with a dark area distally in each web and these are confluent; speculum greenish, but not vivid nor with much sheen; the bluish of median and lesser coverts is tinged slate gray; wing lining and axillars as ♀ Def. Basic except more (and generally darker) gray in primary coverts.

▶   ♀ Juv. Plumage (entire feathering), timing as ♂. In general, like ♂ Juv. but av. differences include: **upperparts** scapulars duskier and with less contrasting edges; **underparts** tend to be more narrowly streaked; **wing** more dusky, the innermost secondaries have outer web nearer olive than dark green and their overlying coverts are sepia edged tan. Wing compared to ♀ Basic wing: secondaries and all upper coverts small, narrow, somewhat pointed; greater secondary coverts over speculum have their very tips white and, well back from the end, a whitish line or narrow mark that is nearly transverse or, when it extends across both webs, may be angled only slightly (or occasionally acutely?) with apex at shaft and pointed toward distal end of feather; see text and illus. of C. W. Dane (1968).

NOTES   Few specimens of ♀ Juv. have been examined, but it is obvious that the rather buffy Juv. head–neck molts very soon into gray Basic I.

The ♀ Juv. generally shows a much more distinct light area at side base of bill than does the ♂ Juv.

It is quite common for flying birds in about mid-Sept. to have the entire venter still in Juv. feathering after the head–neck and dorsum are entirely in Basic I.

▶   ♂ Basic I Plumage (all feathering, excepting all but innermost feathers of wing), generally acquired in LATE AUG. or EARLY SEPT. and retained until late FALL or even into early winter.

This is the gray-headed, typically white-bellied, Plumage of young drakes in fall.

Sides of **head** and sides and front of neck white or very pale gray with fine broken markings; throat white; **upperparts** dark feathers have very pale (even whitish) margins and are plain internally or have a single light marking; **underparts** the feathers on sides of breast have very broad internal dark zones, the largest being an inverted U (usually it is lyre-shaped in Def. Basic); much of belly and abdomen white, or same indistinctly blotched or marked dark; the feathers on sides and flanks have a clear-cut pattern of fuscous with pale tan or whitish edging and internal markings; the new **tail** feathers are decidedly broader than in Juv. and are evenly dark with brownish buff lateral margins. **Wing** innermost secondaries quite broad distally, but slightly pointed at their very ends, the outer web and the end margined pale brownish buff or even white. The remainder of the wing is retained Juv. feathering.

▶ ♂ Alt. I Plumage (all feathering, excepting all but innermost feathers of wing), generally acquired beginning in LATE FALL or most of it even not until early winter (Jan.) and retained into SUMMER. There may be some slight av. differences in feather shapes and coloring from later Alts. Best examples of Alt. I are spring birds, after scapulars and tail are fully grown. Some individuals, in April, have more dullish (bluish slate) heads than seen in later Alts. Several examined have comparatively palish underparts with fine dark transverse markings; others vary as to paleness or darkness of ventral ground color and size and amount of spotting. Most of the Juv. wing still is retained and worn with this Plumage.

NOTE A few individuals evidently acquire much Alt. I quite early in fall, but generally it appears that the molting is slowed or halted during migration (or entirely postponed until afterwards?); then rapid growth of Alt. I occurs in early winter.

▶ ♀ Basic I Plumage (inclusive feathering as ♂ Basic I); as in the drake, typically a FALL Plumage. General characteristics: white area at side base of bill, if obvious, appears more sharply defined than in Juv.; **underparts** whitish, lightly to heavily blotched (not streaked) dark; **dorsal feathering** has a clean-cut, scalloped appearance—dark rounded feathers with contrasting brownish buff or paler margins. The feathers of anterior dorsum usually are plain internally, but some have a brownish chevron mark. The flank feathers are much like those of ♀ Def. Basic, but typically are decidedly narrower. The new **tail** feathers are plain darkish with narrow whitish lateral margins. There is considerable individual variation, especially in size of dusky ventral markings; some appear openly and coarsely marked and others vary to densely and finely marked. Most of the Juv. wing is retained.

▶ ♀ Alt. 1 Plumage (inclusive feathering as ♂ Alt. I) acquired, depending on individual, beginning some time well along in SEPT. or even as late as in DEC. and retained until SPRING. **Head** dark markings are fine and sharply delineated, chin white; **upperparts** feathers on anterior dorsum generally with a pale brownish internal marking; **underparts** typically are silvery white (subterminal dusky feather markings concealed), flank feathers have very broad internal dark zones. Most of the Juv. wing is retained.

NOTES As in the drake, acquisition of either Basic I or Alt. I may be interrupted or halted during fall migration.

Occasionally a ♀ in Alt. I still retains some or all of the Juv. tail feathers, others have the Basic I tail, and still others have the very pointed dark Alt. I tail feathers.

At age about 6 mo., scattered small black spots appear on the upper mandible and are prominent until late spring when they become obscure or disappear; see C. W. Dane (1968) for further details.

▶ ♀ Basic II Plumage (entire feathering), the head-body-tail are acquired in SPRING, well before age 1 year (and well before the nesting season). This feathering resembles later Basics. Then, after nesting, the wing (most of it Juv.) is succeeded by the Basic II wing, and most of this is retained nearly a year. The remainder of Basic II is molted in FALL.

Measurements 18 ♂ (17 from conterminous U.S., 1 Alta.): BILL 39–45mm., av. 42.3; WING 179–198, av. 189; TAIL 62–73, av. 67.5; TARSUS 31–34, av. 33; 16 ♀ (13 conterminous U.S., 2 Alta., 1 Sask.): BILL 38–45 mm., av. 40; WING 173–188, av. 180; TAIL 60–67, av. 63; TARSUS 31–34, av. 33 (ETS).

"Adults" 48 ♂ (conterminous U.S., Mexico, W. Indies): BILL 38.2–44.4 mm., av. 40.9; WING (across chord) 177–196, av. 185; TAIL 59.2–69.1, av. 64.7; TARSUS 29.6–38.7, av. 31.7; 28 ♀ (Canada, conterminous U.S., Mexico): BILL 36.7–40.9 mm., av. 38.7; WING (across chord) 168–187, av. 177; TAIL 59.1–66.2, av. 62.8; TARSUS 28.1–33.3, av. 30.7 (H. Friedmann).

Also see R. E. Stewart and Aldrich (1956), the WING meas. across chord, and undoubtedly including some of the birds meas. by Friedmann.

As in waterfowl generally, the Basic wing measures longer than the Juv. wing. This is indicated in the measurement, taken on underside of wing, of entire length of 10th primary "flattened and straightened," from its juncture with bone. Basic WING 20 ♂ 134–140 mm., av. 138.9, variance 8.71, and 7 ♀ 125–135 mm., av. 130.9, variance 13.37; Juv. WING 20 ♂ 131–140 mm., av. 135, variance 7.71, and 20 ♀ 121.5–134, av. 127.9, variance 8.98 (C. W. Dane 1968).

Weight of fall birds, not separated by age-class 105 ♂ av. 0.9 lb. (409 gm.), max. 1.3 (590 gm.); 101 ♀ av. 0.8 lb. (363 gm.), max. 1.2 (545 gm.) (A. L. Nelson and Martin 1953).

Fall birds in Ill.: 4 ♂ "juvenile" av. 1.13 lb. (513 gm.); 5 ♀ "adult" 0.95 lb. (431 gm.) and 13 ♀ "juvenile" also 0.95 lb. (Bellrose and Hawkins 1947).

From Bennett (1938): wt. of "adults" ♂ 7 in winter 300–400 gm., av. 370; 6 in fall 290–415, av. 353; 7 in spring 300–400, av. 359; and 5 in summer 325–370, av. 353; ♀ 6 in winter 325–360 gm., av. 346; 6 in fall 280–360, av. 315; 6 in spring 300–380, av. 356; and 4 in summer 290–340, av. 314; "juveniles" July–Aug. in Iowa 7 ♂ 271.5–365 gm., av. 309; and 6 ♀ 187.5–326, av. 266.

For correlation of wt. cycle with times of molting of captive Bluewings, see R. B. Owen (1970).

On day of hatching, 73 ducklings weighed 10.5–20.4 gm., mean and standard error 15.7 ± 0.14 and standard deviation 1.16 (Smart 1965a). See table in Southwick (1953a) for wt. of captive ducklings at intervals from age 1 day to 6 weeks.

Hybrids seen or taken in the wild (all drakes): × Cinnamon Teal (*A. cyanoptera*)—1 seen near Regina, Sask., in April–May 1970; 1 collected and 2 seen in Cal., 1 collected in Utah, and an old record on authority of Suchetet (for references, see S. W. Harris and Wheeler 1965), mention of a specimen in the M. Hardy collection (Deane 1905), and in S. Am. 1 collected in Colombia (Lehmann V 1957); × Shoveler (*A. clypeata*)—1 seen at Huntington, B.C.; 2 taken in Cal. plus another Shoveler cross with either *A.*

discors or *cyanoptera* (references in F. A. Hall and Harris 1968), 1 taken in Ill., also an apparent hybrid seen in cent. N.Y. (Parkes 1958). Crosses of Bluewing with Cinnamon Teal and with Shoveler, reared in captivity, are fertile. See Gray (1958) for a listing of 4 additional *Anas* species with which the Bluewing has crossed in captivity.

Geographical variation apparently little, if any; there is, however, considerable individual variation in size and overall darkness or lightness of coloring.

Those Bluewings whose apparent center of breeding abundance is the brackish marshes of the Delaware and Chesapeake Bay areas have been regarded as sufficiently distinct in color (darkness) to warrant naming them as a subspecies (R. E. Stewart and Aldrich 1956). "Examinations of large series by several ornithologists do not support such a division, the alleged differences being individual" (Delacour 1964). RSP

FIELD IDENTIFICATION A small fast-flying waterfowl; usually in compact groups. A distinct swishing sound is heard when a flock passes close by. Bluewings often are seen perching on stumps, large tree limbs, or boulders in areas of shallow water. They are quite unwary.

In all flying ages there is a light patch on the wing, generally a clear light blue, which shows conspicuously in flying birds. In strong light it may appear whitish. However, when Bluewings are swimming, walking, or resting ashore or on the water, neither the blue area nor the green speculum is visible. Both may be flashed momentarily if a bird stretches a wing. The drake has a white crescent, present only from mid-Dec. into the following summer, in front of the eye, on a purplish slaty head; the rest of the bird generally appears rather dark, with buffy or brownish cast, and with a white patch on lower side of rump.

The ♀, young birds, and ♂ in Basic in late summer, are small, somewhat patterned, brownish to grayish birds (and so also are Cinnamon Teal in corresponding Plumages). The neck and head are more slender than in the Greenwing, the bill is decidedly longer, and Bluewings appear more elongated overall when swimming or flying. Mature ♀ ♀, especially, may show a circular pale (to white) area at side base of bill (some other species have it also) and, in spring and early summer, a very pale area (where the drake has white) at lower side of rump.

Other comparisons: the breast and belly of flying Bluewings appear brownish, but are conspicuously white in the Greenwing. The latter generally are in larger flocks and tend to maneuver more, swinging high and then low over flats or marshes. The drake Cinnamon Teal is a dark bird, without facial crescent, but this species has the same general wing pattern as the Bluewing. The drake Cinnamon in Basic, young of both sexes, and ♀ ♀ of all ages, are difficult or even impossible to distinguish afield from Bluewings in comparable feathering. The Shoveler also has a blue-winged pattern, but the large spoon-shaped bill, patterned body, and larger size readily distinguish it from the small teals. FCB

VOICE At times silent, but flocks in spring can be decidedly noisy. Various calls as related to displays are given beyond under "Reproduction."

The drake's usual call, although homologous with the Burp call of the Mallard and various other *Anas*, is a rather thin, high-pitched, almost whistled note, variously ren-

471

dered *tseef, tseel,* and *peew.* In some individuals it is lower pitched, with a nasal quality. The drake's Decrescendo call consists of this note followed by a series of more
abbreviated and quieter ones. It is modified to a lisping *peep* or mouselike squeaks
when drakes in a flock are busily feeding. The drake has been heard to call *wik wik wik*
(A. A. Saunders), apparently the same call described by Murray (1931) as an *ugh ugh
ugh* just like the grunt of a small pig.

   The duck has a quacking call, varying with circumstances from faint to high pitched
and coarse. Most of her calls seem to be such variants, rather than anything very different. McKinney (1970) described a number of these variants. In a feeding flock the
quack is modified to a kind of low chittering with occasional definite quacks interspersed. A duck, while brooding her young in the nest, uttered a faint nasal *kunk kunk
kunk* ("attraction notes") and gave them more loudly and rapidly when the family departed (Collias and Collias 1956). Her call when warning her brood may be rendered
wahu wahu (total of 8 to 10 notes), the 2nd note of pairs being lower than the first (A. A.
Saunders). RSP

HABITAT   In **summer** the Bluewing is a bird of marshes, sloughs, and ponds on
rolling prairies. It is more of a shoreline inhabitant than one of open water. It nests in
fairly tall coarse grasses away from water and much of this habitat has been lost to agriculture and drainage. For summer ecology in Sask., see Dirschl (1969). Hayfields are
not the most satisfactory habitat, because of nest losses from mowing; see discussion by
Gates (1965). The Bluewing has fair nesting success on lightly grazed habitat, but not
where it is heavily grazed; see Burgess et al. (1965) for nesting success vs. land use
practices in Iowa.

   This teal is locally common in various Atlantic coastal brackish marshes, nesting
where *Spartina* and mixed *Spartina–Distichlis* stands occur. It is less common and
more local in various marshes in the interior and near the coast where there is plant life
of about the same density and height as *Spartina.*

   As a **migrant** the Bluewing is found on all sorts of shallows in fresh-, brackish-, and
saltwater areas. Some make long flights over the ocean. In **winter** it is a bird of both
shallow interior and tidewater localities. RSP

DISTRIBUTION   (see map.) Unlike some of our waterfowl, usual breeding and
winter ranges of the Bluewing have little overlap. Apparently some recent breeding
records indicate a return to areas where this teal quite probably was plentiful until
about the 1870s. It is a characteristic of the Bluewing for individuals and small groups to
make long flights, so that in all seasons there are scattered occurrences beyond usual
range.

   Breeding   Northern limits include interior Alaska (Tetlin, Minto Lakes, College,
Yukon flats) as reported by Kessel and Springer (1966), n. Mackenzie Dist. (cent. Cop-
permine R. area), near Hudson Bay in n. Man. (Churchill), s. James Bay area, s. Que.
(L. St. John), and sw. Nfld. (Doyles, Grand Codroy R.). This teal is extending its breed-
ing range, particularly in coastal areas, and increasing in numbers in Cal., Ore.,
Wash., and B.C.; in this general area it is most numerous as a breeder in cent. Wash.
(Wheeler 1965). On the Atlantic side, the Bluewing breeds at various places in s. Que.

472

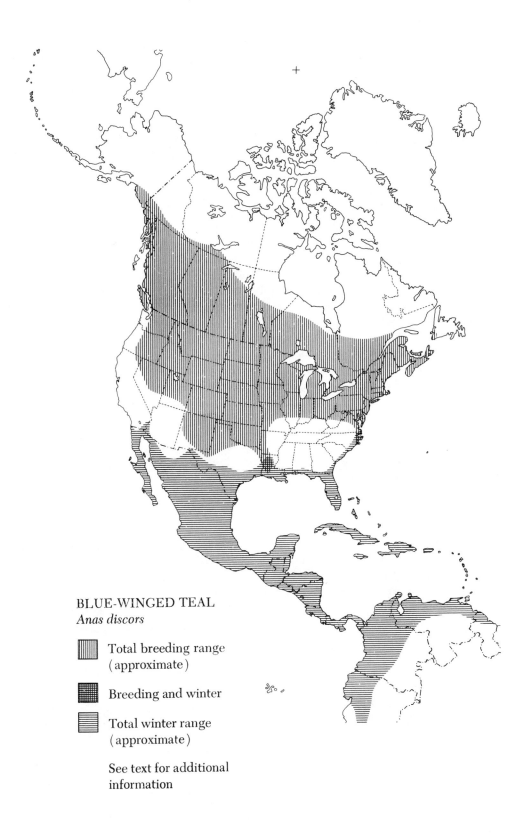

BLUE-WINGED TEAL
Anas discors

Total breeding range
(approximate)

Breeding and winter

Total winter range
(approximate)

See text for additional
information

and in the Maritimes and New England. Various records of local breeding down the Atlantic coast to ne. N.C. (Pea and Bodie Is.) were summarized by Bull (1964). It bred s. of the C. Hatteras area in N.C. in 1969, at W. Onslow Beach, also inland at N. Wilksboro. In 1968 a flock summered at Lakeland, Fla., and a pair had 5 young. A few breed in the Gulf Coast marshes of La. and evidently a variable (sometimes considerably larger) number to the westward in e. Texas. Inland, this teal breeds, or has bred, at scattered quite southerly localities, the farthest se. being Grundy Co. and Mt. Pleasant in Tenn.

Northernmost limits of wintering apparently are in s. Cal., s. Ill., Ohio (Buckeye L.), and N.Y. (Long I.) or possibly Mass.

Peripheral records, not for breeding and mostly not sorted by season, include: Alaska (Norton Sd. region), Mackenzie Dist. (Ft. Simpson, Ft. Norman), e. on the N. Shore of Gulf of St. Lawrence to Augustin, a 1937 record for s. Labrador (Battle Harbor), e. Nfld. (Conception Bay), and sw. Greenland (Godthaab, Frederikshaab, Julianehaab). In Bermuda, regular in fall and there are winter and spring records. Recorded in the Bahamas (New Providence, Grand Bahama). Specimen record for the Dry Tortugas. In the Greater and Lesser Antilles it occurs as a migrant and winterer and has lingered into summer (unconfirmed reports of nesting in Cuba). On the Pacific side, the species was said to have been seen in the Aleutians at Atka I. in July, 1879; an adult ♀, banded in La., was taken on Adak I. on Oct. 15, 1968. In Hawaii, records for Maui, Oahu, and Kauai. The Bluewing has occurred at Clipperton I. off sw. Mexico. In the Galapagos (off Ecuador) most of the various records are within the span Dec.–April.

The Bluewing winters in large numbers in n. S. Am.; **southernmost records** on the Atlantic side are 3 from Argentina and 1 from coastal Uruguay near the Brazilian boundary, and on the Pacific side it is common in n. and cent. Peru and there is a single record for Chile.

In **Britain** and **Europe** it is impossible to distinguish between presumed natural occurrences and those of escaped captives. The older records, which are few, may be acceptable, but this teal now breeds in numbers in various waterfowl collections and the number of reports of birds seen in the wild has increased since about 1960. A young bird banded at Sackville, N.B., on June 7, 1971, was shot on Oct. 9 of that year in Suffolk, England. By 1972 there were over 2 dozen records for the Brit. Isles, plus others for Denmark, Holland, Belgium, France, and Italy.

Recorded as **fossil** from the Pleistocene of Nev., Texas (several localities), Va., and Fla. (6 localities), and from **archaeological sites** in Iowa, Ill. (5 localities), and Ohio; see Brodkorb (1964a) for references. RSP

MIGRATION   The Bluewing goes south early, in late summer–early fall, and arrives back on breeding areas comparatively late. The birds travel farther than any of our other shoal-water ducks. The general direction of flight of the majority is from the prairies of Canada and n. conterminous U.S. to Gulf Coast areas from Mexico and Texas around to w. Fla., with heavy concentration in coastal marshes of La. Formerly, very few remained during winter in La. marshes, but a 1957 hurricane altered the environment drastically so that various duck foods became abundant; then large numbers of Bluewings began, and have continued through the 1960s, to winter in that area.

Most, however, go to Cent. Am. and, especially, to Colombia and Venezuela in n. S. Am. It seems likely that birds from more westerly prairie localities are the ones that winter on the sw. coast of Mexico, in Guerrero and adjoining areas, i.e., they fly southward (rather than southeastward) in fall. A large percentage of breeders on the e. prairies and from the Great Lakes and upper St. Lawrence region move toward the Atlantic coast, reaching it in numbers at points from New Eng. southward; then there is movement down the coastal area to peninsular Fla. and to Caribbean localities and S. Am.

Unlike various other prairie-nesting waterfowl, evidently very few Bluewings go from the interior to Pacific coastal states. The increasing number nesting in B.C., Wash., Ore., and ne. Cal. may account for most of the migrants in and through Cal.

Spring Bluewings begin moving in sw. Mexico in early Jan. and, in overland flights, probably travel quite leisurely at first. Evidently they also begin leaving other southerly areas about that time; in Fla. there is a return movement in late Jan. and relatively high numbers are present until late March. The last generally are gone from S. Am. and most of Cent. Am. by late April, but an occasional bird lingers into May or rarely June. Farther northward, the timetable for peak numbers is roughly as follows: s. third of conterminous U.S.—early March to mid-April; n. third—through April; and in Canada practically all breeders are established on breeding areas on the prairies by around mid-May. They arrive about the last third of May in n. B.C.

The usual social unit in fall is a flock of about 10–40 individuals and unit size appears to be similar in early spring. However, by the time the birds are traveling up through the U.S., many are paired and others are actively engaged in pair formation activities. As a result, there are numerous small groups or even single pairs migrating. They tend to be more scattered than in fall, with pairs stopping at puddles, roadside ditches, or any wet spot.

Summer Many, possibly the majority, of drakes pass the flightless period of molting not far from where their mates nested. But others move away, probably in any compass direction. There is considerable sex segregation as the season wears on, with some drakes molting in gatherings and then going to other places to feed after they have regained flight. The ♀ ♀ (which regain flight later) and the young (after they can fly) move about, some going to places where drakes had preceded them.

Stoudt (in Aldrich 1949) noted that apparently there are segments of the population that have their particular movements; he mentioned one that moved to near Chicago, then some of the birds went northwestward and others northeastward several hundred mi. prior to going southward. Among 3,789 recoveries of birds banded prior to the hunting season in the prairie pothole region, 183 were recovered in the subsequent hunting season due e. in Ont., Que., New Eng., and the Maritimes (B. Sharp 1972).

Fall The flocks come together at staging areas, where they fly about early and late in the day and feed during the middle hours. They form in definite groups that in early morning and in evening engage in various intricate flying and swimming activities and this probably results in more cohesive behavior within a group. Then, in evening, flock after flock departs on migration. For many details of premigratory activity, see R.B. Owen (1968). It is believed that mature drakes are the first to migrate. Also, since many flocks of young migrate unaccompanied by adults, these birds have an innate means of determining direction (Bellrose 1958).

475

Generally there is a heavy flight through Mont., the Dakotas, and Minn. about Sept. 1 and many already are in La. by this time. They begin arriving in Fla. in Aug. and Sept. and numbers continue to increase, the majority of the flocks gathering in assemblies of several thousand individuals; then numbers dwindle in Dec. Bluewings begin arriving in Cuba in early Sept. and in sw. Mexico, Cent. Am., and n. S. Am. by mid-Sept. and others continue arriving at these southerly areas until at least into Nov.

NOTES   Vaught (1964) transferred 377 preflight young from Minn. to Mo., where they were released; 7 were recovered at localities to the north in the year of release.

In the Strait of Yucatan on Nov. 27, 1940, a dozen Bluewings were seen flying due east toward Cuba, not, as one might have expected, in the opposite direction (Wetmore1944).

A banded first-fall bird, released in cent. Ill. in P.M. of Nov. 10 was killed 2 days later in Fla.; 2 other young birds, released in P.M. of Nov. 22, were killed together on Nov. 24 in lower Mobile Bay, Ala. (Bellrose 1958). Traveling 3,000 airline mi. in 30 days is not unusual for Bluewings in their first fall. A young drake, banded in the Athabaska delta in n. Alta., traveled 3,800 mi. to Maracaibo, Venezuela, in exactly one month; another, banded Aug. 19 at Delta, Man., was shot 16 days later at Rio Hacha, Magdalena, Colombia (Glover, in Linduska 1964). A young bird banded Sept. 10, 1969, at Merrymeeting Bay, Me., was shot on Oct. 4 (24 days after banding) at Grande Anse, La Desirade, Guadeloupe, French W. Indies. For speed of travel of young birds for distances of 200–1,000 mi., see fig. 6 in Bellrose (1958).

The longest recorded flight, over 4,000 airline mi., was that of a mature drake, from Oak Lake, Man., to near Lima, Peru, reported by Stoudt (in Aldrich 1949).

From Surinam, in n. S. Am., where the Bluewing is an abundant winterer on lagoons near the coast, Haverschmidt (1970) listed 40 band recoveries from: Alta. 1, Sask. 1, Man. 12, Ont. 6, New Bruns. 1, and S.D. 4, Minn. 6, Iowa 1, Mo. 2, Ill. 2, Mich. 1, N.Y. 2, and Vt. 1. Most had been banded as immatures and were recovered after their first fall migration. RSP

BANDING STATUS   The total number banded through the year 1964 was 356,911 and the total number of recoveries through 1966 was 13,938; main places of banding were Sask., Man., Alta., Minn., N.D., and S.D. Very few have been banded on wintering areas. (Data from Bird Banding Laboratory.) Band-recovery data have not been used very extensively. RSP

REPRODUCTION   This topic was included in Bennett (1938), many later papers were listed by C. W. Dane (1966), and displays and vocalizing were discussed at length by McKinney (1970).

Both sexes **first breed** as yearlings.

Activity leading to **pair formation** occurs from early winter onward, on winter range, but many birds, perhaps mostly those that never have bred, begin displaying in late winter and this continues into spring. Small groups of drakes fly in close pursuit of a duck, crowding her, and each drake also tries to chase other drakes away. The general pattern of aerial activity is very like that of the Mallard, but aerial fighting between drakes is much more frequent in the Bluewing. Such pursuits, however, have largely

476

terminated by the time the birds arrive at nesting places. Contemporaneously with aerial activity, there are displays on the water and on shorelines and mudflats. In nw. Iowa, about 60% of early-arriving Bluewings (in March) already are paired. Pair bond form is **temporary monogamy**.

Displays of the duck INCITING is a very prominent activity, especially of unmated receptive individuals; it consists of head pumping plus chin lifting, while a series of quacking calls is uttered. Especially at evening, in the pairing season, the ♀ utters a series of LOUD REPEATED QUACKS, varying in duration and loudness. TURNING-THE-BACK-OF-THE-HEAD is less developed than in the drake; it is directed toward a particular ♂. LATERAL DABBLING has been observed; the feet are paddled rapidly, various feathers are erected, and the body is oriented broadside toward a particular ♂. SHAKE and BELLY-PREEN, as described below for the drake, have been recorded.

Displays of the drake His BURP call is a very distinctive, thin, whistled *peew*, or a more nasal sounding variant, very unlike the corresponding call of the Cinnamon Teal. CHIN-LIFTING is a response to Inciting by the ♀; also it is done mutually when mates come together after a period of separation, as when the duck joins the drake at his waiting site. LATERAL DABBLING ("mock feeding"), which corresponds to the Grunt-whistle of the Mallard, consists of ritualized dabbling movements, at the same time paddling the feet vigorously but remaining on station, broadside to the ♀; that is, he makes no forward progress on the water such as would occur during actual feeding (compare with Shoveler) and he may conclude with HEAD-DIP (corresponds to Head-up-tail-up of Mallard)—the whole forepart of the body submerged so that his posterior coloring (including that of legs) and pattern are prominently displayed. The feet move vigorously. This display may be given in series. TURNING-THE-BACK-OF-THE-HEAD, which often is linked to (precedes) the next-listed display, is a frequent response to Inciting by the ♀. PREEN-BEHIND-THE-WING varies so little from the usual comfort movement that it is barely distinguishable. SWIMMING-SHAKE is done with body broadside to the ♀; it is stiffly executed. BODY-SHAKE and BELLY-PREEN are done ashore, the ♂ broadside to the ♀ (who may be standing or swimming); the ♂ shakes his body, then bends forward and nibbles his ventral feathering or else passes his bill above his feet without touching his body. PREEN-DORSALLY is very like "normal" preening. The pair bond presumably is established as of the time the duck and drake remain together and the latter drives others away; it is maintained by mutual CHIN-LIFTING.

A JUMP FLIGHT is rare in the Bluewing (compare with Shoveler).

Copulation After a bout of mutual HEAD-PUMPING the drake treads and, at the same time, utters rhythmical wheezing noises or very quiet calls that are difficult to hear. On dismounting, the drake positions himself broadside to the ♀, raises his head fully upward, and with head and neck feathers erected, points his bill downward, raises his wing tips slightly, waggles his tail, paddles his feet, and gives 1 or more distinctive calls—either a single piercing whistled *peew* (or variant nasal low-pitched *pew*) or else his DECRESCENDO CALL (*peew* followed by series of shorter, quieter, low-pitched *pew* notes). The duck bathes. In 1 observation, after the drake called, he swam away while Turning-the-back-of-the-head toward the duck.

Either the birds arrive at a nesting locality already paired (which is usual) or, as soon thereafter as they are paired, they spend much time early and late in the day "prospecting"; in this search for a nest site (or reorientation to a former one) the drake flies close behind the duck and also may stay nearby on the ground while she continues her search there. This activity may terminate soon or it may continue for more than a week sometimes (Glover 1956).

The drake has a **waiting site,** such as a rock protuding above the water, a muskrat house, or a stretch of bare shoreline. Both duck and drake stay within a circumscribed area, which probably is more definite in size early in the season; it may contain several water areas and the drake prefers to wait at the one nearest the nest. If a flying pair of Bluewings approaches the waiting site, the owning drake attacks the intruding ♀ and is, in turn, attacked by her mate (Dzubin 1955). Apparently there is no other aerial defensive activity and other areas thereabouts are used for **communal feeding.** A pair or group may use one of these areas for a few days, then shift to another one. So long as the pair bond is maintained, and regardless of where the pair happens to be, the drake behaves aggressively if other Bluewings approach his mate closely. For details of fighting, see McKinney (1970).

The **nest site** typically is dry and where there is fairly lush plant growth, as in meadows, drier sedge habitat, and hayfields. This provides good cover quite early and, later, the vegetation often forms a canopy over the nest. Location varies from within a few yds. to several hundred yds. from nearest open water; see tabulation in Burgess et al. (1965); the closest recorded apparently are those reported by G. Townsend (1966): successful nests were 17 ± 10 ft. from water in the Saskatchewan R. delta. Depending on number of pairs present and amount of available cover, nests may be as near together as 10 yds. occasionally; a nest per 10–20 acres, however, is a good av. density; see Glover (1956) for details. As noted in small-pond habitat in Sask., pairs are not distributed evenly in what appears to the human eye to be equally suitable habitat; instead, there is a tendency toward grouping—a sort of communal distribution (Dzubin 1955). Thus the Bluewing retains elements of social behavior, as evidenced by communal feeding and clustered nesting, during the reproductive cycle.

The duck scratches a shallow nest bowl, or may make several, and then begins laying immediately at the chosen site or sometimes may delay even as long as a week. Some dry vegetation at the site is added to the bowl. Generally at least 4 eggs are present before any **nest down** is deposited. This down has a conspicuous white center and dark tips; intermingled breast feathers are dark subterminally and very light (lighter than Pintail) proximally; see illus. in Broley (1950). For dimensions of nests, see Glover (1956).

Eggs are laid 1/day, usually in the morning and, after there is down in the nest, the duck uses this to cover the eggs before she departs to join her mate. More down is added, probably until some time early in incubation.

First clutches usually contain 9–13 eggs, av. about 11; G. Townsend's (1966) figure of 9.8 ± 0.4 eggs in 32 first clutches in Saskatchewan R. delta is comparatively low. For many data on clutch size, see especially Bennett (1938), Boyer (1966), C. W. Dane (1966), Glover (1956), Sowls (1955), and G. Townsend (1966). Incubation begins after the last egg is deposited and the duck usually departs to preen and rest 3 times a day. **Incubation period** 23–24 days, which is longer than usually stated (C. W. Dane 1966).

The duck loses wt. at a rate of over 6 gm./day from the time of laying the 7th egg until the 5th day of incubation and thereafter the rate of loss declines (H. J. Harris 1970). (A loss, beginning some time during laying and continuing through incubation that av. about 1% of residual wt./day probably is usual in shoal-water ducks.)

One egg each from 20 clutches from widely scattered parts of breeding range: **size** length 46.58 ± 1.42 mm., breadth 33.46 ± 0.85, radii of curvature of ends 13.58 ± 0.79 and 10.32 ± 0.72; **shape** approximately subelliptical, elongation 1.38 ± 0.048, bicone −0.004, asymmetry +0.136 (FWP). Bent (1923) gave av. meas. of 93 eggs as 46.4 × 33.4 mm. In nw. Iowa, 142 eggs: length 38–51 mm., mean 47.1 ± 0.75, and breadth 30–37, mean 33.9 ± 0.37 (Glover 1956). The shell is smooth and with slight gloss, **color** creamy tan and with very little individual variation.

Yearlings and older cohorts nest within the same span of time; that is, the peak of laying of those first breeding is not later than that of older birds (C. W. Dane 1966). Going from n. to s., the **laying period** is as follows. Saskatchewan R. delta—some eggs in last week of April, but most in the period May 13–June 9, then a rapid decline (G. Townsend 1966). Delta, Man.—May 10–June 10 for first clutches, with peak in late May (C. W. Dane 1966). New Bruns.–N.S. border—early clutches are started around May 20 (Boyer 1966). Nw. Iowa—first egg April 27, set of 9 not much incubated as late as July 21, and laying peak the last week in May (Glover 1956). Chesapeake Bay area—5 eggs in a nest on April 25 and other clutches to June 16 (R. E. Stewart 1962). N.C. (Pea and Bodie Is.)—apparently nest, on av., about a week earlier than in nw. Iowa; peak of hatching June 1–15 (Parnell and Quay 1965).

Nest parasitism Bennett (1938) reported that the Ring-necked Pheasant (*Phasianus colchicus*) lays in a small percentage of Bluewing nests; W. J. Hamilton III (1953) found 2 eggs of the Brown-headed Cowbird (*Molothrus ater*) in a Bluewing nest near Delta, Man.

Drakes commonly maintain station near their mates until first clutches have been incubated 2 weeks or longer. Thus they are gone from their waiting sites in nw. Iowa about mid-June (Glover 1956). At least a considerable number of them then form in small aggregations and go elsewhere to molt. In early successful nestings the drake sometimes still is present at hatching and there are a few observations of a drake associating with a duck and brood but, as pointed out by Dzubin (1955), it is not known whether the 2 adults were mates earlier in that season.

If a duck loses her clutch she nests again, or even may make several renesting attempts, often within 50 yds. of her first-chosen site (Glover 1956). **Replacement clutches** are smaller the later they are initiated, as discussed in detail by C. W. Dane (1966). Probably few yearlings attempt to nest a second time.

There is considerable published information on **nesting success** (% of nests in which 1 or more eggs hatch), **hatching success** (number of eggs/clutch that hatch), and some information on number of young that survive to flying age. The various data are not entirely comparable and the influence of the observers on nest-losses is an unknown and probably variable factor. In most studies, the number of nests that fail (because of natural predation, also mowing, grazing, etc.) is high, the number of eggs/clutch that hatch in successful nests is high (as in most waterfowl), and the number of young reared in proportion to the total number of pairs that attempted to nest is low. These 1949 data

479

from nw. Iowa, from Glover (1956), are fairly typical: 21% of 140 pairs were successful nesters; mean brood size was 5.1 "juveniles"; total number reared was 189 young (an av. of only 1.35 young for each of the 140 pairs that attempted to nest) and there were 123 young present on Sept. 1. (See especially Burgess et al. 1965 for additional data for Iowa.)

The **ducklings** leave the nest on day of hatching or may remain overnight. The duck and her brood tend to remain on a water area near where the young were hatched. However, if it dries up, they move to some more permanent water nearby; this shifting about results in concentrations of broods on scattered deeper ponds. As the season advances and ♀ ♀ that have successfully bred depart to molt, preflight young of various ages join in bands of 20 to 30 or even more individuals, with or without an adult in attendance. See Bennett (1938) for some information on activities of Bluewings during this stage. Captive-reared young first flew when 38–49 days old (Hochbaum 1944), but **age at first flight** in the wild is probably about 42 days. After they are on the wing the young probably scatter, though it seems likely that broodmates are occasionally present in the same flock of fall migrants. RSP

SURVIVAL Bellrose and Chase (1950) analyzed the records of 307 individuals banded at various ages in Ill. and subsequently recovered. Their data indicated an annual mortality rate of about 53% (Farner, in Wolfson 1955). Based on data from various regions, estimated mean annual adult survival rate was calculated as 0.55 ± 0.4 (Boyd, in Le Cren and Holdgate 1962). DSF

HABITS The highly sociable Bluewing travels in compact bunches or flocks containing a score or two of individuals; these gather in huge assemblies at some places along main migration corridors and in parts of winter range. Especially in local flights, a flock changes direction frequently, wheeling about so that the blue on their wings alternately shows and disappears. They are not as fast fliers as Greenwings and the speed, especially of a lone bird, is deceptive and easily overestimated.

This teal associates readily with other birds—the N. Am. Black Duck, Pintail, Shoveler, Cinnamon Teal, Am. Coot, gallinules, etc. In the summer range of the Black Duck, single Bluewings and small groups seem to have a decided preference for the company of this much larger species. The wary Black serves as a lookout for its small relative in the same way that the Black, in turn, is served by Canada Geese as lookouts. When by themselves, small bunches of Bluewings in fall are markedly tame, quite like Ruddies, for example. It is fortunate that they migrate early, thus escaping considerable hunting pressure during the legal season, because a flock will return repeatedly to the same decoys until the last survivor has been shot. On winter range, sometimes the shoal waters where these teal have been congregating gradually shrink; then the surface seems to be covered with Bluewings and a single charge of shot can kill many of them. Often on shallow waters in winter a vast gathering of waterfowl is comprised almost entirely of Bluewings. They are scattered when feeding; if disturbed, they combine in smallish flocks and take wing.

In summer, flightless molting adults do not, unlike some other ducks, sneak ashore if disturbed; instead, they move to open water in compact groups (Oring 1964).

The Bluewing prefers to feed in very shallow water where there is floating and shallowly submerged vegetation plus abundant small aquatic animal life. The birds glean from the surface to a considerable extent. Sometimes they swim with heads immersed up to the eyes and they up-end to obtain food deeper down. They seldom dive. Betweentimes they rest or sun themselves on rocks, stumps, mudflats, and trunks or limbs of fallen trees on or even considerably above the water; sometimes they are lined up on a tree trunk, evenly spaced, with occasional Chin-lifting if one bird moves too close to another.

Bluewings were considered to be abundant in the northeasterly part of their range until about 1880, with a drastic decline afterward; there has been considerable recovery in this area, probably beginning some time in the 1950s. In the Mississippi drainage and elsewhere in the midcontinental portion of the conterminous U.S., much breeding habitat has been lost because of drainage and various agricultural practices. The vast majority nest in rolling prairie country, where there are numerous scattered ponds, in western Canada. This teal still is one of our more numerous shoal-water ducks. It would be difficult even to estimate the total population, however, because the birds can be confused with Cinnamon Teal and because there are no census figures for important segments of the widespread winter range.

For further information see J. C. Phillips (1923b) and especially Bennett's (1938) book on this species. RSP

FOOD Vegetable matter, comprising about 70%, consists mainly of seeds of grasses and sedges, and seeds, stems, and leaves of pondweeds. The bulk of the animal matter, about 30%, is comprised of mollusks and insects plus a few crustaceans (Mabbott 1920). These results are based on 319 stomachs collected in every month except Jan., in 29 states and 4 Canadian provinces.

Vegetable Grasses: panic grass (*Panicum*), foxtail (*Chaetochloa*), wild rice (*Zizania aquatica*), rice cut-grass (*Homalocenchrus oryzoides*), cultivated rice (*Oryza sativa*), and *Monanthochloe littoralis* 12.3%; sedges: chufa (*Cyperus*), spike rush (*Eleocharis*), *Fimbristylis*, bulrushes (*Scirpus*), saw grass (*Cladium effusum*), and *Carex* 18.8%; pondweeds: *Potamogeton*, wigeon grass (*Ruppia maritima*), naiads (*Najas flexilis* and *N. maritima*), and horned pondweed (*Zannichellia palustris*) 12.6%; smartweeds (*Polygonum*) 8.2%; algae: muskgrass (*Chara*) and duckweed (*Lemna*) 3%; waterlilies (Nymphaceae) 1.4%; and miscellaneous vegetable items 14.2% (Mabbott 1920).

The vegetable food in the 61 gullets and gizzards from the upper Chesapeake region consisted mainly of the seeds of *Scirpus validus*, *S. olneyi*, *Polygonum punctatum*, *P. arifolium*, *Echinochloa walteri*, *Cuscuta* sp., *Acnida cannabina*, and *Sparganium americanum* (R. E. Stewart 1962). The 129 gizzards from Ill. contained 83.63% plant and 16.37% animal matter. The 3 most important plant foods were *Cyperus* spp. 47.54%, *Echinochloa* spp. 6.36%, and *Ceratophyllum* spp. 9.73%, (H. G. Anderson 1959). Nineteen birds from Mo. had eaten 70% plant and 30% animal matter. The principal plants were *Polygonum* spp., *Echinochloa* spp., and *Setaria* spp. (Korschgen 1955).

Principal foods taken in Mexico in midwinter were *Chara, Scirpus*, and *Potamogeton* (Bennett 1938). Ducklings in Iowa in July–Aug. fed chiefly on *Scirpus, Potamogeton, Cyperus, Carex, Polygonum, Lemna*, and *Chara* (Bennett 1938).

Animal   Mollusks, principally snails (*Amnicola, Physa, Lymnea*, and *Planorbis*), bivalves (*Sphaerium* and *Pisidium*) 16.8%; insects, larvae of caddis flies (Phryganoidea), nymphs of damselflies (Zygoptera) and dragonflies (Anisoptera), larvae of flies (Diptera), beetles (Coleoptera), and bugs (Heteroptera and Homoptera) 10.4%; crustaceans (Amphipoda, Decapoda, and Ostracoda) 2%; miscellaneous, arachnids, hydrachnids, and fishes 0.3% (Mabbott 1920).

Twenty Fla. specimens contained shells of *Amnicola floridana* and *Truncatella subcylindrica* (F. C. Baker 1890). A crayfish (*Cambarus propinquus*) 1.5 in. long found in a stomach in Ohio (Trautman 1940). Gastropoda (*Littoridinops* sp.), Pelecypoda (*Volsella demissa*), Coleoptera, and larvae and pupae of Libelluloidea were consumed in the upper Chesapeake region. The animal food in Ill. consisted of Hemiptera (*Corixa*) and Chironomidae; in Mo., long-horned grasshoppers (Tettigonidae) 17%, Crustacea and Gastropoda 10.5%, and Corixidae and Coleoptera 2.6%. AWS

POSTSCRIPT   There are data in Keith (1961) for food of adults and young, late spring–early fall in se. Alta.; they are not easily summarized, since various waterfowl species are combined in some of the tables. Dirschl (1969) reported on summer foods of adults in the Saskatchewan R. delta; the teal were shoreline feeders and animal foods (Gastropoda, Hirudinea) reached a peak in consumption in July. Swanson and Bartonek (1970) examined the digestive tracts of 67 birds (adults and flying young) in spring–early fall in N.D. They found that soft foods (chironomids, snails, and the like) break down very rapidly in the esophagus and so are missed unless birds are collected when actually feeding and the digestive tract is put immediately in a preservative. There was about 3 times as much animal food in esophagi as in gizzards. This is an indication of the magnitude of the discrepancy between what ducks eat and what has been reported in the past from gizzard analyses. RSP

Cinnamon Teal

Anas cyanoptera

Rather diminutive duck; size and general proportions of Blue-winged Teal. Bill usually appears larger distally (or somewhat constricted basally), an incipient Shoveler condition. Upper wing coverts mostly blue; speculum green with buffy (not white) narrow trailing edge (which fades). The sexes differ markedly in eye coloring, a condition shared with the Shoveler group (but not occurring in the Bluewing). The drake in Alt. Plumage (most of the year) is largely some variant of deep brownish red (a dominant color also in drakes of the Shoveler group) which is mostly plain or, in n. S. Am., spotted dark (spotting is also a Bluewing characteristic). Unlike both the Bluewing and members of the Shoveler group, the drake has no white patch on side of rump. Other stages of both ♂ and ♀ tend to have a rather reddish overall cast (it fades), rather coarse dark markings, and general shade of side of head of ♀ quite often matches that of side of breast, but head is paler in many individuals. Individual variation in ♀ ♀, at least in N. Am., includes a gradient of light to darkish birds. The ♀ cannot always be distinguished from ♀ Bluewing; the same also may apply to certain predefinitive stages of drakes of the 2 species.

The drake's tracheal bulla is roughly ellipsoidal, 16–20 mm. in longest diam. and 13 mm. in minor axis; it faces to the left and surrounds the left bronchus; it is 2–3 times as large as in the Bluewing and rather differently shaped (J. C. Phillips 1923b).

The one subspecies in our area: bill of ♂ usually 44–47 mm., ♀ 42–44 (compare with Bluewing); length 15–17 in., wingspread 23–26 (♂ av. larger within these spans), wt. usually under 1 lb. There are 4 extralimital subspecies, in S. Am.; av. sizes vary from slightly smaller to considerably larger than in birds of our area.

DESCRIPTION *A. c. septentrionalium* of N. Am. Two Plumages/cycle in both sexes. No complete description of this teal ever has been published; information given here is somewhat sketchy, for lack of opportunity to assemble and examine adequate series of both sexes in all ages and seasons. There is much individual variation in various Plumages of both sexes. As in Bluewing and Northern Shoveler, Basic I is retained by both sexes for a relatively long time.

▶ ♂ Def. Alt. Plumage (all feathering except, in wing, only a few innermost feathers), acquired from LATE SUMMER into or through FALL (being fully developed when the long scapulars are grown), retained until EARLY SUMMER, and then succeeded by Def. Basic over a period of some weeks.

Bill black, the mandible sometimes pinkish proximally; **iris** vivid scarlet, at least in fall–spring (it has been described as golden yellow or orange without mention of season). **Head** nearly black from bill over crown and more or less on nape, also chin blackish; the remainder of head, the neck (except commonly some dark barring on hindneck), sides, and much of **underparts** commonly reddish brown (but individuals vary to palish); abdomen dusky brownish or black in about 85% of individuals (Snyder and Lumsden 1951), but some others have indistinct wavy dark crossbars; a few drakes are somewhat intermediate between Alt. and Basic, since they have scattered breast feathers and even a few on sides have a round black spot in the distal portion of each web; under tail coverts black. **Upperparts** forward portion of mantle more or less barred with some variant of sepia on a tawny base; the shorter scapulars are dark with cinnamon-rufous edging and markings; the long scapulars are nearly black with sharply defined median stripe that is cinnamon-rufous, paling distally; the 2 outermost long scapulars are largely the same blue as the upper wing coverts; upper tail coverts fus-

♀ Def. Alt.   ♂ Def. Alt.

cous edged tawny. The **tail** feathers are pointed, very dark, and margined pale buffy tan. Legs and **feet** muted yellow or somewhat toward orange, joints and webs dusky.

In the **wing** the very long innermost secondaries have outer webs black with sharply defined narrow tan edging, inner webs dark brown (paler at ends), and shafts very light; the overlying greater coverts are very dark, terminally and laterally suffused with bluish; remainder of wing is retained Basic feathering (described below).

In some individuals this Plumage is fully grown (long scapulars have attained full length and extend to within say 20 mm. of tips of folded wing) some time in Sept., but in others not until in Oct. or even Nov. These scapulars become much worn and frayed by spring.

▶ ♂ Def. Basic Plumage (entire feathering), head–body–tail are acquired beginning usually in EARLY JUNE, the old wing quills (Juv. or Basic, depending on age of bird) are dropped in July (then a flightless period, probably about 21 days) and, while the new Basic wing grows, or beginning not long afterward, the remainder of that Plumage is being succeeded by Alt. feathering from some time in JULY onward.

Most of the feathering that is brownish red in Alt. is some variant of pale cinnamon or tawny in Basic. **Head** the pale coloring is nearly plain on chin and upper throat, but streaked very dark on cheeks and neck; **underparts** on breast and sides and flanks the feathers have wide tan or tawny margins and fuscous to blackish internal zones (the alternating wide dark and narrow light zones of feathers of sides and flanks tend not to be sharply defined); there is much individual variation of belly and abdomen— commonly the feathers are white margined or ended and the internal dark markings vary from a round spot on each web, to these coalesced, to a single large dark subterminal area; under tail coverts pinkish buff with large internal dusky areas; **upperparts** the mantle feathers are between fuscous and sepia, broadly margined pinkish cinnamon; the scapulars are shorter than in Alt., with broadly rounded ends, and are very dark with tan margins and shaft stripes; tail feathers are broader distally (not as narrowly tapering to a point as in Alt.) and margined buffy tan.

484

In the **wing** the innermost secondaries have rounded ends and are plain, the outer web very dark and inner one appreciably paler; median and lesser coverts are palish turquoise-cobalt; the distal greater coverts are very dark with white ends that form a bar, which increases greatly in width outwardly along the anterior border of the speculum and beyond in ♂ (it does not widen in the ♀); speculum emerald with an almost hairline whitish trailing edge (it wears off); primaries olive-brownish; wing lining white with zone of fuscous along leading edge; axillars white.

NOTES   The abdomen generally is whitish buff at first, but becomes spotted or blotched dark if the feather ends wear off.

More or less of this Plumage has been found on specimens dating from May to Oct. inclusive (Snyder and Lumsden 1951) and additional specimens show that a few Basic feathers on sides and flanks sometimes remain even into Dec.

▶ ♀ Def. Alt. Plumage (all feathering except, in wing, only a few innermost feathers), acquired in LATE SUMMER–FALL and retained until into MARCH or EARLY APRIL (very little spring material seen).

So very like ♀ Def. Alt. Blue-winged Teal that numerous individuals cannot be identified to species with certainty. **Bill** slaty; **iris** hazel; **feathering** has more somber coloring and less (or even no) rufescent cast such as is typical of the drake Cinnamon in Def. Basic; individual variation in coloring ranges from rather pale (much of head and venter whitish) to moderately dark (much of head, breast, and sides toward tawny); sides of head are paler than sides of breast in some individuals; feathers on chin often partly blackish; the long feathers of flanks have internal light zones that are V-shaped (rather than U-shaped) or are lacking. **Wing** long innermost secondaries blackish brown, paling on inner part of inner web, and outer web narrowly margined creamy, their longest overlying coverts evenly dark and narrower distally than in Basic; the remainder is retained Basic feathering (described below).

▶ ♀ Def. Basic Plumage (entire feathering), head–body–tail and innermost feathers of wing acquired in SPRING and retained well into summer; the remainder of the wing that is part of this Plumage is acquired in LATE SUMMER (after a flightless period) in the early part of the span of molting which concludes with acquisition of Alt. head–body–tail; then the Basic wing is retained nearly a year.

In general, this Plumage has a blended and somewhat "washed out" appearance (not clear-cut as in Alt.), head, neck, ventral surface, and feather edges on dorsum generally toward palish buff, becoming somewhat browner on breast and sides.

Head and neck variable dark streaking, but generally the streaks are longer and wider than in Alt. (coarser patterning); chin and throat white, in some a hint of buff; **dorsum** the feathers broadly rounded, the scapulars even quite squarish ended sometimes, and sooty or fuscous, bordered (wider than in Alt.) buffy to palish tan; **underparts** vary with individual, the breast usually toward tan and remainder whitish and the feathers palish fuscous internally (pattern varies from spotted to blotchy to rather streaked when feather margins become abraded); under-tail pattern generally diffuse (not clear-cut and contrasty). **Wing** innermost secondaries have rounded ends and are nearly unicolor darkish, but outer web has narrow white edge; their longer overlying coverts are evenly dark; the wing has a blue area (as in ♂); the greater coverts are narrowly white on their exposed borders; the speculum area is dark with at least a hint of greenish and the outer webs of the ends of most of the secondaries are narrowly and inconspicuously white (or sometimes slightly buffy, but fade); wing lining white with zone of grayed fuscous along leading edge and these feathers are margined white (broadest at tip, about 1–1½ mm.).

AT HATCHING   See col. pl. facing p. 370. Eye stripe usually broken between bill and eye; bill noticeably long; a dusky "shadow" on side of face; yellow areas pale; dark of legs and feet usually restricted to joints and webs.

▶   ♂ Juv. Plumage (entire feathering), fully developed at about age 7 weeks and most of it lost rapidly soon afterward, except most of the wing retained nearly a year. This Plumage generally is quite buffy tan overall, with all of underparts marked (blotched or streaked).

Iris dark brown at first; by age 8 weeks it has become orange or scarlet (Spencer 1953). **Head** there are some brown markings in the dark of crown; cheeks and neck buffy, but in some creamy, and still others have some tan on face; **upperparts** feathers narrow, rounded at ends, darkish, margined buffy tan (distal margins are quite wide on the long scapulars); **underparts** breast warm brownish or, in some, a rich tan, streaked fuscous; belly and abdomen blotchy to streaked fuscous on whitish; flank feathers narrow, soft, tapering, internally plain darkish on some individuals (but others have internal buffy and tan markings) and widely margined buffy tan; the distal dark area in long under tail coverts generally twice the width of the white margins; **tail** feathers narrow, notched at ends, fuscous, narrowly edged white on outer web.

Wing innermost secondaries have both webs blackish brown and their buffy tan margins (widest on outer web) are not sharply delineated; compared with Basic, the general coloring of the wing is somewhat muted, the upper coverts narrower and rounder ended, etc.; in the lining the darkish feathers toward the leading edge are more broadly (2–3 mm.) margined white than in ♀ Def. Basic, at least in material examined.

NOTE   On a preflight Juv. from Utah, the still growing ventral feathers had very large round dark spots with white borders, especially on breast, but also most of underparts.

▶   ♀ Juv. Plumage (entire feathering), timing, etc., as of ♂ Juv., except most of the wing is retained a few weeks longer in the year after hatching. Not much material examined.

Iris dark brownish. Feathering much as in ♂ Juv. **Underparts** generally more heavily marked dark than in ♂, but individuals vary to narrow dark streaking on pale background; none seen that had a rich tan breast (such as occurs in some ♂ ♂); flank feathers variable as in ♂; **wing** general coloring muted, innermost feathers as in ♂, white bar along leading edge of speculum narrower than in ♂ and does not widen distally; wing lining as ♂.

▶   ♂ Basic I Plumage (all feathering except, in wing, only a few innermost feathers), rapidly succeeds corresponding Juv. feathering beginning about the time the drake attains flight, but molt of tail sometimes is delayed into late fall or even early winter. This is the "first-FALL Plumage" of this teal. Most of the Juv. wing is retained.

Head and neck have more sharply defined and shorter dark streaks than Juv.; **upperparts** various feather margins usually palish buff (not tan); long scapulars have poorly defined tan zone on inner part of inner web and their margins usually are whitish buff and sharply defined; **underparts** are near white with less dark marking than Juv.; the concealed portions of feathers of belly and abdomen have well-defined broad dark markings and, with wear, they become exposed; flank feathers larger and broader than in Juv., with paler margins, and the internal dark area generally contains at least 2 well-defined light (tan) zones; under tail coverts appear predominantly white, the dark internal areas being smaller, darker, and more sharply defined than in Juv. (more contrasty pattern); **tail** very similar to Def. Basic (and often a pause in molting before it is acquired); **wing** elongated innermost secondaries have outer web darkest (to velvety black) and its margin is narrowly and sharply defined buffy tan (margin widens distally).

NOTES   One very tan drake, while still in preflight stage, already was molting from Juv. into Basic I.

By sometime in fall, all soft-part colors approximate those of older age-classes at same season.

In some S. Am. populations of this teal, Basic I is a barred and spotted Plumage.

▶   ♂ Alt. I Plumage (all feathering except, in wing, only a few innermost feathers), generally acquired in LATE FALL–EARLY WINTER of year of hatching; retained into the following SUMMER. This is the last drake Plumage with which the Juv. wing is worn. In material examined, this Plumage was not distinguishable from later Alts., but its presence was indicated by the retained, worn, Juv. wing.

▶   ♀ Basic I Plumage, inclusive feathering, timing, etc., evidently as in ♂ Basic I. The "first-FALL Plumage." Most of the Juv. wing is retained.

Head pale cheeks and the neck have shorter, more clear-cut dark markings than in ♀ Juv.; **upperparts** much as ♂ Basic I; **underparts** breast quite variable, but differs markedly from Juv., since the feathers have a large wide internal dark marking; flank feathers have 2–3 buff markings in dark area of upper web; under tail coverts as ♂ Basic I; **tail,** often acquired late, as in ♀ Def. Basic.

NOTE   Some Basic I feathering, especially on breast, appears on some individuals even before they attain flight.

▶   ♀ Alt. I Plumage (all feathering except, in wing, only a few innermost feathers), acquired in LATE FALL–EARLY WINTER and worn until some time in SPRING. Evidently as later Alts.; most of the wing, however, is retained Juv. feathering.

▶   ♀ Basic II Plumage (entire feathering), all except most of the wing acquired in SPRING (before age 1 year) and retained into LATE SUMMER. As later Basics. The last ♀ Plumage with which the Juv. wing is worn.

NOTE   Although it has been claimed that there are color phases in the ♀ Cinnamon Teal, individuals of both sexes vary from palish through intermediates to darkish overall. They have a wider range of individual variation in coloring than many of our other waterfowl species.

Measurements of specimens in definitive feathering; 12 ♂ (Cal., Utah, Texas): BILL 42–49 mm., av. 45.5; WING 184–197, av. 191; TAIL 65–79, av. 69.5; TARSUS 32–36, av. 34;   12 ♀ (Cal. Utah): BILL 40–45 mm., av. 42.8; WING 170–187, av. 181; TAIL 61–70, av. 67.8; TARSUS 31–34, av. 21 (ETS).

For data on a larger series, evidently the chord (short meas.) of WING given, see

Snyder and Lumsden (1951). For an additional 12 ♀, chord of WING, see Wetmore (1965).

Weight of fall birds, age-classes not distinguished: 26 ♂ av. 0.9 lb. (408 gm.), max. 1.2 (549 gm.); 19 ♀ av. 0.8 lb. (363 gm.), max. 1.1 (499 gm.) (A. L. Nelson and Martin 1953).

Hybrids with the Bluewing (*Anas discors*)—all drakes—seen or taken in the wild, are listed under Blue-winged Teal. A Cinnamon Teal–Mallard cross was taken in Cal. (Maillard 1902). Another hybrid from Cal. was a Shoveler cross with either Cinnamon or Bluewing (Swarth 1915). A pair of wild-taken Shoveler–Cinnamon Teal crosses in s. Cal., plus a captive-reared cross of similar parentage, are similar in pattern, except for less white on upper breast, to the New Zealand Shoveler (*A. rhynchotis*), as mentioned in the last chapter in Delacour (1964). For photo of a ♂ *cyanoptera* × ♀ *clypeata* hybrid, apparently in Basic I Plumage, see J. M. Harrison and Harrison (1965). The tracheal bulla of captive-reared crosses of Cinnamon Teal with Garganey (*A. querquedula*) vary in shape; see Beer (1968).

Geographical variation in the species. There are very large gaps between portions of breeding range. N. Am. population—individuals of each sex are fairly homogeneous in size; Alt. Plumaged ♂ has relatively more yellow component in the reddish brown areas, which are unspotted. In tropical lowland Colombia the smallest birds occur, dark in general coloring, sexes virtually identical in size, and ♂ spotted in all Alt. Plumages. In the highlands there the birds are somewhat larger, with considerable sex disparity in av. size, the drake is spotted in Alt. I and also in about 50% of individuals in succeeding Alts. In arid Bolivian highlands and n. Peru the birds are so large as to have virtually no overlap in size with those of other populations; apparently the ♂ is unspotted, at least beginning with Alt. II, and ♀ has notably heavy streaking on much of head and neck. In Argentina and most of Chile, size is about as in N. Am. (intermediate), the ♂ in Alt. I is nearly unspotted and in succeeding Alts. has, in 1 out of 3 individuals, spots on breast and upper sides. See Snyder and Lumsden (1951) for some further details. RSP

SUBSPECIES   **in our area** *septentrionalium* Snyder and Lumsden—as described above. **Extralimital** *cyanoptera* Vieillot—n. Chile, Paraguay, and s. Brazil s. to include Tierra del Fuego and the Falklands; *orinomus* (Oberholser)—high elevations from s. Peru and Bolivia into n. Chile; *borreroi* Snyder and Lumsden—Andean highlands of Colombia; *tropica* Snyder and Lumsden—Colombian lowlands. RSP

FIELD IDENTIFICATION   In N. Am. Small trim duck; both sexes in all flying ages have a large palish blue area that extends back from leading edge of the wing. Various activities of this teal are reminiscent of those either of the Bluewing or Northern Shoveler, and both of these are among the species with which the Cinnamon readily associates at times. Like the Bluewing, it flies rather fast, often in small compact flocks. Drakes most of the year (Def. Alt. Plumage) appear entirely dark, usually being reddish brown; the blue wing patch is concealed unless the wing is spread; in flight this patch reflects the light and appears almost white at times. The wing lining is mostly white. The drake hardly could be mistaken for the drake Ruddy, which has white

488

cheeks. Even well into molt in summer the drake usually is quite reddish brown. Drakes in their first fall and ♀ ♀ in all flying ages apparently are indistinguishable from young and ♀ Bluewings. The drake Cinnamon, after about 2 months old, has orange or scarlet eyes; those of the Bluewing are dark in both sexes in all flying ages. LGS

VOICE   Seldom noisy, often silent. The drake's usual call, though weak, is stronger than that of the Bluewing. R. A. Ryder (1959) mentioned a monotonous chattering or rattling by drakes as several of them swam around a duck during display. The drake's calling during pursuit flights has been described as chattering squeaks. The duck makes a rattling sound when Inciting and also has a simple and rather weak quack. J. Munro (1945) described the ♀ of a pair as uttering a "thin, nasal quacking almost continuously for 20 min. This was of two distinct sounds, the first soft, the second harsh, as suggested by the syllables *coo-ack, coo-ack*. At times the first sound was gut-tural, as *cow-ack, cow-ack*. Again the two sounds slurred together into the conven-tional duck quack." H. E. Spencer (1953) described the call of the drake as a weak whistling *peep* and that of the duck as a low-pitched, harsh *karrr karrr karrr*. Some additional information, including calls in context with displays, are given beyond under "Reproduction." LGS

HABITAT   In N. Am. In all seasons prefers shallow lake margins, also marshes, ditches, borrow pits, lagoons, and ponds. Like the Northern Shoveler, it does not shun alkaline habitat. Displaying birds in n. Utah used all sizes of freshwater impound-ments; on larger lakes, however, they usually stayed within 50 yds. of shore (H. E. Spencer 1953). For nesting habitat, see "Reproduction." Broods and flightless adults require good escape cover. Broods in n. Utah favored small water bodies margined with emergents such as *Scirpus* (H. E. Spencer 1953). Wintering birds probably use brackish marshes at times.

The diversity of habitat of the various subspecies in S. Am. "is not duplicated" in the habitat of the Cinnamon Teal in N. Am. (Snyder and Lumsden 1951). LGS

DISTRIBUTION   (See map.) *A. c. septentrionalium*. **Breeding**   Center of abun-dance is in conterminous U.S., w. of the Rocky Mts., in the Great Basin and in Pacific coastal states. In Mexico the Cinnamon Teal is a widespread local breeder s. into Jalisco and Tamaulipas; small numbers breed in the highlands of Baja Cal.

Postbreeding dispersal includes areas beyond breeding range, such as indicated on map.

Winter   A considerable number of birds remains within conterminous U.S., mostly in areas where the species also breeds, but largest concentrations are in Mexico, notably in Jalisco on the Pacific side and in Veracruz on the Atlantic side. Beginning not far beyond these areas, records of occurrence of this teal in any season become scarce.

Straggler   In Alaska several sightings in the 1960s; in May, 1970, a ♂ with a ♀ (probably ♀ Cinnamon but possibly Bluewing) near Juneau and perhaps the same drake shortly afterward at Gustavus Airport; May 19, 1972—pair in Ketchikan area; June 9, 1973—pair near Anchorage. In Canada this species has been recorded (Godfrey 1966) as occurring n. to Quesnel in B.C.; at Edmonton, Alta.; at 6 localities in

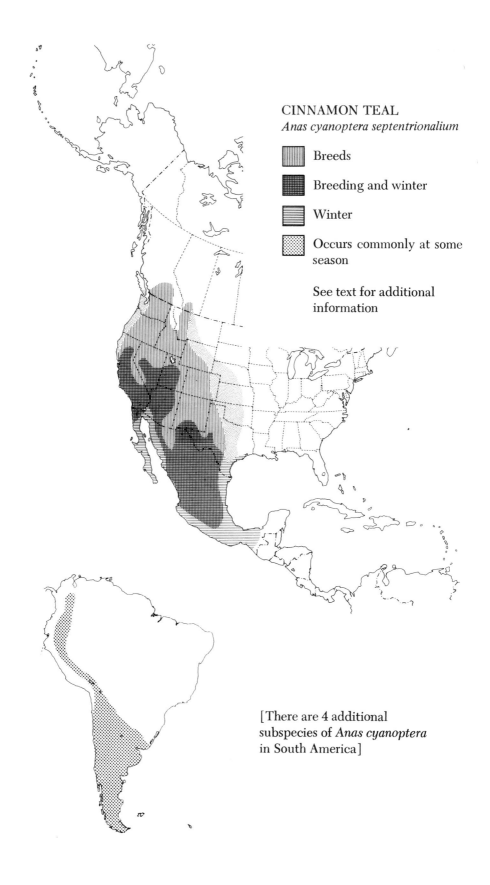

CINNAMON TEAL
Anas cyanoptera septentrionalium

Breeds

Breeding and winter

Winter

Occurs commonly at some season

See text for additional information

[There are 4 additional subspecies of *Anas cyanoptera* in South America]

Sask.; as rare in s. Man.; 2 records for Ont.; and sightings at 3 localities in Que. In conterminous U.S. there are surprisingly few records east of the area of postbreeding dispersal, on the prairies, and the bird becomes quite rare e. of the Mississippi. There are scattered locality records in La. and at least 6 for Fla. This teal has been recorded in Minn., Mo., Ohio, w. N.Y., and in both Carolinas (includes 3 sightings in N.C.). Beyond the Atlantic coast there is a sighting in Dec. on Grand Bahama (Paterson 1968) and 5 winter records for Cuba. On the other side of a wide area for which records are lacking, and although there are records for Nicaragua and Costa Rica, Wetmore (1965) listed the following for the Republic of Panama: 1 taken in early Nov. (it had been banded in Idaho) and 2 in Jan. (1 banded in Cal., the other in Utah); in addition, a bird taken in June was not proven to be from either N. or S. Am. According to Meyer de Schauensee (1966), migrants from N. Am. occasionally reach S. Am.—Colombia (bird taken in Santa Marta region had been banded in Ore.), Venezuela, and possibly Ecuador.

The **fossil** record of the species consists only of occurrences in the Pleistocene of N. Am. at a locality in Ore. and at least 2 in Cal.; see Brodkorb (1964a) for details.

Extralimital subspecies The map is rather generalized for S. Am., to indicate approximate inclusive range of the various subspecies named from that continent; the southerly birds there are migratory. RSP

MIGRATION The Cinnamon Teal in N. Am. has a rather limited distribution and performs comparatively short migrations. (It is also migratory in s. S. Am., but may have only local seasonal movements in northerly parts of that continent.)

Limited band-recovery data indicate a main flight from w. conterminous U.S. se. to Mexico and even to S. Am. Spring migration is the reverse of this. Some evidently remain in Cal. all year, or move only to n. and cent. Mexico for the winter. Another general trend, apparently, is from Utah and ne. periphery or range southwesterly toward the Pacific coast (see G. H. Jensen and Smith, in Aldrich 1949).

Spring migration is relatively late, but first arrivals have been reported in Feb. in Death Valley and Rio Grande Valley and apparently there is movement in Cal. in this month. Migrants seem to require open water and to be intolerant of low temperatures. They have been observed flying in small flocks of 10–20 individuals at altitudes under 500 ft. in n. Utah. Av. arrival in the Great Basin of Utah was first week of March and with peak in third week in April. Sex ratio appeared balanced. H. E. Spencer (1953) believed this teal to be generally a diurnal migrant. Peak of migration in e. Wash. was mid-May (S. W. Harris 1954). The same author noted a nearly even sex ratio early in migration, then a sharp increase in ♂ ♂ at peak.

Summer ♀ ♀ molt locally, where they are rearing broods; the drakes, in small groups, molt in the same general vicinity so far as known.

Fall migration is relatively early and almost all the birds have left the n. part of breeding range by mid-Oct. Peak of fall migration in e. Wash. was late Aug. (S. W. Harris 1954). Migration in n. Utah started in early Aug. The first migrants apparently were drakes, after their flightless period of molting; these formed flocks of less than 150 birds which departed by mid-Sept. (H. E. Spencer 1953).

An "immature" ♀ banded July 31, 1947, at Ogden Bay Refuge (Utah) was shot near

Mexico City on Aug. 15 of the same year; the av. distance/day traveled was 114 mi. (H. E. Spencer 1953).

For various arrival and departure dates, see Bent (1923). LGS

BANDING STATUS   The total number banded in N. Am. was 16,777 through 1964 and there were 656 recoveries through 1961; main places of banding were Cal., Utah, Nev., and Ore. (data from Bird Banding Laboratory). RSP

REPRODUCTION   Both sexes **first breed** as yearlings. The great majority of those that are going to breed are paired already when they arrive at nesting areas, hence pair formation generally must occur in winter/early spring.

Known **displays** and accompanying calls have much in common with those of the better known Northern Shoveler (*Anus clypeata*). Various homologous displays were listed in a table by McKinney (1970), but he had few observations (and only of Cinnamon Teal in captivity) and no attempt is made here to include and describe each of the named ritualized activities he mentioned. As in the Shoveler (and various other ducks), the initial, or social, stage of displays leading to pair formation has evolved from social feeding. Several drakes gather near a ♀. A drake's response to INCITING by the ♀ consists of repeated CHIN-LIFTING (with bill often angled slightly upward) and bouts of PUMPING the neck up and down (typically not as full a movement as in Mallard); his accompanying call has been described as low rattling, chattering notes (Wetmore 1920) and as a creaky *chuck-chuck-chuck* sound reminiscent of a call of the drake Northern Shoveler (Johnsgard 1965). It is very different from the homologous call of Shoveler or Bluewing and probably most similar to that of the Garganey (*Anas querquedula*). (It is of interest that the Introductory shake, a prelude to major displays in various *Anas* species, is unknown in the Cinnamon Teal.) Spells of Chin-lifting alternate with ritualized feeding actions (Lateral dabbling, etc.), silently, in Shoveler fashion; at times the drake makes swimming movements, without much forward motion, near or alongside the ♀ and with his body oriented laterally toward her, and often terminates his overt response by UP-ENDING. Sometimes he TURNS-THE-BACK-OF-THE-HEAD toward an Inciting ♀ and swims ahead of her (Johnsgard 1965); that is, he may try to lead her from the nearby presence of other unmated drakes. At times he also takes station broadside to the ♀, PREENS-BEHIND-THE-WING, performs ritualized feeding movements, and then Up-ends. To return to Chin-lifting, a form of this (with bill angled upward) occurs in various hostile situations. Instances of the drake threatening in this fashion and otherwise behaving aggressively toward ♂ Bluewings have been observed (H. E. Spencer 1953, L. B. Keith). Very short DISPLAY-FLIGHTS, of the Jump flight type performed by the ♂ Shoveler, undoubtedly occur in this teal but McKinney (1970) saw it only once in captive birds. It functions to attract a ♀'s attention. The actual circumstances at the time the pair bond is initiated remain unknown.

PURSUIT FLIGHTS by a number of drakes chasing a ♀ resemble those of other *Anas* species; short chattering squeaks are heard from the flying drakes (H. E. Spencer 1953). W. Anderson and Miller (1953) reported a ♂ Cinnamon and a ♂ Bluewing both pursuing a ♀ of one of these species (not identifiable as to which).

The ♀ Incites in Shoveler fashion, or perhaps more nearly in Garganey fashion,

492

Pumping and Chin-lifting, seldom with any lateral motion of the head. The accompanying call is a rattling *Rrrr*, uttered as the head is raised in Chin-lifting. Her DE-CRESCENDO CALL, seldom heard (it is uttered in all seasons), is a weak *gack-gack-ga-ga*, much like the ♀ Shoveler's, with last 1–2 syllables often muffled or omitted.

Territoriality Maintenance of a "seasonal home range" was studied in Utah by H. E. Spencer (1953) and R. I. Smith (1955). The drake becomes antisocial (aggressive) toward other members of his species (his mate excepted) when the nest site has been selected, in late April or early May in Utah (Spencer, Smith), by late April in e. Wash. (Johnsgard 1955). The focal point, from which defense is launched, is the drake's waiting site or activity center, which usually is situated at a stretch of water not over 100 yds. from the nest (Spencer). The drake pursues intruding drakes, also pairs. The drake is less "mobile" than, for example, Mallard or Pintail; the defended area of the Cinnamon Teal is even smaller than is typical of Shoveler and Gadwall. Distances between activity centers of neighboring drakes were only 10–30 yds. along a channel (Smith); a defended area is rarely over 30 × 30 yds in extent (Spencer). Overt aggressive behavior of a drake includes repeated Chin-lifting (bill angled upward, a rattling call uttered) prior to pursuit.

Copulation usually occurs in close proximity of the drake's activity center, but also at places where the pair feeds; it was observed as late as 2nd week of incubation in 2 pairs, but was most frequent during the laying period (R. I. Smith 1953). Mounting may be preceded by Head-pumping (bill angled downward) by both ♂ and ♀; it is not as prolonged as the homologous behavior of the Mallard (C. Wilson, R. I. Smith); sometimes precopulatory display is omitted entirely (Smith). The drake, on dismounting, adopts a bill-down stance (angled down about 60°), with body close and lateral to the ♀, and erects the feathers of his head and neck; he utters a rather quiet call. (There still is incomplete information on copulatory behavior.)

At the Bear R. Refuge (Utah), 50% of nests were in salt grass (*Distichlis spicata*), but important **nesting cover** also consisted of weeds, hardstem bulrush (*Scirpus acutus*), and other sedges (C. S. Williams and Marshall 1938c). At Ogden Bay (Utah), H. E. Spencer (1953) found salt grass preferred, with salt grass–forb mixtures and forbs also commonly utilized. In a later study at Ogden Bay, R. A. Ryder (1961) found "three-square" and "rush" and "mixed weeds" the most important nesting cover. At Knudson Marsh (Utah), where salt grass flooded during the early part of the nesting season, Wingfield and Low (1955) found 63 nests in *Scirpus acutus*, 75 in *S. olneyi*, and 7 in *Typha* spp. In Honey Lake valley (Cal.), E. G. Hunt and Naylor (1955) found that nesting cover varied in 2 different years: in 1951 most nests were in rye grass, some in salt grass; in 1953 almost all were in Baltic rush. In 1951, 59% of nests were on dykes, 18% on uncultivated land, and the remainder in island, marsh, and agricultural habitats; in 1953, 89.6% were in marsh and 8% on uncultivated land. The change was attributed to greater availability of marsh habitat in 1953. H. E. Spencer (1953) reported that nests rarely were more than 75 yds. from water and most were much closer; in w. Mont., according to Girard (1941), the av. distance from water of 22 nests was 61 yds. (max. 220, min. 3).

In Utah, Spencer found 65 nests on 357 acres (over 5 acres/nest), but if only the nesting cover within the area were used in calculating density, it would exceed 1 nest/acre.

At Tule Lake and Lower Klamath (Cal.), A. W. Miller and Collins (1954) found pre-ferred nesting habitat to be islands with nettle cover under 12 in. high. There, along with the Mallard, sites over water were used more commonly than by other dabbling ducks. All Cinnamon Teal nests, however, were less than 50 yds. from water and 40% were within 3 yds. At Humboldt Bay (Cal.), most of the nests were in grasses and grasslike plants, lower cover than used there by Mallards (Wheeler and Harris 1970).

The **nest site** is selected by the ♀, while accompanied by her mate. She scratches out a shallow depression and lines it with some dead grasses or other plant materials pres-ent at the site. Typically it is very well concealed. In cover types such as *Eleocharis* and *Scirpus*, the duck burrows under the dead growth of previous years, so that the nest is completely under cover and the bird enters and leaves through tunnels under vegeta-tion. In salt grass, the nest is built in a dense clump of the previous year's growth. Average diam. of nest bowl is 18 cm. and depth 7 cm. The **nest down**, added mostly during early incubation, varies considerably in amount, but enough usually is accumu-lated to form a rim of about 5 cm. width to the nest (H. E. Spencer 1953). As in ducks generally, it is darker than the Alt. (winter) down; it is much like that of the Bluewing, lighter than in the Greenwing, drab brownish with large conspicuous white centers; any intermingled feathers are dusky with buffy edges and tips or dusky with whitish central markings (Bent 1923). Nests may be built up (raised) by addition of material when threatened by rising water (H. E. Spencer 1953, W. Anderson 1956).

Laying begins in late April or early May in Utah (H. E. Spencer 1953), early May in n. Cal. (W. Anderson 1956, 1957). Peak of clutch initiation at Ogden Bay, Utah, was May 6–12 and 77% of clutches were started between May 6 and June 2; the spread for the season was April 15–June 24 (R. A. Ryder 1961). Early in the season, laying may be irregular; that is, when first 3 or 4 eggs are being laid, intervals between them vary 1–3 days. After the 4th egg, the usual rate is 1/day. Later in the season, 1 egg/day is usual. Most eggs are laid in the morning, about 8 to 10 A.M. (Summarized from H. E. Spencer 1953.)

Clutch size In Utah, Spencer found 22 clutches av. 9.6 eggs and, in another year, 52 av. 9.7.; these figures include only successful and unparasitized nests; the extremes of clutch size were 4 and 16 eggs. At Knudson Marsh (Utah), 47 successful clutches included 4 (with 3 eggs each), 5(4), 5 (5), 5 (6), 6 (7), 5 (8), 5 (9), 5 (10), 5 (11), 1 (12), and 1 (13); some of them may have been reduced as a consequence of the Redhead (*Aythya americana*) adding eggs to the nests (B. Wingfield). At Tule—Lower Klamath, A. W. Miller and Collins (1954) reported an av. of 10.2 eggs in 32 successful, unparasitized, clutches. In Honey Lake valley (Cal.), E. G. Hunt and Naylor (1955) recorded aver-ages of 10.4 eggs (12 nests) and 9.1 (64 nests). At the same place in 1963, 7 successful nests had 72 eggs (av. 10.3) and 68 (av. 9.7) hatched (W. Anderson 1965).

One **egg** each from 20 clutches (11 Cal., 7 Utah, 2 Ore.) **size** length 46.87 ± 1.12 mm., breadth 34.08 ± 0.86, radii of curvature of ends 13.20 ± 1.02 and 10.57 ± 0.78, **shape** elongation 1.37 ± 0.053, bicone −0.040, asymmetry +0.106 (FWP). The shell is smooth, with slight gloss, **color** some variant of pale buffy to nearly white. Ninety eggs in various collections av. 47.5 × 34.5 mm., with extremes of length being 44–53 mm. and breadth 30–37 (Bent 1923). The 46 eggs in 6 clutches in Utah av. 46.4 × 34.6 mm., with extremes of length being 44–50 mm. and breadth 33.3–35; and the av. wt. of

11 fresh eggs was 26.98 gm. (H. E. Spencer 1953). The same author found a single "runt" egg among about 3,000 eggs examined.

Nest parasitism The Redhead commonly lays in Cinnamon Teal nests. In 2 seasons in Utah, 29% of 59 nests and 22% of 170 nests also contained Redhead eggs. Mallard, Shoveler, and Ruddy Duck eggs also have been found in nests of this teal which, in turn, has laid eggs in nests of Mallard, Redhead, and Ruddy (Wingfield 1951). Parasitized Cinnamon Teal nests often have smaller clutches and desertion is more frequent. For further details see H. E. Spencer (1953) and Weller (1959).

Incubation by the ♀ usually begins within 24 hrs. after the clutch is complete. The **incubation period** varies from 21 to 25 days (Spencer 1953). During early incubation, the duck joins the drake at his activity center several times a day, staying for an hour or longer each time (R. I. Smith 1955). H. E. Spencer (1953) noted that ♀ ♀ often leave the nest between 3 and 5 P.M. to feed and drink, staying away for a maximum of 2 hours. They cover their eggs with down before departing. The bond between mates is maintained during most of the incubation period; drakes often defend territories until a few days prior to hatching of the clutch (R. I. Smith 1955). As time passes, the ♀ becomes very strongly attached to the nest and will perform a distraction display if flushed from it, as she does also when disturbed with her brood. If the duck leaves the nest while her mate is not in the general vicinity, drakes of neighboring pairs approach and attempt to rape her; the duck takes wing and there is a Pursuit flight. When her mate gains position close to her in flight, the other male(s) cease pursuing.

Hatching success Data must be used cautiously because there are several types of bias in duck-nesting studies (R. A. Ryder 1961). A partial listing of recorded information on percentage of nests in which at least some eggs hatched follows: at Knudson Marsh (Utah), in 41% (of 34 unparasitized nests) and 32% (of 107 parasitized) (Wingfield 1951); and 44% (of 18 unparasitized) and 26% (of 23 parasitized) (Weller 1959); in 49 successful nests the av. number of eggs that hatched was 6.6 (Wingfield); at Bear R. (Utah), of 524 nests found, 62% hatched and the av. hatch was 6.8 (C. S. Williams and Marshall 1938c); in w. Mont.; 72% of 22 nests were successful, with 4.7 eggs hatched per clutch (Girard 1941); at Tule–Lower Klamath (Cal.), 75.7% of 37 nests were successful, with 7.0 (89.9%) eggs hatched per clutch (Rienecker and Anderson 1960). For much additional information see, for Utah, H. E. Spencer (1953); for various localities in Cal., W. Anderson (1956, 1957, 1965), E. G. Hunt and Naylor (1955), A. W. Miller and Collins (1954), and Wheeler and Harris (1970). In most nesting studies, predation caused heavy losses; the California Gull (*Larus californicus*) is an important predator in Utah (H. E. Spencer 1953); skunks, brown rats (*Rattus norvegicus*), and raccoons were chief predators in the Sacramento Valley, Cal. (W. Anderson 1957).

That a drake, presumably the mate of earlier in the season; sometimes associates with the ♀ and her brood has been known for decades; the older information was summarized by J. C. Phillips (1923b); also see Bent (1923). The matter becomes less clear from the observation of J. G. Tyler (in Bent) of 3 drakes with a single duck accompanied by 10 downy young; all the drakes showed "great distress" at the close presence of man, while the duck had a "most unconcerned" manner. Drakes associating with brood-rearing ♀ ♀ have been noted recently by Chura (1962) and B. Wingfield. The summer molt into Basic of many drakes begins sufficiently late so that at the time when a considerable number of early broods have appeared the ♂♂ are not yet ready to go elsewhere and become flightless.

Renesting In an experimental study in Lassen Co., Cal., it was found that, in general, the earlier the first clutch was taken, the shorter the interval before the 2nd was begun; and av. clutch size dropped from 10 to 8.3 eggs; details in E. G. Hunt and Anderson (1966). R. I. Smith (1955) believed that, since the drake remains a comparatively long time with the duck, another drake may not be needed (compare with Mallard) to insure fertilization for a replacement clutch.

The number of clutches **hatching** reaches a peak in mid-June in Utah and hatching continues until Aug. 12 (H. E. Spencer 1953); in Cal., hatching dates extend from mid-May to mid-Aug. (A. W. Miller and Collins 1954), but W. Anderson (1956, 1957) found that most clutches hatch in June and July. In the Humboldt Bay area (Cal.), the nesting season lasted 135 days in 1964 and 115 days in 1965; peak of hatch late May–early June; details in Wheeler and Harris (1970). In w. Mont. the peak (69% of clutches studied) was the month of July (Girard 1941).

Ducklings The duck leads her brood to water, to a place where a good growth of emergent vegetation provides protective cover. Broods may move as far as a mile in a few days but, if cover and feeding conditions are good, activities center within an area of a few acres (H. E. Spencer 1953).

In Utah, **brood size** av. 10 ducklings (9 broods) at age of less than a week, and 4.5 (3 broods) at 8 weeks; in another year, broods less than ⅓ grown av. 8.7 (23 broods), between ⅓ and ⅔ grown they av. 6.6 (17 broods), and when over ⅔ grown 4.7 (11 broods) (H. E. Spencer 1953). In the Klamath Basin (Cal.), Chattin et al. (1949) recorded av. brood sizes (all ages) in 2 years as 5.8 (27 broods) and 6.6 (68 broods). At Tule–Lower Klamath, A. W. Miller and Collins (1954) found that, in the first week posthatching, brood size av. 6.6 (74 broods); main brood mortality was thought to occur during the first week; since av. hatch was 9.5; predation by gulls was suspected as causing this decrease. At Humboldt Bay (Cal.), brood size was 10.7 at hatching and 5.8 near time of flying; details in Wheeler and Harris (1970).

The young **attain flight** at age about 7 weeks (H. E. Spencer 1953).

In s. temperate S. Am., the Cinnamon Teal occurring there breeds in the austral spring and summer; just above the Equator, in Colombia, there appear to be 2 breeding seasons, each correlated with a rainy season (Snyder and Lumsden 1951). FM LGS

HABITS *A. c. septentrionalium.* Prenesting birds in Utah fed in early morning and late afternoon; during midday they loafed and sunned. As the season advanced, nest-site hunting was a midday activity. They loafed on small ponds on warm, calm, days and, when the weather was cool and windy, they sought the lee side of dikes and channels (H. E. Spencer 1953).

H. C. Bryant (1914) stated that, in paired birds, the ♀ is first to show alarm and take wing. Lateral head shaking and some up-down motion of the head are preflight movements, in both sexes. Weller (1959) demonstrated that the ♀ has a stronger attachment to her nest than the ♀ Redhead, Canvasback, and Mallard. Near the end of incubation she remains in the vicinity of the nest and, if disturbed, usually has an elaborate distraction display (H. E. Spencer 1953). Nesting ♀♀ apparently show no hostility toward other members of their species or other ducks nesting nearby. R. A. Ryder (1959) described Cinnamon Teal–American Coot (*Fulica americana*) conflicts in Utah; the latter species dominated in 91 encounters and the 2 exceptions involved ♀ teal with broods.

Postbreeding drakes gather in small flocks for molting and afterward such unisexual flocks are on the move earlier than gatherings of postnesting ♀ ♀, of young in their first fall, or of these intermixed.

The flight speed of a Cinnamon Teal, timed from an automobile, increased from 32 to 59 mph; another was clocked at 49 mph (M. T. Cooke 1933).

Aside from some information on greater numbers of this teal occurring at various localities decades ago, as summarized by J. C. Phillips (1923b), there is almost no information on any changes in numbers. There are no records of unusual fluctuations. The birds migrate early in fall, hence escape considerable hunting mortality. Conversion of land to agriculture, drainage of marshes, creation of water impoundments, etc., certainly have affected the local status of this teal. There seems to be no available evidence, however, that any agent, including man, has affected significantly either overall numbers of this bird in N. Am. or the size of its N. Am. range. A. C. Martin et al. (1951) indicated that the range has been reduced 60%, but supporting evidence is lacking.

The Cinnamon Teal usually feeds where the water is shallow. The well-developed lamellae serve as a strainer for separating out small food items. Occasionally the birds feed close to water on dry land. In an aviary they have been seen to dive for food to a depth of 5 ft. (H. E. Spencer 1953). In social feeding, a bird swims on an irregular (often circular) course, following another feeding bird and straining food out of water already agitated by the one ahead; this even carries over into situations in which the lead bird is some other waterfowl species. LGS

FOOD *A. c. septentrionalium.* Examination of 41 stomachs in the U.S. Biological Survey showed 80% of vegetable matter, largely seeds and other parts of sedges, pondweeds, and grasses; and 20% of animal matter about equally divided between mollusks and insects (Mabbott 1920).

Vegetable Sedges: bulrushes (*Scirpus*, mainly *paludosus*), spike rush (*Eleocharis*), and *Carex*, 34.3%; pondweeds: true pondweeds (*Potamogeton*), wigeon grass (*Ruppia maritima*), and horned pondweed (*Zannichellia palustris*), 27.0%; grasses (*Monanthochloë littoralis*) 7.8%; seeds of smartweeds (*Polygonum lapathifolium* and *P. persicaria*), and dock (*Rumex*), 3.2%; seeds of mallow (Malvacae), pigweed (*Chenopodium*), and water milfoil (*Myriophyllum*), 3.0%; and miscellaneous items (*Sparganium, Amaranthus, Ranunculus, Medicago, Rhus, Heliotropium, Galium,* and *Chara*) 4.5%.

Animal Predacious diving beetles (Dytiscidae), water scavenger beetles (Hydrophilidae), leaf beetles (Chrysomelidae), and snout beetles (Curculionidae), 5.4%; water boatmen (Corixidae), 3.0%; damselflies and dragonflies (Anisoptera), flies (Diptera), larvae mainly, chiefly midges (Chironomidae), soldier flies (Stratiomyiidae), flower flies (Syrphidae), brine flies (Ephydridae) and caddis flies (Phryganeidae), 1.8%; snails and small bivalves, 8.7%; miscellaneous, including water mites (Hydrachnidae) and seed shrimps (Ostracoda), 1.3%. AWS

Northern Shoveler

Anas clypeata Linnaeus

Shoveler or Common Shoveler of authors; the Northern Hemisphere member of the Shoveler group. A middle-sized duck with an elongated spatulate bill (twice as wide distally as at base) having an exposed and rather conspicuous comblike strainer (very fine, long lamellae). Median and lesser upper wing coverts are blue or bluish; the speculum area varies from iridescent green (♂ Def. Basic) to sepia (♀ Juv.), bordered white at forward and at trailing edges. Legs and feet are some variant of orange beginning very early in life. The sexes are very different in Alt. Plumage (♂ green headed, white breasted, and rusty bellied; ♀ somewhat like ♀ Mallard) and quite different even in Basic. The various Plumages are described below.

The drake's tracheal apparatus has been described and/or illustrated many times, beginning in 1678. The left-sided bulla is smaller, more like that of the Greenwing (*A. crecca*) than of the Mallard (*A. platyrhynchos*). It is shown in 3 positions in fig. 121 in Schiøler (1925).

Length' ♂ 18–21 in., ♀ 17–20; wingspread ♂ 29–33, ♀ 27–31; usual wt. of ♂ about 1½ lb., ♀ about 1¼.

No subspecies.

DESCRIPTION Two Plumages/cycle in both sexes. In definitive cycles, the Prealt. ("fall") molt is rather late and often protracted in both sexes, and in the ♀ that part of the Definitive Prebasic molt that has been termed the "spring molt" also varies in timing and duration. In the predefinitive cycle, Basic I Plumage in both sexes is worn in its entirety for a relatively long time (as in the Garganey). The predefinitive molts, particularly of the drake, are variable in length, quite often being protracted, so that individuals in some stage of molting may be found through fall, winter, and spring. The predefinitive Plumages of the ♀ have not been understood heretofore, apparently through supposition that observed differences were individual variation in fewer rather than overlapping succession of more feather generations.

▶ ♂ Def. Alt. Plumage (all feathering, excepting almost all of the wing), acquired mainly through FALL, usually beginning in late Aug. or in Sept.; head–body and often part of tail come in first, the remainder of the tail, the long scapulars, and innermost feathers of wing usually are fully grown by some time in Oct.; in some individuals either the whole process is gradual and prolonged or the major portion of it occurs late, the scapulars and tail not being fully developed until some time in Dec. or even Jan. Drakes commonly still are in full Alt. well into JUNE, later than in most of our shoal-water ducks.

Bill upper mandible black, lower nearly black; **iris** vivid yellow. Most of **head** and the neck dark greenish with, depending on lighting conditions, green to blue to ultramarine-violet iridescence; the forepart of the face, including chin and part of throat, sometimes blackish or toward fuscous; **upperparts** feathers of mid-portion of mantle nearly black and margined brownish; shorter scapulars white; longer ones narrow, tapering, pointed, whitish mottled fuscous on inner web and the outer web of some is greenish black and of others bluish (which may include the distal portion of

498

inner web also); lower back to tail black with greenish sheen; **underparts** base of neck and all of breast (also forward sides) white; belly, abdomen, sides and flanks tawny-rufous or brownish red or even toward chestnut (individual variation), many of the feathers having their very tips whitish (these soon wear off) and the flank feathers have fine wavy black lines; a white area on side of rump; the area from vent to tail grades rapidly to black with greenish sheen; **tail** central feathers nearly black, with white on outer half of webs (very little at tips), the others progressively with more white, outermost pair nearly all white except darkish shaft streak; legs and **feet** scarlet-orange to scarlet, including webs.

Wing innermost secondaries elongated, acutely pointed, black with greenish sheen, often frosted white; their longer overlying coverts black, or same suffused with bluish and unspotted. Remainder of wing is retained Basic Plumage (described below).

NOTE See last paragraph under ♂ Alt. I Plumage.

▶ ♂ Def. Basic Plumage (entire feathering); in southerly N. Am. breeding range the molt into Basic begins rarely as early as April, but in most of breeding range it usually does not become evident until about MID-JUNE and, on the individual, then continues for at least 3 weeks; then the wing quills are dropped (flightless period estimated at 23–26 days) and usually not until some time after the new quills are fully grown does the drake begin a fairly prolonged molt back into Alt. head–body–tail and innermost feathers of wing. Most of the Basic wing is retained into the following SUMMER.

Somewhat ♀-like, but differs in many respects. **Head** forehead to nape very dark, the feathers edged brownish; most of remainder of head and the neck white or pale buff, heavily marked dark olive-brownish except chin–throat usually plain; on much of **upperparts** the feathers are olive-brownish or darker, margined buffy brown; the scapulars are short, broadly rounded, and brownish black with broad tan margins; lower back to tail very dark with slight greenish cast; **underparts,** including breast, mostly tawny-buff or a darker, grayed, tawny (individual variation), each feather with a large subterminal dark area (shape variable); the long flank feathers have an internal U-shaped buffy area, next a broad dark zone, and then wide brownish margins; the under-tail area is mixed buffy tan and dark, or sometimes mostly white vermiculated black; **tail** feathers broader distally than in Alt. and light areas usually off-white and reduced in size; legs and **feet** rather "washed out" orange.

Wing the innermost secondary has dark brownish inner and greenish black outer web and very tip rounded; the next 2 have inner web browner than in Alt., with larger area that is nearly white, and their very tips rounded; their longest overlying coverts are black with some blue in outer web; middle and lesser coverts pale bluish or the same grayed somewhat (concealed portions of the feathers are quite brownish); the small coverts toward leading edge of wing occasionally have creamy edging; the greater coverts over the speculum are dark brownish, broadly tipped white (broadest on distal feathers); the speculum is vivid iridescent green and the feathers comprising it are tipped white (narrow white line at trailing edge of wing); primaries and their upper coverts toward sepia; wing lining white with some brownish toward leading edge, axillars white.

NOTE   Specimens of ♀♀ in Def. Basic were dated July 2 to Aug. 23.

▶   ♀ Def. Alt. Plumage (all feathering, excepting almost all of wing), acquired beginning in LATE SUMMER or EARLY FALL and completed by LATE FALL or EARLY WINTER. Usually retained until EARLY SPRING.

In general, more toward gray than brown; part of venter very light and unmarked. **Bill** most of upper mandible olive-grayish or brownish, grading toward greenish distally, and with scattered fine dark dotting which disappears after death (i.e., is absent from museum specimens); edges of upper and almost all of the lower mandible more or less orange; **iris** brownish yellow (not pure yellow as ♂, nor hazel as sometimes stated). Most of **head**–neck some variant of buff, with forehead to nape toward fuscous and the feathers have some light edging; a dark (toward fuscous) stripe through eye; and remainder finely streaked dark except for unmarked chin. Feathers of **upperparts** mostly toward blackish brown, with clear-cut internal markings and also margins that are pale (usually pinkish buff, which fades); **underparts** somewhat brownish on breast and elsewhere buffy or pinkish tan, any visible dark internal portions of the feathers forming a more nearly spotted than streaked pattern on breast, and scalloped effect on sides and especially flanks; abdomen usually unmarked; vent to tail longitudinally streaked dark. **Tail** central pair of feathers very dark (sepia), the other darkish gray-brown edged and internally marked pinkish buff, with former progressively more reduced and latter expanded toward outer pair of feathers (and this fades to nearly white). Legs and **feet** some variant of orange.

Wing innermost secondaries brownish, quite widely margined white; their overlying greater coverts have broadly rounded ends and are blackish brown with well-defined white edging. Remainder of wing is retained Basic feathering (described below).

NOTE   A ♀ still largely in Alt. was collected while tending a brood of 8 downies, July 10, 1958, at Tununuk, N.W.T.

▶   ♀ Def. Basic Plumage (entire feathering) head–body–tail usually acquired quite

500

rapidly in SPRING, but in some individuals during midwinter; then the molt is interrupted until well along in SUMMER when it is completed by loss of any remaining old tail feathers and the wing (then a flightless period estimated at 23–26 days). Most of the Basic is succeeded by Alt. during FALL, sometimes later, except almost all of the Basic wing is retained nearly a year.

More brownish coloring and more blended pattern than Def. Alt.; dark markings generally show on all of underparts, even in new feathering. **Bill** tends to be more evenly neutral-colored in summer and the dark spotting decreases or disappears temporarily. Differences from Def. Alt. include: broader pale buff edging on feathers of forehead to nape; wider and shorter dark markings on sides of **head** and the neck; on **upperparts** the pale feather margins soon wear off, leaving the anterior dorsum and center of back plain dark, and there are no markings within the dark internal portions of the feathers; the dark portions of the long scapulars are very slightly greenish; **underparts** ground color warm buff or slightly brownish, in some paling to off-white on abdomen, and the darker internal portion of the feathers usually consists of a single area (includes most of the feather); the dark is more pronounced and uneven after the ♀ has been incubating; from vent to tail a more subdued streaky pattern; **tail** feathers a variant of sepia, edged and marked pinkish buff, the outermost pair almost entirely pinkish buff.

Wing innermost secondaries have broader edging, usually somewhat buff; their overlying coverts dark with pale edging; the speculum area (of secondaries) is darkish gray or muted greenish without much sheen and the feathers have white tips (form white line at trailing edge of wing); the overlying greater coverts are near sepia with plain white ends (fairly wide white line within the wing); the middle and lesser coverts are a grayed blue or, rather rarely, palish gray, with more or less creamy buff edging (it wears off, while the blue or gray fades); in some, also, at least the middle and lesser coverts have a pale internal marking; primaries and their upper coverts sepia; wing lining and axillars as ♂ Def. Basic.

AT HATCHING   See col. pl. facing p. 370; pattern nearer that of Pintail than Mallard, but coloring of lighter areas nearer Mallard (more or less yellowish buff); edges of upper mandible brownish orange and same coloring is present on part of legs and feet. The bill is longish at hatching and, by age 2 weeks, is becoming spatulate. For a detailed written description of downies, see Payn (1941).

▶   ♂ Juv. Plumage (entire feathering), begins to appear on scapulars and flanks at age about 2 weeks, the belly is feathered at 3 weeks, the flight feathers of wing are visible at 4 weeks, and the bird is largely feathered at 5 weeks (Southwick 1953a), fully feathered except for wing at 6 weeks (Payn 1941), and the wing also is fully grown at about 8 weeks. A LATE SUMMER or EARLY FALL Plumage, worn briefly.

Dullish, blended coloring; all of underparts with darkish markings (streaks, large spots). **Bill** upper mandible palish slaty blue medially, yellowish laterally; lower mandible mostly yellowish. **Iris** changes from brownish toward muted yellowish. **Head–neck** have light brownish ground color, forehead to nape very dark brownish, some indication of a dark stripe through eye (present at least from bill to eye), and remainder finely streaked dark brownish or dusky. **Upperparts** much of mantle dark brownish, the feathers edged slightly to considerably paler; the shorter scapulars edged rather

501

yellowish and generally have 2 internal transverse bars of same; longer scapulars are tapering, rounded, brown with some greenish gloss and margined fairly vivid yellowish; lower back and rump dark with slightly paler feather margins. **Underparts** muted buffy or brownish with darkish (brownish sepia) markings that are streaky on breast, more toward large spots on abdomen and sides, and again streaky from vent to tail. **Tail** feathers narrow, ashy brown edged and marked whitish buff, with notched tips; legs and **feet** muted orange-yellow, the webs quite dusky.

Wing innermost secondaries not elongated, rather blunt ended, brownish or olive-brownish with very narrow white tips; the longest coverts over them are very dark brownish; middle and lesser coverts light grayish to blackish blue (individual variation); greater coverts over the speculum have oval dusky spotting in their white ends; the speculum area is green and the feathers usually have white tips on their outer webs; primaries and their coverts somewhat more brownish than in Def. Basic.

▶ ♀ Juv. Plumage (entire feathering), development presumably as described above for ♂, perfected at age about 8 weeks. Worn briefly, except most of wing long retained.

Differences from ♂ Juv. include: **bill** upper mandible generally has dark spotting laterally; **iris** more brownish. **Wing** innermost secondaries as ♂ Juv.; their longest overlying coverts either plain brownish or same very narrowly edged white distally; greater coverts over the speculum white with smallish dusky spots near their ends; median and lesser coverts more muted, even brownish compared with ♀ Def. Basic, and some have buffy edging; speculum area generally some variant of sepia, but occasionally dark gray with greenish sheen, and these feathers are tipped white on outer web.

▶ ♂ Basic I Plumage (all feathering, except all but innermost feathers of wing), usually begins to appear (on head, mantle, and breast) soon after the Juv. Plumage is perfected in late summer and is the usual Plumage from about MID-SEPT. through NOV. The new tail may be complete by early Oct. or as late as early winter. The innermost secondaries usually come in late.

A distinct, but variable, Plumage. **Iris** yellowish or even toward orange. **Bill** changes from at first largely brownish orange to, as this Plumage is succeeded by incoming Alt. I, olive-brownish or quite gray and with yellowish laterally on upper mandible. Ground color of **head**–neck varies with individual from buffy to white, forehead to nape nearly black, a prominent dusky stripe through eye, and remainder rather coarsely streaked dusky. **Upperparts** feathers blackish brown, without internal markings, and inconspicuously edged tan; the long scapulars are rounded, margined buffy tan, and usually a single long feather is black with greenish sheen plus some white distally astride the shaft across the end; lower back to tail mostly dark with some greenish sheen; the feathers on upper sides of rump are barred whitish (broadly) and very dark (rather narrowly), uniquely in this Plumage. Much of **underparts** yellowish brown to brick red (individual variation), and on the breast and forward sides a very dark subterminal U on each feather shows prominently; the flank feathers also are distinctly zoned broadly dark and narrowly pinkish buff, including their margins; vent to tail some variant of reddish brown, posteriorly with transverse darker barring; **tail** feathers as ♂ Def. Basic; legs and **feet** pale yellowish to a slightly grayed orange.

Wing innermost secondary rounded at tip and plain dark (outer web darkest); the next 2 have some white along shaft and on outer margin and the longest overlying coverts are plain dark; remainder is retained Juv. feathering.

NOTES   The drake not only has a quite different appearance at different stages of molting into and out of this Plumage, but there is also great individual variation in the perfected condition (usually in late fall) of Basic I. In one variant, for example, head–neck are finely marked sepia or dusky on brownish buff (densest on crown) and all of underparts are medium brownish with sepia or darker crescents on breast and some longitudinal markings of same dark color on longer under tail coverts.

Schiøler (1925) understood this Plumage and the 2 lower rt. figs. on his pl. 50 show it well in color; Tougarinov (1941) labeled it "Juvenal"; J. M. Harrison and Harrison (1959) showed it in monochrome, the figs. being labeled "first year transition drake."

Some fall specimens in collections that are labeled "♀" are drakes in Basic I.

▶   ♂ Alt. I. Plumage (all feathering, excepting all but innermost feathers of wing), commonly acquired in JAN., sometimes earlier or later. It is retained into SUMMER.

As this feathering comes in, the **head**–neck become green; the breast at first shows a mixture of dark-scalloped feathers among the incoming white ones, and finally the **breast** becomes all white or with only a few dark-scalloped feathers included; the feathers on anterior **dorsum** and midportion of back commonly are white edged (this wears off); **underparts** as ♂ Def. Alt., although feathers just beyond the vent more often are vermiculated black on white. In the **wing** the several innermost secondaries are somewhat broader distally (i.e., not as narrowly tapering) but patterned as in Def. Alt.

NOTES   Apparently an occasional drake does not acquire full Alt. I, but instead still retains traces of Basic I until the time (in summer) when Alt. I is succeeded by Basic II.

As the drake acquires the dark head of Alt. I, the last of the antecedent Basic I on head frequently occurs briefly as a palish patch or more or less transverse area down the forepart of the face, the same locus that remains light in Def. Alt. Plumage of the Australian Shoveler (*A. rhynchotis*) and is a crescent in the Bluewing (*A. discors*). See discussion in Delacour (1956) and by J. M. Harrison and Harrison (1959). The same phenomenon is not rare during Prealt. molt of older drakes. Also see pl. 53 in Schiøler (1925), showing a ♂ in full Def. Alt. with a white bar on forepart of cheek.

▶   ♀ Basic I Plumage (all feathering, excepting all but innermost feathers of wing), usually succeeds the Juv. beginning soon after the latter is fully grown and typically is retained through FALL.

Usually quite buffy brown overall, but **head**–neck sometimes toward grayish; feathers on dorsum lack internal markings; underparts coarsely and evenly marked (not streaked) darkish.

Upperparts feathers of mantle are evenly rounded (not slightly tapering as Juv.) and have even, palish buff, margins (paler than in ♀ Def. Basic); longest scapulars have palest edging—whitish buff; **underparts** the dark markings are large on the breast, i.e., each feather dark except for margin, and on lower sides and abdomen typically are coarse and are quite evenly arranged (but rarely are fine, numerous, and randomly patterned); vent to tail area quite evenly streaked dark. Legs and **feet** yellow, webs more brownish. **Wing** the 2 innermost secondaries are dark with narrow white edging

503

on outer margin, the next one pales to white at margins, and the longer overlying coverts are plain dark; remainder of wing is retained Juv. feathering.

▶ ♀ Alt. I Plumage (all feathering, excepting all but innermost feathers of wing), succeeds Basic I in LATE FALL or early winter and is retained until SPRING.

The earliest Plumage in which the belly is unmarked. Soft parts as Def. Alt. On the **head** and neck the streaking is heavier and darker and forehead-to-nape darker than in Basic I; feathers of **mantle** and rump have light internal markings, their edges very sharply defined and gray-buff; longer scapulars margined whitish buff to white; **underparts** some variant of buffy brownish, the feathers of breast with broad internal dark markings; those along sides and on flanks vary with individual from plain buffy brownish to same with few and large internal darker brownish areas; the feathers just beyond the vent have more or less circular exposed dark areas and the longer under tail coverts have narrow and very dark median longitudinal stripes. In the **wing** the innermost secondaries have clearly defined white margins on outer web; the longest overlying coverts very dark, some with bluish on outer web; remainder of wing is retained Juv. feathering.

▶ ♀ Basic II Plumage (entire feathering), acquired by an interrupted molt (like all succeeding Basics); the head–body, part or all of tail, and the nest down are acquired through SPRING; much later, after nesting, the molt is completed by the Basic II wing succeeding the very worn Juv. wing. Basic II is worn from some time in SPRING (before age 1 year) until at least well along in SUMMER.

Measurements of specimens from conterminous U.S., 12 ♂ : BILL 62–67 mm., av. 65.5; WING 235–253, av. 244; TAIL 79–92, av. 84; TARSUS 37–41, av. 39; 12 ♀ : BILL 58–66 mm., av. 62; WING 222–233, av. 227; TAIL 75–80, av. 76.5; TARSUS 35–38, av. 37 (ETS).

Another series 69 ♂ "adult" (from Alaska, Canada, conterminous U.S., Mexico, Costa Rica, Jamaica, Europe, Japan, China, Siberia): BILL 56.2–70.1 mm., av. 64; WING (across chord) 219–252, av. 237.1; TAIL 65.6–90.1, av. 75.8; TARSUS 33.2–40.2, av. 37.5; 34 ♀ "adult" (Alaska, Canada, conterminous U.S., Mexico, Costa Rica, Europe, China, Japan, Formosa): BILL 55.6–65.2 mm., av. 60.5; WING (across chord) 209–241, av. 222.4; TAIL 65.4–81.4, av. 72.3; TARSUS 31.3–39.4, av. 35.6 (H. Friedmann).

For additional series, see table compiled by Winterbottom and Middlemiss (1960).

The difference in length between Juv. and Basic flattened WING is shown by these meas. from Schiøler (1925): ♂ 49 Juv. 215–247 mm., av. 232, and 9 Basic 232–243, av. 237; ♀ 29 Juv. 211–224 mm., av. 219, and 14 Basic 215–232, av. 222.

Weight in fall in Ill.: ♂ 16 "adult" av. 1.52 lb. (690 gm.) and 45 "juvenile" 1.48 (672 gm.); ♀ 6 "adult" av. 1.37 lb. (622 gm.) and 35 "juvenile" 1.30 (590 gm.) (Bellrose and Hawkins 1947).

Fall birds, age-classes not separated: 90 ♂ av. 1.4 lb. (636 gm.), max. 2 lb. (908 gm.); 71 ♀ av. 1.3 lb. (590 gm.), max. 1.6 (726 gm.) (A. L. Nelson and Martin 1953).

Fifteen newly hatched ducklings weighed 20.6–25.3 gm., mean and standard error 22.7 ± 0.37 gm., and standard deviation 1.43 (Smart 1965a).

For the U.S.S.R. there are considerable wt. data, by sex, age, and locality, in Dementiev and Gladkov (1952).

504

Hybrids in the wild in N. Am. include a number of crosses with the Bluewing *(A. discors)*; see summary under that species, where also is mention of a cross with either Bluewing or Cinnamon Teal *(A. cyanoptera)*. In spring in N.D. a drake Shoveler was seen, on several occasions, attempting to displace the ♂ of a pair of Bluewings (Martz 1964); some of the published items on capture of hybrids also mention observations of close association of Shovelers and Bluewings in the wild. Presumed natural hybrids with the Muscovy Duck *(Cairina moschata)* also have been taken.

In Eurasia the Shoveler has crossed in the wild with at least these *Anas* species: Greenwing *(crecca)*, Mallard *(platyrhynchos)*, Garganey *(querquedula)*, Gadwall *(strepera)*, and Pintail *(acuta)*. All the above were listed by Gray (1958), plus the following crosses among captives: 2 additional species of *Anas* (a now incomplete listing), also allegedly with *Aix sponsa* and *Aythya nyroca*.

A pair consisting of ♂ Shoveler and ♀ Mallard was seen in Iceland (G. Timmermann 1949).

The tracheal bulla of an *A. penelope* × *clypeata* hybrid was illus. by Beer (1968).

Geographical variation none reported.

It was postulated by Delacour and Mayr (1945) that the Shoveler group (3 geographically separated species in the S. Hemisphere, 1 only in N. Hemisphere) originated through repeated derivation of large size and large bill from ancestral "blue-winged duck" stock. There is less prospect of agreement on this than on the surmise that the closest S. Hemisphere relative of the Northern Shoveler is the essentially nondimorphic Cape Shoveler *(A. smithi)* of s. Africa. On morphological grounds it seems very probable that the former was derived from the same stock as the latter. The northern bird *(clypeata)* has evolved the most striking sexual dimorphism, the most spatulate bill, and has much the largest geographical range of any member of the shoveler group. The 2 birds of the Americas *(clypeata* of N. Am. and the Red Shoveler, *A. platalea,* of S. Am.) appear to be less closely akin than is the former to *smithi* of Africa.

It is of interest, although a phenomenon already known in several Anatid genera, that, when a captive Northern × Red Shoveler pair produced a first-generation ♂ hybrid, this drake showed certain characteristics of a species other than either parent, notably a pale facial crescent quite like that of the Australasian Shoveler *(A. rhynchotis)* and Blue-winged Teal *(A. discors)*. See J. M. Harrison and Harrison (1963a), text and photos. Also see earlier in this account under ♂ Alt. I. RSP

FIELD IDENTIFICATION In N. Am. A medium-sized duck. The Shoveler flies faster than most dabbling ducks, but not as fast as the small teals; like the latter, however, its course often is erratic. More commonly than most of our ducks, it flies in twos, threes, and small companies, but gatherings of up to several hundred also occur during spring migration.

The long spoon-shaped bill resembles a proboscis, thereby lending a distinctive appearance regardless of sex or Plumage. At rest and in flight the bill is carried angled downward, as if it were too heavy to be supported horizontally by the short thick neck. Because of the disproportionate size of the bill, the wings of a flying Shoveler appear to be abnormally far back on the body.

The drake in Alt. Plumage (late fall or later into following summer) is strikingly marked—dark green head, white breast, rusty sides and belly, very dark upperparts, and white patch on side of rump. Because the drake generally is late in molting out of the somewhat ♀ -like Basic Plumage (of summer–early fall), most drakes during fall still appear quite like ♀ ♀ , as also do the young in that season. The ♀ (all year) is brownish, Mallard-like, except for the powder blue forewing and green speculum which are almost identical with those of Blue-winged and Cinnamon Teals. Like the larger Mallard, however, the Shoveler has white outer tail feathers and orange to somewhat reddish legs and feet. FCB

VOICE   Shovelers commonly are silent until after they have finished molting in autumn, but become rather noisy from winter onward through spring. The common call of drakes, on water or in flight, is a nasal, querulous *chugh chugh* or a more gutteral sound, rendered in its several variants as *took took* or *totook took* or *took-a took-a* or any of these notes in longer series. This gutteral call is loud, very distinctive, and quite far carrying. The ♀ has a low-pitched quack, not commonly uttered except in alarm. Additional calls are described under "Reproduction" in their relation to displays.

The rattling sound from the wings, which is a conspicuous element of fluttering display or Jump flight, is not limited to occurrence during display toward a ♀ . Drake Shovelers have a near-vertical takeoff like teal and, at least from fall through spring, it often is accompanied by a loud rattle of the wings. The ♀ also rises abruptly, but without this sound. RSP

HABITAT   In N. Am. In **breeding season** open marshy areas with shallow waterways, abundant aquatic vegetation, and surrounding dry meadows for nesting. The water areas, which may become stagnant or even so dried out as to be mostly mud, produce an abundance of seed-bearing plants, algae, tiny mollusks, aquatic beetles, midge larvae, etc. The Shoveler is not particular as to whether the water is clean and clear, muddy, flowing or stagnant, considerably alkaline, or even heavily polluted with sewage or industrial waste. As J. C. Phillips (1925) pointed out, filth is not essential, but soft slimy mud is what the Shoveler seems to require. It is a filter feeder, below and at the surface, seldom on the bottom, i.e., not in the same niche preferred by the Greenwing and Mallard.

At Delta, Man., 28% of 65 nests were in *Scolochloa festucacea*, 26% in *Spartina pectinata*, 20% in *Agropyron repens*, 18% in *Poa pratensis*, 4% in mixed sedges, 3% in annual weeds, and 1% in *Hordeum jubatum*. Of 37 nests found in Utah, C. S. Williams and Marshall (1938b) reported 24 in *Distichlis spicata*, 7 in *Scirpus acutus*, 3 in *S. paludosus*, 2 in weeds, and 1 in *Salix* sp. In Mont., Girard (1939) found 56% of 132 Shoveler nests in short grasses (*Agropyron smithii*, *Poa pratensis*, *Phleum prateus*, and *Hordeum jubatum*), 13% in *Salsola pestifer*, *Cirsium arvense*, and *C. muticum*, and 23% in tall grasses (*Agropyron repens*, *Calamagrostis canadensis*, *Poa palustris*, and others).

Various breeding habitats include: large marshy areas with interspersion of various

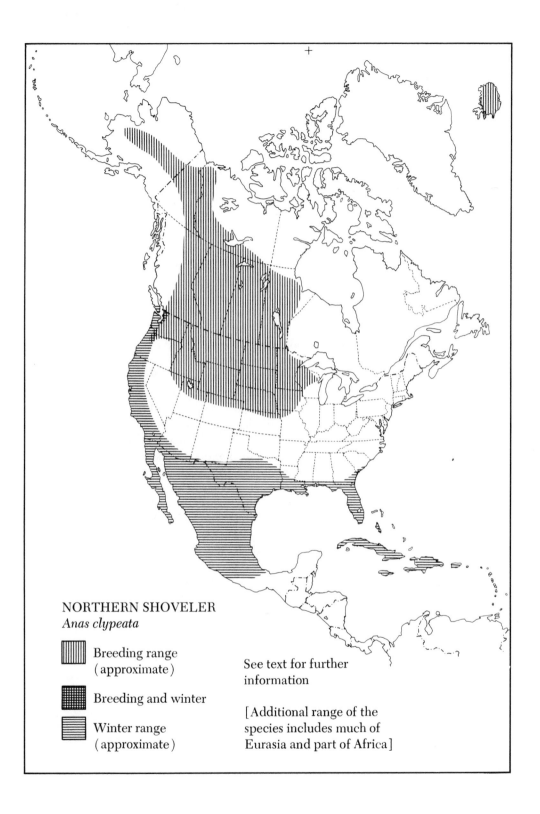

NORTHERN SHOVELER
Anas clypeata

⁝ Breeding range
   (approximate)

▦ Breeding and winter

≡ Winter range
   (approximate)

See text for further
information

[Additional range of the
species includes much of
Eurasia and part of Africa]

vegetative types; barren grounds, such as tundra, near open waters; small glacially formed potholes and small sloughs and their vicinity; marshland on both Atlantic and Pacific coasts.

Dry or fairly dry resting areas, such as unvegetated shorelines or mudbanks, are required.

In **migrations** most numerous on shallow lakes and ponds with extensive mudflats. In **winter** mainly shallow lagoons and upper reaches of other tidal waters where aquatic invertebrates are plentiful.

Occasionally with other waterfowl on marine shores. LKS

DISTRIBUTION (See map.) For detailed summary of older data for entire range of the species, see J. C. Phillips (1925). In both N. Am. and Eurasia, the extent of overlap of breeding and winter ranges is relatively small compared with some waterfowl species. The Shoveler, however, like the Gadwall and Ruddy Duck, nests at scattered localities a considerable distance s. of usual breeding range. In N. Am. there also have been a considerable number of such occurrences to the east, especially since about 1945.

Breeding and summer Nfld.—no proof of breeding. New Bruns.—has bred at 2 localities. In nw. Canada—breeds northward down the Mackenzie drainage and vicinity nearly to the arctic coast. For other Canadian peripheral data, see Godfrey (1966). First record above the Canadian mainland: drake shot on sw. Victoria I. in early June 1971 (T. G. Smith 1973). In mainland Alaska there are records (not breeding) n. to Barrow; the Shoveler has bred at Umiat on the arctic slope and has been recorded in summer beyond to the arctic coast; in w. Alaska, in addition to regular breeding range, there are scattered occurrences in summer out onto the Alaska Pen., St. Lawrence I., and Pribilofs. Amchitka—various occurrences. Attu—known to the natives there. Commander Is.—possibly breeds on Bering, but proof lacking.

Fall Now regular in small numbers in the Aleutians.

Winter At Adak in cent. Aleutians—several records for Nov. and 1 as late as Dec. 5. Upper limits in N. Am. are near coasts, farthest n. on the Pacific side (very large numbers in Cal. and elsewhere). Bermuda—fall and winter occurrences. In the Caribbean—occurs regularly on several larger is. and there are scattered records for various smaller ones around the perimeter s. to include Trinidad. The species is mapped as occurring throughout Mexico and Cent. Am., but there are sizable areas unsuited to it and for which records are lacking. Mexico—occurs in the interior and, on coasts, is more numerous on the Pacific side; winter concentrations as far s. as coastal lagoons in Oaxaca and Chiapas (over 30,000 in Laguna de Joya, Chiapas, in Jan. 1962), and it seems quite probable that such southerly winterers fly overland to these destinations rather than all going down the Pacific coast. Beyond, in Cent. Am., few records: Panama—1, Colombia—several.

In the Pacific Ocean, the following may pertain to birds from N. Am.: Hawaii —regular in winter in the main island group plus winter–spring occurrences at Sand I. and Laysan in the Leeward group, and recorded from Midway; farther s. at Christmas I.—seen March to April or May; Canton I. (Phoenix group)—pair in summer of 1953.

Recorded as **fossil** from the Pleistocene of N. Am. in Ore., Cal. (4 localities), Nev.,

Kans., and Fla. (3 localities). Identified from **archaeological sites** in Iowa and Ill. For full references to all these, plus others in the Palearctic region, see Brodkorb (1964a).

Extralimital data of interest Atlantic area—in Iceland, apparently a recent immigrant and has bred from the 1930s onward (G. Timmermann 1949) and is increasing (Gudmundsson 1951). Nests at 1 or more localities in n. Norway. Bering Sea region—2 records for s. coastal Chuckchee Pen., 1 being for a pair in late June (Portenko 1972). Pacific—there are records far distant from N. Am. (Marianas, Carolines, Marshalls), presumably of birds from Asia. Australia—Frith (1967) accepted only a single record, dating from 1839 in New S. Wales. New Zealand—one shot in May 1968 (P. J. Howard 1968). South Africa—there are several acceptable records of drakes; attempts to discount them by postulating that the local *A. smithi* occasionally acquires an Alt. Plumage like that of *A. clypeata* are unsatisfactory. RSP

MIGRATION In N. Am. Spring movement is late and quite prolonged; fall movement begins early and also is prolonged; in both seasons, however, some of the birds cover long distances rapidly. The bulk of the birds travel via flight "corridors" (of Bellrose 1968) from the n. prairies over the plains to inland areas and sheltered waters around part of the Gulf of Mexico. Another important movement is somewhat diagonal, from Alta. to Mont. to Utah and then to Cal. The largest segment of birds wintering on the Atlantic coast also have a diagonal corridor, via Ill. southeastward to S.C., where easterly breeders probably also go. Birds that go to certain breeding areas may be widely scattered in winter. For example, many from Alta. go to Cal., while others go toward the Gulf of Mexico or down into Mexico. It seems probable that those wintering in Chiapas, far down on the Pacific side of Mexico, come via the continental interior rather than down the Pacific slope.

Spring Main time of passage through the conterminous U.S. is March–April, with peak movement usually in last half of March (s. ⅔) and first 3 weeks of April (n. ⅓). There are late lingerers far southward, at least through May. The bulk of migration in interior Canada occurs from late April to past mid-May and probably continues in n. Canada and in Alaska into June.

Summer Compared with some other dabblers, Shoveler drakes tend to remain longer with their incubating mates which, in turn, are not early nesters. Mainly in the latter part of June and in July, the drakes, already in Prebasic head–body molt, gather in small groups and move away to local waters where they become flightless. Many, however, fly some distance, i.e., have a molt migration to some area of shallow open water and marsh. There seems to be no scattering of drakes in summer to places well n. of breeding localities (such as occurs, for example, in the Pintail), nor any evidence of any sort that Shovelers fly a long distance in any direction to molt. A noted gathering place of molting drakes is Beaverhills L., e. of Edmonton, Alta.

Fall Shovelers begin moving early in n. parts of breeding range. Most of them leave the Peace–Athabaska delta before the end of Aug. (Soper 1951). At the mouth of the Bear R., Utah, the birds begin to congregate after Sept. 1 and tens of thousands are present by the end of the month. By mid-Sept., some already have crossed the plains to the Gulf of Mexico coast. Migration in conterminous U.S. is heavy from about then through Oct. and continues, diminishing, through Nov. and into Dec. in s. half of U.S.

An exception, however, is the Pacific slope, where heavy migration sometimes continues late, until at least mid-Dec. It continues into late Dec. in Mexico and apparently there is movement in that month of a very few birds along the island perimeter of the Caribbean.

Winter In Fla., according to Chamberlain, Jr. (1960), Shovelers possibly move southward of the cent. and s. part of the state prior to Oct. and reappear in Nov. with a rather noticeable increase in Jan. and peak numbers in Feb. "It has been particularly noted" that Jan. migrants into cent. Fla. are normally single-sex flocks, apparently with ♂ flocks moving northward a few days ahead of ♀♀.

The above short account omits some known details. There are, however, great gaps in existing information, such as where various winterers breed, whether unisexual winter flocks may be of prebreeders, etc.

NOTE On Oct. 3, 1968, a ♀ Shoveler was hit, at 13,000 ft. altitude, by an aircraft en route from Bombay to Bangkok (J. G. Harrison 1969). RSP

BANDING STATUS The total number banded in N. Am. through 1964 was 33,894, the total number of recoveries through 1966 was 2,388, and main places of banding were Sask., Alta., Cal., and Utah (data from Bird Banding Laboratory). RSP

REPRODUCTION N. Am. data are emphasized here, but some Palearctic data on several topics (mainly displays) are included. Shovelers of both sexes **first breed** when approaching age 1 year. Unlike Tufted Ducks, yearling ♀ Shovelers are as successful at nesting as older ones and their ducklings survive just as well (Mihelsons et al., in Mihelsons and Viksne 1968). Pairs are formed beginning in winter and continuing throughout spring.

The social phase of **display**, an outgrowth of social feeding, appears to be more formalized than in our other *Anas:* the drakes display more or less in turn. A composite outline of events from this group phase through to completion of pair formation, based on Lorenz (1941), Lebret (1958a), Hori (1962), Johnsgard (1968a), and McKinney (1970) is as follows.

Several drakes gather around a ♀, keeping a few yds. away, stopping and moving when she does. When she stops, or if she Incites, the nearest drake turns full broadside or, additionally, TURNS-THE-BACK-OF-THE-HEAD toward her and begins to move away slowly, looking back and stopping repeatedly to see if she is following. The various drakes thus try to lead the ♀ away. As intensity of activity increases, a drake tries to induce the duck to follow him in flight. He turns broadside, then away, and springs from the water in a short, ritualized, fluttering flight ("JUMP FLIGHT" of Lebret) of a few yds. His repeated *took, totook,* or *took-a* call (these are variants, the first 2 often intermingled in a series) is uttered as this display begins. The flight is a special hovering type, accompanied by a distinctive noisy rattling sound from the wings (the mechanics of this sound production are not known). The drake lands near the ♀ and often Up-ends immediately. He may perform this display flight several times, or another drake may supplant him. The ♀ may not show any positive response, or may show a weak one (by also fluttering a short distance), or she may fly with the drake (thus indicating her preference for him) to another location. If they continue to remain together, the pair bond is formed for the season. Hori described an instance in which a ♀ was with 3 ♂♂, one

510

being her mate; she Incited toward the other drakes but, after 2 fluttering flights by her mate, she flew away with him. Presumably they had become paired very recently.

To return to **the duck,** her INCITING consists of repeatedly raising the head (with bill generally angled slightly upward) and jerking it downward, with or without quacking, and without lateral movement. She also quacks in various other circumstances, including postcoital phase of copulatory activity. Her grating DECRESCENDO CALL is slightly descending and ends with 1 or 2 muffled notes. Other ♀ displays include TURNING-THE-BACK-OF-THE-HEAD, SHAKE (of the body) and BELLY-PREEN, all resembling the same ♂ displays.

Displays of the drake include the following. REPEATED CALLS *took-took* (series of these doubles) or *took* (in series) or may start or finish with a wheezing sound. FAST CALLS short burst of rapid *tooks*, as when 2 pairs come together, or during Lateral dabbling, or before a Jump flight. LATERAL DABBLING (also called Display-feeding, Mock-feeding, and Gabbling) appears to be homologous with Drinking of various *Anas;* the body broadside to the ♀, various feathers erected, while the drake paddles rapidly but without forward movement; he may give Fast calls. HEAD-DIP briefly. UP-END as in feeding, the feet paddled rapidly. SWIMMING-SHAKE stiffly, broadside to ♀. BODY-SHAKE ashore, broadside to ♀. BELLY-PREEN after a Body-shake, ♂ bends forward in posture of nibbling the venter, or else waves bill across venter but without contact. PREEN-DORSALLY occasional. PREEN-BEHIND-THE-WING occasional. These last 2 are very similar to normal comfort movements. BATHE and WING-FLAP several dipping movements and then a stiffly executed flap, or only the latter; the drake swims in a tight circle, then flaps; the wings make a clapping noise on the final flap and the bird utters several *took* notes. DRINKING exaggerated movements.

Copulation Both birds, with bills angled downward, engage in a bout of Precopulatory head-pumping; then the ♂ treads while uttering quiet wheezing noises or *took* calls; then he dismounts, remains broadside, points his bill down, erects various feathers, waggles his tail, paddles while maintaining station, and gives a single *paay* call or ♂ DECRESCENDO (*paay* plus series of *took* notes). Sometimes he orients his body facing the ♀; at other times he partly or completely circles around her, occasionally with Turning-the-back-of-the-head or with a head-jerking action. The ♀ bathes.

In HOSTILE PUMPING, as in response to the near proximity of another drake, the bill is held high and loud *took* calls are uttered. In actual fighting, the birds move in a tight circle. Shovelers show much aerial and overt aggression and so partially isolate themselves in pothole areas, but several pairs tend to utilize one pothole to the exclusion of apparently similar ones nearby.

The Shoveler is one of the last shoal-water ducks to arrive on breeding grounds. Generally the birds come in small flocks (large ones are of transients, bound elsewhere) which disintegrate within a few days as mated pairs establish (or reoccupy) fairly fixed home ranges. In the early hours of daylight especially, the ♀ (followed by her mate) begins search flights over nesting cover. She alights here and there, continuing her search by walking about; McKinney (1967) saw penned birds at this stage pull vegetation over themselves in the same fashion that they form a canopy over the nest later on. Established breeders have a marked tendency to return to the same nest site year after year.

During the prelaying period copulations are frequent; also, the ♀ has much the same

511

"persistent quacking" behavior as the Mallard. In the drake's defended area, which includes some water as well as land, he feeds and waits at a loafing site (commonly a mudbank) for his mate to return from laying or from a span of incubating; copulation also occurs in defended area.

A preferred **nest site** is quite close to water, in low grass, often with little conceal-ment early in the season. In 52 nests at Delta (Man.), distance from water was 0–50 yds. (65% of the nests), 50–100 yds. (26%), 100–200 (4%), and 200–300 (5%). In 35 nests at Tule and Lower Klamath refuges (Cal.), 28.3% were over 50 yds. from water and a larger percentage was over 100 yds. distant than in any other waterfowl nesting there (A. W. Miller and Collins 1954). At Bombay Hook Refuge (Del.), nests were in salt marsh, mostly in patches of dead *Spartina patens,* close to tidal guts (Griffith 1946).

The duck shapes a nest bowl, lines it with some vegetation gathered at the site, and lays her clutch usually at the rate of 1 egg/day. Beginning some time during laying, she also adds **nest down**. It is much like that of the Pintail and Baldpate, dark with light centers, but the intermingled feathers differ; breast feathers are small, with an evenly dark subterminal area; side and flank feathers are some variant of fuscous, with buffy tan margins and at least 1 similarly colored transverse band. The duck covers her eggs carefully before she departs; during incubation she generally leaves twice daily and joins her mate (if he still is nearby) to preen and rest.

All types of pursuit flight described for the Mallard apparently also occur among Shovelers. Three-bird flights, which are seen first during laying or early in incubation, differ from those of the Mallard in that the drake Shoveler always defends his mate from the interloping drake, by repeatedly interposing himself between his mate and the pursuer, or even buffeting the latter (Hori 1963).

Dates for full **first clutches** vary considerably depending on season at any locality, but may be expected in an "average" season about as follows: Bombay Hook (Del.)— early April to early May; Flathead Valley (w. Mont.)—last third of April to late May; Tule–Klamath (nw. Cal.)—mid–April to early June; Delta (Man.)—last third of April to June. Also see Bent (1923).

One **egg** each of 20 clutches (2 Pa., 6 Sask., 1 Mackenzie delta, 7 N.D., 1 Utah, 1 Ore., 1 Cal., 1 Scotland): **size** length 52.85± 1.80 mm., breadth 37.20± 1.18, radii of curvature of ends 14.59± 0.88 and 10.19±1.41; **shape** tends toward elliptical (slender for a duck), elongation 1.41± 0.046, bicone −0.050, asymmetry +0.169 (FWP). For 177 eggs from "various collections," Bent (1923) gave length as 48–58 mm., av. 52.2, and breadth as 34.5–39, av. 37. The data for 275 eggs in Schönwetter (1961) presuma-bly include those in Bent and the figures are nearly identical. In **color** they usually are buffy with greenish tinge.

Clutch size in presumed first clutches at Delta (Man.): 13 eggs (1 nest), 12 (6), 11 (6), 10 (5), and 9 (3). Most published information includes all clutches found through the season, for example: Tule–Klamath in 1952—35 nests had 389 eggs (av. 10.7) and at the same locality in 1957—63 nests had 657 eggs (av. 10.4); in the Flathead Valley in Mont. clutch size av. between 8 and 9 in 132 nests (Girard 1939). For decrease in clutch size through the season, in Alta., see data in Keith (1961); in Latvia, yearling ♀ ♀ began laying a little later than older ones and had a smaller av. clutch size (Mihelsons et al. in Mihelsons and Viksne 1968). A smaller (Sowls 1955) **replacement clutch** is laid in a new nest if the first is lost; perhaps occasionally a ♀ renests if she hatches a brood early and loses it.

Incubation begins after the last egg is laid. The incubation period evidently varies considerably under natural conditions. A stated period of only 22–24 days, which dates from Naumann in the previous century, has been widely quoted. Hochbaum (1944) gave 21–25 days, av. 21–22, for artificially incubated eggs; Heinroth and Heinroth (1928) gave 22–23 days for birds in the Berlin Zoological Garden; McKinney (1967) estimated it to average, in penned birds, between 22 and 25 days. Havlin (1964), however, stated that, both in nature and when artificially incubated, the period was 25–27 days, this being the same as given for wild birds by Noll (1959). At L. Engure in Latvia, incubation period of 21 days (4 clutches), 22 (9), 23 (8), 24 (8), 25 (3), 26 (1), and 27 (1) (Mednis, in Mihelsons and Viksne 1968). Sowls (1955) stated that, when clutches failed to hatch, one ♀ incubated 42 days and another 45. At least during the normal incubation period the ♀ usually leaves the nest 2 or 3 times/day; her absences total several hrs.

Hatching success In N. D. in 1936 and 1937, 59% and 62% of eggs in nests studied hatched (Kalmbach 1938); in Mont., 70% of 1,135 eggs (Girard 1939); in Utah, 80% of 189 eggs (C. S. Williams and Marshall 1938b); and at Tule–Klamath in nw. Cal. in 1952, 91.5% of 389 eggs (A. W. Miller and Collins 1954), and in 1957 the figure was 94.4% for 657 eggs (Rienecker and Anderson 1960).

If the nesting season is early, the drake sometimes is with the ♀ and **brood** for a few days, but most observers have reported that the brood is led to water and tended solely by the ♀. She prefers to keep her ducklings close to shore or near areas of emergent plants, where the family feeds in the shallows. That is, few broods are seen since they tend to hide in shoreline vegetation, especially when very young; older broods prefer larger bodies of permanent water. In captivity, av. wt. of ducklings was as follows: 1 day 23 gm. (6 birds), 1 week 53 gm. (6), 2 weeks 135 gm. (6), 3 weeks 242 gm. (6), 4 weeks 303 gm. (4), and 5 weeks 370 gm. (2) (Southwick 1953a).

Various data on **brood survival** indicate that mortality is heaviest the first week and then decreases greatly. Twenty-five broods in w. S.D. in 1950 av. 7.6 ducklings at 1 week and 6.1 at flying age, and 23 in 1951 av. 8.0 at 1 week and 7 at flying age (Bue et al. 1952); at Tule–Klamath in 1952, brood size declined from an av. of 7.3 at 1 week to 4.9 at 5 weeks, then (from combining of remnants of older broods) rose to 7.5 at 8 weeks (A. W. Miller and Collins 1954). In Man., Sask., and Alta., in 1936 plus 1938–42 inclusive, a tally of over 192,000 young of unstated ages gave annual averages of brood size ranging from 5.5 to 6.49 (Cartwright 1944), or about 6 for an overall figure.

Young Shovelers **attain flight** in 52–60 days (Hochbaum 1944) and presumably are independent from about that time onward.

NOTE For a fairly comprehensive comparison of reproductive behavior of the Cape Shoveler (*A. smithi*) of Africa with the Northern Shoveler, see Siegfried (1965). LKS

SURVIVAL Except for some information on decrease through the season in av. brood size, given above, there are no published N. Am. data. For Britain, based on unpublished data, the mean annual adult survival rate was estimated at 0.56 ± 0.06 by Boyd (in Le Cren and Holdgate 1962). At L. Engure in Latvia, the av. yearly survival

513

rate was estimated for adult ♀ ♀ at no less than 38%, most probably 40–45% (Mihelsons et al., in Mihelsons and Viksne 1968). RSP

HABITS   Except when nesting, the Shoveler is decidedly gregarious; the groups typically are small and compact. Especially during migrations, it also is social and the groups accompany other fast-flying and highly manueverable shoal-water species, notably the Bluewing, Cinnamon Teal, Gadwall, and Baldpate. According to Meinertzhagen (1955), flapping rate is 302/min. cruising and 351/min. rising. Shovelers usually feed in very shallow water, more or less continuously moving about with head and neck submerged much of the time, skimming above the bottom or filtering the water to obtain small animal life and seeds. Social or group feeding, with the birds moving in a circular pattern, has been described a number of times, most recently by Simms (1970). Unlike the Pintail, Shovelers seldom up-end to feed and very rarely dive. They do not ordinarily go to fields to feed. They are most active early and late in the day and, when the sun is high, they rest in groups, by themselves or with other waterfowl, on mud or sand at the water's edge.

Still lacking, at least for N. Am., is a detailed study of habits and behavior of this interesting waterfowl at some place where its numbers are concentrated in winter. In fact, the best extant summary of information for all seasons except breeding remains that of J. C. Phillips (1925). FCB

FOOD   Plants of many families including grasses, sedges, pondweeds, waterlilies, algae, and smartweeds. Examination of 70 stomachs, Aug. to April inclusive, showed 65.8% vegetable and 34.2% animal matter. Approximately ⅔ of the latter consisted of mollusks (McAtee 1922).

Vegetable   Sedges: chufa (*Cyperus*), spike rush (*Eleocharis*), *Fimbristylis*, bulrushes (*Scirpus*), twig rushes (*Mariscus (Cladium)*), *Carex* 16%; pondweeds: true pondweeds (*Pontamogeton*), bushy pondweed (*Najas flexilis*), horned pondweed (*Zannichellia palustris*), wigeon grass (*Ruppia maritima*) 11.3%; grasses: panic grass (*Panicum*), foxtail grass (*Chaetochloa*), rice cut-grass (*Leersia oryzoides*), cultivated rice (*Oryza sativa*), beach grass (*Monanthochloe littoralis*) 8.3%; algae (*Chara*) 6.5%; waterlilies (*Brasenia, Castalia*) 2.5%; duckweeds (*Lemna*)) 1.7%; smartweeds (*Polygonum*) 1.1% (McAtee 1922).

Twelve specimens from the upper Chesapeake region had consumed chiefly the seeds of *Scirpus olneyi*, *Ruppia maritima*, *Distichlis spicata*, and the vegetation of *Chara* sp. (R. E. Stewart 1962). An Ohio bird taken in Nov. had fed extensively on duckweeds (*Lemna, Spirodela*) and seeds of smartweed (Trautman 1940). The 62 gizzards from Ill. contained 82.4% plant and 17.6% animal matter. The principal vegetable matter was seeds of *Cyperus* 31.67%, *Cephalanthus occidentalis* 16.74%, *Zea mays* 11.26%, and *Ceratophyllum demersum* 9.23% (H. G. Anderson 1959). In Mo. 30 gizzards contained mainly the seeds of *Leersia oryzoides* 57.7%, *Polygonum* spp. 12.6%, and *Zea mays* 9.7% (Korschgen 1955). At Reelfoot Lake, Tenn., the 21 gizzards showed 77.36% plant and 22.62% animal matter. The utilization of the seeds of bald cypress (*Taxodium distichum*) was high 23.57%. Other items of importance were

514

the seeds of *Decodon verticillatus* 9.54%, *Oryza sativa* 7.38%, and *Polygonum* spp. 6.67% (Rawls 1958).

The vegetable food in w. Europe consists of buds, stems, and seeds of *Glyceria fluitans, Scirpus, Phragmites, Carex, Potamogeton,* and *Lemna* (in Witherby 1939).

Animal Freshwater univalves (*Amnicola, Neretina, Lymnaea, Planorbis, Physa*) 19%; insects: water boatmen (Corixidae), back swimmers (Notonectidae), water tigers (Dytiscidae), larvae and cases of caddis flies (Trichoptera), dragonfly (Odonata) nymphs, larvae of mayflies (Ephemerida) and several genera of flies (Diptera) 4.6%; crustaceans, chiefly ostracods, and crayfishes 7.6%; fishes 3% (McAtee 1922).

Five stomachs from the Pribilof Is. contained solely the larvae of midges (Chironomidae) (Preble and McAtee 1923). In Cal. (Owens Lake) fed extensively on larvae and pupae of the alkali fly (*Ephydra hians*) (A. K. Fisher 1893). In fall at Great Salt Lake, Utah, thousands of Shovelers fed almost entirely upon brine shrimp (*Artemia fertilis*) and larvae and pupae of alkali flies (Wetmore 1917a). All of 10 Fla. specimens contained shells of *Rissoina pulchra* (F. C. Baker 1890). Among the fishes, carp (*Cyprinus carpio*) and gizzard shad (*Dorosoma cepedianum*) have been identified. In the upper Chesapeake region, fishes (chiefly Poeciliidae), and Gastropoda (*Littoridinops* sp.), and Copepoda; in Mo. Corixidae 4.4% the principal animal item; and at Reelfoot Lake Insecta 14.3%, and Glastropoda 5.5%.

The principal animal items recorded for w. Europe are Mollusca (*Littorina, Rissoa, Hydrobia, Planorbis*), crustaceans (Amphipoda, Copepoda), Insecta (Coleoptera, Hymenoptera), tadpoles, spawn, and worms (in Witherby 1939).

Animal food predominates in Russia and consists mainly of small mollusks and crustaceans, particularly *Daphnia*. On filtering algae (*Conferva*) the birds obtain diatoms, ostracods, and rotifers at the Naurusumk Lakes. Twelve species of mollusks were found in 94.7% of the stomachs from the estuary of the Kama R., e. Russia. At the Rybinsk Reservoir in May, mollusks, mainly *Planorbis contortus*, formed 47% of the food, *Ostracoda* 17%, larvae of aquatic insects 25.2%, Chironomidae, Odonata, and Trichoptera 6%, and seeds 4.8%. Mollusks increased to 74.8% in July–Aug. when, besides *Planorbis*, Viviparidae became important. Seeds rose to 13%. The food in Sept.–Oct. consisted of mollusks 62%, larvae of aquatic insects 31%, and seeds 6.5%.

On the Mologa R. in spring, animal food amounted to 30%, the remainder being *Lemna, Elodea,* and *Ceratophyllum*. Plankton crustaceans formed 75% of food of the young. Mollusks in spring formed the fundamental diet at the mouth of the Volga where plankton occur sparsely. On the Barabinsk steppe, mollusks were found in 71.4% of the stomachs, insects in 35.7%, and arachnids in 7.1%. In winter in Transcaucasia, seeds predominated over animal food. (Summarized from Dementiev and Gladkov 1952). AWS

List of literature cited in this volume
is combined with that of vol. 3
and precedes the index in vol. 3.

Index

Numbers in **boldface** refer to caption pages facing color plates.

519